W9-BOL-730

FIFTH EDITION

SOCIAL GERONTOLOGY

A MULTIDISCIPLINARY PERSPECTIVE

Nancy R. Hooyman

University of Washington

H. Asuman Kiyak

University of Washington

Allyn and Bacon

Boston   London   Toronto   Sydney   Tokyo   Singapore

Series Editor: Sarah L. Kelbaugh
Editor in Chief: Karen Hanson
Editorial Assistant: Jennifer Muroff
Editorial-Production Service: Chestnut Hill Enterprises, Inc.
Manufacturing Buyer: Megan Cochran
Cover Administrator: Linda Knowles

Copyright © 1999, 1996, 1993, 1991, 1988 by Allyn & Bacon
A Viacom Company
160 Gould Street
Needham Heights, MA 02194

All rights reserved. No part of the material protected by this copyright notice may be reproduced or utilized in any form or by any means, electronic or mechanical, including photocopying, recording, or by any information storage and retrieval system, without written permission from the copyright holder.

Internet: www.abacon.com

Between the time Website information is gathered and published, some sites may have closed. Also, the transcription of URLs can result in typographical errors. The publisher would appreciate notification where these occur so that they may be corrected. Thank you.

Library of Congress Cataloging-in-Publication Data
Hooyman, Nancy R.
    Social gerontology : a multidisciplinary perspective / Nancy
Hooyman, H. Asuman Kiyak. — 5th ed.
        p.   cm.
    Includes bibliographical references (p.   ) and index.
    ISBN 0–205–27772–1 (hard)
    1. Gerontology.   2. Aging.   3. Aged—United States.   I. Kiyak, H.
Asuman, 1951–   . II. Title.
HQ1061.H583   1998
305.26—dc21   98-17314
                                                        CIP

Printed in the United States of America

10   9   8   7   6   5   4   3   2   1   RRD-VA   03   02   01   00   99   98

Photo credits
Photo credits may be found on page xviii, which should be considered an extension of the copyright page.

To Valerie Higgins and Fred Cox,
for their assistance
and for their own modeling of successful aging
To Mani, who wanted to help with "THE BIG BOOK"

—NRH

To my father, who epitomized ego integrity
To Joe, for his love and encouragement, . . . and to Lara,
who has made it all worthwhile

—HAK

Nancy R. Hooyman

Nancy R. Hooyman is professor and dean at the School of Social Work at the University of Washington in Seattle. Her Ph.D. is in sociology and social work from the University of Michigan. She is nationally recognized for her scholarship in aging, issues related to family caregiving, gender inequities in caregiving, feminist social work practice, and administration. In addition to this textbook, Dean Hooyman is the coauthor of *Taking Care of Aging Family Members,* and *Feminist Perspectives on Family Care: Policies for Gender Justice,* and has edited *Feminist Social Work Practice in Clinical Settings.* She has published over 80 articles and chapters related to gerontology and women's issues. Her research interests are in family caregiving of persons with chronic disabilities, feminist practice models, and older women's issues. She is a Fellow in the Gerontological Society, and, in 1998, she received the Career Achievement Award from the Association for Gerontology in Social Work Education.

H. Asuman Kiyak

H. Asuman Kiyak is Director of the Institute on Aging, professor in the School of Dentistry, and adjunct professor in the Departments of Architecture and Psychology at the University of Washington. She obtained her Ph.D. in psychology at Wayne State University. Professor Kiyak has been the recipient of major research grants from NIH, AOA, and private foundations in the areas of health promotion and health service utilization by older adults, and in person-environment adaptation to Alzheimer's disease by patients and their caregivers. She has published over 80 articles and 30 chapters in these areas and is known nationally and internationally for her research on geriatric dental care and the application of psychological theory to health promotion.

CONTENTS

CHAPTER **2**

HISTORICAL AND CROSS-CULTURAL ISSUES IN AGING   35

PART TWO   # THE BIOLOGICAL AND PHYSIOLOGICAL CONTEXT OF SOCIAL AGING   51

CHAPTER **3**

THE SOCIAL CONSEQUENCES OF PHYSICAL AGING   55

CHAPTER **4** # Managing Chronic Diseases and Promoting Well-Being in Old Age   93

PART THREE # The Psychological Context of Social Aging   129

CHAPTER **5** # Cognitive Changes with Aging   133

PART FOUR   THE SOCIAL CONTEXT OF AGING   225

CHAPTER **8**   SOCIAL THEORIES OF AGING   229

CHAPTER **9**   THE IMPORTANCE OF SOCIAL SUPPORTS: FAMILY, FRIENDS, AND NEIGHBORS   247

CHAPTER **10**

LIVING ARRANGEMENTS AND SOCIAL INTERACTIONS   287

CHAPTER **11**

PRODUCTIVE AGING: PAID AND NONPAID ROLES AND ACTIVITIES   319

CHAPTER 12

DEATH, DYING, BEREAVEMENT, AND WIDOWHOOD   365

CHAPTER 13

THE RESILIENCY OF OLDER ETHNIC MINORITIES   391

PREFACE

Aging is a complex and fascinating process, one which we will all experience. It is complex because of its many facets—physiological, emotional, cognitive, economic, and interpersonal—that influence our social functioning and well-being. It is a fascinating process because these changes will occur differently in each one of us. There is considerable truth to the statement that, as we grow older, we become more unlike each other.

Aging is also a process that attracts the attention of the media, politicians, business and industry, and the general public, largely because we live in a rapidly aging society. Changes in the numbers and proportion of older people in our population have numerous implications for societal structures, including the family, health and social services, long-term care, pension and retirement practices, political processes, recreational services, and housing. In addition, these changes are of growing concern because of the problems of poverty, inadequate housing, and chronic disease faced by some older people, particularly women, ethnic minorities, the oldest-old, and those living alone. Public officials as well as individuals in the private sector are faced with the challenge of planning for a future when there will be more people over age 65 than ever before.

These changes have also meant that most colleges and universities now offer courses in *gerontology,* the study of aging. The goal of some of these courses is to prepare students to understand the process of aging and the diversity among older people and to work effectively with older adults. These programs also attempt to enhance students'

personal understanding of their own and others' aging. Frequently, students take such a course simply to meet a requirement, not realizing how relevant the aging process is in their own lives. Thus, instructors are often faced with the need to help students see the connection between learning about aging and understanding their own behavior, the behavior of their relatives, and often the behavior of their clients.

This book grew out of our experiences in teaching gerontology courses to undergraduate students. In doing so, we were unable to locate a textbook that conveyed the excitement and relevance of understanding the aging process or one that adequately addressed the biological, physiological, psychological, and social aspects of aging. For years, we were frustrated by the lack of a text that was comprehensive, thorough, and current in its review of the rapidly growing research on older adults. As a sociologist/social worker and psychologist, we have been committed to developing a text that could be useful to a wide range of disciplines, including nursing, social work, sociology, psychology, health education, and the allied health professions.

AIMS AND FOCUS

The primary focus of this book is *social* gerontology. As the title implies, however, our goal is to present the diversities of the aging experience and the older population in a multidisciplinary manner. It is our premise that an examination of the social lives of older people requires a basic understanding of the historical, cultural, biological, physiological, psychological, and social contexts of aging. It is important to understand the changes that occur within the aging individual, how these changes influence interactions with social and physical environments, and how the older person is, in turn, affected by such interactions. Throughout this book, the impact of these dynamic interactions between older people and their environments on their quality of life is a unifying theme.

Social gerontology encompasses a wide range of topics with exciting research in so many domains. This book does not cover all these areas, but rather highlights major research findings that illuminate the processes of aging. Through such factual information, we intend to dispel some of the myths and negative attitudes about aging. We also hope to encourage the reader to pursue this field, both academically and for the personal rewards that come from gaining insight into older people's lives. Because the field is so complex and rapidly changing, more recent research findings may appear to contradict earlier studies. We have attempted to be thorough in presenting a multiplicity of theoretical perspectives and empirical data to insure that the reader has as full and accurate a picture of the field as possible.

FEATURES

This book begins by reviewing major demographic, historical, and cross-cultural changes, and their implications for the development of the field of social gerontology, as well as methods used to study aging and older people. We then turn to the major biological and physiological changes that affect older people's daily functioning, as well as their risk of chronic diseases and consequent utilization of health and long-term care services. The third section considers psychological changes, particularly in learning and memory, personality, mental health, and sexual-

ity. Given our emphasis on how such physical and psychological changes affect the social aspects of aging, the fourth section examines social theories of aging, the social context of the family, friends, and other intergenerational supports, new living arrangements, productivity in the later years, and the conditions under which people die. Throughout the book, the differential effects that these changes have on women and ethnic minorities are identified, with two chapters focusing specifically on such differences. We conclude by turning to the larger context of social, health, and long-term care policies and future implications for the field. To highlight the application of research findings to everyday situations, each chapter integrates discussions of both the policy and practice implications of the aging process. Vignettes of older people in different situations bring to life many of the concepts introduced in these chapters.

NEW TO THIS EDITION

The positive response of students and faculty to the first four editions suggests that we have been successful in achieving our goals for this book. Based on the responses of faculty who have used this book in different colleges across the United States, the fifth edition represents a major change. The book is designed to be completed in a 16-week semester, but readers can proceed at a faster pace through the chapters. The chapter on social theories has been expanded and updated to include recent theoretical developments, including feminist and social constructionist perspectives. New research findings are presented on extending healthy life, achieving successful aging, and encouraging productivity through both paid and unpaid activities. Both the strengths and challenges facing older women and ethnic minorities are presented. Given the dramatically changing political arena, the chapters on social, health, and long-term care policies have been rewritten to reflect contemporary policy debates, to address the need for home and community-based care alternatives to institutionalization, and to take account of the increasing diversity of the older population. The increased attention given to differences in the aging process by gender, ethnicity, and socioeconomic status, and to social, health, and long-term policy debates in this edition is a reflection of the dramatic demographic and economic changes facing us as we enter the twenty-first century.

ANNENBERG/CPB TELECOURSE

Social Gerontology is being offered as part of the Annenberg/CPB college-level telecourse *Growing Old in a New Age,* broadcast on PBS.

Growing Old in a New Age is a thirteen-part public television series and college-level course that provides an understanding of the processes of aging, of old age as a stage of life, and the impact of aging on society. The television series and course respond to the demographic wave that is sweeping our nation and our world, exploring questions about what roles people will play in their eighth, ninth, and tenth decades, and how institutions may evolve to address their needs. *Growing Old in a New Age* also offers opportunities for the student and viewer to examine personal attitudes toward aging and older people. Material contributed by outstanding social scientists, medical professionals, and clinicians provides a multidisciplinary, multicultural approach. Extensive interviews with older people themselves support this cross-cultural and comprehensive introduction to gerontology.

In addition to *Social Gerontology,* a student *Telecourse Study Guide* is available through most college bookstores. A *Telecourse Faculty Guide* is available without charge to those who license the telecourse. The programs may be purchased on videocassettes by calling the Annenberg/CPB Collection at 1-800-LEARNER. Off-air taping licenses may be acquired from either the Annenberg CPB Collection or the PBS Adult Learning Service. Colleges and universities may license the use of

Growing Old in a New Age as a telecourse for college credit through the PBS Adult Learning Service (1-800-257-2578; in Virginia, 703-739-5363).

ACKNOWLEDGMENTS

We are grateful to the many people who have contributed significantly to the successful completion of the fifth edition of *Social Gerontology*. In particular, we thank Valerie Higgins, Fred Cox, Asantewa DeFrietas, Jonas Louie, Jane Braziunas, and Carol Dean for assisting us with library research and the technical aspects of the revisions. Their willingness to "pitch in" and do whatever tasks were necessary was a tremendous support. Our families, Gene, Kevin, and Christopher Hooyman, and Joe and Lara Clark, have been the mainstay of support throughout the preparation of all five editions of this book. And Gnanamani Hooyman, who joined the Hooyman family during the last edition, has never known her mother not to be working on THE BIG BOOK! We would also like to thank Sarah Kelbaugh and Jennifer Muroff at Allyn & Bacon for their continued encouragement in completing this edition.

We appreciate the assistance from the staff associated with the Center on Aging, University of Hawaii at Manoa, who have chosen our text for the first national telecourse on aging, *Growing Old in a New Age*. We are grateful to Dr. Anthony Lenzer, Telecourse Project Director/Executive Producer, for providing us with the opportunity to work with him and his committed, enthusiastic telecourse staff: Dr. Joan Dubanoski, Assistant Project Director/Senior Producer; Rebecca Goodman, Project Coordinator/Writer; Jay Curlee, Director; Ellen Roberts, Field Evaluator; Floriana Cofman, Researcher; and in particular, Dr. Kathryn Braun, author of the student and faculty guides, who has worked closely with us in making major changes to the Student Guide to reflect the changes made in the fifth edition.

We want to thank the following reviewers of the fourth edition for their helpful comments: Jeanne E. Bader, California State University; Karen

A. Roberto, University of Northern Colorado; Kris Bulcroft, Western Washington University; Perry G. Thompson, University of Arkansas at Little Rock; Donald McTavish, University of Minnesota; Brenda J. Moretta, Our Lady of the Lake University; and Dale A. Lund, The University of Utah.

In addition, the following reviewers of the fifth edition made many valuable suggestions: Roberto Socas, Essex County College; William Hays, Wichita State; Margaret Dosch, University of Wisconsin, Lacrosse; Pamela Brangan, Old Dominion University; and Susan Weeks, Sam Houston State University.

Photo Credits:

Pages 14, 27, 63, 101, 108, 116, 236, 311, 341, 406, 410, 501, H. Asuman Kiyak;
Pages 38, 43, 46, 173, 194, 420, c Ed Ross; Page 68, Kevin Horan/Stock Boston;
Page 83, Amy C. Etra/Stock Boston; Page 104, Nita Winter/The Image Works;
Page 119, A. Ramey/PhotoEdit; Page 137, P. Gontier/The Image Works; Page 144,
Gary A. Connor/PhotoEdit; Page 163, Paul Berger/Tony Stone Images; Page 171,
Richard B. Levine; Page 181, Dr. David Nochlin, University of Washington;
Page 185, Martha Tabor/Impact Visuals; Page 191, Donna Binder/Impact Visuals;
Page 207, Spencer Grant/Stock Boston; Page 215, Bill Aronson/PhotoEdit;
Page 219, Frank Siteman/ Stock Boston; Page 234, Paul Stepan/Photo Researchers;
Page 238, Gale Zucker/ Stock Boston; Page 249, Robert Brenner/PhotoEdit;
Page 255, James D. Wilson/ Woodfin Camp & Associates; Page 271, Tony
Freeman/PhotoEdit; Page 275, Michael Siluk/The Image Works; Page 292, Myrleen
Ferguson/PhotoEdit; Page 304, John Neubauer/PhotoEdit; Page 308, Susan
Duncan/ADAptations, Inc.; Page 320, Walter Hodges/Tony Stone Images; Page 344,
R. Lord/The Image Works; Page 354, Frances M. Roberts; Page 367, Mark
Richards/PhotoEdit; Page 370, Patrick James Watson/The Image Works; Page 383,
Elizabeth Crews; Page 395, Hella Hammid/Photo Researchers, Inc.; Pages 400, 459,
Bob Daemmrich/The Image Works; Page 412, Michael McGovern/ The Picture
Cube; Page 432, A. Ramey/Woodfin Camp & Associates; Page 449, Diana
Walker/The Gamma Liaison Network; Page 456, Scott Ryder Photography;
Page 463, Tony Freeman/PhotoEdit; Page 475, Steve Liss/The Gamma Liaison
Network; Page 478, Sarah Putnam/The Picture Cube; Page 484, Gerd Ludwig/
Woodfin Camp & Associates; Page 496, AP Photo/Wide World Photos; Page 506,
Don Smetzer/Tony Stone Images; Page 514, Michael Newman/PhotoEdit.

PART one

THE FIELD OF SOCIAL GERONTOLOGY

1

THE GROWTH OF SOCIAL GERONTOLOGY

TOWARD UNDERSTANDING AGING

From the perspective of youth and middle age, old age seems a remote, and, to some, an undesirable period of life. Throughout history, humans have tried to prolong youth and to delay aging. The attempts to discover a substance to rejuvenate the body and mind have driven explorers to far corners of the globe, and have inspired alchemists and scientists to search for ways to restore youth and extend life. Indeed, the discovery of Florida by Ponce de Leon in 1513 was an accident, as he searched for a fountain in Bimini whose waters were rumored to bring back one's youth. Medieval Latin alchemists believed that eating gold could add years to life and spent many years trying to produce a digestible form of gold. In the seventeenth century, a popular belief was that smelling fresh earth each morning could prolong one's youth. The theme of prolonging or restoring youth is evident today in advertisements for skin creams, soaps, vitamins, and certain foods; in the popularity of cosmetic surgery; in books and movies that feature attractive, youthful-looking older characters; and even in medical research that is testing technological methods to replace depleted hormones in older people in an attempt to rejuvenate aging skin and physical and sexual functioning.

All these concerns point to underlying fears of aging. Many of our concerns and fears arise from misconceptions about what happens to our bodies, our minds, our status in society, and our social lives as we reach our seventies, eighties, and beyond. They arise, in part, from negative attitudes toward older people within our own culture. These attitudes are sometimes identified as manifestations of **ageism,** a term that was coined by Robert Butler, the first Director of the National Institute on Aging, to describe stereotypes about old age. As is true for sexism and racism, ageism attributes certain characteristics to all members of a group solely because of a characteristic they share—in this case, their age. In fact, ageism is one prejudice that we are all likely to encounter sooner or later, regardless of our gender, ethnic minority status, social class, or sexual orientation. A frequent result of ageism is discriminatory behavior against the target group (i.e., older persons). For example, some aging advocates have argued that older, experienced workers are encouraged to retire early rather than laying off younger, less experienced workers because of stereotypes about older people's abilities and productivity.

To distinguish the realities of aging from the social stereotypes surrounding this process requires an understanding of the "normal" changes that can be expected in the aging body, in mental and emotional functioning, and in social interactions and status. Aging can then be understood as a phase of growth and development—a universal biological phenomenon. Accordingly, the normal processes due to age alone need to be differentiated from pathological changes or disease. As life expectancy increases, as the older proportion of our population grows, and as more of us can look forward to becoming older ourselves, concerns and questions about the aging process continue to attract widespread public and professional attention.

THE FIELD OF GERONTOLOGY

The growing interest in understanding the process of aging has given rise to the multidisciplinary field of **gerontology,** the study of the biological, psychological, and social aspects of aging. Gerontologists include researchers and practitioners in such diverse fields as biology, medicine, nursing, dentistry, physical and occupational therapy, psychology, psychiatry, sociology, economics, political science, and social work. These individuals are concerned with many aspects of aging, from studying and describing the cellular processes involved, to seeking ways to improve the quality of life for older people. **Geriatrics** is focused on how to prevent or manage the diseases of aging. The field has become a specialty in medicine, nursing, and dentistry, and is receiving more attention with the increase in the number of older people who have long-term health problems.

Gerontologists view aging in terms of four distinct processes, which will be examined throughout this book.

1. *Chronological aging* is the definition of aging on the basis of a person's years from birth. Thus, a 75-year-old is chronologically older than a 45-year-old. Chronological age is not necessarily related to a person's biological or physical age, nor to their psychological or social age, as we will emphasize throughout this book. For example, we may remark that someone "looks younger (or older)" or "acts younger (or older)" than her or his age. This implies that the individual's *biological* or *psychological* or *social* age is incongruent with the *chronological age.*

2. *Biological aging* refers to the physical changes that reduce the efficiency of organ systems, such as the lungs, heart, and circulatory system. A major cause of biological aging is the decline in the number of cell replications as an organism becomes chronologically older. Another factor is the loss of certain types of cells that do not replicate. This type of aging can be determined by measuring the efficiency and functional abilities of an individual's organ systems, as well as physical activity levels. Indeed, some have referred to this as *functional aging* (Hayflick, 1996).

3. *Psychological aging* includes the changes that occur in sensory and perceptual processes, mental functioning (e.g., memory, learning, and intelligence), adaptive capacity, and personality. Thus, an individual who is intellectually active and adapts well to new situations can be considered psychologically young.

4. *Social aging* refers to an individual's changing roles and relationships in the social structure—with family and friends, in both paid and unpaid productive roles, and within organizations such as religious and political groups. As people age chronologically, biologically, and psychologically, their social roles and relationships also alter. The social context, which can vary considerably for different people, determines the meaning of aging for an individual and whether the aging experience will be primarily negative or positive.

Social gerontologists study the impact of changes on both older people and social structures. They also study social attitudes toward aging and the effects of these attitudes on the older population. For example, as a society, we have tended to undervalue older people and to assume that most older adults are less intelligent, unemployable, nonproductive, uninterested in interacting with younger people, forgetful, and asexual—assumptions not supported by facts. As a result, activities open to older people, particularly jobs in fields that require technical skills, have been limited.

With the growth in the number and diversity of older persons, societal myths and stereotypes have been challenged. The public has become increasingly aware of older citizens' strengths and contributions. Accordingly, the status of older people in our society and the way that other groups view them are changing. Contemporary advertising, for example, reflects the changing status of older people from a group that is viewed as weak, ill, and poor, to one perceived as politically and economically powerful, and, therefore, a growing market.

As older people have become more politically active and as advocacy groups have emerged in support of seniors' rights, they have influenced not only public perceptions, but also age-based policies and programs such as Social Security and Medicare. In the past 50 years, organized groups of older people have helped to bring changes in retirement and pension policies, housing options, health and long-term care policy, education, and other services. Such political and attitudinal changes, which can profoundly transform the condition of older people, are also important issues in the study of social gerontology.

Equally significant in this area of study are the social and health problems that continue to affect a large percentage of older people. Even though older adults today are financially better off than they were 50 years ago, almost 11 percent still fall below the U.S. government's official poverty line. Poverty is an even greater problem for women, ethnic minorities, those living alone, and the oldest of the old. Although less than 5 percent of the older population resides in a nursing home at any given time, the number who will require long-term care at some point in their lives is increasing. Growing percentages of older people in the community face chronic diseases that may limit their daily activities. At the same time, however, health and long-term care costs have grown dramatically. In general, older people pay a higher proportion of their income for health and long-term care than they have at any time in the past, and often lack access to publicly supported home and community-based services. Therefore, many gerontologists are also concerned with developing public policy and practice interventions to address these problems.

SOCIAL GERONTOLOGY

The purpose of this book is to introduce you to *social gerontology.* This term was first used by Clark Tibbitts in 1954 to describe the area of gerontology that is concerned with the impact of social and sociocultural conditions on the process of aging and with the social consequences of this process. This field has grown as we have recognized the extent to which aging differs across cultures and societies.

Social gerontologists are interested in how the older population and the varieties of aging experiences both affect and are affected by the social structure. As we will discuss later in this chapter, older people are now the fastest-growing population segment in the United States. This fact has far-reaching social implications for the areas of health and long-term care, workplace, pension and retirement practices, community facilities, and patterns of government spending. Already, it has led to new specialties in health care and long-term care; the growth of specialized services such as retirement housing, assisted living, adult day health programs; and a leisure industry aimed at the older population. Changes in the sociopolitical structure, in turn, affect characteristics of the older population. For example, the greater availability of secondary and higher education, health promotion programs, and employment-based pensions offers hope that future generations of older people will be better educated, healthier, and economically more secure than the current generation.

WHAT IS OLD AGE?

Contrary to the messages on birthday cards, aging does not start at age 40 or 65. Even though we are less conscious of age-related changes in earlier stages of our lives, we are all aging from the moment of birth. Younger stages are generally referred to as *development* or *maturation,* because the in-

dividual develops and matures, both socially and physically, from birth through adolescence. After age 30, additional changes occur that reflect normal declines in all organ systems. This is called *senescence.* Senescence happens gradually throughout the body, ultimately reducing the viability of different bodily systems and increasing their vulnerability to disease. This is the final stage in the development of an organism.

Our place in the social structure also changes throughout our life span. Every society is *age-graded;* that is, it assigns different roles, expectations, opportunities, status, and constraints to people of different ages. For example, there are common social expectations about the appropriate age to attend school, begin work, have children, and retire—even though many people deviate from these expectations, and some of these expectations change over time. To call someone a *toddler, child, young adult,* or *old person* is to imply a full range of social characteristics. As we age, we pass through a sequence of defined stages, each with its own social norms and characteristics. In sum, age is a social construct with social meanings and social implications.

The specific effects of age grading, or age stratification, vary across different cultures and historical time periods. A primitive society, for instance, has very different expectations associated with stages of childhood, adolescence, and old age from our contemporary American cultures. Even within our own culture, those who are old today have different experiences of aging than previous or future groups of older people. The term **cohort** is used to describe groups of people who were born at approximately the same time and therefore share many common experiences. For example, current cohorts of older persons have experienced the Great Depression, World War II, and the Korean War. These experiences have shaped their lives. Its members include large numbers of immigrants who came to the United States in the first third of the twentieth century, and many who have grown up in rural areas. Their average levels of education are lower than those of later generations. Such factors set today's older population apart from other cohorts and must be taken into account in any studies of the aging process.

A DIVERSE POPULATION

Throughout this book, we will refer to the phenomenon of aging and the population of older people. These terms are based, to some extent, on chronological criteria, but, more importantly, on individual differences in social, psychological, and biological functioning. In fact, each of us differs somewhat in the way we define old age. You may know an 80-year-old who seems youthful and a 50-year-old whom you consider old. Older people also define themselves differently. Some individuals, even in their eighties, do not want to associate with "those old people," whereas others readily join age-based organizations and are proud of the years they have lived. There are significant differences among the "young-old" (ages 65 to 74), the "old-old" (ages 75 to 84), and the "oldest-old" (85 and over) (Riley & Riley, 1986). In addition, there is diversity even within these divisions.

Older people vary greatly in their health status, their productive activities, and their family situations. Some are still employed full- or part-time; most are retired. Most are healthy; some are frail, confused, or home-bound. Most still live in a house or apartment; a small percentage are in nursing homes. Some receive large incomes from pensions and investments; many depend primarily on Social Security and have little discretionary income. Most men over age 65 are married, whereas women are more likely to become widowed and live alone as they age. For all these reasons, it is impossible to consider the social aspects of aging without also assessing the impact of individual variables such as physiological changes, health status, psychological well-being, socioeconomic class, gender, and ethnic minority status. Recognizing this, many chapters in this book focus on biological, physiological, health, psychological, gender,

and ethnic characteristics of older persons that influence their social functioning.

It is likewise impossible to define aging only in chronological terms, since chronological age only partially reflects the biological, psychological, and sociological processes that define life stages. Although the terms *elderly* and *older persons* are often used to mean those over 65 years in chronological age, this book is based on the principle that aging is a complex process that involves many different factors and is unique to each individual. Rather than chronological age, the more important distinctions may be between the ability to function independently or not; that is, the ability to perform activities of daily living that require cognitive and physical well-being.

A PERSON-ENVIRONMENT PERSPECTIVE ON SOCIAL GERONTOLOGY

Consistent with the perspective of the interaction of physiological, psychological, and social changes with aging, this textbook will approach topics in social gerontology from a person-environment perspective. A **person-environment perspective** suggests that the environment is not a static backdrop but changes continually as the older person takes from it what he or she needs, controls what can be manipulated, and adjusts to conditions that cannot be changed. Adaptation thus implies a dual process in which the individual adjusts to some characteristics of the social and physical environment (e.g., completing the numerous forms required by Medicare), and brings about changes in others (e.g., lobbying to expand Medicare benefits to cover dental care).

Environmental Press

One useful way to view the dynamic interactions between the person's physical and psychological characteristics with the social and physical environment is the **competence model.** This model was first proposed by Lawton and Nahemow (1973), and examined further by Lawton (1989) and by Parmelee and Lawton (1990). *Environment* in this model, which is shown in Figure 1.1, may refer to the larger society, the community, the neighborhood, or the home. **Environmental press** refers to the demands that social and physical environments make on the individual to adapt, respond, or change. The environmental press model can be approached from a variety of disciplinary perspectives. A concept fundamental to social work, for example, is that of human behavior and the environment, and the need to develop practice and policy interventions that achieve a better fit between the person and his or her social environment. Health care providers are increasingly aware of the necessity to take account of social and physical environmental factors in their assessments of health problems.

Architects and advocates for persons with disabilities are developing ways to make physical environments more accessible for older people. Psychologists are interested in how physical and social environments may be modified to maximize the older person's ability to learn new tasks and perform familiar ones such as driving, taking tests, and self-care. Sociologists study ways that the macro-environment (larger political and economic structures) affects and is affected by an individual's interactions with it. Because the concepts of this model are so basic to understanding the position of older people in our society and to developing ways to improve the quality of their lives, such environmental interactions will be referred to throughout this text.

We encourage the reader to identify ways to apply this model to diverse settings where older

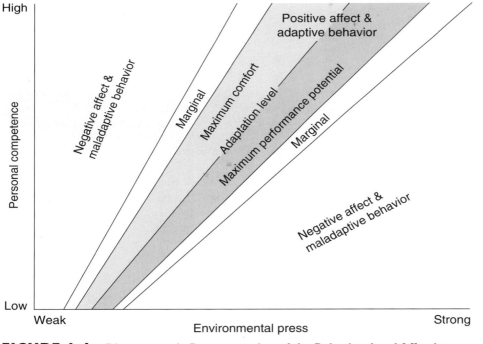

FIGURE 1.1 **Diagrammatic Representation of the Behavioral and Affective Outcomes of Person-Environment Transactions**

SOURCE: M. P. Lawton and L. Nahemow, Ecology and the aging process. In C. Eisdorfer and M. P. Lawton (Eds.), *Psychology of adult development and aging* (Washington, D.C.: American Psychological Association, 1973), p. 661. Copyright 1973 by the American Psychological Association. Reprinted by permission of the author and publisher.

people interact. The environmental press in such settings can range from minimal to quite high. For example, very little environmental press is present in an institutional setting where an individual is not responsible for self-care, such as grooming and housekeeping, and has few resources to stimulate the senses or challenge the mind. Other environments can create a great deal of press, for example, a multigenerational household in which the older person plays a pivotal role. Living in a familiar setting with few visitors generates low levels of environmental press. An increase in the number of people sharing the living arrangement or a move to a new home increases the environmental demands. As the demands change, the individual must adapt to the changes in order to maintain one's sense of competence. Individuals perform at their maximum level when the environmental press slightly exceeds the level at which they adapt. In other words, the environment challenges them to test their limits but does not overwhelm them. If the level of environmental demand becomes too high, the individual experiences excessive stress or overload. When the environmental press is far below the individual's adaptation level, sensory deprivation, boredom, learned helplessness, and dependence on others may result. However, a situation of mild to moderate stress, just below the person's adaptation level, results in maximum comfort. It is important to challenge the individual in this situation as well, to prevent a decline to boredom and inadequate stimulation. In either situation—too much or too little environmental press—the person or the environment must change, if the individual's adaptive capacity is to be restored and quality of life enhanced.

Another concept central to this model is *individual competence*. This is defined by Lawton and Nahemow (1973) as the theoretical upper limit of an individual's abilities to function in the areas of health, social behavior, and cognition. Some of the abilities needed to adapt to environmental press include good health, effective problem solving and learning, skills, job performance, and the ability to manage the basic activities of daily living such as dressing, grooming, and cooking (Parmelee and Lawton, 1990). As suggested by the model in Fig-

ure 1.1, the higher a person's competence, the higher the levels of environmental press that can be tolerated. Thus, an older person with multiple physical disabilities and chronic illnesses has reduced physical competence, thereby limiting the level of social and physical demands with which he or she can cope.

Environmental Interventions

The competence model has numerous implications for identifying interventions to enhance the lives of older individuals. Most services for older people are oriented toward minimizing environmental demands and increasing supports. These services may focus on changing the physical or the social environment, or both. Physical environmental modifications, such as ramps and hand-rails, and community services, such as Meals-on-Wheels and escort vans, are relatively simple ways to reestablish the older person's level of adaptation and to ease the burdens of daily coping. Such arrangements are undoubtedly essential to the well-being of some older people who require supports in the form of environmental adaptations or occasional assistance from family and paid caregivers to enhance their independence. For example, many older people with chronic conditions are able to remain in their own homes because of environmental modifications such as emergency systems that allow them to call for help, vans equipped for wheelchairs, and computers that aid them with communication, and medication reminders. Other examples of both environmental and individual interventions to enhance older people's choices are considered throughout this text.

A fine line exists, however, between minimizing excessive environmental press and creating an unstimulating or "too easy" environment. Well-intentioned families, for example, may do too much for the older person, assuming responsibility for daily activities, so that their older relative no longer has to exert any effort and may no longer feel he or she is a contributing family member. Likewise, professionals and family members may try to shield the older person from experiencing too many changes. For example, they may presume that an older person is too set in her or his ways to adjust to sharing a residence, thereby denying the person the opportunity to learn about and make an independent decision on home-sharing options. Well-intentioned nursing home staff may not challenge residents to perform such daily tasks as getting out of bed or going to the dining hall. Protective efforts such as these can remove necessary levels of environmental press, with the result that the person's social, psychological, and physical levels of functioning may decline. Understimulating conditions, then, can be as negative in their effects on older people as those in which there is excessive environmental press.

ORGANIZATION OF THE TEXT

This book is divided into five parts. Part One is a general introduction to the field of social gerontology and the demographics of an aging society, and includes a brief history of the field, the growth of the older population, a discussion of research methods and designs, and aging in other historical periods and cultures.

Part Two addresses the physiological changes that influence social aging. It begins with a review of normal age-related changes in the body's major organ systems, including changes in the sensory system and their social/environmental effects. It also discusses the chronic diseases that occur most frequently among older people, how these diseases can be managed, factors that influence health care behavior (e.g., when and why older people are likely to seek professional care), and health promotion programs aimed at improving physical, psychological, and social functioning among older people.

In Part Three, we move to the psychological context of aging, including normal and disease-related changes in cognitive functioning (learning, intelligence, and memory), theories of personality development and coping styles, mental health issues of importance to the older population, and the use of mental health services, as well as love, intimacy, and sexuality in the later years.

The social issues of aging are explored in Part Four, beginning with a discussion of current social theories of aging, the importance of family, friends, and neighbors as social supports, and how the array of housing arrangements for older adults affects their social interactions and sense of competence. Issues related to productivity, employment, retirement, and income are next explored, followed by a review of nonpaid productive roles in the community, in education, in religious institutions, and in politics. This part concludes with topics related to death, dying, and widowhood. The last two chapters of Part Four present the challenges and strengths of older ethnic minorities and women.

Part Five goes beyond the individual's social context to address societal perspectives, particularly social, health, and long-term care policy issues of importance to the older population, and contemporary policy debates. The Epilogue focuses on emerging trends in aging and society's responses to future generations or cohorts of older people, especially the aging of the baby boomers.

Each part begins with an introduction to the key issues of aging that are discussed in that section. In order to emphasize the variations in physiological, psychological, social, and societal aspects of aging, vignettes of older people representing these differences are presented. Throughout each chapter, the diversity of the older population and of the aging process itself is highlighted in terms of chronological age, gender, culture, ethnic minority status, and sexual orientation. Where appropriate, the dynamic interaction between older people and their environment is emphasized. How age-related changes are measured and methods for improving measurement in this field are also discussed. Each chapter concludes with a glossary of key terms that were introduced in that chapter.

WHY STUDY AGING?

As you begin this text, you may find it useful to think about your own motivations for learning about older adults and the aging process. You may be in a required course, questioning its relevance, and approaching this text as something you must read to satisfy requirements. Or you may have personal reasons for wishing to learn about aging. You may be concerned about your own age-related changes, wondering whether reduced energy or alterations in physical features are inevitable with age. After all, since middle and old age together encompass a longer time span than any other stage of our lives, it is important that we understand and prepare for these years. Perhaps you are looking forward to the freedom made possible by retirement and the "empty nest." Through increased knowledge about the aging process, you may be hoping to make decisions that can enhance your own positive adaptation to aging and old age. Or perhaps you are interested in assisting aging relatives, friends, and neighbors, wanting to know what can be done to help them maintain their independence, what housing options exist for them, and how you can improve your caregiving abilities.

Learning about aging not only gives us insight into our own interpersonal relationships, self-esteem, competence, and meaningful activities as we grow older; it also helps us comprehend the aging process of our parents, grandparents, clients, patients, and friends. It is important to recognize that change and growth take place throughout the life course, and that the concerns of older people are not distinct from those of the young, but represent a continuation of earlier life periods. Such understanding can improve our effectiveness in communicating with relatives, friends, or professionals. In addition, such knowledge can help change any assumptions we may hold about behavior appropriate to various ages.

Perhaps you wish to work professionally with older people, but are unsure how your interests can fit in with the needs of the older population. In the final chapter of this book, the Epilogue, you will find a discussion of careers in gerontology. If you are already working with older people, you may genuinely enjoy your work, but at the same time be concerned about the social and economic problems facing some older adults and thus feel a responsibility to change these negative social conditions. As a professional or future professional working with older people, you are probably eager to learn more about policy and practice issues that can enhance their quality of life and life satisfaction.

Regardless of your motivations for reading this text, chances are that, like most Americans, you have some misconceptions about older people and the aging process. As products of our youth-oriented society, we have all sensed the pervasiveness of negative attitudes about aging, although our own personal experiences with older people may counter many stereotypes and myths. By studying aging and older people, you will not only become more aware of the older population's competence in many areas, but also be able to differentiate the normal changes that are associated with the aging process from pathological or disease-related changes. Such an understanding may serve to reduce some of your own fears about aging, as well as positively affect your professional and personal interactions with older people. Our challenge as educators and authors is to present you with the facts and the concepts that will give you a more accurate picture of the experience of aging in U.S. society. We also want to convey to you the excitement and importance of learning about the field of aging. We hope that by the time you have completed this text, you will have acquired information that strengthens positive attitudes toward living and working with older people and toward your own experience of aging. First, we will turn to the demographic changes that are resulting in the largest population of people aged 65 and older in history, not just in the United States, but throughout the world.

GROWTH OF THE OLDER POPULATION

As we noted earlier, the single most important factor affecting current interest in the field of gerontology is the growing size of the older population. In 1900, people over 65 accounted for approximately 4 percent of the United States population—less than one in twenty-five. By 1996, 33.9 million, or 12.8 percent of the population, was 65 or older (U.S. Bureau of the Census, 1997). This represents an eleven-fold increase in the older population during this period, compared with a three-fold increase in the population under age 65. During the next 12 years, however, the population over 65 is expected to grow more slowly than it did between 1950 and 1995. After 2010, as the baby boom generation begins to reach old age, the population over 65 will again increase significantly. Thus, by 2030 the population aged 65 and older will increase to 69 million, or more than twice the current number, compared with a 30 percent growth in the total population.

Changes in Life Expectancy

Why have these changes in the older population occurred? Chiefly because people are living longer. In 1900, the average **life expectancy** at birth in the United States (i.e., the average length of time one could expect to live if one were born that year) was 47 years. At that time, there were approximately 772,000 people between the ages of 75 and 84 in the United States, and only 123,000 aged 85 and older. In 1996 there were over 3.8 million in the oldest group. The average life expectancy is now much longer. Females born in 1996 can expect to reach age 79.5, and men, age 72.5. Life expectancy at age 65 is an additional 19.2 years for women and 15.5 years for men (AARP, 1997). About four out of five individuals can now expect to reach age 65, at which point there is a better than 50 percent chance of living past age 80.

According to the Census Bureau, life expectancy at birth is expected to increase from the current 76.1 years to 77.6 in 2005 and to 82.6 in 2050. Sex differences in life expectancy have declined since 1980, when females born that year could expect to live 7.4 years more than men; in 1995, the difference was less than 7 years. Projections by the Census Bureau assume a fairly constant 7-year difference in life expectancy well into the future. Therefore, females born in 2005 are ex-

pected to reach age 81; males in that birth cohort will reach age 74. Even in the year 2050, however, male life expectancy will be less than 80 years, whereas women will achieve 84.3 years (U.S. Bureau of the Census, 1996b). Of course, these projections do not take into account potentially new diseases that could differentially increase mortality risks for men and women. For example, if AIDS continues to be a fatal disease that infects younger men more than women, there could be a much greater sex differential in life expectancy. On the other hand, death rates due to hypertension and heart disease have already started to decline because of lifestyle changes. Since both conditions are somewhat more likely to affect men, these factors may narrow the sex differential and increase life expectancy even more, for both men and women. Nevertheless, the trend illustrated in Figure 1.2, where women outnumber men at every age after 55, will continue well into the twenty-first century.

Most of the gains in life expectancy have occurred in the younger ages. For example, during the period from 1900 to 1993, the average life expectancy at birth increased from 47 years to 76 years. In contrast, gains in life expectancy beyond age 65 during this same period have been relatively modest, from about 12.3 to 17.3 years between 1900 and 1993. Gender differences are particularly striking; older men added 3.3 years and women 6.8 years to their life expectancy from 1900 to 1993. The gains that have occurred in the early years of life are mostly attributable to the eradication in this century of many diseases that caused high infant and childhood mortality. On the other hand, we may find significant increases in survival beyond age 65 in future cohorts, when heart disease and cancer become more chronic and less fatal diseases in adulthood. Already there has been an acceleration of years gained. Between 1900 and 1960 only 2.4 years were gained beyond age 65, while the gain since 1960 has been 3.0 years.

The reasons for this shift have to do with advances in medicine. A hundred years ago, adults generally died from acute diseases, with influenza

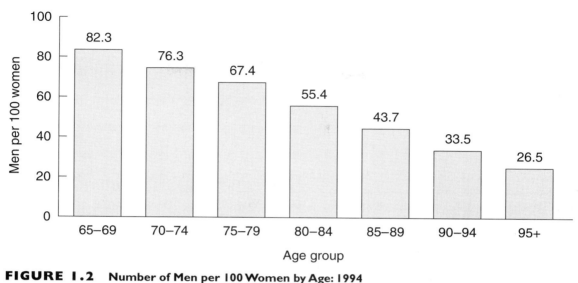

FIGURE 1.2　Number of Men per 100 Women by Age: 1994
SOURCE: U.S. Bureau of the Census, 1994.

and pneumonia the principal killers. Few people survived these diseases long enough to need care for chronic or long-term conditions. Today, death from acute diseases is rare. Maternal, infant, and early childhood death rates have also declined considerably. The result is a growing number of people who survive to old age, often with one or more health problems requiring long-term care. The evidence from epidemiological studies suggests that older Americans are receiving better health care than their counterparts in other developed countries. As a result, white Americans age 80 have a greater life expectancy (women = 9.1 years, men = 7 years) than 80-year-olds in Sweden, Japan, France, and England, even though life expectancy at birth is higher in Sweden and Japan (Manton and Vaupel, 1995).

Maximum Life Span

It is important to distinguish life expectancy from **maximum life span.** While life expectancy is a probability estimate based on environmental conditions such as disease and health care, as described previously, maximum life span is the maximum number of years a given species could expect to live if environmental hazards were eliminated. There appears to be a maximum biologically determined life span for cells that comprise the organism, so that even with the elimination of all diseases, we could not expect to live much beyond 120 years. For these reasons, more and more persons will expect to live longer, but the maximum number of years they can expect to live will not be increased in the foreseeable future unless, of course, some extraordinary and unanticipated biological discoveries occur (Fries, 1980; Fries and Crapo, 1981).

Perhaps the most important goal of health planners and practitioners should be to approach a rectangular survival curve, i.e., the "ideal curve." That is, as seen in the survival curve in Figure 1.3, developments in medicine, public hygiene, and health have already increased the percentage of people surviving into the later years. The ideal situation is one where all people would survive to the maximum life span, creating a "rectangular curve." The survival curves of developed countries serve as a model for developing countries; that is, about half of all babies born today in developed

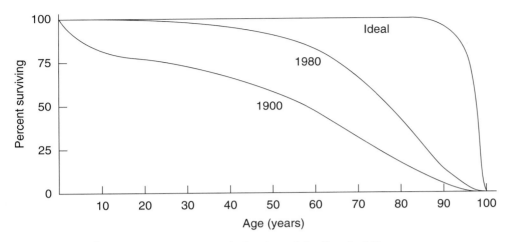

FIGURE 1.3   **Increasing Rectangularization of the Survival Curve**
SOURCE: Adapted from L. Hayflick, The cell biology of human aging. *Scientific American*, 1980, 242, p. 60, by permission of the publisher.

countries will reach age 80, or two-thirds of the maximum life span of 120 years (Hayflick, 1996). We are approaching this ideal curve, but it will not be achieved until the diseases of youth and middle age—including cancer, heart disease, diabetes, and kidney diseases—can be totally prevented or at least managed as chronic conditions.

THE OLDEST-OLD

Ages 85 and Older

The population aged 85 and older, also referred to as the "oldest-old," has grown more rapidly than any other age group in our country. In 1996, of the 33.9 million persons aged 65 and over in the United States, 11.4 million or 33 percent were age 75 to 84, while 3.8 million or almost 11 percent were age 85 and over (AARP, 1997). Since World War II, mortality rates in adulthood have declined significantly, resulting in an unprecedented number of people who are reaching advanced old age and who are most likely to require health and social services (Suzman, Willis, and Manton, 1992).

For these reasons, the population of "oldest-old" Americans has increased by a factor of 23, compared to a twelve-fold growth in the 75–84 age group and an eight-fold increase in the population aged 65–74. Those over 85 have increased by 300 percent from 1960 to 1995. Their numbers are expected to reach 4.3 million in 2000, and about 8.5 million in 2030. Projections vary depending on predictions about changes in chronic disease morbidity and mortality rates (U.S. Bureau of the Census, 1996b).

This tremendous growth in the oldest-old will take place *before* the influx of baby boomers reaches old age, because this latter group will not begin to turn age 85 until after 2030 (i.e., the baby boom generation is generally accepted as those born between 1946 and 1964). By the year 2050, when the survivors of this generation are age 85 and older, they are expected to number 19 million, or 5 percent of the total U.S. population (U.S. Bureau of the Census, 1996b). This represents a 500 percent increase within 60 years. The impact of such a surge in the oldest-old on the demand for health services, especially hospitals and long-term care settings, will be dramatic.

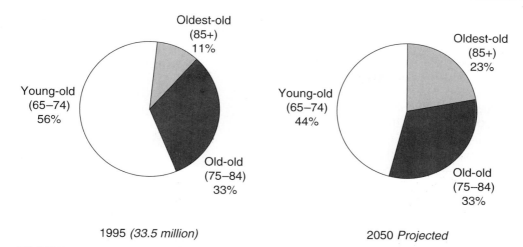

FIGURE 1.4   **Percentage of Older Americans by Age Group**
SOURCE: U.S. Bureau of the Census, 1996b.

It is also important to consider the distribution of selected age groups now and in the future. As noted previously, the young-old (ages 65–74) currently represent 56 percent of the older population; those over 85 make up almost 11 percent of this population. In contrast, the corresponding proportions in 2050 are projected to be 44 percent young-old and 23 percent oldest-old. (See Figure 1.4).

Who are the oldest-old? Not surprisingly, the great majority are women (70 percent). Their educational level is lower than for their younger counterparts aged 65 to 74 (8.6 years vs. 12.1 in 1990), and most are widowed, divorced, or never married (77.2 percent vs. 62 percent). It is not surprising, therefore, that the mean personal income for the oldest-old is lower than for other older adults, and that a high proportion live below or near poverty. The current cohort of oldest-old includes 15 percent who are foreign born. Many immigrated from Italy, Poland, Russia, and other European countries in the early 1900s, while others are later immigrants from China, Japan, the Philippines, and Mexico. The usual problems of aging may be intensified for these non-native speakers of English as they try to communicate with health care providers. Misdiagnosis of physical, psychological, and cognitive disorders may occur in such cases.

Because they are more likely to have multiple health problems that often result in physical frailty, and because up to 50 percent of the "oldest-old" may have some form of cognitive impairment, this group is disproportionately represented in the institutionalized population (nursing homes, group homes, and hospitals) (Carr, Goate, Phil, and Morris, 1997). Almost 25 percent live in an institutional setting, and they make up more than 50 percent of the population of nursing homes. However, the rate of institutionalization among African Americans aged 85 and older is only about half this rate (12 percent). The oldest-old blacks are far more likely to be living with relatives other than a spouse (40 percent). Very few of the oldest-old (regardless of ethnic minority status) live with a spouse, compared with 50 percent of all people over age 65 (U.S. Administration on Aging, 1996). Even among those living in the community, functional health is more impaired in the oldest-old. However, as we will see in later chapters, future cohorts of the oldest-old are likely to be healthier and more active than today's population.

Centenarians

Projections by the Census Bureau (1992) also suggest a substantial increase in the population of "centenarians," people aged 100 or older. In 1994 it was estimated that almost 50,000 Americans were aged 100 or older. These numbers are expected to grow to 75,000 by the year 2000, and to 477,000 by 2030. Even with this twelve-fold increase, however, the population over 100 will still represent less than 1 percent of the U.S. population in 2030. Baby boomers are expected to survive to age 100 at rates never before achieved; one in 26 will live to be 100 by 2025, compared with one in 500 at the turn of the century.

As more and more Americans become centenarians, there is growing interest in their genetics and lifestyle that may have influenced their longevity. The work of Perls (1995) in the New England Centenarian Study points to genetic factors that determine how well the older person copes with disease. As shown in Figure 1.5, this model suggests that the oldest-old are hardy because they have a higher threshold for disease and show slower rates of disease progression than their peers who develop chronic diseases at a younger age and die earlier. Perls illustrates this

A growing number of multigenerational families are headed by centenarians.

hypothesis with the case of a 103-year-old man who displayed few symptoms of Alzheimer's disease; however, at autopsy this man's brain had a

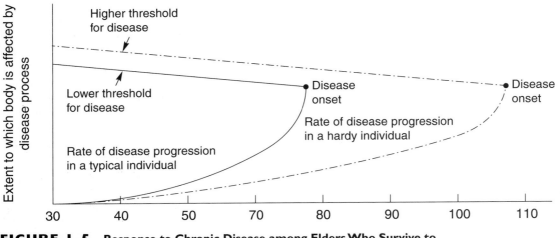

FIGURE 1.5   **Response to Chronic Disease among Elders Who Survive to Age 100 vs Non-Survivors**
SOURCE: Adapted from Perls, 1995.

high level of neurofibrillary tangles that are a hallmark of this disease.

Older men who survive to age 90, in particular, represent the hardiest segment of their birth cohort. Between ages 65 and 89, women score higher on tests of cognitive function. However, after age 90, men perform far better on these tests. Even at age 80, 44 percent of men who had survived to this age were found to be robust and independent, compared with 28 percent of women. Contrary to the belief prevalent in gerontology only a few years ago that dementia is a concomitant of advanced age, it appears that as many as 30 percent of centenarians have no memory problems, 20 percent have some memory problems, and 50 percent have serious problems (Suzman, Willis, and Manton, 1992). Further evidence for the robustness of centenarians comes from the New England study; of the 79 people aged 100 and older in this study, all lived independently into their early 90s and, on average, took only one medication. Centenarians appear to be healthy for a longer period than their shorter-lived peers, but death generally occurs quickly rather than lingering. Indeed, a recent study of medical expenditures for the last two years of life found the average cost to be $22,600 for those who died at age 70, versus $8300 for those who live past 100 (Lubitz and Riley, 1993).

Population Pyramids

The rise in longevity is partly responsible for an unusually rapid rise in the *median age* of the U.S. population—from 28 in 1970 to 35 in 1997—meaning that half the population was older than 35 and half younger in 1997. From an historical perspective, a 5-year increase in the median age over a 20-year period is a noteworthy demographic event (Social Security Administration, 1990). The other key factors contributing to this rise include a dramatic decline in the birth rate after the mid-1960s, high birth rates in the periods from 1890 to 1915 and just after World War II (these "baby boomers" are now all older than the median), and the large number of immigrants who arrived here before the 1920s.

As stated earlier in this chapter, the "baby boom" generation (currently aged 34 to 52) will dominate the age distribution in the United States well into the next century. In fact, by the early part of the twenty-first century, between 2010 and 2030, they will form the "senior boom" and swell the ranks of the 65-plus generation to the point that one in five Americans will be old. The projected growth in the older population will raise the median age of the U.S. population from 35 in 1996 to 36 by the year 2000 and to age 37 by the year 2010. If current fertility and immigration levels remain stable, the only age groups to experience significant growth in the next century will be those older than 55 (U.S. Bureau of the Census, 1996b).

One of the most dramatic examples of the changing age distribution of the American population is the shift in the proportion of older adults in relation to the proportion of young persons, as illustrated in Figure 1.6. In 1900, when approximately 4 percent of the population was age 65 and over, young persons aged 0 to 17 years made up 40 percent of the population. By 1994, reduced birthrates in the 1970s and 1980s had resulted in a decrease of young persons to 25 percent of the population. The U.S. Census Bureau predicts that, by 2030, the proportion of young and old persons will be almost equal, with those aged 0 to 17 forming 22 percent of the population and older adults forming 21 percent. Indeed, in 1990 the proportion of people under age 14 was the same as those aged 60 or older (U.S. Bureau of the Census, 1993c). After the year 2030, if current trends continue, the death rate will be greater than the birth rate.

One way of illustrating the changing proportions of young and old persons in the population is the *population pyramid*. Figure 1.7 contrasts the population pyramid for 1975 and the projected pyramids for the years 2010, 2030, and 2050. Each horizontal bar in these pyramids represents a 10-year *birth cohort* (i.e., people born within the same 10-year period). By comparing these bars, we can determine the relative proportion of each birth cohort. As you can see in the first graph, the distribution of the population in 1975 had already moved

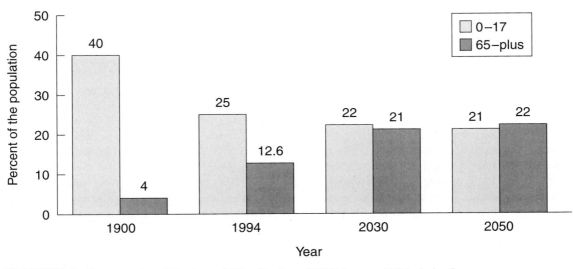

FIGURE 1.6   **Actual and Projected Distribution of Children and Elderly in the Population: 1900–2050**

SOURCE: G. Spencer, U.S. Bureau of the Census, Projections of the population of the United States, by age, sex, and race: 1983–2080. *Current Population Reports,* Series P-25-1104, U.S. Government Printing Office, Washington, DC, 1993.

from a true pyramid to one with a bulge in the 10–30 year-old group; this represents the large group of baby boomers. This pyramid grows more column-like over the years, as shown in the other three graphs. These changes reflect the aging of the baby boomers (note the "pig in a python" phenomenon as this group moves up the age ladder), combined with declining birth rates and reduced death rates for older cohorts.

DEPENDENCY RATIOS

One aspect of the changing age distribution in our population that has raised public concern is the so-called *dependency ratio,* or "elderly support ratio." The way this ratio has generally been used is to indicate the relationship between the proportion of the population that is employed (defined as "productive" members of society) and the proportion that is not in the work force (and is thus viewed as "dependent"). This rough estimate is obtained by comparing the proportion of the population aged 18 to 64 (the working years) to the proportion un-

der age 18 (yielding the childhood dependency ratio) and over 65 (yielding the old-age dependency ratio). This ratio has increased steadily, such that there appear to be proportionately fewer employed persons to support older persons today. In 1910, the ratio was less than .10 (i.e., 10 working people per older person), compared with .21 in 1995 (i.e., 5 working people per older person). Assuming that the lower birth rate will continue, this trend will continue into the early twenty-first century, as the baby boom cohort reaches old age. By the year 2020, a ratio of .28 (or fewer than 4 working people per retired person) is expected (U.S. Administration on Aging, 1997). These changes since 1960, along with projections through 2050, are illustrated in Figure 1.8.

There are problems with such a crude measure, however. It is flawed by the fact that many of the younger and older persons are actually in the labor force and not dependent, while many people of labor-force age may not be employed. A number of analysts have criticized the use of dependency ratios that do not take account of the labor-force participation rates of different groups;

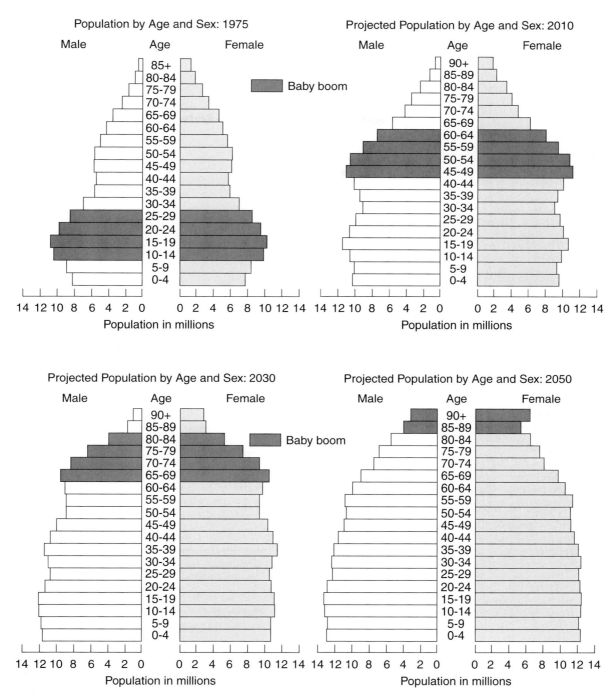

FIGURE 1.7 **Projected Population Figures**

SOURCES: U.S. Bureau of the Census, Preliminary Estimates of the Population of the United States by Age, Sex, and Race: 1970–1981. *Current Population Reports,* Series P-25, No. 917. U.S. Government Printing Office, Washington, DC, 1982.   Jennifer C. Day, U.S. Bureau of the Census, Population Projections of the United States by Age, Sex, Race, and Hispanic Origin: 1993–2050. *Current Population Reports,* P-25-1104. U.S. Government Printing Office, Washington, DC, 1993 (middle series projections).

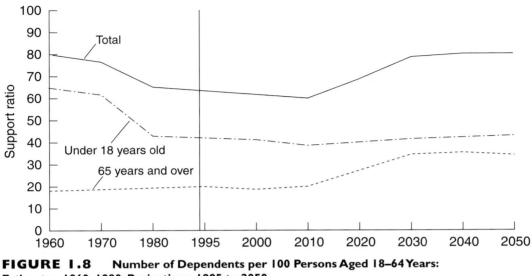

FIGURE 1.8   Number of Dependents per 100 Persons Aged 18–64 Years: Estimates, 1960–1980; Projections, 1995 to 2050
SOURCE: U.S. Bureau of the Census, Current Population Reports, Series P-25, No. 1130, 1996.

for example, the labor-force participation rates of women aged 16 and older are expected to increase into the twenty-first century, while those of men are projected to remain steady. When these variations are taken into account, studies have found that although the total dependency ratio increases as the population ages, even in the year 2050 it will remain lower than recent historical levels. Moreover, despite population aging, those under the age of 16 will continue to constitute the largest "dependent" group well into the twenty-first century. Therefore, we need to be cautious when we hear policy makers predict "burdens" on the younger population and blame rising costs of public pension programs primarily on the changing dependency ratio (Quinn, 1996).

POPULATION TRENDS

In addition to the proportional growth of the older population in general, other demographic trends are of interest to gerontologists. These include statistics related to the social, ethnic, gender, and geographic distribution of older populations. In this section, we will review some of these trends, be-

ginning with the demographics of ethnic minorities in the United States.

Ethnic Minorities

Today, ethnic minorities comprise 15 percent of the population over age 65; they include a smaller proportion of older people and a larger proportion of younger adults than the white population. In 1995, 14 percent of whites, but only 8 percent of African Americans and 5.6 percent of Hispanics were age 65 and over. The difference results primarily from the higher rates of fertility and higher mortality rates among the nonwhite population under age 65 than among the white population under 65. However, beginning in the early part of the twenty-first century, the proportion of older persons is expected to increase at a *higher* rate for the nonwhite population than for the white population, partly because of the large proportion of children in these groups, who, unlike their parents and especially their grandparents, are expected to reach old age. Figures 1.9 and 1.10 illustrate these differential patterns of growth for whites, African Americans, Hispanics, and other races. A more detailed description of ethnic minority populations is provided in Chapter 13.

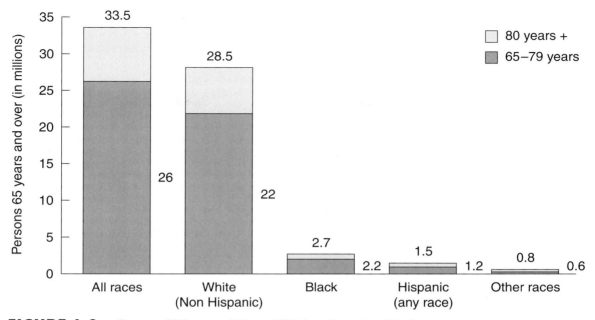

FIGURE 1.9   **Persons 65 Years and Over: 1995 (numbers in million).**
SOURCE: U.S. Bureau of the Census, modified and actual age, sex, race, and Hispanic origin Data, 1996.

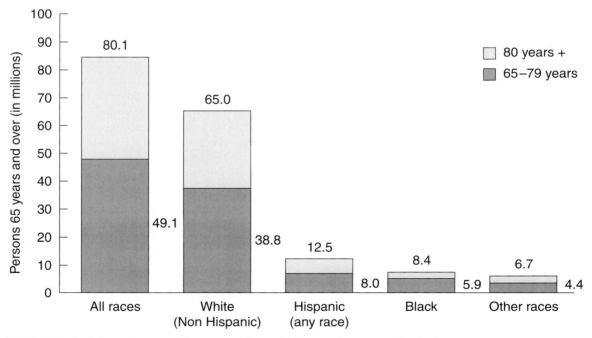

FIGURE 1.10   **Persons 65 Years and Over: 2050 (numbers in million). Hispanics are also included in racial group totals.**
SOURCE: U.S. Bureau of the Census, Middle series projections (1993).

Geographic Distribution

Demographic information on the location of older populations is important for a variety of reasons. For example, the differing needs of rural and urban older people may affect research designs as well as local government policy decisions. Statistical information on older populations state-to-state is necessary in planning for the distribution of federal funds. Comparison of demographic patterns in different nations and cultures may provide insights into various aspects of the aging process. The following are some of the most salient statistics on the geographic distribution of older adults today. The implications of these changes will be considered in later chapters, including the impact of these differences on living arrangements, social, health and long-term care policies, and cross-cultural issues.

Although older adults live in every state and region of the United States, they are not evenly distributed. More live in metropolitan areas; in 1994, 74 percent lived in these communities. About 30 percent of the older population lives in cities, 44 percent in suburbs, and 26 percent in rural areas. Despite their low distribution in rural communities, older adults make up a greater percentage of rural populations than in the general population (i.e., 15 percent of all rural residents vs. 12.8 percent of the total U.S. population) (U.S. Bureau of the Census, 1993c).

The Northeast continues to be the region with the oldest population; those over 65 represent 13.7 percent of its population, compared to 10.9 percent of western states, and 12.8 percent nationally (U.S. Bureau of the Census, 1997). In 1996, about 50 percent of all persons 65 and older lived in nine states: California (with more than 3 million older residents), Florida, New York (over 2 million in each state), Pennsylvania, Texas, Ohio, Illinois, Michigan, and New Jersey (1 million each). This does not necessarily mean that all these states have a higher proportion of older Americans than the national average, but their absolute numbers are large. Some states have a much higher proportion of residents over 65 than the national average. For

example, in 1996 they represented 18.5 percent of the population in Florida, almost 16 percent in Pennsylvania and Rhode Island, and almost 15 percent in West Virginia, Iowa, Arkansas, North and South Dakota, and Connecticut. This contrasts with just 5.2 percent in Alaska and 8.8 percent in Utah (U.S. Bureau of the Census, 1997). It is therefore not surprising that Florida has the highest median age in the United States (37.6 years), and Utah the lowest (26.8 years). In some cases, such as that of Florida, migration of retired persons to the state explains the increase, whereas in others, such as West Virginia and South Dakota, migration of younger persons out of the state leaves a greater proportion of older people. More than 20 percent of some rural counties in these states are over age 65. Other states may simply reflect the generalized "graying of America." These regional differences are expected to continue into the next century, when the median age for the Northeast is projected at 37.6 in the year 2000, versus 36 nationally. Florida will continue to have the highest median age (41.2), and Utah the lowest (27.0). Utah will also have the distinction of being the only state in the year 2000 that will have more than 50 percent of its population under age 30, due to its continued high birth rate.

Residential relocation is relatively rare for older people in the United States. In a typical year, this population accounts for less than 5 percent of all people who move (Naifeh, 1993). The movement that occurs tends to be within the same region of the country and the same types of environment; that is, people over age 65 generally move from one metropolitan area to another or from one rural community to another. These trends and their implications for well-being in the later years will be described further in Chapter 10.

Educational and Economic Status

In 1960, less than 20 percent of the population over age 65 had finished high school. By 1995, 64 percent of the new cohort aged 65 and older had completed high school, with only slight gender differences. However, racial and generational differences are striking. Among whites who were age 65 and older in 1993, the median level of education was 12.5 years, compared with 10 years for African Americans and 8 years for Hispanics in this age group (U.S. Bureau of the Census, 1996a). Because of historical patterns of discrimination in educational opportunities, a disproportionate ratio of older minorities today have less than a high school education. Thus, 63 percent of African Americans and 70 percent of Hispanics in this age group did not complete high school, compared with only 33 percent of white elders (AARP, 1997). Because educational level is so closely associated with economic well-being, these ethnic differences have a major impact on poverty levels of older members of different ethnic minority groups. Other implications of these gaps in educational attainment will be discussed further in Chapter 13.

Not surprisingly, people aged 65 to 69 are more educated today than the old-old (ages 75 and older). Two-thirds of the former (67 percent) have at least a high school education, compared with 52 percent of their older peers. For this reason, the median educational level today is 12.1 years for the young-old, 10.5 years for the old-old, and 8.6 years for the oldest-old (age 85+). Women in all older cohorts of whites and African Americans (but not Hispanics) are more likely than men to have completed high school. The situation shifts for college education. Because of cultural values in previous generations, fewer white women age 65 and older have college degrees than do white men. Among African Americans the pattern is mixed; for those 70 and older, more black women than men have completed college while for the 65–69-year-olds, fewer have completed college (U.S. Bureau of the Census, 1996a). It is noteworthy that an even greater proportion of people over 25 today (75 percent) have at least a high school education. This suggests that future generations of older people will be better educated, many with college degrees, than their grandparents are today. The implications of this shift for political activism,

employment, and societal expectations about productive roles will be explored in the Epilogue.

In 1995 only 16 percent of men and 8 percent of women aged 65 and older were in the labor force. This represents a steady decline in labor-force participation, even with the removal of mandatory retirement from most jobs in 1986. However, part-time work is an increasingly attractive option, with over 50 percent of retired workers (49 percent of men and 63 percent of women) employed in a part-time or temporary capacity (AARP, 1997; U.S. Bureau of Labor, 1994).

Social Security remains the major source of income for old age, not earnings from employment or private pensions. In fact, increases in Social Security benefits along with annual cost-of-living adjustments are primary factors underlying the improved economic status of the older population. Currently, almost 11 percent of older people subsist on incomes below the poverty level, compared to 35 percent in the late 1950s, and equal to the poverty rate of Americans aged 18–64 (AARP, 1997). However, this improved economic status masks the growing rates of poverty among older women, ethnic minorities, the oldest-old, and those living alone, as well as the high percentage who live just above the poverty line. For example, in 1994 the median income for a white married couple aged 65 and older was $25,603, compared with $10,280 for white unmarried females, $6,905 for black unmarried females, and $6,418 for Hispanic unmarried females in this age group. Furthermore, 7.6 percent of older Americans are classified as "near-poor" with income levels between poverty and 125 percent of the poverty level (AARP, 1997; Social Security Administration, 1996). The current and projected economic status of the older population is discussed in detail in Chapter 11.

WORLDWIDE TRENDS

All world regions are experiencing an increase in the absolute and relative size of their older populations. The number of persons age 65 or older in the world is expected to increase from 357 million in 1990 to 761 million in 2025. This will result in a world population in which one out of every seven people will be 65 years of age or older by the year 2025 (U.S. Bureau of the Census, 1993b).

There are substantial differences in the current numbers and expected growth of the older population between the industrialized and developing countries. Currently 55 percent of older adults live in developing countries, projected to increase to 65 percent by 2020. For example, in 1994, 13.7 percent of the population of Western Europe was aged 65 or older; almost 3 percent were 80 or older. The older population represented 18 percent in Sweden; 5 percent were 80 or older. In contrast, Sub-Saharan Africa and South Asia each counted only 3 percent of their population aged 65 or over. The median age of Western Europe in 1990 was 37, compared with a median age of 23.5 worldwide, 32 in the United States, and about 20 in Latin America. In Africa, with continued high fertility and high mortality rates, the median age will continue to be around 20 in the year 2020 (U.S. Bureau of the Census, 1993b).

However, the less developed regions of the world expect to show a nearly fivefold increase in their oldest population, from 3.8 percent in 1975 to 17 percent in 2075. An even greater rise in the proportion of the old-old (ages 75–84) and oldest-old (85+) is expected in these countries, from the current 0.5 percent to 3.5 percent in 2075. Reasons for this increase in developing countries include improved sanitation, medical care, immunizations, and better nutrition. By the year 2020, only 35 percent of the world's older adults are expected to reside in industrialized nations, while 65 percent will live in developing countries (U.S. Bureau of the Census, 1993b). It is important to note, however, that the less developed regions of the world are currently coping with the tremendous impact of high fertility rates. Even with the continued high infant mortality rates in these countries, children under 15 represent 37 percent of the population in less developed regions, compared with 22 percent in more developed regions.

Today the fertility rate of industrial nations is less than 2.0 children per woman, or less than the rate necessary to maintain a steady population level.* In fact, the birthrate in Japan is now the lowest of any country at 1.57. In 1990, for example, Japan experienced 11.1 live births per 1000 population, compared with 15.7 per 1000 in the United States and much higher rates in less developed countries such as Mexico (29 per 1000) and Egypt (40.7 per 1000). For this reason, Japan is experiencing the most rapid rate of population aging in the world; 7 percent of its population was 65 or older in 1970, and increased to 15 percent in 1996. This group will make up 26 percent of Japan's population by 2020. Japan also has the highest life expectancy at birth; more than 86 years for girls and slightly more than 80 for boys born in 1996.

Combined with the improved life expectancy in industrial nations (which has increased by 6 years for men and 8.5 years for women since 1953), this has resulted in a dramatic increase in the older population. The rate has grown more rapidly over the past 20 years, with a significant impact on the availability of workers to support retired persons. That is, the dependency ratio for older retired persons will drop from 3.5 workers to support one retiree in 1990 to about 2 in 2030 in the industrialized countries of Europe. In Japan, the pyramid will become even more rectangular, with a decline from 4 to 2 workers in the next 30 years. In contrast, the ratio in the United States will drop from the current 5 workers to 3 during this same period. These changes will place tremendous demands on the social security systems, government-subsidized health care, and pension programs of these nations. They may need to develop incentives for later retirement, which may be difficult, considering the trend toward early retirement in most industrial nations. It may also be necessary for developed countries to permit more immigration of young workers

*For purposes of this discussion, "industrial nations" include the United States, Canada, the United Kingdom, France, Germany, Japan, and Australia.

from the developing world and provide training in the technology required by these countries. However, this is a controversial proposal for countries where immigrants often are not easily assimilated because of languages, religions, and cultures divergent from those of the host country. For example, in Singapore a more radical approach to caring for a growing older population has emerged. In 1997 the government opened a special court where older persons can bring legal claims against their children for not providing assistance in their old age.

IMPACT OF DEMOGRAPHIC TRENDS IN THE UNITED STATES

As will be discussed later in this book, the growth of older populations has wide-ranging implications. The impact of demographic changes in the United States is most striking when we look at patterns of federal spending. The growth in numbers and proportions of older people has already placed pressures on our health, long-term care, and social service systems, as discussed in Chapters 15 and 16.

The increase in life expectancy also has brought with it a change in expectations about the quality of life in late adulthood. Increasingly in our society, those facing retirement anticipate living 20 to 30 years in relatively good health, with secure and adequate retirement incomes. When these expectations are not met, because of catastrophic medical costs, widowhood, or a retirement income eroded by inflation, older adults may not be prepared to manage a change in their lifestyles. For other segments of the older population, particularly women and ethnic minorities, old age may represent a continuation of a lifetime of poverty or near-poverty. Fortunately, for most older people, the problems associated with old age, particularly chronic illness and the attendant costs, are forestalled until their seventies and eighties. As noted, however, the particularly rapid growth in numbers of frail elders, the majority of whom are women,

may severely strain the health and income systems designed to provide resources in old age.

LONGEVITY IN HEALTH OR DISEASE?

Future cohorts of older people may be healthier and more independent well into their eighties and nineties. A strong argument has been put forth to this effect by Fries (1980, 1990), who has suggested that more people will achieve the maximum life span in future years because of healthier lifestyles and better health care during their youth and middle years. Furthermore, Fries argues that future cohorts will have fewer debilitating illnesses and will, in fact, experience a phenomenon he labelled **compression of morbidity** (i.e., experiencing only a few years of major illness in very old age). These older adults of the future may therefore expect to die a "natural death," or death due to the natural wearing out of all organ systems by approximately age 100. If this process does occur, it will have a significant impact both on the type of health and long-term care services needed by future generations of older people and on their ability to experience productive aging. Long-term care needs may be reduced, with more subacute care facilities and short-term home health services being required.

Indeed, there is some evidence from a review of large national health surveys that the older population today is generally healthier than in previous cohorts. An analysis of two large longitudinal health surveys—the Longitudinal Study on Aging and the National Health Interview Survey (NHIS)—from 1982 through 1993 for respondents who were age 70 and older in each year, reveals that rates of disability are declining or stabilizing. At the same time, recovery from acute disabilities (e.g., due to falls) appears to be improving. This may be due to more aggressive rehabilitation efforts for older adults in recent years (Crimmins, Saito, and Reynolds, 1997), and is consistent with the findings of another analysis of national health surveys. In a comparison of responses to the National Long-term Care Survey from 1982 through 1994, there was a 3.6 percent decline in disability rates, especially among the young-old (Manton, Corder, and Stallard, 1997). This means that future generations of the oldest-old may have lower health care expenditures and less reliance on long-term care services.

The concept of **active versus dependent life expectancy** (Katz et al., 1983) may be useful in this context. These authors distinguish between merely living a long life and living a healthy old age. This can also be conceptualized as adding life to years, not just years to life. Instead of death, they define the endpoint of "active" life expectancy as the loss of independence or the need to rely on others for most activities of daily living. For example, a 65-year-old woman today has approximately 18.6 years remaining, 12.6 in active life expectancy, 6 in dependency. In contrast, a 65-year-old man can look forward to living 14.4 more years, 2.4 of these in a dependent state. Thus, life expectancy has increased beyond age 65, but about a quarter of the years lived will be in a dependent state (Manton and Stallard, 1991). Not surprisingly, differences in life conditions of older persons with inadequate income and those above the median income in the United States have led to the conclusion that there is a major discrepancy of 1 to 2.5 years in active life expectancy between the poor and nonpoor. Therefore, as Kane, Ouslander, and Abrass (1989) state, there may be a growing bimodal distribution of older people remaining healthier and free of disease (as predicted by Fries), and another, probably larger distribution of older adults surviving diseases that would have been fatal years ago, but living with "battle scars." This latter group may be the segment of the population that is distorting projections for compressed morbidity; as we have seen in the reviews of NHIS findings, this latter group also appears to be increasing in size. This is probably the segment of the older population that will require long-term care in the coming century.

HOW AGING AND OLDER ADULTS ARE STUDIED

You are undoubtedly aware that more researchers are studying older people and the process of aging now than at any time in the past. Some of the concerns that have motivated this increasing professional interest in the field have probably influenced your own decision to study gerontology. In this section we will turn to the question of how the older population is studied: What are the particular challenges of social gerontological research, and how are they addressed? Methods of conducting research in this field will be described. The net effect of this information is to give you a basic orientation to the field of aging, how it has developed, and methods of studying the older population.

Development of the Field

Although the scientific study of social gerontology is relatively recent, it has its roots in biological studies of the aging processes and in the psychology of human development. Biologists have long explored the reasons for aging in living organisms. Several key publications and research studies can be identified as milestones in the history of the field.

One of the first textbooks on aging, *The History of Life and Death*, was written in the thirteenth century by Roger Bacon. With great foresight, Bacon suggested that life expectancy could be extended if health practices, such as personal and public hygiene, were improved. The first scientist to explain aging as a developmental process, rather than as stagnation or deterioration, was a nineteenth-century Belgian mathematician–statistician named Adolph Quetelet. His interest in age and creative achievement preceded the study of these issues by social scientists by 100 years. His training in the field of statistics also led him to consider the problems of **cross-sectional research;** that is, the collection of data on people of different ages at one time, instead of **longitudinal research,** the study of the same person over a period of months or years. These problems will be examined in greater detail in the next section of this chapter.

One of the first laboratory studies of aging was undertaken in the 1920s by the Russian physiologist Ivan Pavlov. Pavlov is best known for his research with animals, which has provided the foundation for stimulus-response theories of behavior. Recognizing that the ability of older animals to learn and distinguish a response differed from that of younger animals, Pavlov explored the reasons for these differences in the brains of these animals. The work of Raymond Pearl and colleagues in the 1920s established the insect species *Drosophila* as an ideal animal model for studying biological aging and longevity. During this era, in 1922, American psychologist G. Stanley Hall published one of the first books on the social-psychological aspects of aging in the United States. Titled *Senescence, the Last Half of Life*, it remains a landmark text in social gerontology because it provided the experimental framework for examining changes in cognitive processes and social and personality functions.

Historical Forces of the Late Nineteenth and Early Twentieth Centuries

Two important forces led to the expansion of research in social gerontology in the late nineteenth and early twentieth centuries: the growth of the population over age 65 (as described earlier), and the emergence of retirement policies. Changes in policies toward older adults were first evident in many European countries (e.g., Germany) where age-based social services and health insurance programs were developed. In the United States, these changes did not occur until the 1930s. At the turn of the century, the focus on economic growth and the immediate problems of establishing workers' rights and child welfare laws took precedence over interest in the welfare of older people. The prevailing belief in this country had been that families should be responsible for their aging members. However, the Great Depression of the 1930s

brought to policy makers the stark realization that families struck by unemployment and homelessness could not be responsible for their elders. The older segments of society suffered a disproportionate share of the economic blight of the Depression. New concern for the special needs of the aging population was exemplified by the Social Security system, established in 1935 to help people maintain a minimal level of economic security after retirement. Early work in social gerontology dealt largely with social and economic problems of aging. For example, E. V. Cowdry's *Problems of Ageing*, published in 1939, focused on society's treatment of older people and on their particular needs. It seems amazing to us today that the second edition of this book, published in 1942, contained all the research knowledge available on aging at that time!

FORMAL DEVELOPMENT OF THE FIELD

As society grew more aware of issues facing the older population, the formal study of aging emerged in the 1940s. In 1945, the Gerontological Society of America (GSA) was founded, bringing together the small group of researchers and practitioners who were interested in gerontology and geriatrics at that time. Today, this organization numbers its membership between 6000 and 7000, and it is the major professional association for people in diverse disciplines in the field of aging. The GSA's mission is "to add life to years, not just years to life." This emphasizes the goal of most gerontologists, to enhance quality of life in the later years, not just to extend life. Gerontology became a division of the American Psychological Association in 1945 and, later, of the American Sociological Association.

The *Journal of Gerontology,* which the GSA began publishing in 1946, served as the first vehicle for transmitting new knowledge in this growing field. In 1988 it became two journals, reflecting the growth of this field. Today numerous others are devoted to the study of aging and to the concerns of those who work with older people. An indicator of the knowledge explosion in the field is that the literature on aging published between 1950 and 1960 equalled that of the previous 115 years (Birren and Clayton, 1975). An effort to compile a bibliography of biomedical and social research from 1954 to 1974 produced 50,000 titles (Woodruff, 1975). Today, the burgeoning periodicals in diverse disciplines focused on gerontology have resulted in an exponential growth of research publications in this field. Gerontology has become increasingly more interdisciplinary; that is, specialists in diverse areas of the basic, clinical, behavioral, and social sciences are working together on research projects focused on specific aspects of aging (Birren, 1996).

Major Research Centers Founded

Research in gerontology took on growing significance after these developments, and an interest in the social factors associated with aging grew in the late 1950s and early 1960s. In 1946, a national gerontology research center, headed by the late Nathan Shock, a leader in geriatric medicine, was established at Baltimore City Hospital by the National Institutes of Health. This federally funded research center undertook several studies of physiological aspects of aging, using a cross-sectional approach.

In 1958, Dr. Shock and his colleagues began a longitudinal study of physiological changes in healthy, middle-aged and older men living in the community, by testing them every two years on numerous physiological parameters. They later started to examine the cognitive, personality, and social-psychological characteristics of these men. Much later, in 1978, older women were included in their samples. Known as the **Baltimore Longitudinal Studies,** these assessments of changes associated with healthy aging are still continuing, now under the direction of the National Institute on Aging. More than 2200 volunteers, men and women, aged 20 to 90, have participated or are currently participating in this ongoing study of the basic processes of aging. On average, these volun-

teers remain in the study for 13 years. More recently, ethnic minorities have been recruited as subjects; 13 percent are African Americans, mostly in the younger cohorts. The results of this ongoing research effort continue to provide valuable information about normal age-related changes in physiological and psychological functions. As more ethnic minorities in this longitudinal study grow older, they will provide valuable insights into the process of normal, age-related changes versus disease in these populations.

Concurrently with the Baltimore Longitudinal Studies, several university-based centers were developed to study the aging process and the needs of older adults. One of the first, the Duke University Center on Aging, began in 1955 by one of the pioneers in gerontology, Ewald Busse. This center focused initially on physiological aging and on the mental health of older people, but has also examined many social aspects of aging. The University of Chicago, under the direction of Robert Havighurst, developed the first research center devoted exclusively to the social aspects of aging. The Kansas City studies of adult development, discussed in Chapters 6 and 8, represent the first major social-psychological studies of adult development, and were conducted by researchers from the Chicago center. Research and training centers on aging have since evolved at many other universities, generally stimulated by government sponsorship of gerontological research through the National Institute on Aging (established in 1975), the National Institute of Mental Health (which established its center for studies of the mental health of the aging in 1976), and the Administration on Aging (established in 1965).

RESEARCH METHODS

Before moving on to an examination of the issues and areas of special concern to social gerontologists, let us first consider the ways in which such information about the aging process is gathered. The topic of research methodologies in gerontology may seem an advanced one to introduce in a basic text, but in fact, it is essential to understanding the meaning and validity of information presented throughout this book.

The study of aging presents particular conceptual and methodological difficulties. A major one is how research is designed and data interpreted regarding age changes. A point that complicates research in aging and also produces some misleading interpretations of data is how to distinguish *age changes* from *age differences*. This differentiation is necessary if we are to understand the process of aging and the conditions under which age differences occur. If we wish to determine what changes or effects are experienced as an individual moves from middle age to old age and to advanced old age, we must examine the same individual over a period of years, or at least months. In order to understand age changes, longitudinal research is necessary; that is, the repeated measurement of the same person over a specified period of time.

Unfortunately, the time and cost of such studies prevent many researchers from undertaking longitudinal research. Instead, much of the research in this field focuses on age differences, by comparing people of different chronological ages at the same measurement period. These studies, cross-sectional in nature, are the most common ones in gerontology.

Many older adults participate in research that could benefit others.

The unique problems inherent in how gerontological research is designed and how data are interpreted are evident in the following question: Given that aging in humans is a complex process that proceeds quite differently among individuals in varied geographic, cultural, and historic settings, and that it takes place over a time span as long as 100 to 120 years, how does one study it? Obviously, scientists cannot follow successive generations—or even a single generation of subjects—throughout their life span. Nor can they be expected to address the entire range of variables that affect aging—including lifestyle, social class, cultural beliefs, public policies, and so on—in a single study.

The Age/Period/Cohort Problem

The problem in each case is that of distinguishing *age differences* (ways that one generation differs from another) from *age changes* (ways that people normally change over time). This has been referred to as the "age/period/cohort" problem. (The word *cohort,* you will recall, refers to those people born at roughly the same time. *Period* refers to the effects of the specific historical period involved.) The concept of cohort is an important one in gerontology because historical events differentiate one cohort from another in attitudes and behaviors. Those people in the same cohort are likely to be more similar to each other because of comparable social forces acting on them during a given era.

Cross-Sectional Studies

As noted earlier, the most common approach to studying aging is cross-sectional; that is, researchers compare a number of subjects of different ages on the same characteristics in order to determine age-related differences. One reason that cross-sectional studies are frequently used is that, compared to other designs, data can be readily gathered. Some examples might include a comparison of the lung capacity of men aged 30 with those who are aged 40, 50, 60, 70, and 80, or a study comparing church attendance by American adults under age 65 with those over age 65. The average differences among different age groups in each study might suggest conclusions about the changes that come with age.

The danger with such cross-sectional studies is that these differences might not be due to the process of aging, but rather to particular cultural and historical conditions that shaped each group of subjects being studied. For example, a higher rate of church attendance among today's older adults than among younger adults probably reflects a change in social attitudes during this century toward attending church, as opposed to an increased need for spiritual and religious life as one grows older.

Even in studies of biological factors, such as lung capacity, there may be many intervening variables that threaten the validity of comparative results. In this case, they include the effects of exercise, smoking, and other lifestyle factors, genetic inheritance, and exposure to pollution (this, in turn, might be a product of work environments and social class) on relevant outcome variables.

The major limitation of cross-sectional studies has been when differences among younger and older respondents were erroneously attributed to growing old; for example, some researchers have found that the older the respondent, the lower his or her score on intelligence tests. As a result, cognitive abilities have been misinterpreted as declining with age. In fact, such differences may be due to the lower educational levels and higher test anxiety of this cohort of older compared to younger adults, not to age. This is an example of *confounding*, or a joint effect of two variables on an outcome of interest. In this case, age effects are confounded by the impact of cohort differences. Because many issues in social gerontology center on distinguishing age from cohort effects, a number of research designs have emerged that attempt to do this. They include "longitudinal" and "sequential" designs.

Longitudinal Studies: Design and Limitations

Longitudinal designs permit inferences about *age changes*. They eliminate cohort effects by studying

TABLE 1.1   Alternative Research Designs in Aging

Cohort Born in	TIME OF MEASUREMENT			
	1970	1980	1990	2000
1920	A_1	A_2		
1930		B_1	B_2	
1940		C_1	C_2	C_3
1950				D_4

Cross-sectional: Cohorts A, B, and C are measured in 1980. *Longitudinal:* Cohort A is measured in 1970 and 1980; or Cohort B is measured in 1980 and 1990; or Cohort C is measured in 1980, 1990, and 2000. *Cohort-sequential:* Cohort A is measured in 1970 and 1980; Cohort B is measured in 1980 and 1990. *Time-sequential:* Cohorts B and C are measured in 1980; Cohorts C and D are measured in 2000. *Cross-sequential:* Cohorts B and C are both measured in 1980 and 1990.

SOURCE: Adapted from K. W. Schaie, (Ed.), *Longitudinal studies of adult psychological development* (New York: Guilford Press, 1983).

the same people over time. Each row in Table 1.1 represents a separate longitudinal study in which a given cohort (e.g., A, B, or C) is measured once every 10 years. Despite the advantages of longitudinal designs over the cross-sectional approach, it still has limitations. First, the longitudinal method does not allow a distinction between age and time of testing. For example, if a sample of 55-year-old workers had been interviewed regarding retirement policies in 1975, before mandatory retirement was changed to age 70, and again in 1995, long after mandatory retirement was eliminated, it would be difficult to determine whether the changes found in their attitudes toward retirement came about as a result of their increased age and proximity to retirement, or as a result of the modifications in retirement laws during this period. Longitudinal designs cannot separate the effects of events extraneous to the study that influence people's responses in a particular measurement period.

Another problem with longitudinal studies is the potential for practice effects. This problem occurs in studies that administer aptitude or knowledge tests, where repeated measurement with the same test improves the test-taker's performance because of familiarity or practice. For example, a psychologist who is interested in age-related changes in intelligence could expect to obtain improvements in people's scores if the same test is administered several times, with a brief interval (e.g., less than one year) between tests. In such cases, it is difficult to relate the changes to maturation unless the tests can be varied or parallel forms of the same tests can be used.

Longitudinal studies also present the problem of *attrition*, or dropout. Individuals in experimental studies and respondents in surveys that are administered repeatedly may drop out for many reasons—death, illness, loss of interest, or frustration with poor performance. To the extent that people who drop out are not different from the original sample in terms of demographic characteristics, health status, and intelligence, the researcher can still generalize from the results obtained with the remaining sample. However, more often it is the case that dropouts differ significantly from those who stay until the end. As we shall see in Chapter 5, those who drop out of longitudinal studies tend to be in poorer health, score lower on intelligence tests, and are more socially isolated. In contrast, those who remain are the more educated, healthy, successful, and motivated older participants.

This is known as the problem of *selective dropout*. While many researchers have pointed to the potential bias introduced by selective dropout, others have suggested that the results of such longitudinal data provide a positive developmental image about aging (Cooney, Schaie, and Willis, 1988; Schaie, 1996).

Sequential Designs

Some alternative research designs have emerged in response to the problems of cross-sectional and longitudinal methods. One is the category of **sequential research designs** (Schaie, 1967, 1973, 1977, 1983). These include the cohort-sequential, time-sequential, and cross-sequential methods, which are illustrated in Tables 1.1 and 1.2.

A *cohort-sequential* design is an extension of the longitudinal design, whereby two or more cohorts are followed for a period of time, so that measurements are taken of different age groups at different points in time. Thus, for example, an investigator may wish to compare changing attitudes toward federal policies among the cohort born in 1920 and the cohort born in 1930 and follow each one for 10 years, from 1970 to 1980 for the first cohort, and from 1980 to 1990 for the second. This approach is useful for many social gerontological studies in which age and cohort must be distinguished. However, it still does not separate

TABLE 1.2 **Potential Confounding Effects in Developmental Studies**

	CONFOUNDING EFFECT		
Design	Age × Cohort Confounded	Age × Time of Measurement Confounded	Cohort × Time of Measurement Confounded
Cross-sectional	Yes	No	No
Longitudinal	No	Yes	No
Cohort-sequential	No	No	Yes
Time-sequential	Yes	No	No
Cross-sequential	No	Yes	No

SOURCE: Adapted from M. F. Elias, P. K. Elias, and J. W. Elias, *Basic processes in adult developmental psychology* (St. Louis: C. V. Mosby, 1977).

the effects of cohort from historical effects or time of measurement. As a result, historical events that occurred just before one cohort entered a study but later than another cohort entered may influence each cohort's attitude scores differently.

The *time-sequential* design is useful for distinguishing between age and time of measurement or historical factors. It can be used to determine if changes obtained are due to aging or to historical factors. The researcher using this design would compare two or more cross-sectional samples at two or more measurement periods. For example, a group of 70-year-olds and a group of 60-year-olds might be compared in 1970; the latter could be compared with a new group of 60-year-olds in 1980. Time-sequential designs do not prevent the confounding of age and cohort effects, but it is acceptable to use this method where one would not expect age differences to be confused with cohort differences.

The third technique proposed by Schaie (1983) is the *cross-sequential* design, which combines cross-sectional and longitudinal designs. Thus, for example, the researcher could compare people who were age 40 and 50 in 1980, and again in 1990 when they were age 50 and 60 respectively. This would permit the assessment of cohort and historical factors, because the same cohorts are being compared at two different times, with one providing information on changes from age 40 to 50, and the other representing changes from age 50 to 60. This approach is an improvement over both the traditional cross-sectional and longitudinal designs, but it still confounds age and time of measurement effects. These three sequential designs are becoming more widely used by gerontological researchers, especially in studies of intelligence. Table 1.2 summarizes potential confounding effects in each of these methods.

Despite the growth of new research methods, much of social gerontology is based on cross-sectional studies. For this reason, it is important to read carefully the description of a study and its results in order to make accurate inferences about age changes as opposed to age differences, and to

determine whether the differences found between groups of different ages are due to cohort effects or to the true effects of aging.

Selecting Older Persons as Research Subjects

Accurate sampling can be difficult with older populations. If the sample is not representative, the results are of questionable validity. However, comprehensive lists of older people are not readily available. Membership lists from organizations such as the American Association of Retired Persons tend to overrepresent those who are healthy and financially secure. Studies in institutions, such as nursing homes and adult day centers, tend to overrepresent those with chronic impairments. Reaching older ethnic minorities through organizational lists can be especially difficult.

The problem of selective survival affects all samples of older people. Over time, the birth cohort loses members, so that those who remain are not necessarily representative of all in the original group. Those who survive, for example, probably were healthiest at birth, and maintained their good health throughout their lives—all variables that tend to be associated with higher socioeconomic status.

Even when an adequate sample is located, older respondents may vary in their memories or attention spans; such variations can interfere with conducting interviews or tests. Ethical issues and unique difficulties arise in interviewing frail elders. Currently there are no ethical guidelines specifically aimed at research with older adults. The issue of informed consent becomes meaningless when dealing with a confused or a severely medically compromised older person. In such cases, family members or guardians must take an active role in judging the risks and benefits of research for frail older persons. An additional problem is that studies of the old-old may be influenced by *terminal drop,* a decline in some tests of intelligence shortly before death (Botwinick, 1984; White and Cunningham, 1988). Since death becomes increasingly likely with age, terminal drop will manifest as a gradual decline in performance test scores with age in cross-sectional designs. In longitudinal studies, this problem may result in an overestimation of performance abilities in the later years because those who survive are likely to represent the physically and cognitively most capable older individual (Schaie, 1996). This problem will be explored further in Chapter 5.

Further refinement of research methodologies is a challenging task for social gerontologists. As progress is made in this area, the quality of data with which to study aging will continually improve.

SUMMARY AND IMPLICATIONS

A primary reason for the growing interest in gerontology is the increase in the population over age 65. This growth results from a reduction in infant and child mortality and improved treatment of acute diseases of childhood and adulthood, which in turn increases the proportion of people living to age 65 and beyond. In the United States, average life expectancy from birth has increased from 47 years in 1900 to 78 in 1995, with women continuing to outlive men. The growth in the population over age 85 has been most dramatic, reflecting major achievements in disease prevention and health care since the turn of the century. More recently, there has been increased attention on centenarians. Those who live to be 100 and older may have greater tolerance to stress and therefore fewer chronic illnesses than their peers who die younger. Ethnic minority groups in the United States and developing nations have had a smaller growth in the proportion of people living beyond age 65 than whites and industrialized nations do, but population projections anticipate a much higher rate of growth for these groups by the early part of the twenty-first century.

The growth in the numbers and proportions of older people, especially the oldest-old, will require that both public and private policies affecting employment and retirement, health and long-term care, and social services be modified to meet the needs and improve the quality of life of those who are living longer. Fundamental issues will have to be resolved about who will receive what societal resources and what will be the roles of the private and public sectors for sharing responsibilities of elder care.

Gerontology has grown as a field of study since early philosophers and scientists first explored the reasons for changes experienced with advancing age. Roger Bacon in the thirteenth century, Adolph Quetelet in the early nineteenth century, Botkin in the late nineteenth century, and Ivan Pavlov and G. Stanley Hall in the early twentieth century made pioneering contributions to this field. During the early 1900s, in Europe and the United States, the impact of an increasing aging population on social and health resources began to be felt. Social gerontological research has expanded since the 1940s, paralleling the rapid growth of the older population and its needs.

The growing older population and associated social concerns have stimulated great interest in gerontological research. However, existing research methodologies are limited in their ability to distinguish the process of aging per se from cohort, time, and measurement effects. Cross-sectional research designs are most often used in this field, but these can provide information only on age differences, not on age changes. Longitudinal designs are necessary for understanding age changes, but they suffer from the possibility of subject attrition and the effects of measuring the same individual numerous times. Newer methods in social gerontology, known as cohort-sequential, time-sequential, and cross-sequential designs, test multiple cohorts or age groups over time. They also are limited by possible confounding effects, but represent considerable improvement over traditional research designs.

Because research methods in gerontology have improved, today there is a better understanding of many aspects of aging. Research findings to date provide the empirical background for the theories and topics to be covered in the remaining chapters. Despite the recent explosion of knowledge in gerontology, there are many gaps in what is known about older people and the aging process. Throughout the text, we will call attention to areas in which additional research is needed.

GLOSSARY

active versus dependent life expectancy   a way of describing expected length of life, the term *active* denoting a manner of living which is relatively healthy and independent in contrast to being *dependent* on help from others

ageism   attitudes, beliefs, and conceptions of the nature and characteristics of older persons which are prejudicial, distorting their actual characteristics, abilities, etc.

Baltimore Longitudinal Studies of Aging   a federally funded longitudinal study that has examined physiological, cognitive, and personality changes in healthy, middle-aged and older men since 1958, and in women since 1978

cohort   a group of people of the same generation sharing a statistical trait such as age, ethnicity, or socioeconomic status (for example, all African American women between the ages of 60 and 65 in 1999)

competence model   a conception or description of the way persons perform, focusing on their abilities vis-á-vis the demands of the environment

compression of morbidity   given a certain length of life, this term refers to relatively long periods of healthy, active, high quality existence and relatively short periods of illness and dependency in the last few years of life

cross-sectional research   research that examines or compares characteristics of people at a given point in time and attempts to identify factors associated with contrasting characteristics of different groupings of people

environmental press   features of the social, technological, natural environment that place demands on people

geriatrics   clinical study and treatment of older people and the diseases that affect them

gerontology   the field of study that focuses on understanding the biological, psychological, social, and political factors that influence older people's lives

life expectancy   the average length of time persons, defined by age, sex, ethnic group, and socioeconomic status in a given society, are expected to live

longitudinal research   research that follows the same individual over time, to measure change in specific variables

maximum life span   biologically programmed maximum number of years that each species can expect to live

person-environment (P-E) perspective   a model for understanding the behavior of people based on the idea that persons are affected by personal characteristics, such as health, attitudes, and beliefs, as they interact with and are affected by the characteristics of the cultural, social, political, and economic environment

sequential research designs   research designs that combine features of cross-sectional and longitudinal research designs to overcome some of the problems encountered in using those designs

REFERENCES

American Association of Retired Persons (AARP). *A profile of older Americans: 1997*. Washington, DC, 1997.

Birren, J. E. History of gerontology. In J. E. Birren (Ed.), *Encyclopedia of gerontology*, Vol. 1. San Diego: Academic Press, 1996.

Birren, J. E., and Clayton, V. History of gerontology. In D. S. Woodruff and J. E. Birren (Eds.), *Aging: Scientific perspectives and social issues*. New York: Van Nostrand, 1975.

Botwinick, J. *Cognitive processes in maturity and old age* (3d ed.). New York: Springer, 1984.

Carr, D. B., Goate, A., Phil, D., and Morris, J. C. Current concepts in the pathogenesis of Alzheimer's disease. *American Journal of Medicine*, 1997, *103*, 3S–10S.

Cooney, T. M., Schaie, K. W., and Willis, S. L. The relationship between prior functioning on cognitive and personality dimensions and subject attrition in longitudinal research. *Journals of Gerontology*, 1988, *43*, P12–17.

Crimmins, E. M., Saito, Y., and Reynolds, S. L. Further evidence on the prevalence and incidence of disability among older Americans from two sources: The LSOA and the NHIS. *Journals of Gerontology: Social Sciences*, 1997, *52B*, S59–S71.

Fries, J. F. Aging, natural death, and the compression of morbidity. *New England Journal of Medicine*, 1980, *303*, 130–135.

Fries, J. F. The compression of morbidity: Near or far? *Milbank Quarterly,* 1990, *67,* 208–232.

Fries, J. F., and Crapo, L. M. *Vitality and aging.* San Francisco: W. H. Freeman, 1981.

Hayflick, L. *How and why we age* (2nd ed.). NY: Ballantine Books, 1996.

Kane, R. L., Ouslander, J. G., and Abrass, I. B. *Essentials of clinical geriatrics,* (2nd ed.). New York: McGraw Hill, 1989.

Katz, S., Branch, L. G., Branson, M. H., Papsidero, J. A., Beck, J. C., and Greer, D. S. Active life expectancy. *New England Journal of Medicine,* 1983, *309,* 1218–1224.

Lawton, M. P. Behavior-relevant ecological factors. In K. W. Schaie and C. Scholar (Eds.). *Social structure and aging: Psychological processes.* Hillsdale, NJ: Erlbaum, 1989.

Lawton, M. P., and Nahemow, L. Ecology and the aging process. In C. Eisdorfer and M. P. Lawton (Eds.), *Pychology of adult development and aging.* Washington, DC: American Psychological Association, 1973, 619–674.

Lubitz, J. D., and Riley, G. F. Trends in Medicare payments in the last year of life. *New England Journal of Medicine,* 1993, *328,* 1092–1096.

Manton, K. G., Corder, L., and Stallard, E. Chronic disability trends in elderly U.S. populations: 1982–1994. *Proceedings of the National Academy of Sciences,* 1997, *94,* 2593–2598.

Manton, K. G., and Stallard, E. Cross-sectional estimates of active life expectancy for the U.S. elderly and oldest-old populations. *Journals of Gerontology,* 1991, *46,* S170–182.

Manton, K. G., and Vaupel, J. W. Survival after the age of 80 in the United States, Sweden, France, England, and Japan. *New England Journal of Medicine,* 1995, *333,* 1232–1235.

Naifeh, M. L. *Housing of the elderly: 1991.* Current Housing Reports, series 123/93–1, 1993.

Parmelee, P. A., and Lawton, M. P. The design of special environments for the aged. In J. E. Birren and K. W. Schaie (Eds.), *Handbook of the psychology of aging* (3rd ed.). San Diego: Academic Press, 1990.

Perls, T. T. The oldest old. *Scientific American,* 1995, 70–75.

Quinn, J. *Entitlements and the federal budget: Securing our future.* Washington, DC: National Academy on Aging, 1996.

Riley, M. W., and Riley, J. Longevity and social structure: The potential of the added years. In A. Pifer and L. Bronte (Eds.), *Our aging society: Paradox and promise.* New York: W.W. Norton, 1986.

Schaie, K. W. Age changes and age differences. *The Gerontologist,* 1967, *7,* 128–132.

Schaie, K. W. *Intellectual development in adulthood.* Cambridge: Cambridge University Press, 1996.

Schaie, K. W. (Ed.), *Longitudinal studies of adult psychological development.* New York: Guilford Press, 1983.

Schaie, K. W. Methodological problems in descriptive developmental research on adulthood and aging. In J. R. Nesselroade and H. W. Reese (Eds.), *Lifespan developmental psychology: Methodological issues.* New York: Academic Press, 1973.

Schaie, K. W. Quasi-experimental research designs in the psychology of aging. In J. E. Birren and K. W. Schaie (Eds.), *Handbook of the psychology of aging.* New York: Van Nostrand Reinhold, 1977.

Social Security Administration, Office of Research and Statistics. *Income of the Population 5 and Older, 1994.* SSA Publications, No. 13–11871, January 1996.

Social Security Administration, U.S. Department of Health and Human Services. *Social Security bulletin: Annual statistical supplement.* Washington, DC: U.S. Government Printing Office, 1990.

Suzman, R. M., Willis, D. P., and Manton, K. G. (Eds.), *The oldest old.* New York: Oxford University Press, 1992.

U.S. Adminstration on Aging. National Aging Information Center, *Aging in the twenty-first century.* Washington, DC: 1996.

U.S. Administration on Aging Web Page, http://www.aoa.dhhs.gov/aoa/stats/96pop/percentxstate.html October 1997.

U.S. Bureau of the Census. American housing survey for the United States in 1991. *Current Housing Reports,* Series H150/91, 1993a.

U.S. Bureau of the Census. An Aging World II. *International Population Reports,* Series P. 95, No. 92–3, 1993b.

U.S. Bureau of the Census. Educational Attainment in the U.S.: March 1995. *Current Population Reports,* P. 20, No. 489. Washington, DC: U.S. Government Printing Office, 1996a.

U.S. Bureau of the Census. Growth of America's oldest-old population. *Profiles of America's elderly.* U.S. Department of Commerce, 1992.

U.S. Bureau of the Census. Population projections of the U.S., by age, sex, race, and Hispanic origin data: 1993 to 2050. *Current Population Reports.* Series 1104, U.S. Department of Commerce, 1993c.

U.S. Bureau of the Census. Population projections of the U.S., by age, sex, race, and Hispanic origin data: 1995 to 2050. *Current Population Reports,* P. 25, No. 1130. Washington, DC: U.S. Government Printing Office, 1996b.

U.S. Bureau of the Census Web Page, http://www.census.gov/ October 1997.

U.S. Bureau of Labor Statistics. *Employment and earnings,* January 1994.

White, N., and Cunningham, W. R. Is terminal drop pervasive or specific? *Journals of Gerontology,* 1988, *44,* S141–144.

Woodruff, D. Introduction: Multidisciplinary perspectives of aging. In D. Woodruff and J. Birren (Eds.), *Aging: Scientific perspectives and social issues.* New York: Van Nostrand, 1975.

2

HISTORICAL AND CROSS-CULTURAL ISSUES IN AGING

The experience of aging is not the same today as it was in earlier historical periods. The social and economic roles of older persons, their expectations of the social system, as well as what society expects of them, are in many ways profoundly different today from previous generations. Until relatively recently, only a minority of people lived long enough to be considered old. As the number of older people has grown and as social values have changed, the authority and power of older adults in society have also shifted.

The experience of aging differs cross-culturally as well as historically. That is, in addition to historical changes, there are significant cultural variations that affect the social position of older persons. Perhaps the greatest differences in the status of older adults are between traditional societies and those of the modern Western world, with its rapidly changing values and norms. Examining the different ways that other societies, both historical and contemporary, have dealt with issues affecting their elders can shed light on the process of aging in our society. The emergence of "comparative sociocultural gerontology" or an "anthropology of

aging" has served to refute some of the myths of the "good old days" presumed to exist in historical times and in contemporary nonindustrial societies. It begins to differentiate what aspects of aging are universal or biological as opposed to which factors are largely shaped by the sociocultural system (Sokolovsky, 1997). Understanding how aging in contemporary American society differs from that experienced elsewhere, and which factors are socioculturally determined, can also suggest strategies for developing better environments in which to grow old.

This chapter briefly examines the extent to which older people were valued in stable, preliterate, or primitive societies and in some other nonwestern cultures. Changes in the social roles of older persons, society's expectations of them, and their expectations of society are considered. In addition, contrasting perspectives are reviewed regarding the impact of modernization on the relationship between older persons and the larger society. These influences are examined first historically and then cross-culturally. Within the constraints of this one chapter, we can only glance at a few other cultures. For a more complete view, we urge you to turn to the expanding literature on the anthropology of aging (Fry, 1996; Sokolovsky, 1997). While this chapter explores aging cross-culturally and historically, Chapter 13 focuses on the cultural diversity represented by older ethnic minorities within contemporary American society.

OLD AGE HISTORICALLY

Old Age in Ancient Cultures

Although our knowledge of aging in prehistoric and primitive societies is limited, we know that people of advanced age were rare, with most dying before the age of 35. Nevertheless, there were always a few people perceived to be old, although they were probably chronologically relatively young, since maturity and death came quickly in the lives of people struggling to survive in harsh environments. Those few elders were treated with respect, in a manner that reflected a sense of sacred obligation. During ceremonial occasions, elders were seated in positions of high honor and served as the clan's memory. The belief that an older person was a mediator between this world and the next gave added prestige to elders by conferring on them the role of witch-doctors or priests.

Even though positive attitudes toward the young-old were widespread, nonsupportive or death-hastening behavior was shown toward those who survived beyond an "intact" stage of life. This stage of old-old age was often referred to as the "sleeping period." No longer able to contribute to the common welfare and look after themselves, older people were then viewed as useless, "overaged," or "already dead," and were sometimes treated brutally. Those who outlived their usefulness were a heavy burden in societies that existed close to the edge of subsistence, particularly those in harsh climates with little agriculture, or with no system of **social stratification** (Barker, 1997; Glascock, 1997) In some rural areas of ancient Japan, for example, older people were carried into the mountains and left there to die. It was not unusual for aged Eskimos to walk off into the snow when famine and disease placed great burdens on the tribe. This practice of **geronticide** or **senecide**—the deliberate destruction of older community members—was viewed as functional and, for many traditional societies, often performed with great reverence or ceremony. In a minority of primitive tribes, the frail were killed outright; in most, they were abandoned, neglected, or encouraged to commit suicide, and the burial place was converted into some sort of shrine. Ritual sacrifice was used to kill the oldest members perceived to be a burden among the Ojibwa Indians of Lake Winnipeg and the Siriono of the Bolivian rain forest. Consistent with the coexistence of positive attitudes toward the old along with their nonsupportive treatment, geronticide in many societies often occurred under the older person's direction and by a close relative, usually a son. Examples of geronticide, abandonment, and forsaking support to the oldest-old have been reported in remote cultures even in the twentieth century (Glascock, 1997).

Old Age in Greek and Roman Cultures

In Greek and Roman classical cultures, 80 percent of the population perished before reaching the stage of life that we now consider to be middle-age. Nevertheless, our chronological conception of age, with *old* defined as age 65 and over, began during this period. Age implied power in the ancient cities, which were ruled by councils of elders who derived their authority from their years. Within the family, the eldest male's authority was nearly absolute, and the young were dependent on the old by custom and by law. However, only the elite members of society, not the peasants, benefited from the respect accorded age by the community.

Some idea of the changing status of older people in ancient Greek society can be obtained by analyzing how old and young were depicted in Greek tragedy. In her book, *Time in Greek Tragedy,* de Romilly (1968) points to an evolution of views about age from Aeschylus in the late sixth and early fifth centuries B.C., to Euripides in the mid- to late fifth century B.C. For Aeschylus, age brought with it wisdom, especially about justice and prudence. Although he refers to the destructive influences of age, particularly loss of physical strength, Aeschylus insists that such physical decline has no impact on the older person's mind or spirit. In contrast, Sophocles' tragedies, which were written during the middle of the fifth century, depict old age as distasteful, a time of decline in physical and mental functioning. For Sophocles, youth is the only period of life of true happiness. Later, in Euripides' plays, older people are both wise and weak. Older characters of Euripides long for eternal youth; old age is described as miserable, bitter, and painful. The shift from Aeschylus' admiration of old age to the exaltation of youth and denigration of old age by Sophocles and Euripides may be a reflection of the growth of democracy in fifth-century Greece (and, consequently, a growing belief in social equality) as well as the heroism of young men in the wars of that era.

This coincided with the Classical period, when beauty, youth, and strength were idealized in the visual arts. Greek mythology also depicts the old as tyrannical and wicked, the ultimate enemy in many myths. The gift of immortality was cherished only if it meant rejuvenation or eternal youth. Greek and later Roman mythology contrasted the eternal youthfulness of the gods with the gradual deterioration of mortals. In the myth of Eos and Tithonus, Eos (or Aurora), the goddess of dawn, fell in love with Tithonus, a mortal. She prevailed on Zeus to grant him immortality but forgot to ask that he remain eternally young like her. She left him when he became very old and frail, and eventually turned him into a grasshopper. Presumably this was a better fate for the ancient Greeks and Romans than remaining a feeble old man.

During the Hellenistic era (third and second centuries B.C.), the old regained political power; their increased prestige was reflected by more flattering depictions of elders in art and mythology. The Roman world continued this tradition of greater authority vested in old men; older women were far less powerful than men in both Roman and Greek society (Minois, 1989).

Old Age in Medieval Europe

Little is known about the role of older people during the medieval period, except that life expectancy was even shorter than in the Greek and Roman eras. To a large extent, increasing urbanization and related problems of sanitation and disease were responsible for the high death rates before people reached old age. Nevertheless, older people were more likely than the young to survive the Black Plague and other epidemics, creating a disproportionate population of elders in many communities and arousing bitterness among the young. This also resulted in more extended family living arrangements (Minois, 1989).

The nobility lived longer than the common people during the Middle Ages, mostly because of better standards of living. Furthermore, the general populace was more likely to die of war or the numerous diseases that plagued this era. The nobility had the freedom to flee such conditions. For the small proportion of poor who did manage to survive, old age was a cruel period of life.

To the extent that the prevailing attitudes toward older persons in that historical period can be inferred from art, one would have to conclude that old age was depicted as ugly, weak, and deceptive. During the Renaissance, artists and poets reestablished links with Classical Greece, contrasting the beauty of youth with the unattractiveness and weakness they, like the ancient Greeks, saw in old age. Even later, Shakespeare's description of the seven ages of man in his play *As You Like It* also portrays such a contrast. Youth evolves from an impulsive boy to soldier, to the fifth age "full of wise saws and modern instances." The sixth age is depicted as weak, with "his big manly voice, turning again toward childish treble." The seventh and final stage "is second childishness and mere oblivion, sans teeth, sans eyes, sans taste, sans everything." Thus, Shakespeare's view of old age is that of decline and uselessness; this may reflect the attitude of sixteenth-century Europe that the old were a burden to a community struggling with food shortages and high death rates among its infants and young soldiers. Perhaps most striking is Shakespeare's attribution of wisdom and perspective to middle age, in contrast to the beliefs of pre-Classical and Hellenistic Greek playwrights and philosophers that old age is the time of greatest wisdom.

Old Age in Colonial America

In seventeenth- and eighteenth-century America, old age was treated with deference and respect, in part because it was so rare. This attitude has been described as one of veneration, an emotion closer to awe than affection and a form of worship deeply embedded in the Judeo-Christian ethic of early America. The Puritans, for example, viewed old age as a sign of God's favor and assumed that youth would inevitably defer to age. Old men occupied the highest public offices, as well as positions of authority within the family, until they

Older people in traditional societies symbolize power and wisdom.

died; fathers waited until their sixties before giving their land to their eldest son. Church seats were given to the old. The primary basis of the power enjoyed by older people in colonial times was their control of property, especially productive farmland. In this agricultural society, such control amounted to the ability to dominate all key institutions—the family, the church, the economy, and the polity.

Even though the old were exalted by law and custom in colonial times, they received little affection or love from younger people; in fact, most were kept at an emotional distance. In reserving power and prestige for older persons, society in many ways created this separation between young and old. Elders frequently complained that they had lived to become strangers in their communities. Old age was not a time of serenity, but rather anxiety about adequately fulfilling social obligations and keeping faith with God (Achenbaum, 1996).

This pattern persisted until about 1770, when attitudes toward the older population began to change and the relative status of youth was elevated. There are a number of indications of this change: church-seating arrangements that had favored the old were abolished; the first mandatory retirement laws for legislators were passed; and the eldest son no longer automatically inherited the family property. New fashions were introduced that flattered youth rather than the white wigs and broadwaisted coats that favored older men. Words that negatively portrayed elders, such as *codger* and *fuddy-duddy,* appeared in dictionaries in the nineteenth century. In family portraits, all members of the family were placed on the same horizontal plane rather than positioning the oldest male members to stand over women and children (Fischer, 1978).

A major demographic change occurred in approximately 1810, when the median age began to rise, creating a greater percentage of the population older than the typical "old" age of 40 or 50. This was due primarily to a declining birth rate, not a falling death rate. After 1810, the median age advanced at a constant annual rate, approximately 0.4 percent per year, until about 1950

(Fischer, 1978); this has been attributed to reductions in the impact of diseases. A dramatic change was that parents began to live beyond the period of their children's dependency, for the first time historically experiencing health at the time their children left the family home.

THE EFFECTS OF MODERNIZATION

As the foregoing historical examples suggest, definitions of old age, as well as the authority that older people exercised, largely rested on the material and political resources controlled by older members of society. Examples of these resources are traditional skills and knowledge, security from property rights, civil and political power, food from communal sharing, information control, and general welfare from routine services performed by older people such as child care. Within the constraints set by the social environment and its ideology, older people's social rank was generally determined by the balance between the cost of maintaining them and the societal contributions they were perceived to make. As age became a less important criterion for determining access to and control of valued resources, older members of society lost some of their status and authority.

A number of explanations have been advanced for the declining status of the old in our society. One major explanation is **modernization** theory. One of the first comparative analyses that raised this issue was reported by Leo Simmons in *The Role of the Aged in Primitive Society* (1945). He noted that the status of older persons, as reflected in their resources and the honor bestowed upon them, varied inversely with the degree of technology, social and economic diversity, and occupational specialization (or modernization) in a given society. As society becomes more modernized, according to this theory, older people lose political and social power, influence, and leadership. These social changes also may lead to disengagement of aging persons from community life. In addition, younger and older generations become increasingly separated socially, morally, and intellectually. Youth is glorified as the embodiment of progress and achievement, as well as the means to attain such progress.

Modernization theory has been advanced primarily by Cowgill (1974a, 1974b, 1986). Modernization is defined by Cowgill (1974a) as:

> The transformation of a total society from a relatively rural way of life based on animate power, limited technology, relatively undifferentiated institutions, parochial and traditional outlook and values, toward a predominantly urban way of life, based on inanimate sources of power, highly differentiated institutions, matched by segmented individual roles, and a cosmopolitan outlook which emphasizes efficiency and progress (p. 127).

The characteristics of modernization that contribute to lower status for older people were identified by Cowgill as (1) health technology, (2) scientific technology as applied in economic production and distribution, (3) urbanization, and (4) literacy and mass education.

According to Cowgill, the application of *health technology* has reduced infant mortality and maternal deaths, and prolonged adult life, thereby increasing the number of older persons in the population. With more older people in the labor market, competition for jobs between generations has intensified, and retirement has developed as a means of forcing older people out of the labor market.

Scientific technology creates new jobs primarily for the young, with older workers more likely to remain in traditional occupations that become obsolete. The rapid development of industries that rely on high technology in the twentieth century and the gap between generations in the use of computers illustrate this phenomenon. Unable to perform the socially valued role of contributors to the workforce, many retirees feel marginal and alienated.

In the early stages of modernization, when the society is relatively rural, young people are attracted to urban areas, whereas older parents and grandparents remain on the family farm or in rural communities. The resulting residential segregation of the generations has a dramatic impact on family interactions. The geographical and occupational mobility of the young, in turn, leads to increased social distance between generations and to a reduced status of the old.

Finally, modernization is characterized by efforts to promote *literacy and education,* which tend to be targeted toward the young. As younger generations acquire more education than their parents, they begin to occupy higher status positions. Intellectual and moral differences between the generations increase, with older members of society experiencing reduced leadership roles and influence (Cowgill, 1974a, 1974b).

Some social historians have criticized modernization theory, arguing that it idealizes the past and ignores the fact that older people in many pre-industrial societies were treated harshly and at the whim of younger family members (Albert and Cattell, 1994; Kertzer and Laslett, 1994). However, there is considerable empirical support for this theory. For example, rapid urbanization in many developing countries has dislodged the tradition of family support for many older people. Modern migration programs in India, while providing resources for young and old, have resulted in younger people obtaining more education and creating a sense of superiority over their illiterate elders. Rapid urbanization has left almost 30 percent of old people in rural areas in India without family nearby to care for them (Dandekar, 1996; Vincentnathan and Vincentnathan, 1994). Meanwhile, families who eke out a meager living in urban areas have little to assist their elders who live with them. For example, 33 percent of older women in Mexico's urban areas have been found to have no personal income, and 12 percent earn $5.00 or less per month (Bialik, 1992). Even in the economically more successful countries of east Asia, such as Japan and Taiwan, older people may live in three-generational households but do not necessarily feel welcome in these settings. Evidence of such intergenerational conflict is reflected in suicide rates among older women. Although the rate among women in the United States drops from 11.6 per 100,000 among those aged 40–50, to 6.6 per 100,000 among women over 65, the suicide rate more than triples in Japan (from 11.6 to 39.3 per 100,000) and Taiwan (from 10.4 to 34.6 per 100,000) in this same age range (Hu, 1995).

Occupation and education, however, have had a reversed J-shaped relationship to modernization; that is, in the early phases of rapid social change (illustrated by nations such as Turkey and the Philippines), the occupational and educational status of older adults declined, but then later improved (exemplified by New Zealand, Canada, and the United States). This suggests that, as societies move beyond an initial state of rapid modernization, status differences between generations decrease and the relative status of older people may rise, particularly when reinforced by social policies such as Social Security. Similarly the financial status of older Americans has steadily improved since World War II. It may be that societies in advanced stages of modernization become more aware of the older population's devalued status. Thus, through public education, social policies, and the media, they attempt to create more opportunities and positive images of older people. This has already begun in the United States, with advertising and television programs increasingly portraying older persons as vital, active, and involved, and with many local governments encouraging employers to hire older workers.

Alternatives to Modernization Theory

More recent analyses of older people's status in non-industrial societies have found that conditions for high status did not always apply. For example, differences often existed between the prestige of the old and the way they were actually treated; over 60 percent of the 41 non-industrial societies examined by Glascock (1997) had some form of non-supportive treatment (ranging from insults to killing) for the old, even though older members were also respected in many of these cultures. Death-hastening activities are often justified in these societies by claims that they are directed toward those elders who are no longer active and productive, and are a liability to society and their families. Most societies have some norms of favorable treatment toward their elders, but considerable variability exists in practice. For example, filial piety in China and Taiwan was not always manifest, but affected by family resources and number of living children (Ikels, 1997). The coexistence of high status and bad treatment in many traditional societies can be partially explained in terms of differential behavior toward the young-old versus old-old, noted in our earlier discussion of traditional societies that abandoned or murdered their frail elders (Keith, 1990).

Class and sex differences also come into play. For instance, the norms of filial piety were more often practiced by the well-to-do in traditional rural China. Despite the Confucian reverence for age, older people in lower class families had fewer resources to give them status. The importance of women's household responsibilities throughout life may explain their relatively higher status in old age than men's (Cool and McCabe, 1987).

Turning to contemporary China, there has been a major transformation of life for older people in that country. The "political economy" has had an impact on elders' status as government policies have been altered. For example, women have benefited from changes such as not having to submit to arranged marriages or having their feet bound. Their work opportunities have expanded by opening up more jobs to women. National social insurance has also been developed to benefit older Chinese citizens. But not all changes have had positive effects. Rules limiting family size and the breaking up of communes have had negative consequences for the childless older population in particular. These effects are expected to continue as future cohorts of older people contend with fewer children to care for them in times of need. These changes will also impact multigenerational living arrangements in China (Ikels, 1997).

Another alternative to modernization theory is that the development of state or nation represented a shift in older people's roles (Dickerson-Putnam, 1994; Fry, 1996). With the movement from kin-based societies to modern states and capitalist economies in the nineteenth century, labor became a commodity that was sold in exchange for economic security rather than for the security of an extended family. Such marketplace exchanges also created competition between old and young for jobs; this led to the emergence of retirement laws in nineteenth-century Europe that served to formally remove older people from competition for jobs. The emergence of social security programs in capitalist economies was intended to provide a safety net for retired people that could reduce their dependence on kin and prevent the older person from re-entering the job market. At the same time, social security and pension plans that emerged later have provided a stabilizing effect for older people and their families (Achenbaum, 1993, 1996).

Ideal of Equality versus Status of Age in America

Fischer (1978) has formulated reasons other than modernization for explaining changes between generations in American society. He argues that these changes cannot be attributed to modernization, because the decline in older people's status occurred before industrialization and urbanization. He also contends that the increase in numbers of older people does not fully explain the shifts in attitudes toward the old. Instead, he suggests that the emphasis on youthfulness that characterizes our society can be partially attributed to our cultural values of liberty and equality. Both of these values run counter to a hierarchy of authority based on age.

According to Fischer, the elevated status of older persons in earlier historical periods gradually became supplanted in the late eighteenth and early nineteenth centuries by an emerging ideal of age equality. The fundamental change was caused by the social and intellectual forces unleashed by revolutions in America and France. The spirit of equality was dramatically expressed in public fetes borrowed from the French Revolution, where a symbolic harmony of youth and age was celebrated in elaborate rituals of young and old exchanging food (Fischer, 1978).

However, although our society's ideology was egalitarian, economic inequalities actually grew in the nineteenth century. For example, economic status became the basis of seating arrangements in public meetings. Individualistic pursuits of wealth created countervailing forces to a sense of community that had previously been founded on the power of elders. Thus, the age equality that had initially replaced veneration of elders was later supplanted by a celebration of youthfulness and a derogation of age. Inequalities based on age reemerged, but this time to the advantage of youth. Growing contempt toward older people in the mid-1800s is vividly illustrated by Thoreau's (1856) conclusion, "Age is no better, hardly so well qualified for an instructor of youth, for it has not profited as much as it has lost." Heroes and legends centered on younger men, such as Daniel Boone. Social trends in the early twentieth century, such as the development of retirement policies, mass education, and residential segregation of generations, furthered perceptions of older people as useless, with the cult of youth reaching its peak in the 1960s. One irony was that as the economic and social conditions of many older adults declined in modern America, their ties of family affection, especially between grandparents and grandchildren, often grew stronger (Fischer, 1978).

Other Perspectives on Historical Change

Historians and gerontologists have questioned whether a critical turning point in age relations occurred between 1770 and 1830 (Achenbaum, 1996). Achenbaum, for example, has taken a position somewhere between Fischer's view and modernization theory regarding the change in status of older adults in the United States. He has identified social trends similar to those documented by Fischer, stating that prior to the middle of the nineteenth century, elders were venerated because of their experiences and were actively involved in socially useful roles. A decline in their status, Achenbaum asserts, occurred during the post-Civil War era. The growing empha-

sis on efficiency and impersonality in bureaucracies, along with increased misperceptions about senility, furthered a perception of old age as obsolescence. Both Fischer and Achenbaum suggest that it is not possible to establish a firm relationship between modernization and older people's status; rather, they maintain that Americans have always been ambivalent about old age. Shifting beliefs and values are viewed as more salient in accounting for loss in status than changes in the economic and political structures that occurred with modernization.

These contrasting perspectives of social gerontologists and anthropologists suggest that there is not a simple "before and after" relationship in the meaning and significance of old age between pre-industrial and modern societies (Achenbaum, 1996). People in pre-industrial societies who, by reason of social class, lacked property and power undoubtedly suffered from loss of status, regardless of their age. For such persons, modernization brought less improvement in status than for older people who were better educated and of higher socioeconomic background. Such inequities continue to be problematic, particularly among ethnic minorities within our society. Cultural gerontologists have emphasized that modernization is not a linear process, but proceeds at different rates and through varied stages, each of which may have a different impact on older people's status (Albert and Cattell, 1994; Fry, 1996).

In addition, cross-cultural evidence shows that cultural values can mitigate many of the negative effects of modernization on older people. This is illustrated in modern, industrialized, and urban Japanese society where Confucian values of filial piety and ancestor worship have helped to maintain the relatively high status of older persons and their integration in family life, as well as their leadership in national politics. Traditional values of reciprocity and lifelong indebtedness to one's parents are a major reason for continued three-generational households in Japan (Akiyama, Antonucci, and Campbell 1997).

Political ideology may also be an intervening variable, as illustrated by the effect of Communist

Many older women in China continue in self-employed positions.

party policies in Maoist China which at first villified older people but eventually sought them to work with the young to promote the Cultural Revolution. Despite their emphasis on collectivization, the Communist leaders did not provide a comprehensive welfare program for older people, especially those in rural China. Families were expected to provide care for their elders, except for those who were childless in their old age. However, as modernization and especially urbanization continued in China after the 1950s, societal views of and governmental benefits to older persons improved (Ikels, 1997).

In sum, the effects of modernization historically do not appear to be uniform nor unidirectional. As shown in the next section, many contemporary cultures are still struggling to define satisfying roles for their rapidly increasing populations of older people. Changing values and declining resources result in conflicting attitudes toward their older members in many transitional societies.

A CROSS-CULTURAL VIEW OF OLD AGE IN CONTEMPORARY SOCIETIES

As we have discussed, every society defines people as old on some basis, whether chronological, func-

tional, or generational, and assigns that group a particular set of rights, privileges, and duties that differ from those of its younger members. For example, older persons in our society today qualify for Social Security and Medicare on the basis of their age. In some religious groups, only the oldest members are permitted to perform the most sacred rituals. Societies generally distinguish two classes of elders: (1) those who are no longer fully productive economically, but are physically and mentally able to attend to their daily needs; and (2) those who are totally dependent, who require custodial care, and who are regarded as social burdens and thus may be negatively treated. A third group of older people exists in many societies: those who continue to participate actively in the economy of the social system, through farming or self-employment, care of grandchildren, or household maintenance, while younger adults work outside the home.

Older people who can no longer work but who control resources essential to fulfill the needs of younger group members generally offset the societal costs incurred in maintaining them. In some social systems, political, judicial, or ritual power and privileges are vested in older people as a group, and this serves to mediate social costs. For instance, in societies such as those of East Africa, politically powerful positions are automatically assigned to men who reach a certain age (Keith, 1990). In other societies, the old do not inherently have privileges, but gain power as individuals, often through diplomatic skills and contacts with powerful others. The following examples from other cultures illustrate the balance between the costs and contributions made by older adults.

In the subsistence society of the Chipewyan Indians of Canada, older men are accorded low status, and old age is despised and feared. This is primarily because older men, who are no longer able to hunt, are perceived as unproductive, costing society more than they contribute. Dependent on the contributions of each tribal member, the Chipewyans have sometimes been forced to abandon their old when faced with a choice between the death of older men and that of the entire tribe. Unlike older men, Chipewyan older women are still able to perform customary domestic and gathering tasks that do not require physical vigor. As a result, aging does not produce as substantial a decline in the status of older women as in that of older men (Sharp, 1981).

Unlike Chipewyan men, older men among the Asmats of coastal New Guinea are able to assert political leadership in kinship and local groups even after their hunting skills have deteriorated. The primary reason for this difference is that the Asmat economy is less precarious, so that older men can still acquire resources to protect their position in old age (Amoss and Harrell, 1981).

In other cultures, respect toward intact elders may be promoted, but a subtle acceptance of benign neglect may result in the demise of older persons who are physically and/or cognitively impaired. An ethnographic analysis of Niue, an independent Polynesian island, revealed significant discrepancies between the status of older people who were in good health and had important social and political functions, and of those who were too frail to care for themselves. Although medical services are free on Niue, families and neighbors did not summon visiting doctors and public health nurses, even for infected sores, painful joints, and other treatable conditions in these frail elders. The basic needs of cognitively impaired elders were even more frequently ignored. This may stem from values of reciprocity. Like other societies where reciprocity is crucial for intergenerational exchanges, the frail elders of Niue can no longer contribute to the group's well-being (Barker, 1997). Therefore, such neglect may be seen as a way of merely hastening the inevitable death of these weaker members of that society (Glascock, 1997).

Importance of Social Position and the Control of Property

The control of property is a means of achieving power in most societies. Both in past and present times, older people have used their rights over property to guarantee their security by compelling others to support them or to provide them with goods and services. For example, among the Etal Islanders in Micronesia, the old try to keep enough property to ensure continued care by younger members who hope to inherit it (Nason, 1981). In the Gwembe Tonga tribe in Zambia, males were formerly able to secure their position by accumulating land and livestock. As their lineage land became covered by water, however, forced relocation cost many older people their exclusive control of property, and the old became dependent on sons and nephews, who acquired better land at the time of flooding (Colson and Scudder, 1981).

In other societies, the leadership of males derives from their positions within the family. The traditional Chinese extended household is an example. The position of the aging father in the Chinese family depends almost entirely on the political and economic power he wields (Harrell, 1981). Elders in wealthy Chinese households and those with substantial pensions to contribute to family expenses enjoy higher status within the family and are better able to control the lives of their adult children than those in poor households (Olson, 1990). Both China and India illustrate substantial class differences in the elders' power, as well as the persistence of the extended family structure that confers status on older members, even in the face of modernization. As economic resources decline and class differences disappear in these cultures with increasing modernization, the traditions of filial piety may become undermined. For example, the growing pressures of limited housing and low income in China appear to be having a negative effect on younger generations' attitudes toward old people. In such instances, increased provision of public housing, health care, an old age pension plan, and policies that support family care of elders may serve to reduce tensions between generations (Chow, 1983).

Older persons from traditional cultures who immigrate to Western countries face even more problems adjusting to the loss of power. In the past 25 years, waves of Indochinese refugees have come to the United States from countries experiencing political strife and unrest. Older people who arrived with younger family members have had more difficulties in becoming part of the culture. Property and other resources in their native lands which afforded them importance and power have been stripped from them. Being in the United States has brought them a different life than the one they might have expected for their later years. These older refugees do not have the ability to provide material goods, land, or other financial support which has traditionally given them status (Yee, 1997). Traditional power has been eroded as families have started new lives in this culture. Indeed, financial self-sufficiency has been found to be the major determinant of adjustment to life in the United States among older Indochinese refugees, regardless of education, gender, and English proficiency (Tran, 1992). Recent refugees from Eastern Europe are also struggling with the adjustment to the loss of property and status in their host country.

Knowledge as a Source of Power

Control over knowledge, especially ritual and religious knowledge, is another source of power. The aged Shaman is an example, revered in many societies for knowledge or wisdom. The importance of older members of society in maintaining cultural values is illustrated in India, where traditional Hindu law prescribes a four-stage life cycle for high-caste men: student, householder, ascetic, and mendicant. In the last two stages, older religious men are expected to renounce worldly attachments to seek enlightenment in isolated retreats. This practice ensures that the pursuit of the highest form of knowledge is limited to older men of higher castes (Sokolovsky, 1997). As another example, the !Kung Bushmen value the storytelling ability of people age 45 and over, because the stories are considered to contain the accumulated knowledge of the people. Information and stories are the older person's resource which can be exchanged for food and security (Biesele and Howell, 1981).

Knowledge as the basis of older people's power has been challenged in many traditional societies

by Western technological and scientific expertise (Cowgill, 1974a). For example, the aged farmer who passes on to his children traditional methods of growing crops may be dismayed to find that they ignore this advice and rely on new agricultural methods and products. Examples in which the relevance of traditional knowledge declines with modernization abound in many fields: farming, fishing, construction, housekeeping, even child-rearing. They include the Tong elders of Zambia who lost status due to the flooding of their old habitat and the outmoding of their specialized knowledge (Colson and Scudder, 1981), older people in Taiwan who are less knowledgeable in new commercial and industrial contexts (Harrell, 1981), and many native North American groups faced with changing patterns of production and consumption. Among Western Irish peasants, the once dignified movement of the older couple to the sacred "west room" of the house, which signified high esteem, has been replaced by "warehousing" of elders in institutions (Scheper-Hughes, 1987).

Women in Ganga in Papua, New Guinea have assumed a larger role in local coffee production. However, these changes in their work lives have affected their control over the rituals of education and initiation for younger girls, traditionally an important part of their knowledge base and power. What was once provided by a group of older women is now acted out by a young girl's closest relatives. Consequently the power base of older women in shaping the lives of young women has eroded (Dickerson-Putman, 1994).

Among some cultural groups, however, such as the Coast Salish Indians of Washington, a revival of interest and pride in native identity and religion has occurred, thus raising the esteem of elders who possess ritual knowledge (e.g., they are the only ones who know the words and dance steps) (Amoss and Harrell, 1981; Keith, 1990). Knowledge of the group's culture, particularly traditional arts and handicrafts, and of native songs and epics has enhanced the social status of older persons in these societies; furthermore, the traditions of reverence for old age and wisdom remain strong, overriding the impact of modernization on older people's roles. The timing of such a revival is critical, however. A similar revival among Plains Indians did not have comparable positive consequences for the tribe's older members who were no longer expert in traditional ways (Keith, 1990).

The growing desire for ethnic or tribal identity among many Native Americans, which has led to a conscious restoration of old forms, illustrates that modernization does not automatically erode the status of the elders. Similarly, the search for one's heritage or roots has led to increased contacts between younger generations seeking this information from older persons who often are a great repository of family histories.

Cultural and historical factors can also mitigate the presumed negative consequences of modernization for older people. For example, in Samoa, despite the influx of U.S. aid, industries, and educational programs designed to promote modernization, the cultural system has been flexible enough to maintain older persons as a viable part of society. This has largely been due to the persistence of the traditional *matai* family system, which involves the elders in leadership roles within large bilateral kinship groups, and a village council that accords older Samoans respect and power (Holmes and Rhoads, 1987). The traditional family system has combined with Samoan values of reciprocity in social relationships and an acceptance of dependency in old age to retain high status among Samoan elders.

Indeed, modernization has not resulted in the disintegration of extended families in most non-Western societies, including the rapidly developing Asian and Third World countries. Extended families in rural Thailand and Zimbabwe have adapted to the need for adult children to migrate to the cities for jobs by creating "skip-generation households," where grandparents remain in their rural homes, caring for grandchildren, while their adult children work in urban settings. This reciprocal dependency has also proved useful for many Asians and Eastern European refugee families in the United States where grandparents have immigrated with their adult children in order to provide regular child care to grandchildren in the extended family (Hashimoto, 1991, 1993; Martin, 1989).

Older grandparents in rural China serve a vital role as full-time caregivers for their grandchildren.

The way that older people react to change can serve to maintain or improve their position. Among the Sherpa in Tibet, for example, as younger sons move away from the community, and are not available to share households and care for the old, the old resist the traditional division of property and tend to keep the younger sons' shares for themselves. The elderly Sherpa are also becoming proponents of birth control; since they cannot count on sons to take care of them as they wish, they prefer to share their property among fewer children, keeping more for themselves (Keith, 1990).

EFFECTS OF CULTURE AND MODERNIZATION ARE STILL CHANGING

In other situations, the buffering effects of culture on modernization are less distinct. For example, the issue of modernization and aging in contemporary Japan is particularly complex. Palmore

(1975a, 1975b), and Palmore and Maeda (1985) have described the high status and prestige of older adults in Japan. Values adopted from Confucianism have been viewed as linking the old to a family system that emphasizes filial devotion, in which the dependence of elders in this "second privileged period" is accepted (Ogawa and Retherford, 1993). This perspective has been criticized as being based on cultural values and census figures that reflect intergenerational harmony rather than systematic anthropological or social research (Sokolovsky, 1997).

Indeed, the rapid demographic shifts in Japan that have made it one of the world's oldest populations (as described in Chapter 1) and the growth in the numbers of working women (41 percent currently) have altered traditional conceptions of old age and reduced the positive influences of cultural values on intergenerational relations. For instance, the modernization of Japanese society has resulted in increased economic demands on the nuclear family. This is compounded by the fact that the unprecedented numbers of older people in Japan today have increased the societal costs of maintaining older members of society, and have created dilemmas for younger family members responsible for their support.

The majority of middle-aged persons in Japan still believe that care of older parents is the children's responsibility. Indeed, negligence toward one's parents is a source of great public shame in Japan. Society also assumes responsibility for the care of Japan's elders; all those over 70 receive free basic medical services. The Japanese government provides incentives for home care by families; they can receive subsidies to remodel their homes in order to accommodate joint households as well as a tax credit for providing elder parent care (Maeda and Shimizu, 1992). For these reasons, the proportion of older parents living in multigenerational households is higher than in any other industrialized nation. In 1994, 60 percent of people over age 65 lived with their children and grandchildren, but this is a decline from 1985, when 69 percent of older households were multigenerational. Meanwhile, there has been a growth of households consisting only of the older couple;

in 1994 they made up 24 percent of older households, compared with 19 percent in 1985 (Jenike, 1997).

The number of nursing homes and long-stay hospitals in Japan has also grown rapidly. These trends suggest that traditional customs of caring for aging parents in adult children's homes are slowly changing in Japan, while the percentage of parents living with children has declined, due to urbanization, industrialization, the growing numbers of employed women, and the declining number of children since 1950. Nevertheless, institutionalization in any form is viewed as abandonment by many older people. As a result, most elder care still takes place in private homes. In 1990, 81 percent of people surveyed who were caring for an older person in their homes were middle-aged women (average age of 56) with other life stresses (Lock, 1993). As more older adults live longer, they may increasingly require goods and services at the perceived expense of younger members and may place even greater demands on middle-aged women in Japanese society.

With the increased proportion of educated women who have professional jobs and newer cohorts who have been influenced more by Western values than by Confucianism, many women do not want to leave their jobs to become caregivers to their parents or parents-in-law. As a result, some social researchers predict that Japanese families in the future will expect better long-term care options from the government than are currently available (Freed, 1990).

SUMMARY AND IMPLICATIONS

These brief examples from diverse cultures around the world illustrate how each society responds to its aging members within the constraints set by both the natural environment and the larger human environment of social and technological change. A basic principle governing the status of older adults appears to be the effort to achieve a balance between older people's contributions to the society and the costs of supporting them. As will be discussed in detail in Chapter 9, however, the family plays an important role in supporting the old in most societies. Historical and cross-cultural evidence also suggests that maximum social participation of older adults in society results in greater acceptance and respect of elders by the young in most cultures.

The extent to which older citizens are engaged in society appears to vary with the nature of their power resources, such as their material possessions, knowledge, and social authority. In most of their exchanges, older people seek to maintain reciprocity and to be active independent agents in the management of their own lives. That is, they prefer to give money, time, or other resources in exchange for services or materials. This theoretical perspective, which will be described in more detail as social exchange theory in Chapter 8, suggests that modern society should seek ways of increasing older people's exchange resources so that they are valued by society. For example, maximizing the social value and productivity of the old in our society might include retraining and educational programs and part-time employment (see Chapter 11).

Control of resources as a basis for social interactions between members of a society is important throughout the life cycle. However, it becomes even more crucial in old age, because retirement generally results in a decline in one's level of control over material and social resources. As their physical strength diminishes and their social world correspondingly shrinks, many older people face the challenge of altering their environments and using their capacities in ways that will help them to maintain reciprocal exchanges and to protect their competence and independence. This may be an even greater problem for older refugees who may still have full physical and cognitive functions, but have lost material resources in their homeland that would have given them power and prestige.

These attempts to maintain control over one's environment in the face of changing personal capacities and resources are consistent with the person-environment model presented in Chapter 1.

This issue will be discussed in detail in subsequent chapters on biological, psychological, and social changes with aging.

GLOSSARY

geronticide (or senecide)   inducing the death of old persons, as practiced in some ancient cultures

modernization   advances in technology, applied sciences, urbanization, and literacy which, in this context, are related to a decline in the status of older people

social stratification   divisions among people (e.g., by age, ethnic group) for purposes of maintaining distinctions between different strata by significant characteristics of those strata

REFERENCES

Achenbaum, W. A. Historical perspectives on aging. In R. H. Binstock and L. K., George (Eds.), *Handbook of aging and the social sciences* (4th ed.). San Diego: Academic Press, 1996.

Achenbaum, W. A. Old age. In M. K. Cayton, E. J. Garn, and P. W. Williams (Eds.), *Encyclopedia of American social history*, Vol. 3. New York: Charles Scribner's Sons, 1993.

Akiyama, H., Antonucci, T. C., and Campbell, R. Exchange and reciprocity among two generations of Japanese and American women. In J. Sokolovsky (Ed.), *The cultural context of aging*(3rd ed.). Westport, CT: Bergin and Garvey, 1997.

Albert, S. M., and Cattell, M. G. *Old age in global perspective.* New York: G.K. Hall and Co., 1994.

Amoss, P., and Harrell, S. (Eds.) *Other ways of growing old.* Stanford, CA: Stanford University Press, 1981.

Barker, J. C. Between humans and ghosts: The decrepit elderly in a Polynesian society. In J. Sokolovsky (Ed.), *The cultural context of aging.* Westport, CT: Bergin and Garvey, 1997.

Bialik, R. Family care of the elderly in Mexico. In J. Kosberg (Ed.), *Family care of the elderly.* Newbury Park, CA: Sage, 1992.

Biesele, M., and Howell, N. The old people give you life: Aging among !Kung hunters-gatherers. In P. Amoss and S. Harrell (Eds.), *Other ways of growing old.* Stanford, CA: Stanford University Press, 1981.

Chow, N. The Chinese family and support of the elderly in Hong Kong. *The Gerontologist,* 1983, *23,* 584–588.

Colson, E., and Scudder, T. Old age in Gwemba District, Zambia. In P. Amoss and S. Harrell (Eds.), *Other ways of growing old.* Stanford, CA: Stanford University Press, 1981.

Cool, L., and McCabe, J. The "scheming hag" and the "dear old thing." The anthropology of aging women. In J. Sokolovsky (Ed.), *Growing old in different cultures.* Acton, MA: Copley, 1987.

Cowgill, D. Aging and modernization: A revision of the theory. In J. F. Gubrium (Ed.)., *Late life communities and environmental policy.* Springfield, IL: Charles C. Thomas, 1974a.

Cowgill, D. *Aging around the world.* Belmont, CA: Wadsworth, 1986.

Cowgill, D. The aging of populations and societies. In F. Eisele (Ed.), *Political consequences of aging. The annals of the American Academy of Political and Social Science,* 1974b, *415,* 1–18.

Dandekar, K. *The elderly in India.* Thousand Oaks, CA: Sage, 1996.

de Romilly, J. *Time in Greek tragedy.* Ithaca, NY: Cornell University Press, 1968.

Dickerson-Putnam, J. Old women at the top: An exploration of age stratification among Bena Bena women. *Journal of Cross-Cultural Gerontology,* 1994, *9,* 193–205.

Fischer, D. H. *Growing old in America.* Oxford: Oxford University Press, 1978.

Freed, A. O. How Japanese families cope with fragile elderly. *Journal of Gerontological Social Work,* 1990, *15,* 39–54.

Fry, C. L. Age, aging, and culture. In R. H. Binstock and L. K. George (Eds.), *Handbook of aging and the social sciences* (4th ed.). San Diego: Academic Press, 1996.

Glascock, A. P. When is killing acceptable: The moral dilemma surrounding assisted suicide in America and other societies. In J. Sokolovsky (Ed.), *The cultural context of aging* (3rd ed.). Westport, CT: Bergin and Garvey, 1997.

Harrell, S. Growing old in rural Taiwan. In P. Amoss and S. Harrell (Eds.), *Other ways of growing old.* Stanford, CA: Stanford University Press, 1981.

Hashimoto, A. Family relations in later life: A cross-cultural perspective. *Generations,* 1993, *17,* 24–26.

Hashimoto, A. Living arrangements of the aged in seven developing countries. *Journal of Cross-Cultural Gerontology,* 1991, *6,* 359–381.

Holmes, L., and Rhoads, E. Aging and change in Samoa. In J. Sokolovsky (Ed.), *Growing old in different societies.* Acton, MA: Copley, 1987.

Hu, Y. H. Elderly suicide risk in family context: A critique of the Asian family care model. *Journal of Cross-Cultural Gerontology,* 1995, *10,* 199–217.

Ikels, C. Long-term care and the disabled elderly in urban China. In J. Sokolovsky (Ed.), *The cultural context of aging* (3rd ed.). Westport, CT: Bergin and Garvey, 1997.

Jenike, B. R. Gender and duty in Japan's aged society: The experience of family caregivers. In J. Sokolovsky (Ed.), *The cultural context of aging* (3rd ed.). Westport, CT: Bergin and Garvey, 1997.

Keith, J. Age in social and cultural context: Anthropological perspectives. In R. Binstock and L. George (Eds.), *Handbook of aging and the social sciences* (3rd ed.). New York: Academic Press, 1990.

Kertzer, D., and Laslett, P. (Eds.). *Demography, society and old age.* Berkeley: University of California Press, 1994.

Lock, M. Ideology, female midlife, and the greying of Japan. *Journal of Japanese Studies,* 1993, *19,* 43–78.

Maeda, D., and Shimizu, Y. Family support for elderly people in Japan. In H. Kendig, A. Hashimoto, and L. Coppard (Eds.), *Family support for the elderly; The international experience.* Oxford: Oxford University Press, 1992.

Martin, L. Living arrangements of the elderly in Fiji, Korea, Malaysia and the Philippines. *Demography,* 1989, *4,* 627–633.

Minois, G. *History of old age.* Cambridge, England: Polity Press, 1989.

Nason, J. D. Respected elder or old person: Aging in a Micronesian community. In P. Amoss and S. Harrell (Eds.), *Other ways of growing old.* Stanford, CA: Stanford University Press, 1981.

Ogawa, N., and Retherford, R. Care of the elderly in Japan: Changing norms and expectations. *Journal of Marriage and the Family,* 1993, *55,* 585–597.

Olson, P. The elderly in the People's Republic of China. In J. Sokolovsky (Ed.), *The cultural context of aging* (2nd ed.). New York: Bergin and Garvey, 1990.

Palmore, E. *The honorable elders.* Durham, NC: Duke University Press, 1975a.

Palmore, E. The status and integration of the aged in Japanese society. *Journal of Gerontology,* 1975b, *30,* 199–208.

Palmore, E., and Maeda, D. *The honorable elders revisited.* Durham, NC: Duke University Press, 1985.

Scheper-Hughes, N. Deposed kings: The demise of the rural Irish gerontocracy. In J. Sokolovsky (Ed.), *Growing old in different societies.* Acton, MA: Copley, 1987.

Sharp, H. Old age among the Chipewyan. In P. Amoss and S. Harrell (Eds.), *Other ways of growing old.* Stanford, CA: Stanford University Press, 1981.

Sokolovsky, J. (Ed.) *The cultural context of aging* (3rd ed.). Westport, CT: Bergin and Garvey, 1997.

Thoreau, H. D. *Walden.* New York: New American Library, 1856, Chapter 1, p. 8.

Tran, T. V. Adjustment among different age and ethnic groups of Indochinese in the United States. *The Gerontologist,* 1992, *32,* 508–518.

Vincentnathan, S. G., and Vincentnathan, L. Equality and hierarchy in untouchable intergenerational relations and conflict resolutions. *Journal of Cross-Cultural Gerontology,* 1994, *9,* 1–19.

Yee, B. W. K., The social and cultural context of adaptive aging by Southeast Asian elders. In J. Sokolovsky (Ed.), *The cultural context of aging* (3rd ed.). Westport, CT: Bergin and Garvey, 1997.

two

THE BIOLOGICAL AND PHYSIOLOGICAL CONTEXT OF SOCIAL AGING

If we are to understand how older people differ from younger age groups, and why the field of gerontology has evolved as a separate discipline, we must first review the normal changes in biological and physiological structures as well as diseases that impair these systems and affect the day-to-day functioning of older persons. Part Two provides this necessary background. Normal changes in major organ systems and how they influence the older person's ability to perform activities of daily living and to interact with their social and physical environments are described in Chapter 3. This area of research has received considerable attention as scientists have explored the basic processes of aging. Numerous theories have been developed to explain observable changes such as wrinkles, gray hair, stooped shoulders, and slower response time, as well as changes in other biological functions that can only be inferred from tests of physiologic function. These include changes in the heart, lungs, kidneys, and bones. There are many normal changes in these organ systems within the same person that do not imply disease,

but in fact may slow down the older person. Furthermore, significant differences have been observed among people and among organ systems within the same person in the degree of change experienced. The implications of these changes for the maximum life span of humans are discussed.

Age-related changes in the five major senses are also discussed in Chapter 3. Because sensory functions are so critical for our daily interactions with our social and physical environments, and because many of the normal declines observed in sensory systems are a model of changes throughout the body, it is useful to focus on each sensory system and its role in linking individuals with their environments. Recommendations are made for modifying the environment and for communicating with older people who are experiencing significant declines in vision, hearing, taste, smell, touch, and kinesthetic functioning.

Chapter 4 focuses on secondary aging, i.e., diseases of the organ systems described in Chapter 3, and how these diseases can affect older people's social functioning. Acute and chronic diseases are differentiated, and the impact of these diseases on the demand for health and social services is presented. The growing problem of AIDS among older persons and implications for long-term care are discussed. Moreover, since automobile accidents among older people often result because of psychomotor changes associated with aging, methods to reduce auto fatalities through new programs in driver training and through better environmental design are considered in this chapter. Chapter 4 also provides some striking statistics on older people's use of health services, barriers to their use, and recommendations for enhancing utilization. Most existing medical, dental, and mental health services do not adequately address the special needs of the older population. As a result, older people who could benefit most from the services fail to use them. Health promotion has proven successful in maintaining and even improving older people's health in many areas, including exercise, prevention of falls and osteoporosis, and nutrition. Chapter 4 describes some of these programs and the research evidence for the benefits of health promotion.

Throughout Part Two, the tremendous variations in how people age physically are emphasized. Because of genetic, lifestyle, and environmental factors, some people will show dramatic declines in all their organ systems at a relatively early age. Most older people, however, will experience varied rates of decline in different systems. For example, some people may suffer from chronic heart disease, yet at the same time maintain strong bones and muscle strength. In contrast, others may require medications for painful osteoarthritis, but their heart and lungs remain in excellent condition. The following vignettes illustrate these variations:

A Healthy Older Person

Mrs. Hill is an 84-year-old widow. She has been slightly deaf all her life, has some recent loss of vision, and has to watch her blood pressure, primarily by paying attention to her diet. Despite her minor physical limitations, Mrs. Hill is able to get around to visit her many friends, neighbors, and family in the community. She is still able to drive, walk to the local grocery store almost daily, and take bus trips to visit her grandchildren. Active in the local senior center, she was one of the first participants in a health promotion project for older adults at the center. Now she helps teach an exercise class at the center three times a week. She rarely visits the doctor except for an annual check-up. She does admit to getting frustrated by her reduced energy and the need to slow down, but for the most part, she accepts these changes and adjusts her physical activities accordingly. Her son-in-law has made some minor modifications in her home, especially in the height and location of kitchen shelves, so that her daily routines do not place her at risk for a fall or tire her out too much. Friends and relatives are frequently telling her how she does not look her age; she, in turn, becomes impatient with older people who stay home all the time, watch TV, and complain. She is usually optimistic about her situation, and believes that each person can control how well or poorly they face old age.

An Older Person with Chronic Illness

Mr. Jones, age 69, had a stroke at age 64 and is paralyzed on his left side, so he is unable to walk. The stroke has also left him with slightly slurred speech and some personality changes. His wife states that he is not the kind, gentle man she used to know. He has to be lifted from bed to chair and recently became incontinent. His wife first tried to care for him at home, but after he became incontinent, she felt she could no longer handle the responsibility and made the difficult decision to move him to a nearby nursing home. Both Mr. and Mrs. Jones are having difficulty adjusting to the nursing home placement. Since Mr. Jones remains mentally alert and aware of all the changes, he continually expresses his frustration with his physical limitations and with his forced retirement and reduced income. Their children live in another state and have been unable to help their mother with the daily care or the financial burden of the nursing home. In fact, the children are critical of their mother's decision to institutionalize their father because they think she should have kept him at home, no matter what. As their financial resources dwindle, Mr. and Mrs. Jones are facing the need to apply for Medicaid to cover nursing home costs. Mr. Jones starts to cry easily, sobbing that he is losing control of his life and that his life was never meant to be like this. Mrs. Jones feels angry that her caregiving efforts have not been appreciated and that her husband is so difficult.

These two vignettes point to the complexity of physiological aging. Chronological age is often a poor predictor of health and functional status, as illustrated by Mrs. Hill's excellent functional and emotional health, and Mr. Jones's situation of physical dependency, even though he is 15 years younger than Mrs. Hill. Part Two describes these variations in physiological aging, contrasts these with changes due to disease, and presents factors that influence health care status in the later years.

3

THE SOCIAL CONSEQUENCES OF PHYSICAL AGING

When asked to describe the physical aspects of aging, most people think only of the visible signs—graying hair, balding among some men, wrinkled skin, stooped shoulders, and a slower walk or shuffling gait. Although these are the most visible signs of old age among humans, there are numerous other changes that occur in our internal organs—the heart, lungs, kidneys, stomach, bladder, and central nervous system. These changes are not as easy to detect because they are not visible. In fact, X rays and computer-assisted images of organ systems are not very useful for showing most changes that take place. It is primarily by measuring the functional capacity of these systems (i.e., the performance capacity of the heart, lungs, kidneys, and other organs) that their relative efficiency across the life span can be determined.

As noted in Chapter 1, biological aging, or senescence, can be defined as the normal process of changes over time in the body and its components. It is a gradual process common to all living organisms that eventually affects an individual's functioning vis-à-vis the environment but does not necessarily result in disease or death. This process is gradual and common to all living organisms. It is not, in itself, a disease, but aging and disease are often linked in most people's minds, since declines in organ capacity and internal protective mechanisms do make us more vulnerable to sickness. Because certain diseases such as Alzheimer's, arthritis, and heart conditions have a higher incidence with age, we may erroneously equate age with disease. However, a more appropriate conception of the aging process is a gradual accumulation of irreversible functional losses to which the average person tries to accommodate in some socially acceptable manner. Conversely, people may attempt to alter their physical and social environments by reducing the demands placed on their remaining functional capacity (e.g., relocating to a one-story home or apartment to avoid stairs, driving only during the day, avoiding crowds). This is consistent with the person-environment model of aging; as their physical competence declines, older people may simplify their physical environment to re-establish homeostasis or their comfort zone.

Individual differences are evident in the rate and severity of physical changes, as illustrated by the vignettes of Mrs. Hill and Mr. Jones. Not all people show the same degree of change in any given organ system, nor do all the systems change at the same rate and at the same time. Individual aging depends largely on genetic inheritance, nutrition and diet, physical activity, and environment. Thus, while one 78-year-old feels "old" because of aches and pains due to arthritis but uses her excellent cognitive skills at work every day, another 78-year-old may retain her physical ability but be institutionalized due to advanced dementia.

In this chapter, normal age-related changes in major organ systems of the human body are reviewed. The implications of these changes for older people's ability to interact with their social and physical environments, and the impact of system deterioration and disease on life expectancy, are examined within the context of personal competence vis-à-vis the environment. In the next chapter, the diseases of aging that may impair organ functions more than would be expected from normal aging will be discussed. First, it is useful to examine the major theories of biological aging that have been advanced to explain the changes in all living organisms over time.

BIOLOGICAL THEORIES OF AGING

The process of aging is complex and multidimensional, involving significant loss and decline in some physiological functions, and minimal change in others. Scientists have long attempted to find the causes for this process. A theme of some theories is that aging is a process that is programmed into the genetic structure of each species. Other theories state that aging represents an accumulation of stimuli from the environment that produce stress on the organism. Any theory of aging must be based on the scientific method, using systematic tests of hypotheses and empirical observations. In addition, Bernard Strehler (1986) has proposed

four requirements that biological theories must meet before they can be considered viable:

1. The process must be universal; that is, all members of a species must experience the phenomenon.
2. The process must be deleterious, or result in physiological decline.
3. The process must be progressive, i.e., losses must be gradual over time.
4. Finally, the loss must be intrinsic, i.e., they cannot be corrected by the organism.

These guidelines are helpful for excluding biological phenomena that are different from aging per se. For example, they help to distinguish disease from normal aging; while diseases are often deleterious, progressive, and intrinsic, they are not universal (e.g., not all older adults will develop arthritis or Alzheimer's disease). Each of the following theories meets these criteria, although the evidence to support them is not always clear. Even though these theories help our understanding of aging, none of them is totally adequate for explaining what *causes* aging.

The **Wear and Tear Theory** suggests that, with time, the organism simply wears out (Wilson, 1974). In this model, aging is a pre-programmed process; that is, each species has a biological clock that determines its maximum life span and the rate at which each organ system will deteriorate. This process is compounded by the effects of external stress on the organism (e.g., nutrient deficiencies). Cells continually wear out, and existing cells cannot repair damaged components within themselves. This is particularly true in tissues that are located in the striated skeletal and heart muscle and throughout the nervous system; these tissues are composed of cells that cannot undergo cell division. As we will see later, these systems are most likely to experience significant decline in their ability to function effectively with age.

One of the earliest theories of biological aging, the **Autoimmune Theory**, proposes that aging is a function of the body's immune system becoming defective and attacking not just foreign proteins, bacteria, and viruses, but also producing antibodies against itself. This explanation of the immune system is consistent with the process of many diseases that increase with age, such as cancer, diabetes, and rheumatoid arthritis (Walford, 1969). Nevertheless, this theory does not explain why the immune system becomes defective with age; only the *effects* of this change are described. For example, the thymus gland, which controls production of disease-fighting white blood cells, shrinks with aging, but the reasons for both this reduction in size and why *more* older people do not suffer from autoimmune diseases are unclear.

The **Cross-Linkage Theory** (Bjorksten, 1974) focuses on the changes in the protein called *collagen* with age. Collagen is an important connective tissue found in most organ systems; indeed, about one-third of all the protein in our body is collagen. As a person ages, there are clearly observable changes in collagen, for instance, wrinkling of the skin. These changes lead to a loss of elasticity in blood vessels, muscle tissue, skin, the lens of the eye, and other organs, and to slower wound healing. Another visible effect of changes in collagen is that the nose and ears tend to increase in size. Proponents of this theory argue that these changes are due to the binding of essential molecules in the cells through the accumulation of cross-linking compounds, which in turn slows the process of normal cell functions and shows signs of aging. These cross-links are necessary to join together the parallel molecules of collagen. However, in older animals and humans these links increase, making the tissue less pliable and rigid, as seen in wrinkled skin.

A special case of the cross-linkage theory is the **Free Radical Theory** of aging (Harman, 1956, 1981). Free radicals are highly reactive molecules that break off in cells and possess an unpaired electron. Produced normally by the use of oxygen within the cell, they interact with other cell molecules and may cause DNA mutations, cross-linking of connective tissue, changes in protein behavior, and other damage. Such reactions continue until

one free radical pairs with another or meets an *antioxidant*. These are chemical inhibitors that can safely absorb the extra electron and prevent oxygen from combining with susceptible molecules to form free radicals. It has been proposed that the ingestion of antioxidants such as vitamin E and beta carotene can inhibit free radical damage; this can then slow the aging process by delaying the loss of immune function and reducing the incidence of many diseases associated with aging (Cutler and Cutler, 1983; Harman, 1981).

Nevertheless, it appears that free radicals are not totally destroyed. Those that survive in the organism damage the proteins needed to make cells in the body by interacting with the oxygen used to produce protein. As a result, free radicals may destroy the fragile process of cell-building and the DNA strands that transmit messages of genes. Some have argued that this continuous pounding by dangerous oxidants wears away the organism over time, not just by interfering with cell-building but also by requiring antioxidants to be ever-vigilant. This damage to cell tissue by free radicals has been implicated in normal aging, as well as in the development of some cancers, heart disease, Alzheimer's disease, and Parkinson's disease.

Molecular biologists have explored this theory further by splicing genes to measure the cumulative effects of free radicals in cells, with the goal of developing ways to counter these effects. It may be that synthetic antioxidants can be developed and administered to older people as the body's natural supply is depleted. Animal studies have shown dramatic enhancements of memory and physical activity with high doses of antioxidants. It may be that the free radical theory holds the greatest promise for slowing the aging process in the future. However, while increasing the intake of antioxidants may eventually result in more people achieving their life expectancy, there is no evidence that the maximum life span of 120 years would increase (Hayflick, 1996).

The **Cellular Aging Theory** suggests that aging occurs as cells slow their number of replications. Hayflick and Moorehead (1961) first reported that cells grown in culture (i.e., in controlled laboratory environments) undergo a finite number of replications, approaching 50 doublings. Cells from older subjects replicate even fewer times, as do cells derived from individuals with *progeria,* and Werner Syndrome, both rare genetic anomalies in which aging is accelerated and death may occur by age 15 to 20 in the former, and by 40 to 50 in the latter condition. It appears that cells are programmed to follow a biological clock and stop replicating after a given number of times. In addition, proponents of this theory point out that each cell has a given level of DNA that is eventually depleted. This in turn reduces the production of RNA, which is essential for producing enzymes necessary for cellular functioning. Hence, the loss of DNA and subsequent reduction of RNA eventually result in cell death (Goldstein and Reis, 1984).

Of all the theories of physiological aging, the *cellular* theory appears to explain best the causes and processes of aging. The role of cell replication and RNA production in aging is widely accepted in the scientific community. It should not be assumed, however, that the step from understanding to reversing the process of aging will be achieved soon. It is often erroneously assumed that scientific discoveries of the *cause* of a particular physiological process or disease can immediately lead to *changing* or reversing that condition. Unfortunately, that step is a difficult one to make, as evidenced by progress in cancer research. Scientists have long observed the structural changes in cancer cells, but the reasons for these changes are far from being understood. Without a clear understanding of *why* a particular biological process takes place, it is impossible to move toward reversing that process.

CAN AGING BE REVERSED OR DELAYED?

Growth Hormones

Nevertheless, genetic researchers have made great strides in the past 30 years in their understanding of the aging process. Indeed, contrary to our long-held assumptions about aging, many scientists have become convinced that aging is *reversible.* This may be achieved by introducing new hormones into the body to replace the depleted hormones in genes that serve as chemical messengers. Researchers at the National Institute on Aging, Veterans Administration centers, and universities around the country are testing the effects of injecting growth hormones into aging animals and humans. So far many startling discoveries have been made, such as increased lean muscle mass and vertebral bone density, and reduced fat levels. These changes in turn led to increased activity and vigor. While these effects are short-lived, it may not be long before a human growth hormone is marketed that can safely be administered on a regular basis, like daily doses of vitamins.

One promising compound that is being tested by U.S. and French researchers is the hormone dehydroepiandrosterone, or DHEA. This hormone is secreted by the adrenal glands and the body converts it into testosterone and estrogen. Production of DHEA increases from age 7 to 30, when it stabilizes, then begins to decline. By the age of 80, the body has less than 5 percent of the level of DHEA it produced in its peak. Animal studies have shown that administering DHEA to adult mice results in increased activity levels and learning speed. Human studies are just beginning. Preliminary studies in which DHEA was given orally have shown improved sleep, greater energy, increased sexual activity, and greater tolerance of stress. It may also increase production of an insulin-like growth factor that stimulates cell growth and cell division. The effects were sustained up to three months in these studies (Morales et al., 1995; Mortola and Yen, 1990). However, there is insufficient research evidence to recommend the regular, long-term use of DHEA. Side effects in these short-term studies included liver problems, growth of facial hair in women, and enlarged prostate and breasts among some men, especially at higher doses. Those effects may be due to DHEA's stimulation of testosterone and estrogen. While these and other experiments with growth hormones and other compounds are still in their infancy, they offer promise of extending active life expectancy for future cohorts of older adults. That is, they may not add years to the human life span, but will more likely add life to the years available to each individual.

Caloric Restriction

Several studies using animal models (mice, fruit flies, fish) have demonstrated that reducing caloric intake by 65 percent increased the life span of experimental animals by as much as 35 percent. Dietary restriction did not, however, include limiting nutrients in these studies. Caloric restriction that was accomplished mostly through reducing fat intake has been found to be most successful in extending the life of experimental animals without causing malnutrition. Yet, it is evident from these studies that restriction of fat, protein, or carbohydrate intake alone is not sufficient; total caloric intake must also be reduced. Nor have the same benefits been found from merely increasing the intake of antioxidants or specific vitamins. The benefits of caloric restriction are greatest when it is initiated at birth; however, even when mice were placed on such diets in middle age, their maximum lifespan increased by 10 to 20 percent (Weindruch, 1996). Until the results of longitudinal studies with primates are available, these conclusions are not generalizable to humans. The first such major study with primates is an ongoing one by researchers at the Baltimore Longitudinal Studies Gerontology Research Center (Weed et al., 1997; Lane et al., 1997; Lane et al., 1996, 1995). This study has examined the effects of feeding Rhesus monkeys 30 percent less than their normal caloric intake. After 6 years on this diet, these monkeys showed higher activity levels, lower body temperature, improved glucose metabolism, and a slower decline in DHEA levels produced by the adrenal glands than an age-matched control group of monkeys that were fed ad libitum (i.e., freely, with no caloric restrictions). These results provide the first evidence in primates that caloric restriction may have anti-aging effects by improving energy metabolism and maintaining the production of

adrenal steroids such as DHEA without artificially replacing it. These studies have also found that caloric restriction reduces the growth of tumors, delays kidney dysfunction, decreases loss of muscle mass, and slows other age-related changes ordinarily found in these animals. It also delays the onset of autoimmune disease, hypertension, cataracts, glaucoma, and cancers in these animals. These studies offer further support that caloric restriction may be useful for humans in improving their active life expectancy (Li and Wolf, 1997; Ausman and Russell, 1990; Masoro, 1990).

RESEARCH ON PHYSIOLOGICAL CHANGES WITH AGE

It is difficult to distinguish normal, age-related changes in many human functions from changes that are secondary to disease or other factors. Until the late 1950s, much of our knowledge about aging came from cross-sectional comparisons of healthy young persons with institutionalized or community-dwelling older populations who had multiple health problems. These comparisons led to the not-surprising conclusion that the organ systems of older persons function less efficiently than those of younger persons.

Since the 1950s, a series of longitudinal studies have been undertaken with healthy younger and middle-aged persons who have been followed for several years to determine changes in various physiological parameters. The first of these studies began in 1958 at the Gerontology Research Center in Baltimore, as described in Chapter 1 (Shock, 1962). The initial sample of 600 healthy males between the ages of 20 and 96 was expanded in 1978 to include females. Today, many of the people in the original sample are still participating in the study. Another longitudinal study was undertaken in 1955 at Duke University's Center for the Study of Aging, with a sample composed entirely of older adults. Some of these individuals were followed every two years for more than 20 years (Palmore, 1985, 1974). Many other researchers around the country are now examining physiological functions longitudinally. The information in this chapter is derived from their work.

Aging in Body Composition

Although individuals vary greatly in body weight and composition, there is a general decline in the proportion of body weight contributed by water for both men and women: on the average, from 60 percent to 54 percent in men, and from 52 percent to 46 percent in women (Blumberg, 1996). Lean body mass in muscle tissue is lost, whereas the proportion of fat increases (see Figure 3.1). This decline in muscle mass and increase in fat is known as "sarcopenia." Because of an increase in fibrous material, there is a loss of elasticity and flexibility in muscle tissue. After age 50, the number of muscle fibers steadily decreases; muscle mass declines by 40 percent between ages 30 and 80 (Kohrt and Holloszy, 1995). However, as described in Chapter 4, older people who maintain a vigorous exercise pro-

gram can prevent a significant loss of muscle tone. The loss of muscle mass and water, and increase in fat tissue, all have a significant effect on older people's ability to metabolize many medications. Some medications are processed by muscle tissue, some in fat, and some in water throughout the human body. With the changes in body composition described here, these medications may remain in fat tissue longer than needed, or may be too concentrated relative to the available water and muscle volume.

These changes also are associated with weight changes, from increased weight for some people in the middle years, until the later years when there is a tendency toward lower weight and lower calorie intake. This is why we rarely see people in their eighties and nineties who are obese. The balance of sodium and potassium also changes, with the ratio of sodium increasing by 20 percent from age 30 to 70. Changes in body composition also have implications for the diets of older people; although older people generally

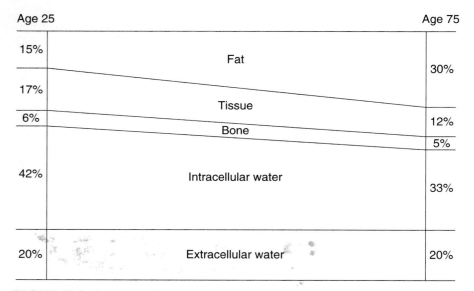

FIGURE 3.1   Distribution of Major Body Components
SOURCE: Reprinted with permission from the American Geriatrics Society. Speculations on vascular changes with age, by R. J. Goldman (*Journal of the American Geriatrics Society*, Vol. 18, p. 766, 1970).

need fewer total calories per day than active younger people, it is important for them to consume a higher proportion of protein, calcium, and vitamin D (Blumberg, 1996). However, many older individuals do not change their diet during the later years unless advised specifically by a physician. Others, especially those living alone, eat poorly balanced meals.

Changes in the Skin

As stated at the beginning of this chapter, changes in the appearance and texture of skin and hair are often the most visible signs of aging. These also tend to have deleterious consequences on how older people view themselves and are perceived by others. The human skin is unique among all other mammals in that it is exposed directly to the elements, with no protective fur or feathers to shield it from the direct effects of sunlight. In fact, ultraviolet light from the sun, which damages the elastic fibers beneath the skin's surface, is probably most directly responsible for the wrinkled, dried, and tougher texture of older people's skin, known as photoaging or extrinsic aging. Indeed, UV radiation may be the main culprit in skin aging. Experiments in which human skin cells collected from exposed parts of the body and from areas protected by the sun (e.g., underarms) found that the former type of cell grew much more slowly (Klingman, Grove, and Balin, 1985). This is evident when one compares the appearance of the skin of two 75-year-olds: one a retired farmer who has worked under the sun most of his life, the other a retired office worker who has spent most of his years indoors. The farmer generally will have more wrinkles; darker pigmentation known as **melanin,** which has been produced by the body to protect it from ultraviolet rays; and drier skin with a leathery texture. He is also more likely to have so-called *age spots* or *liver spots*—harmless from a health standpoint but of concern sometimes for their appearance. As one might expect, people who spend most of their lives in sunny climates are more prone to these changes. There is now growing concern about the negative consequences of extensive exposure to the sun.

Besides these environmental factors, the human body itself is responsible for some of the changes in the skin with age. The outermost layer of skin, the **epidermis,** constantly replenishes itself by shedding dead cells and replacing them with new cells. As the person gets older, the process of cell replacement is slowed, up to 50 percent between ages 30 and 70. More importantly, the connective tissue that makes up the second layer of skin, the *dermis,* thins because the number of dermal cells diminishes and makes it less elastic with age. This results in reduced elasticity and thickness of the outer skin layer, longer time for the skin to spring back into shape, and increased sagging and wrinkling. Women often experience these problems earlier than men, sometimes in their twenties and thirties. This is because women tend to have less oil in the sebaceous glands. However, there is considerable variation in the process of skin change, depending on the relative amount of oil in the glands, exposure to the sun, and heredity. Despite its changing appearance, the skin can still perform its protective function throughout old age.

Wound healing is also slower in older persons. Thus, people over age 65 require 50 percent more time than those under age 35 to form blisters as a means of closing a wound, and more time to form new epithelial tissue to replace blistered skin (Gilchrest, 1982).

The sebaceous and sweat glands, located in the dermis, generally deteriorate with age. Changes also occur in the deepest, or *subcutaneous,* skin layers, which tend to lose fat and water. The changes in subcutaneous skin are compounded by a reduction in the skin's blood circulation, which can damage the effectiveness of the skin's temperature regulatory mechanism and make older people more sensitive to hot and cold temperatures. As a result, older persons' comfort zone for ambient temperature is generally three to five degrees warmer than that for younger persons. It also takes longer for an older person to adjust after being exposed to either hot or cold extreme

SYMPTOMS OF HYPOTHERMIA AND HYPERTHERMIA

Hypothermia is defined as body temperatures below 95°F over a long period. It occurs when an individual's shivering response cannot be activated because of systemic changes or because it is ineffective after prolonged exposure to cold. Symptoms of hypothermia can appear in just a few hours, or over several days. These include confusion and forgetfulness, problems with speaking or breathing, shivering, sleepiness, poor coordination, a puffy face, and a stomach that is cold to touch in the early stages. In the late stages, the skin becomes very cold, pupils become fixed, and the body becomes more rigid. Body heat is lost faster than it can be replaced, resulting in an ability to raise one's body heat, loss of functional capacities, confusion, disorientation, and, in extreme cases, death. Older people who cannot afford to keep their homes heated above 68°F in the winter are at higher risk for hypothermia (Avery, 1984).

Hyperthermia, on the other hand, occurs when body temperature rises above normal and cannot be relieved by sweating, which results in heat exhaustion, heat stroke, heart failure, and stroke. Dizziness, nausea, vomiting, dry skin, cramps, fainting, and confusion may be initial symptoms. The problem is aggravated in older persons because of a reduced efficiency in their sweating response. Those who are overweight or have kidney problems, high blood pressure, poor circulation, diabetes, or emphysema are more vulnerable to hyperthermia than healthy older people. Older people with low income levels who live in houses with no air conditioning are at great risk for hyperthermia in climates where temperatures exceed 90°F with high humidity for several days in a row (Macey and Schneider, 1993).

temperatures. This leaves the older individual much more vulnerable to **hypothermia** (low body temperature, sometimes resulting in brain damage and death) and **hyperthermia** (heat stroke), as evidenced by reports of increased accidental deaths among older adults during periods of extremely cold winter weather and during prolonged heat spells. For example, the long heat wave in Chicago during July 1995 resulted in more than 500 deaths; most of these were older victims who lacked adequate ventilation in their homes (*Chicago Tribune,* July 31, 1995). To prevent hypothermia, it is recommended that indoor temperatures be set above 68°F in older people's homes, and that humidity be minimized; even though some older people are concerned about conserving energy and money by lowering their thermostats below 68°F, especially at night (Macey and Schneider, 1993; Macey, 1989; Collins, 1986).

Changes in the Hair

As we age, we also experience changes in the appearance and texture of our hair. Hair is thickest in early adulthood and decreases by as much as 20 percent in diameter by age 70. This is why so many older people appear to have fine, limp-looking hair. This change is compounded by the increased loss of hair with age. Although we lose up to 60 strands of hair daily during youth and early adulthood, the hair is replaced regularly through the action of estrogen and testosterone. As we age, however, more hairs are lost than replaced, especially in men. Some men experience rapid hair loss, leading to a receding hairline or even complete baldness by their mid-forties. Reasons for the observed variation in hair loss are not clear, but genetic factors appear to play a role.

Gray hair is a result of loss of pigment in the hair follicles. As we age, there is less pigment produced at the roots, so that eventually all the hair becomes colorless, or white in appearance. The gray color of some people's hair is an intermediate stage of pigment loss. In fact, some people may never experience a total loss of pigment production, but will live into an advanced old age with relatively dark hair. Others may experience graying in their twenties. In our society, graying of hair tends to have more stigma associated with it for women than for men.

Changes in the Musculoskeletal and Kinesthetic System

Stature or height declines an average of 3 inches with age, although the total loss varies across individuals and between men and women. Indeed, the Baltimore Longitudinal Studies found that a gradual reduction in height begins around age 30, about 1/16 inch per year on average. We reach our maximum size and strength at about age 25, after which our cells decrease steadily in number and size. This decline occurs in both the trunk and the extremities, and may be attributable to the loss of bone mineral. This loss of bone mineral density is, in turn, attributed to a decline in estrogen levels with menopause in women. Recent studies suggest that a decline in testosterone may explain the similar but less dramatic loss of bone mineral in older men (Rudman et al., 1991). The spine becomes more curved, and discs in the vertebrae become compacted. Such loss of height is intensified for individuals with **osteoporosis,** a disease that makes the bones less dense, more porous, and hence more prone to fractures following even a minor stress. For older people who have no natural teeth remaining, it is not unusual to lose a considerable volume of bone in the jaw or alveolar bone. This results in a poor fit of dentures and a painful feeling when chewing or biting with dentures. The loss

of bone mass characteristic of osteoporosis is *not* a normal process of aging, but a disease that occurs with more frequency among older women, as will be discussed in Chapters 4 and 14.

Another normal change with aging is that shoulder width decreases as a result of bone loss, weakened muscles, and loss of elasticity in the ligaments. Crush fractures of the spine cause the vertebrae to collapse, such that over time, some older people (especially women) appear to be stoop-shouldered or hunched—a condition known as **kyphosis.** Stiffness in the joints is also characteristic of old age; this occurs because cartilage between the joints wears thin and fluid that lubricates them decreases. Strength and stamina also decline with aging. Maximum strength at age 70 has been found to be 65 to 85 percent of the maximum capacity of a 25-year-old. This drops to 50 percent by age 80, although older persons who maintain an active physical fitness program show much less decline in strength. Grip strength declines by 50 percent in men between age 30 and 75, and to a lesser degree in women.

Although the incidence of mobility problems is greater among older people, aging per se is not the cause of motor disabilities. Disease states such as arthritis, stroke, some cardiac disorders, and damage to the kinesthetic sense may affect both the peripheral and central mechanisms responsible for mobility. Other factors limiting mobility include stiffness of joints, reduced ability to raise or turn the neck, and difficulty in gait and posture. Arthritis is a common chronic disease in older people that has a major impact on daily functioning, as we will discuss in the next chapter.

The **kinesthetic system** lets an individual know his or her position in space; adjustments in body position become known through kinesthetic cues. Because of age-related changes in the central nervous system, which controls the kinesthetic mechanism, as well as in muscles, older people demonstrate a decreased ability to orient their bodies in space and to detect externally induced changes in body position. Other physiological and disease-related changes, such as damage to the inner ear, may exacerbate this problem. Researchers who

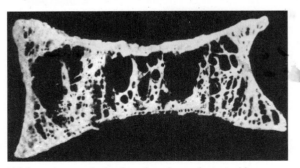

With osteoporosis, both trabecular and cortical bones become more brittle and lace-like.

have compared old and young subjects have found that older persons need more external cues to orient themselves in space, and can be incorrect by 5 to 20 degrees in estimating their position. If both visual and surface cues of position are lost, older people experience postural sway or inability to maintain a vertical stance (Teasdale, Stelmach, and Breunig, 1991).

Not surprisingly, these changes in motor functioning and in the kinesthetic system result in greater caution among older persons, who then tend to take slower, shuffling, and more deliberate steps. Older people are more likely to seek external spatial cues and supports while walking. As a result, they are less likely to go outside in inclement weather for fear of slipping or falling. Some may complain of dizziness and vertigo. These normal, age-related changes combine with the problems of slower reaction time, muscle weakness, and reduced visual acuity to make it far more likely for older people to fall and injure themselves. However, recent attempts to improve balance through general and aerobic exercise through alternative approaches such as Tai Chi, and through systematic programs to increase visual cues, have been successful in enhancing the postural stability of healthy older persons (Hu and Woollacott, 1994). Other advantages of exercise programs for older adults will be discussed in Chapter 4.

Changes in the Sense of Touch

Somesthetic or touch sensitivity also deteriorates with age. This is partially due to changes in the skin and partially to a loss with age in the number of nerve endings. Reduced touch sensitivity is especially prevalent in the fingertips and palms, and in the lower extremities. Age differences in touch sensitivity of the fingertips have been found to be much more dramatic than in the forearm. Using two-point discrimination tests (i.e., the minimum distance at which the subject detects the two points of a caliper), researchers have found that older persons need two to four times the separation of two points that younger persons do. This has significant implications for daily tasks that re-

quire sensitivity of the fingertips, such as the use of Braille by older blind persons (Stevens, 1992).

An important aspect of touch sensitivity is pain perception. Older people are less able to discriminate among levels of painful stimuli pain than young respondents. One reason for this may be that nerve cells in the skin become less efficient with age. As a result, burns are often more serious in older people because they do not respond to the heated object or flame until it is too late. Studies of age differences in threshold levels of pain, however, have produced mixed results (Harkins and Warner, 1980).

It is important to distinguish between pain perception and pain behavior. Tolerance for pain is a subjective experience, which may be related to cultural and personality factors. In older people, increased complaints of pain may be a function of depression and psychosomatic needs. On the other hand, some people may attempt to minimize their pain by not reporting above-threshold levels of unpleasant stimuli. This is consistent with a frequently observed attitude among many older persons that pain, illness, and discomfort are necessary corollaries of aging. In fact, most older adults probably underreport actual pain experienced. For example, an older person may not report symptoms of a heart attack unless or until it is severe. This has significant implications for health-seeking behaviors, as described in Chapter 4.

These musculoskeletal and kinesthetic changes may make it difficult for older people to perform some tasks of daily living, such as getting out of a chair or bed, or reaching up or deep inside a cabinet located overhead. The older person may attempt to accommodate to the latter situation by climbing on a chair or footstool in the kitchen to reach objects on top shelves. This is a dangerous way to solve the problem, because of the loss of balance and the increased brittleness of bones that some older people experience. These changes contribute to a higher incidence of falls and hip fractures in older people, which in turn may produce long-term disability and even death. This may indicate a growing incongruence between aging individuals and their physical environment: Poor lighting, uneven stairs and ground surfaces, high cabinets, and slippery bathroom floors are often found in older people's homes. Minor modifications around the home can reduce the risk of falls, such as installing handrails and grab bars, lowering cabinet height, and making sure that surfaces are smooth but not slippery.

Aging in the Respiratory System

Almost every organ system shows some decline in **functional** or **reserve capacity** with age, as illustrated by several physiological indices in Figure 3.2. It is important to keep in mind that this graph is based on *cross-sectional* data collected from healthy men in these age groups; results from the Baltimore Longitudinal Studies of Aging show more variability when longitudinal data for each cohort are examined. On average, many organ systems show a functional decline of about one percent per year after age 30. Complex functions that require the integration of multiple systems experience the most rapid decline. For example, maximum breathing capacity—which requires coordination of the respiratory, nervous, and muscular systems—is greatly decreased. Accordingly, normal changes in the respiratory and cardiovascular system become most evident with age. These changes are responsible for an individual's declining ability to maintain physical activity for long periods and the increasing tendency to fatigue easily. With aging, the muscles that operate the lungs lose elasticity so that respiratory efficiency is reduced. **Vital capacity,** or the maximum amount of

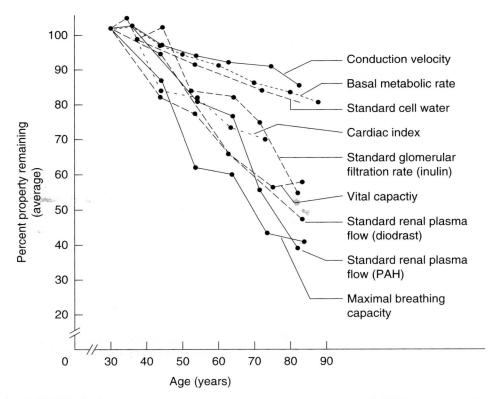

FIGURE 3.2   Aging in Organ Systems
SOURCE: N. W. Shock, The physiology of aging. *Scientific American, 206,* 110.

oxygen that can be brought into the lungs with a deep breath, declines. In fact, it has been estimated that the average decline for men is 50 percent between ages 25 and 70, or a decline from 6 quarts of air to 3 quarts. Breathing may become more difficult after strenuous exercise or after climbing up several flights of stairs, but it does not necessarily impair the older person's daily functions. It may simply mean that the person has to move more slowly or rest on the stairway landing. However, the rate of decline in vital capacity has been found to be slower in physically active men than in sedentary healthy men. In a longitudinal study that followed well-trained endurance athletes (average age 62 at baseline) and a control group of sedentary men (average age 61 at baseline) over 8 years, the maximum volume of oxygen they could take in declined by only 5.5 percent in the "master athletes," compared with 12 percent in sedentary men (Rogers et al., 1990). This suggests that aging per se plays only a small role in the decline of the respiratory system.

Of all the body systems, the respiratory system suffers the most punishment from environmental pollutants and infections. Therefore, it is difficult to distinguish normal, age-related changes from pathological or environmentally induced diseases. **Cilia,** which are hairlike structures in the airways, are reduced in number and are less effective in removing foreign matter; this diminishes the amount of oxygen available. This, combined with declining muscle strength in the chest that impairs cough efficiency, makes the older person more susceptible to chronic bronchitis, emphysema, and pneumonia. Older people can avoid serious loss of lung function by remaining active, pacing their tasks, and taking part in activities that do not demand too much exertion. Avoiding strenuous activity on days when the air quality is poor can also reduce the load on an older person's lungs.

Cardiovascular Changes and the Effects of Exercise

Structural changes in the heart and blood vessels include a reduction in bulk, a replacement of heart muscle with fat, a loss of elastic tissue, and an increase in collagen. Within the muscle fibers, an age pigment composed of fat and protein, known as *lipofuscin,* may take up 5 to 10 percent of the fiber structure (Pearson and Shaw, 1982). These changes produce a loss of elasticity in the arteries, weakened vessel walls, and **varicosities,** or an abnormal swelling in veins that are under high pressure (e.g., in the legs). In addition to loss of elasticity, the arterial and vessel walls become increasingly lined with lipids (fats), creating the condition of **atherosclerosis,** which makes it more difficult for blood to be pumped through the vessels and arteries. It should be noted that this buildup of fats and lipids occurs to some extent with normal aging, but it is exacerbated in some individuals whose diet includes large quantities of saturated fats. In Chapter 4, such lifestyle risk factors for heart disease are reviewed.

Blood pressure is expressed as the ratio of **systolic** to **diastolic pressure.** The former refers to the level of blood pressure (in mm.) during the contraction phase (systole), whereas the latter refers to the stage when the chambers of the heart are filling with blood. For example, a blood pressure of 120/80 indicates that the pressure created by the heart to expel blood can raise a column of mercury 120 mm. During diastole, in this example, the pressure produced by blood rushing into the heart chambers can raise a column of mercury 80 mm. In normal aging (i.e., no signs of cardiovascular disease), systolic blood pressure increases somewhat, but the diastolic blood pressure does not (see Figure 3.3). As with changes in the heart, extreme elevation of blood pressure is not normal and is associated with diet, obesity, and lifestyle, all of which have cumulative effects over the years (Lakatta, 1990). The harmful effects of abnormally high or low blood pressure are examined in Chapter 4.

The maximum heart rate achievable by sustained exercise is directly associated with age; an easy way to calculate this is: 220 minus age in years. For example, a 25-year-old could expect a maximum heart rate of 195 (220–25), whereas a 70-year-old could achieve 150 (220–70) beats per

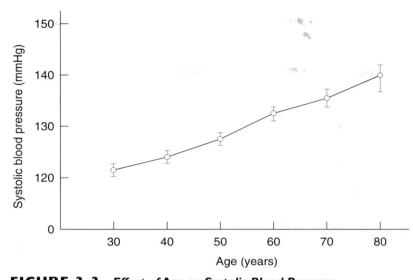

FIGURE 3.3   **Effect of Age on Systolic Blood Pressure**
SOURCE: J. D. Tobin, Physiological indices of aging. In D. Danon, N. W. Shock, and M. Marois
(Eds.), *Aging: A challenge in science and society*, Vol. I (New York: Oxford University Press,
1981).

minute. However, there is some variation across individuals, with the heart rate remaining relatively high in physically active older persons. Resting heart rates also decrease with aging, although physically well-conditioned older people tend to have heart rates more similar to the average younger person.

These changes in the heart and lungs result in less efficient utilization of oxygen. This, in turn, reduces an individual's capacity to maintain physical activity for long periods. Nevertheless, physical training for older persons can significantly reduce blood pressure and increase their aerobic capacity (O'Brien and Vertinsky, 1991). Studies of older persons described as "master athletes"—individuals who have continued to participate in competitive, aerobic exercise (running, bicycling, swimming) into the later years—have shown that physical training results in a greater volume of oxygen, more lean body weight, lower levels of low density lipoprotein (LDL) cholesterol, also known as "bad cholesterol," and higher levels of high density lipoprotein (HDL), or good cholesterol, than is

found in sedentary older persons (Yataco, Busby-Whitehead, Drinkwater, and Katzel, 1997; Rogers et al., 1990). However, these levels in master athletes are worse than in younger athletes, underscoring the reality that normal changes in the body's physiology and its operation cannot be eliminated completely. For example, world-class sprinters are generally in their late teens or early twenties, but marathon winners are normally in their late twenties or early thirties because strength and neuromuscular coordination peak earlier than stamina. After age 30, running speed declines by a few percent each year (Hayflick, 1996).

Nevertheless, moderate exercise, such as a brisk walk three to four times per week, appears to slow down these age-related changes. Researchers have found a significant increase in aerobic capacity, as measured by maximum volume of oxygen intake, and a reduction in fat composition among sedentary older persons after 6 months of low-intensity exercise training (e.g., walking for 20 to 30 minutes), followed by 6 months of high-intensity training (e.g., jogging for

Walking provides many physical and emotional benefits.

20 to 30 minutes). High-intensity exercise resulted in significant weight loss, but low-intensity exercise did not. However, high-intensity training resulted in more orthopedic injuries than did low-intensity training among older participants. For this reason, walking is often the best exercise. Both high- and low-intensity programs have been found to increase significantly the volume of oxygen consumed and to reduce blood pressure among women aged 67 to 89 (O'Brien and Vertinsky, 1991; Foster et al., 1989). These studies, however, suggest that exercise may not be sufficient for reducing cholesterol and triglyceride* levels in the blood, both of which have been associated with heart disease. Instead, reduced intake of animal fats, tropical oils, and refined carbohydrates appears to be essential for lowering these elements in the blood. Although there are limitations, such findings justify optimism that physical health can be considerably improved

---

*Triglyceride is a molecular compound made up of three fatty acids synthesized from carbohydrates.

through lifestyle changes, even after age 65. Aerobic exercise and a healthy lifestyle can significantly increase active life expectancy by postponing and shortening the period of **morbidity** (e.g., days of sickness) that one can expect in the later years. The significance of certain lifestyle habits for maintaining good health in old age is discussed further in Chapter 4.

Changes in the Urinary System

Both kidney and bladder functions change with age. The kidneys play an important role in regulating the body's internal chemistry by filtering blood and urine through an extraordinary system of tubes and capillaries, known as glomeruli. As blood passes through these filters, it is cleaned, and the necessary balance of ions and minerals is restored. In the process, urea (e.g., water and waste materials) is collected and passed through the ureter and the bladder, where it is excreted in the form of urine. With age, the kidneys decrease in volume and weight, and the total number of glomeruli correspondingly decreases by 30 percent from age 30 to age 65. As a result, **renal function**, defined by the rate at which blood is filtered through the kidneys, declines by up to 50 percent with age. These changes have significant implications for an older person's tolerance for certain medications such as penicillin, tetracycline, digoxin, and others that are cleared by glomerular filtration. These drugs remain active longer in an older person's system and may be more potent, indicating a need to reduce drug dosage and frequency of administration.

The kidneys also lose their capacity to absorb glucose, as well as their concentrating and diluting ability, contributing to increased problems with dehydration and **hyponetremia** (i.e., a loss of salt in the blood). Of any organ system, renal function deteriorates most dramatically with age, irrespective of disease.

Compounding this problem, bladder function also deteriorates with age. The capacity of the bladder may be reduced by as much as 50 percent in some persons older than age 65. At the same time, however, the sensation of needing to empty the bladder is delayed. The latter condition may be more a function of central nervous system dysfunction than changes in the bladder. As a result, **urinary incontinence** is common in older adults. It has been estimated that as many as 15 to 30 percent of older people living in the community and at least half of those in nursing homes suffer from difficulties with bladder control. The problem may be made worse by a stroke, dementia, or other diseases associated with the nervous system, such as Parkinson's (Cramer, 1993).

Because of these changes in the kidney and the bladder, older people may be more sensitive to the effects of alcohol and caffeine. Both of these substances inhibit the production of a hormone that regulates urine production. Ordinarily, this hormone, known as antidiuretic hormone (ADH), signals to the kidneys when to produce urine in order to keep the body's chemistry balanced. When it is temporarily inhibited by the consumption of alcohol, coffee, or tea, the kidneys no longer receive messages and, as a result, produce urine constantly. This, in turn, dehydrates the body. It appears that ADH production is slowed with aging, so substances that inhibit its production increase the load on the kidneys and the bladder. Because of these changes, older people may start to avoid social outings, even a trip to the grocery store, out of fear that they may not have access to a bathroom. Possible treatments for urinary incontinence, as well as ways that older people can alter their daily habits to accommodate bladder problems, are discussed more fully in Chapter 4.

Sexual Changes

Men and women experience changes in their sexual organs as they age, but these do not necessarily lead to sexual incapacity. The normal physiological changes that characterize aging alter the nature of the sexual response, but do not interfere with sexual pleasure. These changes are discussed in detail in Chapter 7.

Changes in the Gastrointestinal System

The gastrointestinal system includes the **esophagus**, stomach, intestines, colon, liver, and biliary tract. Although the esophagus does not show age-related changes in appearance, there are some changes in its function in older people. These may include a decrease in contraction of the muscles and more time for the cardiac sphincter (a valve-like structure that allows food to pass into the stomach) to open, thus taking more time for food to be transmitted to the stomach. The result of these changes may be a sensation of being full before having consumed a full meal. This in turn may reduce the pleasure a person derives from eating, and result in inadequate nutrient intake. This sensation also explains why older people may appear to eat such small quantities of food at mealtimes.

Secretion of digestive juices in the stomach apparently diminishes after age 50, especially among men. As a result, older people are more likely to experience the condition of **atrophic gastritis,** or a chronic inflammation of the stomach lining. Gastric ulcers are more likely to occur in middle age than in old age, but older people are at greater risk for colon and stomach cancer. Because of this risk, older people who complain of gastrointestinal discomfort should be urged to seek medical attention for the problem, instead of relying on home remedies or over-the-counter medications.

As with many other organs in the human body, the small and large intestines decrease in weight after age 40. There are also functional changes in the small intestine, where the number of enzymes is reduced, and simple sugars are absorbed more slowly, resulting in diminished efficiency with age. The smooth muscle content and muscle tone in the wall of the colon also decrease. Anatomical changes in the large intestine are associated with the increased incidence of chronic constipation in older persons.

However, behavioral factors are probably more important than organic factors in the development of constipation, as will be discussed in more detail in Chapter 4. Spasms of the lower intestinal tract are an example of the interaction of physiological with behavioral factors. Although they may occur at any age, such spasms are more common among older persons. These spasms are a form of functional disorder, that is, a condition without any organic basis, often due to psychological factors. Many gastrointestinal conditions that afflict older people are unrelated to the anatomical changes described previously. Nevertheless, they are very real problems to an older person who experiences them.

The liver also grows smaller with age, by about 20 percent, although this does not appear to have much influence on its functions. However, there is a deterioration in the ability to process medications that are dependent on liver function. Jaundice occurs more frequently in older people, and may be due to changes in the liver or to the obstruction of bile in the gall bladder. In addition, high alcohol consumption may put excessive strain on the older person's liver.

Changes in the Endocrine System

The endocrine system is made up of cells and tissues that produce a variety of hormones. One of the most obvious age-related changes in the endocrine system is **menopause,** resulting in a reduced production of two important hormones in women—**estrogen** and progesterone. There is strong evidence from a variety of studies that estrogen in particular protects women from heart disease, and more recently has been shown to decrease the risk of Alzheimer's disease. Replacing it can improve cognitive performance in women with this disease (Henderson, 1997; Henderson et al., 1994; Paganini-Hill and Henderson, 1996, 1991). Estrogen replacement therapy has many important benefits, but it also can increase the risk of endometrial and breast cancer in some women. These issues are discussed further in Chapter 4.

Many other hormones besides estrogen and progesterone have been found to decline with aging. These include **testosterone,** thyroid, growth hormones, and insulin. Changes in insulin levels with aging may affect the older person's ability to metabolize **glucose** in the diet efficiently, resulting in high blood sugar levels. It is unclear if the changes in hormone production are a cause or an effect of aging. Nevertheless, much of the research aimed at reversing or delaying aging has focused on replacing other hormones whose levels decline with aging. There is some support for this in animal studies; for example, by stimulating the hypothalamus in the brain (which produces growth hormones) of old female rats, researchers have stimulated the development of eggs and increased the synthesis of protein in these animals. Researchers have also administered thyroid hormones to old rats, thereby increasing the size of the thyroid and the efficiency of their immune system (Hayflick, 1996).

Changes in the Nervous System

The brain is composed of billions of neurons, or nerve cells, and billions of **glial cells** that support these. We lose some of both types of cells as we grow older. Neuronal loss begins at age 30, well before the period termed *old*. It is compounded by alcohol consumption, cigarette smoking, and breathing polluted air. The frontal cortex has been found to experience a greater loss of cells than other parts of the brain. A moderate degree of neuronal loss does not create a major decline in brain function, however. In fact, contrary to popular belief, we can function with fewer neurons than we have, so their loss is not the reason for mild forgetfulness in old age. Even in the case of Alzheimer's disease and other **dementias,** severe loss of neurons may be less significant than changes in brain tissue, blood flow, and receptor organs (Thomas et al., 1996).

Other aging-related changes in the brain include a reduction in its weight by 10 percent, an accumulation of lipofuscin (i.e., an age pigment composed of fat and protein), and slower transmission of information from one neuron to another. The reduction in brain mass occurs in all species, and is probably due to loss of fluids. The gradual buildup of lipofuscin, which has a yellowish color, causes the outer cortex of the brain to take on a yellow-beige color with age. As with the moderate loss of neurons, these changes do not appear to alter brain function in old age. That is, difficulties in solving problems or remembering dates and names cannot be attributed to these slight changes in the size and appearance of the brain.

In contrast, the change in neurotransmitters and in the structure of the **synapse** (the junction between any two neurons) does affect cognitive and motor function. Electroencephalograms, or readings of the electrical activity of the brain, show a slower response in older brains than in the young. These changes may be at least partially responsible for the increase in reaction time with age. Researchers with the Baltimore Longitudinal Studies of Aging (BLSA) have found that reaction time slows by as much as 20 percent between age 20 and age 60 (Hayflick, 1996). Other hypotheses include neuronal loss and reduced blood flow; however, available data are inconclusive. Reaction time is a complex product of multiple factors, primarily the speed of conduction and motor function, both of which are slowed by the increased time needed to transmit messages at the synapses. The reduced speed with which the nervous system can process information or send signals for action is a fairly widespread problem, even in middle age when people begin to notice lagging reflexes and reaction time. As a result, such tasks as responding to a telephone or doorbell, crossing the street, completing a paper and pencil test, or deciding among several alternatives generally take longer for older people than for the young. Most people adjust to these changes by modifying their physical environment or personal habits, such as taking more time to do a task and avoiding rush situations; for example, an older person may compensate by leaving the house one hour before an appointment instead of the usual 15 minutes, shopping for groceries during times when stores are not crowded, or shopping in smaller stores. Such adaptations are perhaps most pronounced in the tasks associated with driving. The older driver tends to be more cautious, to slow down well in advance of a traffic signal, to stay in the slower lane, and to avoid freeways during rush hour. Many choose to drive larger cars that can survive collisions better than compact cars. Despite this increased cautiousness, accident rates are high among older drivers, as we will discuss in the next chapter.

Changes in the central nervous system that accompany aging also affect the senses of hearing, taste, smell, and touch. Despite these changes, intellectual and motor function apparently do not deteriorate significantly with age. The brain has tremendous reserve capacity that takes over as losses begin. It is only when neuronal loss, inadequate function of neurotransmitters, and other structural changes are severe that the older person experiences significant loss of function. The changes in the brain that appear to be associated with Alzheimer's disease will be discussed in Chapter 6.

Changes in Sleep Patterns with Aging

One of the most common complaints of older people is that they can no longer sleep well, with up to 40 percent of older persons in community surveys complaining of sleep problems. These complaints have a basis in biological changes that occur with aging. Results of laboratory studies of sleep–wake patterns of adults have consistently revealed age-related changes in **EEG** patterns, sleep stages, and circadian rhythms (Vitiello, 1996).

Sleep progresses over five stages. The first four stages occur when no rapid eye movements take place (non-**REM** sleep); the fifth stage is that of rapid eye movements (**REM sleep**). Stage 4 is when deep sleep takes place. Sleep stages occur in a linear pattern from stage 1 through stage 4, then REM sleep, stage 5. Each cycle is repeated four or five times through the night. Brain wave activity differs in a characteristic pattern for each stage.

With normal aging, even in the absence of any predisposing diseases, there is a slowing down of many of these brain waves; the length of time in each stage changes. In particular, lab tests have shown a decline in total sleep time in stages 3, 4, and 5, and sleep is lighter. Older people have shorter cycles from stages 1 to 4 and REM sleep, with the latter stage occurring earlier in the cycle.

During these stages older people, more so than the young, are easily awakened, apparently by environmental stimuli that would not disturb a younger person (Vitiello and Prinz, 1991).

Changes in circadian rhythms, or the individual's cycle of sleeping and waking within a 24-hour period, are characterized by a movement from a two-phase pattern of sleep (awake during the day, asleep during the night) to a multiphasic rhythm that is more common in infants, i.e. daytime napping and shorter sleep cycles at night. These changes may be associated with changes in core body temperatures in older people discussed earlier in this chapter.

The older person may compensate by taking more daytime naps, which can lead to further disruptions in night sleep. More often, older people who report sleep disturbances to their primary physician are prescribed sleeping pills or sedative hypnotic medications; this age group represents the highest users of such medications, receiving almost one half of all sedative hyponotic drugs prescribed in the United States. Yet medications do not necessarily improve their sleep patterns, especially if used long-term (Vitiello, 1996; Ohayon and Caulet, 1995; Mullan, Katona, and Bellew, 1994). Both the incidence of sleeping difficulties and the use of sleeping pills are more common in older women than in older men. In fact, these normal, age-related changes in sleep patterns need not be disruptive to the older person's well-being. It may be disturbing for people accustomed to normal sleep in their youth to have a lighter, shorter, and more disrupted sleep pattern as they age, but individuals can adjust to these changes just as they do to other normal physiological changes without resorting to medications. Many hypnotics used to treat sleep disorders can produce a paradoxical effect by resulting in insomnia if used for a long time. Sleep disturbances can be alleviated by improving one's **sleep hygiene.** These include behaviors such as increasing physical exercise, reducing the intake of caffeine and other medications, avoiding napping during the day, as well as improving the sleeping environment (e.g., a quieter

bedroom with heavy curtains to block out the light) (Vitiello, 1996).

There are a few true *disorders of sleep* that can occur with aging; these include respiratory problems, **sleep apnea,** which is defined as a 5- to 10-second cessation of breathing, and **nocturnal myoclonus,** which is a neuromuscular disturbance affecting the legs during sleep. These must be treated with medications. More often, however, sleep disturbance is generally associated with poor physical health and depression (Foley et al., 1995; Livingston, Blizard, and Mann, 1993).

CHANGES IN SENSORY FUNCTIONS

Our ability to see, hear, touch, taste, and smell has a profound influence on our interactions with the social and physical environment. Recognizing this relationship between our sensory and social functioning, and the gradual decline in our sensory abilities with aging, it is critical that we understand these changes and how they can influence our social capabilities as we age. There is a popular belief that, as we get older, we cannot see, hear, touch, taste, or smell as well as we did when we were younger. This appears to be true. The decline in all our sensory receptors with aging is normal; in fact, it begins relatively early. We reach our optimum capacities in our twenties, maintain this peak for a few years, and gradually experience a decline, with a more rapid rate of decline after the ages of 45 to 55. Having said this, we should note that there is tremendous diversity among individuals in the rate and severity of sensory decline, as illustrated earlier by Mrs. Hill and Mr. Jones. Some older persons may have better visual acuity than most 25-year-olds; there are many 75-year-olds who can hear better than most younger persons. Think about the wine taster who, in old age, may still be considered the master of this trade, performing a job that requires excellent taste discrimination.

Although age per se does not determine deterioration in sensory functioning, it is clear that many internal changes do occur (the older person who has better visual or hearing acuity than a 25-year-old probably had even better sensory capacities in the earlier years). It is important to focus on *intraindividual* changes with age, not *interindividual* differences, when studying sensory and perceptual functions. Unfortunately, most of the research on sensory changes with age is cross-sectional, that is, based on comparing different persons who are older and younger. For this reason, the reader needs to be aware that there are tremendous individual differences in how much and how severely sensory functions deteriorate with age.

Changes in different senses vary within the same individual. Thus, the person who experiences an early and severe decline in hearing acuity may not have any deterioration in visual functioning. Some sensory functions, such as hearing, may show an early decline, yet others, such as taste and touch, change little until well into advanced old age. Over time, however, sensory changes affect an older person's interactions with the social and physical environments.

Because these changes are usually gradual, people adapt and compensate by using other, still-intact sensory systems. For example, they may compensate by standing closer to objects and persons in order to hear or see, by using nonverbal cues such as touch and different body orientations, or by utilizing technical devices such as bifocals or hearing aids. To the extent that people can control their environment and make it conform to their changing needs, sensory decline need not be incapacitating. However, if the environment does not allow for modification to suit individual needs, if the decline in any one system is severe, or if several sensory systems deteriorate at the same time, it becomes much more difficult for individuals to use compensatory mechanisms. Such problems are more likely to occur in advanced old age.

Before reviewing the major changes in sensory processes that accompany aging, it is helpful to clarify some terminology. **Sensation** is the process of taking in information through the sense organs. **Perception** is a higher function in which the infor-

mation received through the senses is processed in the brain. **Sensory threshold** is the minimum intensity of a stimulus that a person requires in order to detect the stimulus. This differs for each sensory system. **Recognition threshold** is the intensity of a stimulus needed in order for an individual to identify or recognize it. As might be expected, a greater intensity of a stimulus is necessary to recognize than to detect it. **Sensory discrimination** is defined as the minimum difference necessary between two or more stimuli in order for a person to distinguish between them. There is considerable evidence that, with normal aging, a decline occurs in all sensory systems. That is, sensory and recognition thresholds increase, and discrimination between multiple stimuli demands greater distinctions between them.

Changes in Vision

Although the proportion of blind persons in old age is not significantly higher than among younger persons, the rates of impairments that affect some aspects of visual functioning increase with age. Vision problems increase with age; when we compare 55- to 64-year-olds with those over age 85, there is a fourfold increase in the rate of visual impairments, from 55 per 1000 people to 225 per 1000 (Bognoli and Hodos, 1991). As a result, older persons are more likely to experience problems with daily tasks that require good visual skills, such as reading small print or signs on moving vehicles, locating signs, or adapting to sudden changes in light level. In addition, impaired vision caused by untreated cataracts or glaucoma is much more likely to result in problems with activities of daily living than is hearing impairment (Rudberg et al., 1993).

EFFECTS OF STRUCTURAL CHANGES IN THE EYE
Most age-related problems in vision are attributable to changes in parts of the eye (see Figure 3.4). However, these problems are aggravated by changes in the central nervous system which block the transmission of stimuli from the sensory

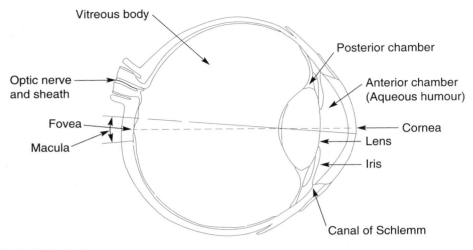

FIGURE 3.4 **The Eye**

organs. Changes in the visual pathways of the brain and in the visual cortex may be a possible source of some of the alterations that take place in visual sensation and perception with age.

The cornea is usually the first part of the eye to be affected by age-related changes. The surface of the cornea thickens with aging, and the blood vessels become more prominent. The smooth, rounded surface of the cornea becomes flatter and less smooth, and may take on an irregular shape. The older person's eye appears to lose its luster and is less translucent than it was in youth. In some cases, a fatty yellow ring, known as the *arcus senilis,* may form around the cornea. This is not a sign of impending vision loss; in fact, it has no impact on vision. It is sometimes associated with increased lipid deposits in the blood vessels.

At its optimal functioning, the pupil is sensitive to light levels in the environment, widening in response to low light levels and contracting when light levels are high. With aging, the pupil appears to become smaller and more fixed in size. The maximum opening of the pupil is reduced in old age, commonly to about two-thirds the original maximum. That is, the older person's pupil is less able to respond to low light levels by dilating or opening to the extent needed. The eye also re-sponds more slowly to changes in light conditions. This problem is compounded by a slower shift from cones to rods under low-light conditions. As a result, the older person may have considerable difficulty functioning in low-light situations, or in adjusting to significant changes in ambient light. In fact, older people may need three times more light than younger persons to function effectively; for example, highway signs must be 65 to 75 percent closer than for younger drivers to be readable at night. These changes may also reduce the older person's ability to discern images in conditions of poor light contrast (e.g., driving at twilight or under foggy or rainy conditions), and to detect details in moving objects. Even among healthy older persons who are still driving, age-related visual changes may significantly alter their abilities under marginal conditions. For example, a survey of participants aged 22 to 92 in the Baltimore Longitudinal Studies (described in Chapter 1) revealed that age was highly correlated with reports of problems with sudden merging of other vehicles, judging their own and other vehicles' speed, driving under glare and hazy conditions, and reading street signs while driving (Kline et al., 1992).

For these reasons, older people may choose to avoid such activities, especially driving among fast-moving traffic on freeways at night when bright headlights create glare against asphalt surfaces, and in rain. Although this is a safe approach for coping with age-related difficulties in low-light situations, older people must be encouraged to maintain their activity level and not become isolated because of declines in visual function. In such instances, families and professionals may have to encourage older people to use other forms of transportation, such as buses and taxis, thereby avoiding the problem of too little environmental stimulation relative to the person's competence.

As another illustration, many older people may feel frustrated when they go to a special restaurant for an evening dinner, only to find that the tables are lit by candles. This makes it difficult to read the menu, to see the way to the table, and even to have eye contact with companions. Family and friends may be frustrated in such situations if they do not understand that the older person's complaints about the restaurant stem from these changes in vision, not from their lack of appreciation for their efforts. Some older people cope with these problems by avoiding such restaurants altogether or going there only during daylight hours.

PROBLEMS RELATED TO OXYGEN AND FLUID LEVELS
Problems in rod and cone function may be related to a reduced supply of oxygen to the retina. Some researchers have suggested that this may be due to a deficiency of vitamin A. However, there is little research evidence to suggest that increased intake of vitamin A in old age can improve visual functioning under low-light conditions.

As stated earlier, there are two fluid-filled chambers in the eye: aqueous humour fills the anterior or front portion of the eye, and vitreous humour is found in the posterior chamber, behind the lens. The aqueous humour drains through the Canal of Schlemm. In the disease state known as **glaucoma,** there may be less efficient drainage, or perhaps excessive production of the aqueous humour. Glaucoma occurs more frequently after middle age and can be managed with regular medications. More severe cases may require surgery or, more recently, the use of laser treatment. In its

later stages, glaucoma may result in tunnel vision, which is a gradual narrowing of an individual's field of vision, such that peripheral vision is lost and the individual can focus only in the center. Untreated glaucoma is the third leading cause of blindness in the United States, the United Kingdom, and Canada (Accardi, Gombos, and Gombos, 1985), and increases in frequency with age. Among African Americans, glaucoma is the leading cause of blindness, with a prevalence rate in middle-class blacks 15 times that of whites. Even when socioeconomic differences and access to health care are controlled, glaucoma is both more prevalent and more difficult to treat in blacks (Sommer, Tielsch, and Katz, 1991; Wilson, 1989).

Unlike the aqueous humour, which drains and is replenished throughout life in healthy persons, the vitreous humour remains constant. With aging, it may thicken and shrink. Lumps of collagen, the primary content in this fluid, may be formed. Older persons who complain of "floaters" in the eye are responding to these free-floating formations in the front chamber of the eye. These changes, which cannot be prevented or stopped, are often upsetting to individuals. Those who experience them should be assured that floaters do not cause blindness. Frequent examinations by an ophthalmologist are useful in the later years to check for such conditions and to determine if they may be caused by other diseases.

EFFECTS OF AGING ON THE LENS
Perhaps the greatest age-related changes in the eye occur in the lens. In fact, it has been suggested that the lens is a model system for studying aging because it contains some of the oldest cells in the body, formed during the earliest stages of the development of the embryo. Furthermore, the lens is a relatively simple structure biochemically; all of its cells are of the same type, composed of protein.

Collagen is the primary protein in the lens, and makes up 70 to 80 percent of the total tissue composition of the entire body. As it ages, collagen thickens and hardens. This change in collagen makes the lens less elastic, thereby reducing its ability to change form (i.e., from rounded to elongated and flat) as it focuses from near to far. Muscles that help stretch the lens also deteriorate with age, thereby compounding the problem of changing the shape of the lens. This process, known as **accommodation,** begins to deteriorate in middle age and is manifested in increasing problems with close vision. (We all are familiar with people even in their forties and fifties who need to hold their reading material at arm's length.) As a result, many persons in their forties may need to use reading glasses or bifocals. By age 60, accommodative ability is significantly deteriorated. Decrements in accommodation may cause difficulties for the older person when shifting from near to far vision; for example, when looking across a room, walking up or down stairs, reading and looking up, and writing notes while looking up at a blackboard or a lecturer.

The hardening of the lens due to changes in collagen tissue does not occur uniformly. Rather, there is differential hardening, with some surfaces allowing more light to enter than others. This results in uneven refraction of light through the lens and onto the retina. When combined with the poor refraction of light through the uneven, flattened surface of the cornea, extreme sensitivity to glare often results. This problem becomes particularly acute in environments with a single source of light aimed at a shiny surface, such as a large window at the end of a long, dark corridor with highly polished floors, occasional street lights on a rain-slicked highway, or a bright, single, overhead incandescent light shining on a linoleum floor. These conditions may contribute to older people's greater caution and anxiety, while driving or walking.

From childhood through early adulthood, the lens is a transparent system through which light can easily enter. With normal aging, the lens becomes more opaque, and less light passes through (especially shorter wavelengths of lights); these changes compound the problems of poor vision in low light that were described earlier. Some older persons experience a more severe opacification (clouding of the lens) to the point that the lens prevents light from entering. This condition, known

as a **cataract,** is a leading cause of blindness in the United States and the primary cause of blindness worldwide (Sperduto, 1994). In a survey of white and black older persons in Baltimore, unoperated age-related cataracts accounted for 27 percent of all blindness among African Americans, compared with 13 percent among whites (Sommer et al., 1991). Researchers in the Framingham eye study have examined the incidence of cataracts, i.e., the development of the condition in the same individual over a number of years. In a re-examination of survivors of the original Framingham eye study 13.6 years later, the incidence rate was 50 percent for people aged 55 to 59 at the beginning of the study. It jumped to 80 percent for older adults who had been age 70 to 74 at the start (Milton and Sperduto, 1991). Its prevalence increases tenfold between ages 52 and 85. There is strong evidence for a relationship between the development of cataracts with age and the lack of antioxidants such as vitamins A, C, and E (Jacques, Chylack, and Taylor, 1994; Seddon et al., 1994b).

A cataract may occur in any part of the lens—in the center, the peripheral regions, or scattered throughout. A scattered cataract produces extreme opacity in various parts of the lens and causes light to refract at varying densities, resulting in severe problems with glare. If the lens becomes totally opaque, cataract surgery may be required to extract the lens. One of the most frequently performed types of eye surgery, it carries relatively little risk, even for very old persons, and can significantly enhance the older person's quality of life. Indeed, this is the most common surgical procedure performed on people over age 65, with about 1.35 million extractions performed per year, usually as an outpatient procedure (AHCPR, 1993). A lens implant in place of the extracted lens capsule is the most common treatment, but a contact lens is an alternative treatment. The advantage of the implant is that it does not require the older person to have good finger dexterity to put the lens in the eye and take it out. The implant is particularly useful for the person who still has one natural lens, because it allows an image to form at the same distance from the retina in both eyes. When the older person first obtains a substitute lens, it takes some time to adjust to performing daily activities, especially if the artificial lens is not an implant, and the images form on different planes for the two eyes. Researchers have found that patients who receive a lens implant show improvement not just in visual function, but also in objective assessments of activities of daily living and manual function within 4 to 12 months (Applegate et al., 1987).

In addition to getting harder and more opaque, the lens becomes yellower with age. This is also due to changes in the collagen tissue that makes up the lens. The increasingly more opaque and yellowing lens acts as a filter to screen out wavelengths of light, thus reducing the individual's color sensitivity and ability to discriminate among colors that are close together in the blue-green range. Changes in the lens are especially noticeable after age 60 (Cooper, Ward, Gowland, and McIntosh, 1991; Weale, 1988). Older people may have problems selecting clothing in this color range, sometimes resulting in their wearing poorly coordinated outfits. Deterioration in color discrimination may also be due to age-related changes in the visual and neural pathways.

The physical environment can be redesigned to accommodate the older person's competence in this area. For example, older people can benefit from rooms and hallways that use widely contrasting colors on opposite ends of the color spectrum, such as red and yellow, green and orange. Generally, blue and green should not be used to define adjoining spaces, such as stairs and stair landings, floors and ramps, and curbs and curbcuts. This is particularly important when the junction of those spaces represents different levels, so that not seeing these color distinctions leaves a person at risk of an accident.

OTHER CHANGES IN VISION   Depth and distance perception also deteriorate with aging, because of a loss of convergence of images formed in the two eyes. This is caused by differential rates of hardening and opacification in the two lenses, uneven refraction of light onto the retina, and reduced visual acuity in aging eyes. (The problem of depth perception becomes compounded for people who have had cataract surgery in one eye and must use a contact lens in that eye, but nothing in the other eye). As a result, there is a rapid decline after age 75 in the ability to judge distances and depths, particularly in low-light situations and in the absence of orienting cues. Examples of situations with inadequate cues include stairs with no color distinctions at the edges and pedestrian ramps or curbcuts with varying slopes and no cues to guide the user. The older driver who is undergoing changes in depth perception experiences increased problems when driving behind others, approaching a stop sign, or parking between other cars.

Another change in the visual system that normally occurs with age is narrower peripheral vision (the ability to see on either side without moving the eyes or the head). The field of vision may be as wide as 270° in some young persons, and as narrow as 120° in some older adults. This is because the fovea (or blind spot) increases in size between ages 60 and 90, and retinal metabolism deteriorates, especially in the peripheral region where there are fewer nerve endings. The problem of reduced peripheral vision becomes particularly acute when driving. An older person may not see cars approaching from the left or right at an intersection. Combined with reduced reaction time and age-related musculoskeletal changes that make turning the neck difficult, older drivers experience greater risks. These changes are often of great concern to family and friends who worry about whether and how to convince an older person to stop driving.

Some older persons experiencing age-related macular degeneration (AMD) may have the opposite problem: loss of the central visual field. The macula is that point in the retina with the best visual acuity, especially for seeing fine detail, because it has the highest concentration of cones. **Macular degeneration,** the fourth major cause of blindness in the United States, occurs if the macula receives less oxygen than it needs, resulting in destruction of the existing nerve endings in this region. The incidence of macular degeneration, like cataracts, increases with age, but even more dramatically.

People over age 80 have 15 times the likelihood of developing AMD than people aged 60. There is evidence for both a genetic basis and environmental risk factors for age-related macular degeneration. Like cataracts, AMD may be associated with a lack of antioxidants. Studies that have supplemented older people's diets with carotenoid rich foods, and some that used zinc supplements, have found positive effects on visual activity of AMD patients (Allikmets et al., 1997; Blumberg, 1996; Seddon et al., 1994a).

The early stages of macular degeneration may begin with a loss of detail vision; then central vision gradually becomes worse, so that in severe cases, the older person has poor central vision, but adequate peripheral vision. Total blindness rarely occurs. Older persons with this condition may compensate by using their remaining peripheral vision. They may then appear to be looking at the shoulder of someone they are addressing, but actually be relying on peripheral vision to see the person's face. Laser treatment in the early stages of this disease has been effective in preventing the loss of central vision in many cases.

Some older people experience reduced secretion of tears, often associated with diseases such as Sjögren's Syndrome. These individuals, most often post-menopausal women, complain of "dry eyes" that cause irritation and discomfort. Unfortunately, this condition has no known cure, but it does not cause blindness and it can be managed with artificial tears to prevent redness and irritation. Artificial tears can be purchased at most drugstores.

The muscles that support the eyes, similar to those in other parts of the body, deteriorate with age. In particular, two key muscles atrophy. These are the elevator muscles, which move the eyeball up and down within its socket, and the ciliary muscle, which aids the lens in changing its shape. Deterioration of the elevator muscles results in a reduced range of upward gaze. This may cause problems with reading overhead signs and seeing objects that are placed above eye level, such as on high kitchen shelves. Weakening of the ciliary muscles contributes to the problem of poor accommodation in the later years.

Assisting Adaptation and Quality of Life through Environmental Modifications

Many older adults report significant impairments in their activities of daily living, including reading small print, functioning in and adjusting to dimly lit environments, tracking moving targets, and locating a sign in a cluttered background (Kosnick et al., 1988). This may mean that an older person feels compelled to give up valued social activities, such as playing cards, participating in reading clubs, driving, cooking, and hobbies such as sewing, leathercrafts, and stamp collecting. Abandoning these activities often produces a sense of loss and isolation. Furthermore, the environment outside the home can become too demanding and difficult to negotiate safely. Family and friends can assist by providing encouragement and by improving the physical environment to support rather than hinder an older person who is experiencing these changes.

In terms of maintaining person-environment congruence and psychological well-being, an aging person should be encouraged to maintain social contacts, even if new activities must be substituted for old. Older people can take advantage of large-print newspapers and books, audio tapes of books that are available in community libraries, playing cards with large letters and, more recently, larger fonts on flat-screen computer monitors that are designed to reduce glare. Local agencies serving the visually impaired often provide low-vision aids at minimal cost. These include needle threaders for sewing; templates for rotary telephones, irons, and other appliances; large-print phone books, clocks, and calendars; and magnifying glasses for situations where large-print substitutes are unavailable.

Family and friends also can help by improving the physical environment inside and around an older person's home. These changes may be as simple as replacing existing lightbulbs with higher wattage and 3-way bulbs, rearranging furniture so that low tables and footstools are outside the traffic flow, and putting large-print labels on prescription bottles, spices, and cooking supplies. Other environmental modifications may be more costly or require the use of a professional architect. Contrasting color strips on stairs, especially on carpeted or slippery linoleum stairs, aid the older person's depth perception. Color and light coding of ramps and other changes in elevation also can be valuable. To the extent possible, changes in floor surfaces such as door sills should be removed or well demarcated. Increasing the number of light sources, installing nonslip and nonglossy floor coverings, and using a flat paint instead of glossy finishes can reduce the problem of glare. Venetian and vertical blinds can also help the older person control glare throughout the day. An even better architectural solution is to use indirect or task lighting (e.g., reading lamps, countertop lamps) rather than ceiling fixtures, and adding dimmer switches to the rooms used most by older people.

All these solutions can enhance the competence of a person who is experiencing gradual declines in visual functions. Age-related changes in vision need not handicap people if they can be encouraged to adapt their usual activities and their environment to fit their current level of visual functioning and their needs. An older person who is having difficulty adjusting to losses produced by vision decrements may initially resist such changes. One way to address this resistance is for family members and service providers to involve the older person in decisions about environmental modifications and alternative activities.

Changes in Hearing

In terms of survival, vision and hearing are perhaps our most critical links to the world. Although vision is important for negotiating the physical environment, hearing is vital for communication. Because hearing is closely associated with speech, its loss disrupts a person's understanding of others and even the recognition of one's own speech. Consider some ways in which we rely on our hearing ability in everyday life: in conversations with family, friends, and co-workers; in localizing the sound of approaching vehicles as we cross the street or drive; and in interpreting other people's emotions through their tone of voice and use of language.

How does a person function if these abilities gradually deteriorate? Clearly, an older person who is experiencing hearing loss learns to adapt and make changes in behavior and in social interactions, so as to reduce the detrimental social impact of hearing loss. Many younger hearing-impaired persons learn sign language or lip reading. But these are complex skills requiring extensive training and practice, and are less likely to be learned by those who experience gradual hearing loss late in life.

THE ANATOMY AND PHYSIOLOGY OF THE EAR
It is useful to review the anatomy of the ear in order to understand where and how auditory func-

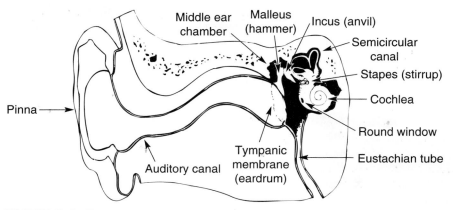

FIGURE 3.5 The Ear

tion deteriorates with age. The auditory system has three components, as illustrated in Figure 3.5. The outer ear begins at the **pinna**, that visible portion that is identified as the ear. The **auditory canal** is also part of the outer ear. Note the shape of the pinna and auditory canal; it is a most efficient design for localizing sounds.

The eardrum, or **tympanic membrane**, is a thin membrane that separates the outer ear from the middle ear. This membrane is sensitive to air pressure of varying degrees and vibrates in response to a range of loud and soft sounds. In the **middle ear** are located three bones: the malleus, the incus, and the stapes, more commonly known as the hammer, the anvil, and the stirrup (so named because of their shapes). These very finely positioned and interrelated bones carry sound vibrations from the middle ear to the **inner ear**— that snail-shaped circular structure called the cochlea. Amplified sounds are converted in the cochlea to nerve impulses, which are then sent through the internal auditory canal and the cochlear nerve to the brain, where they are translated into meaningful sounds. The cochlea is a fluid-filled chamber with thousands of hair cells that vibrate two parallel membranes to move sound waves. High-pitched sounds stimulate hair cells at the base of the cochlea; low-pitched sounds stimulate hair cells at the apex. The vibration of these hair cells is one of several factors involved in the perception of pitch (or frequency) and loudness (intensity) of a sound.

AGE-RELATED CHANGES The pinna appears somewhat elongated and rigid in some older adults. These changes in the outer ear, however, have no impact on hearing acuity. The supporting walls of the external auditory canals also deteriorate with age, as is true for many muscular structures in the human body, including, as we have seen, the muscles of the eye. Arthritic conditions may affect the joints between the malleus and stapes, making it more difficult for these bones to perform their vibratory function. Otosclerosis is a condition in which the stapes becomes fixed and cannot vibrate. It is sometimes

found in young persons, but more frequently occurs in the later years.

The greatest decline with age occurs in the cochlea, where structural changes result in **presbycusis**, or age-related hearing loss. Changes in auditory thresholds can be detected by age 30 or even younger, but the degeneration of hair cells and membranes in the cochlea is not observed until much later. Tests of pure tone thresholds (i.e., the level at which a tone of a single frequency can be detected) have revealed a steady decline in longitudinal studies over 15 years. Changes in the high-frequency range were found to be about 1 dB per year. In the range of speech, changes were slow until age 60, then accelerated to a rate of 1.3 dB per year after age 80 (Brant and Fozard, 1990). These declines may be even worse for the general population, since this study excluded people with diseases of the ear and with self-reported hearing difficulties. It is estimated that about 39 percent of the population age 65 and older in the United States have some loss of hearing, and 13 percent suffer from advanced presbycusis (Gordon-Salant, 1996).

As with studies regarding changes in the visual system, researchers in the area of auditory perception have suggested that changes in the brain with aging are primarily responsible for the deterioration in auditory functioning. These may include cellular deterioration and vascular changes in the major auditory pathways to the brain. However, aging and disease-related pathological changes can damage the auditory system itself. Together with exposure to environmental noise over a lifetime, these factors can cause presbycusis (Gordon-Salant, 1996).

Tinnitus is another problem that affects hearing in old age. This is a high-pitched "ringing" that is particularly acute at night or in quiet surroundings. It may occur bilaterally or in one ear only. The incidence increases threefold between youth and middle age, and fourfold between youth and old age. Tinnitus may be related to occupational noise exposure; for example, men with tinnitus have been found to have 20 to 30 years of exposure to noisy work environments. This condition may be aggravated by other types of hearing loss (Rosenhall and Karlsson, 1991). It cannot be cured, but people suffering from tinnitus can generally learn to manage it. Alternative approaches such as accupuncture have been found to reduce the ringing, however (Micozzi, 1997).

In contrast to visual changes, hearing loss appears to be significantly affected by environmental causes. People who have been exposed to high-volume and high-frequency noise throughout their lives (e.g., urban dwellers and factory workers) experience more hearing decrements in old age

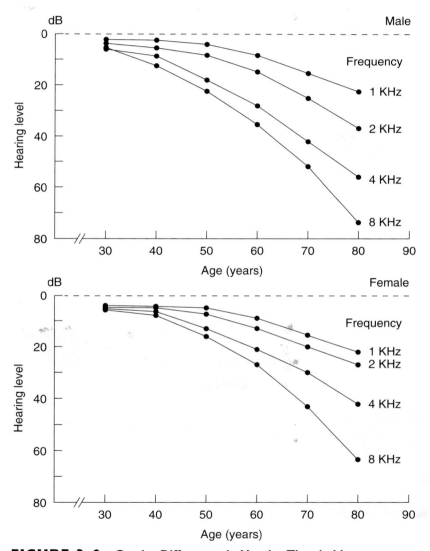

FIGURE 3.6   Gender Differences in Hearing Thresholds
SOURCE: J. M. Ordy, K. R. Brizzee, T. Beavers, and P. Medart. Age differences in the functional and structural organization of the auditory system in man. In J. M. Ordy and K. R. Brizzee (Eds.), *Sensory systems and communication in the elderly* (New York: Raven Press, 1979), p. 156. Reprinted with permission of the author and publisher.

than do those from rural, low-noise environments. Women generally show less decline than men (see Figure 3.6). It is interesting to speculate why these sex differences appear. Are they due to variations in noise exposure or to hormonal differences between men and women? The fact that severe hearing loss is found in some women suggests that the former hypothesis may be more likely.

Hearing loss may also be caused by excess ear wax, which seems to accumulate more rapidly in some older people. A thorough audiology exam should be done after a physician removes the ear wax in these cases.

COMPENSATION AND ADAPTATION Hearing loss can be of several types, involving limited volume and range or distortion of sounds perceived. Older persons who have lost hearing acuity in the range of speech (250–3000 Hz.) have particular difficulties distinguishing the sibilants or high-frequency consonants such as *z, s, sh, f, p, k, t,* and *g.* Their speech comprehension deteriorates as a result, which may be the first sign of hearing loss. In contrast, low-frequency hearing loss has minimal impact on speech comprehension. As Figure 3.6 illustrates, higher frequency sounds can be heard better by raising the intensity. Studies of speech perception have increased the recognition of consonants (*p, t, k, b, d, g*) by 50 to 90 percent among older persons by raising their intensity (Guelke, 1987).

Thus, an individual experiencing increased problems with hearing may compensate by raising the volume of the TV and radio, moving closer to the TV, or even listening to other types of music made by lower pitched instruments such as an organ. When this occurs, it is imperative to determine whether a hearing loss exists, to identify the cause, and to fit the individual with an appropriate hearing aid, if that is possible. A hearing aid increases the volume of sound. This may compensate for loss of higher-frequency sounds, but hearing aids cannot completely obliterate the problem of presbycusis. In fact, they often result in such major adaptation problems that many older persons stop wearing them after several months of frustrated attempts to adjust to the device. A major difficulty with conventional hearing aids is that the volume of background noise is raised, in addition to the sound that the user of the device is trying to hear. There is also a greater social stigma associated with wearing a hearing aid than with wearing glasses. These are undoubtedly some of the reasons why only about 20 percent of people with hearing loss use them (Liston, Solomon, and Banerjee, 1995).

If an older person feels stigmatized by the hearing aid, emotional support from others can be useful in easing the adjustment. If the hearing aid does not appear to fit an older person's needs, a replacement should be sought. Fortunately, developments in hearing aid technology are resulting in digital hearing aids with tiny computer chips that filter sounds to match each user's hearing loss profile, without amplifying background noises. These newer designs also are less obtrusive and fit well inside the ear. However, they can cost about twice as much as conventional hearing aids and are not covered by most health insurance plans.

Other means of compensating for hearing loss are to design environments that dampen background noises or to select such settings for communicating with older persons. Sound levels should not exceed 80 decibels in settings where older persons are found. Soundproof rooms are beneficial, particularly if housing for older people is built on busy streets or near freeways, but this is a costly alternative. Clinics and offices of health professionals should have at least one quiet area where an older patient can communicate with professionals without being distracted by background noises. Older people who are experiencing auditory decline can also benefit from new designs in telephones with volume adjusters and lights that blink when the phone rings.

When conversing with people who are experiencing age-related hearing loss, the following hints can help both younger and older persons enjoy their communication (Kiyak, 1996).

1. Face an older person directly and maintain eye contact.

2. Sit somewhat close and at eye level with the older person.
3. Do not cover the face with hands or objects when speaking.
4. Speak slowly and clearly, but without exaggerating speech.
5. Do not shout.
6. Avoid distracting background noises by selecting a quiet, relaxing place away from other people, machines, and traffic sounds.
7. Speak in a lower, but not monotonic, tone of voice.
8. Repeat key points in different ways.
9. If specific information is to be transmitted (e.g., how to take medications), structure the message in a clear, systematic manner.

One of the most frustrating experiences for some older people is the simultaneous deterioration of both hearing and vision. Although it is relatively rare for aging to result in significant declines in both these functions, family members, friends, and professionals must be especially sensitive to the communication techniques described earlier. When talking with an older person who is impaired in both hearing and vision, touching his or her hand, arm, or shoulder may aid communication.

Changes in Taste and Smell

Although older people may complain that food does not taste as good as it once did, these complaints are probably not due to an age-associated generalized loss of taste sensitivity. It was once thought that age brought dramatic decreases in the number of taste buds on the tongue, that this loss of receptor elements led to functional loss that was experienced as a dulling of taste sensation, and that these changes accounted for older people's reduced enjoyment of food (Mistretta, 1984). Recent studies, however, have challenged each link in this chain of reasoning.

Early research on taste anatomy reported taste-bud loss (Arey, Tremaine, and Monzingo, 1935), but subsequent studies have shown that the number of taste buds does not decline with age (Miller, 1988). Early studies of taste function found large age-related changes in taste thresholds (Murphy, 1979). However, later studies found much smaller age-related declines in threshold sensitivity (Cowart, 1989). Moreover, there are improved measurement techniques in this field that control for differences between generations in the way they respond to demand characteristics of the task. This has led to the conclusion in more recent studies that threshold loss almost never involves more than one of the four basic taste qualities.

Thresholds reflect the ability of the sensory system to detect weak stimuli, but this aspect of taste function may be less relevant to the enjoyment of food than the ability to appreciate taste intensity. For example, older people with decreased taste threshold sensitivity will require more salt to know if there is any salt on their vegetables. But to determine *how* salty the vegetables are requires a different taste mechanism that may still be functioning. This ability to appreciate the strength of a taste stimulus can be assessed by modern direct scaling techniques. Studies using these techniques have demonstrated that taste-intensity perception is remarkably robust with age (Tylenda and Baum, 1988).

The notion that various functions decline differentially has replaced the belief that older people

Cooking with spices can enhance olfactory and taste sensitivity.

AN OLDER PERSON WITH MULTIPLE SENSORY IMPAIRMENTS

Mrs. Wilson is an 82-year-old widow who has lived on her own for the past 20 years since her husband died. She had cataract surgery 12 years ago in her left eye, and began wearing a hearing aid 10 years ago. She has adjusted quite well to these changes in her vision and hearing, and maintains her quality of life by remaining active. The only situations she avoids are large gatherings, such as lunch at the senior center where it always seems to be too noisy for her to enjoy conversations with her friends. More recently, Mrs. Wilson has stopped driving at night because of increasing sensitivity to glare and problems with finding her way on the poorly lit rural roads near her home. She enjoys gardening and is proud of her rose garden with its varied fragrances in the summer. Recently she has no-ticed a slight loss of her well-honed skills in telling apart one variety of rose from another by their fragrances, but she remains better at it than her children and grandchildren! She also plants aromatic herbs in her garden so she can use them to perk up her cooking with herbs and spices for herself and her friends. Mrs. Wilson realizes that her vision, hearing, taste, and smell have all declined as she has aged, but she is determined to make the best use of her remaining abilities in these senses. The changes she has made in her environment, such as avoiding night driving and using more herbs in cooking, are examples of Mrs. Wilson's attempts to maintain person-environment congruence.

experience a generalized taste loss. The research task now is to specify *which* aspects of taste function remain intact and which decline with normal aging or disease. Although the taste function of older people does not undergo a general decline in strength, it demonstrates changes that are specific in a variety of ways (Weiffenbach, 1990). For example, although the relationship between taste intensity and stimulus strength is age-stable, judgments of taste intensity become less reliable with age. Even this change in reliability is specific. It affects salt but not sugar judgments (Weiffenbach, Cowart, and Baum, 1986). It is also important to note that in studies where the average performance of the older individuals is poorer, some older persons perform as well as, or better than, many younger persons.

Appreciation of food does not depend on taste alone. The sense of smell clearly is involved. We have all experienced changes in the way food "tastes" while ill with a head cold and a stuffy nose. These changes, which you can mimic by holding your nose, suggest that sensitivity to airborne stimuli plays a key role in the perception of foods. There is considerable evidence for age-related decline in the sense of smell. Older people perceive airborne stimuli as less intense than younger persons, and do less well on odor identification. External factors such as smoking and medications contribute to these differences, but even after accounting for these factors, age differences are dominant (Ship and Weiffenbach, 1993; Weiffenbach and Bartoshuk, 1992). When parallel assessments are made in the same subject, age-related declines for smell are greater than for taste. This suggests that one way to increase older people's enjoyment of eating is to provide them with enhanced food odors.

Certain problems are associated with reduced sensitivity to taste and smell. For example, declines in the recognition and identification of odors, especially the odor of gas, are observed in people over age 80. This raises an important safety concern with this age group. Some older people compensate for losses in taste sensitivity by increasing their salt intake. This is not only harmful for individuals with hypertension, but it is also ineffective if the lack of taste is really due to reduced sensitivity to the smell of food. Other older people may find that food is so unappetizing that they lose interest in it, and eat only when they are very hungry. This is risky because it may result in poor nutrition. A better approach is to enhance the flavor of foods with herbs and spices, and with pleasant aromas (e.g., basil, tarragon, and cinnamon) that do not disturb the older person's digestive system, and may actually enhance the digestive process. Classes in cooking with herbs and spices can be valuable for older people who are experiencing changes in their taste and olfactory abilities. Along with cooking techniques, the nutritional value of each ingredient, and the benefits and potential harm of each spice and herb should be reviewed in these classes. These activities can also help older people in sharpening their sensitivity to tastes and odors, and enhancing quality of life.

SUMMARY AND IMPLICATIONS

As shown by this review of physiological systems, the aging process is gradual, beginning in some organ systems as early as the twenties and thirties, and progressing more rapidly after age 70, or even 80, in others. Even with 50 percent deterioration in many organ systems, an individual can still function adequately. The ability of human beings to compensate for age-related changes attests to their significant amount of excess reserve capacity. In most instances, the normal physical changes of aging need not diminish a person's quality of life if person-environment congruence can be maintained. Since many of the decrements are gradual and slight, older people can learn to modify their activities to adapt to their environments—for example, by pacing the amount of physical exertion throughout the day. Family members and professionals can be supportive by encouraging modifications in the home, such as minimizing the use of stairs, moving the focus of the older person's daily activities to the main floor of the home, and reinforcing the older person's efforts to cope creatively with common physical changes.

There are significant differences in the rate and severity of decline in various organ systems, with the greatest deterioration in functions that require coordination among multiple systems, muscles, and nerves. Similarly, there are wide variations

across individuals in the aging process, springing from differences in heredity, diet, exercise, and living conditions. Many of the physiological functions that were once assumed to deteriorate and to be irreversible with normal aging are being reevaluated by researchers in basic and clinical physiology, as well as by health educators. Even people who begin a regular exercise program late in life have experienced significant improvements in their heart and lung capacity. The role of preventive maintenance and health promotion in the aging process will be discussed in Chapter 4.

Sleep patterns do, however, change with normal aging. Lab studies have revealed changes in EEG patterns, sleep stages, and circadian rhythms with advancing years, even in the absence of disease. Sedative hypnotic drugs are widely used by older people who complain of sleep disturbance. However, improving sleep hygiene by increasing physical exercise, reducing the intake of alcohol, caffeine, and some medications, and improving the sleep environment are generally more effective methods than sleeping pills for long-term use. Only in the case of true sleep disorders, such as sleep apnea and twitching legs during sleep, are medications useful.

Changes in sensory function with age do not occur at a consistent rate in all senses and for all people. Some people show rapid declines in vision while maintaining their hearing and other sensory abilities. Others experience an early deterioration in olfactory sensation, but not in other areas. All of us experience some loss in these functions with age, but interindividual differences are quite pronounced.

Normal age-related declines in vision reduce the ability to respond to differing light levels; to function in low-light situations; to see in places with high levels of glare; to discern color tones, especially in the green-blue-violet range; and to judge distances and depth. Peripheral vision becomes somewhat narrowed with age, as does upward and downward gaze. Older people have more diseases of the eye, including glaucoma, cataracts, and macular degeneration; if these diseases are not treated, blindness can result. Visual impairments generally result in more problems with activities of daily living than do hearing impairments. Therefore, older persons who experience significant declines in visual function with age should be encouraged to maintain former levels of activity, either by adapting the environment to fit changing needs or by substituting new activities for those that have become more difficult. Some older people prefer to withdraw from previous activities, thereby becoming more isolated and at risk of depression and declining quality of life.

Decline in auditory function generally starts earlier than visual problems, and affects more people. Significant impairments in speech comprehension often result. Although hearing aids can frequently improve hearing in the speech range by raising the intensity of speech that is in the high frequency range, many older people feel uncomfortable and even stigmatized when using them. Hence, the solutions to communicating with hearing-impaired older people may lie mostly within the environment, not within older persons themselves. These include changes in communication styles, such as speaking directly at an older person in a clear voice, but not shouting; speaking in a lower tone; repeating key points; and sitting closer to a hearing-impaired person. Environmental aids such as soundproof or quiet rooms and modified telephones can also be invaluable for older people who are experiencing significant hearing declines.

Although many older people complain that food does not taste as good as it once did, there are only minimal changes with age in taste acuity. The decline in olfactory receptors with age is more significant than in taste receptors, and may be responsible for the perception of reduced taste acuity. These changes are more pronounced in people who smoke or drink heavily, but the use of medications has only modest effects. There is less change in people who have sharpened their taste and olfactory sensitivity, such as professional winemakers and perfumers. This pattern suggests that older people should be encouraged to participate in activities that enhance their taste and olfactory functions.

As we have seen in previous chapters, normal aging does not lead to disability. However, the changes that occur with normal aging, as noted here and elsewhere, are likely to result in a slowing of functions, increased caution, and a reduction of physical activity. This should not be considered a sign of disease but a recognition of the older person's sensory and physical limitations and capabilities.

Older people should be encouraged to maximize use of all their functions, so that deterioration does not occur more rapidly than necessary. Unfortunately, the fear of not being able to hear, see, or maintain their balance keeps many older people tied to their homes and increases the risk of social isolation. It is important for people of all ages to maintain and perhaps even increase their activity levels because those who use their neuromuscular functions, sensory capacities, and cognitive skills regularly can prevent premature deterioration of these functions. Hence, the recognition and use of one's capacities to the fullest should begin early in life and continue into advanced old age.

As we learn more from studies of normal physiological changes with aging, reports that once appeared definitive are found to be less so, and a complete understanding of some areas is shown to be lacking. This is particularly true in the areas of taste, smell, and pain perception. Research is needed to distinguish normal changes in these areas from those that are related to disease, and those that can be prevented. Longitudinal research would help to answer many of these questions. Finally, research that examines the impact of sensory deterioration on the older person's interactions with the environment is also needed.

GLOSSARY

accommodation   ability of the lens of the eye to change shape from rounded to flat, in order to see objects that are closer or farther from the lens

atherosclerosis   accumulation of fats in the arteries and veins, blocking circulation of the blood

atrophic gastritis   chronic inflammation of the stomach lining

auditory canal   the portion of the outer ear between the pinna and the ear drum

autoimmune theory of aging   the hypothesis that aging is a function of the body's immune system becoming defective, producing antibodies against itself

cataract   clouding of the lens of the eye, reducing sight and sometimes leading to blindness; requires surgical extraction of the lens

cellular aging theory of aging   the hypothesis that aging occurs as cells slow their number of replications, based on the observation that cells grown in controlled laboratory environments are able to replicate only a finite number of times

cilia   hair-like structures in the airways of the lungs and bronchia

cross-linkage theory of aging   the hypothesis that aging is a function of the reduction of collagen with age, causing loss of elasticity in most organ systems

dementia   diminished ability to remember, make accurate judgments, etc.

diastolic blood pressure   the level of blood pressure during the time that chambers of the heart are filling with blood

electroencephalogram (EEG)   readings of the electrical activity of the brain

epidermis   the outermost layer of skin

esophagus   the tube leading from the throat to the stomach

estrogen   a female sex hormone that declines significantly with aging; can be replaced alone (ERT) or in combination with progesterone, another female sex hormone (HRT)

free radical theory of aging   a special case of the cross-linkage theory of aging which posits that free radicals, highly reactive molecules, may produce DNA mutations

functional (or reserve) capacity   the ability of a given organ to perform its normal function, compared with its function under conditions of illness, disability, and aging

glaucoma   a disease in which there is insufficient drainage or excessive production of aqueous humor, the fluid in the front portion of the eye

glial cells   cells that support nerve tissue in the brain

glucose   one of the sugars in food, especially fruit; used as an energy source by living organisms

hyperthermia   body temperatures several degrees above normal for prolonged periods

hyponatremia   loss of salt in the blood

hypothermia   body temperatures several degrees below normal for prolonged periods

inner ear   the cochlea or snail-shaped structure that converts sound into nerve impulses and sends it on to the brain

kinesthetic system   the body system that signals one's position in space

kyphosis   stoop-shouldered or hunched condition caused by collapsed vertebrae as bone mass is lost

macular degeneration   loss of vision in the center of the visual field

melanin   skin pigmentation

menopause   one event during the climacteric in a woman's life when there is a gradual cessation of the menstrual cycle, which is related to the loss of ovarian function; considered to have occurred after 12 consecutive months without a menstrual period

middle ear   the location of three bones, the malleus, incus, and stapes, that transmit sound from the eardrum to the inner ear

morbidity   sickness, ill health

neurons   nerve cells in the brain

neurotransmitters   chemical messengers such as acetylcholine that transmit messages across neurons

nocturnal myoclonus   a neuromuscular disturbance affecting the legs during sleep

orthopedic injuries   injuries to the bones, muscles, and joints

osteoporosis   a dramatic loss in calcium and bone mass resulting in increased brittleness of the bones and increased risk of fracture, more frequently found in white, small stature women

perception   the process through which the information received through the senses is processed in the brain

pinna   the visible portion of the outer ear

presbycusis   age-related hearing loss

recognition threshold   the intensity of a stimulus needed in order for an individual to identify or recognize a sensation

REM   one of the stages of sleep during which rapid eye movement (REM) occurs

renal function   kidney function, defined by the rate at which blood is filtered through the kidneys

senescence   biological aging, i.e., the gradual accumulation of irreversible functional losses to which the average person tries to accommodate in some socially acceptable way

sensation   the process of taking in information through the sense organs

sensory discrimination   the minimum difference necessary between two or more stimuli in order for a person to distinguish between them

sensory threshold   the minimum intensity of a stimulus that a person requires in order to detect a stimulus

sleep apnea   5- to 10-second cessation of breathing, which disturbs sleep in some older persons

sleep hygiene   behaviors associated with sleep, e.g., location, lighting, regular vs. irregular bedtime, use of drugs that promote or hinder sleep

synapse   the junction between any two neurons

systolic blood pressure   the level of blood pressure during the contraction phase of the heart

testosterone   a male sex hormone

tinnitus   high pitched ringing in the ear

triglyceride   one of the fatty acids synthesized from carbohydrates and stored in fat tissues of humans

tympanic membrane   the ear drum

urinary incontinence   diminished ability to retain urine; loss of bladder control

varicosities   abnormal swelling in the veins, especially the legs

vital capacity   the maximum volume of oxygen intake through the lungs with a single breath

wear and tear theory of aging   one of the biological theories of aging; states that aging occurs because of the system simply wearing out over time

REFERENCES

Accardi, F. E., Gombos, M. M., and Gombos, G. M. Common causes of blindness: A pilot survey in Brooklyn, New York. *Annals of Ophthalmology,* 1985, *17,* 289–294.

Agency for Health Care Policy and Research (AHCPR). *Management of Cataract in Adults: Clinical Prac-tice Guidelines. AHCPR Publication No. 93–0543, Rockville, MD, 1993.

Allikmets, R., Shroyer, N. F., Singh, N., Seddon, J. M., and Lewis, R. A. Mutation of the Stargardt disease gene (ABCR) in age-related macular degeneration. *Science,* 1997, *277,* 1805–1807.

Applegate, W. B., Miller, J. T., Elam, J. T., Freeman, J. M., Wood, T. O., and Gettlefinger, T. C. Impact of cataract surgery with lens implantation on vision and physical function in elderly patients. *Journal of the American Medical Association,* 1987, *257,* 1064–1066.

Arey, L., Tremaine, M., and Monzingo, F. The numerical and topographical relations of taste buds to human circumvallate papillae throughout the life span. *Anatomical Record,* 1935, *64,* 9–25.

Ausman, L. M., and Russell, R. M. Nutrition and aging. In E. L. Schneider and J. W. Rowe (Eds.), *Handbook of the biology of aging* (3rd ed.). San Diego: Academic Press, 1990.

Avery, W. M. Hypothermia and heat illness. *Aging,* 1984, *344,* 43–47.

Bjorksten, J. Crosslinkage and the aging process. In M. Rockstein, M. L. Sussman, and J. Chesky (Eds.), *Theoretical aspects of aging.* New York: Academic Press, 1974.

Blumberg, J. B. Status and functional impact of nutrition in older adults. In E. L. Schneider and J. W. Rowe (Eds.), *Handbook of the biology of aging* (4th ed.). New York: Van Nostrand, 1996.

Bognoli, P., and Hodos, W. *The changing visual system: Maturation and aging in the central nervous system.* New York: Plenum Press, 1991.

Brant, L. J., and Fozard, J. Age changes in pure-tone hearing thresholds in a longitudinal study of normal human aging. *Journal of the Acoustical Society of America,* 1990, *88,* 813–820.

Chicago Tribune: Alone in life, unclaimed in death. July 31, 1995, p. 1, 6.

Collins, K. J. Low indoor temperatures and morbidity in the elderly. *Age and Ageing,* 1986, *15,* 212–220.

Cooper, B. A., Ward, M., Gowland, C. A., and McIntosh, J. M. The use of the Lanthony New Color Test in determining the effects of aging on color vision. *Journals of Gerontology,* 1991, *46,* 320–324.

Cowart, B. J. Relationships between taste and smell across the life span. In C. Murphy, W. S. Cain, and D. M. Hegsted (Eds.), Nutrition and the chemical senses in aging: Recent advances and current research needs. *Annals of the New York Academy of Sciences.* New York: New York Academy of Sciences, 1989.

Cramer, D. Promoting continence: Strategies for success. *Perspectives in Health Promotion and Aging,* 1993, *1,* 1–3.

Cutler, E. D., and Cutler, R. G. Tissue auto-oxidation, antioxidants, and life span potential. *The Gerontologist,* 1983, *23* (Special Issue), 194.

Foley, D. J., Monjan, A. A., Brown, S. L., Simonsick, E. M., Wallace, R. B., and Blager, D. G. Sleep complaints among elderly persons: An epidemiological study of three communities. *Sleep,* 1995, *18,* 425–432.

Foster, V. L., Hume, G. J. E., Byrnes, W. C., Dickinson, A. L., and Chatfield, S. J. Endurance training for elderly women: Moderate vs. low intensity. *Journals of Gerontology,* 1989, *44,* M184–M188.

Gilchrest, B. A. Skin. In J. W. Rowe and R. W. Besdine (Eds.), *Health and disease in old age.* Boston: Little, Brown, 1982, 381–392.

Goldstein, S., and Reis, R. J. S. Genetic modifications during cellular aging. *Molecular and Cellular Biochemical,* 1984, *64,* 15–30.

Gordon-Salant, S. Hearing. In J. E. Birren (Ed.), *Encyclopedia of gerontology,* Vol. 1. San Diego: Academic Press, 1996.

Guelke, R. W. Consonant burst enhancement: A possible means to improve intelligibility for the hard of hearing. *Journal of Rehabilitation Research and Development,* 1987, *24,* 217–220.

Harkins, S. W., and Warner, M. H. Age and pain. In C. Eisdorfer (Ed.), *Annual review of gerontology and geriatrics* (vol. 1). New York: Springer, 1980.

Harman, D. A theory based on free radical and radiation chemistry. *Journal of Gerontology,* 1956, *11,* 298.

Harman, D. The aging process. *Proceedings of the National Academy of Science,* 1981, *78,* 7124–7128.

Hayflick, L. *How and why we age.* New York: Ballantine Books, 1996.

Hayflick, L., and Moorehead, P. S. The serial cultivation of human diploid cell strains. *Experimental Cell Research,* 1961, *25,* 285–621.

Henderson, V. W. The epidemiology of estrogen replacement therapy and Alzheimer's disease. *Neurology,* 1997, *48,* S27-S35.

Henderson, V. W., Paganini-Hill, A., Emanuel, C. K., Dunn M. E., and Buckwalter, J. G. Estrogen replacement therapy in older women. *Archives of Neurology,* 1994, *51,* 896–900.

Hu, M. H., and Woollacott, M. H. Multisensory training of standing balance in older adults. *Journals of Gerontology,* 1994, *49,* M52–M71.

Jacques, P. F., Chylack, L. T., and Taylor, A. Relationships between natural antioxidents and cataract formation. In B. Frei (Ed.), *Natural antioxidants in human health and disease.* San Diego: Academic Press, 1994.

Kiyak, H. A. Communication in the practitioner-aged patient relationship. In P. Holm-Pedersen and H. Loe (Eds.), *Textbook of geriatric dentistry* (2nd ed.). Copenhagen: Munksgaard, 1996.

Kline, D. W., Kline, T. J. B., Fozard, J. L., Kosnik, W., Schieber, F., and Sekuler, R. Vision, aging, and driving: The problems of older drivers. *Journals of Gerontology,* 1992, *47,* M27–34.

Klingman, A. M., Grove, G. L., and Balin, A. Aging of human skin. In C. E. Finch and E. L. Schneider (Eds). *Handbook of the biology of aging.* New York: Van Nostrand, 1985.

Kohrt, W. M., and Holloszy, J. O. Loss of skeletal mass with aging: Effect on glucose tolerance. *Journals of Gerontology: Biological and Medical Sciences,* 1995, *50,* 68–72.

Kosnick, W., Winslow, L., Kline, D., Rasinski, K. and Sekuler, R. Visual changes in daily life throughout adulthood. *Journals of Gerontology,* 1988, *43,* M63–70.

Lakatta, E. Heart and circulation. In E. L. Schneider and J. W. Rowe (Eds), *Handbook of the Biology of Aging* (3rd ed.). San Diego: Academic Press, 1990.

Lane, M. A., Baer, D. J., Rumpler, W. V., Weindruch, R., Ingram, D. K., Tilmont, E. M., Cutler, R. G., and Roth, G. S. Calorie restriction lowers body temperature in rhesus monkeys. *Proceedings of the National Academy of Sciences,* 1996, *93,* 4159–4164.

Lane, M. A., Ball, S. S., Ingram, D. K., Cutler, R. G., Engel, J., Read, V., and Roth, G. S. Diet restriction in Rhesus monkeys lowers fasting and glucose-stimulated glucoregulatory end points. *American Journal of Physiology,* 1995, *268,* 941–948.

Lane, M. A., Ingram, D. K., Ball, S. S., and Roth, G. S. Dehydroepiandrosterone sulfate: A biomarker of primate aging slowed by calorie restriction. *Journal of Clinical Endocrinology and Metabolism,* 1997, *82,* 2093–2096.

Li, Y. and Wolf, N. S. Effects of age and long-term caloric restriction on the aqueous collecting channel in the mouse eye. *Journal of Glaucoma,* 1997, *6,* 18–22.

Liston, R., Solomon, S., and Banerjee, A. K. Prevalence of hearing problems, and use of hearing aids among a sample of elderly patients. *British Journal of General Practice,* 1995, *45,* 369–370.

Livingston, G., Blizard, B., and Mann, A. Does sleep disturbance predict depression in elderly people? *British Journal of General Practice,* 1993, *43,* 445–448.

Macey, S. M. Hypothermia and energy conservation: A tradeoff for elderly persons? *International Journal of Aging and Human Development,* 1989, *29,* 151–161.

Macey, S., and Schneider, D. Deaths from excessive heat and excessive cold among the elderly. *The Gerontologist,* 1993, *33,* 497–500.

Masoro, E. J. Animal models in aging research. In E. L. Schneider and J. W. Rowe (Eds.), *Handbook of the biology of aging* (3rd ed.). San Diego: Academic Press, 1990.

Micozzi, M. Exploring alternative health approaches for elders. *Aging Today,* 1997, *18,* 9–12.

Miller, I. J. Human taste bud density across adult age groups. *Journals of Gerontology,* 1988, *43,* B26–30.

Milton, R. C., and Sperduto, R. D. Incidence of age-related cataract: 13.6 year follow-up in the Framingham eye study. *Investigations in Ophthalmic Vision Science,* 1991, *32,* 1243–1250.

Mistretta, C. M. Aging effects on anatomy and neurophysiology of taste and smell. *Gerodontology,* 1984, *3,* 131–136.

Morales, A. J., Nolan, J. J., Nelson, J. C., and Yen, S. S. Effects of replacement dose of dehydroepiandrosterone in men and women of advancing age. *Journal of Clinical Endocrinology and Metabolism,* 1995, *80,* 2799.

Mortola, J., and Yen, S. S. The effects of oral dehydroepiandrosterone on endocrine-metabolic parameters in postmenopausal women. *Journal of Clinical Endocrinology and Metabolism,* 1990, *71,* 696–704.

Mullan, E., Katona, C., and Bellew, M. Patterns of sleep disorders and sedative hypnotic use in seniors. *Drugs and Aging,* 1994, *5,* 49–58.

Murphy, C. The effect of age on taste sensitivity. In S. Han and D. Coons (Eds.), *Special senses in aging.* Ann Arbor: Institute of Gerontology, University of Michigan, 1979.

O'Brien, S., and Vertinsky, P. Unfit survivors: Exercise as a resource for aging women. *The Gerontologist,* 1991, *31,* 347–357.

Ohayan, M. M., and Caulet, M. Insomnia and psychotropic drug consumption. *Progress in Neuropsychopharmacology, Biology and Psychiatry,* 1995, *19,* 421–431.

Paganini-Hill, A., and Henderson, V. W. Estrogen deficiency and risk of Alzheimer's disease in women. *American Journal of Epidemiology,* 1991, 256–261.

Paganini-Hill, A., and Henderson, V. W. Estrogen replacement therapy and risk of Alzheimer's disease. *Archives of Internal Medicine,* 1996, *156,* 2213–2217.

Palmore, E. (Ed.). *Normal aging II: Reports from the Duke Longitudinal Study,* 1970–1973. Durham, NC: Duke University Press, 1974.

Palmore, E. (Ed.). *Normal aging III: Reports from the Duke Longitudinal Study.* Durham, NC: Duke University Press, 1985.

Pearson, D., and Shaw, S. *Life extension.* New York: Warner Books, 1982.

Rogers, M. A., Hagberg, J. M., Martin, W. H., Ehsani, A. A., and Holloszy, J. O. Decline in VO2 max with aging in master athletes and sedentary men. *Journal of Applied Physiology,* 1990, *68,* 2195–2199.

Rosenhall, U., and Karlsson, A. K. Tinnitus in old age. *Scandinavian Audiology,* 1991, *20,* 165–171.

Rudberg, M. A., Furner, S. E., Dunn, J. E., and Cassel, C. K. The relationship of visual and hearing impairments to disability. *Journals of Gerontology,* 1993, *48,* M261–M265.

Rudman, D., Drinka, P. J., Wilson, C. R., Mattson, D. E., Scherman, F., Cuisinier, M. C., and Schultz, S. Relations of endogenous anabolic hormones and physical activity to bone mineral density in elderly men. *Clinical Endocrinology,* 1991, *40,* 653–661.

Seddon, J. M., Ajani, U. A., Sperduto, R. D., Hiller, R., Blair, H. N., and Burton, T. C. Dietary carotenoids, vitamins A, C, and E, and advanced age-related macular degeneration. *Journal of the American Medical Association,* 1994a, *272,* 1413–1420.

Seddon, J. M., Christen, W. G., Manson, J. E., Lamotte, F. S., Glynn, R. J., Buring, J. E., and Hennekens, C. H. The use of vitamin supplements and the risk of cataract among U.S. male physicians. *American Journal of Public Health,* 1994b, *84,* 788–792.

Ship, J. A., and Weiffenbach, J. M. Age, gender, medical treatment, and medication effects on smell identification. *Journals of Gerontology,* 1993, *48,* M26–M32.

Shock, N. W. The physiology of aging. *Scientific American,* 1962, *206,* 100–110.

Sommer, A., Tielsch, J. M., and Katz, J. Racial difference in the cause-specific prevalence of blindness in East Baltimore. *New England Journal of Medicine,* 1991, *325,* 1412–1417.

Sperduto, R. D. Age-related cataracts: Scope of problem and prospects for prevention. *Preventive Medicine,* 1994, *23,* 735–739.

Stevens, J. C. Aging and spatial acuity of touch. *Journals of Gerontology,* 1992, *47,* B35–40.

Strehler, B. L. Genetic instability as the primary cause of human aging. *Experimental Gerontology,* 1986, *21,* 283.

Teasdale, N., Stelmach, G. E., and Breunig, A. Postural sway characteristics of the elderly under normal and altered visual and support surface conditions. *Journals of Gerontology,* 1991, *46,* B238–B244.

Thomas, T., Thomas, G., McLendon, C., Sutton, T., and Mullan, M. Beta-amyloid-mediated vasoactivity and vascular endothelial damage. *Nature,* 1996, *380,* 168–171.

Tylenda, C. A., and Baum, B. J. Oral physiology and the Baltimore Longitudinal Study of Aging. *Gerodontology,* 1988, *7,* 5–9.

Vitiello, M. V. Sleep disorders and aging. *Current Opinions in Psychiatry,* 1996, *9,* 284–289.

Vitiello, M. V., and Prinz, P. N. Sleep and sleep disorders in normal aging. In M. J. Thorpy (Ed.), *Handbook of sleep disorders.* New York: Marcell Decker, 1991.

Walford, R. L. *The immunological theory of aging.* Baltimore: Williams and Wilkins, 1969.

Weale, R. A. Senescence and color vision. *Journal of Gerontology,* 1988, *41,* 635–640.

Weed, J. L., Lane, M. A., Roth, G. S., Speer, D. L., and Ingram, D. K. Activity measures in rhesus monkeys on long-term calorie restriction. *Physiology and Behavior,* 1997, *62,* 97–103.

Weiffenbach, J. M. Assessment of chemosensory functioning in aging: Subjective and objective procedures. In E. L. Schneider and J. W. Rowe (Eds.), *Handbook of the biology of aging.* San Diego: Academic Press, 1990.

Weiffenbach, J. M., and Bartoshuk, L. M. Taste and smell. *Clinics in Geriatric Medicine,* 1992, *8,* 543–555.

Weiffenbach, J. M., Cowart, B. J., and Baum, B. J. Taste intensity perception in aging. *Journal of Gerontology,* 1986, *41,* 460–468.

Weindruch, R. Caloric restriction and aging. *Scientific American,* 1996, *274,* 46–52.

Wilson, D. L. The programmed theory of aging. In M. Rockstein, M. L. Sussman, and J. Chesky (Eds.), *Theoretical aspects of aging.* New York: Academic Press, 1974, 11–21.

Wilson, M. R. Glaucoma in blacks: Where do we go from here? *Journal of the American Medical Association,* 1989, *261,* 281–282.

Yataco, A. R., Busby-Whitehead, J., Drinkwater, D. T., and Katzel, L. I. Relationship of body composition and cardiovascular fitness to lipoprotein lipid profiles in master athletes and sedentary men. *Aging,* 1997, *9,* 88–94.

4 Managing chronic diseases and promoting well-being in old age

No aspect of old age is more alarming to many of us than the thought of losing our health. Our fears center not only on the pain and inconvenience of illness, but also on its social-psychological consequences, such as loss of personal autonomy and economic security. Poor health, more than other changes commonly associated with aging, can reduce a person's competence in dealing with his or her environment.

This chapter examines social and psychological factors that affect perceptions of health and use of health services, looking first at definitions of good health and how the social context, especially stress, affects it. Chronic and acute health problems are then differentiated, followed by a discussion of the most common chronic diseases experienced by older people and some of their social consequences. The remainder of the chapter is devoted to utilization of health care by older adults and their health behavior. Health promotion programs are described as a way to reduce the incidence of chronic diseases, primarily through altering health behaviors.

Defining health

It is not necessary to argue that good health is valued, but what do we mean by **good health?** Most people would agree that health is something more than the mere absence of disease or infirmity. As defined by the World Health Organization, health is a state of complete physical, mental, and social well-being. Thus, health implies an interaction and integration of body, mind, and spirit, a perspective that is reflected in the growth of health promotion programs with older adults.

As used by health care workers and researchers, the term **health status** refers to: (1) the presence or absence of disease, and (2) the degree of disability in an individual's level of functioning. Thus, activities that older people can do, or think they can do, are useful indicators of both how healthy they are and the services and environmental changes they need in order to cope with their impairments. Older people's ability to function independently at home is of primary concern. The most commonly used measure of *functional* *health,* termed the **Activities of Daily Living (ADL)**, summarizes an individual's performance in personal care tasks such as bathing, dressing, using the toilet, eating, getting in or out of a bed or chair, caring for a bowel control device, as well as instrumental activities of daily living such as home management, managing money, shopping, light housework, meal preparation, making a phone call, and taking medications.

The World Health Organization defines **disability** as impairments in the ability to complete multiple daily tasks. Slightly more than 20 percent of older people are estimated to have a mild degree of disability in their ADL. Only a small proportion—approximately 4 percent—are severely disabled. The more disabled older population is limited in their amounts and types of major activities and mobility, such as eating,

dressing, bathing, or toiletry. Severely disabled persons are often unable to carry on major activities without the assistance of family or professionals. The extent of disabilities and need for help in personal care activities increase with age and differ by gender, as shown in Figure 4.1. Women aged 90 and older are twice as likely to be disabled and to require assistance than those aged 70 to 74. Men are less likely to have ADL limitations in both age groups and show a smaller increase in disability with age (NCHS, 1995). This may be because men who survive to 70, and especially to age 90, have a genetic advantage and are hardier than men who die of similar conditions earlier in life.

In 1995, approximately 7.1 million persons 65 years or older needed some assistance in order to remain in the community (including 10.5 per-

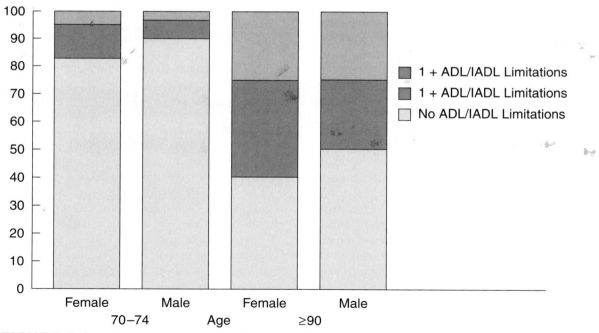

FIGURE 4.1   Comparing ADL and IADL Limitations among Men and Women, Young-Old and Oldest-Old
SOURCE: National Center for Health Statistics, 1997.

cent of those aged 65–79 and 51 percent of those over age 85). This figure is expected to reach 8.5 million by the year 2000, 12 million by 2020, and 17 million by 2040. Another way to describe these projections is to state that the proportion of persons over age 65 with one or more activity limitations will increase from the current 19 percent to 21 percent by the year 2040. About 20 percent of this group will have severe limitations in ADLs (U.S. Administration on Aging, 1997).

QUALITY OF LIFE IN HEALTH AND ILLNESS

Societal values affect our attitudes toward loss of health. In our own culture, the attitudes tend to be negative. The importance placed by our culture on being independent and highly active may underlie our relative inability to accept illness graciously. Such values may also partially explain why healthy older people often do not want to share housing or recreational activities with those who have mental or physical disabilities.

Yet the fear of declining health may trouble us more than the actual experience of it. Although younger people assume that health issues are older people's greatest preoccupation, most elders appear to be fairly positive about their health. The 1994 National Health Interview Survey found that almost 72 percent of older respondents in the community described their health as excellent, very good, or good compared to their age peers, while only 9 percent reported their health as poor (NCHS, 1995). Even institutionalized older persons tend to rate their health positively. These positive ratings, despite health problems, have been explained in terms of a comparison with peers, a sense of accomplishment from having survived to old age, a perception of competence to meet environmental demands, and a broad definition of quality of life to include social and economic factors. A reliable evaluation of health takes into account not only a physician's assessment of a patient's physical condition, but also the older person's self-perceptions, observable behavior, and

life circumstances. Most older people appear to adjust their perceptions of their health in response to the aging process. Perceived health is influenced largely by limitations in activities of daily living and the number of medications an older person consumes, especially among older women (Johnson and Wolinsky, 1994).

Older people who must take multiple medications, who are experiencing chronic pain, or have limitations in their ADLs and in their interpersonal relations, are more likely to report lower quality of life. On the other hand, those who have recently had a successful medical or surgical intervention to *alleviate* the symptoms of their chronic conditions are more likely to report improved quality of life. It is noteworthy that physicians rate the quality of life of older persons with diabetes, arthritis, or even ischemic heart disease lower than do these elders themselves. This may indicate greater adaptation to disabling conditions among patients than physicians expect, or may suggest that medical professionals' definitions of quality of life are more constrained by health factors than are definitions by patients themselves. However, a national survey of 9,000 adults with chronic diseases revealed that people with arthritis, heart disease, and chronic lung disease reported the greatest impairments in quality of life; those with hypertension reported the least (Stewart et al., 1989).

Social and psychological factors also influence people's assessments of their physical well-being. An older person's position in the social structure—for example, whether one is male or female, black or white, high or low income—affects perceptions of health. Thus, while more than 72 percent of white persons age 65 and older rate their health as good or excellent, only 52 percent of blacks and less than 50 percent of Hispanics that age do so. In the 1992 National Health Interview Survey, 17.6 percent of African American elders rated their health as poor, compared with only 8.3 percent of whites. About 5.4 percent of persons aged 65 and older with incomes over $35,000 rate their health as poor, compared with 14 percent of their peers who have incomes less than $10,000. However, older women do not rate their health more poorly than men, even though they have more chronic diseases and are more likely to be institutionalized (NCHS, 1994).

Perceptions of good health tend to be associated with other measures of well-being, particularly life satisfaction. Older persons who view themselves as reasonably healthy tend to be happier, more satisfied, more involved in social activities, and less tense and lonely. In turn, lower life satisfaction is associated with lower levels of self-perceived health. It has also been found that self-ratings of health are correlated with mortality. That is, older people who report poorer health, especially poorer functional abilities, are more likely to die in the next three years than those who perceive their functional health to be good (Bernard et al., 1997).

EFFECTS OF STRESS ON HEALTH

As the previous discussions suggest, health status involves the dynamic interplay among physical, social, and psychological forces. Environmental factors affect both perceptions of and actual degree of physical well-being. One of the most significant environmental factors is stress.

Individuals are subject to different degrees of stress from their environments, with diverse consequences for their overall physical and mental health. In this context, **stress** can be defined as the gamut of social-psychological stimuli that produce physiological responses of shallow, rapid breathing, muscle tension, increased blood pressure, and accelerated heart rate. The literature on social stress and health emphasizes that stress has broad physiological effects on the body and can predispose the individual to a wide range of diseases. Hypertension, cardiovascular disease, and cancer have been correlated with particular risk factors, such as stressful lifestyles, cigarette smoking, drinking, and being overweight. How people cope with stress, however, affects the likelihood of deleterious consequences, as will be seen in the discussion of adaptation in Chapter 6. Health risk

factor analyses move beyond assessments of possible differences in genetics and in health care to variations in health behaviors and lifestyles that can affect the outcome of stressful life events. Health promotion interventions to minimize stress are also discussed later in this chapter.

Studies concerning stressful life events and health are especially relevant to older people. As people age, they are more likely to experience events involving loss. In addition, the cumulative amount of stress they have experienced may increase. This can tax their declining physiological and psychological capacities to the limit, leading to illness, disease, and death. On the other hand, older people today are the survivors of their cohort. Many have experienced significant personal and societal tragedies such as world wars and the Great Depression. It may be that the psychological resources gained through older people's life experiences mediate the effects of stress in these survivors. More research is needed to determine how aging or the life course may influence responses to stress.

CHRONIC AND ACUTE DISEASES

As noted in Chapter 3, the risk of disease and impairment increases with age; however, the extreme variability in older people's health status, as illustrated by Mrs. Hill and Mr. Jones in the vignettes in Chapter 3, shows that poor health is not necessarily a concomitant of aging. The incidence of acute or temporary conditions, such as infections or the common cold, decreases with age. Those **acute conditions** that occur, however, are more debilitating and require more care, especially for older women. The average number of days of restricted activity due to acute conditions is nearly three times greater for people age 65 and over than it is for those 17 to 44 years old. Among the older population, 33 days per year are restricted activity days, of which 14 are spent in bed (NCHS, 1995). An older person who gets a cold, for example, faces a greater risk of pneumonia or bronchitis because of changes in organ systems (described in Chapter 3) which reduce his or her resistance and recuperative capacities. Thus, older people are more likely to suffer restrictions on their social activities as a result of temporary health problems.

In some cases, an acute condition that merely inconveniences a younger person may result in death for an older person. For example, respiratory infection rates are similar in young and old people, but people aged 65 and older account for 89 percent of all deaths due to pneumonia and influenza (CDC, 1995). This is why it is important for older people to be vaccinated against pneumonia and influenza. These vaccines can reduce the risk of pneumonia by 67 percent and of flu by 50 percent among older people. In addition, vaccination against pneumonia can save medical costs and increase days of healthy living for older adults. Yet recent surveys reveal that less than one-third obtain a pneumococcal vaccination and only one-half receive annual vaccines against influenza (Sisk et al., 1997; CDC, 1996; Govaert, Thijs, and Masurel, 1994). Recent changes in Medicare to cover the full cost of vaccinations may increase these rates.

Older people are also much more likely than the young to suffer from **chronic conditions.** Chronic health conditions are long-term (more than three months), often permanent, and leave a residual disability that may require long-term management or care rather than cure. More than 80 percent of persons age 65 and over have at least one chronic condition, with multiple health problems being common in older adults (NCHS, 1995). Chronic problems are often accompanied by continuous pain and/or distress. At the very least, the individual is inconvenienced by the need to monitor health and daily activities, although ADLs may not always be limited. National surveys have found that almost 40 percent of older persons with chronic diseases report limitations in their ability to perform basic ADLs (Guralnick and Simonsick, 1993).

Although the nature and the severity of any chronic condition vary with the individual, most older persons are capable of carrying out their normal daily routines. For example, chronic heart problems may limit an older person's capacity to jog five miles a day, but he or she may still be able to live at home, visit with friends, and take a daily walk. Only about 2 percent of those age 65 and over are confined to bed by their chronic conditions, and most older people with chronic conditions are not dependent on others for managing their daily routines. On the other hand, the small percentage who do need assistance with care have placed enormous pressures on formal health and long-term care services as well as on informal caregivers, as discussed in Chapters 9 and 16.

The most frequently reported chronic conditions causing limitation of activity in persons age 65 and over are shown in Figure 4.2 for women and Figure 4.3 for men. Arthritis, hypertension, hearing impairment, and heart disease are the leading chronic conditions. The most common heart condition for both men and women is ischemic heart disease. Not surprisingly, most chronic conditions increase in prevalence with age (NCHS, 1995).

For example, people age 65 and over are twice as likely to suffer from arthritis as those age 45 to 64. Other conditions, such as heart disease and diabetes, show lower rates in the oldest-old, probably because of the higher mortality associated with these diseases. Gender differences are also evident in the prevalence of these chronic conditions. Older women were more likely to report a diagnosis of arthritis, hypertension, sinusitis, or cataracts in the 1994 National Health Interview Survey; whereas older men more often reported heart disease, hearing impairment, tinnitus, and visual impairment. In addition to these top ten chronic conditions, aging is associated with a dramatic increase in diseases of the prostate in men (especially **benign hypertrophy of the prostate**), increasing six-fold between ages 45–64 to 75 and older. For women, varicose veins in the legs increase five-fold between ages 45–64 and 65–74 (NCHS, 1995).

Interactive Effects

Even though the majority of chronic conditions are not severely limiting, they can nevertheless

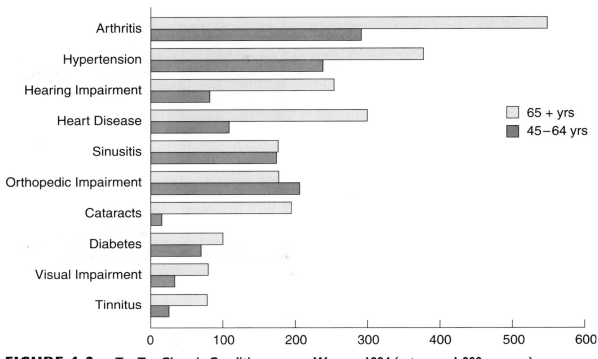

FIGURE 4.2 **Top Ten Chronic Conditions among Women: 1994 (rates per 1,000 persons)**
SOURCE: National Center for Health Statistics. Current estimates from the National Health Interview Survey: 1994. *Vital and Health Statistics*, Series 10, #193, 1995.

make life difficult and lower older people's resistance to other illnesses. As noted earlier, the functional limits imposed by a chronic illness interact with the social limits set by others' perceptions of the illness to influence an older person's daily functioning. Therefore, it is important to look beyond the statistics on the frequency of chronic conditions to the nature of chronic illnesses, the interaction of physical changes with emotional and sociocultural factors, and the physiological differences between younger and older people.

Certain types of chronic diseases (e.g., cancer, anemia, and toxic conditions) may be related to older people's declining **immunity,** that is, reduced resistance to environmental carcinogens, viruses, and bacteria. The accumulation of long-term, degenerative diseases may mean that a chronic condition, such as bronchitis, can have different and

more negative complications than the same disease would have in a younger person. With reduced resistance to physical stress, an older individual may be less able to respond to treatment for any acute disease, such as a cold or flu, than a younger person would. The cumulative effect of chronic illness and an acute condition may become the crisis point where the older person becomes dependent on others for care.

Sociocultural factors also are apparently related to the incidence and severity of chronic conditions; the prevalence of disability is higher among nonwhites, people with low socioeconomic and education status, and those in nonfarm rural areas. Disabling chronic illnesses tend to occur earlier among African Americans, Mexican Americans, and American Indians than among whites, resulting in higher rates of hospitalization, longer hospital stays, and a shorter life expectancy (Can-

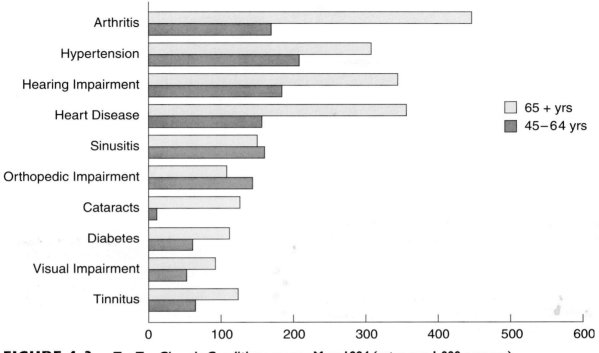

FIGURE 4.3   Top Ten Chronic Conditions among Men: 1994 (rates per 1,000 persons)
SOURCE: National Center for Health Statistics. Current estimates from the National Health Interview Survey: 1994. *Vital and Health Statistics,* Series 10, #193, 1995.

tor, 1991; Kickbush, 1989). Poorer self-assessments of health and lower life expectancies have been explained as products of discriminatory policies, where nonwhites have had lower incomes and inadequate nutrition throughout their lifetimes. An additional factor is that ethnic minorities, because of their cultural values and negative experiences with formal services, may be less likely to utilize the health care system. (The effects of ethnic minority status on the incidence and treatment of chronic conditions are further discussed in Chapter 13.)

Psychological factors also influence how a person reacts to chronic physical problems. For example, people with a pessimistic outlook toward their health and aging tend to have less physiological reserve capacity, as illustrated by comments such as, "She lost her will to live," or "He stopped fighting and gave up." There are nu-

merous examples of the impact of an optimistic attitude on the outcome of disease, perhaps best exemplified by Norman Cousins' (1979) accounts of the positive effects of humor on curing his potentially fatal disease. Thus, the impact of any chronic condition appears to be mediated by the physiological changes that occur with age, the sociocultural context, and the person's mental and emotional outlook.

Unfortunately, well-intentioned family members and health care professionals may assume that all chronic conditions are disabling or that a certain degree of disability is inevitable with aging. As a result, they may prematurely restrict a person's independence or not use the same treatments that they might administer to younger adults. The following anecdote illustrates how others' perceptions of health typical of old age can be unnecessarily limiting.

A 101-year-old man went to see a doctor about a pain in his left leg. The doctor said, "It is just a sign of aging," to which the man replied, "But my right leg is the same age, and it feels just fine."

In sum, disabling health changes occur at different rates in different individuals and are not inevitable with age. We turn now to an examination of the chronic conditions that are the most common causes of death in older people.

CAUSES OF DEATH IN OLDER ADULTS

Heart disease, cancer, and strokes account for over three-quarters of all deaths among people over age 65, as shown in Table 4.1 (Van Nostrand, Furner, and Suzman, 1993). Even though there have been rapid declines over the past 30 years, heart disease remains the major cause of death. It is the number-one risk factor among adults age 65 and over, killing twice as many people as do all forms of cancer combined, and accounting for 20 percent of adult disabilities. Heart disease accounts for 18 percent of hospital admissions, and over 45 percent of deaths that occur among older people, with the highest rates among the oldest old. Although death rates from cancer, especially lung cancer, continue to rise, it is esti-

mated that eliminating cancer as a cause of death would extend the average life span by less than two years at age 65. Eliminating deaths due to major cardiovascular diseases, however, would add an average of 14 years to life expectancy at age 65. The benefits of eliminating cardiovascular diseases would be especially significant for older white women (17.4 years) and non-white women (22 years). This would also lead to a sharp increase in the proportion of older persons in the total population (Hayflick, 1996). In contrast to heart disease, stroke has been decreasing as a leading cause of death among the older population over the past 30 years (NCHS, 1995).

Men have higher rates of heart disease and cancer than women. In fact, gender differences in mortality are due mainly to the greater incidence of the principal fatal chronic diseases among men. However, as shown in Figures 4.2 and 4.3, women experience more nonfatal chronic conditions, including arthritis, hiatus hernia, incontinence, osteoporosis, and cataracts, than do men (NCHS, 1995). These diseases are less likely to result in death than cancer and heart disease, but they may lead to nearly as many days spent in bed. In other words, older women are more likely to be bothered by chronic conditions and to be functionally disabled, but they are less likely to face life-threatening diseases than are older men.

TABLE 4.1   Mortality Rates for Older Women and Older Men, from the Four Leading Causes: 1992

	DEATHS PER 100,000 POPULATION PER YEAR, 1987		
	65–69	75–79	85+*
Diseases of heart	820	2098	7179
Malignant neoplasms (cancer)	736	1188	1612
Cerebrovascular diseases (strokes)	116	422	1763
Chronic obstructive pulmonary disease (COPD)	114	271	363

*For the population aged 85+, strokes are the second leading cause of death, pneumonia and influenza the fourth, and COPD the sixth leading cause of death.

SOURCE: Van Nostrand, Furner, and Suzman, 1993.

COMMON CHRONIC CONDITIONS

Heart Disease and the Cardiovascular System

Heart disease is a condition in which blood to the heart is deficient because of a narrowing or constricting of the cardiac vessels that supply it. This narrowing may be due to *atherosclerosis,** in which fatty deposits (plaque formation) begin early in life and accumulate to reduce the size of the passageway of the large arteries. A number of factors have been found to increase the risk of atherosclerosis. These include: hypertension or high blood pressure, elevated blood lipids (resulting from a dietary intake of animal products high in cholesterol), cigarette smoking, diabetes mellitus, obesity, inactivity, stress, and family history of heart attack. People in industrialized nations have higher levels of atherosclerosis, but the extent to which this is due to lifestyle factors in developed countries is unknown.

As the reduced blood flow caused by atherosclerosis becomes significant, angina pectoris may result. The symptoms of angina are shortness of breath and pain from beneath the breastbone, in the neck, and down the left arm. For older individuals, these symptoms may be absent or may be confused with signs of other disorders, such as indigestion or gallbladder diseases. Treatment includes rest and nitroglycerine, which serves to dilate the blood vessels.

If deficient blood supply to the heart persists, heart tissue will die, producing a dead area known

---

*The terms *atherosclerosis* and **arteriosclerosis** are often used interchangeably, causing confusion regarding their distinction. Arteriosclerosis, a generic term, sometimes called hardening of the arteries, refers to the loss of elasticity of the arterial walls. This condition occurs in all populations, and can contribute to reduced blood flow to an area. In atherosclerosis, the passageway of the large arteries narrows as a result of the development of plaques on their interior walls; atherosclerosis has been found to be age-related and of higher incidence in industrialized populations. Arteriosclerosis and atherosclerosis can be superimposed, but there is not a causative relationship between the degree of atherosclerosis and the loss of elasticity (arteriosclerosis).

as an *infarct.* In other words, coronary artery disease can lead to a myocardial infarction, or heart attack. **Acute myocardial infarction** results from blockage of an artery supplying blood to a portion of the heart muscle. The extent of heart tissue involved determines the severity of the episode. Heart attacks may be more difficult to diagnose in older people, since their symptoms are often a generalized state of weakness, dizziness, confusion, or shortness of breath rather than the chest and back pain or numbness in the arms that characterizes heart attacks in younger people. Symptoms in older people may also merge with other problems, so that a heart attack may not be reported or treated until it is too late for effective help. Although women are less likely to have heart attacks than men prior to menopause, their rates are similar after age 65. As noted in Chapter 3, hormone replacement therapy (HRT) after menopause has been found to reduce the incidence of heart disease. This may be due to improved ratios of "good" cholesterol (HDL) to "bad" cholesterol (LDL) and increased pliability of blood vessels following regular use of HRT. However, some women may increase their risk of cancer with HRT, as discussed later in this chapter. Even at younger ages, women who develop a myocardial infarction fare less well than men, as evidenced by their higher mortality within the first year.

The term *congestive heart failure,* or heart failure, indicates a set of symptoms related to the impaired pumping performance of the heart, so that one or more chambers of the heart do not empty adequately during the heart's contractions. Heart failure does not mean that the heart has stopped beating, but that its pumping efficiency has decreased. This results in shortness of breath, reduced blood flow to vital body parts, including the kidneys, and a greater volume of blood accumulating in the body tissues, causing edema (swelling). Treatment involves drugs, dietary modifications (e.g., salt reduction), and rest.

Most cardiovascular problems can be treated with diet, exercise, and medications. They should not prevent older people from carrying out most ADLs. Preventive steps are most important, however. For example, *hypertension,* or high blood pressure, has been found to be the major risk factor in the development of cardiovascular complications and can be affected by preventive actions. As shown in Figure 4.2, the risk of hypertension is greater for women than men after age 65 (NCHS, 1995). This may partially explain why the incidence of coronary heart disease and strokes increases with age among women, although women on the average still live longer than men.

As noted in Chapter 3, systolic blood pressure often increases with age, from an average of 120/80 to between 130/80 and 140/80, but increases greater than this represent a definite hazard. Among older adults, risk of coronary heart disease, kidney disease, stroke, and death rises progressively with increasing blood pressure. The rates of *hypertension* are higher among African Americans than whites, but it is unclear whether this difference is due to lifestyle or genetic factors.

Significant increases in blood pressure should never be considered normal. In some isolated, primitive populations, a rise in pressure with age does not occur. Although genetic factors may come into play, this difference suggests that individuals can make lifestyle changes that may reduce their vulnerability to high blood pressure. The preventive measures most likely to reduce cardiovascular risk are weight control; daily physical activity; treatment of diabetes; reduced intake of salt, saturated fats, and cholesterol; increased intake of fruits and vegetables (rich in magnesium), fruits rich in potassium (e.g., bananas, oranges), and foods high in calcium; and avoidance of cigarette smoking and excessive alcohol intake. For most people, hypertension can be controlled by improving these health habits, although some must also use antihypertensive medications (National Heart, Lung and Blood Institute, 1997).

Another cardiovascular problem, which is less frequently addressed than hypertension, is *hypotension,* or low blood pressure. Yet hypotension, characterized by dizziness and faintness from exertion after a period of inactivity and frequently related to anemia, is actually very common among older adults. Problems with hypotension may be more pronounced after sitting or lying down for a long time (postural hypotension) or suddenly standing, after which a person may appear to lose balance and sway. Hypotension is not in itself dangerous, but can increase the risk of falls. Older people who have a history of low blood pressure or who are taking some types of antihypertensive medications need to move more slowly.

Strokes and Other Cerebrovascular Problems

We have seen how heart tissue can be denied adequate nourishment because of changes in the blood vessels that supply it. Similarly, arteriosclerotic and atherosclerotic changes in blood vessels that serve the brain can reduce its nourishment and result in the disruption of blood flow to brain tissue and malfunction or death of brain cells. This impaired brain tissue circulation is called *cerebrovascular disease.* When a portion of the brain is completely denied blood, a cerebrovascular accident (CVA), or stroke, occurs. The severity of the stroke depends on the particular areas as well as the total amount of brain tissue involved. Many older adults who have heart problems also are at risk for cerebrovascular disease.

CVAs represent the fourth leading cause of death following accidents. Of the 200,000 deaths from strokes each year, 80 percent occur among persons aged 65 and over (NCHS, 1995). African American elders are at greater risk for strokes than whites or other minority groups.

Atherosclerotic changes, in which fatty deposits gradually obstruct an artery in the brain or neck, are a common underlying condition. The most frequent cause of strokes in older persons is a cerebral thrombosis, a blood clot that either diminishes or closes off the blood flow in an artery of the brain or neck. Another cause of stroke is cerebral hemorrhage, in which a weak spot in a blood vessel of the brain bursts. Cerebral hemorrhage is less common in older adults, although more likely to cause death when it does occur. The risks of stroke appear to be related to social and personal factors, most prominently hypertension, but also age, previous lifestyle, diet, and activity patterns. Regular, sustained exercise and lowfat diets are associated with the reduction of fatty particles that clog the blood stream. New findings about the benefits of common drugs like aspirin and warfarin in preventing blood clots are also reducing the risk of strokes. Indeed, the death rate from strokes has dropped by 40 percent in the last 20 years, especially among the older population, because of these preventive measures and improved and immediate treatment of strokes (Gorelick, Shanmugam, and Pajeau, 1996).

The area of the brain that is damaged by a stroke dictates which body functions may be affected. For instance, if the speech center of the brain dies, then the stroke victim may be unable to speak or understand speech (aphasia). Another possible effect is paralysis of one side of the body (hemiplegia), which also may be associated with blindness in half of the victim's visual field (heminanopsia).

The treatment for strokes is similar to that for heart attacks and hypertension: modulated activity and supervised schedules of exercise and drugs. Stroke victims often require physical, occupational, and speech therapy, and their recovery process can be slow, frustrating, and emotionally draining for the victim and his or her family. It is important to assess carefully the effect of a stroke on a given individual and determine what functions can be retrained (Gresham, Duncan, and Stason, 1995). Newer, more aggressive and immediate rehabilitation methods have been effective in reducing the rates of residual impairments following a stroke. Within a year after the stroke, about half have regained most of their motor function, but more people report residual non-motor impairments such as problems with vision, speech, and loss of balance (Ferrucci, Kittner, Corti, and Guralnik, 1995; Pinsky et al., 1990).

Rehabilitation must address not only physical conditions, but also the psychosocial needs for support and respite of stroke patients and their families. The recognition of this wider range of rehabilitation has led to the creation of stroke support groups in many communities, organized by

stroke patients and their families, or by local hospitals and senior centers.

Cancer

Among those 65 years old and over, 21 percent of deaths are due to cancer, especially cancers of the stomach, lungs, intestines, and pancreas. In fact, these malignancies in old age are the second leading cause of death, and 50 percent of all cancer occurs and is diagnosed after age 65. Cancer of the bowel is the most common malignancy in those age 70 and over, and is second to lung cancer in cancer-related deaths. Lung cancer has its highest incidence in men age 65 and over, but appears to be associated more with smoking than with age. Cancer of the colon is more common in women, whereas rectal cancer is more frequent in men. Women also face increasing risks of breast and cervical cancers with age (NCHS, 1995). Both the incidence and mortality rates due to cervical and breast cancer are greater in older African American women than in older white women, primarily because of lower use of cancer screening services (Caplan, Wells, and Haynes, 1992).

The greater risk of cancer with age may be due to a number of factors, such as the effects of a slow-acting carcinogen, prolonged "development time" necessary for growth to be observable, extended pre-exposure time, and failing immune capacity that is characteristic of increased age. Some cancers which have a high prevalence in the middle years and again in old age may have a different etiology. For example, breast cancer in premenopausal women appears to have a genetic basis and is related to family history, while that in postmenopausal women may have more external or environmental causes. Certain diet and lifestyle factors may also be related to cancer in older people. Diagnosing cancer in old age is often more difficult than at earlier life stages, because of the existence of other chronic diseases and because symptoms of cancer, such as weight loss, weakness, or fatigue, may be inaccurately attributed to aging, depression, or dementia. In addition, the current older generation's fear of cancer may be so great that they do not seek medical help to address their suspicions and fears.

Arthritis

Although not a leading cause of death, arthritis is the most common chronic condition affecting older people and is a major cause of limited activity. In fact, all persons over age 60 have been estimated to have some physical evidence of arthritis, with over 70 percent having some musculoskeletal complaint (NCHS, 1995). Because arthritis is so common and the symptoms are so closely identified with the normal aging process, older people may accept arthritis as an inevitable accompaniment of a long life. If so, they may fail to seek treatment or to learn strategies to reduce pain and support their independent functioning. Although many treatments are used to control arthritic symptoms, little is known about ways to postpone or eliminate these disorders.

Arthritis is not a single entity, but includes over 100 different conditions of inflammations and degenerative changes of bones and joints. **Rheumatoid arthritis,** a chronic inflammation of the membranes lining joints and tendons, is characterized by pain, swelling, bone dislocation, and limited range of motion. It afflicts two to three times more women than men and can cause severe crippling. Rheumatoid arthritis is not associated with aging per se; many young people also have this condition, with initial symptoms most commonly appearing between 20 and 50 years of age. Symptoms of rheumatoid arthritis include malaise, fatigue, loss of weight, fever, joint pain, redness, swelling, and stiffness affecting many joints. The disease is characterized by acute episodes followed by periods of relative inactivity. The cause of rheumatoid arthritis is unknown; treatment includes a balance of rest, exercise, and use of aspirin, which provides relief from pain, fever, and inflammation. Use of other anti-inflammatory agents, antimalarials, and corticosteroids, as well as surgical procedures to repair joints and correct various deformities, have been found to be effective for some people. There are some important new developments in drug therapy for rheumatoid arthritis, many of which will be available before the end of the century.

Osteoarthritis, which is presumed to be a universal corollary of aging, is a gradual degeneration of the joints that are most subject to stress—those of the hands, knees, hips, and shoulders. Pain and disfigurement in the fingers are manifestations of osteoarthritis, but are generally not disabling. Osteoarthritis of the lower limbs, however, can limit mobility. Heredity as well as environmental or lifestyle factors—particularly obesity, occupational stresses, and wear and tear on the joints—have been identified as causes of osteoarthritis. Some progress has been made in minimizing inflammation and pain through the use of anti-inflammatory drugs, steroids, mild exercise, heat and cold, and reduction of strain on weight-bearing joints through weight loss and the use of weight-bearing appliances. Surgical procedures may restore function to the hips and knees, but cannot cure the arthritic condition.

The pervasive and unpredictable nature of the pain of arthritis can dominate a person's life and result in frustration and depression. Even on "good days" when pain subsides, an older arthritic may live with the fear of the inevitable "bad day" and may structure daily activities to avoid pain. Each day may seem to consist of a succession of obstacles, from getting out of bed and fastening

Gentle massage can relieve the pain of arthritis.

clothing, to opening packages, dialing the phone, and handling dishes for meals. Concentrating on coping with one obstacle after another in the completion of tasks can be exhausting, even when minimal physical exertion is involved in each task.

The prime danger for people with arthritis is reducing their physical activity in response to pain. Movement stimulates the secretion of synovial fluid, the substance that lubricates the surfaces between joints and increases blood flow to joint areas. Movement also tones the muscles that hold joints in place and that shield joints from excessive stress. When someone tries to avoid pain by sitting still as much as possible, the losses in lubricating fluid and muscular protection make movement still more painful. Eventually, the muscles surrounding immobilized areas lose their flexibility, and affected joints freeze into rigid positions called **contractures.** For these reasons, older people need to be encouraged to maintain physical activity in spite of pain. The adage "use it or lose it" has special meaning to an arthritis victim! The environment may need to be restructured in these cases, so that a person with arthritis is able to walk around and keep up with daily activities, but is not burdened by extreme press or demands. For example, a smaller home on one level, such as that selected by Mrs. Fox in our earlier description of multiple chronic diseases, can reduce the environmental press for older people with arthritis.

Osteoporosis

The human body is constantly forming and losing bone through the metabolism of calcium. As noted in Chapter 3, osteoporosis involves a more dramatic loss in bone mass. The increased brittleness of the bones associated with this condition can result in diminished height, slumped posture, backache, and a reduction in the structural strength of bones, making them susceptible to fracture. Compressed or collapsed vertebrae are the major cause of kyphosis, or "dowager's hump," the stooped look that many of us associate with aging.

Osteoporosis apparently starts well before old age (perhaps as young as age 35) and is more than four times more common in women than in men. The causes of osteoporosis are unclear, although it may be associated with loss of calcium and estrogen in menopausal women, a sedentary lifestyle, cigarette smoking, excessive alcohol and caffeine consumption, long-term dieting or fasting, inadequate fluoride intake, or a genetic factor that determines bone density. For example, Caucasian women are more likely to develop this condition than African American women (Looker, Johnston, and Wahner, 1995).

The primary risk posed by osteoporosis is a fracture of the neck of the femur, or thigh. Many of the falls and associated hip fractures of old age actually represent an osteoporotic femoral neck that broke from bearing weight, causing the individual to fall. Osteoporosis and its less serious counterpart, **osteopenia** (a significant loss of calcium and reduced bone density but without the risk of fractures), together affect about 25 million Americans, 80 percent of whom are women. It results in 1.5 million fractures per year; 40 percent are spinal, 25 percent are hip, and 15 percent are wrist fractures (Looker et al., 1995; OWL, 1994). Many older people have undiagnosed osteoporosis, often showing no symptoms until a fall or fracture occurs. Typically, no immediate preceding event can be identified as the cause of the fracture.

Some 20 percent of white women experience fractures by age 65, increasing to more than 30 percent by age 90. Although both sexes lose bone mass with aging, it is rare for men to develop symptomatic osteoporosis before age 70. White men are far less likely than white women to experience hip fractures; African American men and women have even lower rates of fractures than white men. Risk factors for hip fractures among white women with osteoporosis are age (especially over 70), family history of hip fractures, low body weight, use of medications that affect balance, not using estrogen, and disabilities or weakness of the lower extremities (LaCroix, 1997).

Hip fractures are of concern because of their impact on morbidity and mortality; it is estimated that 15 to 20 percent of people with a hip fracture die from it or from surgical complications (Josephson et al., 1991). Even when the older person does not die from a hip fracture, falls that result in hip fractures can cause long-term disability and are responsible for more days of restricted activity among older people than any other health problem. The costs to society are also high; it has been estimated that yearly costs associated with treating fall-related fractures alone, not including long-term care, are as high as 7 to 10 billion (Berg and Cassels, 1992; Kosorek, Omenn, and Diehr, 1992). With the growth of the older population, it is predicted that more than $45 billion will be spent over the next ten years to care for white women in the United States who sustain a fracture (Chrischilles et al., 1994).

However, not all falls and fractures among older people result from osteoporosis. Cardiovascular disease underlies approximately one-half of them. Others are due to a decline in postural control, produced by impairments of the senses and the central nervous system, changes previously discussed in Chapter 3.

PREVENTING OSTEOPOROSIS: THE CASE FOR AND AGAINST ESTROGEN   The goal in treating osteoporosis is to prevent further bone loss. Increased intake of dietary calcium, vitamin D, fluoride, moderate weight-bearing exercise such as vigorous walking and strength-training to help retain calcium, and estrogen have been used as therapies (Nelson et al., 1994). In the years immediately following menopause, the rate of bone loss can be as high as 5 percent compared to a normal rate of 1 or 2 percent. For women entering menopause, reduced estrogen, not calcium, is the primary cause of bone loss in the first 5 years after menopause. Accordingly, hormone replacement therapy (HRT) can decrease the risk of hip fractures by 25 to 50 percent, and of spinal crush fractures by 50 to 75 percent. Since estrogen blocks the process of bone reabsorption, it can help the bones absorb dietary calcium and thereby increase bone density 3 to 5 percent in the first year. However, the effects may not be permanent, and benefits may be lost after discontinuing HRT (OWL, 1994). Although HRT is the best medical means of preventing osteoporosis and bone fractures, especially when started soon after menopause and continued for several years, it has been found in some cases to be associated with breast and endometrial cancer. The combination of synthetic progesterone (progestin) with estrogen can reduce the chances of endometrial cancer. For some women, however, progestin has unpleasant side effects such as a recurrence of monthly periods or breakthrough bleeding, breast tenderness, bloating, cramps, and mood swings.

HRT is far less effective if begun long after the menopause than immediately after it. Small, short-stature women who are postmenopausal, have high caffeine intake, smoke cigarettes, and have a family history of osteoporosis appear to be most at risk of cancer associated with hormone treatments. An additional problem is that when hormone replacement therapy is discontinued, bone loss is more rapid than prior to treatment. On the other hand, HRT actually reduces the incidence of coronary heart disease by 50 percent and has no effect on the risk of strokes. This conclusion is based on a large-scale, 16-year study of postmenopausal women and on several studies of women over age 70 (Stampfer et al., 1991; Henderson et al., 1991; Stampfer and Colditz, 1991). Cardiovascular disease is a greater risk for women after age 50 than is breast cancer; it accounts for 52 percent of all deaths of women over age 50 in 1990, compared with 5 percent for breast cancer. Most women without family history of breast cancer and other risk factors for cancer would appear to benefit from estrogen replacement. Evidence from the Framingham study suggests that HRT must take place at least 7 years continuously to demonstrate these benefits. Other studies suggest that use of estrogen supplements should be limited to ten years or less to reduce the risk of breast cancer (Steinberg et al., 1992). Despite its proven benefits, only about 15 percent of postmenopausal women are currently undergoing HRT (Bush, 1990). This low utilization rate may be due in part to misinformation or lack of information available to women who are faced with the decision about

TABLE 4.2   **Advantages and Disadvantages of Estrogen Replacement Therapy**

PROVEN BENEFITS	LIKELY BENEFITS	PROVEN RISKS	LIKELY RISKS
Relieves menopausal symptoms (e.g. hot flashes, night sweats)	Reduces risk of heart disease	Increases risk of endometrial cancer	Increases risk of breast cancer (especially if family history)
Relieves vaginal dryness	Reduces risk of colon cancer	Increases risk of benign fibroid tumors in uterus	Weight gain
Slows rate of bone loss	Reduces sudden shifts in mood	Premenstrual symptoms reappear (fluid retention, tender breasts)	Blood clots
	Improves cognitive abilities	May cause menstrual bleeding if combined with progesterone	Increases risk of gallstones
	Slows cognitive decline in Alzheimer's disease		Headaches may increase

whether to use HRT. Table 4.2 illustrates the potential benefits and risks of HRT.

For women who cannot or choose not to undergo HRT, new drugs have been approved by the Food and Drug Administration. Some of these drugs have been found to slow the rate of bone loss and prevent vertebral fractures. However, none of these medications eliminates the need for increased intake of calcium and Vitamin D among older women. Combinations of fluoride and calcium treatments have also been given, but may have negative side effects of gastrointestinal and rheumatic complaints.

Scientists are working on new forms of estrogen that will have the benefits of current forms without the risks. These "designer estrogens," or selective estrogen receptor modulators, appear to improve bone density and reduce levels of LDL (bad) cholesterol while increasing the levels of HDL (good) cholesterol, but do not have harmful effects on breast tissue.

CALCIUM AND EXERCISE TO PREVENT OSTEO-POROSIS   Certain dietary and exercise habits may help prevent osteoporosis, especially increasing the amount of calcium after age 40. A 1994 consensus conference at the National Institutes of Health concluded that women should consume 1500 mg. of calcium daily if they are

not on HRT, and 1000 mg per day if they are on HRT. This is higher than previously recommended; 1500 mg of calcium is equivalent to five 8-ounce glasses of milk daily, far more than most women are accustomed to consuming. Calcium is absorbed better when combined with Vitamin D. For this reason, milk in the United States is fortified with Vitamin D. Unfortunately, many older women do not consume enough milk or milk products to obtain Vitamin D in that manner. It is also produced by the human body after 15 to 20 minutes of exposure to sunlight each day, but many older women avoid the sun or are unable to get outside every day. There is strong evidence from a large study of 3000 older women in France that daily supplementation with Vitamin D (800 international units) and calcium (1200 mg) can reduce hip fractures by 43 percent and spinal fractures by 32 percent (Chapuy et al., 1992). For this reason, older women who do not obtain an adequate intake of fortified milk or sunshine should take daily multivitamins with at least 400 IUs of Vitamin D (600 IUs for those over age 70).

Although increased calcium appears to be an important preventive measure, low dietary calcium may be only partly responsible for osteoporosis (Arnaud and Sanchez, 1990). Therefore, increasing calcium intake may not prevent frac-

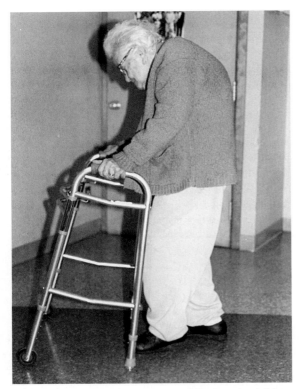

Osteoporosis can make movement difficult and painful.

postmenopausal women (Nelson et al., 1994; Notelovitz, Martin, and Tesar, 1991). The strength-training program was combined with estrogen therapy in the former study, but not in the latter study. Another study demonstrated that simple, vigorous walking on a daily basis reduced hip fractures by 30 percent in older women (Cummings et al., 1995). These recent clinical experiments demonstrate that high-intensity (i.e., twice weekly), strenuous exercise not only maintains, but also *increases* bone mineral density in older women (up to age 70 in both studies). The strength-training program implemented by Nelson and colleagues also resulted in increased muscle mass, muscle strength, balance, and spontaneous physical activity. Because of the increased attention to osteoporosis today, many entrepreneurial clinics are offering bone density testing to postmenopausal women. These tests show the obvious results; that most women over 50 have less bone mass than younger women. However, they do not provide a comparison with any baseline data for a specific individual. These tests might be helpful if obtained before menopause in women at risk for osteoporosis, then redone when these women are in their sixties, seventies, and eighties.

Chronic Obstructive Pulmonary Disease or Respiratory Problems

Chronic *bronchitis, fibrosis, asthma,* and *emphysema* are manifestations of chronic obstructive pulmonary diseases (COPD) that damage lung tissue. They increase with age, develop slowly and insidiously, and are progressive and debilitating, often resulting in frequent hospitalizations, major lifestyle changes, and death. In fact, by age 90, most people are likely to have some signs of emphysema, with shortness of breath and prolonged and difficult exhalation. Getting through daily activities can be extremely exhausting under such conditions. Causes of COPD are both genetic and environmental, especially prolonged exposure to various dusts, fumes, or cigarette smoke. Three to four times as many men as women have these diseases, probably due to a combination of normal

turing after bone loss has occurred. One reason is that an estimated 40 percent of osteoporotic women have a deficiency of the enzyme that is needed to metabolize calcium (lactose), thus making calcium less easily absorbed. An additional problem is that once one fracture is present, a patient has a 70 to 80 percent chance of developing another fracture.

A combination of calcium and exercise (twice-weekly brisk walks and once-weekly aerobics) appears to reduce bone loss over a 2-year period more than exercise alone. This combined regimen is not as effective as moderate exercise combined with hormone replacement therapy, which actually *increases* bone density almost 3 percent per year (Prince et al., 1991). Two longitudinal studies have shown that high-intensity strength-training using exercise machines for one year can significantly *increase* bone mineral density in age changes in the lung and a greater likelihood of smoking and exposure to airborne pollutants. This is especially true in older cohorts; men in the oldest-old group are three times more likely to die of COPD than their female counterparts, as shown in Table 4.1. Treatment is usually continuous, and includes drugs, respiratory therapy, breathing exercises to compensate for damage, and the avoidance of respiratory infections, smoking, pollution, and other irritants.

Allergic reactions to bacterial products, drugs, and pollutants also increase with age. The greater incidence of drug allergies may be a function of both decreases in physiological capacities and the increased use of many drugs, such as sedatives, tranquilizers, antidepressants, and antibiotics.

Diabetes

Compared with other systems of the body, the endocrine glands do not show consistent and predictable age-related changes, other than the gradual slowing of functioning. However, insufficient insulin, produced and secreted by the pancreas, can lead to *diabetes mellitus*. Diabetes mellitus is characterized by above-normal amounts of sugar (glucose) in the blood and urine, resulting from an inability to use carbohydrates. Diabetics may go into a coma when their blood sugar levels get very high. Low blood sugar (hypoglycemia) can also lead to unconsciousness.

Older diabetics include: (1) those who have had the disease since youth; (2) those who develop it in late middle age and incur related cardiovascular problems; and (3) those who develop it late in life and generally show mild pathologic conditions. The last type is most common in older persons, and can often be managed without medication. The incidence of newly diagnosed adult-onset diabetes is highest in the 60- to 80-year-old category (NCHS, 1995). Although diabetes can occur at any age, diabetic problems related to the body's lessened capability to metabolize carbohydrates can be particularly severe in older adults. Many cases are associated with being overweight, especially due to changes in fat/mus-

cle ratio and slower metabolism with aging. This is particularly true among older African American women, who have a higher rate of obesity and diabetes than do older white women (NCHS, 1995). Glucose tolerance and the action of insulin are often compromised by poor diet, physical inactivity, and coexistent diseases.

Symptoms of diabetes include excessive thirst, increased appetite and urination, fatigue, weakness, loss of weight, and decreased wound healing. These symptoms may not be present in older people, however. Instead, diabetes among the older population is generally detected incidentally through eye examinations, hospitalization, and testing for other disorders. Since blood glucose may be temporarily elevated under the stress of illnesses such as stroke, myocardial infarction, or infection, people should not be labeled as diabetic unless the high glucose level persists under conditions of reduced stress.

The cumulative effect of high blood glucose levels can lead to complications in advanced stages of diabetes. These include infections, nerve damage, blindness, renal disorders, stroke, cognitive dysfunction, harm to the coronary arteries, skin problems, and poor circulation in the extremities, leading to gangrene. The interaction of diabetes with ordinary age-related physical problems such as hypertension can result in serious health difficulties and consequent limitations on daily activities. Atherosclerosis and coronary heart disease, for example, are more common in diabetics than in nondiabetics.

Diabetes cannot be cured, but it can generally be managed at home through a diet of reduced carbohydrates and calories; regular exercise; proper care of feet, skin, teeth, and gums; and monitored insulin intake for those who require it. To minimize forgetfulness and treatment errors, older people, especially those who acquire diabetes late in life, may need instruction regarding the importance of diet, daily examination of their bodies, urine testing, and the correct dosage of insulin or other drugs. With proper management, diabetics can live long and useful lives. Some promising results from studies with Rhesus monkeys offer potential approaches to preventing diabetes in humans. As described in Chapter 3, diets that provide 30 percent fewer calories but the same level of nutrition have been found to lower blood glucose and insulin levels compared to an age-related increase in these markers of diabetes in a control group of Rhesus monkeys (Kemnitz et al., 1994). Changes made to Medicare in 1997 provide for education in self-care of diabetes.

Problems with the Kidneys and Urinary Tract

The various diseases and disorders of the urinary system characteristic of old age tend to be either acute infections or chronic problems resulting from the gradual deterioration of the structure and function of the excretory system with age. As we have seen in Chapter 3, the kidneys shrink in size, and their capacity to perform basic filtration tasks declines, leading to a higher probability of disease or infection. One of the most common age-related problems for women is the inability of the bladder to empty completely. This often results in cystitis, an acute inflammatory state accompanied by pain and irritation. Cystitis can generally be treated with antibiotics.

Older men face an increased risk of diseases of the prostate gland, with cancer of the prostate being the most frequent malignancy of older men. For this reason, the American Cancer Society and the American Urological Association recommend annual prostatic evaluations for men aged 50 and older by both a digital rectal exam and a new test to determine levels of prostate-specific antigen (PSA) in the blood. Cancer of the prostate frequently spreads to the bones, but surgery is rarely recommended for men over age 70 because the disease usually progresses slowly in this age group. Instead, more conservative treatment and more frequent monitoring are usually the treatment of choice (Albertsen, Fryback, and Storer, 1995).

INCONTINENCE A more difficult, noninfectious, and chronic urinary problem is **incontinence** (i.e., inability to control urine and feces), which

has been estimated to occur in 5 to 19 percent of men and 7 to 38 percent of women over age 65 and living in the community (Cramer, 1993; Ouslander and Abelson, 1990). Since older people and their families often consider incontinence a taboo topic, they tend to be unaware of methods to cope with and treat it. Most older adults do not discuss the problem with their doctors, and only a small percentage use any protective devices. Many health care providers, in turn, do not ask their older patients about problems with incontinence. This widespread reluctance to acknowledge incontinence as a problem can have serious psychological and social implications, particularly on the decision to institutionalize an older person. Accordingly, about half of the older population living in nursing homes experience at least one episode of incontinence daily.

There are two primary types of incontinence: (1) *urge incontinence,* where the person has a strong urge to urinate and is unable to hold urine long enough to reach a toilet, and (2) *stress incontinence,* where leakage occurs during physical exertion or when sneezing or coughing, a phenomenon that can also occur among younger women. Many cases of incontinence represent a combination of these two types, referred to as mixed incontinence. Incontinence sometimes results from a specific precipitating factor, such as acute illness, infection, or even a change in residence. It can be treated if the cause is known. Temporary incontinence can be caused by bladder or urinary tract infections which may be treated with antibiotics. Prescribed medications can also cause urgent and frequent urination. If informed of the detrimental effects of medication on an older person, a physician may reduce the drug dosage. With age, the bladder and urethra in women commonly descend, resulting in stress incontinence; leaking then occurs with the increased abdominal pressure brought on by coughing, sneezing, laughing, lifting, or physical exercise. Another type of incontinence, known as *functional incontinence,* often results from neurological changes and accompanies other problems, such as Parkinson's disease and organic brain syndrome. Other physical causes that should be investigated medically are prostate problems, pernicious anemia, diabetic neuropathy, and various cancers.

Since the types and causes of incontinence vary widely, thorough diagnosis and individualized treatment programs are critical. Even habitual incontinence should not be assumed to be irreversible; it may be treated or partially controlled through drugs, surgery, dietary changes, exercises, or behavioral management techniques, such as reducing fluid intake when bathroom access is limited. Although some physicians prescribe medications to increase bladder capacity or reduce urine production, these often have unpleasant side effects such as blurred vision and dry mouth. Noninvasive treatment, such as frequent access to toilet facilities, restriction of fluid intake before bedtime, and systematic exercise of the pelvic muscle is often just as effective. Even incurable problems can be managed through protective products (e.g., absorbent pads) and catheters (tubes draining the bladder) to reduce complications, anxiety, and embarrassment. In fact, only about 25 percent of older persons with incontinence are so severely disabled that they are unlikely to regain continence and require a catheter or other external appliances to cope with the conditions (Cramer, 1993). Physical exercise designed to promote and maintain sphincter muscle tone can also be a means to prevent or reduce age-related incontinence, particularly among older women. All possible treatments, especially behavioral techniques, exercise, and biofeedback, should be explored, since older people's embarrassment and humiliation over their difficulties may result in their avoiding social gatherings out of fear of having their incontinence detected. Support groups, such as *Help for Incontinent People (HIP),* have chapters nationwide.

Problems with the Intestinal System

Many older people experience problems in digestion and continuing gastrointestinal distress, due particularly to age-related slowing down of the digestive process. Most intestinal problems are, in fact, related to unbalanced diets or diets with limited fiber content. **Diverticulitis** is one of the most common difficulties, affecting up to 50 percent of persons aged 80 and over, and especially women (Greenwald and Brandt, 1996). It is a condition in which pouches or sacs (diverticula) in the intestines (especially in the colon) result from weakness of the intestinal wall; these sacs become inflamed and infected, leading to symptoms of nausea, abdominal discomfort, bleeding, and changes in bowel function. Management includes a high-fiber diet and antibiotic therapy. Diverticulitis, which is increasing in industrialized nations, may be associated with a highly refined diet lacking in fiber.

Many older people worry about constipation, but this is not an inevitable outcome of aging, as noted in Chapter 3. Causes of constipation include overuse of cathartics, lack of exercise, psychological stress, gastrointestinal disease, and an unbalanced diet with respect to bulk. Constipation may be a symptom of an underlying disease or obstruction. If this is not the case, treatment commonly includes physical activity, dietary modification, and increased fluid intake. Because many older people are overly concerned about having regular bowel movements, they may become dependent on laxatives, which can, over time, cause problems, such as irritating the colon and decreasing the absorption of certain vitamins. Some older people may become preoccupied with bodily functions, often boring or frustrating family members with detailed accounts.

Hiatus hernia appears to be increasing in incidence, especially among obese women; this occurs when a small portion of the stomach slides up through the diaphragm. Symptoms include indigestion, difficulty in swallowing, and chest pain that may be confused with a heart attack. Medical management includes weight reduction, elevation of the upper body when sleeping, changes in the size and frequency of meals, and medication. Although hiatus hernia in itself is not especially severe, it may mask the symptoms of more serious intestinal disorders, such as cancer of the stomach.

The incidence of gall bladder disease, especially with gallstones, also increases with age and is indicated by pain, nausea, and vomiting, with attacks increasing in number and severity. Most cases in older adults are asymptomatic, and physicians debate whether to perform surgery or follow a more conservative course of medical management. Medical treatment usually involves a program of weight reduction, avoidance of fatty foods, and use of antacids.

Oral Diseases

Because of developments in preventive dentistry, newer cohorts of older people have better oral health than any preceding cohort. According to the most recent National Health and Nutrition Exam Survey (NHANES III), only 30 percent over age 65 today are completely **edentulous** (i.e., no natural teeth remaining). As one might expect, edentulism increases with age, from 26 percent of the young-old to 44 percent of the old-old. This change is due entirely to historical differences in dental care delivery, not because of the aging process. Ethnic minority differences in tooth loss are minimal in the young-old, but increase in the oldest-old, such that 43 percent of whites, 44 percent of Mexican Americans, and 53 percent of African Americans age 75 and older were found to be missing all their teeth in the NHANES III survey (Marcus, Drury, Brown, and Zion, 1996).

The common problems of tooth decay and periodontal diseases also appear to increase with age, although the evidence is limited and less clear. In NHANES III, the rate of root caries (cavities that develop on exposed root surfaces) was found to be more than three times greater among subjects over age 65 than in those under age 45; rates of decay on the enamel surfaces of teeth, however, are not much higher among 65- to 74-year-olds compared with 35- to 44-years-olds. Differences are much greater when the older group is compared with people aged 18 to 24, who have only about 10 percent of their tooth surfaces decayed or filled, compared with 31 percent of people aged 65–74 (Winn et al., 1996). These differences reflect changes over time in preventive dental care, such as the widespread use of water fluoridation.

NHANES III also found an age-related increase in the incidence of periodontitis or gum disease. Most of the increase occurs in middle age, after age 45 (Brown, Brunelle, and Kingman, 1996).

In contrast, cancers of the lip, tongue, mouth, gum, pharynx, and salivary glands increase with advanced age, regardless of ethnic minority status or sex. In North America and Western Europe, cancer of the lip is the most frequent and has the highest survival rates among those listed previously (between 65 and 90 percent over a five-year period). Smoking and heavy alcohol use are strongly linked to oral cancer.

AIDS in the Older Population

While it cannot be classified as a chronic disease in the same way as diabetes or chronic obstructive pulmonary disease is, the growing number of older adults with AIDS (Acquired Immune Deficiency Syndrome) and the increasing time between infection, diagnosis, and death make this an important public health issue in gerontology. Over the next few years, AIDS will place greater demands on long-term care, especially home-based services. Since it is mandatory to report AIDS cases, the Centers for Disease Control and Prevention (CDC) receive reports from all state and territorial health departments on all diagnosed cases of AIDS. Because of stereotypes that older people are not sexually active, many physicians and HIV-testing programs do not routinely test older adults for AIDS (El-Sadr and Gettler, 1995; Gueldner, 1995). In 1995, of the more than one-half million diagnosed cases of AIDS, 10 percent were age 50 or older. There was an increase in diagnosed cases of 17 percent between 1990 and 1995 in this age group, compared to less than 10 percent for people under age 40. Almost one-third (29 percent) of this older group was over age 60 (CDC, 1995). Although men are at greater risk today in all age groups, older women are also at increased risk. For example, among all persons over age 50 who were diagnosed with AIDS in 1995, 12 percent were women; but among those aged 65 and older, 21 percent were women (CDC, 1995). The most common risk factor for men between ages 50 and 65 is homosexual or bisexual behavior. After age 65, blood transfusions are the primary risk factor (representing 25 percent of cases), followed by homosexual, then heterosexual behavior. Although widespread testing of blood products began in 1988, this has not totally eliminated the infection rate (Gaeta, Lapolla, and Melendez, 1996). Intravenous drug use is much less common in the population aged 50 and older compared with younger groups; therefore their risk of contracting AIDS in this manner is much lower.

In a study of families of transfusion-infected AIDS patients, slightly more wives (18 percent) than husbands (8 percent) of AIDS patients were seropositive (i.e., the HIV antibody was detected in their blood). In addition, seropositive wives were older than seronegative wives (median age 62 versus 54 respectively) (Peterman et al., 1988). Older women are also becoming infected through heterosexual transmission by their male partners who were infected in other ways. These results lend support to the argument that older persons are more vulnerable to infection with the AIDS virus because their immune system deteriorates with aging, as described earlier in this chapter. Furthermore, the progression from HIV to AIDS is more rapid among older people—62 percent compared with 21 percent of younger people. Their remaining lifespan after the diagnosis is also less (6.3 months versus 16.5 months for younger AIDS victims) (Ferro and Salit, 1992). Another reason why older women may be more likely to become infected are the vaginal changes after the menopause. In particular, there is a thinning of the vaginal walls due to loss of estrogen as described in Chapter 7. This leads to mucosal disruption and tearing of the vaginal wall, and thus makes it more susceptible for the HIV to enter the bloodstream. Furthermore, older adults are far less likely to use condoms during intercourse than are younger persons (Gaeta et al., 1996).

For these reasons, it is important to educate older adults about *their* risk for AIDS. Even those who know something about this disease may feel that it cannot affect them if they are not engaging in homosexual activity or intravenous drug use. Many older people have relied on the media for their knowledge in this area. Unfortunately, there have been few reports in the media of *older* adults contracting AIDS through heterosexual intercourse or through blood transfusions. It is therefore not surprising that many older people are unaware that they may be infected. They are also less willing to be tested for the virus, and once diagnosed, are less likely to seek out AIDS support groups or other forms of emotional support. At the same time, ageist attitudes may prevent health providers from encouraging sexually active elders to be tested for this virus or even asking questions about their sexual history as part of a routine health screening (Emlet, 1993, 1997; Gueldner, 1995).

Accidents among Older People

Although mortality statistics suggest that older people are less likely than the young to die of accidents (only 7 per 10,000 deaths compared with 10 per 10,000 among people 21 and younger), these numbers mask the true incidence of deaths due to accident-related injuries. For example, if an older person breaks a hip after falling down a flight of stairs or breaks a leg in an auto accident, she enters a hospital, often is discharged to a nursing home, and soon after may die from pneumonia. Pneumonia is then listed as the cause of death, when in fact this acute condition was brought on by the patient's problems in recovering from the accident.

Despite this underestimate, the risk of death from physical injuries is about four times greater for 80-year-olds than for 20-year-olds, due probably to their greater physical vulnerability (Evans, 1991; Maher, 1990). In addition, people over age 65 have the highest rates of auto injury-related hospitalization and death of any age group except teenagers. Although driving fatalities for all age groups have declined in the past decade, fatalities among drivers 65 and older have increased (Waller, 1991). This may be due to the increase in absolute numbers of older drivers as well as their greater vulnerability.

Older drivers are less likely to drive in bad weather, at night, in freeway traffic, or in rush hour. In fact, they drive fewer miles per year than younger drivers. Nevertheless, they have more accidents per mile driven. This higher rate of accidents may be attributed to changes in eye-hand coordination, slower reaction time, impaired vision (especially diminished night vision and sensitivity to glare), and hearing impairments, as described in Chapter 3. Changes in cognitive function that may impair driving abilities are described in Chapter 5. Even though most accidents by older drivers occur at low speeds, age-related declines in organ systems and brittle bones (see Chapter 3) make the older person more vulnerable to injuries and even death as a result of accidents. In addition, some medications—especially those given for insomnia or anxiety—that have a long half-life in the bloodstream have been found to increase the risk of motor vehicle crashes in older adults by as much as 45 percent. This is a major risk, since many older people are prescribed these medications (Hemmelgarn et al., 1997).

It may be useful for state licensing departments to test all adults annually on some of the relevant physiological and cognitive abilities, and to retrain older drivers who are experiencing significant declines in these areas. The American Association of Retired Persons, National Safety Council, and the Automobile Association of America have developed such courses. For example, AARP estimates that some 500,000 older drivers enroll in their "55 Alive/Mature Driving" program each year. This 8-hour course is offered through retirement homes, senior centers, shopping malls, libraries, and churches throughout the United States. Older persons can obtain discounts of 5 to 10 percent on their auto insurance in many states after completing such courses.

Older drivers also can be assisted by improved environmental design. For example, older people have more accidents while making left turns; these could be avoided by designing better left-turn intersections with special lanes and left arrow lights. Road signs that are clearer and redundant could reduce the high number of violations received by older drivers for improperly changing lanes or entering and exiting highways. Automobiles with right sideview mirrors, enlarged rearview mirrors, less complicated dashboards, airbags, and better protection on doors could also reduce accident rates among older individuals.

FALLS AND THEIR PREVENTION

As noted earlier, older people are at a greater risk of falls than the young. Up to 30 percent of older adults in the community, and even more in long-term care settings, experience a fall in a given year. Many older people who fall become more fearful of falling and therefore restrict their activity levels. They may also become more rigid or overly cautious in walking. This may, in turn, increase the likelihood of subsequent falls. Therefore it is important to identify risk factors for falls and try to prevent them.

Risk factors for falls include inactivity, visual impairment, multiple diseases and medications (e.g., cardiac conditions and medications that cause postural hypotension), and gait disorders that are common among older persons. Lighting levels and hazards in the environment such as slippery floors, loose area rugs, and poorly demarcated stairs can also precipitate a fall. Among nursing home residents, risk factors for recurrent falls (i.e., a second or third fall several months after the first one) appear to be older age (≥ 75), needing assistance with several activities of daily living, and balance and behavioral problems (Thapa, Gideon, Fought, and Ray, 1995).

Many interventions to prevent falls have been successful. In one study, environmental modifications of the homes of older people who had experienced multiple falls in the past resulted in a 72 percent decrease in falls (Tideiksaar, 1990). In a large study of 14 nursing homes, 50 percent of the homes (the experimental group) had major modifications made to their physical environment, in wheelchair safety, and in use of psychotropic medications. No changes were made in the other seven homes (control group). A significant decline in recurrent falls occurred among older residents of the experimental homes compared with the control group. That is, 19 percent of those with environmental modifications versus 54 percent in the control group fell in the following 2 years (Ray et al., 1997). Other studies have tested methods to teach older women how to control their balance and thereby prevent falls and have focused on reducing the use of psychotropic medications (Ray et al., 1997; Tinetti et al., 1994).

USE OF PHYSICIAN SERVICES BY OLDER PEOPLE

The increased incidence of many chronic and acute diseases among the older population would seem to predict a striking growth with age in the use of health care services. As shown in Table 4.3, there is some support for a differential pattern of utilization. The probability of seeing a doctor at least once in the previous year increases slightly with age; 73 percent of people aged 25 to 44 reported doing so in 1994, compared with 78 percent of those aged 65 to 74 and 90 percent of those persons 75 years or older. However, the major difference across age groups is in frequency of use. In 1994 people aged 65 and older made an average of 11.3 physician visits per person, compared with 5.5 visits for those aged 25 to 44 and 7.3 visits for people aged 45 to 64 (NCHS, 1995). When they do visit physicians, both younger and older people do so primarily for acute symptoms and to receive similar diagnostic and therapeutic services. However, the larger number of yearly visits by older persons may indicate that they are seeking care for chronic conditions as well. It is noteworthy that only a small proportion of older adults are high users of all health services. In a longitudinal study of over 2000 older adults, only 3 percent were consistently high users of physician services over a 6-year period, while 40.5 percent were consistently low to medium users, i.e., six or fewer annual physician visits (Stump, Johnson, and Wolinsky, 1995).

Use of Other Health Services

Hospital utilization apparently reflects older people's need for health care more accurately than do elective visits to physicians' offices. Older people are more frequently hospitalized and for longer periods of time than younger populations, accounting for about 30 percent of all short-stay hospital days of care (NCHS, 1995). However, the average length of stay has been reduced since the introduction of **Diagnostic Related Groupings (DRGs)** for Medicare patients in 1983 (see Chapter 16). While DRGs prompted a transfer of care from inpatient hospital settings to outpatient settings, home-based care after a hospitalization health utilization by older people has decreased overall since 1985, reflecting more stringent eligibility and reimbursement criteria rather than a diminishing need for care.

TABLE 4.3 **Physician Utilization Rates by Age: 1994**

AGE	VISITS PER YEAR*	INTERVAL SINCE LAST VISIT	
		<1 year	5+ years
25–44	5.5	73.4%	4.6%
45–64	7.3	76.8%	4.7%
65–74	10.3	78.0%	4.7%
75+	13.5	89.8%	2.5%

*Includes office and emergency room physician contacts

SOURCE: NCHS, *Vital and Health Statistics,* Series 10, # 193, 1995.

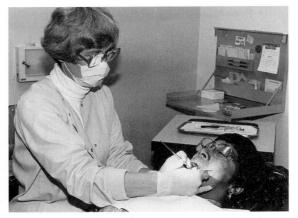

Health professionals need to be sensitive to cultural differences when caring for older patients.

The use of prescription medications may also be an indication of the older person's need for health care. Although representing only 12 percent of the population, older people purchased approximately 30 percent of all prescription drugs and 40 percent of all over-the-counter drugs in 1994. About 25 percent of older people take three or more prescription drugs a day, compared to 9 percent of younger people (Piraino, 1995). It has been estimated that some older people take as many as 12 to 15 different medications simultaneously (French, 1996). Not surprisingly, because of the higher likelihood of their having many chronic conditions, nursing home residents take more prescription drugs than do community-dwelling elders. Many older people may be taking either too many medications or inappropriate drugs. Overmedication is a concern for older people because the less efficient excretion of drugs by the kidney and liver, and the changing proportions of fat and muscle tissue throughout the older person's body, as discussed in Chapter 3, may prolong the effects of some drugs. Furthermore, combinations of medications can cause adverse drug reactions. As many as 30 percent of all hospital admissions of older people result from such adverse reactions, and many of the falls and sudden impairment in cognitive function may be due

to inappropriate medication or overmedication (Lamy, 1989; Kusserow, 1989).

The higher rate of medication use among older persons also may result in reporting errors and in incorrect use of these drugs. Older people admitted to a hospital have been found to give inconsistent medication reports. For example, medication histories provided by older patients at admission differed from their reports to a research assistant within two days in 83 percent of the cases; 46 percent had three or more inconsistencies. Fully 22 percent of the drugs included in the medication history were denied by older patients in the subsequent interviews (Beers, Munekata, and Storrie, 1990).

An area of elective health care, ignored even more than routine medical care, is the use of professional dental services. Although the rate of preventive dental service utilization has risen significantly over the past 20 years among younger cohorts, the use of dental services by older adults has increased only slightly. In the latest national survey, older persons continued to be the lowest utilizers of professional dental care; 57 percent had not seen a dentist in the past year, and 33 percent had not obtained care in the past five years (Gift and Newman, 1993; U.S. Dept. of Health and Human Services, 1992). This rate is incongruent with the level of oral diseases that require professional attention in older persons. Yet, once older persons enter the dental care system, their average number of visits is similar to that of younger people. The current state of Medicare reimbursement, where physician visits are covered but dental care is not, plays an important role in this differential pattern of utilization.

The use of mental health services is even lower than that of dental care in the older population. Some reasons for this low level of utilization will be discussed in Chapter 6.

HEALTH PROMOTION WITH OLDER PEOPLE

Health promotion has been defined as a combination of health education and related organizational, political, and economic changes aimed at improving health. This emphasis on the variety of interventions acknowledges the complex social, biological, cultural, and economic factors that influence health and health behavior. Accordingly, this definition includes altering individual health practices, such as diet and exercise, as well as trying to create healthier environments and to change cultural attitudes and expectations toward health. Health promotion represents a shift from a biomedical model that emphasizes the physician's responsibility to treat disease, to a model where individuals are responsible for and feel more in control of their own health and can optimize their quality of life. Health promotion thus makes explicit the importance of people's environments and lifestyles as determinants of their health status.

In 1989, the federal government facilitated the collaboration of numerous expert working groups, representing 300 national organizations, the health departments of all states, and the Institute of Medicine of the National Academy of Sciences to develop health goals for the nation. This report established several health objectives that Americans should attempt to achieve by the year 2000. Labeled *Healthy People 2000,* this document has been used widely by policy makers and practitioners as a blueprint for health promotion programs. Three broad goals of this report are relevant for older adults: (1) increase the span of *healthy* life (i.e., compressed morbidity); (2) reduce health disparities among Americans; and (3) improve access to preventive services for all Americans (U.S. Public Health Service,1989).

The primary rationale for health promotion programs for older adults is to reduce the incidence of *disabling chronic diseases,* and thereby to enhance the older person's functional independence and overall quality of life, not merely to prolong life. Health promotion is also a recognition that chronic conditions cannot be "cured" but can be prevented from causing disability. As suggested in our earlier discussion of disease, as many as 80 percent of the chronic illnesses that afflict older individuals are estimated to be related to social, environmental, and behavioral factors, particularly

poor health habits. In addition, 90 percent of fatal and near-fatal episodes of strokes and heart attacks are believed to be preventable. For example, heart disease has been linked to daily stress, sedentary living, weight gain, smoking, and high-cholesterol diets. Yet all of these risk factors can be reduced, even in later life, through changes in health habits (e.g., controlling blood pressure and weight, stopping cigarette smoking, reducing cholesterol levels, and engaging in regular, moderate exercise). A viable health care goal, as noted in Chapter 1, is therefore the "compression of morbidity," delaying the age at which chronic illness and the infirm period of life begins (Berg and Cassells, 1992; Fries, 1980, 1984). This goal of improvement in chronic disease rates seems feasible, given the evidence that individuals over age 75 who followed seven health-enhancing behaviors achieved the same health index ratings as those 30 years younger who followed few or none of these behaviors (Paffenberger et al., 1986). Other evidence is shown by studies of male master athletes in their 60s. These athletes experience very little decline in their cardiovascular functions, including maximum heart rate and maximum volume of oxygen used during exercise, especially when compared with age-matched sedentary men. Furthermore, HDL cholesterol levels are higher and their triglycerides are lower than in age-matched sedentary men, and are comparable to healthy young men (Yataco, Busby-Whitehead, Drinkwater, and Katzel, 1997; Rogers et al., 1990).

As stated succinctly by the Surgeon General's Report on Health Promotion and Aging (1988), prevention not only improves one's quality of life, but also may save dollars in the long run. Growing awareness of these benefits is not reflected in the allocation of health dollars, however, since only 6 percent of the national health care dollar is spent on prevention and early detection services (Brown, 1994). Medicare and most private health insurance plans do not typically pay for preventive services, although the 1997 changes in Medicare have resulted in more coverage of preventive services than in the past. An encouraging sign is the number of health maintenance organizations, health care clinics, universities, and work sites that are offering health promotion programs. Some of these programs have been carried into senior centers and assisted living, retirement, and nursing homes.

The Relationship of Health Practices to Health Outcomes

Considerable research demonstrates the relationship of personal health habits to health status and life satisfaction. The following factors have been identified to be related to good health status: not smoking, limiting alcohol consumption, maintaining one's weight in the ideal range, sleeping seven to eight hours per night, and maintaining moderate levels of aerobic exercise. These relationships have been found to be cumulative and independent of age, sex, and economic status (Rakowski, 1994).

Additional epidemiological evidence demonstrates links between specific health habits and decreased longevity and/or increased health risks. These specific lifestyle factors, discussed briefly below, include alcohol consumption, cigarette smoking, diet, and exercise.

The relationship between drinking alcohol and physical health in old age is U-shaped, with the least healthy tending to be those who drink heavily and those who abstain, although abstainers may include former heavy drinkers who have damaged their systems. Light drinking may have some benefits to the heart. Excessive drinking (five or more drinks at a single sitting) has been found to contribute to poorer than average physical health, more frequent hospitalizations, decreased cognitive function, poorer metabolism of prescription medications, and premature death (Wattis and Seymour, 1994; Cummings, 1993).

The effects of cigarette smoking, especially in interaction with other risk factors, on heart disease, emphysema, and lung cancer have been extensively documented (Harris, 1994). Smokers who use oral contraceptives, are exposed to asbestos, have excessive alcohol consumption, or are at risk for hypertension have a greater chance of experiencing nonfatal myocardial infarction and are at significant risk for cancers of the oral cavity and lung, and for osteoporosis (Goldberg, 1988). Even those who have smoked for years can benefit from smoking cessation. Six years after quitting smoking, older men and women have been found to have lower death rates than their peers who continue smoking (Rimer, 1988; Hermanson, 1988).

Poor diet has been determined to be related to obesity, cancer, and heart disease. Obesity carries an increased risk of cardiovascular and pulmonary difficulties, aggravates other conditions such as hypertension, arthritis, and diabetes, and adds risk to surgery. Interpretation of the relationship between obesity and morbidity and mortality is difficult, however, since obesity is correlated with other risk factors, such as high blood pressure.

The relationship between diet, blood cholesterol, coronary heart disease, and stroke has also been suggested in numerous studies. As noted earlier, diets high in fat, sugar, and salt and low in fiber have been found to be associated with a high incidence of coronary heart disease, hypertension, diabetes, obesity, tooth decay, and certain cancers common among older people. Most of such evidence, however, is from epidemiologic studies that demonstrate an association between diet and disease, but do not necessarily prove causation. For example, some environmental factors that influence the likelihood of disease are also linked to poor nutrition. These include low socioeconomic status, ill-fitting dentures, eating alone, or a sedentary way of life. Nevertheless, recent clinical studies have identified the effects of specific dietary behaviors on health outcomes. It appears that a moderate reduction in dietary fat consumption, to 26 percent of total calories, may be more beneficial than a severe reduction (18 percent fat) in reducing cholesterol levels (Knopp et al., 1997). Indeed, among men with high levels of LDL (bad cholesterol) and triglycerides (a type of fat found in blood), those who reduced their fat intake to 26 percent showed the greatest reduction in LDL and triglycerides, while maintaining their HDL (good cholesterol) levels. When fat intake decreased to 18 percent, HDL levels also declined.

Older people with all levels of ability can benefit from exercise.

Another nutritional problem of older adults is insufficient intake of certain nutrients. Researchers have found that as many as 40 percent of older people have diets that are deficient in three or more nutrients. Up to 15 percent may have vitamin B_{12} deficiency, which is necessary for the production of blood cells and healthy functioning of the nervous system. These deficiencies are in part due to inadequate intake of milk, eggs, vegetables, fruit, and other sources of these nutrients. They may also result from poorer absorption of nutrients by the gastrointestinal (GI) system in older adults, especially those on multiple medications that affect GI absorption (Wallace, 1997).

There is considerable evidence of the relationship between regular, moderate exercise and reduction in a person's chances of dying from heart disease and cancer, as well as hospital admissions for serious illness (LaCroix et al., 1996; Sherman, D'Agostino, Cobb, and Kannel, 1994.) Up to 50 percent of physical changes in older people that are mistakenly attributed to aging may be due to being physically unfit. Physically inactive people age faster and look older than physically fit persons of the same age, in part because of what has been termed **hypokinesia,** a disease of "disuse," or the degeneration and functional loss of muscle and bone tissue (O'Brien and Vertinsky, 1991).

The goal of remaining physically active with advancing age is to delay the declines in functional capacity with aging. Because the body's adaptability to exercise remains unimpaired by aging, exercise can slow the decline of physiological functions. In particular, cross-training that includes aerobic exercise three times per week, as well as stretching and weight training, can maintain cardiovascular and respiratory functioning; it can restore and maintain muscular strength and joint flexibility (especially in the lower body, which is important for preventing falls), and reduce the risk of bone loss and fractures. It appears to benefit even those with coronary artery disease, diabetes, hypertension, and pulmonary disorders by causing weight loss; reducing blood sugar, blood fat, and high blood pressure; and improving circulation (Clark, 1996; Jette et al., 1996; Tinetti et al., 1994).

Despite the known benefits of exercise, a major goal of *Healthy People 2000,* i.e., 50 percent participation by individuals 65 years and older in "appropriate" physical activity, is far from being met. It has been estimated that less than 30 percent have achieved this goal. New activity objectives that all adults and children over age 6 should exercise regularly have now been established. But current activity levels among most older adults are so low that meeting objectives for the year 2000 will mean significant behavioral changes among the general public, up to a four-fold increase in activity levels (Pate, Pratt, and Blair, 1996).

Nevertheless, there are indications of improvements in Americans' health behaviors. For example, the National Survey of Self-Care and Aging, conducted in the early 1990s, asked older adults to describe the type and frequency of their personal health care behaviors. Researchers then examined the association between these behaviors and subsequent hospitalization rates and Medicare reimbursements. They found that older adults who maintained a healthy weight, never smoked, participated in regular physical exercise, worked in their garden, and regularly checked their pulse and blood pressure were less likely to enter the hospital and had lower Medicare reimbursements (i.e., lower rates of medical service use). Older people who modified their homes to prevent falls (e.g., removing throw rugs, installing extra lighting on stairs) also reduced their Medicare costs, but these differences were not significant (Stearns et al., 1997). The dramatic impact of self-care behaviors on hospital and physician use is an important indicator of the benefits for both individuals and society of a healthy lifestyle in the later years.

Psychosocial conditions, particularly a loss of control, excessive stress, and the absence of social supports, have also been linked to decreased longevity and/or poor health. As discussed in Chapter 9, there is relatively strong epidemiologic evidence that persons who are married, have close contacts with friends and relatives, and share common religious, ethnic, or cultural interests with others experience lower morbidity and greater longevity than those without such ties. Social networks apparently act to buffer the negative effects of stress. Translating the results of research on social supports into health services has been slow, partly because they do not fit the traditional biomedical model of disease and treatment.

Health Promotion Guidelines

Given the growing evidence about the relation of health practices to health status, most health promotion programs include components on injury prevention, nutrition, exercise, and stress management. Oral health promotion has also been implemented in geriatric dentistry. An underlying theme is taking greater responsibility for one's own health, rather than relying on medical professionals. Some programs also include educating participants to change the larger social environment, perhaps through collective action. Several components of health promotion programs are briefly summarized.

1. NUTRITION   Although information on older people's dietary needs is incomplete and often contradictory, the basic principles are:

(a) Consume a wide variety of foods, especially fruits and vegetables.

(b) Increase consumption of unprocessed foods containing complex carbohydrates (starch and fiber), such as whole grains and legumes.

(c) Restrict intake of sugar, fat, and cholesterol-containing foods.

Unfortunately, there are a number of barriers to adequate nutrition. Some of these result from physiological and social changes common to aging and include an inability to chew and swallow due to no teeth, missing teeth, or loose-fitting dentures; problems with taste or smell; poor digestion of certain foods; and emotional barriers, such as loneliness, that deprive mealtime of its social satisfactions and may diminish appetite. Others result from societal conditions, such as the expense of particular foods or lack of access to them. Any nutritional assessment of an older person must take account of such factors that can affect the amount and type of food consumed.

2. EXERCISE   Exercise programs need to be tailored to take account of variability in physical function and fitness levels. Past exercise programs for older people may have been overly cautious; instead, older adults need to be challenged to obtain the full benefits of an appropriately designed exercise program. Beyond the benefits of aerobic fitness, a variety of physical activities are important to maintain overall muscle strength and endurance, joint mobility, balance, upright posture, and management of specific chronic diseases (Cress and Green, 1996).

Prior to beginning an exercise program, older people should have a thorough medical examination, including a treadmill or other exercise tolerance test, to determine their baseline for physical fitness. An ideal exercise program begins with a low level of activity and includes an initial warm-up, with stretching, light calisthenics, and leisurely walking, more strenuous exercise for 20 minutes or more, and a relaxing cool-down period of 5 to 10 minutes of light exercise, at least three times each week. Brisk walking is one of the safest and best exercises for older people. Most ambulatory older persons, even those at a lower level of fitness, can build up their walking to one or more miles daily, and at a speed of three or four miles per hour. Indeed, even older adults with multiple chronic conditions have shown significant improvements in their speed of walking, gait, balance, and grip strength following a year of low-intensity exercise and weight training (Sharpe et al., 1997). There is evidence that greater physiological benefits, such as fat loss and cardiovascular change, require more intense and vigorous exercise, such as jogging or bicycling, which can be safely undertaken by healthy older people.

3. STRESS MANAGEMENT Stress-related disorders include emotional disturbances, psychosomatic complaints, headaches, insomnia, hypertension, and certain types of rheumatic or allergic afflictions as well as cardiovascular and kidney diseases. As noted earlier, older people may be more susceptible to such negative effects because of the body's decreased ability to adapt to stress and increased vulnerability to physiological changes induced by the stress response itself. This means that the aging process may be accelerated by repeated exposure to stress at a time of diminished adaptability. Health care professionals have shown increasing interest in ways to reduce such potential negative effects through stress management techniques, such as stress alleviation, progressive muscle relaxation, and clinical biofeedback.

Another important outcome of physical activity is stress reduction, which is linked to other benefits such as better sleep, muscle relaxation, positive mood, and improved self-image and self-concept. Overall, exercise appears to act as a buffer in many stress-illness relationships, possibly through biochemical interactions linking mind and body. More research is needed, however, on which particular modalities of stress reduction are most helpful to older people.

Oral Health Promotion

Only a few health promotion programs include preventive dentistry. One reason for this is that dental disease and tooth loss are frequently assumed to be natural concomitants of aging. Once an individual has lost many teeth from poor oral health in the middle years, it is presumed there is little to promote and maintain. Despite this skeptical attitude, held by professionals and older people alike, some oral health promotion efforts have been found to be successful (Kiyak, 1996).

With increased preventive dentistry in youth and middle-age, more people are retaining their natural teeth into old age, as noted earlier in this chapter (Marcus, Drury, Brown, and Zion, 1996). This suggests that individuals with teeth remaining should perform regular oral health care, including brushing, flossing, and regular visits to a dentist or hygienist. Older people are not only less inclined to use professional dental services, but also less likely to know and value techniques of preventive dentistry (Kiyak, 1996). Therefore, prevention must be defined differently by age. In younger persons, the initiation of dental disease and tooth loss can be prevented; in older adults, the goals are to prevent *further* tooth loss and diseases that are secondary to other medical conditions and/or medications (e.g., dry mouth caused by some medications that are used to treat hypertension and depression).

Limitations of Health Promotion

Health promotion programs have been criticized for their emphasis on individual responsibility for change, which minimizes the societal factors that underlie individual health practices and use of services, such as income and access to affordable health care (Walker, 1994). Likewise, some educational efforts ignore the roles of policy makers, health care providers, food manufacturers, and the mass media in creating social and economic environments that may counter health promotion interventions. In addition to educating individuals to adopt healthy habits, the broader social environment must be changed, for example, through training older people in advocacy and political action.

To the extent that interventions focus primarily on individual change, their relevance is questionable for low-income and ethnic minority populations, whose health problems often stem from situational factors such as poverty over which individuals have little control. Accordingly, low-income populations, preoccupied with meeting basic needs, may view exercise and healthy foods as luxuries. Participation in a regular physical exercise regimen and walking program is lower among older adults with less than eight years of education and among African Americans (Clark, 1995). Few health promotion efforts have been effectively implemented with low-income or ethnic minority groups. The programs that have been tried have had problems with recruitment and retention (Yee and Weaver, 1994).

In general, organized health promotion programs have difficulty recruiting more than 50 percent of the target population; even those focused on rehabilitation of post-myocardial infarct patients and managing high blood pressure through exercise have had recruitment difficulties. Attrition is also high, with rates of 30 to 60 percent. Older people most likely to participate in organized health promotion are those with a preventive attitude (e.g., regular users of physicians and dentists for check-ups, nonsmokers, exercisers, and users of seat belts and smoke alarms) and those with higher participation rates in community services generally (Carter et al., 1991; Wagner et al., 1991).

Another limitation is that, although the value of health promotion is widely publicized, individuals often do not act on this information. Think about the number of people who continue to smoke despite the empirical evidence linking smoking to lung cancer, or the small proportion of women over age 45 who have a Pap smear and breast exam on a regular basis even though such tests are important in detecting cancer. As another example, despite the widely known benefits of exercise, less than 25 percent of people over age 65 engage in appropriate levels of physical

activity. As we are all aware, people do not always engage in healthy behaviors, even when they know that they should! The gap between health knowledge and health practices can be large. On the other hand, older people are more likely to change their health behaviors after learning new self-care topics than are younger people (Yusuf et al., 1996).

Even when individual behavioral change is a legitimate goal, sustaining health practices over time is difficult in the face of years of habit. In fact, little is known about the long-term changes resulting from many health promotion interventions, because most evaluations have been conducted soon after program completion, with follow-ups of less than two years. Health promotion demonstration programs have not been long-lasting or widely replicated. Longitudinal research is needed to assess the long-range (ten years or more) consequences of health promotion interventions for individuals and for health care costs, especially since programs to modify health-related behaviors may initially be very costly before they achieve long-run savings.

On the other hand, it is encouraging that short-term educational programs aimed at improving older participants' knowledge and preventive health behaviors in the areas of cancer, heart disease, and oral diseases have shown significant improvements at their termination (Kiyak, 1996; Keintz et al., 1988). The most effective prevention appears to come from two approaches: eliminating iatrogenic disease that is induced in the patient by medical care, especially with regard to the side effects of medications, and preventing the transformation from disease to disability. Health promotion is clearly a growing area, especially in light of pressure from the federal government and insurers to reduce rising health care costs, and it raises numerous opportunities for policy and program development and research. One of the major conclusions of the 1995 White House Conference on Aging was that preventive health care and exercise among older people can save $260 billion in health care costs.

SUMMARY AND IMPLICATIONS

Although older persons are at risk of more diseases than younger people, most older people rate their own health as satisfactory. Health status refers not only to an individual's physical condition, but also to her or his functional level in various social and psychological domains. It is affected by a person's social surroundings, especially the degree of environmental stress and social support available. Although stress has been found to increase the risk of certain illnesses, such as cardiovascular disease, older people are generally less negatively affected by stress; this may reflect maturity, self-control, or a lifetime of developing coping skills.

Older people are more likely to suffer from chronic or long-term diseases than from temporary or acute illnesses. The majority of older persons, however, are not limited in their daily activities by chronic conditions. The impact of such conditions apparently varies with the physiological changes that occur with age, the individual's adaptive resources, and his or her mental and emotional perspective. The type and incidence of chronic conditions also vary by gender.

The leading causes of death among persons over age 65 are heart disease, cancer, accidents, and stroke. Diseases of the heart and blood vessels are the most prevalent. Since hypertension or high blood pressure is a major risk in the development of cardiovascular problems, preventive actions are critical, especially weight control, dietary changes, appropriate exercise, and avoidance of cigarette smoking. Cancers, especially lung, bowel, and colon cancers, are the second most frequent cause of death among older persons; the risk of cancer increases with age. Cerebrovascular disease, or stroke, is the third leading cause of death among older persons. It may be caused by cerebral thrombosis, or blood clots, and by cerebral hemorrhage. Healthy lifestyle practices are important in stroke prevention.

Arthritis, although not fatal, is a major cause of limited daily activity and is extremely common among older persons. Osteoporosis, or loss of bone mass and the resultant increased brittleness of the bones, is most common among older women, and may result in fractures of the hip, spine, and wrist. Chronic respiratory problems, particularly emphysema, increase with age, especially among men. Diabetes mellitus is a frequent problem in old age, and is particularly troubling because of the many related illnesses that may result. Problems with the intestinal tract include diverticulitis, constipation, and hiatus hernia. Cystitis and incontinence are frequently occurring problems of the kidneys and urinary system. Although the majority of older persons have some type of incontinence, many kinds can be treated and controlled.

The growth of the older population, combined with the increase in major chronic illnesses, has placed greater demands on the health care system in this country. Nevertheless, older people seek outpatient medical, dental, and mental health services at a slightly lower rate than their incidence of chronic illnesses would predict. Like younger people, the older population is most likely to seek health services for acute problems, not for checkups on chronic conditions or for preventive care. Beliefs that physicians, dentists, and mental health professionals cannot cure their chronic problems may deter many older people from seeking needed care. The problem may be compounded by the attitude of some health care providers who have not been trained in geriatrics that older people are poor candidates for health services. More university and continuing education classes are needed to provide training in geriatrics and gerontology for staff in health care settings and to address their attitudes toward older people.

Health promotion has proven to be effective in improving the well-being and enhancing the quality of life of older people. The elimination or postponement of the chronic diseases that are associated with old age is a major goal for health promotion specialists and biomedical researchers. Treatment methods for all these diseases are changing rapidly with the growth in medical technology and the increasing recognition given to such environmental factors as stress, nutrition, and exercise in disease prevention. If health promotion efforts to modify lifestyles are successful, and if aging research progresses substantially, the chronic illnesses that we have discussed will undoubtedly be postponed and disability or loss of functional status will be delayed until advanced old age.

GLOSSARY

ADL Activities of Daily Living summarizes an individual's performance in personal care tasks such as bathing or dressing, as well as such home management activities as shopping, meal preparation, and taking medications

acute condition short-term disease or infection, often debilitating to older persons

acute myocardial infarction loss of blood flow to a specific region of the heart, resulting in a necrosis of the myocardium

arteriosclerosis loss of elasticity of the arterial walls

benign hypertrophy of the prostate enlargement of the prostate gland in older men, without signs of cancer or other serious disease; may cause discomfort

chronic condition long-term (more than three months), often permanent, and leaving a residual disability that may require long-term management or care rather than cure

contracture the loss of flexibility or freezing of a joint due to lack of use

Diagnosis related groups (DRGs) a system of classifying medical cases for payment on the basis of diagnoses; used under Medicare's prospective payment system (PPS) for inpatient hospital services

diverticulitis a condition in which pouches or sacs (diverticula) in the intestinal wall become inflamed and infected

disability an impairment in the ability to complete multiple daily tasks

edentulous the absence of natural teeth

good health more than the mere absence of infirmity, a state of complete physical, mental, and social well-being

health promotion a model where individuals are responsible for and in control of their own health, in-

cluding a combination of health education and related organizational, political, and economic changes conducive to health

health status the presence or absence of disease as well as the degree of disability in an individual's level of functioning

hiatus hernia a condition where a small portion of the stomach slides up through the diaphragm

hypokinesia the degeneration and functional loss of muscle and bone due to physical inactivity

immunity resistance to environmental carcinogens, viruses, and bacteria

incontinence the inability to control urine and feces; two types: urge incontinence, where a person is not able to hold urine long enough to reach a toilet, and stress incontinence, where leakage occurs during physical exertion, laughing, sneezing, or coughing

osteopenia a significant loss of calcium and reduced bone density not associated with increased risk of fractures

rheumatoid arthritis a chronic inflammation of the membranes lining joints and tendons, characterized by pain, swelling, bone dislocation, and limited range of motion; can occur at any age

stress the gamut of social-psychological stimuli that produce physiological responses of shallow, rapid breathing, muscle tension, increased blood pressure, and accelerated heart rate

REFERENCES

Albertsen, P. C., Fryback, D. G., and Storer, B. E. Long-term survival among men with conservatively treated localized prostate cancer. *Journal of the American Medical Association*, 1995, *274*, 626–631.

Arnaud, C. D., and Sanchez, S. D. The role of calcium in osteoporosis. *Annual Review of Nutrition*, 1990, *10*, 397–414.

Beers, M. H., Munekata, M., and Storrie, M. The accuracy of medication histories in the hospital medical records of elderly persons. *Journal of the American Geriatrics Society*, 1990, *38*, 1183–1187.

Berg, R. L., and Cassels, J. S. (Eds). *The second fifty years: Promoting health and preventing disability*. Washington, DC: Institute of Medicine, National Academy Press, 1992.

Bernard, S. L., Kincade, J. E., Konrad, T. R., Arcury, T. A., Rabiner, D. Predicting mortality from community surveys of older adults: The importance of self-rated functional ability. *Journals of Gerontology: Social Sciences,* 1997, *52,* S155–S163.

Brown, L. J., Brunelle, J. A., and Kingman, A. Periodontal status in the United States: Prevalence, extent, and demographic variation. *Journal of Dental Research,* 1996, *75,* 672–683.

Brown, R. E. *National expenditures for health promotion and disease prevention and activities in the United States.* Washington, DC: The Medical Technology Assessment and Policy Research Center, 1994.

Bush, T. L. The epidemiology of cardiovascular disease in postmenopausal women. *Annals of the New York Academy of Sciences,* 1990, *592,* 264–230.

Cantor, M. Family and community: Changing roles in an aging society. *The Gerontologist,* 1991, *31,* 337–346.

Caplan, L. S., Wells, B. L., and Haynes, S. Breast cancer screening among older racial/ethnic minorities and whites. *Journals of Gerontology,* 1992, *47* (Special Issue), 101–110.

Carter, W. B., Elward, K., Malmgren, J., Martin, M. L., and Larson, E. Participation of older adults in health programs and research: A critical review of the literature. *The Gerontologist,* 1991 *31,* 584–592.

Centers for Disease Control and Prevention (CDC). *HIV/AIDS Surveillance Report: Year-End Edition.* Atlanta: CDC Publications, 1995, 7.

Centers for Disease Control and Prevention (CDC). National Center for Chronic Disease Prevention and Health Promotion. *Physical activity and health: A report of the Surgeon General.* Atlanta: CDC Publications, 1996.

Centers for Disease Control and Prevention (CDC). Pneumonia and influenza death rates: United States 1979–1994. *Morbidity and Mortality Weekly Reports,* 1995, *44,* 535–537.

Centers for Disease Control and Prevention (CDC). Pneumonia and influenza vaccination levels among adults aged greater than or equal to 65 years: United States 1993. *Morbidity and Mortality Weekly Reports,* 1996, *45,* 859.

Chapuy, M. C., Arlot, M. E., Duboeuf, F., Brun, J., and Crouzet, B. Vitamin D3 and calcium to prevent hip fractures in elderly women. *New England Journal of Medicine,* 1992, *327,* 1637–1642.

Chrischilles, E., Shireman, T., and Wallace, R. Costs and health effects of osteoporotic fractures. *Bone,* 1994, *15,* 377–386.

Clark, D. O. The effect of walking on lower body disability in blacks and whites. *American Journal of Public Health,* 1996, *86,* 57–61.

Clark, D. O. Racial and educational differences in physical activity among older adults. *The Gerontologist,* 1995, *35,* 472–480.

Cousins, N. *Anatomy of an illness.* New York: Bantam Books, 1979.

Cramer, D. Promoting continence: Strategies for success. *Perspectives in Health Promotion and Aging,* 1993, *1,* 1–3.

Cress, M. E., and Green, F. A. Exercise and aging: Physical fitness. In M. A. Stenchever (Ed.), *Health care for the older woman.* New York: Chapman and Hall, 1996.

Cummings, N. A., Chemical dependency among older adults. In F. Lieberman and M. F. Collen (Eds.), *Aging in good health: A quality lifestyle for the later years.* New York: Plenum Books, 1993.

Cummings, S. R., Nevitt, M. C., Browner, W. S., Stone, K., Fox, K. M., and Ensrud, K. E. Risk factors for hip fractures in white women. *New England Journal of Medicine,* 1995, *332,* 767–773.

El-Sadr, W., and Gettler, J. Unrecognized human immunodeficiency virus infection in the elderly. *Archives of Internal Medicine,* 1995, *155,* 184–186.

Emlet, C. A., HIV/AIDS in the elderly: A hidden population. *Home Care Provider,* 1997, *2,* 22–28.

Emlet, C. A., Service utilization among older people with AIDS. *Journal of Case Management,* 1993, *2,* 119–124.

Evans, L. *Traffic safety and the driver.* New York: Van Nostrand Reinhold, 1991.

Ferro, S., and Salit, I. E. HIV infection in patients over 55 years of age. *Journal of Acquired Immune Deficiency Syndromes,* 1992, *5,* 348–355.

Ferrucci, L., Kittner, S. J., Corti, M. C., and Guralnik, J. M. Neurological conditions. In J. M. Guralnick, L. P. Fried, E. M. Simonsick, J. D., Kaspar, and M. E. Lafferty (Eds.), *The women's health and aging study.* Bethesda: NIH/NIA, 1995.

French, D. G. Avoiding adverse drug reactions in the elderly patient. *Nurse Practitioner,* 1996, *21,* 90–105.

Fries, J. F. Aging, natural death, and the compression of morbidity. *New England Journal of Medicine,* 1980, *303,* 130–135.

Fries, J. F. The compression of morbidity: Miscellaneous comments about a theme. *The Gerontologist,* 1984, *24,* 354–359.

Gaeta, T. J., Lapolla, C., and Melendez, E. AIDS in the elderly. *Journal of Emergency Medicine,* 1996, *14,* 19–23.

Gift, H., and Newman, J. How older adults use oral health care services: Results of a national interview survey. *Journal of the American Dental Association,* 1993, *124,* 89–93.

Goldberg, A. Health promotion and aging: Physical exercise. Surgeon General's Workshop, *Health Promotion and Aging,* March 1988.

Gorelick, P. B., Shanmugam, V., and Pajeau, A. K. Stroke. In J. E. Birren (Ed.), *Encyclopedia of gerontology,* Vol. 2. San Diego: Academy Press, 1996.

Govaert, T. M., Thijs, C. T., and Masurel, N. The efficacy of influenza vaccination in elderly individuals. A randomized double-blind placebo-controlled trial. *Journal of the American Medical Association,* 1994, *272,* 1661–1665.

Greenwald, D. A., and Brandt, L. J. Gastrointestinal system: Function and dysfunction. In J. E. Birren (Ed.), *Encyclopedia of gerontology,* Vol. 1. San Diego: Academy Press, 1996.

Gresham, G. E., Duncan, P. W., and Stason, W. B. *Poststroke rehabilitation: Assessment, referral, and patient management.* Rockville, MD: USDHHS, Agency for Health Care Policy and Research, 1995.

Gueldner, S. H. The elderly: The silent population. *Journal of the Association of Nurses in AIDS Care,* 1995, *6,* 9–10.

Guralnik, J. M., and Simonsick, E. M. Physical disability in older Americans. *Journals of Gerontology,* 1993, *48,* 3–10.

Harris, J. The health benefits of health promotion. In M. P. O'Donnell, and J. Harris (Eds.), *Health promotion in the workplace.* Albany, NY: Delmar, 1994.

Hayflick, L. *How and why we age.* New York: Ballantine Books, 1996.

Hemmelgarn, B., Suissa, S., Huang, A., Boirin, J. F., and Pinard, G. Benzodiazepine use and the risk of motor vehicle crash in the elderly. *Journal of the American Medical Association,* 1997, *278,* 27–31.

Henderson, B. E., Paganini-Hill, A., and Ross, R. K. Decreased mortality in users of estrogen replacement therapy. *Archives of Internal Medicine,* 1991, *151,* 75–78.

Hermanson, B. Beneficial six-year outcome of smoking cessation in older men and women with coronary artery disease: Results from the CAS registry. *New England Journal of Medicine,* 1988, *320,* 1365–1369.

Jette, A. M., Harris, B. A., Sleeper, L., Lachman, M. E., Heislein, D., and Georgetti, M. A homebased exercise program for nondisabled older adults. *Journal of the American Geriatrics Society,* 1996, *44,* 644–649.

Johnson, R. J., and Wolinsky, F. D. Gender, race, and health: The structure of health status among older adults. *The Gerontologist,* 1994, *34,* 24–35.

Josephson, K. R., Fabacher, D. A., and Rubenstein, L. Z. Home safety and fall prevention. *Clinics in Geriatric Medicine,* 1991, *7,* 707–731.

Keintz, M. K., Rimer, B., Fleisher, L., and Engstrom, P. Educating older adults about their increased cancer risk. *The Gerontologist,* 1988, *28,* 487–490.

Kemnitz, J. W., Roccer, E. B., and Weindruch, R. Dietary restriction increases insulin sensitivity and lowers blood glucose in Rhesus monkeys. *American Journal of Physiology,* 1994, *266,* E540–E547.

Kickbush, I. Healthy cities: A working project and a growing movement. *Health Promotion,* 1989, *4,* 77–82.

Kiyak, H. A. Measuring psychosocial variables that predict older persons' oral health behavior. *Gerodontology,* 1996, *13,* 69–75.

Knopp, R. H., Walden, C. E., Retzlaff, B. M., McCann, B. S., Dowdy, A. A., Albers, J. J., Gey, G. O., and Cooper, M. N. Long-term cholesterol-lowering effects of 4 fat-restricted diets in hypercholesterolemic and combined hyperlipidemic men. The dietary alternatives study. *Journal of the American Medical Association,* 1997, *278,* 1509–1515.

Kosorek, M. R., Omenn, G. S., Diehr, P. Restricted activity days among older adults. *American Journal of Public Health,* 1992, *82,* 1263–1267.

Kusserow, R. P. *Drug use among the elderly. Report of the Inspector General.* Department of Health and Human Services, January 1989.

LaCroix, A. Z. *Health promotion for older Adults: Osteoporosis.* NWGEC Curriculum Modules, University of Washington, 1997.

LaCroix, A. Z., Leveille, S., Hecht, J., Grothaus, L., and Wagner, E. Does walking reduce the risk of cardiovascular disease and death in older adults? *Journal of the American Geriatrics Society,* 1996, *44,* 113–120.

Lamy, P. P. Pharmacotherapeutics in the elderly. *Morbidity and Mortality Weekly,* 1989, *38,* 144–148.

Looker, A. C., Johnston, C. C., Wahner, H. W., Dunn, W. L., and Calvo, M. S. Prevalence of low femoral bone density in older U.S. women from NHANES III. *Journal of Bone Mineral Research,* 1995, *10,* 796–802.

Maher, M. C. Driving difficulties increase with age, *Washington Post,* Oct. 30, 1990.

Marcus, S. E., Drury, T. F., Brown, L. J., and Zion, G. R. Tooth retention and tooth loss in the permanent dentition of adults: United States, 1988–1991. *Journal of Dental Research,* 1996, *75,* 684–695.

National Center for Health Statistics. Current estimates from the National Health Interview Survey: U.S. 1992. *Vital and Health Statistics,* Series 10, #189, 1994.

National Center for Health Statistics. Current estimates from the National Health Interview Survey: U.S. 1994. *Vital and Health Statistics,* Series 10, #193, 1995.

National Heart, Lung, and Blood Institute. *Sixth report of the Joint National Committee on Prevention, Detection, Evaluation and Treatment of High Blood Pressure.* NIH: NHLBI Publications, Nov. 1997.

Nelson, M. E., Fiatarone, M. A., Morganti, C. M., Trice, I., Greenberg, R. A., and Evans, W. J. Effects of high intensity strength training on multiple risk factors for osteoporotic fractures. *Journal of the American Medical Association,* 1994, *272,* 1909–1914.

Notelovitz, M., Martin, D., and Tesar, R. Estrogen therapy and variable resistance weight training increase bone mineral in surgically menopausal women. *Journal of Bone Mineral Research,* 1991, *6,* 583–590.

O'Brien, S. J. and Vertinsky, P. A. Unfit survivors: Exercise as a recourse for aging women. *The Gerontologist,* 1991, *31,* 347–357.

Ouslander, J. G., and Abelson, S. Perceptions of urinary incontinence among elderly outpatients. *The Gerontologist,* 1990, *30,* 369–372.

OWL (Older Women's League). *A status report on osteoporosis: The challenge to midlife and older women.* Washington, DC: 1994.

Paffenberger, R., Hyde, R., Wing, A., and Hsied, C. Physical activity, all-cause mortality and longevity of college alumni. *The New England Journal of Medicine,* 1986, *314,* 605–613.

Pate, R. R., Pratt, M., and Blair, S. N. Physical activity and public health. *Journal of the American Medical Association,* 1996, *273,* 402–407.

Peterman, T. A., Stoneburner, R. L., Allen J. R., Jaffe, H. W., and Curran, J. W. Risk of human immunodeficiency virus transmission from heterosexual adults with transfusion-associated infections. *Journal of the American Medical Association,* 1988, *259,* 55–58.

Pinsky, J. L., Jette, A. M., Kannel, W. B., and Feinleib, M. The Framingham disability study: Relationship of various coronary heart disease manifestations to disability in older adults living in the community. *American Journal of Public Health,* 1990, *80,* 1363–1376.

Piraino, A. J. Managing medication in the elderly. *Hospital Practice,* 1995, *30,* 59–64.

Prince, R. L., Smith, M., Dick, I. M., Price, R. I., Webb, P. G., Henderson, K., and Harris, M. P. Prevention of postmenopausal osteoporosis. *New England Journal of Medicine,* 1991, *325,* 1189–1195.

Rakowski, W. The definition and measurement of prevention, preventative health care, and health promotion. *Generations,* 1994, *18,* 18–23.

Ray, W. A., Taylor, J. A., Meador, K. G., Thapa, P. B., and Brown, A. K. A randomized trial of a consultation service to reduce falls in nursing homes. *Journal of the American Medical Association,* 1997, *278,* 595–596.

Riggs, B. L., Hodgson, S. F., O'Fallon, W. M., Chao, E. Y., Wahner, H., et al. Effects of fluoride treatment on the fracture rate in postmenopausal women with osteoporosis. *New England Journal of Medicine,* 1990, *322,* 802–809.

Rimer, B. Health promotion and aging. Smoking among older adults: The problems, consequences and possible solutions. In Surgeon General's Workshop, *Health Promotion and Aging,* March 1988.

Rogers, M. A., Hagberg, J. M., Martin, W. H., Ehsani, A. A., and Holloszy, J. O. Decline in vo_2 max with aging in master athletes and sedentary men. *Journal of Applied Physiology,* 1990, *68,* 2195–2199.

Sharpe, P. A., Jackson, K. L., White, C., Vaca, V. L., Hickey, T., Gu, J., and Otterness, C. Effects of a one year physical activity intervention for older adults at congregate nutrition sites. *The Gerontologist,* 1997, *37,* 208–215.

Sherman, S. E., D'Agostino, R. B., Cobb, J. L., and Kannel, W. B. Physical activity and mortality in women in the Framingham heart study. *American Heart Journal*, 1994, *128*, 879–884.

Sisk, J. E., Moskowitz, A. J., Whang, W., Lin, J. D., Fedson, D. S., and McBean, A. M. Cost-effectiveness of vaccination against pneumococcal bacteremia among elderly people. *Journal of the American Medical Association*, 1997, *278*, 1333–1339.

Stampfer, M. J., and Colditz, G. A. Estrogen replacement therapy and coronary heart disease: A quantitative assessment of the epidemiologic evidence. *Preventive Medicine*, 1991, *20*, 47–63.

Stampfer, M. J., Colditz, G. A., Willett, W. C., Manson, J. E., Rosner, B., Speizer, F. E., and Heinnekens, C. H. Postmenopausal estrogen therapy and cardiovascular disease: Ten-year follow-up from the Nurses' Health Study. *New England Journal of Medicine*, 1991, *325, 756*–762.

Stearns, S. C., Bernard, S. L., Konrad, T. R., Schwartz, R. J., and Defriese, G. H. *Medicare use and costs in relation to self-care practices.* Poster presented at annual meetings of the Association for Health Services Research, 1997.

Steinberg, K. K., Thacker, S. B., Stroup, D. F., Zack, M. M., Flanders, W. D., and Berkelman, R. L. A meta-analysis of the effect of estrogen replacement therapy on the risk of breast cancer. *Journal of the American Medical Association*, 1992, *265*, 185–199.

Stewart, A. L., Greenfield, S., Hays, R. D., Wells, K., Rogers, W. H., Berry, S. D., McGlynn, E. A., and Ware, J. E. Functional status and well-being of patients with chronic conditions. *Journal of the American Medical Association*, 1989, *262*, 907–913.

Stump, T. E., Johnson, R. J., and Wolinsky, F. D. Changes in physician utilization over time among older adults. *Journals of Gerontology*, 1995, *50B*, S45–S58.

Surgeon General's Workshop: *Health Promotion and Aging: Proceedings.* Washington, DC: U.S. Government Printing Office, 1988.

Thapa, P. B., Gideon, P., Fought, R. L., and Ray, W. A., Psychotropic drugs and risk of recurrent falls in ambulatory nursing home residents. *American Journal of Epidemiology*, 1995, *142*, 202–211.

Tideiksaar, R. Environmental adaptations to preserve balance and prevent falls. *Topics in Geriatric Rehabilitation*, 1990, *5*, 78–84.

Tinetti, M. E., Baker, D. I., McAvay, C., Claus, E. B., Garret, P., and Gottschalk, M. A multifactorial intervention to reduce the risk of falling among elderly people living in the community. *New England Journal of Medicine*, 1994, *331*, 821–827.

U.S. Administration on Aging Webpage. Oct. 1997. http://www.aoa.dhhs.gov//aoa/stats/aging21/table19.html

U.S. Department of Health and Human Services, Dental Services and Oral Health: United States. *Vital and Health Statistics.* DHHS Publication Number PHS 93–1511, Series 10, No. 183, 1992.

U.S. Public Health Service. *Promoting health/preventing disease: Year 2000 objectives for the nation.* Washington, DC: U.S. Department of Health and Human Services, 1989.

Van Nostrand, J. F., Furner, S. E., and Suzman, R. (Eds.), Health data on older Americans: United States, 1992. *Vital and Health Statistics*, Series 3: Analytic and Epidemiological Studies, No. 27, DHHS Publication 93–1411. Hyattsville, MD: NCHS, 1993.

Vogt, T. Cost-effectiveness of prevention programs for older people. *Generations*, 1994, *18*, 63–68.

Wagner, E. H., Grothaus, L. C., Hecht, J. A., and LaCroix, A. Z. Factors associated with participation in a senior health promotion program. *The Gerontologist*, 1991, *31*, 598–602.

Walker, S. Health promotion and prevention of disease and disability. *Generations*, 1994, *18*, 45–49.

Wallace, J. I. *Health promotion for older adults: Nutrition.* NWGEC Curriculum Modules, University of Washington, 1997.

Waller, P. F. The older driver. *Human Factors*, 1991, *33*, 499–505.

Wattis, J. P., and Seymour, J. Alcohol abuse in elderly people: Medical and psychiatric consequences. In R. R. Watson (Ed.), *Handbook of nutrition in the aged* (2nd ed.) Boca Raton, FL: CRC Press, 1994.

Winn, D. M., Brunelle, J. A., Selwitz, R. H., Kaste, L. M., Oldakowski, R. J., Kingman, A., and Brown, L. J. Coronal and root carries in the dentition of adults in the United States. *Journal of Dental Research*, 1996, *75*, 642–651.

Yataco, A. R., Busby-Whitehead, J., Drinkwater, D. T., and Katzel, L. I. Relationship of body composition and cardiovascular fitness to lipoprotein lipid profiles in master athletes and sedentary men. *Aging*, 1997, *9*, 88–94.

Yee, B., and Weaver, G. Ethnic minorities and health promotion: Developing a culturally competent agenda. *Generations*, 1994, *18*, 39–44.

Yusuf, H. R., Croft, J. B., Giles, W. H., Anda, R. F., Casper, M. L., Casperson, C. J. Leisure-time physical activity among older adults. *Archives of Internal Medicine*, 1996, *156*, 1321–1326.

three

THE PSYCHOLOGICAL CONTEXT OF SOCIAL AGING

The dynamic interactions between people and their environments as they age, the population trends that have made gerontology such an important concern in the late twentieth century, and the historical background of social gerontology were discussed in Part One. Part Two focused on the normal biological and physiological changes that take place with aging. The types of chronic and acute health problems that afflict older people and influence their social functioning were presented. The older population's use of the health care system was reviewed. Part Two concluded with a discussion of the growing field of health promotion, and how improved health behaviors can help people achieve successful aging.

In this section, the focus is on psychological changes with aging—both normal and abnormal—that influence older people's social behavior and dynamic relationships with their physical and social environments. As we have already seen, many changes take place in the aging organism that make it more difficult to perform activities of daily living and to respond as quickly and easily to external demands as in youth. Many older people have chronic health problems, such as arthritis, diabetes, or heart disease, that compound the normal changes that cause people to slow down. In a similar manner, some changes in cognitive functioning, personality, and sexuality are a function of normal aging. Other psychological changes may be due to the secondary effects of diseases.

Many researchers have examined changes in intelligence, learning, and memory with aging. The literature in this area, reviewed in Chapter 5, suggests that normal aging does not result in significant declines. Although older subjects in the studies described do not perform as well as younger subjects, their scores are not so poor as to indicate significant impairments in social functioning. Laboratory tests also may be less than ideal as indicators of cognitive function in older people. Suggestions for improving memory in the later years are discussed. The chapter concludes with a review of what is known about wisdom and creativity in old age.

Chapter 6 describes personality development in the later years, the importance of maintaining self-esteem, and threats to self-esteem that result from changes in social roles. This chapter also focuses on coping and successful adaptation to the changes associated with aging. Given the normal age-related changes in physiological, sensory, and cognitive functions, in personality styles, and in older individuals' social networks, some gerontologists have argued that older people experience more stress in a given time period than the young. Furthermore, there has been considerable debate about whether aging results in the use of different types of coping strategies. However, there is insufficient longitudinal research in this area to conclude with any certainty that aging is associated with more stressful life events than young adulthood.

Some forms of psychopathology, such as sociopathic behavior, are more common in youth than in old age. However, as described in Chapter 6, some older people are at high risk for major depression, paranoia, and some forms of dementia. In the case of dementia, such as Alzheimer's disease, memory and problem-solving abilities decline quite dramatically, sometimes within a few years, other times over many years. Older individuals with a diagnosis of dementia experience significant impairments in their ability to interact with other people and to control their physical and social environments. To the extent that older people do not seek mental health services for treatable disorders such as depression or paranoia, their social interactions will deteriorate. Some may become reclusive and, in the case of severely depressed older persons, at greater risk of suicide. Despite the growing number of studies that support the benefits of therapeutic interventions for older adults, the older population, especially ethnic minorities, underutilizes mental health services. Most of the mental health care provided to older people takes place in hospitals, not in community mental health centers nor in private practice. And most therapy is provided by family doctors who generally do not have special expertise in geriatric medicine or psychiatry.

An important aspect of personality is sexuality, the individual's ability to express intimate feelings through a wide range of love and pleasurable experiences. Chapter 7 addresses the influence of social attitudes and beliefs, normal physiological changes, and diseases on older people's sexuality. Contrary to popular belief, aging need not reduce sexual pleasure and capacity. More often, older people withdraw from sexual activity because of societal expectations and stereotypes. As societal attitudes become more enlightened and sexual taboos are reduced, older people will express their sexuality more easily.

Perhaps the most important knowledge to be gained in Part Three is that aging does not affect all people's psychological functions in the same way. Normal cognitive changes generally are not so dramatic as to impair older people's social functions. However, some people report mild forgetfulness, a condition known as "benign senescent forgetfulness." A relatively small segment of the older population experiences Alzheimer's disease or other types of dementia. Personality and patterns of coping also do not change so dramatically as to impair social functioning, although some sex-typed behaviors become less pronounced with age. Coping and adaptation skills do not become impaired with normal aging; styles of coping vary widely among older people. Indeed, aging results in increasing differences in psychological functioning among people, not greater similarity. Some older people age successfully despite chronic diseases and deterioration in cognitive function, while others experience poor adaptation to these normal and secondary changes of aging. The following vignettes illustrate the contrasts in psychological aging.

An Older Person with Intact Cognitive Abilities

Mr. Wallace, age 85, is a retired professor in a midwestern community. He retired 20 years ago, after teaching history in a large state university for 40 years. He remains active by doing volunteer work in the local historical society, teaching part-time at the university, and traveling to Europe with his wife for three months every summer, occasionally leading groups of other retirees in tours of medieval European towns. Mr. Wallace's major project that he wishes to complete before he dies is an historical novel about Charlemagne. This is a topic about which he has lectured and read extensively, and one he enjoys investigating in detail during his trips to Europe. Mrs. Wallace often remarks that he is busier these days than he was before his retirement. During the first few months after retirement, Professor Wallace experienced a mild bout of depression; it was relieved as he became involved in group therapy with other retirees. Mr. Wallace enjoys intellectual challenges today as much as he did when he was employed, in fact, more so, because he is pursuing these activities without the pressures of a day-to-day job. He vows to keep up his level of activity until he "runs out of energy."

An Older Person with Good Coping Skills

Mrs. Johnson, age 83, has suffered numerous tragedies throughout her life. Born to a poor farming family in Mississippi, she moved North with her mother and eight older sisters and brothers as a child, after her father died and the family farm was lost. The family supported itself through hard work in the factories. Mrs. Johnson married young; she and her husband struggled through the years to own their home and raise their three children. Her husband died 20 years ago, leaving her with a small pension. She worked at a manual labor job until she was 70 years old, when her arthritis made it painful for her to do the heavy work needed on the job. During the past three years, Mrs. Johnson has experienced a series of losses: her son and daughter-in-law died in an auto accident; her last surviving sister died; and her oldest granddaughter, the one on whom she could most depend, moved West to attend medical school. Mrs. Johnson admits these losses are painful, but that it is "God's will" that she experience them. Her strong faith in God helps her accept these changes in her life and her deteriorating health as part of a "Master Plan." When she becomes too distraught, she turns to the Bible, and looks forward to visits from her grandchildren and great-grandchildren to keep her busy.

An Older Person with Dementia

Mr. Adams is age 64. Several years ago he started showing signs of confusion and disorientation. He was diagnosed as having Alzheimer's disease at age 60, five years before his planned retirement. He and his wife had made plans to travel around the world during retirement; now all their plans have completely changed. While there have been some brief periods during the past four years where he has seemed to be better, Mr. Adams now is extremely agitated and disoriented, wanders during the night, and is occasionally abusive to people near him. He often does not know who his wife and children are. The slightest change in routine will upset him. In his lucid moments, Mr. Adams cries and wonders what has happened to his life; at some points, he can also carry on short conversations. His wife is determined to keep him at home, even though he often verbally abuses her and does not recognize or appreciate all that she does for him. She is able to take him to an adult day-care center during the day, where the staff try to keep him active and stimulated. Mrs. Adams also attends meetings of a support group for family caregivers of Alzheimer's disease patients. She enjoys these meetings because she can express her feelings about how hard things are and then be supported for her efforts by other caregivers. Mr. Adams expresses great fear at the thought of a nursing home, but his wife worries about how long she can manage him at home.

The next three chapters describe how the aging process influences cognitive abilities, personality styles, mental health, and intimacy and sexuality as well as responses to major life events. They emphasize the wide variations in these processes with aging. The vastly different psychological states of Mr. Wallace, Mrs. Johnson, and Mr. Adams result in significant variations in the social aspects of their lives.

5 COGNITIVE CHANGES WITH AGING

One of the most important and most studied aspects of aging is cognitive functioning; that is, intelligence, learning, and memory. These are critical to an individual's performance in every aspect of life, including work and leisure activities, relationships with family and friends, and productive roles in the community. Older people who have problems in cognitive functioning will eventually experience stress in these other areas as well, along with an increasing incongruence between their competence levels and the demands of their environments. Researchers have attempted to determine whether normal aging is associated with a decline in the three areas of cognitive functioning and, if so, to what extent such a decline is due to age-related physiological changes. Much of the research on these issues has evolved from studies of cognitive development across the life span. Other studies have been undertaken in response to concerns expressed by older persons or their families that they cannot learn as easily as they used to, or that they have more trouble remembering names, dates, and places than previously.

This chapter reviews the research on cognition and normal aging, the problems of determining why observed changes occur, some of the social consequences of age-related cognitive changes, and some techniques that older persons can use to improve their learning and memory. We examine the three key elements of intellectual processes—intelligence, learning, and memory—and briefly discuss the issue of creativity.

INTELLIGENCE AND AGING

The first of the three components of cognition, intelligence, is difficult both to define and to measure. Of all the elements of cognition, it is the least verifiable. We can only infer its existence and can only indirectly measure individual levels. **Intelligence** is defined as the "theoretical limit of an individual's performance" (Jones, 1959, p. 700). The limit is determined by biological and genetic factors; however, the ability to achieve the limit is influenced by environmental opportunities, such as a challenging educational experience, as well as by environmental constraints, such as the absence of books or other intellectual stimulation. Intelligence encompasses a range of abilities, including the ability to deal with symbols and abstractions, to acquire and comprehend new information, to adapt to new situations, and to understand and create new ideas. Alfred Binet, who developed the first test of intelligence, emphasized the operational aspects of intelligence: "to judge well, to comprehend well, to reason well, these are the essentials of intelligence" (Binet and Simon, 1905, p. 106). **Intelligence quotient** (or IQ) refers to an individual's relative abilities in some of these areas compared to others of the same chronological age.

Most theorists agree that intelligence is composed of many different components. Perhaps the most complex model is Guilford's (1967, 1966) three-dimensional structure of intellect (see Figure 5.1). The three dimensions represent the content of knowledge (e.g., figures, symbols, and words), the operations that an individual must perform with this knowledge (e.g., memorize, evaluate, and come up with single or multiple solutions), and the products that are derived from these operations (e.g., relations, systems, and implications). This is probably the most complete model, yielding 120 separate components. Such a model is difficult to test. Nevertheless, a multidimensional structure of intelligence, although not identical to Guilford's model, is assumed by most contemporary measures of intelligence. Most tests of intelligence today measure a subset of intellectual abilities known as "primary mental abilities," which generally include:

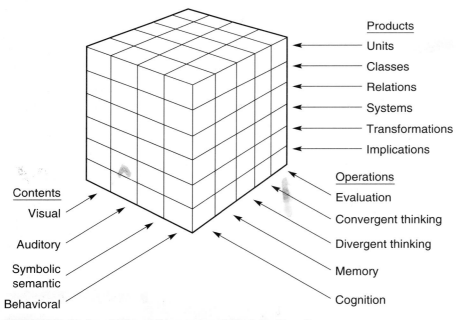

FIGURE 5.1 **A Three-Dimensional Model of Intellect**
SOURCE: J. P. Guilford, *The nature of human intelligence* (New York: McGraw-Hill, 1967) and J. P. Guilford, *Way beyond the IQ* (Buffalo, NY: Creative Education Foundation, 1977). Reprinted by permission of the author, McGraw-Hill, and the Creative Education Foundation.

1. Number or mathematical reasoning;
2. Word fluency or the ability to use appropriate words to describe the world;
3. Verbal meaning or vocabulary level;
4. Inductive reasoning or the ability to generalize from specific facts to concepts; and
5. Spatial orientation or the ability to orient oneself in a three-dimensional space.

A useful distinction has been made between **fluid intelligence** and **crystallized intelligence** (Horn, 1982, 1970; Horn and Donaldson, 1980; Cattell, 1963). These two types of intelligence include some of the primary mental abilities described above. Fluid intelligence consists of skills that are biologically determined, independent of experience or learning, and may be similar to what is popularly called "native intelligence." It involves processing information that is not embedded in a context of existing information for the individual. It requires flexibility in thinking. These skills may be measured by tests of spatial orientation, abstract reasoning, and perceptual speed. Crystallized intelligence refers to the knowledge and abilities that the individual acquires through education and lifelong experiences. Some indicators are verbal comprehension, word association, and social judgment. These two types of intelligence have been found to show different patterns with aging, as shown in the next section.

There has been considerable controversy regarding intelligence in the later years (Schaie, 1996a). Many researchers have found significant differences between young and old persons on intelligence tests in cross-sectional studies, with older persons performing at a much lower level. Even when the same cohort is followed longitudinally, there is a decline in some intelligence tests that is independent of generational differences (Schaie and Hertzog, 1986). Others have concluded that aging is not really associated with a decline in intelligence, but that standardized IQ tests and the time pressures on test-takers are more detrimental to older persons than to the young. Still others have pointed to methodological problems in conducting research in this area. Unfortunately, these mixed research findings have served to perpetuate the stereotype that older people are less intelligent than the young.

Many older persons are concerned that their intelligence has declined from when they were young. This concern may loom so large for them that merely taking part in a study intended to "test their intelligence" may provoke sufficient anxiety to affect their performance on the test. Such anxieties may also influence the older person's daily functioning. Older people who are told by friends, family, test-givers or society in general that they should not expect to perform as well on intellectual tasks because aging causes a decline in intelligence may, in fact, come to perform more poorly.

The most widely used measure of adult intelligence is the Wechsler Adult Intelligence Scale (WAIS). It consists of 11 subtests, 6 of which are described as Verbal Scales (which measure, to some extent, crystallized intelligence), and 5 as Performance Scales (providing some measure of fluid intelligence). Verbal scores are obtained by measuring an individual's ability to define the meaning of words, to interpret proverbs, and to explain similarities between words and concepts. In this way, accumulated knowledge and abstract reasoning can be tested. Performance tests focus on an individual's ability to manipulate unfamiliar objects and words, often in unusual ways. These include tests of spatial relations and abstract reasoning, and may require an individual to put puzzles together to match a picture, match pictures with symbols or numbers, or arrange pictures in a particular pattern. Both psychomotor and perceptual skills are needed in performing these tasks. In addition, the performance tests on the WAIS are generally timed; the verbal tests are not.

A consistent pattern of scores on these two components of the WAIS has emerged in numerous studies; it has been labeled the *Classic Aging Pattern*. People beyond the age of 65 in some studies, and even earlier in other studies, perform significantly worse on Performance Scales (i.e., fluid intelligence), but their scores on Verbal Scales (i.e., crystallized intelligence) remain stable. The tendency to do worse on the performance tasks with aging may reflect age-related changes in noncognitive functions, such as sensory and perceptual abilities, and in psychomotor skills. As we have seen in Chapters 3 and 4, aging results in a slowing down of the neural pathways and of the visual and auditory functions. This slower reaction time, and the delay in receiving and transmitting messages through the sense organs, explain poorer performance on subtests requiring such capabilities. Some researchers have therefore argued for the elimination of time constraints in performance tasks. Studies that have not measured speed of performance have still found significant age differences in these subtests (Salthouse, 1996). There appears to be a decline in performance-related aspects of intellectual function, independent of psychomotor or sensory factors. Speed of cognitive processing, such as the time to perform simple math problems, also declines with age and, in turn, slows an individual's responses on tests of performance.

Turning to verbal skills, the Classic Aging Pattern suggests that the ability to recall stored verbal information and to use abstract reasoning tends to remain constant throughout life. Declines, where they exist, tend not to show up until advanced old age, or, in the case of cognitive impairment such as the dementias, to begin early in the course of the disease.

Cognitive studies of older adults reveal that, when given logically inconsistent statements, older subjects analyze these inconsistencies on the basis of their own knowledge, whereas younger adults tend to ignore the logic and attempt to reach conclusions quickly. Older subjects have also been found to reject simplified solutions and to prefer a complex analysis of the problem. This finding from laboratory-based research is supported by surveys of attitudes and beliefs among respondents of varying ages. Younger respondents are more willing to provide a direct response, whereas many older persons attempt to analyze the questions and give more contingency re-

sponses; that is, analyzing the question and stating that the answer could be x in one situation and y in another, rather than an all-encompassing response. For example, on a measure of environmental preference, the respondent may be asked, "How much privacy do you generally prefer?" A younger respondent is more likely to focus on the "general" situation, whereas the older respondent will be more likely to consider situations both in which privacy is preferred and where it is not. It thus appears important to review older persons' responses to tests of problem solving and abstract reasoning from other perspectives beyond the traditional approaches that are grounded in cognitive theories developed with younger populations. Most tests of intelligence do not reward test-takers who provide the more analytic or complex responses typical of some older people.

Problems in the Measurement of Cognitive Function

A major shortcoming of many studies of intelligence in aging is their use of cross-sectional research designs rather than longitudinal approaches. As we saw in Chapter 1, the former method is used to compare at a single point in time, two or more groups defined by age or other characteristics. The latter approach is used to examine the same group (or groups) several times over a period of weeks, months, or years. Age differences that are obtained in cross-sectional studies may be a reflection of cohort or generational differences rather than actual age changes. In particular, changes in educational systems and the development of television, computers, and high-speed travel have had a profound impact on the experiences of today's youth when compared with those of people who grew up in the early twentieth century. These historical factors may then have a greater effect on intelligence scores than age per se.

Another problem is subject attrition, or dropout from longitudinal studies of intelligence. There is a pattern of selective attrition, whereby the people who drop out tend to be those who have performed less well, who perceive their performance to be poor, or whose health status and ambulatory abilities are worse than average. The people who stay in the study (i.e., "the survivors") performed better in the initial tests than did dropouts. This is consistent with our earlier observation that older persons often become unduly anxious about poor performance on tests of intellectual function. Hence, the results become biased in favor of the superior performers, indicating stability or improvement over time, and do not represent the wider population of older adults, whose performance might have shown a decline in intelligence (Schaie, 1996b).

Longitudinal Studies of Intelligence

Several major longitudinal studies have examined changes in intellectual function from youth to old age (Schaie, 1996a; 1983). The Iowa State Study tested a sample of college freshmen in 1919 and retested them in 1950 and 1961 (Cunningham and Owens, 1983; Owens, 1966, 1953). The researchers found general stability in intellectual functioning through middle age, with a peak in their late forties and fifties. Declines were observed after age 60 in many men, but the degree of change varied widely among the men and across variables. The New York State Study of Aging Twins began in 1946 and followed this group through 1973 (Kallmann and Sander, 1949). Average performance declined significantly on timed tests, but, as with the Iowa State Study, individual differences were pronounced. Among the individuals who were healthy enough to complete the final follow-up, performance on nonspeeded intelligence tests remained stable until they reached their ninth decade. The greatest declines were observed in the test of hand-eye coordination and in fluid intelligence. Both studies had less than 25 percent of the original sample available at the final follow-up, which raises questions whether survivors are representative of their cohort in cognitive functioning.

The Seattle Longitudinal Study began in 1956 and collected data on Thurstone's primary mental abilities every 7 years over 28 years (Schaie,

Intellectual stimulation can help sustain higher level cognitive skills.

1996a). At each follow-up assessment, individuals who were still available from the original sample were retested, along with a new, randomly selected sample from the same population. The 1984 cycle included a test of some older people who had previously participated in a cognitive retraining program (Willis and Schaie, 1986). This study has provided the basis for the development of sequential research models, described in Chapter 1. Peak performance varied across tests and between men and women, ranging from age 32 on the test of Numbers for men and age 39 on the test of Reasoning for women, to age 53 for Educational Aptitude. A review of age changes for the 128 people who were observed over the entire course of this study reveals age decrements after age 60 on tests of word-fluency, space, and numbers that became progressively worse in later years. Tests of spatial abilities and inductive reasoning, both indicators of fluid intelligence, showed greater decline with age. However, other primary mental abilities, such as verbal meaning and reasoning, showed no declines until the mid-seventies. These results are consistent with cross-sectional results using the WAIS, as we have seen earlier. They are supported by other, shorter longitudinal studies that have found little change over three years (Zelinski, Gilewski, and Schaie, 1993). The findings suggest that the Classic Aging Pattern holds up in both cross-sectional and longitudinal studies, and that some performance aspects of intelligence may begin to deteriorate after age 60, although major changes are generally rare until the mid-seventies.

In all these studies, most of the significant declines have been found in intellectual abilities that are less practiced. Schaie (1996b) concludes that the changes observed in the Seattle Longitudinal Study indicate a normative developmental transition from stability in general intelligence in the middle years, to a gradual decline that begins around age 60. Most people maintained their abilities in one or more areas well into their advanced years, as shown in Figure 5.2. However, Schaie and colleagues found no linear decline in all five primary mental abilities for any participants as old as age 88 (Schaie 1996a, 1996b, 1989).

The Duke Longitudinal Studies, described in Chapter 1, assessed intelligence and memory, in addition to many health variables. This series of three longitudinal samples, each measured several times, provides useful information about the relationship between intellectual function and health

status, especially cardiovascular disease (Palmore, 1985, 1974; Siegler, 1983). The findings regarding age changes generally are consistent with the other longitudinal studies described in this section; declines in cognitive function were not observed until individuals reached their seventies. Scores on performance tests were found to decline earlier than scores on verbal measures. Another longitudinal study in Sweden has examined cognitive functioning among the oldest-old (ages 84 to 90 in this study). A two-year follow-up revealed that participants who had scored high on tests of memory, attention, orientation, and ability to follow instructions continued to perform well at follow-up. However, average performance declined slightly on all these tests (Johansson, Zarit, and Berg, 1992).

FACTORS THAT MAY INFLUENCE INTELLIGENCE IN ADULTHOOD

Researchers who have compared intelligence test scores of older and younger persons have found

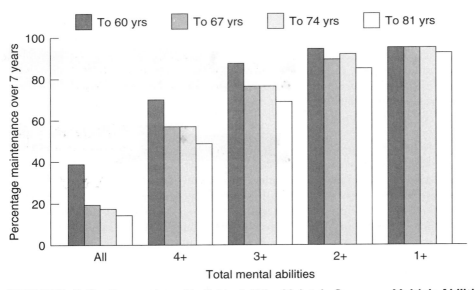

FIGURE 5.2   **Proportion of Individuals Who Maintain Scores on Multiple Abilities**
SOURCE: Schaie, K. W. The hazards of cognitive aging. *The Gerontologist,* 1989, *29,* 484–493. Reprinted with permission.

wide variations in scores of both groups. As described earlier, older test-takers generally have obtained poorer scores, but age per se is only one factor in explaining intellectual functioning.

As mentioned earlier, there is also a biological factor in intelligence, such that some people are innately more intelligent than others. However, it is difficult to determine the relative influence of biological factors, because it is impossible to measure the specific mechanisms of the brain that account for intelligence. There are structural changes in the brain and in neural pathways with aging, as we have seen in Chapter 3. However, these changes are generally diffuse and not focused in a particular region of the brain. It is therefore impossible to determine what specific changes in the brain and its pathways may account for the age-related deterioration that is observed.

Other variables that have been examined are educational attainment, involvement in complex versus mechanistic work, cardiovascular disease, hypertension, and sensory deficits. Some studies have found cohort differences on tests of intelligence, with newer cohorts of older people performing better than previous cohorts who took the same test at about the same age. These differences emerge on tests of crystallized *and* fluid intelligence (represented by verbal meaning and inductive reasoning tests), even when comparing adult children and their parents (Schaie and Willis, 1995; Schaie et al., 1992). The advantage of newer cohorts has been attributed to higher educational attainment. Therefore, it is important to control statistically for educational differences when analyzing the relationship between age and intelligence. Significant positive effects of education have been found on all tests of cognitive function when comparing healthy independent adults aged 70 to 79 with different educational levels. In particular, participants with the highest level of education (12+ years) did three times better on a test of abstract thinking than did people with seven or fewer years of education (Inouye et al., 1993).

Occupational level, which is generally correlated with educational level, also influences intel-ligence test scores. Older people who still use their cognitive abilities in jobs or activities that require thinking and problem-solving (such as Mr. Wallace in the introductory vignette) show less decline on cognitive tests than those who do not use these skills. This is because most of the observed declines in intellectual abilities occur in highly challenging, complex tasks. In addition, people whose occupations demand more verbal skills (e.g., lawyers and teachers) may continue to perform very well on these aspects of intelligence tests, whereas those who use more abstract and fluid skills in their occupations (e.g., architects and engineers) may do well on the performance tests of the WAIS, even into their seventies and eighties. In general, older people who do not participate in any intellectual pursuits perform worse on intelligence tests than do their peers who are "cognitively engaged" (Gold et al., 1995; Baltes, 1993; Inouye et al., 1993; Dutta, 1992).

The effects of declining physical health and sensory losses on intelligence become more severe in the later years, and these factors may displace any positive influence due to education and occupation for people who are 75 years and older. Several studies have identified poorer performance on intelligence tests by older people in poor health. Older people with cardiovascular problems tend to do worse on tests of intelligence than those without such disorders, particularly in tests that demand psychomotor speed (Hultsch, Hammer, and Small, 1993). In the Seattle Longitudinal Study, participants with cardiovascular disease declined at younger ages on all tests of mental abilities than did people with no disease (Gruber-Baldini, 1991). Older people with severe or uncontrolled hypertension performed worse on these tests than did those with no hypertension. Interestingly, however, older adults with borderline hypertension showed the least decline. This may be because mild elevations of blood pressure in older persons are useful for maintaining sufficient blood circulation to the brain (Sands and Meredith, 1992). Nutritional deficits may also impair an older person's cognitive functioning. One study of community dwelling, healthy older persons (ages

66 to 90) examined their performance on multiple tests of cognitive functioning and nutritional status longitudinally. Older people with low intake of Vitamins E, A, B_6, and B_{12} at baseline performed worse on visuospatial and abstraction tasks 6 years later; those who used vitamin supplements did better. Dietary intake of thiamine, riboflavin, niacin, folate, and protein also correlated with performance on these cognitive tests (Larue, et al., 1997). These findings reinforce the results of research on the impact of nutritional deficiencies on performance, described in Chapter 4. Depression, or even mild dysphoria (i.e., feeling "blue" or "down in the dumps," but not clinically depressed), is a psychological variable that can influence cognitive function. Indeed, in a large study of people aged 50 to 93 that controlled for the effects of age, education, and occupation, older people with worse scores on a measure of depression had significantly lower scores on tests of both crystallized and fluid intelligence (Rabbitt et al., 1995). Given the prevalence of depression in the older population, it is important to consider this as a cause of poorer cognitive performance rather than aging per se.

As we noted in Chapter 3, hearing loss is common in older persons, especially moderate levels of loss that affect their ability to comprehend speech. Visual deficits become more severe in advanced old age. It appears that poorer performance by some test takers who are very old is due primarily to these sensory losses, not to a central cognitive decline. Older persons with hearing or vision loss do especially poorly on tests of verbal meaning and spatial relations (Lindenberger and Baltes, 1994).

Another physical health factor that appears to be related to intelligence test scores is an apparent and rapid decline in cognitive function within five years of death. This phenomenon is known as the *terminal drop* or **terminal decline hypothesis,** first tested by Kleemeier (1962). In longitudinal studies of intelligence, older subjects whose test scores are in the lower range to start with, and who decline more sharply, have been found to die sooner than good performers. This has been observed on many different tests, especially in vocabulary and word fluency (Berg, 1996; Cooney, Schaie, and Willis, 1988). This suggests that time since birth (i.e., age) is not as significant in intellectual decline as is proximity to death.

Finally, anxiety may negatively affect older people's intelligence test scores. As shown in the following section, older people in laboratory tests of learning and memory are more likely than the young to express high test anxiety and cautiousness in responding. These same reactions may occur in older people taking intelligence tests, especially if they think that the test really measures how "intelligent" they are. Anxieties about cognitive decline and concerns about becoming cognitively impaired may make older people even more cautious, and hence result in poorer performance on intelligence tests.

THE PROCESS OF LEARNING AND MEMORY

Learning and *memory* are two cognitive processes that must be considered together. That is, learning is assumed to have occurred when an individual is able to retrieve information accurately from his or her memory store. Conversely, if an individual cannot retrieve information from memory, it is assumed that learning has not adequately taken place. Thus, *learning* is the process by which new information (verbal or nonverbal) or skills are encoded, or put into one's memory. *Memory* is the process of retrieving or recalling the information stored in the brain when needed. Memory also refers to a part of the brain that retains what has been learned throughout a person's lifetime. For example, a person may have learned many years ago how to ride a bicycle. If this skill has been encoded well through practice, the person can retrieve it many years later from his or her memory store, even if he or she has not ridden a bicycle in years. Researchers have attempted to distinguish three separate types of memory: sensory, primary or short-term, and secondary or long-term.

"Sensory memory," as its name implies, is the first step in receiving information through the sense organs and passing it on to primary or secondary memory. It is stored for only a few tenths of a second, although there is some evidence that it lasts longer in older persons because of slower reaction times of the senses. Sensory memory has been further subdivided into **iconic** (or visual) and **echoic** (or auditory) memory. Examples of iconic memory are words or letters that we see, faces of people with whom we have contact, and landscapes that we experience through our eyes. Of course, words can be received through echoic memory as well, such as when we hear others say a specific word, or when we repeat words aloud to ourselves. A landscape can also enter our sensory memory through our ears (e.g., the sound of the ocean), our skin (e.g., the feel of a cold spray from the ocean), and our nose (e.g., the smell of salt water). To the extent that we focus on or rehearse any information that we receive from our sense organs, it is more likely to be passed into our primary and secondary memories.

Despite significant changes in the visual system with aging (as described in Chapter 3), early studies of iconic memory have found only small age differences in the ability to identify stimuli presented briefly. When old and young individuals were tested with seven-letter strings, the former were slower by a factor of 1.3, a rate similar to that found with single letters (Cerella, Poon, and Fozard, 1982). Such modest declines in iconic memory would not be expected to influence observed decrements in secondary or long-term memory. However, some researchers have suggested that even small declines in sensory memory may result in a large decline in long-term memory (Craik and Jennings, 1994).

Although research on iconic memory is limited, there has been even less with echoic memory and less still that has compared older persons with younger. We have all experienced the long-term storage of memories gained through touch, taste, or smell. For example, the odor of freshly baked bread evokes memories in many older people of their early childhood. However, these sensory memories are more difficult to test. As a result, very little is known about any changes experienced with these other modes of sensory memory.

Primary memory is a temporary stage of holding and organizing information, and does not necessarily refer to a storage area in the brain. Despite its temporary nature, primary memory is critical for our ability to process new information. We have all experienced situations where we hear or read a bit of information such as a phone number or someone's name, use that name or number immediately, then forget it. In fact, most adults can recall seven, plus or minus two, pieces of information (e.g., digits, letters, or words) for 60 seconds or less. It is not surprising, therefore, that local phone numbers in most countries are seven digits or less! In order to retain this information in our permanent memory store (**secondary memory**), it must be rehearsed or "processed" actively. This is why primary memory has been described as a form of "working memory" that decides what information should be attended to or ignored, which is most important, and how best to store it (Baddeley, 1986). If we are distracted while trying to retain the information for the 60 seconds that it can last in short-term memory, we immediately forget it, even if it consists of only two or three bits of information. This happens because the rehearsal of such material is interrupted by the reception of newer information in our sensory memory. Most studies of primary memory have found minimal age differences in its storage capacity. Differences that exist may be due to slower reaction time in older persons. It may also be that the encoding process which takes place in primary memory requires some organization or elaboration of the information received. Older persons are less likely than young people to process new information in this manner. Indeed, some have argued that aging leads to a decline in "attentional resources," or mental energy, to organize and elaborate newly acquired information in order to retain it in secondary memory (Smith, 1996; Craik, 1994; Craik and Jennings, 1994; Salthouse and Babcock, 1991).

True learning implies that the material we have acquired through our sensory and primary memories has been stored in "secondary memory." Thus, for example, looking up a telephone number and immediately dialing it does not guarantee that the number will be learned. In fact, only with considerable rehearsal can information from primary memory be passed into secondary memory. This is the part of the memory store in which everything we have learned throughout our lives is kept; unlike primary memory, it has an unlimited capacity.

Older people consistently recall less information than younger people in paired associate tests with retention intervals as brief as one hour or as long as eight months. Age differences in secondary memory appear to be more pronounced than in sensory or primary memory and are often frustrating to older people and their families. Indeed, there appears to be a widespread concern among middle-aged and older people that they cannot remember and retrieve information from secondary memory (Poon, 1985). This perception that one has poor memory can seriously harm older people's self-concept, their performance on many tasks, and may even result in depression. Such concern, growing out of a fear of dementia, is generally out of proportion to the actual level of decline.

Older individuals can benefit significantly from methods to help organize their learning, such as imagery and the use of mnemonics. Examples of such techniques to improve learning and memory are discussed later in this chapter.

THE INFORMATION PROCESSING MODEL

Figure 5.3 presents the **information processing model** of memory. This is a conceptual model; that is, it provides a framework for understanding how the processes of learning and memory take place. It is not necessarily what goes on in the neural pathways between the sense organs and the secondary memory store. Having described each of the components in this model, let us review the steps involved in processing some information that we want to retain. One example is the experience of learning new names at a social gathering. Sensory memory aids in hearing the name spoken, preferably several times by other people, and seeing the face that is associated with that name. Primary memory is used to store that information temporarily, so that a person can speak to others and address them by name (an excellent method of rehearsing this information), or manipulate the information in order to pass it on to secondary

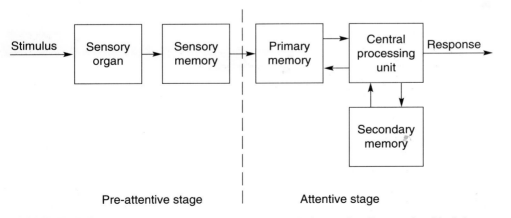

FIGURE 5.3 **Schematic Representation of the Information Processing Model**

memory. This may include repeating the name several times to oneself, trying to isolate some aspect of the person's physical features and relating it to the name, and associating the name with other people one has known in the past who have similar names. In the last type of mental manipulation, information from secondary memory (i.e., names of other people) is linked with the new information. This is a useful method because the material in secondary memory is permanent, and associating the new information with well-learned information aids in its storage and subsequent recall.

During any stage of this cognitive processing, the newly obtained information can be lost. This may occur if the sensory memory is flooded with similar information; in this case, if a person is being introduced to multiple new names and faces at a party, it is almost impossible to distinguish the names or to associate each name with a face. Information may also be lost during the primary memory stage. In our example, if a person is trying to use the newly heard name and is distracted by other names and faces, or receives unrelated but relevant information (e.g., a telephone call) while rehearsing the new name, the name has not been sufficiently processed to pass into secondary memory.

The learning process may also be disrupted because of inability to retrieve information efficiently from secondary memory. For example, a person may associate the newly heard name with someone known in the past; if he or she has difficulty retrieving the stored name from secondary memory, however, this may be so frustrating as to redirect the individual's attention from the new name to the old name. How often have you ignored everything around you to concentrate on remembering a name that is "on the tip of the tongue" (i.e., in secondary memory) but not easily retrievable? As noted above, aging appears to reduce the efficiency of *processing* information in sensory and primary memories, as well as retrieval from secondary memory (i.e., working memory). It does *not* influence the storage capacity of primary or secondary memories. That is, contrary to popular opinion, these memory stores are not physical spaces that become overloaded with information as we age.

FACTORS THAT AFFECT LEARNING IN OLD AGE

One problem with assessing learning ability is that it is not possible to measure the process that occurs in the brain while an individual is acquiring new information. Instead, we must rely on an individual's performance on tests that presumably measure what was learned. This may be particularly disadvantageous to older persons, whose performance on a test of learning may be poor because of inadequate or inappropriate conditions for expressing what was learned (Botwinick, 1984). For example, an older person may in fact have learned many new concepts in reading a passage from a novel, but not necessarily the specific concepts that are called for on a test of learning. Certain physical conditions, such as lighting levels, size of print, tone and loudness of the test-giver's voice in an oral exam, and the time constraints placed on the test-taker, may affect performance and thus lead to underestimates of what the older person has actually learned. The learning environment can be improved, however; such environmental changes as glare-free and direct lighting, lettering of good quality, size, and contrast, a comfortable test-taking situation with minimal background noise, and a relaxed and articulate test-giver can help older learners.

Time constraints are particularly detrimental to older people. Although the ability to encode new information quickly is a sign of learning ability, it is difficult to measure this ability. Instead, response time is generally measured. As we have already seen, psychomotor and sensory slowing with age has a significant impact on the older person's response speed. One of the first researchers to test the effect of these conditions on learning was Canestrari (1963). Using a common test of learning, the paired associates task (i.e., linking two unrelated words, letters, digits, or symbols, such as *cat* and *82*, and asking subjects to respond with the second when the first is mentioned), Canestrari presented the paired associates at varying rates, or allowed individuals to pace the task by controlling the visual apparatus themselves. In comparing people aged 60 to 69 with those aged 17 to 35, he found striking differences between old and young individuals' performance when the task was paced fast, fewer differences in moderate pacing, and the fewest differences in self-paced conditions. Young persons did well in all conditions, but older persons in this study benefited the most from self-pacing. Decline in perceptual speed, which can be measured separately from memory skills per se, may be a major reason why older people do worse on memory tests. Research by Salthouse (1996, 1994a, 1993) has shown that perceptual speed accounts for a significant part of the observed age-related variance in memory performance. Even when older research subjects are given more time to complete tests of memory, their perceptual speed still plays a significant role in their performance.

Research on paired associates tasks has demonstrated that older persons make more *errors of omission* than *errors of commission*. That is, older persons are more likely not to give an answer than to guess and risk being wrong. This phenomenon was first recognized in middle-aged and older adults in tests of psychomotor functioning. The older the respondent, the more likely he or she was to work for accuracy at the expense of speed. This occurs even when the older learner is encouraged to guess and is told that it is acceptable to give wrong answers (i.e., commission errors). Conditions of uncertainty and high risk are particularly difficult for older persons; here they are far more cautious than the young. Low-risk situations elicit less caution from older people and greater willingness to give responses in a learning task. The aging process may create an increased need to review multiple aspects of a problem, probably because of past experiences with similar dilemmas. Errors of omission may be reduced somewhat by giving rewards for both right and wrong answers.

Computers provide oppportunities for active learning.

Verbal ability and educational level are important factors in learning verbal information. Studies that entail learning prose passages have shown age deficits among those with average vocabulary abilities and minimal or no college education. In contrast, older persons with high verbal ability and a college education perform as well as younger subjects in such experiments. This may be due to greater practice and facility with such tasks on the part of more educated persons and those with good vocabulary skills. It may also reflect differences in the ability to organize new information, a skill that is honed through years of education and one that assists in the learning of large quantities of new material (Ratner et al., 1987).

Similarly, older people who have developed manual skills in a particular area have been found to perform just as well on perceptual-motor tests as do younger persons with skills. Two classic studies examined choice reaction time, tapping rate, and accuracy by testing people aged 19 to 72 who varied in typing speed (Salthouse, 1984). These well-designed experiments measured age differences in real-life studies where professional typists were asked to type prose passages as well as random letter series. While the older typists had more years of relevant employment, there were no differences between old and young in the *recency* of this experience (i.e., older typists were just as likely to be using their skills currently). This research demonstrated that typing time remains stable with increasing age, even though choice reaction time increases and tapping rate declines. These findings are consistent with other studies of the basic components of perceptual-motor abilities (McDowd and Craik, 1988).

Such stability in performing familiar perceptual-motor tasks may also occur because the accomplished performer of a specific task makes more efficient moves in completing a task than does a less skilled person. Such differences are evident in many areas demanding skill, from typing and driving to playing a musical instrument or operating a lathe. Therefore, aging workers can overcome the effects of slower psychomotor speed and declines in learning skills by their greater experience in most occupations (Salthouse, 1994a, 1993).

The conditions under which learning takes place affect older persons more than the young, just as test conditions are more critical. Older persons respond differently to varied testing situations; people tested under challenging conditions ("this is a test of your intelligence") are likely to do worse than those in supportive conditions ("the researcher needs your help"). Positive feedback appears to be a valuable tool for eliciting responses from older adults in both learning and test situations.

It is helpful to pace the information so that it is presented at a rate suitable to the older learner and to give him or her opportunities to practice the new information (e.g., writing down or spelling aloud newly learned words). Another condition that supports learning is the presentation of familiar and relevant material compared to material perceived by the older learner to be unimportant. Older people do worse in recalling recently acquired information than do younger people when the new information is unfamiliar or confusing. Age differences also emerge when the material to be learned is low in meaning and personal significance to the learner. Laboratory studies of cognitive functioning often seem artificial and meaningless to older people who are unaccustomed to such research methods, and even more so to those with little academic experience. Many people will complain that such tests are trivial, nonsense, or that these tasks have no connection to the "real world." Indeed, it may appear odd to anyone to be learning meaningless words and symbols on a **tachistoscope** (a screen that is timed to present visual stimuli at a specific pace) or other laboratory device. But for those older people who are unfamiliar with test-taking situations, it may appear particularly foolish and not worth the effort required. This may also serve a useful ego-defensive function for people who feel uncomfortable or threatened by a test-taking situation. It is generally easier for people to blame the environment or the test situation for their poor performance than to accept it as a sign of a decline in their intelligence or their ability to learn.

Spatial memory, that is, the ability to recall where objects are in relationship to each other in space (e.g., when finding one's way around a community or using a map), also appears to decline with aging. It is unclear, however, if older people do worse than the young because they have difficulty encoding and processing the information, or if the problem is in retrieval. It appears that there is an age-related decline in encoding ability for spatial information. Spatial recall was tested in one study following the presentation of a two-dimensional black-and-white map versus a colored map or a three-dimensional model. Older subjects in this study recalled fewer items than the young did under the condition of no visual cues, but no age differences were found when color or 3-D representations were used. (Sharps and Gollin, 1988).

Similarly, older people have more difficulty than younger persons in reading maps that are misaligned relative to the user. For example, when older people stand in front of a "You are here" map that is aligned 180° away from themselves, they take up to 50 percent more time and make 30 percent more errors than younger persons in the same condition. However, when the map is aligned directly with the user, no age differences are observed. This may be attributable to increased problems with mental rotation of external images and with perspective-taking as we age (Aubrey, Li, and Dobbs, 1994; Aubrey and Dobbs, 1990).

AGE-RELATED CHANGES IN MEMORY

As we have seen, learning involves encoding information and storing it into secondary or long-term memory, so that it can be retrieved and used later. Studies of this process have focused on two types of retrieval: recall and recognition. **Recall** is the process of searching through the vast store of information in secondary memory, perhaps with a cue or a specific, orienting question (e.g., "List the capitals of each state." "Describe how to repair a bicycle." "Give the dates when the U.S. Constitution was signed, when the U.N. Charter was signed," etc.). **Recognition** requires less search. The information in secondary memory must be matched with the stimulus information in the environment (e.g., "Which of these three cities is the capital of New York?"). Recall is demanded in essay exams, recognition in multiple-choice tests.

Not surprisingly, most researchers have found age-related deficiencies in recall, but few differences in recognition (Smith, 1996). Recall tasks have been further divided into **free recall** and **cued recall** situations. In the former, no aids or hints are provided for retrieving information from secondary memory. In the latter case, the individual is given some information to aid in the search (e.g., category labels and first letter of a word). Older people tend to do much worse than the young in tests of free recall, but are aided significantly by cueing. In particular, use of category labels (se-

mantic cues) at the learning stage has been found to be more helpful to older persons than the use of structural cues—for example, giving the respondent the first letter of a word to be recalled (Smith, 1996). However, cued recall tests are not as helpful as recognition tests for older learners.

An area of considerable controversy in aging and memory function is the question of whether older people have better recall of events that occurred in the distant past than recent situations. Many events are firmly embedded in secondary memory because they are unique or so important that subsequent experiences do not interfere with the ability to recall them. The birth of a child, one's wedding ceremony, or the death of a parent, spouse, or sibling are events that most people can recall in detail 40 to 50 years later. This may be because the situation had great private significance or, in the case of world events, such as the bombing of Hiroshima or President Kennedy's assassination, had a profound impact on world history. Some distant events may be better recalled because they had greater personal relevance for the individual's social development than recent experiences, or because they have been rehearsed or thought about more. Another possibility is that cues that helped the older person recall events in the past are less effective with recalling recent occasions because of "cue-overload." That is, the same cues that were once helpful in remembering certain information are also used to recall many recent events. But the cues are so strongly associated with one's earlier life experiences that the newer information becomes more difficult to retrieve. For example, older people may have difficulty memorizing new phone numbers because the cues that helped them recall phone numbers in the past may be so closely associated with previous ones that they confuse recent phone numbers with old ones.

One problem in determining whether recall of distant situations is really better than recall of recent events is the difficulty in validating an older person's memories. In many cases, there are no sources that can be checked to determine the accuracy of an older person's recollections. We can all identify with this process of asking an old friend or family member, "Do you remember the time when . . . ?" If others have no recollection of the event, it may make us wonder if the situation really took place, or it may mean that the event was so obscure that it made no impact on other people. Hence, such memories are difficult to measure accurately.

Several theories have been offered to explain *why* older people may have problems with retrieving information from secondary memory. One explanation is that not using the information results in its loss (the **disuse theory**). This theory suggests that information can fade away or decay unless it is exercised, as in the adage, "Use it or lose it." However, this explanation fails to account for the many facts that are deeply embedded in a person's memory store and that can be retrieved even after years of disuse.

A more widely accepted explanation is that new information interferes with the material that has been stored over a period of many years. As we have noted earlier, interference is a problem in the learning or encoding stage. When the older person is distracted while trying to learn new information, this information does not become stored in memory. Poor retrieval may be due to a combination of such distraction during the learning stage and interference by similar or new information with the material being searched in the retrieval stage. Although researchers in this area have not conclusively agreed on any of these explanations, the **interference theory** appears to hold more promise than others for explaining observed problems with retrieval.

IMPROVING COGNITIVE ABILITIES IN OLD AGE

In the Seattle Longitudinal Study described earlier in this chapter, the researchers tested the effects of **cognitive retraining**—teaching research participants how to use various techniques to keep their minds active and maintain good memory skills. This cognitive retraining was based on the premise

of maximizing one's remaining potential, a widely accepted concept in physical aging but only recently applied to cognitive aging. Intellectual activities that involve problem-solving and creativity, such as Scrabble and crossword puzzles, are described by Schaie and colleagues (Willis and Schaie, 1988, 1986; Schaie and Hertzog, 1986) as effective ways for older people to maximize their intellectual abilities. Cognitive performance improved in about 65 percent of participants, and 40 percent who had declined in the preceding 14 years showed a return to their predecline levels. However, the oldest participants benefited least from training, even with booster sessions to assist in the retraining.

There has been considerable experimentation with techniques for improving memory. Some of the most exciting research in this field focuses on developing new drugs that enhance the chemical messengers in neurons or improve the function of neural receptors. Within the next few years there may be some approved memory-enhancing drugs for older adults. Other researchers have examined practical methods such as cognitive aids. Although useful at any age, cognitive aids may be particularly helpful for an older person who is experiencing increased problems with real-world cognitive abilities, such as recalling names, words, phone numbers, and daily chores. Older persons are more likely to use external aids such as notes and lists than they are to use cognitive aids such as imagery and word association. That is, they are more likely to reduce environmental press than to enhance their competence in learning as a means of improving P-E congruence.

Most memory improvement techniques are based on the concept of **mediators**, that is, the use of visual and verbal links between information to be encoded and information that is already in secondary memory. Mediators may be visual (e.g., the method of locations) or verbal (i.e., the use of mnemonics). **Visual mediators**—the method of locations (or loci)—are useful for learning a list of new words, names, or concepts. Each word is associated with a specific location in a familiar environment. For example, the individual is instructed to "walk through" his or her own home mentally. As the person walks through the rooms in succession, each item on the list is associated with a particular space along the way. Older persons using this technique have been found to recall more words on a list than when they use no mediators. One advantage of the method of loci is that learners can visualize the new information within a familiar setting, and can decide for themselves what new concept should be linked with what specific part of the environment. Imaging is a useful technique in everyday recall situations as well. For example, an older person can remember what he or she needs to buy at the grocery story by visualizing using these items while preparing dinner (Camp, 1988).

Another way of organizing material to be learned and to ensure its storage in secondary memory is to use **mnemonics,** or verbal riddles, rhymes, and codes associated with the new information. Many teachers use such rhymes to teach their students multiplication, spelling (e.g., "*i* before *e* except after *c*"), and the calendar ("30 days hath September, April, June, and November/ all the rest have 31, except February alone, and that has 28 days clear/ except every leap year"). There are many other mnemonics that we acquire through experience as well as our own efforts to devise ways to learn a new concept. These can assist older people, especially the young-old, to learn more efficiently, especially if the mnemonics are specific to the memory task at hand (Verhaeghen, Marcoen, and Goossens, 1992). Older people with mild or moderate dementia can also benefit from visual methods of recall (e.g., method of loci), but less from list-making (Yesavage, Sheikh, Friedman, and Tanke, 1990). Whatever method is used, however, it is important to train the older person in the use of a specific mnemonic and to provide easy strategies to help the person apply these techniques to everyday learning events. As an example, one study provided half the sample with a "memory handbook" and 30 minutes of practical instruction, and the other half with just a pamphlet that gave examples of useful mnemonics (but no face-to-face instruction in their use). The former group demonstrated significant improvements in two subsequent memory tests; the pamphlet group did not (Andrewes, Kinsella, and Murphy, 1996).

Other mediators to aid memory include using the new word or concept in a sentence, associating the digits in a phone number with symbols or putting them into a mathematical formula (e.g., "the first digit is 4, the second and third are multiplied to produce the first"), placing the information into categories, using multiple sensory memories, and even combining sensory with motor function. In this last technique, one may write the word (iconic memory), repeat it aloud to oneself (echoic memory), or "feel" the letters or digits by outlining them with one's hand. Unfortunately, many older persons do not practice the use of newly learned memory techniques. They may not be motivated to use the techniques, which often seem awkward, or they may forget and need to be reminded. Perhaps the major problem is that these are unfamiliar approaches to the current generation of older people. As future cohorts become more practiced in these memory techniques through their educational experiences, the use of such strategies in old age should increase.

The most important aspect of memory enhancement may be the ability to relax and to avoid feeling anxious or stressed during the learning stage. As noted earlier, many older people become overly concerned about occasional memory lapses, viewing them as a sign of deterioration and possible onset of senile dementia. Thus, a young person may be annoyed when a familiar name is forgotten, but will probably not interpret the memory lapse as loss of cognitive function, as an older person is likely to do. Unfortunately, society reinforces this belief. How often are we told that we are "getting old" when we forget a trivial matter? How often do adult children become concerned that their parent sometimes forgets to turn off the stove, when in fact they may frequently do this themselves?

In addition to mediators, simple devices or **external aids** are often used by older people to keep track of the time or dates, or to remember to turn the stove on or off. Simple methods like list-making can significantly improve an older person's recall and recognition memory, even if the list is not used subsequently. A list that is organized by topic or type of item (e.g., a chronological "to-do" list or a grocery list that groups produce, meats, dry-goods together) also has been found to aid older people's memory significantly. However, older adults with higher educational attainment and better vocabulary skills benefit even more from list-making methods (Burack and Lackman, 1996). Older people can develop the habit of associating medication regimens with specific activities of daily living, such as using marked pill boxes and taking the first pill in the morning before their daily shower, or just before or after breakfast, taking the second pill with lunch or before their noontime walk, and so on. These behaviors need to be associated with activities that occur every day at a particular time, in order that the pill-taking becomes linked with that routine. Charts listing an individual's daily or weekly routine can be posted throughout the house. Alarm clocks and kitchen timers also can be placed wherever an older person will be while the oven or stove is in operation. This will help in remembering that the appliance is on without having to stay in the kitchen. With the increased availability of home computers, daily activities and prescription reminders could be programmed into an older person's computer. A fire alarm or smoke detector is essential for every older person's home, preferably one for every floor or wing of the house. Finally, for older people who have serious memory problems and a tendency to get lost while walking outdoors, a bracelet or necklace imprinted with the person's name, address, phone number, and relevant medical information can be a lifesaver.

WISDOM AND CREATIVITY

Wisdom and creativity are more difficult to define and measure. Most people have an image of what it means to be wise or creative, but it is impossible to quantify an individual's level of wisdom or creativity. It has been suggested that *wisdom* requires the cognitive development and mastery over a person's emotions that come with age (Butler and Gleason, 1985). Wisdom is a combination of experience, introspection, reflection, intuition, and empathy; these are qualities that are honed over many years and that can be integrated in people's interactions with their environments. Thus, younger people may have any one of these skills, but their integration requires more maturity. Wisdom is achieved by transcending the limitations of basic needs such as health, income, and housing. The individual must have continued opportunities for growth and creativity in order to develop wisdom (Ardelt, 1997; Orwell and Achenbaum, 1993).

Wisdom implies that the individual does not act on impulse and can reflect on all aspects of a given situation objectively. In many cultures, older persons are respected for their years of experience, and the role of "wise elder" is a desired status. But not all older people have achieved wisdom. Wisdom suggests the ability to interpret knowledge, or to understand the world in a deeper and more profound manner. Such reflectiveness and the reduced

In many cultures, old age is viewed as a time of wisdom.

self-centeredness that this requires allow older people to take charge of their lives and become more accepting of their own and others' weaknesses. Indeed, among older men and women in the Berkeley Guidance Study, those who scored high on the three components of wisdom (cognitive, reflective, affective thinking) also scored high on a measure of life satisfaction. This suggests that "successful aging" (described in Chapter 6) is enhanced when wisdom has been attained (Ardelt, 1997). Older people who have achieved this level of wisdom could play a useful role in many businesses and government agencies, where their years of experience and ability to move beyond the constraints presumed by others could help such organizations succeed.

Creativity refers to the ability to apply unique and feasible solutions to new situations, to come up with original ideas or material products. A person may be creative in science, the arts, or technology. Although we can point to creative people in each of these areas (e.g., Albert Einstein in science, Wolfgang Amadeus Mozart and Georgia O'Keeffe in the arts, and Thomas Edison in technology), it is difficult to determine the specific characteristics that make such persons creative. As with intelligence in general, creativity is inferred from the individual's output, but cannot really be quantified or predicted. One measure of creativity is a test of *divergent thinking*, which is part of Guilford's (1967) structural model of intelligence. This is measured by asking a person to devise multiple solutions to an unfamiliar mental task (e.g., name some different uses for a flower). Later still, Torrance (1988) developed a test of creativity that also measures divergent thinking. Children who

scored high on this test were found to be creative achievers as young adults (i.e., the test has good predictive and construct validity), but the test has not been used to predict changes in creativity across the lifespan.

Divergent thinking may be only one component of creativity, however. A creative person must also know much about a particular body of knowledge such as music or art before he or she can make creative contributions to it. However, this neglects the contributions to scientific problem-solving or the arts by people who may have expertise in one area and bring a fresh perspective to a different field. To date, there have been no systematic studies of divergent thinking among people who are generally considered to be creative. Much of the research on creativity has been performed as analyses of the *products* of artists and writers, not on their creative *process* directly. Indeed, no studies have been conducted to compare the cognitive functioning of artists, scientists, technologists, and others who are widely regarded as creative with that of persons not similarly endowed. Researchers who have examined the *quantity* of creative output by artists, poets, and scientists have found that the average rate of output at age 70–80 drops to approximately half that of age 30–40. However, a secondary peak of productivity often occurs in the 60s, although not as high as the first peak (Simonton, 1989; 1991). Indeed, Simonton's analysis of the last works of 172 classical composers in their final years revealed compositions that were judged highly by musicologists in terms of esthetics, melody, and comprehensibility (Simonton, 1989). Mathematicians and theoretical physicists produce their major works

CREATIVITY IN OLD AGE

There are numerous examples of late-life creativity in the arts (e.g., Georgia O'Keeffe, who painted some of her most highly acclaimed pieces in her 80s; and Pablo Picasso, who was productive up to his death at age 91); in the sciences (e.g., Humboldt's last volume of *Cosmos* was completed at age 89); and in gerontology (e.g., Chevreul, who moved from his profession as a chemist to the study of gerontology at age 90 and continued to publish scientific papers at age 100).

in their late twenties and early thirties, whereas novelists, historians, and philosophers reach their peak in their late forties and fifties.

SUMMARY AND IMPLICATIONS

This chapter presented an overview of the major studies on cognitive functioning in the later years. Researchers have examined age-related changes in intelligence, learning, and memory, and what factors in the individual and the environment affect the degree of change in these three areas of cognitive functioning.

Of all the cognitive functions in aging, intelligence has received the greatest attention and controversy. It is also the area of most concern for many older persons. One problem with this area of research is the difficulty of defining and measuring what is generally agreed to be intelligence. In examining the components of intelligence measured by the Wechsler Adult Intelligence Scale (WAIS), fluid intelligence (as measured by performance scales) has been shown to decline more with aging than verbal, or crystallized, intelligence. This may be due partly to the fact that the former tests are generally timed, while the latter are not. However, age differences emerge even when tests are not timed, and when variations in motor and sensory function are taken into account. This decline in fluid intelligence and maintenance of verbal intelligence is known as the Classic Aging Pattern. To the extent that older persons practice their fluid intelligence by using their problem-solving skills, they will experience less decline in this area. In contrast, aging does not appear to impair the ability for remembering word and symbol meanings. This does not imply that the ability to recall words is unimpaired, but when asked for definitions of words, older people can remember their meanings quite readily.

One problem with studying intelligence in aging is that of distinguishing age changes from age differences. To determine changes with age, people must be examined longitudinally. The problems of selective attrition and terminal drop make it diffi-

cult to interpret the findings of longitudinal studies of intelligence. These factors may result in an underestimate of the decline in intelligence with aging. The problem of cross-sectional studies of intelligence is primarily that of cohort differences. Even if subjects are matched on educational level, older persons have not had the exposure to computers and early childhood learning opportunities that have become available to recent cohorts. Other factors, such as occupation, sensory decline, poor physical health, and severe hypertension, have been found to have a significant impact on intelligence test scores.

Learning and memory are cognitive functions that are usually examined because tests of memory are actually tests of what a person has learned. According to the information-processing model, learning begins when information reaches sensory memory, and then is directed via one or more sensory stores to primary memory. It is in primary memory that information must be organized and processed if it is to be retained and passed into secondary memory. Information is permanently stored in this latter region. Studies of recall and recognition provide evidence that aging does not affect the capacity of either primary or secondary memory. Instead, it appears that the aging process makes us less efficient in "reaching into" our secondary memory and retrieving material that was stored years ago. Recognition tasks, in which a person is provided with a cue to associate with an item in secondary memory, are easier than pure recall for most people, but especially for older individuals.

The learning process can be enhanced for older people by reducing time constraints, making the learning task more relevant for them, improving the physical conditions by using bright but glare-free lights and large letters, and providing visual and verbal mediators for learning new information. Helping the older learner to relax and not feel threatened by the learning task also ensures better learning. Such modifications are consistent with the goal of achieving greater congruence between older people and their environment.

Significant age-related declines in intelligence, learning, and memory appear not to be inevitable.

Older people who continue to perform well on tests of intelligence, learning, and memory are characterized by: higher levels of education, good sensory functioning, good nutrition, employment that required complex problem-solving skills, and who continued use of such skills in their later years. People who do not have serious cardiovascular disease or severe hypertension also perform well, although there is some slowing of cognitive processing and response speed. Even such slowing of processing speed is not a problem for older people whose crystallized knowledge in the targeted area is high.

Although there is some agreement that wisdom is enhanced by age and that creativity reaches a second peak for some people in old age, there has been less research emphasis in these areas. Indeed, these concepts are more difficult to measure in young and old persons. These and other issues in cognition must be studied more fully with measures that have good construct validity before gerontologists can describe with certainty cognitive changes that are attributable to normal aging.

GLOSSARY

cognitive retraining   teaching research participants how to use various techniques to keep their minds active and maintain good memory skills

crystallized intelligence   knowledge and abilities one gains through education and experience

cued recall   remembering when some information to aid in the search is provided

disuse theory   the view that memory fades or is lost because one fails to use the information

echoic memory   auditory memory, a brief period when new information received through the ears is stored

external aids   simple devices used by older people to keep track of the time or dates, etc., such as list-making

fluid intelligence   skills that are biologically determined, independent of experience or learning, similar to "native intelligence," requiring flexibility in thinking

free recall   remembering when no aids are provided for retrieving information from secondary memory

iconic memory   visual memory, a brief period when new information received through the eyes is stored

information processing model   a conceptual model of how learning and memory take place

intelligence   the theoretical limit of an individual's performance

intelligence quotient (IQ)   an individual's relative abilities in making judgments, comprehension, reasoning

interference theory   the view that memory fades or is lost because of distractions experienced during learning or interference from similar or new information to the memory sought

mediators   visual and verbal links between information to be memorized and information that is already in secondary memory

mnemonics   the method of using verbal cues such as riddles or rhymes as aids to memory

primary (short-term) memory   a brief storage of newly acquired information; can hold 7±2 stimuli before it is processed into secondary memory or discarded

recall   the process of searching through secondary memory in response to a specific external cue

recognition   matching information in secondary memory with the stimulus information

secondary (long-term) memory   permanent memory store; requires processing of new information to be stored and cues to retrieve stored information

spatial memory   the ability to recall where objects are in relationship to each other in space

tachistoscope   a screen that is timed to present visual stimuli at a specified pace

terminal decline hypothesis   the hypothesis that persons who are close to death decline in their cognitive abilities

visual mediators   the method of locations; memorizing by linking each item with a specific location in space

REFERENCES

Andrewes, D. G., Kinsella, G., and Murphy, M. Using a memory handbook to improve everyday memory in community-dwelling older adults with memory complaints. *Experimental Aging Research,* 1996, *22,* 305–322.

Ardelt, M. Wisdom and life satisfaction in old age. *Journals of Gerontology,* 1997, *52B,* P15–P27.

Aubrey, J. B., and Dobbs, A. R. Age and sex differences in the mental realignment of maps. *Experimental Aging Research*, 1990, *16*, 133–139.

Aubrey, J. B., Li, K. Z. H., and Dobbs, A. R. Age and sex differences in the interpretation of misaligned "You-are-Here" maps. *Journals of Gerontology*, 1994, *49*, P29–P31.

Baddeley, A. *Working memory*. New York: Oxford University Press, 1986.

Baltes, P. B. The aging mind: Potential and limits. *The Gerontologist*, 1993, *33*, 580–594.

Berg, S. Aging, behavior, and terminal decline. In J. E. Birren and K. W. Schaie (Eds.), *Handbook of the psychology of aging* (4th edition). San Diego: Academic Press, 1996.

Binet, A. and Simon, T. Méthodes nouvelles pour le diagnostique du niveau intellectuel des anormaux. *Année Psychologique*, 1905, *11*, 102–191.

Botwinick, J. *Aging and behavior: A comprehensive integration of research findings* (3d ed.). New York: Springer, 1984.

Bruce, P. R., and Herman, J. F. Adult age differences in spatial memory. *Journal of Gerontology*, 1986, *41*, 774–777.

Burack, O. R., and Lackman, M. E. The effects of list-making on recall in young and elderly adults. *Journals of Gerontology*, 1996, *51B*, P226–P233.

Butler, R. N., and Gleason, H. *Productive aging: Enhancing vitality in later life*. New York: Springer, 1985.

Camp, C. J. In pursuit of trivia: Remembering, forgetting, and aging. *Gerontological Review*, 1988, *1*, 37–42.

Canestrari, R. E. Paced and self-paced learning in young and elderly adults. *Journal of Gerontology*, 1963, *18*, 165–168.

Cattell, R. B. Theory of fluid and crystallized intelligence: A critical experiment. *Journal of Educational Psychology*, 1963, *54*, 1–22.

Cerella, J., Poon, L. W., and Fozard, J. L. Age and iconic read-out. *Journal of Gerontology*, 1982, *37*, 197–202.

Cooney, T. M., Schaie, K. W., and Willis, S. L. The relationship between prior functioning on cognitive and personality dimensions and subject attrition in longitudinal research. *Journals of Gerontology*, 1988, *43*, P12–P17.

Craik, F. I. M. Memory changes in normal aging. *Current Directions in Psychological Science*, 1994, *5*, 155–158.

Craik, F. I. M., Jennings, J. M. Human memory. In F. I. M. Craik and T. A. Salthouse (Eds.), *The handbook of aging and cognition*. Hillsdale, NJ: Erlbaum, 1994.

Cunningham, W. R., and Owens, W. A. The Iowa State study of the adult development of intellectual abilities. In K. W. Schaie (Ed.), *Longitudinal studies of adult psychological development*. New York: Guilford Press, 1983.

Dutta, R. *The relationship between flexibility—rigidity and the primary mental abilities*. Unpublished doctoral dissertation. Pennsylvania State University, 1992.

Gold, D. P., Andres, D., Etezadi, J., Arbuckle, T., Schwartzman, A., and Chaikelson, J. Structural equation model of intellectual change and continuity and predictors of intelligence in older men. *Psychology and Aging*, 1995, *10*, 294–303.

Green, R. F. Age-intelligence relationship between ages sixteen and sixty-four. *Developmental Psychology*, 1969, *1*, 618–627.

Gruber-Baldini, A. L. *The impact of health and disease on cognitive ability in adulthood and old age in the Seattle Longitudinal Study*. Unpublished doctoral dissertation. Pennsylvania State University, 1991.

Guilford, J. P. Intelligence: 1965 model. *American Psychologist*, 1966, *21*, 20–26.

Guilford, J. P. *The nature of human intelligence*. New York: McGraw-Hill, 1967.

Horn, J. L. Organization of data on life-span development of human abilities. In L. R. Goulet and P. B. Baltes (Eds.), *Life-span developmental psychology: Research and theory*. New York: Academic Press, 1970.

Horn, J. L. The aging of human abilities. In B. B. Wolman (Ed.), *Handbook of developmental psychology*. Englewood Cliffs, NJ: Prentice-Hall, 1982.

Horn, J. L., and Donaldson, G. Cognitive development in adulthood. In O. G. Brim and J. Kagan (Eds.), *Constancy and change in human development*. Cambridge, MA: Harvard University Press, 1980.

Hultsch, D. F., Hammer, M., and Small, B. J. Age differences in cognitive performance in later life: Relationships to self-reported health and activity lifestyle. *Journals of Gerontology*, 1993, *48*, P1–P11.

Huyck, M. H., and Hoyer, W. J. *Adult development and aging*. Belmont, CA: Wadsworth, 1982.

Inouye, S. K., Albert, M. S., Mohs, R., and Sun-Kolie, R. Cognitive performance in a high-functioning, community-dwelling elderly population. *Journals of Gerontology*, 1993, *48*, M146–M151.

Jarvik, L. F., and Falek, A. Intellectual stability and survival in the aged. *Journal of Gerontology,* 1963, *18,* 173–176.

Johansson, B., Zarit, S. H., and Berg, S. Changes in cognitive functioning of the oldest old. *Journals of Gerontology,* 1992, *47,* P75–P80.

Jones, H. E. Intelligence and problem-solving. In J. E. Birren (Ed.), *Handbook of aging and the individual: Psychological and biological aspects.* Chicago: University of Chicago Press, 1959.

Kallmann, F. J., and Sander, G. Twin studies on senescence. *American Journal of Psychiatry,* 1949, *106,* 29–36.

Kleemeier, R. W. Intellectual change in the senium. *Proceedings of the Social Statistics Section of the American Statistical Association,* 1962, *1,* 290–295.

Labouvie-Vief, G., and Blanchard-Fields, F. Cognitive aging and psychological growth. *Aging and Society,* 1982, *2,* 183–209.

Larue, A., Koehler, K. M., Wayne, S. J., Chiulli, S. J., Haaland, K. Y., and Garry, P. J. Nutritional status and cognitive functioning in a normally aging sample: A 6-year reassessment. *American Journal of Clinical Nutrition,* 1997, *65,* 20–29.

Lindenberger, U., and Baltes, P. B. Sensory functioning and intelligence in old age. *Psychology and Aging.* 1994, *9,* 339–355.

McDowd, J. M., and Craik, F. I. M. Effects of aging and task difficulty on divided attention performance. *Journal of Experimental Psychology: Human Perception and Performance,* 1988, *14,* 267–280.

Orwoll, L., and Achenbaum, W. A. Gender and the development of wisdom. *Human Development,* 1993, *36,* 274–296.

Owens, W. A. Age and mental abilities: A longitudinal study. *Genetic Psychology Monographs,* 1953, *48,* 3–54.

Owens, W. A. Age and mental ability: A second adult follow-up. *Journal of Educational Psychology,* 1966, *57,* 311–325.

Palmore, E. (Ed.). *Normal aging II: Reports from the Duke longitudinal study.* Durham, NC: Duke University Press, 1974.

Palmore, E. (Ed.). *Normal aging III: Reports from the Duke longitudinal study.* Durham, NC: Duke University Press, 1985.

Poon, L. W. Differences in human memory with aging: Nature, causes, and clinical implications. In J. E. Birren and K. W. Schaie (Eds.), *Handbook of the psychology of aging* (2nd ed.). New York: Van Nostrand Reinhold, 1985.

Rabbitt, P., Donlan, C., Watson, P., McInnes, L., and Bent, N. Unique and interactive effects of depression, age, socioeconomic advantage, and gender on cognitive performance of normal healthy older people. *Psychology and Aging,* 1995, *10,* 307–313.

Ratner, H. H., Schell, D. A., Crimmins, A., Mittleman, D., and Baldinelli, L. Changes in adults' prose recall: Aging or cognitive demands. *Developmental Psychology,* 1987, *23,* 521–525.

Rebok, G. W. *Life-span cognitive development.* New York: Holt, Rinehart and Winston, 1987.

Reese, H. W. Models of memory development. *Human Development,* 1976, *19,* 291–303.

Ross, E. Effects of challenging and supportive instructions on verbal learning in older persons. *Journal of Educational Psychology,* 1968, *59,* 261–266.

Salthouse, T. A. Age-related differences in basic cognitive processes: Implications for work. *Experimental Aging Research,* 1994a, *20,* 249–255.

Salthouse, T. A. Aging of working memory. *Neuropsychology,* 1994b, *8,* 535–543.

Salthouse, T. A. Effects of age and skill in typing. *Journal of Experimental Psychology: General,* 1984, *113,* 345–371.

Salthouse, T. A. General and specific speed mediation of adult age differences in memory. *Journals of Gerontology,* 1996, *51B,* P30–P42.

Salthouse, T. A. Speed and knowledge as determinants of adult age differences in verbal tasks. *Journals of Gerontology,* 1993, *48,* P29–P36.

Salthouse, T. A., and Babcock, R. L. Decomposing adult age differences in working memory. *Developmental Psychology,* 1991, *27,* 763–776.

Sands, L. P., and Meredith, W. Blood pressure and intellectual functioning in late midlife. *Journals of Gerontology,* 1992, *47,* P81–P84.

Schaie, K. W. Age changes and age differences. *The Gerontologist,* 1967, *7,* 128–132.

Schaie, K. W. *Intellectual development in adulthood: The Seattle Longitudinal Study.* Cambridge: Cambridge University Press, 1996a.

Schaie, K. W. Intellectual development in adulthood. In J. E. Birren and K. W. Schaie (Eds.), *Handbook of the psychology of aging.* (4th edition). San Diego: Academic Press, 1996b.

Schaie, K. W. The hazards of cognitive aging. *The Gerontologist*, 1989, *29*, 484–493.

Schaie, K. W. The primary mental abilities in adulthood: An exploration in the development of psychometric intelligence. In P. B. Baltes and O. G. Brim, Jr. (Eds.), *Life-span development and behavior* (Vol. 2). New York: Academic Press, 1979.

Schaie, K. W. The Seattle Longitudinal Study: A 21-year exploration of psychometric intelligence in adulthood. In K. W. Schaie (Ed.), *Longitudinal studies of adult psychological development*. New York: Guilford Press, 1983.

Schaie, K. W., and Hertzog, C. Toward a comprehensive model of adult intellectual development: Contributions of the Seattle Longitudinal Study. In R. J. Sternberg (Ed.), *Advances in human intelligence* (Vol. 3). Hillsdale, NJ: Erlbaum, 1986.

Schaie, K. W., and Labouvie-Vief, G. V. Generational versus ontogenetic components of change in adult cognitive behavior: A fourteen-year cross-sequential study. *Developmental Psychology*, 1974, *10*, 305–320.

Schaie, K. W., Plomin, R., Willis, S. L., Gruber-Baldini, A., and Dutta, R. Natural cohorts: Family similarity in adult cognition. In T. Sonderegger (Ed.), *Psychology and aging: Nebraska symposium on motivation*. Lincoln: University of Nebraska Press, 1992.

Schaie, K. W., and Willis, S. L. Perceived family environments across generations. In V. L. Bengston, K. W. Schaie, and L. Burton (Eds.), *Societal impact on aging: Intergenerational perspectives*. New York: Springer, 1995.

Sharps, M. J., and Gollin, E. S. Aging and free recall for objects located in space. *Journals of Gerontology*, 1988, *43*, P8–P11.

Siegler, I. C. Psychological aspects of the Duke Longitudinal Studies. In K. W. Schaie (Ed.), *Longitudinal studies of adult psychological development*. New York: Guilford Press, 1983.

Simonton, D. K. Career landmarks in science: Individual differences and interdisciplinary contrasts. *Developmental Psychology*, 1991, *27*, 119–127.

Simonton, D. K. The swan-song phenomenon: Last works effects for 172 classical composers. *Psychology and Aging*, 1989, *4*, 42–47.

Smith, A. D. Memory. In J. E. Birren and K. W. Schaie (Eds.), *Handbook of the psychology of aging* (4th ed.). San Diego: Academic Press, 1996.

Spearman, C. *The abilities of man: Their nature and measurement*. New York: Macmillan, 1927.

Torrance, E. P. The nature of creativity as manifest in its testing. In R. J. Sternberg (Ed.), *The nature of creativity: Contemporary psychological perspectives*. Cambridge: Cambridge University Press, 1988.

Verhaeghen, P., Marcoen, A., and Goossens, L. Improving memory performance in the aged through mnemonic training: A meta-analytic study. *Psychology and Aging*, 1992, *7*, 242–251.

White, N., and Cunningham, W. R. Is terminal drop pervasive or specific? *Journals of Gerontology*, 1988, *43*, P141–P144.

Willis, S. L., and Schaie, K. W. Gender differences in spatial ability in old age: Longitudinal and intervention findings. *Sex Roles*, 1988, *18*, 189–203.

Willis, S. L., and Schaie, K. W. Training the elderly on the ability factors of spatial orientation and inductive reasoning. *Psychology and Aging*, 1986, *2*, 239–247.

Yesavage, J. A., Sheikh, J. I., Friedman, L., and Tanke, E. Learning mnemonics: Roles of aging and subtle cognitive impairment. *Psychology and Aging*, 1990, *5*, 133–137.

Zelinski, E. M., Gilewski, J. J., and Schaie, K. W. Individual differences in cross-sectional and 3-year longitudinal memory performance across the adult life span. *Psychology and Aging*, 1993, *8*, 176–186.

6

PERSONALITY AND MENTAL HEALTH IN OLD AGE

We have all had the experience of watching different people respond to the same event in different ways. For example, you probably know some students who are extremely anxious about test-taking while others are calm, and some students who express their opinions strongly and confidently while others rarely speak in class at all. All these characteristics are part of an individual's personality.

Personality may be defined as a unique pattern of innate and learned behaviors, thoughts and emotions that influence how each person responds and interacts with the environment. An individual may be described in terms of several personality traits, such as passive or aggressive, introverted or extroverted, independent or dependent. Personality may be evaluated with regard to particular standards of behavior; for example, an individual may be described as adapted or maladapted, adjusted or maladjusted. Personality characteristics affect people's interactions with their environments.

In this chapter we examine normal developmental change and stability in personality across

the lifespan, and then focus on some personality and psychiatric disorders found in older people. Theories of personality that have considered age-related stability and change are examined. The manner in which personality characteristics may change or remain stable through interactions with the social environment are discussed. The following questions are considered: Are personality characteristics both innate and capable of developing throughout life? To what extent do an individual's interactions with the environment change his or her personality or reveal the individual's "true self" that may have been concealed because of social pressures to conform to particular norms? The ways in which self-concept and self-esteem are affected by these normal changes in personality with aging are also reviewed. Conditions that result in successful aging, or help us reach an advanced old age with optimal physical, functional, cognitive, and social skills, are identified.

Although personality remains relatively stable with normal aging, some older people who showed no signs of psychopathology earlier in their lives may experience some types of mental disorders in late life. For other older people, psychiatric disorders that they experienced in their younger years may continue or may re-emerge. In some individuals the stresses of old age may compound any existing predisposition to psychopathology. These stresses may be internal, resulting from the physiological and cognitive changes described in previous chapters, or external, that is, a function of role losses and the deaths of partners, friends, and especially one's children. These conditions significantly impact older people's competence, so that they become more vulnerable to environmental press and less able to function at an optimal level.

Personality styles influence how we cope with and adapt to the changes we experience as we age. The process of aging involves numerous stressful life experiences. How an older person attempts to alleviate such stress has an influence on that individual's long-term well-being. The person-environment congruence model presented in Chapter 1 suggests that our behavior is influenced and modified by the environment, and that we shape the environment around us. An individual's behavior is often quite different from one situation to another, and depends both on the social norms and expectations of each situation and on that person's needs and motives. Unfortunately, few researchers have examined this reciprocal relationship in adult development.

STAGE THEORIES OF PERSONALITY

Erikson's Psychosocial Model

Most theories of personality have emphasized the developmental **stages** of personality and imply that the social environment influences development. As we focus on stages of adult development, however, it is important to avoid the image of rigid, immutable stages and transitions that are inevitable, with no room for individual differences. In fact, people *do* make choices regarding their specific responses to common life changes. This results in numerous expressions of behavior under similar

life experiences such as adolescence, parenting, retirement, and even the management of chronic diseases. There has been disagreement about whether this pattern of development continues through adulthood. Sigmund Freud's focus on psychosexual stages of development through adolescence has had a major influence on developmental psychology. In most of his writings, Freud suggests that personality achieves stability by adolescence. Accordingly, adult behavior is a reflection of unconscious motives and unsuccessful resolution of early childhood stages.

In contrast, Erik Erikson, who was trained in psychoanalytic theory, moved away from this approach and focused on psychosocial development throughout the life cycle. According to his model (Erikson, 1963, 1968, 1982, 1986), the individual undergoes eight stages of development of the ego. Three of these are beyond adolescence, with the final stage occurring in mature adulthood. At each stage the individual experiences a major task to be accomplished and a conflict; the conflicts of each stage of development are the foundations of successive stages. Depending on the outcome of the crisis associated with a particular stage, the individual proceeds to the next stage of development in alternative ways. Erikson also emphasized the interactions between genetics and the environment in determining personality development. His concept of the *epigenetic principle* assumed an innate plan of development in which people proceed through stages as they become cognitively and emotionally more capable of interacting within a wider social radius. Hence, each subsequent stage requires additional cognitive and emotional development before it can be experienced (Erikson, 1963).

As shown in Table 6.1, the individual in the last stage of life is confronted with the task of **ego integrity versus despair**. According to Erikson, the individual at this stage accepts the inevitability of mortality, achieves wisdom and perspective, or despairs because he or she has not come to grips with death and lacks ego integrity. A major task associated with this last stage is to integrate the experiences of earlier stages and to realize that one's

TABLE 6.1   **Erikson's Psychosocial Stages**

	STAGE	GOAL
I	Basic trust vs. mistrust	To establish basic trust in the world through trust in the parent.
II	Autonomy vs. shame and doubt	To establish a sense of autonomy and self as distinct from the parent; to establish self-control vs. doubt in one's abilities.
III	Initiative vs. guilt	To establish a sense of initiative within parental limits without feeling guilty about emotional needs.
IV	Industry vs. inferiority	To establish a sense of industry within the school setting; to learn necessary skills without feelings of inferiority or fear of failure.
V	Ego identity vs. role diffusion	To establish identity, self-concept, and role within the larger community, without confusion about the self and about social roles.
VI	Intimacy vs. isolation	To establish intimacy and affiliation with one or more others, without fearing loss of identity in the process that may result in isolation.
VII	Generativity vs. stagnation	To establish a sense of care and concern for the well-being of future generations; to look toward the future and not stagnate in the past.
VIII	Ego integrity vs. despair	To establish a sense of meaning in one's life, rather than feeling despair or bitterness that life was wasted; to accept oneself and one's life without despair.

life has had meaning, whether or not it was "successful" in a socially defined sense. Older people who achieve ego integrity feel a sense of connectedness with younger generations, and share their experiences and wisdom with them. This may take the form of face-to-face interactions with younger people, counseling, mentoring, sponsoring an individual or group of younger people, or writing memoirs or letters. This latter has been described as *life review*, and has been found to be a useful mode of therapy with older adults, as we describe later in this chapter.

Life satisfaction, or the feeling that life is worth living, may be achieved through these tasks of adopting a wider historical perspective upon one's life, accepting one's mortality, sharing experiences with the young, and leaving a legacy to future generations.[*] Erikson's theory provides a framework for studying personality in late life because it suggests that personality is dynamic throughout the life cycle. Indeed, this theory fits the person-environment model; we interact with a variety of other people in different settings, and our personality is affected accordingly.

Jung's Psychoanalytic Perspective

Carl Jung's model of personality also assumes changes throughout life, as expressed in the following statement from one of his early writings:

> We cannot live the afternoon of life according to the program of life's morning, for what was great in morning will be little at evening, and what in the morning was true will at evening have become a lie (1933, p. 108).

[*]Researchers have found that health, marital, and financial status, as well as the availability of a confidant, are also significant predictors of life satisfaction.

Jung's model emphasizes stages in the development of consciousness and the ego, from the narrow focus of the child to the other-worldliness of the older person. Jung suggests that the ego moves from *extraversion,* or a focus on the external world in youth and middle age when the individual progresses through school, work, and marriage, to *introversion,* or to a focus on one's inner world in old age. Like Erikson, Jung examined the individual's confrontation with death in the last stage of life. He suggested that life for the aging person must naturally contract, that the individual in this stage must find meaning in inner exploration and in an afterlife. In contrast to the young, older persons have "a duty and a necessity to devote serious attention to (themselves). After having lavished its light upon the world, the sun withdraws its rays in order to illuminate itself" (Jung, 1933, p. 109). Jung (1959) also focused on changes in **archetypes** with age. That is, according to Jung, all humans have both a feminine and a masculine side. An archetype is the feminine side of a man's personality (the anima) and the masculine side of a woman's personality (the animus). As they age, people begin to adopt psychological traits more commonly associated with the opposite sex. For example, older men may show more signs of passivity while women may become more assertive as they age, a change that has been observed in some empirical studies of personality and aging.

Empirical Testing of These Perspectives

In testing the validity of these theories, subsequent research has contributed to our understanding of personality development in late adulthood. Many of these studies are cross-sectional; that is, they derive information on age *differences,* not age changes. There are notable exceptions to this approach, including the Baltimore Longitudinal Study (described in Chapter 1) and the Kansas City Studies, which have examined changes in physiological, cognitive, and personality functions in the same individuals over a period of several years. Research by Costa and McCrae (1986; 1994) in the Baltimore Longitudinal Study is re-

lated to Erikson's work in that it has identified changes in *adjustment,* with age, but stability in specific traits (described later in this chapter). Cross-sectional studies by McAdams and De St. Aubin (1995), and by Peterson and Klohnen (1995), have examined age differences in **generativity,** Erikson's seventh stage. These researchers have consistently found middle-aged and older adults to express more generative concerns (i.e., attributing more importance to the care of younger generations than self-development) than young adults. "Generative adults" exhibit concerns not just toward their own children, but toward the young in society.

Other researchers have found support for Jung's observations regarding decreased sex-typed behavior in old age. David Gutmann (1977, 1980, 1992), who has studied personality across the life span in diverse cultures from a psychoanalytic perspective, has found a shift from **active mastery** to **passive mastery** as men age. In contrast, women appear to move from passive to active mastery. That is, young adult males tend to be more achievement-oriented, to take more risks, to be more competitive, and to be concerned with controlling their environments, whereas young adult women tend to be more affiliative and expressive. Gutmann found greater expressiveness, nurturance, and need for affiliation and accommodation among older males than in younger men, whereas older women tended to be more instrumental and to express more achievement-oriented responses than young women. The increased passivity of older men may allow them to explore their inner worlds and move beyond the external orientation of their younger years (Gutmann, 1992). Another longitudinal study that has found support for stage theories of personality is the Grant study of Harvard University graduates (Vaillant, 1977, 1994; Vaillant and Vaillant, 1990). This study followed 268 men, beginning in 1938 when they were students, through age 65 when 173 of the men were still available to take part in these life reviews and qualitative interviews. These men were observed to follow a common pattern of stages—from the establishment of a professional identity in their twenties and thirties, to career consolidation in their forties, to exploration of their inner worlds in midlife (a major transition similar to the stage of ego integrity versus despair that Erikson described as occurring in late life). Men who were most emotionally stable and well adjusted in their fifties and sixties had experienced greater generativity (i.e., responsibility for and care of co-workers, children, charity), were less sex-stereotyped in their social interactions, and were more nurturant and expressive. These changes have implications for contemporary family roles and responsibilities, as discussed in Chapter 9.

The Kansas City Studies

One of the first longitudinal studies of personality in middle and old age was conducted by Neugarten and her associates in the 1950s and 1960s. The "Kansas City Studies of Aging" have contributed to our understanding of many age-related changes in personality and coping. These researchers found that older men became more accepting of their affiliative, nurturant, and sensual side, while women learned to display the egocentric and aggressive impulses that they had always possessed but had not displayed during their younger years. Neugarten, similar to Jung and Gutmann, has suggested that these characteristics always exist in both sexes, but social pressure and societal values encourage the expression of more sex-typed traits in youth.

The Kansas City studies represented the first major attempt to examine personality longitudinally and provided the empirical basis for activity and disengagement theories described in Chapter 8. They found changes in such personality characteristics as nurturance, introversion, and aggressiveness in the later years. Contrary to popular stereotypes, aging was also associated with greater differences (individuation) among individuals; as people aged, they developed more unique styles of interaction. Neugarten and colleagues (1968) suggested that people do not resemble each other more in old age, but in fact become more differentiated because they grow less concerned about societal expectations. Other age-related changes observed in the Kansas City studies included shifts toward greater cautiousness and interiority; that is, a preoccupation with one's inner life and less extroversion, as suggested by Jung.

The Kansas City researchers also observed decreased impulsiveness and a movement toward using more sophisticated ego defense mechanisms with age. For example, older persons tended to use less denial and more sublimation. Attitudes toward the world were also likely to change with age, but these were found to relate closely to personal experiences. For instance, people do not necessarily become more conservative as they age. Based on generational (cohort) differences and personal experiences, some persons become more liberal while others adopt a more conservative social perspective during the later years. These age-related changes in impulsiveness, types of defense mechanisms used, and attitudes have been supported in studies of personality by researchers examining a diverse variety of cultural and ethnic minority groups (Shanan and Jacobowitz, 1982; Gaber, 1983; Thomae, 1992). Many of the changes attributed to personality in old age, such as preference for solitude or slower paced activities, are not personality traits per se, but lifestyle preferences that are influenced by life experiences, opportunities, and functional health status.

Dialectical Models of Adult Personality

Another model of adult personality development has been proposed by Levinson (1977, 1986) and his colleagues (Levinson et al., 1978). This model is based on secondary analyses of American men described in published biographies and in interviews with working-class men. It has also been found to apply to women (Roberts and Newton, 1987). In contrast to Erikson, who focused on stages of ego development, Levinson and colleagues have examined developmental stages in terms of **life structures,** or the underlying characteristics of a person's life at a particular period of time. Of all stage theories of adult development, this model is the most explicit in linking each stage with a specific range of chronological age. Each period in the life structure (defined as "eras" by Levinson) represents developmental stages. Levinson defines four eras, each one lasting about 20 years. These are separated by *transitions* of about 5 years each which generally occur as the individual perceives changes in the self, or as external events such as childbirth and retirement create new demands on one's relationships with others. (See Table 6.2.)

Levinson's model represents an example of a *dialectical approach* to personality development; it proposes that change occurs because of interactions between a dynamic person (one who is biologically *and* psychologically changing) and a dynamic environment. To the extent that an individual is sensitive to the changing self, he or she can respond to changing environmental or societal conditions by altering something within the self or by modifying some expectations from the environment. This process thereby reestablishes equilibrium with the environment. For example, older people who deny the normal biological and physiological changes they are experiencing may have difficulty in modifying their lifestyles and moving into a different developmental phase.

TRAIT THEORIES OF PERSONALITY

Another perspective on personality is to examine characteristic behaviors that reflect specific **traits** within individuals. Traits are relatively stable characteristics of personality; together they make up a constellation that distinguishes each individual. For example, we can describe people along a continuum of personality attributes such as extroverted to introverted, passive to aggressive, and optimistic to pessimistic.

This assumption of stability has led trait researchers to examine personality traits longitudinally in the middle and later years. Proponents of this approach are McCrae and Costa (1984, 1990), who have measured specific traits of participants in the Baltimore Longitudinal Studies (described in Chapter 1). They propose a five-factor model of personality traits, consisting of five primary, independent components: neuroticism, extraversion, openness to experience, agreeableness, and conscientiousness. Within each component are six facets or subcategories of traits. For example, neuroticism consists of anxiety, impulsiveness, self-consciousness, hostility, depression, and vulnerability. People with high neurotic tendencies would score high on these factors also.

TABLE 6.2   Levinson's "Seasons" of Life

Era I	Preadulthood (Age 0–22)
	(An era when the family provides protection, socialization, and support of personal growth)
	Early Adult Transition (Age 17–22)*
Era II	Early Adulthood (Age 17–45)
	(An era of peak biological functioning, development of adult identity)
	Entering the adult world, entry life structure for early adulthood
	Age 30 transition*
	Settling down, culminating life structure for early adulthood
	Mid-Life Transition (Age 40–45)*
Era III	Middle Adulthood (Age 40–65)
	(Goals become more other–oriented, compassionate roles, mentor roles assumed; peak effectiveness as a leader)
	Entering life structure for middle adulthood
	Age 50 transition*
	Culmination of middle adulthood
	Late Adulthood Transition (Age 60–65)*
Era IV	Late Adulthood (Age 60+)
	(An era when declining capacities are recognized, anxieties about aging, loss of power and status begin)
	Acceptance of death's inevitability

*Indicates major transitions to a new developmental era.

SOURCE: D. Levinson, C. M. Darrow, E. B. Klein, M. H. Levinson, and B. McKee, *The seasons of a man's life* (New York: Alfred A. Knopf, 1978). Reprinted with permission of the author and publisher.

Standardized tests such as the Guilford-Zimmerman Temperament Survey (GZTS) are used to compare individuals with population norms on these traits. By administering the GZTS to subjects in the Baltimore Longitudinal Studies, researchers found great stability in the five traits described above. Using a cross-sectional approach, they also identified consistency in these traits in middle-aged and older adults. Both groups differed from young adults on some personality factors (McCrae and Costa, 1984; Costa and McCrae, 1995, 1994). Other studies support the lifelong stability, and even the possible heritability of some personality traits. For example, a study of middle-aged identical and fraternal twins in Sweden found similarities in their personality characteristics, whether they were reared together or apart. In particular, traits of emotionality, activity, sociability, extroversion, and neuroticism varied in the same manner within each pair of twins (Plomin et al., 1988; Pederson et al., 1988).

There is also some evidence of cohort and cultural influences on personality traits. Using a cross-sequential research design (described in Chapter 1), Schaie and Willis (1991) found few changes in specific traits of the same individuals over 7 years, but they did find cohort differences. That is, the oldest group in the first wave were less flexible and adaptable than were the same older persons in the second wave of testing 7 years later. Cultural factors may also play a role in the development of certain traits. For example, traditional societies, including the United States before the women's liberation movement of the 1960s, reinforced "agreeableness" as a trait in women; the associated cluster of personality factors such as altruism, compliance, modesty, and tender-mindedness are viewed in traditional societies as important "feminine" traits. However, as women move into more diverse roles and enter occupations that were once considered "masculine," there is less gender stereotyping of traits. Similarly, as cultural barriers disappear through the globalization of media, music, fashion and food (e.g., the McDonaldization of the world), there appears to be a "universal adolescent" personality that is

Maintaining an active lifestyle can enhance an older person's self-confidence.

emerging. In a major cross-cultural study of 6000 adolescents in ten countries, Offer and colleagues (1988) found high levels of self-confidence, sociability, ability to cope, and caring for others across these widely divergent cultures. Whether such cross-cultural similarities will persist across the life span is, of course, unknown.

SELF-CONCEPT AND SELF-ESTEEM

A major adjustment required in old age is the ability to redefine one's **self-concept** or one's cognitive image of the self as social roles shift and as new roles are assumed. Our self-concept emerges from our interactions with the social environment, our social roles, and accomplishments. Through continuous interactions with the environment, people can confirm or revise these self-images, either by *assimilating* new experiences into their self-concept, or through *accommodating* or adjusting their self-concept to fit the new reality. The latter is more difficult and requires greater adaptive skills

(Whitbourne and Primus, 1996). For example, how does a retired teacher identify himself or herself upon giving up the work that has been that individual's central focus for the past 40 or 50 years? How does a woman whose self-concept is closely associated with her role as a wife express her identity after her husband dies?

Many older persons continue to identify with the role that they have lost (think of those who continue to introduce themselves as a "teacher" or "doctor" long after retiring from those careers). This would represent a type of identity assimilation. Others experience role confusion, particularly in the early stages of retirement, when cues from other people are inconsistent with an individual's self-concept. This may require identity accommodation. Still others may undergo a period of depression and major readjustment to the changes associated with role loss. To the extent that a person's self-concept is defined independently of particular social roles, one adapts more readily to the role losses that may accompany old age. Both assimilation of new social roles to a stable self-concept, and some accommodation to changing realities, are indicators of successful adaptation of one's self-concept.

For an older person whose self-concept is based on social roles and others' expectations, role losses have a particularly significant impact on that individual's **self-esteem**—defined as an evaluation or feeling about his or her identity relative to some ideal or standard. *Self-esteem* is based on an emotional assessment of the self, whereas *self-concept* is the cognitive definition of one's identity. The affective quality of self-esteem makes it more dynamic and more easily influenced by such external forces as retirement, widowhood, health status, and reinforcements (both positive and negative) from others (e.g., respect, deference, or ostracism). Social roles integrate the individual to society and add meaning to one's life. As a result, alterations in social roles and the loss of status that accompanies some of these changes often have a negative impact on an older person's self-esteem. Think, for example, of an older woman whose social roles have included that of caregiver to her family. If she herself be-

comes dependent on others for care because of a major debilitating illness such as a stroke or dementia, she is unwittingly robbed of this "ideal self," and her self-esteem may suffer.

An individual who experiences multiple role losses must not only adapt to the lifestyle changes associated with aging (e.g., financial insecurity or shrinking social networks), but must also integrate the new roles with his or her "ideal self" or learn to modify this definition of "ideal." Older persons who are experiencing major physical and cognitive disabilities simultaneously with role losses, or worse yet, whose role losses are precipitated by an illness (e.g., early retirement due to stroke or institutionalization because of Alzheimer's disease), must cope with multiple problems at a time in their lives when they have the fewest resources to resolve them successfully. Depression is not an uncommon reaction in these cases, as discussed later in this chapter.

Some studies have shown a generalized decrease in self-esteem from age 50 to 80, although many others have found improvement from adolescence through the young-old period. These varied findings may be attributed to the cross-sectional nature of research on self-esteem and age (Giarrusso and Bengtson, 1996). Stressful life events and severe hearing loss can impair self-esteem among older people (Tran, Wright, and Chatters, 1991; Chen, 1994). For example, older people who are socially isolated and have significant physical disabilities have been found to have the poorest self-esteem (Pinquart, 1991). The following personality factors have been suggested as important to maintaining self-esteem in the later years:

1. Reinterpretation of the meaning of self, such that an individual's self-concept and self-worth are independent of any roles he or she has played ("I am a unique individual" rather than "I am a doctor/teacher/wife").

2. Acceptance of the aging process, its limitations, and possibilities. That is, individuals who realize that they have less energy and respond more slowly than in the past, but that they can still participate in life, will adapt more readily to the social and health losses of old age.

3. Reevaluation of one's goals and expectations throughout life. Too often people establish life goals at an early age and are constantly disappointed as circumstances change. The ability to respond to internal and external pressures by modifying life goals appropriately reflects flexibility and harmony with one's environment.

4. The ability to look back objectively on one's past and to review one's failures and successes. *Life review* entails an objective review and evaluation of one's life. An older person who has this ability to review past experiences and how these have influenced subsequent personality development, behavior, and interpersonal relationships can call upon coping strategies that have been most effective in the past and adapt them to changed circumstances.

STRESS, COPING, AND ADAPTATION

The process of aging entails numerous life changes, as noted in this and previous chapters. These changes, both positive and negative, place demands on the aging person's abilities to cope with and adapt to new life situations. Together with health and cognitive functioning, personality characteristics influence coping responses. Self-concept and self-esteem are two important elements that play a role in coping styles, and may help explain why some older people adjust readily to major life changes, while others have difficulty with such transitions. Indeed, self-esteem, health, and cognitive skills all contribute to an individual's sense of competence. Major life events and situations represent environmental stressors that place demands on an individual's competence. These and other factors that influence adaptation in old age are discussed in this section.

Some Useful Definitions

Before examining coping and adaptation in old age, it is important to clarify and define some key concepts. The concept of **life events** (or *life experiences*) forms the basis for this section. These

terms refer to internal or external stimuli that cause some change in our daily lives. They may be positive or negative, gains or losses, discrete or continuous. Examples of internally created events include changes in eating or sleeping habits and the effects of a chronic disease such as arthritis or diabetes. Externally initiated events might include starting a new job, losing one's job, or retirement.

Improvement in one's own health or in a family member's health are examples of positive life events, whereas deteriorating health and death are negative events. Some life experiences may have both positive *and* negative aspects. For example, older workers may view their pending retirement with great joy and make numerous plans for the post-retirement years; however, there are some negative consequences as well, including reduced income, unstructured time, and loss of the worker role.

Another distinction is made between *on-time* and *off-time* events (Neugarten, 1985). This concept distinguishes life experiences that a person can anticipate because of one's stage in the life cycle (on-time) from those that are unexpected at a given stage (off-time). Other researchers have used the terms *normative* and *non-normative* events, suggesting that an individual anticipates some life experiences because they are the norm for most people of a given age. Thus, for example, a man married to a 75-year-old woman is more likely to expect the death of his wife than is the husband of a 35-year-old woman. A 50-year-old woman is more likely than a 35-year-old to anticipate the onset of menopause and its accompanying physiological and psychological changes. As shown later in this chapter, researchers have found differences in how people respond to on-time and off-time events.

The concept of *stress,* as defined in Chapter 4, is also important for this chapter. Since Selye's (1946) introduction of this term, many researchers have explored the antecedents, components, and consequences of stress. In fact, Selye (1970) defined aging as the sum of stresses experienced across one's lifetime. It is important to note that not everyone perceives the same events to be stressful. Lazarus and DeLongis (1983) have introduced the concept of *cognitive appraisal*—the way in which a person perceives the significance of an encounter for his or her well-being. Cognitive appraisal serves to minimize or magnify the importance or stressfulness of an event by attaching some meaning to it. If a situation is construed as benign or irrelevant by an individual, it does not elicit coping responses. On the other hand, if a person appraises a situation as challenging, harmful, or threatening, it becomes a stressor, and calls upon the individual's adaptation responses.

It is useful to distinguish between positive and negative stressors such as life events. The concept of cognitive appraisal suggests that a person who perceives a particular situation as a challenge (i.e., a positive stressor) copes differently with it than one who views it as a threat (i.e., a negative stressor). For example, an older woman who moves voluntarily to a retirement apartment may view it as an exciting and desirable change in her lifestyle, or she may resent the change as too demanding and disruptive. In the former case, she will adapt more readily and will experience less negative stress than in the latter. On the other hand, if this person views the move as totally benign and does not expect it to place any demands on her, she will probably be unpleasantly surprised by the level of stress that she eventually encounters, no matter how minimal.

Aging and Life Events

Life events are identifiable, discrete life changes or transitions that demand adaptation by the individual, because they disrupt one's person-environment balance or homeostasis. Some researchers have made a distinction between life events and chronic stressors, such as poor health and financial difficulties: both types of stressors require adaptive or coping skills (McLeod, 1996). There has been much discussion among researchers about the nature of life events in the later years, the older person's ability to cope with them, and whether old age is associated with more or fewer life events than youth. Many significant life events tend to occur more often in old age, such as widowhood,

retirement, and relocation to a nursing home. The nature of such roles and the novelty associated with assuming a social role for the first time result in major changes in an individual's daily functioning and demand adaptation to the new situation. Few studies have compared the relative stressfulness of role losses, role gains or replacements, and role extensions in old age, although there is extensive research on life stress among younger populations. Chapter 11 examines both paid and unpaid productive roles in the later years in greater detail.

The first systematic studies of the physiological and psychological impact of increased sources and amounts of stress on humans were undertaken by Holmes and colleagues (Holmes and Rahe, 1967; Rahe, 1972; Holmes and Masuda, 1974). They introduced the concept of *life change units*, a numerical score indicating the typical level of change or stress that a particular event produces in an individual's day-to-day life. Indeed, they found a relationship between life change units and physical health. Holmes and Rahe derived the social readjustment rating scale (SRRS), which consists of 43 events, each with an associated change score. Their research with young and middle-aged adults revealed that people who experienced multiple events with life change units totaling more than 200 points within a 2-year period were more susceptible to physical illness.

Potential Problems in Measurement of Stress

It is unclear whether these same life events produce the same level of stress in older persons as they do in younger people. Many of them are less likely to be experienced in old age (e.g., jail term, marriage, assuming a new mortgage, or beginning or ending school). Furthermore, the life change units assigned to some events by the young respondents in Holmes and Rahe's sample may not reflect the degree of stress actually produced by events that they have not yet experienced (e.g., death of a partner). Subsequent researchers have developed and tested life-event scales that are more relevant to older adults (Amster and Krauss, 1974; Muhlenkamp, Gress, and Flood, 1975; Kiyak and Kahana, 1975). Kiyak and Kahana kept many of the original SRRS items, but also added some items that were appropriate for older persons, and compared the weights assigned to these events by older persons and by college students (median ages 70 and 20).

Table 6.3 presents comparisons across some items that were common to all the scales. The relative stress of some items remains constant across the studies; for example, death of spouse received the highest readjustment score in all four. Young and old respondents, however, appear to perceive the stressfulness of an event differently, as illustrated by the significant differences between these groups in Table 6.3; note how marital reconciliation and death of a close friend were perceived to be more stressful by younger respondents. Furthermore, older people who had experienced significant life events such as retirement and death of a spouse assigned lower readjustment scores to these events than other older or younger respondents. These findings suggest that the anticipation of an event is more stressful than the actual experience, and that previous experience with a life event can help the person cope better when a similar event occurs. In addition, older people have developed greater resilience and maturity through their previous experiences coping with life events; they may be the most adaptive members of their

cohort because they have survived beyond the life expectancy predicted for their birth cohort (McLeod, 1996).

Although researchers have focused on the stress produced by major life events, Lazarus and Cohen (1977) have suggested that most people experience stress as a result of "chronic daily hassles." Their "hassles scale" measures such day-to-day problems as feelings of loneliness, lack of energy, regrets over past decisions, and concerns about one's current situation. These are generally not specific events with a beginning or end point, but are chronic and may occur simultaneously with other "hassles." To the extent that an older person feels powerless, lonely, and regretful, feelings of stress will increase, with a corresponding need to adapt to the situation in some way. Lazarus and Cohen have not reported differences in the frequency with which older persons experience such chronic feelings in comparison to younger persons.

One aspect of life events that has not been explored with older adults, but which may influence psychological well-being, is the impact of anticipated events that do not materialize. That is, how do older persons respond after anticipating a major event and then discovering that it will not take place? One can list many such events, both positive and negative, that may result in stress if they do not occur. For example, anticipating relocation to a nursing home from the hospital, an older

TABLE 6.3 **Comparison of Life Change Units**

| EVENT | SRRS | KIYAK AND KAHANA | | AMSTER AND KRAUS | MUHLENKAMP, GRESS, AND FLOOD |
		Young	Old		
Death of spouse	100	88 *	79	125	73
Marriage	50	78 *	64	50	50
Marital reconciliation	45	65 *	47	39	35
Death of a close friend	37	67 *	47	50	52
Change in residence	20	59 *	51	43	39
Financial problems	38	68 *	59	56	43
Improved financial status	38	59 *	48	56	43

person may direct family members to sell his or her home and its furnishings. What happens if a suitable nursing home is not found, and family members put pressure on the person to move in with them? What is the impact of learning just a few days before a major holiday that a family gathering anticipated eagerly by an older person must be canceled? Variables such as an individual's level of anticipation and availability of optional outcomes undoubtedly play a role in reactions to these situations. Research on how people of different ages cope with such "non-events" is needed.

What Determines Stress Responses in Old Age?

The manner in which we respond to life events, role changes, and chronic daily hassles depends on many personal and environmental factors. As noted above, one variable is the cognitive appraisal of a situation by an individual as being stressful or not. The relative desirability or undesirability of an event, whether or not it is anticipated, and previous experiences with similar events may determine how an individual responds to the situation. The availability of social supports also is significant (Coyne and Downey, 1991). A person who must face all challenges alone may use different coping strategies than one who has family and friends to turn to in times of crisis.

Both social and personal factors affect the process of coping with stressful events. The former includes friendships and family support, while the latter includes the individual's functional health, cognitive status, and self-esteem, as well as aspirations, values, vulnerabilities, and needs that mediate between a particular stressful situation and its outcomes. For example, an older woman whose partner has recently died after a long illness will be more likely to rely on others if she has a strong need for dependency *and* if she has family and friends who encourage such dependency. If, on the other hand, she is highly independent and/or has no strong social network on which she

has relied for past help, she will be more likely to use instrumental, self-initiated coping strategies (e.g., find out more about the problem or learn new skills to solve it), and less likely to ask others to assist her in her grieving process.

Personality styles also may influence how people respond to stress. Earlier in this chapter, Gutmann's (1977, 1980, 1992) research on active and passive mastery styles was described. A person with a passive style does not feel powerful enough to directly influence his or her fate, whereas one with an active style tends to rely more on personal abilities and less on others. Differences in responses to stress by older people with these different styles would be expected; however, research has not provided sufficient evidence for such hypothesized variations.

Another personality characteristic that may influence how successfully people respond to stress is *locus of control*. This is the belief by an individual that events in his or her life result from personal actions (internal locus), or are determined by fate or powerful others (external locus). Internal locus of control has been found to be related to successful coping in both young and old, and appears to remain stable in the young-old (Thomae, 1992).

Adaptation in the Later Years

As noted earlier in this chapter, a critical personality feature in the later years is an individual's ability to adapt to major changes in life circumstances, in health and social status, and in social and physical environments. **Adaptation** includes a range of behaviors such as coping, goal setting, problem solving, and other attempts to maintain psychological homeostasis (Ruth and Coleman, 1996). Given older people's numerous experiences with life events, role loss, and environmental changes throughout life, it would appear that adaptation in old age should occur with relative ease. Indeed, in one sense, an individual who has reached age 75 or 80 has proved to be the most adaptable of his or her generation, since the ultimate proof of adaptation is survival. As we have seen thus far, older people continue to face challenges to their well-being in the form of personal and family illness, age-related declines in sensory and physiological functions, and changes in their social and physical environments. To the extent that older people are capable of using coping skills that were effective in youth and middle age, they will continue to adapt to change successfully.

Does coping change with age? Before answering, we must first define and consider the functions of **coping.** Coping is the manner in which a person responds to stress. It includes cognitive, emotional, and behavioral responses made in the face of internally and externally created events. It differs from defense mechanisms in that people are generally conscious of how they have coped in a particular situation and, if asked, can describe specific coping responses to a given stressor. Coping strategies may be described as "planful behavior" in response to a stressful situation. These contrast with **defense mechanisms,** unconscious reactions that an individual adopts to defend or protect the self from impulses and memories that threaten one's identity. Defense mechanisms also have an underlying evaluative quality; some defenses are more primitive or less mature than others (see

Table 6.4). Thus, for example, a young child is more likely to use the defense mechanisms of denial and projection, or to need to view threatening impulses as present in others, not in the self. As people mature, so do the defense mechanisms that they use. The Grant Study of Harvard Graduates, described earlier, found that the men in this sample used fewer primitive mechanisms (e.g., projection) as they reached middle-age, and more mature mechanisms, such as sublimation, suppression, and humor (Vaillant, 1994).

Unlike defense mechanisms, coping styles cannot easily be categorized as primitive or mature. Some forms of coping, however, are aimed not at resolving the problem, but at providing psychological escape, as illustrated by the categories of coping defined by some researchers (see Table 6.5). For example, an older man who is confronted with the news that he has lung cancer may cope by eating or sleeping more, or by taking a vacation to "get away from it all." This response may alleviate the stressful feeling, but it does not aid in the treatment of the cancer.

Our earlier discussion of coping responses to life events and chronic stressors suggests that coping reactions generally serve two functions: to solve a problem that has produced stress for the

TABLE 6.4   Major Ego Defense Mechanisms

DEFENSE MECHANISM	EXAMPLE
1. Denial (a premature defense mechanism)	Denying what one really feels to avoid punishment by the super-ego and rejection by others.
2. Projection	Feeling that others are untrustworthy when one feels unsure about one's own trustworthiness.
3. Repression	Forgetting an event that could disturb the feeling of well-being if brought into consciousness.
4. Reaction formation	Extreme display of love and affection toward someone who is actually hated.
5. Regression and fixation	Returning to a comfortable stage of life and/or way of behaving under conditions of anxiety and stress.
6. Displacement	Taking out one's anger and hostility on family because one is afraid of expressing anger toward one's supervisor at work who has humiliated the individual.

TABLE 6.5   Classification of Coping Responses

GENERAL STRATEGIES OF COPING
(Lazarus, 1975a, 1975b; Lazarus and Launier, 1978; Lazarus and Folkman, 1984)

1. Information search in an attempt to understand the situation
2. Direct action to change the situation
3. Inhibition of action
4. Psychological responses to the emotional arousal created by the situation

COPING RESPONSES TO TERMINAL ILLNESS
(Moos, 1977)

1. Searching for information
2. Setting goals
3. Denying or minimizing the problem
4. Seeking emotional support
5. Rehearsing alternative outcomes

DIMENSIONS OF COPING
(Kahana and Kahana, 1982)

1. Instrumental (taking action, alone or with the assistance of others)
2. Intrapsychic (cognitive approaches, acceptance of the situation)
3. Affective (releasing tensions, expressing emotions)
4. Escape (avoiding or denying the problem, displacement activities such as increased exercise, eating, and smoking)
5. Resigned helplessness (feeling impotent, unable to cope)

individual, and to reduce the emotional and physiological discomfort that accompanies the stressful situation. These have been defined as problem-focused and emotion-focused coping (Lazarus and Folkman, 1984). In some cases, an individual may focus only on solving the problem *or* on dealing with the emotional distress that it creates. Such reactions tend to be incomplete and do not resolve

both the emotional and functional impact of the situation. Coping must fulfill both emotion-regulating and problem-solving functions in order to alleviate stress.

The question of whether coping styles change with age has not been extensively researched. Some early studies of coping among young and middle-aged persons have reported few significant differences, although these groups have generally not been compared with older persons (Folkman et al., 1987). Older (ages 65 to 91) and middle-aged (ages 50 to 64) respondents in McCrae's (1989) study used more mature coping styles (e.g., problem-solving, and seeking the advice of family, friends, and professionals) and fewer escapist strategies than did younger (ages 24 to 49) respondents. Other cross-sectional studies have also found age differences. For example, older persons are less likely than the young to use confrontation as a coping response, especially when the stressor could be defined as a threat. They are more likely to use distancing techniques and to reappraise the situation in a positive light (Folkman et al., 1987; Irion and Blanchard-Fields, 1987). In the Baltimore and the Bonn Longitudinal Studies, cross-sectional differences were greater than intra-individual change. In both studies—the former, examining adults over a 7-year period, the latter over 10 years—coping responses remained quite stable (McCrae, 1989; Thomae, 1992). In particular, coping styles related to the personality characteristic of neuroticism remain stable over 7 years, even though cross-sectional comparisons reveal that older respondents in general use *less* neurotic coping (Costa and McCrae, 1993). These results highlight the importance of examining coping styles within the same individual over time. Indeed, there may be some support for the hypothesis that at least some coping styles are part of an individual's basic personality. The finding of stability in coping styles with age does not imply that older people cannot select the appropriate coping response to a given situation. For example, caregivers of older persons with Alzheimer's disease use a diverse range of coping styles (Kiyak et al., 1985). Similarly, women aged 55 to 65 in stressful

Religious activity can serve a useful coping function.

situations have been found to use a variety of coping responses, including turning to work or religion or ignoring the problem (Griffith, 1983).

Religious coping has been found to be an important coping strategy in several studies of older persons, especially among African Americans (McCrae, 1989, 1984; McFadden, 1996). Indeed, in the Duke Longitudinal Study, 45 percent of the respondents aged 55 to 80 mentioned trust and faith in God, prayer, and seeking help from God as a coping strategy for at least one of the three major life events they had experienced. Over 70 percent of adults have been found to use religion in coping with major life events. Religious coping among church-going adults has been found to significantly predict their recent mental health and perceived general health (Pargament et al., 1990; 1995).

Studies of coping among the old-old have concluded that acceptance of change in one's life (e.g., institutionalization, divorce of children or grandchildren) may be the most adaptive coping response. Control over external events may be-

come less important than the need to make uncontrollable events more acceptable to one's values and beliefs (Ryff, 1989b, 1991). In most cases, the coping styles chosen by an older person are appropriate for the problem at hand and result in successful adaptation. When cognitive deterioration is significant, however, there is a restriction in the range of an individual's coping responses and a tendency to resort to more primitive reactions, such as denying or ignoring the problem. The majority of older people appear capable of using a wide repertoire of coping responses and can call upon the most effective ones for a given situation. In sum, the available research suggests that most people maintain their coping styles into old age, and use appropriate responses for the problem at hand.

SUCCESSFUL AGING

Researchers and clinicians have become increasingly interested in the concept of **successful aging** (Rowe and Kahn, 1987, 1997; Seeman et al., 1994). This interest has been sparked by the growing number of older people who have avoided the chronic health problems and declining cognitive skills that afflict other older adults and have managed to cope effectively in their daily lives. What are the characteristics of such elders who age successfully that distinguish them from their less hardy peers? Successful aging has been defined as a combination of physical and functional health, high cognitive functioning, and active involvement with society. Implicit in this definition is that the successful older person has low risk of disease and disability (i.e., healthy lifestyle factors such as diet, not smoking, physical activity), is actively using problem-solving, conceptualization, and language skills, is maintaining social contacts, and is participating in productive activities (e.g., volunteering; paid or unpaid work). A model of successful aging proposed by Rowe and Kahn (1997), shown in Figure 6.1, integrates these components.

The MacArthur Studies of Successful Aging have examined longitudinally a cohort of men and

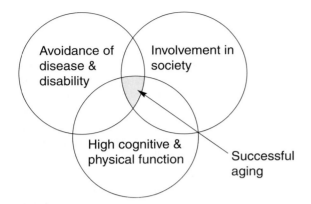

FIGURE 6.1 **A model of successful aging. This model assumes that all three components must exist for successful aging to occur.** SOURCE: Adapted from Rowe & Kahn, 1997.

women (aged 70 to 79 at baseline) in three Eastern U.S. communities. These people were selected because they represented the top third of their age group in several areas of cognitive and physical function. Within this selective group of "robust" older persons, more specific tests of cognitive and physical abilities, as well as physiological parameters, were conducted in 1988 and 1991. Those with the highest performance scores in this group at follow-up and those who survived 3 years later had fewer chronic conditions (especially cardiovascular diseases), better self-rated health, and higher educational and income levels. The majority of these robust older adults reported no problems with activities of daily living such as walking ¼ mile without stopping, lifting a 10-pound weight, and crouching and stooping without help. Three-year follow-ups revealed that the majority (55 percent) maintained their baseline performance levels. Another 23 percent showed a decline on the performance tests, while 22 percent actually *improved* on these tests. Those who declined or died in the interim had greater weekly variability in their physical performance, blood pressure, balance, and gait, and had entered the study with some chronic diseases (Seeman et al., 1994; Nesselroade, Featherman, Agen, and Rowe, 1996).

As noted above, successful aging also implies maintenance of cognitive functioning. In the MacArthur Studies, the best predictor of continued high levels of cognitive ability was educational level (Albert et al., 1995). Rather than innate intelligence, higher educational achievement in those who aged successfully was most likely due to life-long interest in intellectual activities such as reading and solving crossword puzzles, as well as a beneficial effect of education on the development of complex networks in the brain. Other predictors of maintaining cognitive abilities were involvement in strenuous physical activity at home (this may occur because physical exercise appears to increase brain-derived neurotrophic factor in the hippocampus and neocortex, thereby enhancing central nervous system functions). A higher level of self-efficacy, that is, a feeling of competence in one's ability to deal with new situations, was also a significant predictor (Rowe and Kahn, 1997).

The Oregon Brain Aging Study, a longitudinal assessment of a smaller number of optimally healthy persons aged 65 to 74 and 84 to 100, has measured multiple physical, cognitive, neurologic, and sensory functions as indicators of healthy aging (Howieson et al., 1993). This group of older adults was selected because they had no history of diseases affecting brain function, no psychiatric disorders, or medications that could impair cognition. The researchers found very few areas of decline in this group of healthy elders; the oldest-old differed from the youngest-old only on tests requiring visual perception and constructional skills, *not* on tests of memory or reasoning.

A broader perspective on successful aging, one that considers exceptional functioning on measures of physical health, cognitive abilities, and emotional well-being, is represented by the concept of "robust aging" (Vaillant and Vaillant, 1990; Suzman et al., 1992; Garfein and Herzog, 1995). Four important characteristics appear to distinguish robust older adults from their less-robust peers (Garfein and Herzog, 1995): productive involvement (defined as 1500 hours or more of paid or unpaid work, home maintenance, or

Gerontologists have recently focused on identifying the characteristics of people who age successfully.

Erikson describes in the eighth stage of adult development. It requires that older persons continue their active involvement with society that is the hallmark of the seventh stage, i.e., generativity. Research with older adults participating in the Foster Grandparents Program revealed that people who have aged successfully believe they have achieved higher-order needs, such as helping children, making a difference in others' lives, and feeling that one's life has a purpose (Fisher, 1995). These are elements of both generativity and ego integrity, and support the importance of both types of developmental tasks for successful aging.

MENTAL DISORDERS AMONG OLDER PERSONS

The primary affective or emotional disorder of old age is depression, which accounts for a significant number of suicides, especially among older men. Alzheimer's disease and other dementias are cognitive disorders that are far more likely to affect the old than the young. Alcoholism and drug abuse are less common in older individuals, although their effect on the physical health and cognitive functioning of older people is more detrimental than on younger persons. Paranoid disorders and schizophrenia are conditions that are first diagnosed in youth or middle age. Each of these conditions is reviewed in the following sections.

The prevalence of psychiatric disorders among older persons who are living in the community ranges from 15 to 25 percent, depending on the population studied and the categories of disorders examined. Even higher rates can be expected in the institutionalized older population, with estimates of 10 to 40 percent of people with mild to moderate impairments, and another 5 to 10 percent with significant impairments. Twenty percent of all first admissions to psychiatric hospitals are persons over age 65. Older psychiatric patients are more likely to have chronic conditions and to require longer periods of inpatient treatment than are younger patients, as evidenced by the fact that 25 percent of all beds in these

volunteer activity in the past year), absence of depressive symptoms (i.e., high affective well-being), high physical functioning, and no cognitive impairment. In the survey by Garfein and Herzog, the robust group included many in the oldest-old age range. Robust elders reported more social contacts, better physical health and vision, and fewer significant life events (e.g., death of partner, child, close friend) in the past 3 years than did poorly functioning elders.

Fisher (1995) and Ryff (1989a) also have emphasized that a sense of purpose or contribution to society is a critical element of successful aging. They note that this sense of purpose requires more than reflection, acceptance, and ego integrity as hospitals are occupied by older persons. Note the discrepancy between this proportion and the proportion over age 65 in the U.S. population—12.6 percent in 1990. It has been estimated that 100,000 older chronic psychiatric patients live in state mental hospitals, 500,000 in nursing homes, and the remainder (over 1 million) in the community, where they often receive inadequate treatment for their psychiatric condition (Butler, Lewis, and Sunderland, 1991). At the same time, however, older persons are less likely than the young to use community mental health services. Older patients comprise only 4 percent of the load of psychiatric outpatient clinics and less than 2 percent of those served by private practitioners (Butler et al., 1991).

One problem with describing the prevalence of mental disorders of older people is the lack of criteria distinguishing conditions that emerge in old age from those that continue throughout adulthood. In fact, the major classification system for psychiatric disorders, the *Diagnostic and Statistical Manual,* fourth edition (DSM-IV), of the American Psychiatric Association (1994), makes such a distinction only for dementias that begin in late life. No other mental disorders are distinguished for old age, although other diagnostic categories are described specifically for adulthood as separate from childhood or adolescence. The problem of inadequate criteria for late-life **psychopathology** (or psychiatric disorders) is compounded by the lack of age-appropriate psychological tests for diagnosing these conditions. An increasing number of researchers, however, are developing such measures, especially for diagnosing depression and dementia in older people.

Depression

The three most prevalent forms of late-life psychopathology are depression, dementia, and paranoia. Of these, **depression** is the most common. It is important to distinguish *unipolar* depression from *bipolar* disorders (that is, ranging from a depressed to a manic state), as well as severe conditions such as sadness, grief reactions, and other affective disorders. Most of the depressions of old age are unipolar; manic-depressive disorders are rare. Still other cases in late life are *secondary* or *reactive* depressions, which arise in response to a significant life event with which the individual cannot cope. For example, physical illness and the loss of loved ones through death and relocation may trigger depressive reactions in older people (Phifer and Murrell, 1986). The vegetative signs, suicidal thoughts, weight loss, and mood variations from morning to night that are observed in major depression are not found in reactive depression. Studies of older individuals in community settings and in nursing homes suggest that the prevalence of major depression is generally lower than the rates of minor or reactive depression. Estimates of 20 percent for minor depression, 1 percent for major depression, and 0.1 percent for bipolar disorder have emerged from these studies; rates as high as 10 to 15% have been found among institutionalized older adults, however (Parmelee, Katz, and Lawton, 1992; Jefferson and Greist, 1993; Koenig and Blazer, 1996).

As noted earlier in this chapter, most role *gains* (e.g., worker, driver, voter, partner, or parent) occur in the earlier years, whereas many role *losses* may multiply in the later years. As we have seen, loss of roles may be compounded by decrements in sensory abilities, physical strength, and health. Although depression usually does not result from any one of these alone, the combination of several losses in close sequence may trigger a reactive depressive episode. This may be due to changes in the brain caused by multiple stressors that affect the production of mood-regulating chemicals in the brain. It appears that acute life events can lead to a recurrence of major depression, but do not necessarily trigger its first onset (Kessler, 1997). Older people with major physical conditions such as stroke, cancer, or chronic pain, and those who do not have a supportive social network are at greatest risk. Among elders who are hospitalized for physical health problems, 10 percent have been found to have major depression, and 30 percent minor depression (NIH, 1994; Koenig and Blazer, 1996). In addition, older people who have experienced depression in the past are at risk for a recurrence, especially if it is triggered by a major life event (Gurland, 1992).

If the psychiatric symptoms persist beyond six months in these patients, this may indicate the development of a major depressive episode (Nacoste and Wise, 1991). Consistent with the approach of a better fit between the older person and the environment, environmental and social interventions as well as psychotherapy are more effective than antidepressant medications for minor depression; however, medications and sometimes electroconvulsive therapy are necessary to treat major depression and prevent suicide, as described later in this chapter.

Death rates appear to be greater among older persons with a diagnosis of depression, almost twice that for nondepressed people over 20 years (Gurland, 1992). Medical hospital stays are often twice as long for those with depression. In addition, depressed older adults take longer to recover from a hip fracture or stroke (Koenig and Blazer, 1996). Some older persons with depression are more apathetic, less interested in their environments, and more likely to entertain thoughts of suicide than younger depressives.

The most obvious signs of major depression are reports or evidence of sadness and feelings of emptiness or detachment with no precipitating major life event such as bereavement. Also common are expressions of anxiety or panic for no apparent cause, loss of interest in the environment, and neglect of self-care, as well as changes in eating and sleeping patterns. The depressed person may complain of vague aches and pains, either generally or in a specific part of the body. Occasional symptoms or symptoms associated with a specific medication, physical illness, or alcoholism need to be distinguished from the somatic complaints associated with depression. Only when multiple symptoms appear together and persist *for at least 2 weeks* should an individual and his or her family suspect major depression, especially if an older person speaks frequently of death or suicide. The symptoms of a major depression are listed in Table 6.6.

TABLE 6.6 Summary of DSM-IV Criteria for Major Depressive Episode

At least five of the following symptoms are present during the same 2-week period and represent a change from previous function:

1. Depressed mood most of day, nearly every day[*]
2. Markedly diminished interest or pleasure in activities, apathy[*]
3. Significant weight loss or weight gain, or appetite change
4. Sleep disturbance (insomnia or hypersomnia) nearly every day
5. Agitation or retardation of activity nearly every day
6. Low energy level or fatigue nearly every day
7. Self-blame, guilt, worthlessness
8. Poor concentration, indecisiveness
9. Recurrent thoughts of death, suicide

[*]At least one of the symptoms should be these.

SOURCE: Adapted with permission from the *Diagnostic and statistical manual of mental disorders,* 4th ed. Copyright 1994 American Psychiatric Association, 327.

One problem with detecting depression in older people is that they may be more successful than their younger counterparts at masking or hiding symptoms. In fact, many cases of depression in older persons are not diagnosed because the individual either does not express changes in mood or denies them in the clinical interview. A *masked depression* is one in which few mood changes are reported. Instead, the patient complains of a vague pain, bodily discomfort, and sleep disturbance; reports problems with memory; is apathetic; and withdraws from others (Gallo, Anthony, and Muthen, 1994; Lichtenberg, Ross, Millis, and Manning, 1995). This is a common condition in older generations because many of these people were raised in environments that discouraged open expression of feelings.

Health care professionals and family members need to distinguish depression from medical conditions and changes due to normal aging. For example, an older woman with arthritis who complains of increasing pain may actually be seeking a reason for vague physical discomfort that is related to a depressive episode. People with masked depression are more likely to complain of problems with memory or problem-solving. Their denial or masking of symptoms may lead the physician to assume that the individual is experiencing **dementia,** a condition that is generally irreversible. It is for this reason that depression in older persons is often labeled *pseudo-dementia.*

Because of such likelihood of denial, a physician's first goal with an older patient who has vague somatic and memory complaints should be to conduct a thorough physical exam and lab tests. This is important in order to determine if an individual is depressed or has a physical disorder or symptoms of dementia. If the cognitive dysfunction is due to depression, it will improve when the depression is treated. On the other hand, some medical conditions, including Parkinson's, rheumatoid arthritis, thyroid dysfunction, and diseases of the adrenal glands, may produce depressive symptoms. In some cases, depression can co-exist with medical conditions such as heart disease and stroke, compounding the dys-

function associated with these medical problems and delaying the recovery process. Certain medications may also produce feelings of depression; these include antihypertensives, digoxin, corticosteroids, estrogens, some antipsychotic drugs, and antiparkinsonism drugs such as L-dopa. In fact, any medication that has a depressant effect on the central nervous system can produce depressive symptoms in older patients, specifically lethargy and loss of interest in the environment. For these reasons, it is important that older people with depressive symptoms be examined thoroughly for underlying physical illness, hypothyroidism, vitamin deficiencies, chronic infections, and reactions to medications. Physicians must frequently conduct medication reviews to determine if their older patients begin to show side effects to a drug, even after using it for several months or years.

THERAPEUTIC INTERVENTIONS   It is important to treat both major and secondary depressions upon diagnosis, because the older depressed patient is at higher risk of self-destructive behavior and suicide. The first task of physicians or mental health professionals who diagnose depression in an older person is to provide psychological sup-

---

SEEKING A DIAGNOSIS

Often, older people who show symptoms of depression may deny any problems. Family, friends, and professionals who interact with the older person can help get an accurate diagnosis and appropriate treatment. The following actions are recommended.

1. If the symptoms shown in Table 6.6 have persisted long after a negative life event, it is probably not a reaction to the loss. Seek out a medical evaluation by a specialist in geriatric psychiatry or psychology.
2. If the older person resists the initial or subsequent visits to the geriatric mental health specialist, emphasize to the person that depression

is *not* a normal process of aging and can be treated.
3. Explore the most appropriate treatment for each patient; antidepressant medications may be the treatment of choice for one older person, but group psychotherapy may be best for another.
4. Whatever treatment is selected, give it time to work. The patient should not be discouraged if medications do not improve moods immediately, or if they have side effects initially. It may require changing the dosage several times before an ideal level is found for that particular patient.

port for acute symptoms, including empathy, attentive listening, and encouragement of active coping skills. For patients with minor depression, this may be all they need to show a decrease in symptoms. For more severely depressed elders, however, alternative therapies may be required. There is some disagreement, however, about the efficacy of such therapies. Although short-term improvements may be achieved through treatment, the long-range prognosis is not always successful, and some older people will experience a relapse (Gurland, 1992). If the onset of depression occurs before age 70, psychotherapy is generally more successful.

The most common therapeutic intervention with depressed older individuals is pharmacological, which is particularly useful for those experiencing a major depression (NIH, 1994). Therapy with antidepressants is generally long-term. Although antidepressants work well for some older persons, many others cannot use these drugs because of other medications they are taking, such as antihypertensives, or because the side effects are more detrimental than the depression itself. These effects include postural hypotension (i.e., a sudden drop in blood pressure when rising from a prone position), increased vulnerability to falls and fractures, cardiac arrhythmias, urinary retention, constipation, disorientation, skin rash, and dry mouth. Because of these potentially dangerous reactions, it is important to start antidepressant therapy at a much lower dose (perhaps 50 percent lower) in older than in younger patients. Many older persons who turn to a general practitioner for treatment of depression often receive antidepressants as a first line of attack rather than psychotherapy, which may be more appropriate. There is increased evidence that a combination of well-monitored pharmacotherapy and psychotherapy can produce a decrease in symptoms in up to 80 percent of older adults (Koenig and Blazer, 1996).

Older people are just as likely as younger persons to benefit from the insight and empathy provided by a therapist trained in geriatric psychotherapy (Scogin and McElreath, 1994). In particular, secondary depression responds well to supportive psychotherapy that allows the patient to review and come to terms with the stresses of late life. Supportive psychotherapy is useful because it allows older patients to reestablish control and emotional stability. Older depressed persons appear to benefit from short-term, client-centered, directive therapy more than from therapy that is nondirective or uses free association to uncover long-standing personality conflicts. Cognitive-behavioral interventions, such as self-monitoring of negative thoughts about oneself, daily monitoring of moods, and increased participation in pleasant events, have been found to be especially effective with older depressed persons (Teri et al., 1997; DeVries, 1996). These methods can help them overcome the anxieties, fears, guilt, and apathy that are so detrimental to their interpersonal functioning.

As noted above, psychotherapy must be accompanied by **pharmacotherapy** or **electroconvulsive therapy** in severely depressed elders. Despite past controversy about its use, electroshock or electroconvulsive therapy (ECT) is sometimes used in cases of severe depression. ECT is regarded as a quick method for major depression in patients who have not responded to medications, who have a higher risk of suicide, and/or who refuse to eat. Older patients with severe agitation, vegetative symptoms, or feelings of hopelessness, helplessness, worthlessness, and delusions often respond well to ECT. Clinical reports cite the effectiveness of ECT for patients over age 60 (Benbow, 1989). On the other hand, some psychiatrists have avoided using ECT with older patients because of its potentially harmful effects on memory. It also poses risks for patients with a recent myocardial infarction, stroke, or severe hypertension. Risks to memory function apply in particular when bilateral ECT (i.e., shock to both sides of the brain) is administered. Unilateral nondominant hemisphere ECT is often preferred because it is capable of alleviating depression without impairing cognitive functioning (Koenig and Blazer, 1996). It may be necessary to provide maintenance ECT for older depressed persons (as often as once a month), and, in some cases, follow up with antidepressants after a course of ECT to prevent relapse.

Suicide among Older People

It has been estimated that 17 to 25 percent of all reported suicides occur in persons aged 65 and older. In 1994, the national rate was 12 suicides per 100,000 population. The rate for persons over age 65 was over 18 per 100,000, ranging from 15.3 for those aged 65 to 74, to 23 per 100,000 among those over age 85 (Blazer and Koenig, 1996; McIntosh, 1997). The highest suicide rates in the United States are found among older white males. The prevalence of suicide in this population group, 38.9 per 100,000, is more than twice the rate for nonwhite males (15.6), seven times the rate for older white women (5.8), and 14 times the rate for older nonwhite women (2.8). Older white men are at even greater risk than younger men aged 15 to 24, who have the second highest rate of suicide (24.1 per 100,000). Both white and nonwhite older men account for 81 percent of all suicides among the population aged 65 and older. Note that these statistics reflect direct or clearly identifiable suicides. There are probably a significant number of indirect suicides that appear to be accidents or natural deaths (e.g., starvation or gas poisoning), and cases where family members and physicians do not list suicide as the cause of death when the conditions are questionable; therefore these rates may underrepresent the actual incidence of the problem.

One explanation for the higher rates of suicide among older white males is that they generally experience the greatest incongruence between their ideal self-image (that of worker, decision-maker, or holder of relatively high status in society) and the realities of advancing age. With age, the role of worker is generally lost, chronic illness may diminish one's sense of control, and an individual may feel a loss of status. Social isolation also appears to be important; suicide rates among older widowed men have been found to be more than five times greater than for married men, but

no differences have been found between married and widowed women (Li, 1995). This is because older widowed men are most likely to lack strong social support networks. Older men in ethnic minority populations such as African American, Chinese, and Filipino are less likely to commit suicide because of more extensive family support systems. Suicide risk is greatest among white males who are widowed, aged 85 and older, with recurrent major depression, and with chronic pain, cardiopulmonary diseases, or cancer (Zweig and Hinrichsen, 1993; Blazer and Koenig, 1996). However, contrary to popular belief, older suicide victims are no more likely than other older people to have been diagnosed with a terminal illness prior to the suicide.

Suicide rates declined among the older population from 1940 to 1980, but rose by 9 percent from 1980 to 1994, especially among men over age 80. It is difficult to explain this reversal in trends; the growing availability of firearms, greater acceptance of suicide by society, and lack of strong social supports among unmarried older men have been suggested as reasons. There are fewer nonfatal suicide attempts in older men compared to the young. That is, the rate of completed suicides is far greater among older men—one for every eight attempts, compared with one completed suicide for every 100 to 200 attempts by the young. This difference may be due to the use of more lethal methods of suicide such as shotguns; 70 percent of suicides among older men in 1994 involved firearms (Adamek and Kaplan, 1996; McIntosh, 1997).

Because attempts at suicide are more likely to be successful in older men, it is important for family members and health care providers to be sensitive to clues of an impending suicide. In one study of older persons who had committed suicide, 75 percent had seen a primary care physician in the preceding month, but their psychiatric disturbances had not been detected or were inadequately treated. In most cases, these older persons had not sought psychiatric care. This study reported that less than 14 percent of older men who committed suicide had sought treatment from a mental health care provider (Conwell and Caine, 1991). Family members should be aware of risk factors for suicide, such as a serious physical illness with severe pain, the sudden death of a loved one, a major loss of independence, or financial inadequacy. Statements that indicate frustration with life and a desire to end it, a sudden decision to give away one's most important possessions, and a general loss of interest in one's social and physical environment must be attended to closely by those who are familiar with the older person. Since older people are less likely to make threats or to announce their intentions to commit suicide than are young people, it is even more important to watch for subtle cues. Clearly, not all older people displaying such symptoms will attempt suicide, but the recognition of changes in an older family member's or client's behavior and moods can alleviate a potential disaster.*

Dementia

As stated in Chapter 5, normal aging does not result in significant declines in intelligence, memory, and learning ability. Mild impairments do not necessarily signal a major loss but often represent a mild form of memory dysfunction known as **benign senescent forgetfulness.** Only in the case of the diseases known collectively as the dementias does cognitive function show marked deterioration. Dementia includes a variety of conditions that are caused by or associated with damage of brain tissue, resulting in impaired cognitive function and, in more advanced stages, impaired behavior and personality. Such changes in the brain result in progressive deterioration of an individual's ability to learn and recall items from the past. Previously, it was assumed that all these syndromes were associated with cerebral arteriosclerosis ("hardening of the arteries"). In fact, we

now know that a number of these conditions occur independently of arteriosclerosis. Some features are unique to each type of dementia, but all dementias have in common a change in an individual's ability to recall events in recent memory, and problems with comprehension, attention span, judgment, and orientation to time, place, and person. The individual with dementia may experience increased concreteness of thought (i.e., be unable to understand abstract thought or symbolic language; for example, he or she cannot interpret a proverb), particularly in the later stages of the disease.

Although not part of normal aging, the likelihood of experiencing dementia does increase with advancing age. Depending on the criteria used, estimates range from two to three million people over age 65 having some type of dementia; almost 2 million have severe dementia, and up to 5 million are mildly to moderately impaired (Hendrie, 1997; Teri, McCurry, and Logsdon, 1997). Because of problems in differentially diagnosing dementia, and differences in the criteria used by available tests and classification systems, prevalence rates can vary from 3 to 29 percent of the older population (Erkinjuntti, Ostbye, Steenhuis, and Hachinski, 1997). Nevertheless, there is general agreement among epidemiological studies that the incidence of dementias increases with age, especially between ages 75 and 90. For example, it is estimated that 2 percent of the 75 to 79 age group has moderate to severe dementia, while 8.5 percent of 85- to 89-year-olds have this condition (Paykel et al., 1994). As noted in Chapter 1, rates of dementia among "hardy" centenarians may actually be lower than among 85- to 90-year-olds.

The major types of dementias are shown in Table 6.7. Note the distinction between *reversible* and *irreversible* dementias. The first refers to cognitive decline which may be caused by drug toxicity, hormonal or nutritional disorders, and other diseases that may be reversible. Sources of potentially reversible dementias include tumors in and trauma to the brain, toxins, metabolic disorders such as hypo- or hyperthyroidism, diabetes, hypo- or hypercalcemia, infections, vascular lesions, and

*As will be described in Chapter 12, some people believe that suicide for terminally ill older people allows them to maintain control over their death. Groups who adhere to this viewpoint, particularly the Hemlock Society, would be opposed to interventions to stop an older person from choosing suicide.

TABLE 6.7 Major Dementias of Late Life

REVERSIBLE	IRREVERSIBLE
Drugs	Alzheimer's
Alcohol	Vascular
Nutritional deficiencies	Huntington's
Normal pressure hydrocephalus	Pick's disease
Brain tumors	Creutzfeldt-Jacob
Hypothyroidism/Hyperthyroidism	Kuru
Neurosyphilis	Korsakoff
Depression (pseudo-dementia)	

hydrocephalus. Severe depression may produce confusion and memory problems in some older people. Some medications may also cause dementia-like symptoms. This problem is aggravated if the individual is taking multiple medications or is on a dosage that is higher than can be metabolized by the older kidney or liver. An individual who appears to be suffering from such reactions should be referred promptly for medical screening.

Irreversible dementias are those that have no discernible environmental cause and cannot yet be cured. Although there is considerable research on the causes and treatments for these conditions, they must be labeled irreversible at the present time. Some of these are more common than others; some have identifiable causes while others do not. Pick's disease is one of the rarest; in this type, the frontal lobes of the brain atrophy. Of all the dementias, it is most likely to occur in younger persons and to result in significant personality changes. Creutzfeldt-Jacob and Kuru diseases have been traced to a slow-acting virus that can strike at any age. In the former type of dementia, decline in cognitive abilities occurs quite rapidly, as seen in the brief epidemic of "mad cow disease" that was attributed to consuming tainted beef in Great Britain during 1996. The latter type is quite rare. Huntington's Disease is a genetically transmitted condition that usually appears in people in their thirties and for-

ties. It results in more neuromuscular changes than do the other dementias.

Vascular dementia has been estimated to represent 15 to 20 percent of all nonreversible dementias. This is the form of dementia that in the past was identified as "senility." In this type, blood vessels leading to the brain become occluded, with the result that several areas of the brain show infarcts or small strokes. The primary risk factor for vascular dementia is the same as for strokes, that is, hypertension. Because of this, vascular dementia may be prevented by controlling hypertension, although once it occurs, this type of dementia is irreversible (Lis and Gaviria, 1997).

Alzheimer's Disease

The most common irreversible dementia in late life, accounting for 50 to 70 percent of all dementias, is senile dementia of the Alzheimer's type (Alzheimer's disease or AD). Prevalence rates are difficult to obtain, but it has been estimated that 5 to 15 percent of all persons over age 65 and over, and 25 percent in nursing homes have symptoms of AD. The prevalence of Alzheimer's disease appears to increase with age; less than 2 percent of the general population under age 60 are affected, whereas rates of 20 to 50 percent have been estimated for the population over age 80 (Evans et al., 1989; Carr, Goate, Phil, and Morris, 1997; Hendrie, 1997). However, because of selective survival, it appears that men who survive into their nineties become less likely to develop AD after this age (Perls, 1995). Although a distinction was made in the past between pre-senile (i.e., before age 65) and senile dementia, there is now common agreement that these are the same disease. Recent analyses also suggest that AD now ranks third in health care costs, just after cancer and heart disease.

POTENTIAL CAUSES AND RISK FACTORS FOR ALZHEIMER'S DISEASE Several hypotheses have been proposed to explain the causes of Alzheimer's disease. Some researchers have suggested that it may result from a slow virus, or a virus-like agent called a prion, as in Kuru and Creutzfeldt-

Jacob disease (Wurtman, 1985). Others have identified its link with Down syndrome (i.e., a greater frequency in families where Down syndrome has occurred, and a high prevalence in people with Down syndrome by age 40). Multiple occurrences have been found in some families (e.g., two siblings or a parent and child both develop AD), which suggests that chromosomal or other genetic factors may play a role in its etiology. Case control studies that have focused on the incidence or development of AD have not found support for environmental hypotheses, such as a previous head injury, thyroid disease, exposure to therapeutic radiation, anesthesia, or the accumulation of heavy metals (e.g., aluminum) in the brain (Kokmen, Beard, O'Brien, and Kurland, 1996). Even though the abnormal tangles (a web of dead brain cells) found in the neurons of the brain of Alzheimer's victims have been observed to contain much more aluminum than is found in brains of normal controls, it is difficult to determine if such accumulation of aluminum is a cause or outcome of the disease. Older people with diabetes or a history of major depression appear to be at increased risk for dementia in late life (Rocca, 1994; Kokmen et al., 1996).

Another potential risk factor that has drawn more research interest recently is lack of estrogen. Animal studies have revealed that estrogen interacts with neurotransmitter systems to affect the formation and connectivity of synapses. As estrogen secretion declines with aging, proteins associated with neuronal growth decrease, resulting in the synaptic impairments typical of AD. Just as estrogen replacement therapy (ERT) has been found to prevent bone loss and cardiovascular disease in postmenopausal women, there is some evidence from animal studies that it can restore the brain proteins necessary for neuronal growth (Singer 1996a, 1996b). Human studies examining the impact of estrogen replacement therapy have been mostly cross-sectional. In one of the few large-scale longitudinal studies, 248 women with a diagnosis of Alzheimer's or probable Alzheimer's disease were compared with age-matched controls in the same community (Leisure World, in south-

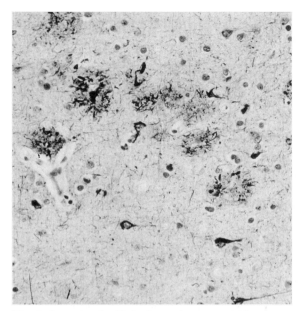

The dark patches in this brain section are neuritic plaques with a core of amyloid protein, characteristic of Alzheimer's disease.

ern California). Both groups had first completed a health questionnaire in 1981, so estrogen use over the subsequent 14 years could be determined. ERT significantly reduced the risk of AD and related dementias; in fact, both higher dosages and longer duration of use were associated with a much lower rate of AD among surviving women (Paganini-Hill and Henderson, 1996). Nevertheless, there may be lifestyle differences between users and nonusers of ERT that may also explain the beneficial effects of ERT. Therefore it may be premature to conclude that replenishing older women's estrogen levels can lower their risk of AD (Henderson, 1997).

The brains of AD patients experience a reduction in the number of cholinergic cells (up to 80 percent loss in some key areas). These brain cells are important for learning and memory because they release an important chemical "messenger," *acetylcholine*, that transfers information from one cell to another. Their loss reduces the acetylcholine available for this important function.

The noradrenergic system is another chemical messenger system that becomes impaired with Alzheimer's disease, further complicating our understanding of why and how these neurochemical systems appear to break down in this disease. Still another neurochemical change observed in Alzheimer brains is the accumulation of *amyloid*, a protein. It appears that there may be a genetic defect in one of the normal proteins located in brain regions responsible for memory, emotions, and thinking. Amyloid is actually a group of proteins found in the neurofibrillary tangles that characterize an Alzheimer brain. The precursor protein to amyloid (Beta-amyloid) is coded by a gene located in chromosome 21, which is also the chromosome responsible for Down syndrome. Researchers have found deposits of amyloid or its precursor Beta-amyloid in the brains of Down patients who die at a younger age with Alzheimer's disease, which provides further evidence of the link between these two conditions. Beta-amyloid may be responsible for the death of brain cells in these patients. As with other changes observed in the brains of AD patients, it is not yet clear whether these Beta-amyloid deposits are the *cause* of AD or secondary to other structural or biochemical changes (Carr et al., 1997).

Recent genetic research has centered on a protein called apolipoprotein, or *apo-E*, which is responsible for transporting cholesterol in the blood. Of the three common allelic variations of apo-E proteins, *E2, E3, E4*, those who inherit an E4 gene from *each* parent have 8 times the risk of developing AD than the general population, and deteriorate more rapidly than AD patients who have lower levels of apo-E4. In addition, AD patients with one or more apo-E4 allele have an increased risk of death due to ischemic heart disease (Carr et al., 1997; Olichney et al., 1997). Those who acquire an E3 gene from each parent also have a greater risk of developing AD, but at a later age than those with two E4 genes (at an average age of 75 versus 68).

As illustrated by Mr. Adams in the introductory vignette, Alzheimer's disease is characterized by deficits in attention, learning, memory, and language skills. An individual with this condition may also have problems in judgment, abstraction, and orientation. These changes in cognitive function appear to be related to structural changes in the brain. For example, the hippocampus is a region in the limbic system deep inside the brain that is involved in learning new information and retrieving old information. It is one of the first regions where plaques and tangles occur, so it is not surprising that patients in the earlier stages of the disease often have difficulties with attention span and with orientation to the environment, increased anxiety and restlessness, and unpredictable changes in mood. Family members may complain that the older person has become more aggressive or, in some cases, more passive than in the past. Depression may set in as the individual realizes that he or she is experiencing these problems. This depression may also be associated with deterioration in the locus ceruleus, a part of the brain that produces a mood-regulating chemical. In the more advanced stages of the disease, as it spreads to the cerebral cortex, which controls language and movement, there may be marked aphasia (i.e., problems recalling appropriate words and labels), perseveration (i.e., continual repeating of the same phrase and thoughts), apathy, and problems with comprehension. Alzheimer's victims at this stage may not recognize their partners, children, and long-time friends. However, it is not unusual for some patients in the moderate stages of AD to describe quite articulately and vividly events that took place many years ago. In the advanced phases, as the neurons in the motor cortex die, the patient may need assistance with bodily functions such as eating and toileting. At autopsy, there is a generalized deterioration of cortical tissue, which appears to be tangled and covered with plaque.

ARE THERE STAGES OF ALZHEIMER'S DISEASE?

There have been some attempts to determine if AD proceeds through a series of stages, such that symptoms become more prevalent and severe. This is a difficult task because the course of AD varies so widely. Some patients may experience a rapid decline in memory while their orientation to time, place, and people may remain relatively intact. Other patients may experience mood and personality changes early, whereas still others maintain their pre-morbid personality for many years after the symptoms first appear.

A broad distinction is often made among early, middle, and advanced stages of AD. These categories are based on the patient's levels of decline in memory, orientation, and activities of daily living. Some psychologists have provided guidelines with the use of assessment tools such as the Mini-Mental Status Exam and the Dementia Rating Scale (Folstein, Folstein, and McHugh, 1975; Mattis, 1976), which give clues to the patients' levels of deterioration on the basis of their test scores. Perhaps the most extensive research to determine the stages of AD has been conducted by Reisberg et al. (1982). Based on their observations of functional and cognitive declines in AD patients, they have developed a Global Deterioration Scale that delineates seven stages of the disease, as shown in Table 6.8.

Because of recent attention by the media and by researchers on Alzheimer's disease, there is some tendency to overestimate its occurrence and to assume that it is the cause of all dementias. It has even created what one neurologist has called "Alzheimer's phobia" in many older people (Fox, 1991). In many ways, it has replaced vascular dementia as a label given without a thorough diagnosis. The most confirmatory diagnosis of Alzheimer's disease today can still only be made at autopsy, when the areas and nature of damaged brain tissue can be identified. However, several psychological measures of cognitive functioning and a thorough physical exam can provide clues to its existence in the earlier stages, or may indicate that the observed changes in behavior and/or personality are due to a reversible condition. Early diagnosis can be made with some certainty with an extensive patient work-up. These include a medical and nutritional history; laboratory tests of blood, urine, and stool; tests for thyroid function; and a thorough physical and psychological examination. In some cases, extensive radiological studies are conducted, including a CT (computerized

TABLE 6.8 Global Deterioration Scale

Stage 1: No cognitive or functional decrements

Stage 2: Complaints of very mild forgetfulness and some work difficulties

Stage 3: Mild cognitive impairment on cognitive battery; concentration problems; some difficulty at work and in traveling alone

Stage 4: Late confusional stage; increased problems in planning, handling finances; increased denial of symptoms; withdrawal

Stage 5: Poor recall of recent events; may need to be reminded about proper clothing and bathing

Stage 6: More advanced memory orientation problems; needs assistance with activities of daily living; more personality changes

Stage 7: Late dementia with loss of verbal abilities; incontinent; loss of ability to walk; may become comatose

SOURCE: B. Reisberg, S. H. Ferris, M. J. De Leon, and T. Crook, The Global Deterioration Scale for assessment of primary degenerative dementia. *American Journal of Psychiatry, 139*, pp. 1136–1139, 1982. Copyright 1982, the American Psychiatric Association. Reprinted by permission.

tomography) scan, a PET (positron emission tomography) scan, or MRI (magnetic resonance imaging), in order to detect any tumors, strokes, blood clots, or hydrocephalus, and to test the response of specific areas of the brain. In fact, it is primarily through a process of elimination of other conditions that some dementias such as AD may be diagnosed. In such diagnoses, it is particularly important to detect depression, drug toxicity, and nutritional deficiencies because, as stated earlier, these conditions may be reversed.

THERAPY FOR PATIENTS WITH ALZHEIMER'S DISEASE Unfortunately, no completely successful treatment for AD is yet available. If the evidence for high levels of certain abnormal proteins in Alzheimer brains proves correct, future treatment might involve the use of drugs that interrupt the production of those proteins and their precursors so they cannot accumulate in brain tissue. Some researchers have focused on nerve growth factor, a naturally occurring protein that replenishes and maintains the health of nerve cells. Animal studies have shown remarkable success in repairing damaged brain cells.

Currently, many researchers are testing medications that may improve the cognitive functioning of victims of dementia. These medications include some drugs that restore the activity of neurotransmitters in the brain and some that even replace lost neurochemicals. In the last few years, two medications have been approved by the Federal Drug Administration to prevent the loss of acetylcholine in the brains of AD patients. These drugs, tacrine hydrochloride (marketed as Cognex) and donepezil (Aricept), are known as "cholinergic enhancers" because they block the enzyme that breaks down acetylcholine. Some researchers have begun to explore the possibility that AD may be related to inflammation of brain tissue. This has led to the hypothesis that non-steroidal anti-inflammatory drugs (NSAIDs), such as ibuprofen, can prevent or delay the onset of AD. Although many older people currently use low doses of NSAIDs to prevent heart attacks, there are few controlled clinical trials testing whether NSAIDs have similar benefits for AD. There is, however, some correlational evidence from the Baltimore Longitudinal Studies of Aging. Older people in this study who reported that they used NSAIDs regularly for 2 or more years had less than half the risk of AD as non-users (Stewart et al., 1997). Another promising pharmacotherapy for AD may be a combination of vitamin E (described in Chapter 3 as an antioxidant that appears to prevent or reduce the symptoms of other chronic diseases) and selegiline hydrochloride (marketed as Eldepryl and generally prescribed for Parkinson's disease). In one clinical trial, patients in the moderate stage of AD who were given this combination did not decline as rapidly as those given a placebo (Sano et al., 1997). As yet, no medication effectively restores cognitive function

in the severely impaired older person for any significant period of time. Nevertheless, researchers have made dramatic strides toward understanding the neurochemical basis of this disease and are rapidly moving toward its treatment.

Medications are often prescribed to manage behavioral problems in some AD patients, including agitation, hallucinations, physical aggressiveness, and wandering. In particular, risperidone, a drug used to treat psychotic symptoms in schizophrenic patients, appears to calm aggressive, delusional behaviors in a significant segment of this population (Goldberg and Goldberg, 1997). Because of their potential side effects, however, it is important to weigh the severity, frequency, and harm caused by these behaviors to the patient and caregivers against the possible side effects of medications. Furthermore, the prescribing physician must regularly re-evaluate the need to continue or reduce the dosage of any drugs used for behavior management, perhaps as frequently as every 3 to 4 months.

As noted earlier, new medications that are being approved by the FDA show some promise of slowing down the rate of decline with AD. To date, however, neither these medications nor psychotherapy can restore the cognitive functions that are lost with most irreversible forms of dementia. Nevertheless, many older persons can benefit from memory retraining and environmental modifications. That is, individual competence can be enhanced somewhat and the environment simplified considerably in an effort to maintain P-E congruence. The individual's social and home environments can be changed in order to maintain some independent functioning. Research has shown, however, that most caregivers of AD patients do not make the necessary environmental changes unless professionals or other friends and family encourage or initiate such changes (Kiyak, 1991). Simple changes such as removing sources of glare and making lighting levels consistent throughout the house, and especially later in the day, can prevent confusion and "sundowning," a condition that affects some AD patients as natural light levels change and they become more fatigued later in

Caregivers play an essential role in the well-being of older people with Alzheimer's disease.

the day. Written schedules of activities, simplified routes from room to room, and written directions for cooking, bathing, and taking medications can aid a person in finding his or her way around and prevent the frustration that results from getting lost or not recognizing once familiar people and places. AD patients can be encouraged to perform more ADLs if their grooming supplies (e.g., toothbrush, toothpaste, comb) are kept visible and in a familiar sequence of use. These items can also help AD patients recognize their own bathroom or bedroom as the disease progresses. It is important to maintain a regular schedule, to keep the patient active, and to prevent withdrawal from daily interactions. However, the frequency and intensity of such activities should not overwhelm or confuse the patient. Wandering is another problem that can be prevented with some environmental changes. These can be as punitive as locking all exterior doors, or more protective, such as providing a safe backyard or garden area for the AD patient to explore, within easy sight of the home's windows and doors to orient the patient. ID bracelets with silent or audible beepers that can help locate the AD patient are becoming more common for use in the home, since their benefits in nursing homes have been demonstrated. Some local chapters of the Alzheimer's Association offer the "safe return" program, which provides ID bracelets for AD patients, maintains records, and assists emergency teams in locating, identifying, and returning home the AD patient who becomes lost in the community (Alzheimer's Association, 1997).

Ultimately, the goal of managing these dementias is to slow the rate of deterioration and to prevent institutionalization for as long as possible. For the AD patient who does enter a nursing home, it is important to find a facility that can maximize the individual's remaining abilities and help them as the disease progresses (i.e., environments that can maintain the patient's P-E congruence). In recent years, there has been a growth in the number of special care units (SCUs) in nursing homes. These units are generally designed for residents with advanced dementia, especially AD, and staffed by nurses and therapists with special training in this field. Many provide a higher staff-to-resident ratio, a safe environment where patients can explore without getting lost, and special services aimed at maintaining the patients' remaining cognitive capacities. They are less likely to use chemical and physical restraints with disruptive residents. However, because there are no national licensing regulations for SCUs, the nature of services and quality of care provided vary widely. That is, the designation of a nursing home unit as a SCU does not necessarily imply richer or more tailored services than non-SCU units that also house AD and other dementia patients (Grant, Kane, and Stark, 1995; Sloane et al., 1995).

CAREGIVER NEEDS One of the most important considerations with Alzheimer's disease and other dementias is to provide social and emotional support to the family as well as the patient. At least half of all people with Alzheimer's disease remain in the community, cared for by a partner.

The stress of caring for this population often results in deterioration of family members' physical and psychological health. Many caregivers feel they must shoulder this responsibility alone, resulting in increasing levels of depression, burden, and declining physical health (Pearson et al., 1993;

CAREGIVER STRESS IN ALZHEIMER'S DISEASE

If is often said that caregivers of AD patients are "the second victims" of this disease. The following vignette illustrates the dilemma faced by these caregivers.

John Jones has had Alzheimer's disease for five years and is cared for by his wife, Mary. Married for 60 years, by all accounts they have had mutual sharing and caring throughout those years. Now Mary does all personal care for John, and it is getting to the point where he does not recognize her. It saddens her when he asks "Where is Mary?" The mutuality of the past relationship is fast disappearing. Yet she takes very seriously the marriage vow to care for him until death. And it is the love and caring of the past that sustains her now.

They have four children, all of whom live out of state. When her children telephone weekly, Mary assures them that all is going well. However, a neighbor called the oldest daughter to inform her that her mother is not doing well. Mary has lost a good deal of weight; she looks at least 10 years older and seems to have "the weight of the world on her shoulders." Mary has a known history of heart troubles. The daughter plans to come home to insist that her mother take care of herself, enlisting home health or institutional care for John. When she mentioned this to her mother on the last phone call, Mary adamantly insisted that it is her responsibility to care for her husband. The daughter is afraid that she will be caring for two patients in the future, as she is most concerned that her mother's health will fail.

Reese et al., 1994; Russo et al., 1995; Vitaliano et al., 1996). As family caregivers assume more responsibility for an AD patient whose functional abilities decline, perceived burden increases. This condition is aggravated and depression becomes more likely if the AD patient also displays more disruptive behaviors such as aggressiveness, frequent wakings during the night, and wandering. Caregivers who experience the most depressive symptoms also report being most disturbed by such behaviors (Pearson et al., 1993). Depression is particularly high among spouse caregivers (Schulz and Williamson, 1991). Several physiological and physical health outcomes of stress have been found among such caregivers. These include higher insulin and glucose levels than age-matched controls, higher levels of lipids in blood, and cardiovascular disease (King, Oka, and Young, 1994; Vitaliano, Russo, and Niaura, 1995; Vitaliano et al., 1996).

Support groups aid their members in coping with the inevitable losses faced by the victims of AD—forgetting where they are when they go for a walk in the neighborhood, not recognizing their own children, agitation and aggressive behavior,

and, in more advanced cases, needing assistance with dressing, eating, bathing, and toileting. These groups, most of which are coordinated by local chapters of the national Alzheimer's Association, also provide caregivers with emotional support and respite. Depression, chronic fatigue, and anger are all common reactions among caregivers of dementia patients. Support groups can alleviate these stress responses for caregivers who begin participating early in the course of the disease so they are able to anticipate problems. Those who attend sessions regularly benefit the most. A longitudinal study that tested the effects of a yearlong weekly support-group program on depression also included individual and family counseling sessions during the first 4 months of the program. Combined individual, family, and support-group intervention was the key to significant declines in depression scores among this experimental group. Spouse caregivers in the control group, who received counseling or referrals only if they requested them (which occurred infrequently), became more depressed during this same period. The multi-pronged intervention was also effective in reducing the number of AD patients who were placed in nursing homes (Mittelman et al., 1993; 1995). The growth of adult day centers has been another response to the need to keep persons with dementia in the community, to help them remain active and retain learned skills, and to provide respite for their family caregivers. The need for publicly funded daycare, respite, and support groups, however, is greater than the availability of services.

Alcoholism

For most older people, alcohol use is associated with socializing and occurs in moderation (i.e., less than once a week, and no more than two drinks each time). However, those who consume four or more drinks per occasion and do so frequently (defined as alcoholism) are more likely to use alcohol as a way to cope with some life events and to help them relax (Krause, 1995; Mockenhaupt and Beck, 1997). It is difficult to obtain accurate statistics on the prevalence of alcoholism in older adults, because of the stigma associated with this condition among older cohorts. Estimates vary, from 2 to 10 percent of all older people living in the community. Alcoholism in older adults is accompanied by depression in 30 percent of cases, and by dementia in 20 percent, although the direction of causality is not always clear (Adams et al., 1993; Osgood, Wood, and Parham, 1995; Koenig and Blazer, 1996). Those at greatest risk are widowers, and well-educated white men who have never married. Older men are four times more likely to have alcohol problems than are older women. Women at greatest risk of alcohol abuse are those who are smokers, not married, not religious, and with little social support (Molgaard et al., 1990; Graham, Carver, and Brett, 1995; Holroyd et al., 1997).

It is important to distinguish lifelong abusers of alcohol from those who began drinking later in life. Alcoholics are less likely to be found among the ranks of persons over age 60 because of higher death rates at a young age among alcoholics. Those who continue to drink in old age tend to decrease their consumption. Surveys of alcoholism rates among older persons have revealed approximately equal proportions of those who began to drink heavily before age 40 and those who began in old age (Miller et al., 1991).

Some older persons who are diagnosed as alcoholics have had this problem since middle age, but increasing age may exacerbate the condition for two reasons. First, the central nervous system (CNS), liver, and kidneys become less tolerant of alcohol with age because of the physiological changes described in Chapter 3 (e.g., loss of muscle tissue, reduction in body mass, and reduced efficiency of liver and kidney functions). For this reason, a smaller dose of alcohol can be more deleterious in the later years. Second, an individual who has been drinking heavily for many years has already produced irreversible damage to the CNS, liver, and kidneys, creating more problems than those due to normal aging alone. Perhaps because of the damage to their CNS, men who began drinking heavily before the age of 35 are more likely to experience depression, restlessness, sleeplessness, and tension than those who started later (Gurnack and Hoffman, 1992). It is difficult to determine the incidence of alcoholism among older persons who have no previous history of this disease. Physiological evidence is lacking, and drinking is often hidden from friends, relatives, and physicians. The older person may justify overconsumption of alcohol on the grounds that it relieves sadness and isolation. Even when family members are aware of the situation, they may minimize it by rationalizing that alcohol is one of the older person's few remaining pleasures. Denial is a common problem among older alcoholics who are influenced by beliefs of the prohibition era that alcoholism is a moral weakness and not a disease. In addition, many older people may feel that they should be able to cope with their alcoholism on their own and not have to rely on health professionals or even on support groups such as Alcoholics Anonymous.

Physicians may overlook the possibility that alcohol is creating a health problem because the adverse effects of alcohol resemble some physical diseases or psychiatric and cognitive disorders that are associated with old age. For example, older alcoholics may complain of confusion, disorientation, irritability, insomnia or restless sleep patterns, heart palpitations, weight loss, depression, or a dry cough. Beliefs held by health care providers that alcoholism does not occur in older people may also prevent its detection. Because of the problems caused by heavy alcohol use in old age, primary-care physicians must screen their older patients by asking questions about the quantity, frequency, and context of drinking. This can help in the diagnosis and referral of older alcoholics to treatment programs, which currently are underutilized by the older population. This can also reduce the emotional, physical, and cognitive deterioration caused by alcoholism in older people and the subsequent hospitalizations and use of emergency medical services for conditions that are secondary to heavy alcohol consumption (Adams, Barry, and Fleming, 1996; Holroyd et al., 1997).

THERAPEUTIC INTERVENTIONS Therapy for older alcoholics has not been differentiated from that for younger alcoholics. However, it is probably more important to focus on older alcoholics' medical conditions because of physical declines that make them more vulnerable to the secondary effects of alcohol. As with younger alcoholics, psychotherapy and occupational and recreational therapy are important for treating older people experiencing alcoholism. Recovery rates for older alcoholics are as high as for younger alcoholics.

Drug Abuse

As noted in Chapter 4, older persons use a disproportionately large number of prescription and over-the-counter (OTC) drugs, representing approximately 30 percent of prescription expenditures. In particular, older people are more likely than the young to be using tranquilizers, sedatives, and hypnotics, all of which have potentially dangerous side effects. Older persons have been found to abuse aspirin compounds, laxatives,

and sleeping pills, often because of misinformation about the adverse effects of too high a dosage or too many pills. It is not unusual to hear older patients state that they took twice or three times as much aspirin as they were prescribed because they did not feel their pain was being alleviated with the lower dose. Yet, changes in body composition, renal, and liver functions that occur with age, combined with the use of multiple medications, make older persons more likely to experience adverse drug reactions. Noncompliance with therapeutic drug regimens is often unintentional; older patients may take too much or too little of a drug because of nonspecific or complicated instructions by the physician, and they may use OTC drugs without reading warning labels about their side effects and interactions with other drugs they are using. Intentional noncompliance generally takes the form of older patients' deciding that they no longer need the medication or that it is not working for them. Such noncompliance has been found to be responsible for approximately 10 percent of all hospital admissions among the older population (Col, Fanale, and Kronholm, 1990).

Fortunately, there is growing awareness of the effects of "polypharmacy" among both health care providers and older people themselves. Older persons do not abuse drugs to the extent that younger populations do, nor use illicit drugs such as heroin, cocaine, and marijuana. Nor do they use hallucinogens, amphetamines, or mood-enhancing inhalants in noticeable numbers.

Paranoid Disorders and Schizophrenia

Paranoia, defined as an irrational suspiciousness of other people, actually takes several forms. In older persons, paranoia may be due to social isolation, a sense of powerlessness, progressive sensory decline, and problems with the normal "checks and balances" of daily life. Still other changes in the aging individual, such as problems with memory, may result in paranoid reactions. It should also be noted that some of the suspicious attitudes of older persons may represent accurate readings of their experiences. For example, an older person's children may in fact be trying to institutionalize him or her in order to take over an estate; a nurse's aide may really be stealing from an older patient; and neighborhood children may be making fun of the older adult. It is therefore important to distinguish actual threats to the individual from unfounded suspicions. To the extent that the individual has some control over his or her environment, the older person's perception of a threatening situation will be reduced. This is consistent with the P-E competence model. The diagnosis of paranoid disorders in older people is similar to that in younger patients; the symptoms should have a duration of at least one week, with no signs of schizophrenia, no prominent hallucinations, and no association to an organic mental disorder (APA, 1994).

Schizophrenia is much less prevalent than depression or dementia in old age. Most older persons with this condition were first diagnosed in adolescence or in middle age and continue to display behavior symptomatic of schizophrenia. However, the severity of symptoms appears to decrease and to change with age; older schizophrenics are less likely to manifest thought disorders and loss of emotional expression (Blazer, George, and Hughes, 1988; Rabins, 1992). Late onset schizophrenia with paranoid features has been labeled *paraphrenia* by some psychiatrists, especially in Europe and in Great Britain (Butler et al., 1991).

Schizophrenics of any age, but especially older patients, need monitoring of their medication regimes and structured living arrangements. However, many of the current cohort of older chronic schizophrenics residing in the community were deinstitutionalized during the early 1960s as part of the national Community Mental Health Services Act of 1963. After spending much of their youth and middle age in state hospitals, these patients were released with the anticipation that they could function independently in the community with medications to control their hallucinations and psychotic behavior. Although this approach has proven effective for many former schizophrenic inpatients, some have not adjusted successfully to deinstitutionalization, as witnessed by the number of homeless older schizophrenics seen on the streets in most major cities.

THERAPEUTIC INTERVENTIONS As with depression, psychotherapy can be useful for paranoid older persons. In particular, cognitive behavioral approaches, in which an individual focuses on changing negative, self-defeating beliefs or misconceptions, may be useful in treating paranoid older persons who often attribute causality to external factors (e.g., the belief that someone took their pocketbook, that they themselves did not misplace it). Psychotherapy with paranoid older individuals may be effective in redirecting beliefs about causality to the individuals themselves. On the other hand, pharmacotherapy with antipsychotic medications is generally most effective for older schizophrenic patients.

Anxiety

Anxiety disorders are another type of functional disorder or emotional problem with no obvious organic cause. Although more common than schizophrenia and paranoid disorders, anxiety disorders are not as common in older populations as they are in the young. This may be because the older person develops more tolerance and better ability to manage stressful events. More likely, however, those who have anxiety disorders in middle age may be less likely to survive to old age. Data from the Epidemiological Catchment Area study revealed a prevalence rate of 5.5 percent among those 65 and older, but late-life anxiety disorders may co-exist with other medical and psychiatric disorders that can mask the underlying anxiety (Regier et al., 1988). The most common forms of anxiety disorders in the older population are generalized anxiety, phobias, and panic disorders. As with other psychiatric disorders that can be masked by physical symptoms, primary-care physicians must probe further when older patients complain of diffuse pain, fast or irregular heart rate, and restlessness. Once the condition is diagnosed, older people can benefit from cognitive-behavioral therapy, psychosocial support, and in some cases, pharmacotherapy (Banazak, 1997).

OLDER ADULTS WHO ARE CHRONICALLY MENTALLY ILL

The plight of older persons who are chronically mentally ill has recently been addressed by mental health advocates. This population is defined as people who suffer mental or emotional disorders that erode or prevent the development of their functional capacities in ADL, self-direction, interpersonal relations, social transactions, learning, and recreation (Light and Lebowitz, 1991). Many chronically mentally ill older persons were institutionalized in their young adult years and released into the community after the deinstitutionalization movement began in 1963, but since then they have been in and out of hospitals as their conditions have become exacerbated. These people have survived major upheavals in their lives under marginally functional conditions.

As noted by Quam and Abramson (1991), who have examined the well-being of chronically mentally ill adults, "it is remarkable that members of this population survive into middle age and old age" despite the social neglect they have experienced. Of course, the social disruption and years of treatment with psychotropic drugs take their toll on many of these people, who are physiologically old in their fifties and sixties. It often becomes difficult for chronically mentally ill persons to obtain medical care for purely physical symptoms because health care providers may dismiss a complaint as hypochondriasis and/or attribute it to the patient's psychiatric disorder. It is important for doctors in this situation to perform a thorough exam to exclude conditions caused by the mental disorder or by aging per se, and to treat any systemic diseases that are diagnosed.

Psychotherapy with Older Persons

Despite early doubts by Freud (1924) and others about the value of psychotherapy for older patients, many researchers and therapists have developed and tested psychotherapeutic interventions specifically for this population, or have modified existing approaches. One problem in working with older individuals may be overcoming the misconceptions held by some older persons about psychotherapy. For this reason, short-term, goal-oriented therapies may be more effective with older patients because they can begin to experience benefits immediately. On the other hand, older patients who are reluctant and unwilling to open up to a therapist may benefit more from long-term treatment in which rapport and trust between the therapist and the client can be established gradually. Several different types of therapy have been explored with this population.

Life review is one therapeutic approach that has been successfully used with older persons. Such therapy encourages introspection through active reminiscence of past achievements and failures, and may reestablish ego integrity in depressed older persons. This method may also be used effectively by social service providers who are not extensively trained in psychotherapy. An alternative form of life review, known as **reminiscence therapy,** has been compared with a more focused, problem-solving therapy. While it has short-term benefits for depressed older people, it is less effective in long-term (i.e., greater than 3 months) reduction of depressive symptoms (Arean et al., 1993).

Group therapy has been advocated for older patients experiencing mental disorders, especially depression. Groups offer the opportunity for peer support, social interaction, and role modeling. Life review may be used effectively as part of group therapy. The opportunity to share life experiences and to learn that others have had similar stresses in their lives appears to enhance insight, self-esteem, and a feeling of catharsis. Group reminiscence therapy appears to reduce symptoms of depression immediately after the

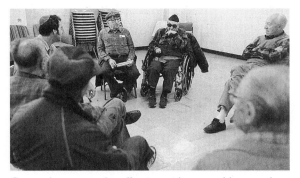

Group therapy can be effective with many older people.

sessions have been completed, but its long-term benefits are unclear (McMurdo and Rennie, 1993). Groups have also been established for improving memory and enhancing cognitive skills. They are an ideal setting for teaching memory skills with the use of games and puzzles as well as reminiscence exercises.

Empirical studies have been conducted to compare the efficacy of alternative therapeutic interventions. For example, *cognitive-behavioral* (i.e., active, structured, and time-limited therapy) and *brief psychodynamic therapy* (i.e., helping the patient to develop ego strength and feelings of control) both appear to be equally effective in alleviating minor depression, even up to 12 months following treatment (Gallagher-Thompson and Steffan, 1994). Psychodynamic therapy uses psychoanalytic concepts such as insight, transference, and the unconscious to relieve symptoms of depression and to prevent its recurrence by understanding why the individual behaves in self-defeating ways. Each type of therapy may be appropriate for different types of older patients. For example, in comparing cognitive-behavioral therapy with brief psychodynamic therapy among depressed caregivers of Alzheimer's disease patients, longer-term caregivers improved more with cognitive-behavioral methods, while shorter-term caregivers benefited more from psychodynamic therapy (Gallagher-Thompson and Steffan, 1994).

The therapeutic interventions just described are more frequently used in community settings than in nursing homes. The latter setting lends itself to more intense, long-term therapies: behavior-change programs, milieu therapy, and remotivation therapy. Behavior-change techniques using operant reinforcement and token economies have been successfully used in long-term care settings with psychiatrically impaired young and old patients. These methods have been found to increase self-feeding and self-care, and have been effective in reducing dependency in older persons. Milieu therapy is consistent with Lawton and Nahemow's competence model described earlier. This approach focuses on improving the therapeutic environment of the nursing home or enhancing an individual's sense of control over some important aspects of life.

Remotivation therapy has been used successfully with less confused elders. Groups of older persons with some cognitive impairment and who are withdrawn from social activities meet together under the guidance of a trained group leader. The purpose is to discuss events and experiences by bringing all group members into the discussion, emphasizing the event's relevance for each member, and encouraging them to share what they have gained from the session. This approach has been found to be effective in psychiatric hospitals and nursing homes, as well as in adult day centers.

Use of Mental Health Services

As noted in Chapter 4, older persons use physician services somewhat more than the young do, and are hospitalized at a much higher rate. In contrast, mental health services are significantly underutilized by older people, especially ethnic minorities. Community-based care is used by older people at a far lower rate than inpatient hospital treatment. It has been estimated that only 4 to 6 percent of patients using community mental health centers are age 65 or older (Butler et al., 1991), far below their representation in the U.S. population and less than the estimated prevalence of mental disorders in this group. An even smaller percentage of users are ethnic minority elders.

Older persons may be more likely to seek help from their primary physicians and to be hospitalized for mental disorders than to seek community mental health services. This may be because medical care does not carry the stigma of mental health services, especially for older ethnic minorities. A disproportionate number of older persons represent the population of patients in state mental hospitals that house the chronically mentally ill. Despite the deinstitutionalization movement of the 1960s, the great majority of all psychiatric services to older people are in hospital settings.

BARRIERS TO OLDER PERSONS' USE OF MENTAL HEALTH SERVICES Older adults are generally unwilling to interpret their problems as psychological, preferring instead to attribute them to physical or social conditions or to normal aging. In addition, the current cohort of older persons may be less oriented to the use of mental health services because of societal stigmas, limited knowledge about mental disorders, and a lack of confidence in mental health workers. This requires a good "psychological ear" on the part of the older person's primary-care physician. As noted earlier, older patients may complain of physical symptoms rather than focus on psychological concerns. Therefore the physician must be attuned to the underlying emotional distress presented by the older patient.

Perhaps the greatest barrier to older individuals' obtaining mental health services is accessibility. In addition to the physical access issues of transportation and architectural barriers, there are significant problems of fragmented services and older people's lack of knowledge about seeking mental health services on their own or obtaining appropriate referrals from physicians or social service providers. Fortunately, many new and innovative programs have arisen to overcome these barriers and respond to the mental health needs of older adults. For example, home

visits by a psychiatrist, social worker, and a nurse are made of low-income, isolated older people in Baltimore through the "Psychogeriatric Assessment and Treatment in City Housing" (or PATCH) program. Rural elders in Iowa are served by mental health professionals through the Elderly Outreach Program (or EOP) of the community mental health system. The Family Services Program of greater Boston offers a community mental health program aimed especially at ethnic minority elders, entitled Services for Older People (or SOP). In Seattle, a mental health team from the community mental health network provides on-site evaluation and therapy to area nursing homes on a regular basis. In many communities, "gatekeepers" (nontraditional referral sources such as meter readers, postal carriers, and apartment and mobile home managers who have contact with isolated older people in the community) are trained to identify older persons who may require psychiatric care. These isolated older adults are typically chronically mentally ill (Raschko, 1991).

Many senior centers employ social workers trained in geriatrics to conduct support groups, education programs, and individualized sessions on coping with grief, loss, loneliness, and on methods to improve memory. Such programs reduce the stigma of psychotherapy by their informal structure in a familiar environment.

Reimbursement for psychological services is also a problem. For example, Medicare Part A pays no outpatient mental health expenditures, but pays for a limited number of days for inpatient treatment. Furthermore, co-payment by the subscriber for mental health services is greater than for physical health services. It should be noted that this discrepancy occurs in many health insurance programs used by younger persons as well. Because of attitudes held by older patients toward mental disorders and by therapists toward older clients, however, these reimbursement issues are greater barriers to older persons' use of mental health services than they are for the young. Future cohorts of older people may be more likely to seek such services in community mental health centers, because of increasing awareness of mental disorders and treatment modalities.

SUMMARY AND IMPLICATIONS

Personality development in adulthood and old age has received increasing attention over the past 30 years. Earlier theories of personality suggested that development takes place only during childhood and adolescence, and stabilizes by early adulthood. Beginning with Erik Erikson, however, several theorists have suggested that personality continues to change and evolve into old age. According to Erikson's theory of psychosocial development, the individual experiences stages of development, with crises or conflicts at each stage, and the outcome of each has an impact on ego development in the next stage. The seventh stage, generativity versus stagnation, takes place mostly during the middle years, but increasingly researchers are finding that continued generativity in old age is important for successful aging. Programs such as foster grandparents encourage older people to experience continued generativity by working with young children. The eighth and last stage of personality development occurs in old age and poses the conflict of ego integrity versus despair in dealing with one's impending death. Both cross-sectional and longitudinal studies have found evidence for these last two stages of development.

The work of Carl Jung also emphasizes the growth of personality across the life span, but does not specify stages of development. Jung's model, like Erikson's, focuses on the individual's confrontation with death in this last stage. In addition, Jung described a decrease in sex-typed behavior with aging. This has been supported in cross-cultural studies by Gutmann (1977, 1980, 1992) and in the longitudinal Kansas City studies. These investigators found that men become more accepting of their nurturant and affiliative characteristics as they age, whereas women learn to accept their egocentric and aggressive impulses. Levinson's life structures model also examines personality from a developmental stage perspective. This model is consistent with the person-environment approach in emphasizing the interaction between the individual and his/her environment as the impetus for change.

Trait theories of personality have been tested systematically in the Baltimore Longitudinal Studies of Aging (Costa and McCrae, 1986, 1994, 1995; McCrae and Costa, 1990). These researchers have tested a five-factor model of personality consisting of five primary traits (neuroticism, extraversion, openness to experience, agreeableness, and conscientiousness), and several subcategories of traits. They have found considerable stability in these traits from middle-age to old age when tested longitudinally, and age differences between young and old when tested cross-sectionally. The development of self-concept and self-esteem in old age has been researched even less. It is recognized that older persons' self-concepts must be redefined as they move from traditional roles of worker, partner, and parent to less well-differentiated roles such as retiree or widow. But the process by which such changes take place and, more important, how they influence life satisfaction and self-esteem in old age is unclear.

Somewhat more research has been devoted to age-related changes in the nature of life events and the stress associated with them. Cognitive appraisal is an important consideration in understanding people's reactions to life events. To the extent that people perceive a situation as a threat, or as a negative stressor, the response may be avoidance or ineffective coping. If a particular life event is viewed as benign or unimportant, coping responses will not be activated. If an event proves to be more stressful than anticipated, an older person will be unprepared to cope with these demands.

Adaptation is influenced by an individual's access to a support network, cognitive skills, and personality traits such as active versus passive "mastery style" and "locus of control." Although ego defense mechanisms have been observed to become more mature in middle and old age, it is difficult to describe coping styles in a similar manner.

Age differences in the use of coping styles have been observed in cross-sectional studies, but longitudinal comparisons reveal considerable stability in coping.

Successful aging may be defined as the ability to avoid disease and disability, to function at a high level cognitively, to remain involved in society, and to cope effectively with life events and chronic hassles. An individual who has survived to the age of 75 or older has proved to be adaptable to new situations. Hence, older people who remain physically, cognitively, and socially active can achieve successful aging.

The prevalence of mental disorders in old age is difficult to determine, although estimates range from 5 to 45 percent of the older population. Research in acute and long-term care institutional settings provides higher estimates than epidemiological studies conducted in the community. This is because many older persons with mental disorders are treated in institutional settings rather than through community mental health services.

The most common mental disorder in late life is depression, although estimates of its prevalence also vary widely, depending on the criteria used to diagnose depression. Bipolar disorders are rare in old age; minor depression is more common than major depression. Reactive or minor depression that is secondary to major life changes is found frequently in older persons. This condition responds well to environmental and social interventions, whereas antidepressant therapy is more effective for major depression, and electroconvulsive therapy for severe depression in older people who do not respond to other forms of therapy. Diagnosing depression in older people is often difficult. Many deny it, while others attribute it to medical conditions. On the other hand, it is important to screen for medical conditions and medications that may produce depressive symptoms as a side effect.

Depression is a risk factor for suicide in older people, particularly for white men over age 85. Life changes that result in a loss of social status and increased isolation may explain why this group is more likely to commit suicide. The increased risk of suicide in the older population highlights the need for family members and service providers to be sensitized to clues of an impending suicide.

Dementia includes numerous reversible and irreversible conditions that result in impaired cognitive function, especially recall of recent events, comprehension, learning, attention, and orientation to time, place, and person. It is essential to perform a complete diagnostic work-up of older people who have symptoms of dementia. A medical history, physical examination, assessment of medications, lab tests, psychological and cognitive testing, as well as neurological testing, will aid in distinguishing "reversible" dementias that can be treated from the "irreversible" dementias such as Alzheimer's disease that currently can be managed but not cured. The biological basis of Alzheimer's disease is being examined in numerous studies; future treatments may involve medications that replace or prevent the loss of brain chemicals. Family members and service providers should be aware of changes in the older person's cognitive functioning and behavior that may signal dementia, and must avoid labeling such changes as normal aging or as—the catchall phrase—"senility."

Although cognitive functioning cannot be restored in irreversible dementias, older persons in the early stages of these conditions often benefit from memory retraining and from psychotherapy to cope with the changes they are experiencing. Environmental modifications that simplify tasks and aid in orienting the patient may slow the rate of deterioration and postpone institutionalization. It is also important to provide emotional and social support to family caregivers of elders with Alzheimer's disease and other dementias. Support groups, adult day care, and other such respite programs are valuable for spouses and other caregivers who assume full-time care for these patients at home, although they are limited by funding constraints.

Alcoholism and drug abuse are less common in older persons than in the young, although accurate estimates of prevalence are difficult to obtain. Physical health and cognitive function are significantly impaired in older alcoholics. Older men with a history of alcohol abuse also have a greater risk of suicide than do younger men or young and old women who are alcoholics. Drug abuse in older persons is rarely associated with illicit drugs, but often takes the form of inappropriate use or overuse of some prescription and over-the-counter drugs. Adverse reactions are more likely to occur in older persons because of age-related physiological changes that impair the ability to metabolize many medications and because of the greater likelihood of polypharmacy.

Paranoia and schizophrenia are far less common than depression and dementia in older persons. Most people with these conditions first developed them in middle age; life changes such as relocation and confusion that result from dementia may trigger paranoid reactions in old age, and may aggravate pre-existing schizophrenic symptoms. Psychotherapy, especially using cognitive behavior strategies, may be effective in treating paranoia, although it is important first to determine and to verify the underlying causes of the condition.

Many researchers have explored the feasibility of psychotherapy with older patients. Both short-term, goal-oriented therapy and long-term approaches have been advocated. Specific modes of therapy with older patients include reminiscence, brief psychodynamic, and cognitive-behavioral techniques. These interventions have been particularly effective with depressed older people in community settings. Nursing homes are ideal settings for long-term, intense therapies using groups, but staff may not have the time or training to implement them. Behavior change and milieu therapy have resulted in significant improvements in short-term experimental interventions.

Despite the demonstrated efficacy of many forms of psychotherapy with older persons, they significantly underutilize mental health services. Most treatments for mental disorders in this population take place in hospitals. Many older people prefer to seek treatment for depression and other mental disorders from a general physician. This may result in an overuse of pharmacological treatment and an underutilization of psychotherapy in cases where the latter may be more effective. Such behavior may be attributed to reluctance among the current cohort of elders to admit they have a psychiatric problem, a lack of knowledge about such conditions and their treatment, as well as problems with accessibility. Attitudes of mental health providers and social service providers about the value of psychotherapy for older persons and, perhaps most important, the lack of effective links between mental health and social services to the older population, have been barriers in the past. As more programs evolve that integrate services, and as future cohorts become aware of mental disorders and their treatment, there will be greater acceptance and use of mental health services by older people.

GLOSSARY

active and passive mastery interactions with one's social environment that are more controlling and competitive, versus more affiliative and docile

adaptation ability to change personal needs, motivations, behaviors, and expectations to fit changing environmental demands or conditions

anxiety disorder functional psychological disorder often triggered by external stress; accompanied by physiological reactivity such as increased heart rate and sleep disorders

archetypes masculine and feminine aspects of personality, present in both men and women

benign senescent forgetfulness mild age-related decline in memory and learning ability; not progressive as in dementia

coping (problem-focused versus emotion-focused) conscious responses to stress, determined by nature of stressor, personality, social support, and health

defense mechanisms unconscious responses to stress, in order to defend the ego from impulses, memories, and external threats

dementia progressive, marked decline in cognitive functions associated with damage to brain tissue; may affect personality and behavior; may be reversible or irreversible type

depression (major versus minor or reactive) the most common psychiatric disorder in old age, diagnosed if several behavioral and affective symptoms (e.g. sleep and disturbances) are present for at least two weeks; bipolar disorders less common in older people than reactive (or minor) and major depression

ego integrity versus despair the eighth and last stage of psychosocial development in Erikson's model; aging individual achieves wisdom and perspective, or despairs because views one's life as lacking meaning

electroconvulsive or electroshock therapy (ECT) a form of therapy for severely depressed patients in which a mild electrical current is applied to one or both sides of brain

generativity the seventh stage of psychosocial development in Erikson's model; goal of middle-aged and older persons is to care for, mentor younger generations, look toward future and not stagnate in past

life events identifiable, discrete life changes or transitions that require some adaptation to re-establish homeostasis

life review a form of psychotherapy that encourages discussion of past successes and failures

life structures in Levinson's model, specific developmental stages consisting of eras and transitions

paranoia a psychiatric disorder characterized by irrational suspiciousness of other people

pharmacotherapy use of medications to treat symptoms of physical or psychiatric disorders

psychopathology abnormal changes in personality and behavior that may be caused or triggered by a genetic predisposition, environmental stress, and/or systemic diseases

reminiscence therapy a type of psychotherapy used with depressed, anxious, sometimes confused older adults, stimulating older person's memory for successful coping experiences and positive events in the past

self-concept cognitive representation of the self; emerges from interactions with social environment, social roles, accomplishments

self-esteem evaluation or feeling about one's identity relative to an " ideal self"; differs from self-concept in being more of an emotional, not cognitive, assessment of self

stage theories of personality development of individual through various stages, each one necessary for adaptation and for psychological adjustment

successful aging achievement of good physical and functional health, cognitive and emotional well-being in old age, often accompanied by strong social support and productive activity

trait theories personality theories that describe individuals in terms of characteristic or "typical" attributes that remain relatively stable with age

REFERENCES

Adamek, M. E., and Kaplan, M. S. Firearm suicide among older men. *Psychiatric Services*, 1996, *47*, 304–306.

Adams, W. L., Barry, K. K., and Fleming, M. F. Screening for problem drinking in older primary care patients. *Journal of the American Medical Association*, 1996, *276*, 1964–1967.

Adams, W. L., Zhong, Y., Barboriak, J. J., and Rimm, A. A. Alcohol-related hospitalizations of elderly people. *Journal of the American Medical Association*, 1993, *270*, 6–9.

Albert, M. S., Savage, C. R., Jones, K., Berkman, L., Seeman, T., Blazer, D., and Rowe, J. W. Predictors of cognitive change in older persons: MacArthur studies of successful aging. *Psychology and Aging*, 1995, *10*, 578–589.

Alzheimer's Association. *Action series: Modifying the environment.* Chicago: Alz. Association, 1997.

American Psychiatric Association (APA). *Diagnostic and statistical manual of mental disorders* (4th ed.). Washington, DC: APA, 1994.

Amster, L. E., and Krauss, H. The relationship between life crises and mental deterioration in old age. *International Journal of Aging and Human Development*, 1974, *5*, 51–55.

Arean, P. A., Perri, M. G., Nezu, A. M., Schein, R. L., Christopher, F., and Joseph, T. X. Comparative effectiveness of social problem-solving therapy and reminiscence therapy as treatments for depression in older adults. *Journal of Consulting and Clinical Psychology*, 1993, *61*, 1003–1010.

Banazak, D. A. Anxiety disorders in elderly patients. *Journal of the American Board of Family Practice*, 1997, *10*, 280–289.

Benbow, S. M. The role of electroconvulsive therapy in the treatment of depressive illness in old age. *British Journal of Psychiatry*, 1989, *155*, 147–152.

Blazer, D. G., George, L. K., and Hughes, D. Schizophrenic symptoms in an elderly community population. In J. A. Brody and G. L. Maddox (Eds.), *Epidemiology and aging: An international perspective*. New York: Springer, 1988.

Blazer, D. G., and Koenig, H. G. Suicide. In J. E. Birren (Ed.), *Encyclopedia of gerontology*. San Diego: Academic Press, 1996.

Butler, R. N., Lewis, M., and Sunderland, T. *Aging and mental health* (4th ed.). New York: Macmillan, 1991.

Carr, D. B., Goate, A., Phil, D., and Morris, J. C. Current concepts in the pathogenesis of Alzheimer's disease. *American Journal of Medicine*, 1997, *103*, 3S–10S.

Chen, H. L. Hearing loss in the elderly: Relation to loneliness and self-esteem. *Journal of Gerontological Nursing*, 1994, *20*, 22–28.

Coblentz, J. M., Mattis, S., Zingesser, L. H., Kasoff, S. S., Wisniewski, H. M., and Katzman, R. Presenile dementia: Clinical evaluation of cerebrospinal fluid dynamics. *Archives of Neurology*, 1973, *29*, 299–308.

Col, N., Fanale, J. E., and Kronholm, P. The role of medication noncompliance and adverse drug reactions in hospitalizations of the elderly. *Archives of Internal Medicine*, 1990, *150*, 841–845.

Conwell, Y., and Caine, E. D. Suicide in the elderly chronic patient population. In E. Light and B. D. Lebowitz (Eds.), *The elderly with chronic mental illness*. New York: Springer, 1991.

Costa, P. T., and McCrae, R. R. Cross-sectional studies of personality in a national sample. Development and validation of survey measures. *Psychology and Aging*, 1986, *1*, 140–143.

Costa, P. T., and McCrae, R. R. Psychological stress and coping in old age. In L. Goldberger and S. Breznitz (Eds.), *Handbook of stress: Theoretical and clinical aspects* (2nd ed.). New York: Free Press, 1993.

Costa, P. T., and McCrae, R. R. Solid ground in the wetlands of personality: A reply to Block. *Psychological Bulletin*, 1995, *117*, 216–220.

Costa, P. T., and McCrae, R. R. Stability and change in personality from adolescence through adulthood. In C. F. Halverson, G. A. Kohnstamm, and R. P. Martin (Eds.), *The developing structure of temperament and personality from infancy to adulthood*. Hillsdale, NJ: Erlbaum, 1994.

Coyne, J. C., and Downey, G. Social factors and psychopathology: Stress, social support and coping processes. *Annual Review of Psychology*, 1991, *42*, 401–425.

De St. Aubin, E., and McAdams, D. P. The relations of generative concern and generative action to personality traits, satisfaction/happiness with life, and ego development. *Journal of Adult Development*. 1995, *2*, 99–112.

DeVries, H. M. Cognitive-behavioral interventions. In J. E. Birren (Ed.), *Encyclopedia of gerontology*, San Diego: Academic Press, 1996.

Erikson, E. H. *Childhood and society* (2nd ed.). New York: Norton, 1963.

Erikson, E. H. *Identity, youth and crisis*. New York: Norton, 1968.

Erikson, E. H. *The life cycle completed: A review*. New York: Norton, 1982.

Erikson, E. H., Erikson, J. M., and Kivnick, H. Q. *Vital involvement in old age*. New York: Norton, 1986.

Erkinjuntti, T., Ostbye, T., Steenhuis, R., and Hachinski, V. The effect of different diagnostic criteria on the prevalence of dementia. *New England Journal of Medicine*, 1997, *337*, 1667–1674.

Evans, D. A., Funkenstein, H. H., Albert, M. S., Scherr, P. A., Crook, N. R., Chown, M. J., Hebert, L. E., Hennakens, C. H., and Taylor, J. D. Prevalence of Alzheimer's disease in a community population of older persons: Higher than previously reported. *Journal of the American Medical Association*, 1989, *262*, 2551–2556.

Fisher, B. J. Successful aging, life satisfaction, and generativity in later life. *International Journal of Aging and Human Development*, 1995, *41*, 239–250.

Folkman, S., Lazarus, R. S., Pimley, S., and Novacek, J. Age differences in stress and coping processes. *Psychology and Aging*, 1987, *2*, 171–184.

Folstein, M., Folstein, S., and McHugh, P. R. Mini-mental state: A practical method for grading the cognitive state of patients for the clinician. *Journal of Psychiatric Research*, 1975, *12*, 189–198.

Fox, J. Broken connections, missing memories. Interviewed in *Time*, April 15, 1991, 10–12.

Freud, S. *Collected papers, Volume I*. London: Hogarth Press, 1924.

Gaber, L. B. Activity/disengagement revisited: Personality types in the aged. *British Journal of Psychiatry*, 1983, *143*, 490–497.

Gallagher-Thompson, D., and Steffan, A. Comparative effectiveness of cognitive-behavioral and brief psychodynamic psychotherapy for treatment of depression in family caregivers. *Journal of Consulting and Clinical Psychology*, 1994, *62*, 543–549.

Gallo, J. J., Anthony, J. C., and Muthen, B. O. Age differences in the symptoms of depression: A latent trait analysis. *Journals of Gerontology*, 1994, *49*, P251–264.

Garfein, A. J., and Herzog, A. R. Robust aging among the young-old, old-old, and oldest-old. *Journals of Gerontology*, 1995, *50B*, S77–S87.

Giarrusso, R., and Bengtson, V. L. Self-esteem. In J. E. Birren (Ed.), *Encyclopedia of gerontology*, Vol. 2. San Diego: Academic Press, 1996.

Goldberg, R. J., and Goldberg, J. Risperidone for dementia-related disturbed behavior in nursing home residents. *International Psychogeriatrics*, 1997, *9*, 65–68.

Graham, K., Carver, V., and Brett, P. J. Alcohol and drug use by older women: Results of a national survey. *Canadian Journal on Aging*, 1995, *14*, 769–791.

Grant, L. A., Kane, R. A., and Stark, A. J. Beyond labels: Nursing home care for Alzheimer's disease in and out of special care units. *Journal of the American Geriatrics Society*, 1995, *43*, 589–576.

Griffith, J. W. Women's stress responses and coping: Patterns according to age groups. *Issues in Health Care of Women*, 1983, *4*, 327–340.

Gurland, B. The impact of depression on quality of life of the elderly. *Clinics in Geriatric Medicine*, 1992, *8*, 377–385.

Gurnack, A. M., and Hoffman, N. G. Elderly alcohol misuse. *International Journal of the Addictions*, 1992, *27*, 867–878.

Gutmann, D. L. The cross-cultural perspective: Notes toward a comparative psychology of aging. In J. E. Birren and K. W. Schaie (Eds.), *Handbook of the psychology of aging*. New York: Van Nostrand Reinhold, 1977.

Gutmann, D. L. Culture and mental health in later life. In J. E. Birren, R. B. Sloane, and G. D. Cohen (Eds.), *Handbook of mental health and aging* (2nd edition). New York: Academic Press, 1992.

Gutmann, D. L. Psychoanalysis and aging: A developmental view. In S. I. Greenspan and G. H. Pollock (Eds.), *The course of life: Psychoanalytic contributions toward understanding personality development. Vol. 3: Adulthood and the aging process.* Washington, DC: U.S. Government Printing Office, 1980.

Henderson, V. W. The epidemiology of estrogen replacement therapy and Alzheimer's disease. *Neurology*, 1997, *48*, S27–S35.

Hendrie, H. C. Epidemiology of Alzheimer's disease. *Geriatrics*, 1997, *52*, S4–S8.

Holmes, T. H., and Masuda, M. Life change and illness susceptibility. In B. S. Dohrenwend and B. P. Dohrenwend (Eds.), *Stressful life events: Their nature and effects*. New York: Wiley, 1974.

Holmes, T. H., and Rahe, R. The social readjustment rating scale. *Journal of Psychosomatic Research*, 1967, *11*, 213–218.

Holroyd, S., Currie, L., Thompson-Heisterman, A., and Abraham, I. A descriptive study of elderly community-dwelling alcoholic patients in the rural south. *American Journal of Geriatric Psychiatry*, 1997, *5*, 221–228.

Howieson, D. B., Holm, L. A., Kaye, J. A., Oken, B. S., and Howieson, J. Neurological function in the optimally healthy oldest old. *Neurology*, 1993, *43*, 1882–1886.

Irion, J. C., and Blanchard-Fields, F. A cross-sectional comparison of adaptive coping in adulthood. *Journal of Gerontology*, 1987, *42*, 502–504.

Jefferson, J. W., and Greist, J. H. *Depression and older people: Recognizing hidden signs and taking steps toward recovery.* Madison, WI: Pratt Pharmaceuticals, 1993.

Jung, C. G. Concerning the archetypes, with special reference to the anima concept. In *C. G. Jung, Collected works*, Vol. 9, Part I. Princeton, NJ: Princeton University Press, 1959.

Jung, C. G. *Modern man in search of a soul.* San Diego: Harcourt Brace and World, 1933.

Kessler, R. C. The effects of stressful life events on depression. *Annual Review of Psychology*, 1997, *48*, 191–214.

King, A. C., Oka, R. K., and Young, D. R. Ambulatory blood pressure and heart rate responses to the stress of work and caregiving in older women. *Journals of Gerontology*, 1994, *49*, M239–245.

Kiyak, H. A. *Adaptation among elderly with Alzheimer's disease.* Final report submitted to the National Institute of Aging. Grant No. R01AG04070, 1991.

Kiyak, H. A., and Kahana, E. F. Life events scaling by college students and the elderly. Paper presented at meetings of the American Psychological Association, New York, 1975.

Kiyak, H. A., Montgomery, R., Borson, S., and Teri, L. Coping patterns among patients with Alzheimer's disease and non-demented elderly. Paper presented at meetings of the Gerontological Society, New Orleans, November, 1985.

Koenig, H. G., and Blazer, D. G. Depression. In J. E. Birren (Ed.), *Encyclopedia of gerontology,* San Diego: Academic Press, 1996.

Kokmen, E., Beard, C. M., O'Brien, P. C., and Kurland, L. T. Epidemiology of dementia in Rochester, Minnesota. *Mayo Clinic Proceedings,* 1996, *71,* 275–282.

Krause, N. Stress, alcohol use, and depressive symptoms in later life. *The Gerontologist,* 1995, *35,* 296–307.

Lazarus, R. S., and Cohen, J. B. *The hassles scale, stress and coping project.* Berkeley: University of California, 1977.

Lazarus, R. S., and DeLongis, A. Psychological stress and coping in aging. *American Psychologist,* 1983, *38,* 245–254.

Lazarus, R. S., and Folkman, S. *Stress, appraisal and coping.* New York: Springer, 1984.

Levinson, D. J. A conception of adult development. *American Psychologist,* 1986, *41,* 3–13.

Levinson, D. J. Middle adulthood in modern society: A sociopsychological view. In G. DiRenzo (Ed.). *We the people: Social change and social character.* Westport, CT: Greenwood Press, 1977.

Levinson, D. J., Darrow, C. M., Klein, E. B., Levinson, M. H., and McKee, B. *The seasons of a man's life.* New York: Knopf, 1978.

Li, G. The interaction effect of bereavement and sex on the risk of suicide in the elderly. *Social Science and Medicine,* 1995, *40,* 825–828.

Lichtenberg, P. A., Ross, T., Millis, S. R., and Manning, C. A. The relationship between depression and cognition in older adults: A cross-validation study. *Journals of Gerontology,* 1995, *50B,* P25–P32.

Light, E., and Lebowitz, B. D. (Eds.) *The elderly with chronic mental illness.* New York: Springer, 1991.

Lis, C. G., and Gaviria, M. Vascular dementia, hypertension, and the brain. *Neurological Research,* 1997, *19,* 471–480.

Mattis, S. Mental status examination for organic mental syndrome in the elderly patient. In R. Bellack and B. Karasu (Eds.), *Geriatric psychiatry.* New York: Grune and Stratton, 1976.

McAdams, D. P., and De St. Aubin, E. A theory of generativity and its assessment through self-report, behavioral acts, and narrative themes in autobiography. *Journal of Personality and Social Psychology,* 1992, *62,* 1003–1015.

McCrae, R. R. Age differences and changes in the use of coping mechanisms. *Journals of Gerontology,* 1989, *44,* P161–Pl64.

McCrae, R. R. Situational determinants of coping responses: Loss, threat and challenge. *Journal of Personality and Social Psychology,* 1984, *46,* 919–928.

McCrae, R. R., and Costa, P. T. *Emerging lives, enduring dispositions.* Boston: Little, Brown, 1984.

McCrae, R. R., and Costa, P. T. *Personality in adulthood.* New York: Guilford, 1990.

McFadden, S. H. Religion, spirituality, and aging. In J. E. Birren and K. W. Schaie (Eds.), *Handbook of the psychology of aging* (4th ed.). San Diego: Academic Press, 1996.

McIntosh, J. L. *U.S.A. suicide: 1994 official final statistics.* 1997. http://oit.iusb.edu/~jmcintos/suicide-stats.html

McLeod, J. D. Life events. In J. E. Birren (Ed.), *Encyclopedia of gerontology,* San Diego: Academic Press, 1996.

McMurdo, M. E., and Rennie, L. A controlled trial of exercise by residents of old people's homes. *Age and Ageing,* 1993, *22,* 11–15.

Miller, N. S., Belkin, B. M., and Gold, M. S. Alcohol and drug dependence among the elderly. *Comprehensive Psychiatry,* 1991, *32,* 153–165.

Mittlelman, M. S., Ferris, S. H., Shulman, E., Steinberg, G., Ambinder, A., Mackell, J. A., and Cohen, J. A comprehensive support program: Effect on depression in spouse-caregivers of AD patients. *The Gerontologist,* 1995, *35,* 792–802.

Mittelman, M. S., Ferris, S. H., Steinberg, G., Shulman E., Mackell, J. A., Ambinder, A., and Cohen, J. An intervention that delays institutionalization of Alzheimer's disease patients: Treatment of spouse-caregivers. *The Gerontologist,* 1993, *33,* 730–740.

Mockenhaupt, R. E., and Beck, K. H. The social context of drinking in mid-life and older persons. Paper presented at annual meeting of the Gerontological Society of America, 1997.

Molgaard, C. A., Nakamura, C. M., Stanford, E. P., Peddecord, M., and Morton, D. M. Prevalence of alcohol consumption among older persons. *Journal of Community Health,* 1990, *15,* 239–251.

Muhlenkamp, A., Gress, L. D., and Flood, M. A. Perception of life change events by the elderly. *Nursing Research,* 1975, *24,* 109–113.

Nacoste, D., and Wise, W. The relationship among negative life events, cognitions and depression within three generations. *The Gerontologist,* 1991, *31,* 397–403.

Nesselroade, J. R., Featherman, D. L., Agen, S. H., and Rowe, J. W. *Short-term variability in physical performance and physiological attributes in older adults: MacArthur successful aging studies.* Unpublished manuscript, University of Virginia, 1996.

Neugarten, B. L., Havighurst, R. J., and Tobin, S. S. Personality and patterns of aging. In B. L. Neugarten (Ed.), *Middle age and aging.* Chicago: University of Chicago Press, 1968.

NIH (National Institutes of Health) Consensus Development Conference. *Diagnosis and treatment of depression.* Washington, DC: 1994.

Offer, D., Ostrov, E., Howard, K. I., and Atkinson, R. *The teenage world: Adolescents' self-image in ten countries.* New York: Plenum, 1988.

Olichney, J. M., Sabbagh, M. N., Hofstetter, C. R., Galasko, D., Grundman, M., Katzman, R., and Thal, L. J. The impact of apolipoprotein E4 on cause of death in Alzheimer's disease. *Neurology,* 1997, *49,* 76–81.

Osgood, N. J., Wood, H. E., and Parham, I. A. *Alcoholism and aging: An annotated bibliography and review.* Westport, CT: Greenwood Press, 1995.

Paganini-Hill, A., and Henderson, V. W. Estrogen replacement therapy and risk of Alzheimer's disease. *Archives of Internal Medicine,* 1996, *156,* 2213–2217.

Pargament, K. I., Ensing, D. S., Falgout, K., Olsen, H., Reilly, B., Van Haitsma, K., and Warren, R. Religious coping efforts as predictors of outcomes to significant negative life events. *American Journal of Community Psychology,* 1990, *18,* 793–824.

Pargament, K. I., Van Haitsma, K., and Ensig, D. S. When age meets adversity: Religion and coping in the later years. In M. A. Kimble, S. H. McFadden, J. W. Ellor, and J. J. Seaber (Eds.), *Aging, spirituality and religion: A handbook.* Minneapolis: Fortress Press, 1995.

Parmelee, P. A., Katz, I. R., and Lawton, M. P. Incidence of depression in long-term care settings. *Journals of Gerontology,* 1992, *47,* M189–M196.

Paykel, E. S., Brayne, C., Huppert, F. A., Gill, C., Barkley, C., Gehlhaar, E., and Beardsold, L. Incidence of dementia in a population older than 75 years in the United Kingdom. *Archives of General Psychiatry,* 1994, *51,* 325–332.

Pearson, J. L., Teri, L., Wagner, A., Truax, P., and Logsdon, R. G. The relationship of problem behaviors in dementia patients to the depression and burden of caregiving spouses. *American Journal of Alzheimer's Disease and Related Disorders and Research,* 1993, *7,* 15–22.

Pederson, N. L., Plomin, R., McClearn, G. E., and Friberg, L. Neuroticism, extroversion, and related traits in adult twins reared apart and reared together. *Journal of Personality and Social Psychology,* 1988, *55,* 950–957.

Perls, T. T. The oldest-old. *Scientific American,* 1995, *272,* 70–75.

Peterson, B. E., and Klohnen E. C. Realization of generativity in two samples of women at midlife. *Psychology and Aging,* 1995, *10,* 20–29.

Phifer, J. E., and Murrell, S. A. Etiologic factors in the outset of depressive symptoms in older adults. *Journal of Abnormal Psychology,* 1986, *95,* 282–291.

Pinquart, M. Analysis of the self-concept of independently living senior citizens. *Zeitschrift für Gerontologie,* 1991, *24,* 98–104.

Plomin, R., Pederson, N. L., McClearn, G. E., Nesselroade, J. R., and Bergeman, C. S. EAS temperaments during the last half of the lifespan: Twins reared apart and twins reared together. *Psychology and Aging,* 1988, *3,* 43–50.

Quam, J. K., and Abramson, N. S. The use of time lines and life lines in work with chronically mentally ill people. *Health and Social Work,* 1991, *16,* 27–33.

Rabins, P. V. Establishing Alzheimer's disease units in nursing homes: Pros and cons. *Hospital and Community Psychiatry,* 1986, *37,* 120–121.

Rabins, P. V. Schizophrenia and psychotic states. In J. E. Birren, R. B. Sloane, and G. D. Cohen (Eds.), *Handbook of mental health and aging* (2nd ed.). New York: Academic Press, 1992.

Rahe, R. H. Subjects' recent life changes and their near future illness reports: A review. *Annals of Clinical Research,* 1972, *4,* 393.

Raschko, R. Spokane community mental health center elderly services. In E. Light, and B. D. Lebowitz (Eds.), *The elderly with chronic mental illness.* New York: Springer, 1991.

Reese, D. R., Gross, A. M., Smalley, D. L., and Messer, S. C. Caregivers of Alzheimer's disease and stroke patients: Immunological and psychological considerations. *The Gerontologist,* 1994, *34,* 534–540.

Regier, D. A., Boyd, J. H., Burke, J. D., Rae, D. S., Myers, J. K., Kramer, M., Robins, L. N., George, L. K., Karno, M., and Locke, B. Z. One month prevalence of mental disorders in the United States: Based on five epidemiologic catchment area sites. *Archives of General Psychiatry*, 1988, *45*, 977–986.

Reisberg, B., Ferris, S. H., De Leon, M. J., and Crook, T. The Global Deterioration Scale for assessment of primary degenerative dementia. *American Journal of Psychiatry*, 1982, *139*, 1136–1139.

Roberts, P., and Newton, P. M. Levinsonian studies of women's adult development. *Psychology and Aging*, 1987, *2*, 154–163.

Rocca, W. A. Frequency distribution and risk factors for Alzheimer's disease. *Nursing Clinics of North America*, 1994, *29*, 101–111.

Rowe, J. W., and Kahn, R. L. Human aging: Usual and successful. *Science*, 1987, *237*, 143–149.

Rowe, J. W., and Kahn, R. L. Successful aging. *The Gerontologist*, 1997, *37*, 433–440.

Russo, J., Vitaliano, P. P., Brewer, D. D., Katon, W., and Becker, J. Psychiatric disorders in spouse caregivers of care recipients with Alzheimer's disease. *Journal of Abnormal Psychology*, 1995, *104*, 197–204.

Ruth, J. E., and Coleman, P. Personality and aging: Coping and management of the self in later life. In J. E. Birren and K. W. Schaie (Eds.), *Handbook of the psychology of aging* (4th ed.). San Diego: Academic Press, 1996.

Ryff, C. D. Beyond Ponce de Leon and life statisfaction: New directions in quest of successful aging. *International Journal of Behavioral Development*, 1989a, *12*, 35–55.

Ryff, C. D. In the eye of the beholder: Views of psychological well-being among middle-aged and older adults. *Psychology and Aging*, 1989b, *4*, 195–210.

Ryff, C. D. Possible selves in adulthood and old age: A tale of shifting horizons. *Psychology and Aging*, 1991, *6*, 286–295.

Sano, M., Ernesto, C., Thomas, R. G., Klauber, M. R., Schafer, K., and Grundman, M. A controlled clinical trial of selegiline, alpha-tocopherol or both as treatment for Alzheimer's disease. *New England Journal of Medicine*, 1997, *336*, 1216–1222.

Schaie, K. W., and Willis, S. L. Adult personality and psychomotor performance. *Journal of Gerontology*, 1991, *46*, P275–P284.

Schulz, R., and Williamson, G. M. A 2-year longitudinal study of depression among Alzheimer's caregivers. *Psychology and Aging*, 1991, *6*, 569–578.

Scogin, F., and McElreath, L. Efficacy of psychosocial treatments for geriatric depression: A quantitative review. *Journal of Consulting and Clinical Psychology*, 1994, *62*, 69–74.

Seeman, T. A., Charpentier, P. A., Berkman, L. F., Tinetti, M. E., Guralnick, J. M., Albert, M., Blazer, D., and Rowe, J. W. Predicting changes in physical performance in a high functioning elderly cohort: MacArthur Studies of Successful Aging. *Journals of Gerontology*, 1994, *49*, M97–M108.

Selye, H. The general adaptation syndrome and the diseases of adaptation. *Journal of Clinical Endocrinology*, 1946, *6*, 117–230.

Selye, H. Stress and aging. *Journal of the American Geriatrics Society*, 1970, *18*, 660–681.

Shanan, J., and Jacobowitz, J. Personality and aging. In C. Eisdorfer (Ed.), *Annual Review of Gerontology and Geriatrics*, 1982, *3*, 148–180.

Singer, C. A., Pang, P. A., Dobie, D. J., and Dorsa, D. M. Estrogen increases gap-43 (neuromodulin) mRNA in the preoptic area of aged rats. *Neurobiology of Aging*, 1996a, *17*, 661–663.

Singer, C. A., Rogers, K. L., Strickland, T. M., Dorsa, D. M. Estrogen protects primary cortical neurons from glutamate toxicity. *Neuroscience Letters*, 1996b, *212*, 13–16.

Sloane, P. D., Lindeman, D. A., Phillips, C., Moritz, D. J., and Koch, G. Evaluating Alzheimer's disease special care units: Reviewing the evidence and identifying potential sources of study bias. *The Gerontologist*, 1995, *35*, 103–111.

Small, G. W., Liston, E. H., and Jarvik, L. F. Diagnosis and treatment of dementia in the aged. *Western Journal of Medicine*, 1981, *135*, 469–481.

Stewart, W. F., Kawas, C., Corrada, M., Metter, E. J., Risk of Alzheimer's disease and duration of NSAID use. *Neurology*, 1997, *48*, 626–632.

Suzman, R. M., Harris, T., Hadley, E. C., Kovar, M. G., and Weindruch, R. The robust oldest old: Optimistic perspectives for increasing healthy life expectancy. In R. M. Suzman, D. P. Willis, and K. G. Manton (Eds.), *The oldest old*. New York: Oxford Press, 1992.

Teri, L., Logsdon, R. G., Uomoto, J., and McCurry, S. M. Behavioral treatment of depression in dementia patients: A controlled clinical trial. *Journals of Gerontology*, 1997, *52B*, P159–P166.

Teri, L., McCurry, S. M., and Logsdon, R. G. Memory, thinking, and aging: What we know about what we know. *Western Journal of Medicine*, 1997, *167*, 269–275.

Thomae, H. Emotion and personality. In J. E. Birren, R. B. Sloane, and G. D. Cohen (Eds.), *Handbook of mental health and aging* (2nd ed.). New York: Academic Press, 1992.

Tran, T. V., Wright, R., and Chatters, L. Health, stress, psychological resources, and subjective well-being among older blacks. *Psychology and Aging*, 1991, 6, 100–108.

Vaillant, G. E. *Adaptation to life*. Boston: Little, Brown, 1977.

Vaillant, G. E. Ego mechanisms of defense and personality psychopathology. *Journal of Abnormal Psychology*, 1994, *103*, 44–50.

Vaillant, G. E., and Vaillant, C. O. Natural history of male psychological health: A 45-year study of pre-dictors of successful aging. *American Journal of Psychiatry*, 1990, *147*, 31–37.

Vitaliano, P. P., Russo, J., and Niaura, R. Plasma lipids and their relationship to psychosocial factors in older adults. *Journals of Gerontology*, 1995, *50B*, P18–P24.

Vitaliano, P. P., Scanlan, J. M., Krenz, C., Schwartz, R. S., and Marcovina, S. M. Psychological distress, caregiving, and metabolic variables. *Journals of Gerontology*, 1996, *51B*, P290–P299.

Whitbourne, S. K., and Primus, L. A. Physical identity. In J. E. Birren (Ed.), *Encyclopedia of gerontology*, San Diego: Academic Press, 1996.

Wurtman, R. J. Alzheimer's disease. *Scientific American*, 1985, *252*, 62–74.

Zweig, R. A., and Hinrichsen, G. A. Factors associated with suicide attempts by depressed older adults: A prospective study. *American Journal of Psychiatry*, 1993, *150*, 1687–1693.

7

LOVE, INTIMACY, AND SEXUALITY IN OLD AGE

The previous chapter focused on personality: who one is and how one feels about oneself. An important aspect of one's personality is sexuality. In fact, **sexuality** encompasses many aspects of one's being as a man or a woman, including one's sexual self-concept, relationships, and functioning (Johnson, 1996). **Sex** is not just a biological function involving genital intercourse or orgasm; it also includes the expression of feelings—loyalty, passion, affection, esteem, and affirmation of one's body and its functioning, which are part of the self in an intimate way (Butler and Lewis, 1993). A person's speech and movement, vitality, and ability to enjoy life are all parts of sexuality. As with other aspects of aging discussed throughout this text, sexuality is thus comprised of biological, emotional, intellectual, spiritual, behavioral, and sociocultural components (Denney and Quadagno, 1992).

Because of the importance of sexuality in people's lives, both older people and professionals who work with them need to understand the normal physiological changes that may affect sexual functioning and the centrality of intimacy across the life span. Since our sexual nature goes far beyond whether we are sexually active at any particular point in life, older individuals need to be comfortable with whatever decisions they make regarding their sexuality. Accordingly, professionals need to respect older adults' choices and values regarding the expression of their sexuality. Although most older individuals can and do engage in intercourse, some older adults genuinely have no desire to engage in the physical aspects of sexual behavior—just as varying patterns of sexual expression are present at all ages.

This chapter begins by examining the prevalent attitudes and beliefs about sex and love in old age that frequently affect an older person's sexuality. It then reviews the age-related physiological changes that may alter the nature of older men and women's sexual response and performance but do not necessarily interfere with their overall experience of sexuality. Other factors that affect sexual activity—chronic illness, psychosocial conditions, and professionals' attitudes—are identified. In many instances, these dynamic contextual factors may exert greater influence than physiological changes as such. Sexual behavior, because of the powerful role it plays in the lives of most people, is especially likely to be affected by the interactions of physiological changes, the larger physical and social environment, the individual's personal learning history, self-concept, and the psychological meaning attached to one's experiences. These factors are examined in terms of both male-female and same-gender relationships, as well as within the larger context of the importance of late-life affection, love, and intimacy. The chapter concludes by identifying implications for professionals who work with older people.

ATTITUDES AND BELIEFS ABOUT SEXUALITY IN LATER LIFE

It is striking that at a time when our society is increasingly tolerant of sexual self-determination for nearly every segment of our population, outdated ideas persist in our approach toward sex and aging (Kaye, 1993). Widespread stereotypes, misconceptions, and jokes about old age and sexuality can powerfully and negatively affect older people's sexual experience. Many of these attitudes and beliefs stem from ageism generally, such as the perceptions of older people as physically unattractive and therefore asexual. Another example of ageism is the perspective that all older people are the same, lacking energy and devoid of sexual feeling, and therefore are not interested in sex. Since sexuality in our society tends to be equated with youthful standards of attractiveness, definitions of older people as asexual are heightened for older women and for individuals with chronic illness and disability.

Other attitudes and beliefs may stem from misinformation, such as the perception that sexual activity and drive do and should decline with old age. Accordingly, older people who speak of enjoying sexuality may be viewed as sinful, exaggerating, or deviant—for example, the "dirty old man." Alternatively, older people who express caring and physical affection for one another may be infantilized, defined as "cute" and ridiculed by professionals, their age peers, and family members. Such public scrutiny and teasing frequently occur among residents and staff of long-term care facilities. The current cohort of older people grew up in periods of restrictive guidelines regarding appropriate sexual behavior and taboos relating to other forms of sexual activity, such as masturbation. Many of these attitudes and beliefs of both older people and their families may reflect a Victorian morality that views sex only as intercourse and intercourse only as appropriate for conception. Sex for communication, intimacy, or pleasure may be considered unnecessary and immoral.

Unfortunately, the widely held attitude in our society that sexual interaction between older persons is socially unacceptable and physically harmful may have negative consequences for older people. Surrounded by those with such beliefs and fearing ridicule or censure, many older people may unnecessarily withdraw from all forms of sexual expression long before they need to, thereby depriving themselves and often their partners of the energy and vitality inherent in sexuality. For many older adults, sexual activity, in the broadest sense of encompassing both physical and emotional interaction, is necessary for them to feel alive, to reaffirm their identity, and to communicate with their partners. Yet, by accepting society's stereotypes, some older individuals may bar themselves from sexual and intimate experiences that could benefit their overall physical and mental well-being (Teitelman, 1990). Understanding the natural physiological alterations in sexual response associated with the aging process is an essential first step toward dispelling such myths. In future years, those myths may change, as the media, gerontologists, and other professionals convey the message that sex is permissible and desirable in old age. In fact, one sign of change is that current cohorts of older people appear more accepting of and permissive in their attitudes toward sexuality and aging than in the past (Johnson, 1996; Steinke, 1994).

MYTHS AND REALITY ABOUT PHYSIOLOGICAL CHANGES AND FREQUENCY OF SEXUAL ACTIVITY

One of the most prevalent societal myths is that age-related physiological changes detrimentally affect sexual functioning. Such misconceptions have been created by the early research on sexuality. In part because of researchers' assumptions that older people do not engage in sex or are embarrassed to talk about it, many early surveys of sexual attitudes did not even question older people about their sexuality. Such avoidance of the topic fostered further misinformation and misconceptions.

Other early studies included questions about sexuality, but focused on changes only in the frequency of sexual intercourse. These researchers thereby overlooked the subjective experience or more qualitative aspects of sexuality in old age. For example, from 1938 to 1948, Kinsey and his colleagues studied primarily 16- to 55-year-olds, and their discussion of respondents over age 60 focused almost exclusively on the frequency of sexual intercourse, not on the meaning of sexuality to older people. Using numbers of **orgasm** or ejaculation as the measure of good sex, they found that by age 70, 25 percent of men experienced sexual dysfunction. Women were portrayed as reaching the peak of their sexual activity in their late twenties or thirties, then remaining on that plateau through their sixties, after which they showed a slight decline in sexual response capability (Kinsey, Pomeroy, and Martin, 1948, 1953). Because Kinsey and his colleagues overlooked the broader psychological aspects of sexuality, they failed to address the subjective experience, meaning, and importance of sex at different ages. Older individuals may have sexual intercourse less often, but it is not necessarily less meaningful than at a younger age. In fact, few age-related physiological changes prevent continued sexual enjoyment and activity in old age.

In addition to the emphasis on frequency of sexual intercourse, early research on sexuality was limited by the non-random and therefore non-representative nature of the sample and by comparing younger and older cohorts at one point in time. For example, the Duke Longitudinal Study, which in 1954 examined the frequency of sexual intercourse and interest in sex, found declining frequencies of sexual activity for older adults compared to their young and middle-aged counterparts, especially for women and unmarried in-

dividuals. The median age for stopping intercourse was 68 in men and 60 in women (Pfeiffer and Davis, 1972). This study had several limitations, however. The definition of sexual activity was limited to heterosexual intercourse, and the respondents constituted a cohort of individuals raised during a period of strict sexual conservatism. As discussed in Chapter 1, we now know that such cross-sectional data fail to give a lifetime picture of an individual's sexual activity. Because the cohort effect was not identified, the low levels of sexual activity reported may have reflected the attitudes, values, and reluctance to report on their activity among a cohort of elders who grew up in the Victorian era of the late 1890s to early 1900s, rather than any age-related physiological changes in sexual functioning (Schiavi and Rehman, 1995).

A subsequent reanalysis of the 1954 Duke Longitudinal Study data to control for a possible cohort effect and the second Duke Longitudinal Study over a six-year period revealed stability of sexual activity patterns from mid- to late life (George and Weiler, 1981). In other words, those who were sexually conservative and inactive in young adulthood and mid-life, perhaps because of their social upbringing, carried that pattern through their later years. Similarly, those who were more sexually active in young adulthood and middle age continued to remain active in old age. A later analysis of the Duke data also found older women to be more interested in sex than older men; however, the rate of sexual activity among older women declined, partly because of the absence of partners and because the husband tended to be the one responsible for curtailing or discontinuing sexual activities. In fact, marital status appears to be more important in influencing women's sexual activity than it is for men's (Matthias et al., 1997). For men, sexual dysfunction or impotence appears to be the main barrier to sexual activity (Wiley and Bortz, 1996).

One of the first large-scale studies that provided evidence for continued sexuality in old age was the work of Masters and Johnson (1981). In their classic study of sexual responsiveness across the life span, Masters and Johnson determined that, while physiological changes occur with age, the capacity for both functioning and fulfillment does not disappear. They concluded that there are no known limits to sexual activity. Later studies have tended to find that most older adults, especially men, even among those over age 80, remain sexually active. As with most behaviors, there is a wide range in sexual activity; some individuals even experience an increase in sexual behavior with increasing age (Matthias et al., 1997; Weg, 1996; Schiavi and Rehman, 1995). In an open-ended questionnaire completed by 800 participants in senior centers, Starr and Weiner (1981) found the majority of respondents to be sexually active. In fact, 99 percent desired sexual relations with varying frequencies if they could engage in sexual activity whenever they wanted. Sexual inactivity appeared to be based upon life circumstances, not lack of interest or desire. Contrary to earlier findings from the 1954 Duke study, sexual frequency did not decline sharply with age, but ranged instead from 1.5 times a week for 60- to 69-year-olds, 1.4 times a week for 70- to 79-year-olds, to 1.2 times a week for the group over age 80. Some later studies have found the average frequency of sexual activity to be four times a month among those aged 65 and older (Steinke, 1994; Marsiglio and Donnelley, 1991).

In sum, age, type of study design (longitudinal versus cross-sectional) and the possible confounding of age with cohort membership may partially account for different outcomes. Older people who remain sexually active do not differ significantly in the frequency of sexual relations compared with their younger selves (longitudinal data). Rather, sexual activity appears to decrease significantly when older people are compared with younger people at the same point in time (cross-sectional data). When a partner is available, the rate of sexual behavior is fairly stable throughout life. And sexually active older people perceive their sex lives as remaining much the same as they grow older. Although good physical and mental health are predictors of sexual activity and satisfaction (Matthias et al., 1997), even older people with chronic health problems, depression, and cognitive dysfunction can still enjoy sexual satisfaction (Richardson and Lazur, 1995; Schiavi and Rehman, 1995).

Rates of activity increase to over 80 percent for men and over 60 percent for women when sexual activity is defined more broadly than intercourse to encompass touching and caressing (Janus and Janus, 1993; Diokno, Brown, and Herzog, 1990). Studies that include open-ended questions have tended to identify the excitement, enjoyment, and pleasure—the passion and romance—of late-life sexuality and the value older adults place on the quality and meaning of intimate relationships. Accordingly, sexual activity and satisfaction have been found to be related to older people's sense of self-worth and competence (Weg, 1996; Marsiglio and Donnelly, 1991).

To review, as our biological clocks change with age, it is not necessarily for the better or worse in terms of either the frequency of activity or the nature of the sexual experience. Individuals who have been sexually responsive all their lives will still be sexual and enjoy sexual satisfaction in their later years, although their experience may differ subjectively from their earlier years (Zeiss, 1997; Bachman and Leiblum, 1991). Yet, this difference can be positive. For example, 75 percent of the respondents in the Starr-Weiner study described earlier (1981) said that sex is the same or better than when they were younger. Although the majority of female respondents considered orgasm essential to a good sexual experience, they also emphasized mutuality, love, and caring as central to a satisfying sexual relationship and willingly varied their sexual practices to achieve satisfaction. Male respondents emphasized that it is not only the physical stimulation of sex that is important, but also that sex is necessary for them to feel alive, to reaffirm their identity, and to communicate with a person they care about. The actual level of activity may be less important than one's satisfaction with the activity (Matthias et al., 1997). Nevertheless, a number of physiological, age-related changes can affect the nature of the sexual response (Kaplan, 1990).

Sexuality and intimacy are important throughout the later years.

WOMEN AND AGE-RELATED PHYSIOLOGICAL CHANGES

With the growing numbers of women in the 45- to 54-year-old age group, increasing attention is being given to menopause. As noted in Chapter 4, the major changes for women as they grow older are associated with the reduction in estrogen and progesterone, the predominant hormones produced by the ovaries, during menopause. The **climacteric**—loss of reproductive ability—takes place in three phases: premenopause, menopause, and postmenopause, and may extend over many years. Premenopause is marked by a decline in ovarian function in which a woman's ovaries stop producing eggs and significantly decrease their monthly production of estrogen. Menopause, in the strictest sense as one event during the climacteric, is a period in a woman's life when there is a gradual cessation of the menstrual cycle, including irregular cycles and menses, which are related to the loss of ovarian function. Menopause is considered to have occurred when 12 consecutive months have passed without a menstrual period. The average age of menopause is 50 or 51 years across most cultures, although it can begin as early as age 40 and as late as age 58. Surgical removal of the uterus—**hysterectomy**—also brings an end to menstruation.

The major physiological changes related to the decrease in **estrogen** in menopausal and postmenopausal women are hot flashes, urogenital atrophy, urinary tract changes, and bone changes. **Hot flashes** are caused by vasomotor instability, when the nerves overrespond to decreases in hormone levels. This affects the hypothalamus (the part of the brain that regulates body temperature), causing the blood vessels to dilate or constrict. When the blood vessels dilate, blood rushes to the skin surface, causing perspiration, flushing, and increased pulse rate and temperature. Hot flashes are characterized by a sudden sensation of heat in the upper body, often accompanied by a drenching sweat and sometimes followed by chills. Gradually diminishing in frequency, hot flashes generally disappear within a year or two. Sleep disturbances can also result from hormonal changes, with sleep deprivation leading to irritability and moodiness often associated with menopause. Although 80 percent of women aged 45 through 55 experience some discomfort such as hot flashes and sweats during menopause, most find that these physiological changes do not interfere with their daily activities or sexual functioning; they also do not cause psychological difficulties, although vasomotor instability does disrupt and reduce sleep (Kaiser, 1996; Weg, 1996).

Estrogen loss combined with the normal biological changes of aging leads to urogenital atrophy—a reduction in the elasticity and lubricating abilities of the vagina approximately 5 years after the menopause. As the vagina becomes drier and the layer of cell walls thinner, the amount of lubricants secreted during sexual arousal is reduced.

Although vaginal lubrication takes longer, these changes have little impact on the quality of orgasms and do not result in an appreciable loss in sensation or feeling. Nevertheless, urogenital atrophy is an important contributor to decline in sexual activity with menopause. Discomfort associated with these changes during intercourse can be minimized by using artificial lubricants such as KY jellies and vaginal creams. In addition, regular and consistent sexual activity, including masturbation, maintains vaginal lubricating ability and vaginal muscle tone, thereby reducing discomfort during intercourse (Bachmann, 1995).

Because of thinning vaginal walls, which results from estrogen degeneration and which offers less protection to the bladder and the urethra, lower urinary tract infections such as cystitis and burning urination may occur more frequently. These problems can be treated and often reversed with hormone replacement therapy, most often estrogen combined with progesterone. Incontinence has been found to inhibit sexual desire and response; unfortunately, many older women are reluctant to discuss incontinence with others, which precludes their finding ways to prevent its negative impact upon sexual activity (Kaiser, 1996).

As discussed more fully in Chapter 4, osteoporosis, which is related to the loss of estrogen during menopause, is caused by a woman's inability to absorb sufficient calcium to strengthen her bones. The reduction in bone mass predisposes older women to fractures. Hormone replacement therapy combined with regular exercise has been found to prevent osteoporosis, and may actually increase bone mass by promoting new bone formation, especially in the hip and spine (PEPI Trial, 1996; Notelovitz, Martin, and Tesar, 1991).

Contrary to stereotypes and taboos regarding menopause, approximately 20 percent of women go through this experience with no intense symptoms such as hot flashes, while 15 percent experience symptoms sufficiently severe to warrant treatment. The majority—65 percent—experience only mild symptoms that do not require any medical intervention. This wide variability in symptoms suggests that there is not an inevitable "menopausal syndrome" (Weg, 1996). The primary medical response to the symptoms of hot flashes and vaginal atrophy has been hormone replacement therapy (HRT), which restores body hormones to levels similar to those before menopause. In 1992, the National Institutes of Health, through the Women's Health Initiative, began a study of 70,000 postmenopausal women ages 50 to 79 to examine the long-term benefits and risks of HRT. As noted in Chapter 4, estrogen does alleviate hot flashes and vaginal changes, including atrophy, dryness, itching, pain during intercourse, lower urinary tract problems, and frequent urination, and appears to be a major factor in the prevention of osteoporosis and cardiovascular diseases. The average amount of time spent on HRT by most women is nearly 10 years, although less than 20 percent of postmenopausal women use estrogen, especially among ethnic minority elders. There is some evidence that beneficial effects of estrogen occur even when it is started after the age of 60. These also include effects on stability of cognitive abilities and skin and hair quality (Jacobs and Hillard, 1996). The benefits and risks of HRT are described in greater detail in Chapters 4 and 6.

Increasingly, nutrition, exercise, and herbal or naturopathic treatments have been found useful in moderating symptoms associated with menopause. In many non-Western cultures, menopause is viewed as a time of respect and status for women. Although our cultural view is that women are expected to have difficulty at this period of life, the incidence of insomnia, depression, and anxiety may be traced to the meaning or psychosocial significance that individuals attach to menopause, as well as the value placed on the role of mother. The findings on whether menopause is more distressing to employed women or to housewives are mixed. Most women view menopause as a potentially positive transition rather than as a loss of fertility or as a cause of depression. It can be a time to focus on future opportunities, for self-accomplishment and new meaning, and for positive changes in life-style toward greater autonomy

(Jones, 1997; Defey, Storch, Cardozo, and Diaz, 1996). Other symptoms reported by menopausal women, such as headaches, dizziness, palpitations, depression, and weight increase, are not caused by menopause itself, but may be due to underlying psychosocial reasons. In sum, menopause, like other transitions that women experience, is affected by physiological and sociocultural factors, personality, and cultural influences.

Despite some of the uncomfortable symptoms, menopause does not impede full sexual activity from a physiological point of view. In fact, many women, freed of worries about pregnancy and birth control, report greater sexual satisfaction after menopause, including after a hysterectomy (Weg, 1996). Generally, an older woman's sexual response cycle has all the dimensions of her younger response, but the time it takes for her to respond to sexual stimulation gradually increases. The subjective levels of sexual tension initiated or elaborated by clitoral stimulation do not differ for older and younger women. The preorgasmic plateau phase, during which sexual tension is at its height, is extended in duration. Contrary to stereotypes, most older women experience and enjoy orgasm. For example, in the classic Starr and Weiner study (1981), the majority of women were orgasmic always or most of the time: 69 percent of those aged 60 to 69, 76 percent of those 70 to 79 years of age, and 68 percent of the group over age 80. These and other data suggest that an older woman's capacity for orgasms may be slowed, but not impaired. The orgasm is experienced more rapidly, somewhat less intensely, and more spasmodically. The resolution phase, during which the body returns to its baseline prearousal state, occurs more rapidly than in younger women.

From a physiological point of view, no impediment exists to full sexual activity for women after menopause. In fact, women experience only a slight decline in their capacity for sexual pleasure throughout their lives. Changes such as the thinning of vaginal walls and loss of vaginal elasticity may render intercourse somewhat less pleasurable, but these effects can be minimized by sexual regu-larity. Instead, older women's sexuality tends to be influenced more by sociocultural expectations than by physiological changes—primarily by the limited number of male partners and the common cultural definition of older women as asexual and unattractive. Low self-image, for example, can be a barrier to intimacy (Haffner, 1994). These psychosocial barriers will be discussed more fully later in this chapter.

MEN AND AGE-RELATED PHYSIOLOGICAL CHANGES

Relatively little attention has been given to men's hormonal rhythms compared to women's. One reason for less attention is that men maintain their fertility and generally do not lose their capacity to father children, making any hormonal and sexual changes less abrupt and visible. There is, however, increasing recognition that **male menopause** or "viropause" does occur and can affect the psychological, interpersonal, social, and spiritual dimensions of a man's life. However, the male climacteric differs from women's in two significant ways: it comes 8 to 10 years later (typically between ages 45 and 54), and progresses at a more gradual rate. This is because the loss of testosterone (approximately 1 percent a year on average), while varying widely among men, is not as dramatic nor as abrupt as the estrogen depletion for menopausal women. Nevertheless, loss of testosterone may reduce muscle size and strength, increase calcium loss in the bones, cause declines in the immune system responses, and lessen sexual response and interest. In addition, men report varied levels of fatigue, irritability, indecisiveness, depression, loss of self-confidence, listlessness, poor appetite, and problems of concentration (Diamond, 1997; Weg, 1996). Some men indicate reduced interest in sex, anxiety and fear about sexual changes, increased relationship problems and arguments with their partners over sex, love, and intimacy, and loss of **erection** during sexual activity. Changes in secondary sexual characteristics also occur; a man's voice may become higher pitched, his facial hair may grow more slowly, and muscularity may give way to flabbiness. Combined with the loss of muscle tissue and weight loss in the later years discussed in Chapter 3, it is not unusual for men to become thinner and less muscular by their seventies. All of these changes require adjustment and adaptation, but in themselves do not necessarily result in reduced sexual enjoyment and desire.

The normal physiological changes that characterize men's aging alter the nature of the sexual response, but do not interfere with sexual performance. The **preorgasmic plateau phase,** or excitement stage, increases in length, so that there is a slower response to sexual stimulation. An erection may take longer to achieve and may require more direct stimulation. For example, in 18-year-old males, full erection is achieved on stimulation for an average of 3 seconds; at age 45, the average time is 18 to 20 seconds, while a 75-year-old man requires 5 minutes or more. Erections tend to be less full with age and the erect penis may be less firm. But these erectile changes do not necessarily alter a man's sexual enjoyment and satisfaction. The frequency and degree of erections can be studied while a man is sleeping. The recording of **nocturnal penile tumescence**—(sleep-related erections)—offers an opportunity to evaluate objectively sexual functioning under relatively controlled conditions. Such studies have found that the volume and force of the ejaculation are decreased in older men as they sleep. The two-stage orgasm—the sense of ejaculation inevitably followed by actual semen expulsion that is experienced by younger males—often blurs into a one-stage ejaculation for older men (Schiavi et al., 1990; Thienhaus, 1988; Masters and Johnson, 1981).

Accordingly, orgasm is experienced more rapidly, somewhat less intensely, and more spasmodically, occurring every second or third act of intercourse rather than every time. The length of time between orgasm and subsequent erections increases; in other words, the **refractory period** after ejaculation, before a second ejaculation is possible, is longer. However, although these changes may alter the nature of the sexual experience, none of them causes sexual inactivity or impotence; whether all or singly, the subjectively appreciated levels of sensual pleasure may not diminish (Katchadourian, 1987; Masters and Johnson, 1981). In recent years, as noted in Chapter 1, there has been increasing attention to hormones such as DHEA, that is produced by the adrenal glands, the brain, and the skin, to revive men's sexual interest.

Although not an inevitable consequence of aging, erectile dysfunction or **impotence** (i.e., an inability to get and sustain an erection) is the chief cause of older men's withdrawing from sexual activity. The Massachusetts Male Aging Study of 1700 men found that erectile dysfunction occurred in more than 50 percent of the men age 40 and over. Older men and their partners need to be informed that sexual dysfunctions are both common and treatable. Although there is not a significant correlation between impotence and lowered testosterone levels, declines in DHEA levels with aging are found to be associated with impotence (Diamond, 1997). An older man may be particularly at risk when he faces the combination of the unexpected onset of involuntary alterations in his established sexual patterns and the negative conditioning of cultural stereotypes related to sexual function and aging. Despite the underlying pathologies associated with impotence, it tends to be underdiagnosed because of the embarrassment and reluctance of older men and their health care providers to discuss sexual matters candidly. Since medical treatments can be effective in altering erectile dysfunction, health care providers must be sure to rule out the physical basis of impotence, which tends to be more important than psychological factors (Kaiser, 1996; Rosen, 1996; NIH Consensus Statement, 1992). These physical risk factors include cardiovascular disease, the effects of drugs (especially antihypertensives, antidepressants, and tranquilizers), diabetes, hypertension, endocrine or metabolic disorders, neurological disorders, depression, alcohol, or prostate disorders. Most types of prostate surgery do not cause impotence, as will be discussed in the next section, "Disease and Sexual Activity."

In recent years, there has been growing attention to new ways to treat impotence. The marketing of a wide range of products, in part, reflects drug companies' awareness of the buying power of Baby Boomers. Treatments for impotence include oral medication that cause erections; pellets that are inserted into the uerthra with an applicator and then dilate the arteries and relax the erectile tissues, thereby triggering involuntary erections; injection therapy; vacuum pumps; **penile implants;** and vascular surgery. Clinical trials of oral medications, such as Sildenafil or Viagra, have found that 60 to 80 percent of the men who have participated and who have varying degrees of impotence have benefited (Leland, 1997). It is important, however, that attention continue to be given to the psychological factors related to intimacy and sexual enjoyment in old age, not just to chemical solutions. As noted above, the concept of sexuality in old age needs to be expanded to include more than erec-

tion and ejaculation during intercourse. For example, health care providers and counselors must encourage couples to communicate their fears about impotence and suggest ways that they can openly enjoy fulfilling sexual experiences and intimacy without an erection.

In summary, the normal physiological changes that characterize men's aging alter the nature of the sexual response, but do not interfere with men's sexual performance. These include (1) slower response to sexual stimulation, with a longer time and direct physical stimulation more often needed for an erection, (2) less full or firm erections, (3) decreased volume and force of ejaculation, (4) occasional lack of orgasm during intercourse, and (5) increased length of time between orgasm and subsequent erections. Impotence, the most common sexual disorder among older men, appears to be influenced more by physiological than psychosocial factors.

Table 7.1 summarizes the physiological changes that affect sexual activities in older people, but do not necessarily alter sexual satisfaction.

TABLE 7.1   Age-Related Physiological Changes in Genital Function

Normal changes in aging women that do not interfere with full sexual activity:

- Reduction in vaginal elasticity and lubrication
- Thinning of vaginal walls
- Slower response to sexual stimulation
- Preorgasmic plateau phase is longer
- Fewer and less intense orgasmic contractions
- After orgasm, rapid return to pre-arousal state

Normal changes in aging men that alter the nature of the sexual response, but do not interfere with performance:

- Erection may require more direct stimulation
- Erection is slower, less full, disappears quickly after orgasm
- Orgasm experienced more rapidly, less intensely, and more spasmodically; decreased volume and force of ejaculation
- Increased length of time between orgasm and subsequent erections (longer refractory period)
- Occasional lack of orgasm during intercourse
- More seepage or retrograde ejaculation

DISEASE AND SEXUAL ACTIVITY

Although normal physiological changes do not inevitably reduce sexual enjoyment, physical well-being does appear to be associated with sexual responsiveness and activity (Schiavi and Rehman, 1995). Not surprisingly, physical health problems, of one's own and/or one's partner, are a frequently cited reason for refraining from sexual activity. Even when an illness does not directly affect the sexual organs themselves, disease can affect sexual function because of physical decline, associated pain, iatrogenic complications of medication, and the partner's fears about causing further injuries to health. Since sexual response depends on the cooperation of multiple systems of the body—hormonal, circulatory, and nervous systems—if any of these are disrupted, sexual functioning can be adversely affected. And because sexual response also depends upon an individual's mental well-being, the distraction of illness may be all-consuming and deplete the psychic energy needed for sexual interest and responsiveness. On the other hand, sexual activity can be an important component of treatment following a major illness or surgery and is minimally risky to a person's health (Kaiser, 1996). In this section, the chronic illnesses that commonly affect sexual functioning—diseases of the prostate, diabetes, heart disease and strokes, and degenerative and rheumatoid arthritis—are briefly discussed.

More than 50 percent of men age 65 and over have some degree of **prostate enlargement,** known as *benign prostatic hypertrophy* or BPH. One out of every three men over age 65 will experience prostate difficulties, usually inflammation or enlargement of the prostate gland, pain in the uro/genital area, and urinary flow dysfunction (Diamond, 1997; Bostwick, MacLennan, and Larson, 1996). Infections may be successfully treated with antibiotics, and new drugs are available to shrink the prostate. Some prostate problems are treatable through simple interventions such as warm baths and gentle massage or through antibiotics. However, when urination is

severely restricted or painful, surgery is necessary. After surgery, semen is no longer ejaculated through the penis, but is pushed back into the bladder and is later discharged in the urine. After healing occurs, the capacity to ejaculate and fertility may return in some men. The feeling of orgasm or climax can still be present, and sexual pleasure is not inevitably lessened.

The rate at which prostate cancer kills men is similar to that of breast cancer in women. The most extreme treatment for prostate cancer is **radical perineal prostatectomy,** when nerves are cut (Kaiser, 1996; Morra and Potts, 1996). Although most forms of prostate surgery do not cause impotence, irreversible impotence and incontinence can result from radical prostatectomy. Fortunately, there are an increasing number of alternatives for early prostate cancer, such as radioactive pellet implantation or some other form of radiation therapy. Nerve-sparing surgery has been developed, and may reduce the incidence of impotence among some men who undergo radical prostatectomy. However, the urologist's priority is to rid the patient of cancer tissue, and nerves very close to the prostate gland must often be severed. New treatments or refinements of treatments, such as penile implants, vacuum pumps, and smooth muscle relaxants that are injected into the penis, are currently being developed, but research on their effectiveness and complications is, in most cases, incomplete (Bostwick et al., 1996). Health care providers must be sensitive to providing older patients with as much information as possible about the implications of surgery for sexual functioning.

Despite the fact that prostate surgery does not cause impotence in the majority of cases, between 5 and 40 percent of men who have undergone such surgery say that they can no longer achieve an erection. In addition, since treatment of prostate cancer often involves methods that lower testosterone levels or block the effects of testosterone, a large percent of men undergoing such treatment feel loss of sexual desire, and up to 40 percent actually experience hot flashes (Diamond, 1997). In such instances, psychological factors need to be addressed through counseling, and couples need to be encouraged to try alternate methods of sexual satisfaction until the man can achieve an erection. In some instances, a man's postoperative "impotence" may be a convenient excuse for not engaging in sexual activity, or may represent fears of additional illness. In instances where impotence is irreversible, partners need to be encouraged to pursue alternate means of sexual pleasure or consider a penile implant. Masturbation, more leisurely precoital stimulation, and use of artificial lubricants can all provide satisfying sexual experiences.

While most older men fear that prostate surgery will interfere with their sexual functioning and satisfaction, women may fear that a **hysterectomy** (surgical removal of the uterus), an ovariectomy (surgical removal of both ovaries), or a **mastectomy** (surgical removal of one or both breasts) will negatively affect their sexual functioning. However, in most instances, women's sexual satisfaction and long-term functioning are not affected by these surgeries, particularly if their partners are sensitive and supportive. On the other hand, some hormonal changes associated with a complete hysterectomy may affect sex drive. When women experience menopause as a result of a hysterectomy, perhaps earlier than the average age of onset for menopause, hormone replacement therapy is advisable except when the hysterectomy was due to cancer.

More common medical causes of male impotence than prostate surgery are arteriosclerosis—the vascular hardening that leads to heart attacks and strokes—and diabetes, particularly for those who have been diabetic most of their lives. Anything that damages the circulatory system—smoking, inactivity, poor diet—can cause erectile dysfunction. Older people who have experienced a heart attack or heart surgery may assume that sexual activity will endanger their lives and give it up. Unfortunately, many health care providers are not sensitive to such fears and fail to reassure individuals that sexual activity can be resumed after they undergo a stress test without pain or arrhythmia (Kaiser, 1996). Another precaution for post-heart attack patients who have been pre-

scribed nitroglycerin is to take their usual dose 15 to 30 minutes before engaging in sexual activity (Schiavi and Rehman, 1995). Stroke patients may also feel compelled to abstain from sexual activity because of an unfounded fear that sex could cause another cerebrovascular accident. In the majority of cases, strokes do not harm the physiology of sexual functioning or the ability to experience arousal (Thienhaus, 1988). However, some antihypertensive drugs can cause impotence or inhibit ejaculation. Fortunately, a new class of antihypertensive drugs, called ACE inhibitors, has been reported to cause fewer side effects on sexual function.

Impotence in life-long diabetics occurs because diabetes interferes with the circulatory and neurologic mechanisms responsible for the supply of blood flowing to the penis for erection. In such instances, a penile implant may be an option. In instances of late-onset diabetes, impotence may be the first observable symptom. However, when the diabetes is under control, potency generally returns. The sexual functioning of women diabetics appears to be relatively unimpaired. When diabetes is controlled through balanced blood chemistry, sexual problems other than impotence that are attributable to the disease should disappear or become less severe. Other less common diseases that may cause impotence are illnesses that affect the vascular and endocrine systems, kidney diseases, and neurological lesions in the brain or spinal cord (Gambert, 1987; Walz and Blum, 1987).

Arthritis does not directly interfere with sexual functioning, but can make sexual activity painful. Some medications used to control arthritic pain may also affect sexual desire and performance. Yet sexual activity can serve to maintain some range and motion of the limbs and joints and thereby help sore joints; it can also stimulate the body's production of cortisone, which is one of the substances used to treat the symptoms of rheumatoid arthritis (Cochrane, 1989). Pain during sexual intercourse can be minimized by experimenting with alternative positions. A warm bath, massage of painful joints, and timing the use of pain-killing medications approximately 30 minutes prior to intercourse may also help to control some of the pain associated with arthritis. As with most chronic diseases, communication with the partner about what is comfortable and pleasurable is essential (Walz and Blum, 1987).

Closely related to the effects of chronic illness upon sexuality are those of drugs, including alcohol. Diagnosing the effects of drugs on sexuality may be particularly difficult, since drugs affect individuals differently, and drug interactions frequently occur. Drugs that inhibit or otherwise alter the performance of any one of the systems of the body can alter sexual response. For men, some medications that are prescribed for chronic conditions may cause impotence, decrease sexual drive, delay ejaculation, or result in an inability to ejaculate. Psychotropic medications used to treat depression and psychosis are particularly likely to impair erectile functioning (Corbett, 1987). Of patients taking thioridazine, 49 percent will experience impaired ejaculation, and 44 percent impotence. Yet this is one of the first drugs that a physician will prescribe for an older person who is agitated, depressed, schizophrenic, or anxious. Similarly, in 40 percent of the cases involving the drug amoxapine for treatment of depression, impotence occurs. As noted above, other types of drugs likely to affect sexual functioning are antihypertensive medications used to treat high blood pressure, drugs to control diabetes, and steroids (Lewis, 1989).

For women, drugs may be associated with decreased vaginal lubrication, reduced sexual drive, and a delay or inability to achieve orgasm (Walz and Blum, 1987). Fortunately, physicians as well as older people are becoming more aware of potential negative effects of drug regimes on sexual functioning. Likewise, more drugs are now available that do not have negative side-effects on sexual desire and/or ability. These include ACE inhibitors among the antihypertensives; fluoxetine, trazodone, and maprotiline among the antidepressants; desipramine among the tricyclic antidepressants; and lorazepam, alprazolam, and buspirone among antianxiety agents (Lewis, 1989).

Alcohol, when used excessively, can act as a depressant on sexual ability and desire. Alcohol consumption affects male sexual performance by making both erection and ejaculation difficult to attain; consequently, a man's anxiety about performance may increase and result in temporary impotence. Prolonged alcoholism may lead to impotence as a result of irreversible damage to the nervous system. Although the effects of alcohol on women's sexual performance have not been extensively researched, some women who abuse alcohol appear to experience less sexual desire and no orgasms.

GAY AND LESBIAN PARTNERS IN OLD AGE

Although most examples of sexual activity in this chapter are presented in terms of **heterosexual** marital relationships, this should not be assumed to always be the case. Older people, their family members, and health and social service professionals must be sensitive to heterosexual relationships outside of marriage as well as to same-gender, or **homosexual** relationships. Such sensitivity includes the discarding of stereotypical views of the nature of **gay** and **lesbian** relationships. Contrary to commonly held images, the varieties of gay and lesbian bonding are similar to those within heterosexual communities—ranging from monogamous life partners and non-monogamous primary relationships to serial monogamy and episodic liaisons. Gay and lesbian life partners face many of the same issues that confront long-term heterosexual spouses, such as fears about the loss of sexual attractiveness, the death or illness of a sexual partner, or diminished interest or capacity for sex because of chronic disease. On the other hand, after a lifetime of discrimination or ostracism from family members, coworkers, or society generally, homosexual couples face additional issues regarding intimacy and sexuality, which are discussed in this chapter and in Chapter 9.

Although there is as much diversity of sexual activity for gay and lesbian older people as for het-

Many lesbian and gay couples maintain long-term commitments to each other.

erosexuals, there is also a consistent pattern of relatively high life satisfaction with being gay, good adjustment to old age, and on-going sexual interest and activity. Older gay individuals who define the meaning of homosexuality in terms of positive self-identity and acceptance have been found to have the fewest psychosomatic complaints (Adelman, 1991). Both lesbians and gays are more likely to report a high level of life satisfaction if they are happily partnered and communicating effectively with one another (Lee, 1990).

Older lesbians have generally practiced serial monogamy throughout their lives and continue in later life to expect to find a new partner, although many of the current cohort of older lesbians remain closeted about their sexual orientation. They usually report positive self-image and feelings about being identified as a lesbian (Deevey, 1990). Older lesbians generally do not fear changes in physical appearance, loneliness, or isolation in old age as much as some heterosexual women do, perhaps because of the strong friendship networks that characterize many lesbian relationships (Dorfman, Walters, Burke, Hardin, Karanik, Raphael, and Silverstein, 1995). Most lesbians remain sexually active, although sexual frequency generally declines. The extent to which sexual activity is considered to be an integral part of a lesbian rela-

tionship varies, although sexuality in a broader sense continues to play an important role in their lives (Kehoe, 1989, 1986). For some, lesbianism is a wider female interdependence and sense of positive self-identity rather than a sexual relationship as such.

The number of gay men with partners increases with age and peaks among those 46 to 55 years old. After age 60, the percent of gay couples decreases because of death, illness, cautiousness, or rejection of the notion of having a single, life-long partner (Pope and Schulz, 1991; Berger, 1984). Older gay men are more likely to be in long-term relationships (with an average length of 10 years) or none at all rather than in short-term relationships of a year or less. Gay men tend to be more concerned about age-related changes in physical appearance than are lesbians, although perhaps no more so than their heterosexual peers, and they may think of themselves as older than their chronological age. Nevertheless, they generally maintain positive feelings about themselves and their appearance in old age (Bennett and Thompson, 1990). Compared with their younger counterparts, older gay men have been found to be similarly involved in the homosexual world, satisfied with their social lives and sexual orientation, and confident in their popularity with other homosexuals. Consistent with the continuity theory of aging, sex appears to be equally important at all phases of a gay man's life. Contrary to the myth of lonely, rejected, depressed older gay men, most gay men are generally sexually active, although frequency does decline with age; they typically are satisfied with their partners and their sex lives; they report a positive sense of self-esteem, well-being, and contentment and adapt fairly well to the aging process. Despite fears of loneliness, most gay men have closer friendships in old age than do heterosexual men, and these friends and confidants may serve to resolve their fear of aging (Dorfman et al., 1995; McDougall-Graham, 1993; Quam and Whitford, 1992; Pope and Schultz, 1991). For many gay men, friendships may replace family ties disrupted by declaration of their homosexuality.

On the other hand, compared with their younger counterparts, older gay men are more likely to fear exposure of their homosexuality, to hide their sexual orientation, to view their relatives, friends, and employers as less accepting of their homosexuality, and to see their sexual orientation as outside of their personal control. However, these differences largely reflect cohort effects, rather than the aging process per se. The social support function of gay and lesbian relationships is discussed further in Chapter 9.

As noted in Chapter 4, there is growing concern about the increase in AIDS among the older population. Despite the risks, most older gay men remain sexually active, although they engage less frequently in one-night encounters and are more knowledgeable about safe sex than comparably aged heterosexual males (Pope and Schulz, 1991). With the growing public awareness about the importance of safe sex, future cohorts of gay men may be less likely to engage in high-risk sexual behavior. Older persons with AIDS have been found to be less likely to use emotional support and mental health services than the younger population. Such services may need to be reconfigured and presented differently in order to meet the emotional needs of the older population diagnosed with AIDS (Emlet, 1996).

PSYCHOSOCIAL FACTORS AND LATE-LIFE AFFECTION, LOVE, AND INTIMACY

In addition to the effects of normal physiological changes and chronic disease upon sexual activity and enjoyment, a number of psychosocial factors affect the ways in which older people express their sexuality.

1. Past history of sexual activity. Those who were most sexually active in middle age generally remain so in old age. As noted above, it appears that sexuality is stable and continuous across the life span.

2. Negative attitudes toward sexual activities other than intercourse such as kissing, petting, holding and being held, dancing, massage, and masturbation interfere with the openness to try new ways of expressing intimacy.

3. Reactions to physiological changes and to illness-induced or doctor-induced changes. For example, if older men subscribe to the myth that in sex, performance counts (how many orgasms, how long an erection), rather than focusing on pleasuring and closeness, they are likely to experience performance anxiety. Since anxiety tends to block sexual interest and response, such older men may be caught in a bind. The more they are concerned about performing well, the harder they try and the more difficult it becomes. In such instances, older men need to be reminded that there is no right way. Rather, sex can be whatever they and their partners find satisfying at the moment.

4. Reactions to the attitudes of others, including the larger society that one is "too old" for sex. Societal misconceptions regarding sexuality in later life can have a powerful effect on one's self-concept and perception of oneself as still being sexually attractive and interesting.

5. Living arrangements. For example, older adults in long-term care facilities face numerous barriers to sexual expression, including lack of privacy and of partners, staff attitudes, and chronic illness (Richardson and Lazur, 1995).

A primary psychosocial factor, especially for women, is the availability of a partner. Although the nature of sexual relationships is becoming increasingly varied, most sexual activity for the current cohort of older people occurs within the context of a marital relationship (Teitelman, 1990). For women in heterosexual relationships, a central problem is differential life expectancy and the fact that most women have married men older than themselves. Because of older women's lower marriage and remarriage rates, the opportunity for sexual activity within heterosexual relationships is dramatically reduced with age, but the capacity for sexual enjoyment is not altered.

The current cohort of older women, for whom sexual activity was tied to marriage, have relatively few options for sexual relationships. Unfortunately, these options are made more difficult because of the lack of socially approved models of sexuality for older women. For many women, their only models for sexuality may be the young. In addition, the pairing of older women with younger men is still rare, largely because of the double standard of aging in which older men are often viewed as distinguished while older women are perceived as unattractive and asexual. Women are also more likely than men to face socioeconomic barriers to meeting new partners, given the higher incidence of poverty among women compared to men. If a woman is preoccupied with financial or health worries, sexual activity may be a low priority.

Gender differences in sexual interest and participation may also be a barrier to finding satisfying intimate heterosexual relationships. Women report that sexual activities of sitting and talking, making oneself more attractive, and saying loving words are more important than do men. Men, however, view sexual activities such as erotic readings and movies, sexual daydreams, and physically intimate activities, such as body caressing, intercourse, and **masturbation,** as more important than do women (Johnson, 1996).

Although an increasing number of older women may discover that they prefer relationships with other women, the frequency that such shifts in sexual orientation occur in later life is unknown. In some instances, developing a close relationship with another woman may not be overtly sexual, but rather a preference for the companionship of the same sex. In addition, fearing isolation from family and friends, some older lesbians may not feel comfortable with being open about their sexual orientation. On the positive side, there is growing acceptance of masturbation as an alternative to a sexual relationship. However, older women may experience some defensiveness or guilt about masturbating, in large part because of the Victorian morality under which most of the current older generation was raised (Ludeman, 1981). In addition, masturbation cannot fully substitute for being valued by someone else.

In contrast, marital status has little or no effect on men's sexual behavior or interest. Rather, the central issue for men appears to be understanding the physiology of impotence and possible treatments or prevention. However, sexual functioning in both men and women is affected by the presence of a partner. Accordingly, a man who has not had sexual intercourse for a long time following the loss or illness of a partner may experience what has been called **widower's syndrome.** He may have both the desire and new opportunities for sexual activity, but his physiological system may not respond and he cannot maintain an erection. If he becomes anxious and fearful about his performance, partial or incomplete impotence may result. A similar condition has been reported among husbands whose wives have Alzheimer's disease (Litz, Zeiss, and Davies, 1990). Fortunately, widower's syndrome can be resolved through unhurried, non-demanding sexual interaction with an understanding partner (Masters and Johnson, 1981).

Similarly, women may face **widow's syndrome.** After a year or more of sexual inactivity, women are likely to experience a reduction in the elasticity of the vaginal walls. With the woman less likely to respond to sexual excitement, vaginal lubrication is slowed and reduced. Although these are all symptoms that arise from estrogen deficiency, they become more severe when there is a long period of no sexual contact. For men and women, frequency of contact is important to ensure sexual responsiveness and comfort. Both men and women who are grieving the loss of a partner are unlikely to have the energy, sensitivity, and interest in someone beyond themselves—all essential features of successful sexual activity (Masters and Johnson, 1981).

Another critical factor in the physical and social environment is whether living arrangements provide opportunities for privacy. Such opportunities are most likely to be limited for those in long-term care facilities. Lack of privacy, negative staff attitudes, administrative difficulties, and the unromantic atmosphere of institutional environments all reduce the incentive of residents to be sexually interested or involved. On the other hand, when conjugal rooms are set aside, residents may be too embarrassed to use them.

Staff attitudes, which tend to reflect those of the larger society, may be the greatest barrier. Staff tend to assume that frail residents no longer need sexual intimacy. If older residents express a desire for sexual activity, staff may ignore, infantilize, tease, or ridicule them, or report it to administrators, thereby adding to a sense of embarrassment. Other staff may believe that chronic illness makes sexual activities impossible or harmful. Despite such obstacles, some residents in such settings are sexually active, and others would be if the opportunity allowed. The institutionalization of older persons does not necessarily mean the end of their sexual interest. Even institutionalized older people with dementia may maintain the competency to initiate sexual relationships (Lichtenberg and Strzepek, 1990). Long-term care facilities need to develop policies to assure privacy, establish conjugal rooms or home visits, evaluate patients' concerns about sexual functioning, encourage varied forms of sexual expression, and educate both staff and residents about sexuality and aging (Richardson and Lazur, 1995).

Table 7.2 summarizes the psychological and social factors that may affect sexual activity among older people.

As noted throughout this chapter, sex encompasses more than intercourse. It is also important to recognize and to convey to older individuals that affection may be expressed in a wide variety of ways other than through sex. As noted above,

TABLE 7.2 Psychosocial Factors That Influence Sexual Activity in Older Adults

- Past history of sexual activity
- Attitudes toward sexual activities other than intercourse
- Reactions to physiological changes or to illness-induced changes
- Reactions to attitudes of others
- Availability of a partner, especially for women
- Performance anxiety; widower's/widow's syndrome
- Opportunities for privacy
- Staff attitudes toward those in institutional settings

intimacy, love, attachment, and friendship are cherished aspects of life, vital to an older person's sense of well-being. When older persons are experiencing assaults on their self-esteem, the need for affection may become even more intense. Without such affection, older individuals may feel lonely, even though they may be surrounded by other people and not physically alone.

Intimacy and attachment can be conveyed through mutuality, openness, commitment, sharing, respect, and enjoyment (Davis, 1985). With age, long-term relationships frequently move toward deeper levels of intimacy expressed in terms of loyalty, security, and mutual emotional interest. This is not the case, however, in relationships characterized by conflict, emotional distance, and emotional or physical abuse throughout the years. On the other hand, many older people dealing with the feelings of loss and loneliness occasioned by the divorce or death of a spouse may find it difficult to invest the energy needed to develop intimate relationships.

An important aspect of most intimate relationships is touch. The need to be touched is lifelong; physical contact through touching and caressing is as powerful in the sixties, seventies, and eighties as in infancy, childhood, and early adulthood. Since the sense of touch is the most basic sense, older individuals may rely upon the sense of touch to a greater extent in their social interactions than other age groups (Weg, 1996). Just beneath an older person's expression of loneliness or of missing a former partner may lie the desire for someone to touch them. A handclasp or hand laid gently on the shoulder or arm, a child's hug, or a back massage can all be vital to addressing an older person's needs for affection and can increase their responsiveness. Staff in long-term care facilities especially need to be sensitive to the life-affirming role of touch for most older people, including those with dementia and those who are withdrawn or disoriented. On the other hand, helping professionals must recognize cultural differences regarding the meaning and appropriateness of touch. They need to be aware that, in some cultures, differ-

Staff in long-term care facilities can provide emotional support through touch.

ential social status, gender, age, and the setting may influence the older person's acceptance of a friendly touch.

Friends are often important sources of intimacy, especially after a major role transition such as death of a spouse, divorce, or retirement. For example, an intimate friendship with a confidant can help prevent the demoralization often produced by widowhood. The presence of a close confidant also appears to be related to life satisfaction and a sense of belonging, worth, and identity (Lowenthal, Thurnher, and Chiriboga, 1975). In any senior center or congregate meal site, gatherings of highly valued same-sex companions are frequent. Among women especially, same-sex companions frequently greet each other warmly with a hug and kiss, may join arms while walking, and spend valued time together. These contacts are non-sexual in the narrow definitions of the term, but can be important to sexual health and to a person's psychological adaptation to aging (Walz and Blum, 1987). The importance of friendship in old age is discussed further in Chapter 9.

FACILITATING OLDER ADULTS' SEXUAL FUNCTIONING

Given the importance of sexuality and sexual satisfaction, the individual's sexual history should be part of the clinical evaluation of older persons, and health care professionals have a critical role in helping the older person understand and adapt to altered sexual needs and capacities. Unfortunately, many health care providers have been taught little or nothing about sexuality and intimacy in late adulthood. Professionals may be uncomfortable or intimidated when asked to respond to the lifelong intimacy needs of people as old as their own parents or grandparents. Physicians are often in a central position to respond to an older person's concerns about sexuality, yet they may be more likely to prescribe treatment for physical symptoms, such as vaginal dryness, than to respond to the older person's emotional concerns or need for information. Often the topic of sexuality or intimacy is just below the surface when an older person is reminiscing or discussing losses and loneliness, such as the death of a partner. The loss of intimacy may underlie other disorders that the physician is treating, such as depression (Genevay, 1990).

When an older person raises concerns about sexual functioning, such as impotence, it is important that the physician first differentiate potential physical causes, including medications, from psychological ones. This can be done through a careful medical and social history, a thorough physical assessment, and basic hormone tests (Haffner, 1994). Such an approach can help to distinguish short-term problems that many individuals experience at various times, such as transitory impotence, from problems that persist under all circumstances with different sexual partners over a prolonged time period.

Health care providers also can encourage and assure continuity of sexual expression for those for whom this has been an important part of their lives. One of the first health professionals to address this issue, Comfort (1980), noted that sexual responsiveness should be fostered but not preached. In an AARP survey of older adults and sexual functioning, older respondents suggested guidelines for health care providers (Johnson, 1997). These included using clear and easy-to-understand terms; being open-minded, respectful, and non-judgmental; and encouraging discussion. What an older person may want most when he or she raises sexual concerns is support, acceptance, and listening. Older people who are concerned about their sexual functioning should be encouraged to focus on giving and receiving pleasure rather than on genital sex. As noted earlier, professionals should convey that intercourse is only one way of relating sexually and that there is no prescribed way for sex to proceed. Rather, many choices can be made regarding sexuality. When a partner is not available, masturbation can be viewed as an acceptable release of sexual tension. Explicit discussion of masturbation with older people may relieve anxiety caused by earlier prohibitions during adolescence and young adulthood. Alternatively, professionals need to be sensitive to the fact that some older people do not want to engage in any sexual activity and must not put undue pressure upon them to be sexually active. What is important is for practitioners to take account of an older person's values, life experiences, and right to autonomy, and support them in making their own choices about sexual behavior and sexuality.

Many older people need to be encouraged to develop alternative definitions of sexual activity that are not performance oriented (i.e., broader than genital intercourse) in order to gain intimacy, joy, and fulfillment through a broad spectrum of sensual interactions. Sex education in general can increase their sexual awareness, knowledge, interest, enjoyment, and range of activities. As noted above, sex education is also important for staff who work with older people. They need to be careful not to impose their values on older people. For example, nursing home employees need to avoid the stereotype of dirty old men and must recognize that the desire for intimacy and closeness continues throughout life. When working with older people who are experiencing memory loss or disorientation, staff need to evaluate the competencies of the older person to engage in intimate relationships. These include assessing the older person's awareness of the relationship, abil-ity to avoid exploitation, and awareness of potential risks.

In the past, sex therapists have focused on working with younger people. Fortunately, this bias is changing, and various therapies for older people who report sexual difficulties have been found to be effective. Sex therapy with older persons should include the following elements: The first step is to eliminate or control medical problems, including drug interference, that may directly impair genital functions or indirectly affect sexual functioning. Psychotherapy and sexual therapy with older adults should include practical behavioral techniques in the form of specifically structured sexual interactions that the couple can conduct in the privacy of their home (Kaplan, 1990). These activities should emphasize intimacy, giving pleasure, communicating with the partner, and letting the partner know when pleasure is experienced. Opportunities should be provided to discuss problems encountered as well as concerns about performance. Increasingly, therapists are recognizing the value of a holistic approach that includes exercise, nutrition, and interventions to build self-esteem.

SUMMARY AND IMPLICATIONS

As discussed throughout this chapter, sexuality is affected by physical, psychological, and disease-related changes. The normal physiological changes that men and women experience in their sexual organs as they age do not necessarily affect their sexual pleasure or lead to sexual incapacity. Even chronic disease does not necessarily eliminate sexual capacity. For example, many older persons, after adequate medical consultation, can resume sexual activity following a heart attack. Contrary to the myths about sexuality in old age, many people in their seventies and eighties participate in and enjoy sexual activities.

Older couples can adapt to age-related changes in sexual functioning in a variety of ways. Simply knowing that such changes are normal may help older people maintain their sexual self-esteem. For both older men and women, long leisurely foreplay can enhance sexual response. Avoiding alcohol use prior to sexual activity can be helpful, since alcohol increases desire, but decreases sexual ability. Health professionals need to be alert to medications that adversely affect sexual functioning, such as antihypertensives, tranquilizers, and antidepressants.

This chapter emphasizes how psychosocial factors also can influence an older person's sexual behavior. Myths, stereotypes, and jokes pervade the area of sexuality in old age. Unfortunately, societal expectations of reduced sexual interest may mean that older people stop sexual activity long before they need to. In future years, these myths may change as the media, gerontologists, and other professionals convey the message that sex is not only permissible but desirable in old age.

In professional work with older partners, definitions of sexuality need to be broadened beyond sexual intercourse. A variety of behaviors, such as touching, kissing, hugging, and lying side by side, can contribute to sexual intimacy and satisfaction, even for institutionalized older persons. Touching older people—a hand clasp or back rub, for example—is especially important in home-bound and institutional settings.

Practitioners need to be sensitive to their clients' values and life experiences and to support them in making their own choices about sexual behavior and sexuality. Many of the current cohort of older persons grew up with taboos relating not only to intercourse but also to other forms of sexual activity, such as masturbation. Hence, older individuals may need encouragement from professional counselors or others if they are to be free to affirm their sexuality and to experience intimacy with others.

GLOSSARY

climacteric in women, the decline in estrogen production and the loss of reproductive ability; in men, the decline in testosterone

erection the swelling of the penis or clitoris in sexual excitement

gay homosexual man

heterosexuality sexual orientation toward the opposite gender

homosexuality sexual orientation toward the same gender

hot flashes a sudden sensation of heat in the upper body caused by vasomotor instability as nerves over-respond to decreases in hormone level during menopause

hysterectomy surgical removal of the uterus

impotence the inability to have or maintain an erection

intimacy feelings of deep mutual regard, affection, and trust, usually developed through long association

lesbian homosexual woman

male menopause a term which suggests a significant change experienced by men as their production of testosterone decreases in later life; although male fertility is maintained, some men experience both psychological and physiological changes

mastectomy surgical removal of one or both breasts, usually in treatment of breast cancer

masturbation erotic stimulation of the genital organs achieved by manual contact exclusive of sexual intercourse

nocturnal penile tumescence in men, sleep-related erections

orgasm climax of sexual excitement

penile implant devices surgically implanted in the penis to reverse impotence and allow an erection

preorgasmic plateau phase in men and women, the phase of love-making prior to orgasm in which sexual tension is at its height

prostate, enlargement of growth of the prostate, due to changes in prostatic cells with age, which can result in pain and difficult urination

radical perineal prostatectomy type of surgical removal of the prostate, usually in treatment for prostate cancer

refractory period in men, the time between ejaculation and another erection

sex in the most narrow sense, a biological function involving genital intercourse or orgasm; in a broader sense, expressing oneself in an intimate way through a wide-ranging language of love and pleasure in relationships

sexuality   feelings of sexual desire, sexual expression, sexual activity

widow(er)'s syndrome   a term coined by Masters and Johnson describing sexual dysfunction following a long period of abstinence due to a spouse's illness and/or death

REFERENCES

Adelman, M. Stigma, gay lifestyles, and adjustment to aging: A study of later-life gay men and lesbians. In *Gay midlife and maturity* (Special Issue). New York: Haworth Press, 1991, 7–32.

Bachmann, G. A. Influence of menopause on sexuality. *International Journal of Fertility and Menopausal Studies,* 1995, *40(1),* 16–22.

Bachmann, G. A., and Leiblum, S. R. Sexuality in sexagenarian women. *Maturitas,* 1991, *13,* 43–50.

Bennet, K. C., and Thompson, N. C. Accelerated aging and male homosexuality. *Journal of Homosexuality,* 1990, 20, 65–75.

Berger, R. M. Realities of gay and lesbian aging. *Social Work,* 1984, *29,* (1), 57–62.

Bostwick, D. G., MacLennan, G. T., and Larson, T. *Prostate cancer: What every man—and his family—needs to know.* New York: Villard, 1996.

Butler, R. N., and Lewis, M. I. *Love and sex after 60* (rev.). New York: Ballantine Books, 1993.

Cochrane, M. Immaculate infection. *Nursing Times,* 1989, 26, 31–32.

Comfort, A. Sexuality in later life. In J. E. Birren and R. B. Sloane. (Eds.), *Handbook of mental health and aging.* New York: Van Nostrand Reinhold, 1980.

Corbett, L. The last sexual taboo: Sex in old age. *Medical Aspects of Human Sexuality,* 1987, *15*(4), 117–131.

Davis, K. E. Near and dear: Friendship and love compared. *Psychology Today,* 1985, *19,* 22–30.

Deevey, S. Older lesbian women: An invisible minority. *Journal of Gerontological Nursing,* 1990, *16(5),* 35–39.

Defey, D., Storch, E., Cardozo, S., and Diaz, O. The menopause: Women's psychology and health care. *Social Science and Medicine,* 1996, *42(10),* 1447–1456.

Denney, N. W., and Quadagno, D. *Human sexuality.* St. Louis: C. V. Mosby, 1992.

Diamond, J. *Male menopause.* Naperville, IL: Sourcebooks, 1997.

Diokno, A. C., Brown, M.B., and Herzog, A. R. Sexual function in the elderly. *Archives of Internal Medicine,* 1990, *150,* 197–200.

Dorfman, R., Walters, K., Burke, P., Hardin, L., Karanik, T., Raphael, J., and Silverstein, E. Old, sad and alone: The myth of the aging homosexual. *Journal of Gerontological Social Work,* 1995, *24,* (1–2), 29–44.

Emlet, C. A. Case managing older people with AIDS: Bridging systems—recognizing diversity. *Journal of Gerontological Social Work,* 1996, *27,* 55–71.

Gambert, S. R. (Ed.). *Handbook of geriatrics.* New York: Plenum Medical Book Company, 1987.

Genevay, B. Being old, sexual and intimate: A threat or a gift? In B. Genevay and C. Katz (Eds.), *Countertransference and older clients.* Newbury Park, CA: Sage, 1990, 148–167.

George, L. K., and Weiler, S. J. Sexuality in middle and late life: The effects of age, cohort and gender. *Archives of General Psychiatry,* 1981, *38,* 919–923.

Haffner, D. Love and sex after 60: How physical changes affect intimate expression. *Geriatrics,* 1994, *49(9),* 20.

Jacobs, S., and Hillard, T. C. Hormone replacement therapy in the aged: A state of the art review. *Drugs and Aging,* 1996, *8(3),* 193–213.

Janus, S. S., and Janus, C. L. *The Janus Report on sexual behavior.* New York: John Wiley and Sons, 1993.

Johnson, B. Older adults' suggestions for health care providers regarding discussions of sex. *Geriatric Nursing,* 1997, *18(2),* 65–66.

Johnson, B. K. Older adults and sexuality: A multidimensional perspective. *Journal of Gerontological Nursing,* 1996, *22(2),* 6–15.

Jones, J. B. Representations of menopause and their health care implications: A qualitative study. *American Journal of Preventive Medicine,* 1997, *13(1),* 58–65.

Kaiser, F. E. Sexuality in the elderly. *Urologic Clinics of North America,* 1996, *23(1),* 99.

Kaplan, H. Sex, intimacy and the aging process. *Journal of the American Academy of Psychoanalysis,* 1990, *18,* 185–205.

Katchadourian, H. *Fundamentals of human sexuality* (4th ed.). New York: Holt, Rinehart, and Winston, 1987.

Kaye, R. A. Sexuality in the later years. *Ageing and Society, 1993, 13,* 415.

Kehoe, M. *Lesbians over 60 speak for themselves.* New York: Harrington Pore Press, 1989.

Kehoe, M. Lesbians over 65: A triple invisible minority. *Journal of Homosexuality, 1986, 12,* 139–152.

Kinsey, A., Pomeroy, B., and Martin E. *Sexual behavior in the human female.* Philadelphia, PA: W. B. Saunders, 1953.

Kinsey, A. C., Pomeroy, B., and Martin, E. *Sexual behavior in the human male.* Philadelphia, PA: W. B. Saunders, 1948.

Lee, J. A. Can we talk? Can we really talk? Communication as a key factor in the maturing homosexual couple. *Journal of Homosexuality,* 1990, *20(3–4),* 143–168.

Leland, J. A pill for impotence. *Newsweek,* November 17, 1997, 62–68.

Lewis, M. Sexual problems in the elderly: Men's vs. women's: A geriatric panel discussion. *Geriatrics,* 1989, *44,* 75–86.

Lichtenberg, P. A., and Strzepek, D. M. Assessments of institutionalized dementia patient's competence to participate in intimate relationships. *The Gerontologist,* 1990, *30,* 117–120.

Litz, B. T., Zeiss, A. M., and Davies, H. T. Sexual concerns of male spouses of female Alzheimer's disease patients. *The Gerontologist,* 1990, *30,* 113–116.

Lowenthal, M., Thurnher, M., and Chiriboga, D. *Four stages of life: A comparative study of women and men facing transitions.* San Francisco: Jossey-Bass, 1975.

Ludeman, K. The sexuality of the older person: Review of the literature. *The Gerontologist,* 1981, *21,* 203–208.

Marsiglio, W., and Donnelley, D. Sexual relations in later life: A national study of married persons. *Journals of Gerontology,* 1991, *46,* S338–344.

Masters, W. H., and Johnson, V. E. Sex and the aging process. *Journal of the American Geriatrics Society,* 1981, *29,* 385–390.

Matthias, R. E., Lubben, J. E., Atcheson, K. B., and Schweitzer, S. O. Sexual activity and satisfaction among very old adults: Results from a community-dwelling Medicare population survey. *The Gerontologist,* 1997, *37,* 6–14.

McCartney, J., Izemen, H., Rogers, D., and Cohen, N. Sexuality in the institutionalized elderly. *Journal of the American Geriatrics Society,* 1987, *35,* 331–333.

McDougall-Graham, J. Therapeutic issues with gay and lesbian elders. Special Issue: The forgotten aged: Ethnic, psychiatric, and societal minorities. *Clinical Gerontologist,* 1993, *14,* 45–57.

Morra, M., and Potts, E. *The prostate cancer answer book.* New York: Avon Books, 1996.

NIH Consensus Statement. National Institutes of Health Consensus Development Conference, 1992, *10(4),* 1–33.

Notelovitz, M., Martin, D., and Tesar, R. Estrogen therapy and variable-resistance weight training increase bone mineral in surgically menopausal women. *Journal of Bone Mineral Research,* 1991, *6,* 583–590.

PEPI Trial Writing Group. Effects of hormone therapy on bone mineral density. *Journal of the American Medical Association,* 1996, *276,* 1389–1396.

Pfeiffer, E., and Davis, G. C. Determinants of sexual behavior in middle and old age. *Journal of the American Geriatrics Society,* 1972, *20,* 151–158.

Pope, M., and Schulz, R. Sexual attitudes and behavior in midlife and aging homosexual roles. *Journal of Homosexuality,* 1991, *20,* 169–177.

Quam, J., and Whitford, G. Adaptation and age-related expectations of older gay and lesbian adults. *The Gerontologist,* 1992, *32,* 367–374.

Richardson, J. P., and Lazur, A. Sexuality in the nursing home patient. *American Family Physician,* 1995, *51(1),* 121–124.

Rosen, R. C. Erectile dysfunction: The medicalization of male sexuality. *Clinical Psychology Review,* 1996, *16(6),* 497–519.

Schiavi, R. C., and Rehman, J. Sexuality and aging. *Urologic Clinics of North America,* 1995, *22(4),* 711–726.

Schiavi, R., Schreiner-Engal, P., Mandati, J., Schanzen, H., and Cohen, E. Healthy aging and male sexual function. *American Journal of Psychiatry,* 1990, *147,* 766–771.

Starr, B. D., and Weiner, M. B. *The Starr-Weiner report on sex and sexuality in the mature years.* New York: Stein and Day, 1981.

Steinke, E. E. Knowledge and attitudes of older adults about sexuality in ageing: A comparison of two studies. *Journal of Advanced Nursing,* 1994, *19(3),* 477–485.

Teitelman, J. Sexuality and aging. In I. Parham, L. Poon, and I. Siegler (Eds.), *Aging curriculum content for education in the social-behavioral sciences.* New York: Springer, 1990.

Thienhaus, J. Practical overview of sexual functions and advancing age. *Geriatrics,* 1988, *43,* 63–65.

Walz, T., and Blum, N. *Sexual health in later life.* Lexington, MA: Lexington Books, 1987.

Weg, R. B. Sexuality, sensuality, and intimacy. *Encyclopedia of gerontology: Age, aging, and the aged,* 1996, 2(L-Z Index), 479–488.

Wiley, D., and Bortz, W. M. Sexuality and aging—Usual and successful. *Journals of Gerontology,* 1996, *51(A),* M142-M146.

Zeiss, A. M. Sexuality and aging: Normal changes and clinical problems. *Topics in Geriatric Rehabilitation,* 1997, *12(4),* 11–27.

THE SOCIAL CONTEXT OF AGING

Throughout the previous three sections, we have identified how changes in the physical and psychological aspects of aging have diverse consequences for older people's cognitive and personality functioning, sexuality, and mental health. We have also seen how social factors (e.g., the presence of strong family and friendship ties) can affect physical changes (e.g., being at risk for certain chronic illnesses) as well as psychological experiences (e.g., the likelihood of suicide). Within this framework of the dynamic interactions among physical, psychological, and social factors, we turn now to a more detailed discussion of the social environment of aging and its congruence with older people's level of functioning.

We begin with a review in Chapter 8 of the major social theories of aging—explanations of changes in social relationships that occur in late adulthood. Congruent with the person-environment perspective throughout the text, these theories address the optimal way for people to relate to their changing social and physical environments as they age. There are substantial differences among the early social gerontological theories, such as role, activity, and disengagement, which were concerned with adaptation to age-related changes, and later theories, including continuity, age stratification, and exchange theory, which recognized the diverse and dynamic nature of the aging experience. The most recent theories have been described as taking a "qualitative leap" over prior theories; these include social phenomenology, social constructionism, and critical and feminist theory, all of which raise fundamental questions about positivist or empirical approaches to studying aging and emphasize the highly subjective nature of the aging experience. These social gerontological theories, then, provide the basis for examining the primary dimensions of older people's social environments: family, friends, and other social supports; housing and community; paid and non-paid productive roles and activities; and changes in one's social network through death and loss. These later theoretical approaches, in particular, recognize how older people's experiences with their social environments can vary by ethnic minority status and gender.

Chapter 9 begins by examining the importance of informal social supports, particularly family, neighbors, and friends, to quality of life. In Chapter 1, we saw how longer life expectancies, combined with earlier marriages and childbearing, have reduced the average span in years between generations. This has also increased the number of three- and four-generation families. The growth of the multigenerational family has numerous ramifications for relationships between spouses, between grandparents and grandchildren, between adult children and older relatives, and among siblings and other extended family members. Generally, these relationships are characterized by reciprocity, with older family members providing resources to younger generations and trying to remain as independent as possible. The normal physical and psychological changes of aging usually are not detrimental to family relationships, although caring for an older relative with a long-term illness can burden family members. Compared to the earlier years, late-life family relationships are more often characterized by losses that demand role shifts and adjustments. A widower may cope with the loss of his wife by remarrying, whereas a widow tends to turn to adult children and friends.

Although there are some older people living alone—including a growing number who are homeless—friends, neighbors, and even acquaintances often perform family-like functions for them. More conducive to reciprocal exchanges, they may be an even more important source of support for an older person than one's family members. As gerontologists have recognized the importance of informal social networks for older people's well-being, programmatic interventions have been developed specifically to strengthen these ties, which are described in Chapter 9.

Where people live—the type of housing, urban–suburban location, and safety of the community—affects their social interactions. Chapter 10 illustrates the importance of achieving congruence between older people's social, psychological, and physical needs and their physical environment. Relocation is an example of a disruption of this congruence or fit between the environment and the older person. Another illustration of a physical environment that no longer fits a person's social needs is when older residents become so fearful of victimization that they dare not leave their homes. Characteristics of the neighborhood can enhance older persons' social interactions and, in some instances, their feelings of safety. Planned housing, home-sharing, congregate housing, assisted-living facilities with multiple levels of care, home health care, and nursing homes are ways to modify the physical environment to support older people's changing and diverse needs. Chapter 10 also includes a discussion of housing policies and social and health services that affect older people, as well as an analysis of the problems of homelessness among the older population.

Throughout our discussion of the social context for aging, the effects of socioeconomic status on types of interactions and activities are readily apparent. Economic status is largely determined by past and current employment patterns and by the resulting retirement benefits. Chapter 11 shows declining rates of labor-force participation among both men and women age 65 and over, due largely to the trend toward early retirement. Most people choose to retire early, provided their public or private pensions will enable them to enjoy economic security. Although most older people apparently do not want to work full-time, many would like the option of flexible part-time jobs, increasingly for economic reasons. For most people, retirement is not a crisis, although for those without good health, adequate finances, or prior planning, retirement can be a difficult transition. Accordingly, women, ethnic minorities, and low-status workers are most vulnerable to experiencing poverty or near-poverty in old age.

Chapter 11 also examines how people's interactions change with age in terms of their non-paid productive roles, including involvement in community, organizational, and religious activities, and political participation. The extent and type of participation are influenced not only by age, but also by gender, ethnic minority status, health, socioeconomic class, and educational level. Therefore, declines in participation may not necessarily be caused by age-related changes but instead represent the influence of other variables. Generally, involvement tends to be fairly stable across the life course; leisure, volunteer and community activities, and roles formed in early and middle adulthood are maintained into later life. This does not mean, however, that older people do not develop new interests and skills. Many people initiate new forms of productivity through senior centers, volunteering, civic organizations, political activism, and education programs.

Chapter 12 examines attitudes toward death and dying and the process of dying. The impacts of social and cultural values, as well as individual factors such as the relationship between the dying person and caregivers, are discussed in reviewing grief and mourning. Recent trends in an individual's right to die and the legal and ethical debates about active and passive euthanasia also are reviewed in this chapter. It concludes by examining the process of widowhood and how people cope with this major life event.

Because of the predominance of social problems faced by older women and ethnic minorities, their special needs and some practice and policy interventions are discussed in Chapters 13 and 14. Economic difficulties experienced in young and middle adulthood by these groups tend to be perpetuated in old age. These are not isolated problems, but rather of increasing concern to gerontologists and policymakers, since women over age 65 form the majority of older people, and older ethnic minorities, although a small percentage of the total older population today, is growing rapidly. These populations nevertheless display considerable strength and resiliency in the face of social problems.

The following vignettes illustrate the diversity of social interactions experienced by older people and set the stage for our discussion of the social context of aging.

An Older Person with Limited Social Resources

Mr. Valdres, age 73, has been separated from his wife for 20 years. He lives in a small room in an inner-city hotel. Since he worked odd jobs all his life, often performing migrant farm labor, he collects only the minimum amount of Social Security. Some months he finds it very hard to get by and has only one meal a day. Although he is not in contact with his former wife or his six children, he does have a group of buddies in the area who watch out for one another and who get together at night to have a beer and watch TV in the hotel lobby. Although he has smoked all his life and suffers from emphysema, he refuses to see a doctor or any other staff at the downtown medical clinic. He also will not apply for any public assistance, such as SSI or food stamps, in part because he does not understand what these programs are, but also because he does not want government "handouts." The hotel manager keeps track of his activities and will occasionally slip him some extra money or food.

An Older Person with Extensive Social Resources

Mrs. Howard, age 78, lives with her husband in a small town. Most of her relatives, including three of her children and eight grandchildren, live in the area, and there are large family gatherings on Sundays and holidays. She is a retired teacher; her husband was a successful local realtor until he retired. Both retired in their early seventies. They have considerable savings; in addition, they always lived simply and frugally, saving for their retirement. They have lived in the same house for the past 42 years, and their home is well maintained and recently modernized. Mrs. Howard enjoys gardening, doing housework, reading, and visiting. In addition, she is very active in her church, serves on the Advisory Board to the Area Agency on Aging, and is involved in the town's politics. She also tutors children with learning disabilities. Her days are filled with housework, talking to friends, neighbors, or relatives, or helping someone out, whether a grandchild or neighbor. Despite all her activity, she occasionally complains of being lonely and useless.

An Older Person Coping with Multiple Losses

Mr. Mansfield is 87 years old. He and his wife had six children. After having been a successful businessman in the Chicago area, he retired to the south when he turned 66. Mr. Mansfield and his wife were active in their church, and enjoyed going to plays and keeping up with their children who had interesting careers all over the United States. He enjoyed his retirement until his wife of 50 years died when he was 80. Mr. Mansfield was heartbroken and thought that his life had ended. He then became involved in a support group offered through his church and started teaching adult education classes. Through that experience, he became involved in the ecumenical life of the small southern town and was very active in putting on an annual conference. Although he still speaks with tears when talking about his relationship with his deceased wife, it has become clear that his life has found new meaning and purpose in his church work, and in becoming a volunteer for the Area Agency on Aging. However, Mr. Mansfield recently faced a new challenge. His youngest and his oldest children have both died. The oldest died in her early fifties of a drug overdose of pills she was taking for chronic pain. The youngest, a son, died 6 months later after a long battle with AIDS. Although

these were wrenching experiences for him, he is now facing these bereavements with a different support network. The pain is still there, but he is able to share it with others. And he continues to be an active volunteer. His own health is beginning to deteriorate, however, and he has started to talk about his own death. He is concerned about his ability to drive, as his eyesight is diminished. His faith and belief system are integral to his dealing with these concerns about death and dying.

These vignettes show the importance of informal social support networks, whether for an apparently isolated person in a low-income hotel such as Mr. Valdres, or for an older person, such as Mr. Mansfield, coping with multiple social losses. We turn now to a review of some of the social theories that attempt to explain successful and satisfying aging.

CHAPTER 8

SOCIAL THEORIES OF AGING

THE IMPORTANCE OF SOCIAL THEORIES OF AGING

All of us develop interpretive frameworks or lenses, based on our experiences, by which we attempt to explain the aging process and answer questions we all wonder about: What makes for successful aging? What should our society be doing with regard to older people? What enhances older people's life satisfaction and well-being? We observe older people in our families and communities and make generalizations about them. For example, some of our stereotypes of older people may be the result of unconscious theorizing about the meaning of growing old. Or we may devise our own recommendations for policies or programs based on our informal and implicit theories. In effect, we are developing theories based on our own experiences.

In contrast to our personal observations about age changes, the scientific approach to theory development is a systematic attempt to explain *why* an age change or event occurs. Theory-building—the cumulative development of

explanation and understanding about observations and findings—represents the core of the foundation of scientific inquiry and knowledge (Bengtson, Burgess, and Parrott, 1997). By using scientific methods, researchers seek to understand phenomena in a manner that is reliable and valid across observations, and then to account for what they have observed in the context of previous knowledge in the field. Scientists never entirely prove or disprove a theory. Instead, through empirical research, they gather evidence that may strengthen their confidence in it or move them closer to rejecting the theory by demonstrating that parts of it are untrue. Scientific theories not only lead to the accumulation of knowledge, but point to unanswered questions for further research and suggest directions for practical interventions. In fact, a good theory is practical! For example, some of the biological theories of aging discussed in Chapter 3 are useful in guiding people's health behaviors. If the theory is inadequate, the research, intervention, or public policy may fail by not achieving its intended goals (Bengtson et al., 1997).

This chapter focuses on social theories of aging—explanations of changes in social relationships that occur in late adulthood. All these theories address implicitly or explicitly the basic issue of what is the optimal way for older people to relate to their environments. Although no one grand, all-encompassing social gerontological theory has emerged, each of the theories discussed here suggests some important factors related to aging or age-related issues and thus serves as a guide for further inquiry and possible intervention in the aging process. They represent different lenses through which to view and explain the phenomenon of aging, and thus lay a groundwork for our discussions of the social aspects of aging in later chapters: social supports, living arrangements, socioeconomic status, and changing employment and retirement roles.

Most of these theories have been developed only since the 1950s and 1960s. This is because early research in the field of gerontology tended to be applied rather than theoretical in nature, attempting to solve problems facing older people. Researchers were concerned with individual life satisfaction and older people's adjustment to the presumably "natural" conditions of old age—retirement, ill health, or poverty. Despite their relative recency, theories of aging can be classified into first, second, and third generations (Bengtson et al., 1997; Hendricks, 1992), or first and second transformations of theoretical development or evolution of new modes of consciousness (Lynott and Lynott, 1996). The order in which they are presented in this chapter basically reflects the temporal dimensions of this intellectual history. Although there is overlap of the central theoretical concepts across time, these theories are distinguished by a shift from a focus on the individual to structural factors to interactive processes, and from largely quantitative methods in the positivist scientific tradition to a range of more qualitative methodologies that seek to understand the meaning of age-related changes among those experiencing them.

SOCIAL GERONTOLOGICAL THEORY BEFORE 1961: ROLE AND ACTIVITY

Much of the early social gerontological research was organized around the concept of adjustment, with the term "theory" largely absent from the literature (Lynott and Lynott, 1996). The perspectives on roles and activities, however, later came to be called theories. Some theories of adjustment have focused on the individual and his/her personal characteristics (health, personality, needs), while others have emphasized society's demands on and expectations of the individual as he/she ages. Growing old was conceptualized as the individual encountering problems of adjustment due to role changes in later life.

Role Theory

One of the earliest attempts to explain how individuals adjust to aging involved an application of **role theory** (Cottrell, 1942). Individuals play a variety of social roles in their lifetimes, such as student, mother, wife, daughter, businesswoman, grandmother, and so on. Such roles identify and describe a person as a social being and are the basis of self-concept. They are typically organized sequentially, so that each role is associated with a certain age or stage of life. In most societies, especially Western ones, chronological age is used to determine eligibility for various positions, to evaluate the suitability of different roles, and to shape expectations of people in social situations. Some roles have a reasonable biological basis related to age (e.g., the role of mother), but many can be filled by individuals of a wider age range (e.g., the role of volunteer). Age alters not only the roles expected of people, but also the manner in which they are expected to play them. For example, a family's expectations of a 32-year-old mother are quite different from their expectations of her at age 62. How well individuals adjust to aging is assumed to depend on how well they accept the role changes typical of the later years.

Age norms serve to open up or close off the roles that people of a given chronological age can play. Age norms are assumptions of age-related capacities and limitations—beliefs that a person of a given age can and ought to do certain things. As an illustration, an older widow who starts dating may be told by family members that she should "act her age." Norms may be formally expressed through social policies and laws (e.g., mandatory retirement policies that existed prior to 1987). Typically, however, they operate informally. For example, even though employers cannot legally refuse to hire an older woman because of her age, they can assume that she is too old to train for a new position. Individuals also hold norms about the appropriateness of their own behavior at any particular age, so that social clocks become internalized and age norms operate to keep people on the time track (Hagestad and Neugarten, 1985). Most people in our society, for example, have expectations about the appropriate age at which to graduate from school, start working, marry, have a family, reach the peak of their career, and retire. These expectations have been shifting among younger cohorts, however, with more persons marrying later, and in middle age entering second or third careers.

Every society conveys age norms through socialization, a life-long process by which individuals learn to perform new roles, adjust to changing roles, relinquish old ones, and thereby become integrated into society. Older adults become socialized to new roles that accompany old age. In addition, they must learn to deal with role losses, such as the loss of the spouse role with widowhood or the worker role with retirement. These losses can lead to an erosion of social identity and self-esteem (Rosow, 1985). Older people may also experience role discontinuity, whereby what is learned at one age may be useless or conflicting with a subsequent period in one's life. For example, learning to be highly productive in the workplace may be antithetical to adjusting to leisure time in retirement. Although institutions or social situations that help older people prepare for such role changes are limited, older people often display a considerable degree of flexibility in creating or substituting roles in the face of major changes in life circumstances. In fact, more recent research has identified a process of **role-exit,** whereby individuals disengage from roles to which they have had a major commitment and which have been central to their identity, such as the employee role. Interventions such as retirement planning can encourage a process of gradually ceasing to identify with the worker role and its demands, slowly adapting to leisure roles (Ekerdt and De Viney, 1993).

With age, roles also tend to become more ambiguous. Guidelines or expectations about the requirement of roles, such as that of nurturing parent, become less clear (Rosow, 1985). Older people have often lacked desirable role options and models. Until recently, few role models existed; those in the media and the public realm have tended to be youthful in appearance and behavior, maintaining middle-age standards which can hinder socialization to old age. In addition, some groups, such as women and minorities, may lack the resources to move into new roles or to emulate younger, physically attractive models. Fortunately, with the growth and visibility of the older population, there are more models of role gains and successful aging as well as alternative roles for older people to play than in the past. There is also increasing recognition that the role of "dependent person" is not inevitable with age. Rather, the life course is characterized by varying periods of greater or lesser dependency in social relationships, with most people being emotionally dependent on others regardless of age. Even a physically impaired older person may still continue to support others and may be able to devise creative adaptations to ensure competence at home. For example, older people who volunteer as "phone pals" in a telephone reassurance program for latchkey children provide valuable emotional support.

In the future, roles appropriate to old age may become clearer, more continuous with past roles, and more satisfying. Cohorts of older people may also be better prepared for the role changes that often accompany the aging process. A growing number of interventions, such as pre-retirement counseling and support groups, can help to smooth role transitions. This is especially useful if the older person has the freedom and autonomy to choose particular roles after retirement (Herzog and House, 1991; Herzog, Kahn, Morgan, Jackson, and Antonucci, 1989).

Activity Theory

Activity theory also attempted to answer how individuals adjust to age-related changes, such as retirement, poor health, and role loss. Based upon Robert Havighurst's analyses of the Kansas City Studies of Adult Life (1963, 1968), it was believed that the well-adjusted older person is one who takes on a larger number and variety of **productive roles** through activities in voluntary associations, churches, and leisure organizations. The more active the older person, the greater his or her satisfaction, positive self-concept, and adjustment in later life will be (Bengtson, 1969). Accordingly, age-based policies and programs were conceptualized as ways to develop new roles and activities, often consistent with middle-age behavior, and to encourage social integration. To a large extent, activity theory is consistent with our society's value system, which emphasizes work and productivity. Many older people themselves have adopted this perspective and believe it helps them to maintain life satisfaction, as illustrated by the following vignettes.

An Older Person Pursuing Leisure Activities

Bob lives in the Northwest region of the United States. He retired at age 62 after 30 years of work in a management position for an aerospace company. He and his wife of 40 years carefully saved money so that they could be very active in their retirement. They now spend their winters as "snowbirds," traveling in their mobile home to the "sun belt." Now at age 69, they have spent 7 years in the same community in Arizona where they are well-known and have made many friends. In the summer, they usually take one extended trip to the mountains. They enjoy good health and believe that keeping active is the key to their zest for life.

Rose was a nurse for 30 years. In her career in direct patient care and teaching, she has held positions of authority. She has always liked learning new things. Now 74 and retired, she is very active in her church and directs the adult education program. She has participated in Elderhostel four times, and has had the opportunity to visit several foreign countries. She has taken two trips with her teenage grandchildren as well. Staying active means learning to her, and she has shared slide shows of her journeys with her retired friends and the women's group at her church.

Activity theory, however, fails to take account of how personality, socioeconomic status, and lifestyle variables may be more important than maturational ones in the associations found between activity and life satisfaction, health, and well-being (Covey, 1981). The value placed by older people on being active probably varies with their life experiences, personality, and economic and social resources. Activity theory defined aging as an individual social problem. A challenge to this perspective was formulated in 1961 as **disengagement theory**, which shifted attention away from the individual to the social system as an explanation for successful adjustment to aging.

THE FIRST TRANSFORMATION OF THEORY

Disengagement Theory

The development of disengagement theory represents a critical juncture as the first public statement wherein social aging theory is treated as a form of scientific activity in its own right, separate from policy and practice applications and information-gathering (Lynott and Lynott, 1996). In fact, disengagement theory was the first comprehensive, explicit, and multidisciplinary theory advanced in social gerontology (Achenbaum and Bengtson, 1994). Cumming and Henry, in their book *Growing Old* (1961), argue that aging cannot be understood separate from the characteristics of the social system in which it is experienced. All societies need orderly ways to transfer power from older to younger generations. Therefore, the social system deals with the problem of aging by institutionalizing mechanisms of disengagement. Accordingly, older people decrease their activity levels, seek more passive roles, interact less frequently with others, and become increasingly preoccupied with their inner lives. *Disengagement* is thus viewed as adaptive behavior, allowing older people to maintain a sense of self-worth while adjusting through withdrawal to the loss of prior roles, such as occupational or parenting roles. Since disengagement is presumed to have positive consequences for both society and the individual, this theory challenges the assumption of activity theory that older people have to be "busy" and engaged in order to be well-adjusted.

Disengagement and Adaptation

Inga was an executive secretary to a highly successful businessman. She has never married. When she retired at age 62, she took a creative writing class, something she had dreamed of all her life but had not had the time to pursue. At 75 she is very content to sit in her rent-controlled apartment which overlooks a park. She has lived there for 15 years. She finds much inspiration in watching life pass before her in the park. Writing poetry and short stories gives her an outlet for her thoughts. She feels that her writing has developed greater depth as she has achieved wisdom and contemplated the meaning of her life.

John worked for 40 years on the assembly line at a factory making cars. He believed that it was a good job which supported his family well, but he had worked many overtime hours and had had little time for leisure. Now 70, he sits in the chair in his living room and watches TV and reads the paper. This has been his pattern since his retirement 5 years ago. Occasionally, he and his wife of 45 years will go out to dinner. John is glad not to have to go to the "rat race" of work every day.

Disengagement theory has been widely discounted by most gerontologists, however. While attempting to explain both system- and individual-level change with one grand theory, it has generally not been supported by empirical research (Achenbaum and Bengtson, 1994). Older people, especially in other cultures, may move into new roles of prestige and power. Likewise, not everyone in our culture disengages, as evidenced by the growing numbers of older people who remain employed, healthy, and politically and socially active. As with activity theory, disengagement theory fails to account for variability in individual preferences, for personality, and for differences in the sociocultural setting and environmental opportunities (Achenbaum and Bengtson, 1994; Marshall, 1994). Likewise, it cannot be assumed that older people's withdrawal from useful roles is necessarily good for society. For example, policies to encourage retirement have resulted in the loss of older workers' skills and knowledge in the workplace. Although disengagement theory has largely disappeared from the empirical literature, as the first attempt to define an explicit multidisciplinary theory of aging, it has had a profound impact upon the field.

Continuity Theory

While challenging both activity and disengagement theory, **continuity theory** maintained the focus on social-psychological theories of adaptation which were developed from the Kansas City Studies. According to continuity theory, individuals tend to maintain a *consistent* pattern of behavior as they age, substituting similar types of roles for lost ones and maintaining typical ways of adapting to the environment. Life satisfaction is determined by how consistent current activities or lifestyles are with one's lifetime experiences (Atchley, 1972; Neugarten, Havinghurst, and Tobin, 1968). Basically, this perspective states that, with age, we become more of what we already were when younger. Central personality characteristics become even more pronounced, and core values

Religious leadership can be continued across the lifespan.

even more salient with age. For example, people who have always been passive or withdrawn are unlikely to become active upon retirement. In contrast, people who were involved in many organizations, sports, or religious groups are likely to continue these activities or to substitute new ones for those that are lost with retirement or relocation. An individual ages successfully and "normally" if she or he maintains a mature, integrated personality while growing old. Continuity theory is difficult to test empirically, since an individual's reaction to aging is explained through the interrelationships among biological and psychological changes and the continuation of lifelong patterns. Another limitation is that by focusing on the individual as a unit of analysis, it overlooks the role of external social factors in modifying the aging process. It thus could rationalize a laissez-faire or "live and let live" approach to solving the problems facing older people.

Continuity and Adaptation

At age 80, Rabbi Green, who has taught rabbinical students for 40 years, still makes the trip from his suburban home into the city to work with students one day per week. He speaks with considerable excitement about the reciprocal relationship between him and his students. When students talk about their relationship with him,

it becomes clear how much they value him as a mentor. Being a "teacher" is who he is now and who he has always been.

Mary, 90, has always been the "cookie jar" mother to her children and their friends. She was there to offer goodies and a listening ear. Now her children and the generation of young persons who were their friends live far away. But a new generation of younger persons has moved into the neighborhood in the small town where she lives. She has become acquainted with many of them and their parents as they stop to talk with her as she works in her beloved yard. Now many will stop by for a cookie and a glass of milk after school. She is fondly called the "cookie jar grandma." Along with giving them cookies, the children say that she always listens to them.

ALTERNATIVE THEORETICAL PERSPECTIVES

Activity, disengagement, and continuity theories have often been framed as directly challenging one another (Lynott and Lynott, 1996; Hochschild, 1975, 1976), even though they differ in the extent to which they focus on individual behavior or social systems/social structure (Marshall, 1996). None fully explains successful aging nor adequately addresses the social structure or the cultural or historical contexts in which the aging process occurs. During this early period of theory development, the factors found to be associated with optimal aging were, for the most part, individualistic—keeping active, withdrawal, "settling" into old age. When macro-level phenomena were considered, they were not conceptualized as structurally linked between the individual and society. Nor were race, ethnicity, and class explicitly identified as social structural variables. A number of alternative theoretical viewpoints have emerged since the 1960s, each attempting to explain "the facts" of aging better than another (Lynott and Lynott, 1996). These alternative viewpoints, many of which placed greater emphasis on a macro-level of structural analysis, include symbolic interactionism or subcultures of aging, age stratification, social exchange, and political economy.

Symbolic Interactionism and Subculture of Aging

Consistent with the person-environment perspective outlined in Chapter 1, these **interactionist** theories focus on the person-environment transaction process, emphasizing the dynamic interaction between older individuals and their social world. It is assumed that older people must adjust to ongoing societal requirements. When confronted with change, whether relocation to a nursing home or learning to use a computer, older individuals are expected to try to master the changing situation while extracting from the larger environment what they need to retain a positive self-concept.

Attempting to bridge the gap between the activity and disengagement points of view, the **symbolic interactionist** perspective of aging argues that the interactions of such factors as the environment, individuals, and their encounters in it can significantly affect the kind of aging process people experience (Gubrium, 1973). This perspective emphasizes the importance of considering the meaning of the activity, such as disengagement, for the individuals concerned. Gubrium argued that in some environments, activity may be valued, while in others it is devalued. Depending upon a person's resources (health, socioeconomic status, social support) as well as the norms in a given environment for interpreting them, there are either positive or negative consequences for life satisfaction (Lynott and Lynott, 1996). Both the self and society are viewed by symbolic interactionists as able to create new alternatives. Therefore, low morale and withdrawal from social involvement are not inevitable with aging, but are one possible outcome of an individual's interactions that can be altered. Policies and programs based on the symbolic interactionist framework optimistically assume that both environmental constraints and individual needs can be changed.

Labeling theory, derived from symbolic interaction theory, states that people derive their self-concepts from interacting with others in their social milieu. In other words, we all tend to think of ourselves in terms of how others define us and react to others. Once others have defined us into distinct categories, they react to us on the basis of these categorizations. As a result, our self-concept and behavior change. For example, an older person who forgets where she or he parked the car is likely to be defined by relatives as showing signs of dementia, while younger people who do so are viewed as busy and distracted.

Subculture of Aging

Roy, 63, has resided in a downtown SRO hotel in the Pacific Northwest for the past 4 years. A logger for many years, he never married, living alone in the woods for most of his work life and coming into town only when he needed supplies. When logging was curtailed, he "retired" early. Now he lives with many other elderly men downtown, having only a nodding acquaintance with them. He is able to make use of a low income clinic for health care, and goes once a week to a downtown church where they serve lunch to older adults in the area.

Proponents of a **subculture of aging theory** believe that older people maintain their self-concepts and social identities through their membership in a subculture (Rose, 1965). It argues that behavior, whether of older persons or others, cannot be evaluated in terms of some overall social standard or norm. Rather, it is appreciated or devalued against the background of its members' expectations. Older people are presumed to interact with each other more than they do with others in society, because they have developed an affinity for each other through shared backgrounds, problems, and interests. At the same time, they may be excluded from fully interacting with other segments of the population, either because of self-segregation in retirement communities or "involuntary" segregation, such as younger people leaving inner city or rural areas and thereby isolating older residents. The formation of an aging subculture is viewed as having two significant consequences for older people: an identification of themselves as old, and thus socially and culturally distant from the rest of our youth-oriented society; and a growing group consciousness that may create the possibility of political influence and social action. Although the interactionist and subculture perspectives have implications for how to restructure the environment, the focus has been primarily on how individuals react to aging rather than on the broader socio-structural factors that shape the experience and meaning of aging in our society.

Age Stratification Theory

Just as societies are stratified in terms of socioeconomic class, gender, and race, every society divides people into categories or strata according to age—"young," "middle-aged," and "old." Age stratification is defined in terms of differential age cohorts. This means that individuals' experiences of aging, and therefore his or her roles, varies with their age strata. An older person's evaluation of life cannot be understood simply as a matter of being active or disengaged. Instead, changes in the system of age stratification influ-

Age stratification theory and the subculture of aging suggest that older people prefer socializing within their own cohorts.

ence how one's experiences affect life satisfaction (Lynott and Lynott, 1996).

The **age stratification** approach challenges the activity and disengagement theories, directing attention away from individual adjustment to that of the age structure of society (Marshall, 1996). It adds a structured time component in which cohorts pass through an age structure viewed as an age-graded system of expectations and rewards (Riley, Johnson, and Foner, 1972). This recognizes that the members of one strata differ from each other in both their stage of life (young, middle-aged, or old) and in the historical periods they have experienced. Both the life course and the historical dimensions explain differences in how people behave, think, and, in turn, contribute to society. Differences due to the historical dimension are referred to as cohort flow. As we saw in our discussion of research designs (Chapter 1), people who were born at the same time period (cohort) share a common historical and environmental past, present, and future. They have been exposed to similar events, conditions, and changes, and therefore come to see the world in a like fashion (Riley, 1971). For example, older people who were at the early stage of their occupational and child-rearing careers during the Depression tend to value economic self-sufficiency and "saving for a rainy day," compared to younger cohorts who have experienced periods of economic prosperity during early adulthood. This may create difficulties across generations in understanding each other's behavior with regard to finances or lifestyle.

Because of their particular relationship to historical events, people in the old-age stratum today are very different from older persons in the past or in the future, and they experience the aging process differently. This also means that cohorts as they age collectively influence age stratification. When there is a lack of fit in terms of available roles, cohort members may challenge the existing patterns of age stratification. For example, as successive cohorts in this century have experienced increased longevity and formal educational levels, this has changed the nature of how they age, how they view aging, and the age stratification system itself. The cohort retiring in the 1990s tends to view retirement and leisure more positively than the cohorts that retired in the 1950s, for example. They also have been more likely to challenge restrictions on their roles as workers and community participants through age discrimination lawsuits, legislative action, and political organization than previous cohorts. These variations, in turn, will affect the experiences and expectations of future cohorts as they age. In other words, as successive cohorts move through the age strata, they alter conditions to such a degree that later groups never encounter the world in exactly the same way, and therefore age in different ways.

Age stratification theory, with its focus on structural, demographic, and historical characteristics, can help us understand the ways in which society uses age to fit people into structural niches in the social world, and how this age structure changes with the passage of time. By viewing aging groups as members of status groups within a social system, as well as active participants in a changing society, stratification theory can provide useful sociological explanations of age differences related to time, period, and cohort.

More recently, the concept of **structural lag** has emerged from the age and society perspective (Riley, Kahn, and Foner, 1994; Riley and Riley, 1994). Structural lag occurs when social structures cannot keep pace with the changes in population and individual lives (Riley and Loscocco, 1994). For example, with the increases in life expectancy, societal structures are inadequate to accommodate and utilize post-retirement elders. Proponents of this perspective argue that an age-integrated society would compensate for structural lag by developing policies, such as extended time off for education or family across the life span, to bring social structures into balance with individuals' lives.

Social Exchange Theory

Social exchange theory also challenged activity and disengagement theory. Drawing upon economic cost-benefit models of social participation,

Dowd (1980) attempts to answer why social interaction and activity often decrease with age. He maintains that withdrawal and social isolation are not the result of system needs or individual choice, but rather of an unequal exchange process between older persons and other members of society. The balance of interactions existing between older people and others determines personal satisfaction. Accordingly, individual adjustment depends on the immediate costs and benefits between persons, although exchange may also be driven by emotional needs and resources, such as social support (Bengtson et al., 1997). Because of the shift in **opportunity structures**, roles, and skills that accompanies advancing aging, older people typically have fewer resources with which to exert power in their social relationships, and their status declines accordingly (Hendricks, 1995). Loss of power or the ability to control one's environment thus explains why older people, left only with the capacity for compliance, may disengage. Society is at an advantage in such power relationships, reflected in the economic and social dependency of older people who have outmoded skills. With fewer opportunity structures and little to exchange in value, some older people are forced to accept the retirement role and to turn to deference and withdrawal in order to balance the exchange equation (Lynott and Lynott, 1996).

Despite their limited resources, most older people seek to maintain some degree of reciprocity and be active, independent agents in the management of their lives. In this model, adaptability is a dual process of influencing one's environment as well as adjusting to it. Although older individuals have fewer resources to bring to the interaction or exchange, they often have non-material resources such as respect, approval, and time for voluntary activities. Similarly, policies and services that are developed for older people might aim to maximize their non-material resources that are valued by our society as well as to increase opportunity structures for older people. For example, the growing number of intergenerational programs recognize the volume of social exchange between generations. Exchange theory is relevant to contemporary debates about intergenerational social support and transfer across generations through public policies such as Social Security and within families through caregiving relationships.

Political Economy of Aging

The focus of exchange theory on power and opportunity structures is related to the **political economy of aging,** a relatively recent macroanalysis of structural characteristics that determine how people adapt in old age and how social resources are allocated. According to the political economy perspective, social class is a structural barrier to older people's access to valued social resources, with dominant groups within society trying to sustain their own interests by perpetuating class inequities (Overbo and Minkler, 1993; Minkler and Estes, 1984; Olson, 1982). Socioeconomic and political constraints, not individual factors, thereby shape the experience of aging, and are patterned not only by age but also by class, gender, race, and ethnicity. These structural factors, often institutionalized and reinforced by economic and public policy, limit opportunities, choices, and experiences of later life (Bengtson et al., 1997). This means that the process of aging and how individuals adapt are not the problem. Rather, the major problems faced by older people are socially constructed in a capitalist society as a result of societal conceptions of aging. In fact, policy solutions, such as Social Security, Medicare, and Medicaid, are viewed as a means of social control that perpetuate the "private" troubles of older people while meeting the dominant needs of the economy (Estes, Linkins, and Binney, 1996; Olson, 1982). Estes et al. (1996) argues that the marginalization of the older population is furthered by the development of the "Aging Enterprise," a service industry of agencies, providers, and planners that reaffirms the out-group status of older adults in order to maintain their own jobs. Policy solutions have tended to focus on integrating and socializing older people to adapt to their status, rather

Both young and old can benefit from the Foster Grandparents program.

than efforts to fundamentally alter social and economic conditions that underlie the problems facing older people.

Life Course Perspective

The **life course perspective** is not necessarily a theory, but a framework pointing to a set of problems requiring explanation (George, 1996). It attempts to bridge sociological and psychological thinking about processes at both the macro (population) and micro (individual) levels of analysis by incorporating the effects of history, social structure, and individual meaning into theoretical models (Bengtson et al., 1997; Marshall, 1996). This approach takes account of the diversity of roles and role changes across the life span, since it suggests that development is not restricted to any one part of the life span, but rather, a lifelong and highly dynamic process. Development cannot be solely equated with steady incremental growth or change but instead is an interactive, non-linear process characterized by the simultaneous appearance of role gains and losses, continuity, and discontinuity. Accordingly, development is multidirectional, with stability in some functions, decline in others, and improvement in others. For example, an older person may experience some decrement in memory but still be very creative. In addition, these patterns of development are not the same in all individuals, as reflected by the considerable heterogeneity of life trajectories and transitions among older individuals. The life course perspective has been used to analyze how caregiving is now a standardized part of the life course, "on-time" for increasing numbers of middle-aged adult children, because more older people are living longer and requiring care by family members (Elder, George, and Shanahan, 1996). As another example, the life course perspective has been used to examine the concept of cumulative disadvantage for women across life, because of their limited opportunities to aggregate savings and private pensions as compared to men (O'Rand, 1996).

In contrast with the more individualistic approach of role theory, the life course perspective attempts to explain how aging is related to and shaped by social contexts, history, cultural meanings, and location in the social structure, and how time, period, and cohort shape the aging process for individuals and social groups (Bengtson and Allen, 1993; George, 1993; Elder, 1992; Baltes, 1987). This approach is also multidisciplinary in content and methods, bringing together seemingly disparate approaches to the life course (Bengtson et al., 1997). While the life course perspective is not explicitly articulated throughout this text, our multidisciplinary person-in-environment approach encompassing biological, psychological, physiological, and social changes draws upon many of the concepts of intra-individual change, inter-individual variability, and historical, social, and cultural contexts or environments.

RECENT DEVELOPMENTS IN SOCIAL GERONTOLOGICAL THEORY: THE SECOND TRANSFORMATION

Social Phenomenologists and Social Constructionists

The "second transformation" in theoretical development, occurring since the early 1980s, has been described as a qualitative leap in gerontological thought (Lynott and Lynott, 1996). Phenomenological theorists have taken issue with the presumed "facts of aging," questioning the nature of age and how it is described and whose interests are served by thinking of aging in particular ways. **Social phenomenologists** and **social constructionists** claim that the approach, orientation, and other subjective features of the researchers and their world are significantly connected to the nature of the data as such. Therefore, the data or facts of aging cannot be separated from the researcher's perceptions about time, space, and self—or those of the individuals being studied. People actively participate in their everyday lives, creating and maintaining social meanings for themselves and those around them. No one, including researchers, directly or objectively sees a fixed reality. Rather, each of us actively constructs meanings that influence what we each call reality (Ray, 1996). For pheomenologists and social constructionists, it is not the objects or facts but rather the assumptions and interpretations of them that is critical (Lynott and Lynott, 1996). For example, this theoretical perspective would attempt to understand how legislators and other policymakers assume certain features about the older population in deciding whether to increase or decrease Medicare or Social Security benefits.

The emphasis of phenomenologists is on understanding, not explaining, individual processes of aging as influenced by social definitions and social structures (Bengtson et al., 1997). Instead of asking how factors such as age cohorts, life stages, or system needs organize and determine one's experience, they reverse the question and ask how individuals, whether professionals or lay persons, draw upon age-related explanations and justifications in how they relate to and interact with one another. Individual behavior produces a "reality," which in turn structures individual lives. This means that social reality shifts over time, reflecting the differing life situations and social roles that occur with maturation (Dannefer and Perlmutter, 1990). For example, Gubrium and Lynott (1983) maintain that whether an individual feels old or not, behaves old or not, or feels satisfied with life or not depends upon their "background experiences" or relevant worlds to interpret later life experiences. Not only do theories construct versions of reality, but people do so in their everyday lives; and in the everyday world, people often use or critique the constructions of theorists (Marshall, 1996). Gubrium (1993a) used life narratives to discern the subjective meanings of quality of care and quality of life for nursing home residents—meanings that cannot be measured by predefined measurement scales such as those used by most survey researchers. Similarly, Diamond (1992) utilized participant observation techniques as a nursing assistant to learn about the social world of nursing homes. He described the social construction of his job, how the meanings of care are constantly negotiated as the invisible work of caring for older residents' emotional needs clashes with the daily tasks of a nursing assistant. The realities of age and age-related concepts are thus socially constructed. For example, labeling older people as dependent, asexual, frail or marginal is defined socially. However, the focus is on how these definitions emerge through social interactions rather than taking account of social structure and power (Kaufman, 1994).

Social constructionists and phenomenologists, such as Gubrium and Diamond, because of their focus on individual interactions, tend to use ethnographic or more qualitative methods to obtain multifaceted views of the aging experience. For example, Diamond (1992), as a participant observer as a nursing assistant, described both the social construction of the job and the negotiation of the position of patient in a nursing home. This contrasts with the **positivist approach** of many of the earlier theories. In order to gather extensive verbal or observational data, their samples of informants are relatively small compared to the more traditional quantitative methods typically used. To positivists, however, social constructionist theories may seem impossible to test, closer to assumptions about meaning than

propositions that can be proved or disproved (Bengtson et al., 1997).

Critical Theory and Feminist Perspectives

Social constructionist theories have influenced other contemporary social gerontology theories, especially critical and feminist theories. **Critical theorists** critique the transformation of the relationships between subjects and objects from being genuine to being alienated, not the research procedures nor the objective state of objects per se. With respect to age conceptualizations and theories of aging, critical theorists are concerned with how they represent a language serving to reify experiences as something separate from those doing the experiencing (Lynott and Lynott, 1996). For example, Tornstam (1996, 1992) argues that conventional gerontology draws on a limited positivist notion of knowledge and science that produces a model of aging based only on social problems. By contrast, a more critical and humane approach would allow older people themselves to define the research questions. Arguing for humanistic discourse in gerontology, Moody (1988) identifies four goals of a critical gerontology approach: (1) to theorize subjective and interpretive dimensions of aging; (2) to focus not on technical advancement but on "praxis," defined as active involvement in practical change, such as public policy; (3) to link academics and practitioners through praxis; and (4) to produce "emancipatory knowledge," which is a positive vision of how things might be different or what a rationally defensible vision of a "good old age" might be (p. xvii). To achieve this knowledge requires moving beyond the conventional confines of gerontology to explore contributions toward theory development from more reflective modes of thought derived from the humanities (Cole, Achenbaum, Jakobi, and Kastenbaum, 1993). Dannefer (1994) suggests that critical gerontology should not merely critique existing theory but create positive models of aging that emphasize strengths and diversity. For example, Atchley (1993) maintains that critical gerontology must question traditional positivistic assumptions and measures to try to understand the multiple dimensions of retirement, including retirement as a freeing stage in the life course. What is yet unknown is what "a good old age" means, as well as how it will be attained and what type of "emancipatory knowledge" is possible. Nevertheless, critical thinking has the potential to expand the field of social gerontology. It can do so by providing insight into, and critical self-reflection on, the continuing effort to understand the aging experience (Lynott and Lynott, 1996).

Because most gerontologists have been trained in the positivist tradition, critical theory, which is very abstract, is not often cited nor yet well understood. Nevertheless, it is becoming a topic of considerable theoretical discourse in contemporary social gerontology (Minkler, 1996; Phillipson, 1996; Cole et al., 1993). By questioning traditions in mainstream social gerontology, critical theory calls attention to other perspectives relevant to understanding aging, especially the humanistic dimension of aging (Gubrium, 1993b), and has influenced feminist theories of aging. In addition, the self-reflexive nature of critical theory constantly challenges gerontologists to understand the impact of social research and policy on older individuals (Tornstam, 1992). With growing attention to ethnographic and other qualitative methodologies, the interpretive approach of critical theory will increasingly be brought to bear on empirical observations of aging, with researchers attempting to integrate critical theory with the strengths of positivist approaches.

From a critical theory perspective, current theories and models of aging are viewed as insufficient because they fail to include gender relations and the experiences of women in the context of aging (Marshall, 1996; Bleiszner, 1993). For example, women have traditionally been ignored in retirement research, often because paid employment is assumed to be unimportant to them (Calasanti, 1993). **Feminist theories** draw upon a number of other theories discussed thus far: political economy by focusing on the economic and

power relations between older men and women; and symbolic interactionism, phenomenology, and social constructionism in their belief that gender must be examined in the context of social structural arrangements. Other common themes are attempts to integrate micro and macro approaches to aging through the links between individuals and social structures, especially regarding power relations and the utilization of both quantitative and qualitative methodologies (Lynott and Lynott, 1996; Ray, 1996; Bury, 1995).

Feminist theorists argue that gender should be a primary consideration in attempts to understand aging and older people, especially since women are the majority of the older population. Because gender is an organizing principle for social interactions across the life span, men and women experience the aging process differently (Bengtson et al., 1997; Marshall, 1996; Ginn and Arber, 1995). Although there is a wide range of intellectual paradigms and political positions within feminism, most feminist theories in aging have drawn on "socialist feminism." This model argues that women occupy an inferior status in old age as a result of living in a capitalist and patriarchal society (Arber and Ginn, 1995, 1991). Socialist feminists point to inequities in the gender-based division of labor and argue for major changes in the way that society defines, distributes, and rewards "work." They attempt to understand women's aging experiences in light of macro-level social, economic, and political forces rather than as isolated results of individual choices. Caregiving, women's retirement, health, and poverty across the life course have all been examined by feminist theorists in light of women's differential access to power throughout their lives in terms of the paid labor force, childrearing, and unpaid housework. Such unequal access leaves women without economic resources and necessary social support for managing problems in later life (Arber and Ginn, 1995; Hooyman and Gonyea, 1995; Calasanti and Hendricks, 1993; Stoller, 1993). Social policy is criticized for defining the problems facing women as private responsibilities, rather than taking account of how existing structural arrangements create women's dependency and limited choices in old age. For example, the lack of retirement pensions for a lifelong career as homemaker and caregiver leaves older women vulnerable to society's whims in identifying social benefits to older adults. The need for feminist theory can also be seen when considering the failure to take domestic labor seriously in life-course analyses of work (Marshall, 1996). As another example of a feminist approach, the consequences of caregiving should not be evaluated on the basis of individual characteristics such as caregiver burden. Instead, the underlying problem for women of all ages is inadequate and gender-based policies; the long-range solution is reorganizing work as a societal rather than an individual responsibility. From a feminist perspective, caring work must be reorganized to be more equitable and humane both for the givers and the receivers (Meyer, 1997; Hooyman and Gonyea, 1995).

A Feminist Perspective on Caregiving

Mrs. Reid grew up with the expectation that she would marry, have children, and take care of her family. She fulfilled this expectation, raising four children, caring for her husband when he suffered a heart attack in his early 60s, and then later caring for both her mother and her mother-in-law. She never held a full-time job, instead working occasionally and part-time in order to supplement her husband's income. When he died at age 65, she was left with only his Social Security. All her years of caregiving work, that had contributed to her family's well-being and to the economy, were not compensated in any way. If her caregiving work were valued by our society, Social Security would be altered to view such in-home care as legitimate work that contributes to society. Accordingly, caregivers such as Mrs. Reid would receive Social Security benefits in their own right in old age.

More recently, there have been efforts to integrate **postmodern theory** into gerontology and feminism, although postmodernism is itself antitheoretical. Postmodernism theory views knowledge as socially constructed and social life as

highly improvisational. Theoretically, modernism challenges positivistic science (Marshall, 1996; Ray, 1996). Postmodernists view the primary task to be the critique of language, discourse, and research practices that constrict knowledge about older women. For example, they approach caregiving not as the result of "natural" tendencies in women toward nurturing, but the outcome of socialization processes and polices which reify gendered patterns of caring by depending on the unpaid labor of women as efficient and cost-effective (Hooyman and Gonyea, 1995; Stoller, 1993; Hooyman, 1992). A postmodern feminist approach in gerontology draws upon a variety of methodologies to understand women's experiences. Researchers acknowledge how their assumptions, values, and beliefs influence the research process; and the research is oriented to changing conditions that face women, conducted to benefit women as well as having women as active participants.

Because feminist theories of aging are new to the field, broad, and often ideologically based, they are less frequently cited than established models of explanation, such as social constructionism, life course, and exchange theories. Nevertheless, they can make significant contributions to gerontology and to the development of feminist theory generally. Not only are they focusing on the needs of the majority of the older population, but they also take account of diversity by race, ethnicity, social class, education, and mental status. Addressing issues that are relevant to the lives of women, they draw explicit linkages to practice. In addition, they provide models for integrating micro and macro levels of analyses and thus encompass both structural and individual levels of theory and change in order to improve the social and economic positions of women as they age. Lastly, they challenge "mainstream" feminist theories to take account of issues of age, since gender shapes everyday experiences throughout the life course (Bengtson et al., 1997; Meyer, 1997). The merger of feminist and aging scholarship has the potential for formulating politically sustainable solutions that permit women and men, young and old, to balance the burdens and satisfactions of caregiving work and paid work (Meyer, 1997).

SUMMARY AND IMPLICATIONS

This review of theoretical perspectives has highlighted the multiplicity of lenses through which to view and explain the aging process. Although we have emphasized the importance of utilizing explicit theoretical perspectives to build, revise, and interpret how and why phenomena occur, it is apparent that no one theory can explain all aging phenomena (Marshall, 1994). Instead, these theories or conceptual frameworks vary widely in their emphasis on individual adjustment to age-related changes, their attention to social structure, power, and economic conditions, the methodologies utilized, and their reflective nature on the meaning of the aging experience. As noted in the introduction, they represent different times or historical periods in the development of social theories. Some, such as disengagement theory, have been largely rejected by empirical data, while others, such as critical theory and feminist theory, are only now evolving and capturing the attention of a new generation of gerontological researchers. Other earlier perspectives, such as social exchange and symbolic interactionism, still influence research questions and social policy. As a whole, these theoretical perspectives point to new ways of seeing aging phenomena and new modes of analysis, laying the framework for future research directions (Hendricks, 1992). As the social, economic, and political conditions affecting older people change, new theoretical perspectives must develop or former ones must be revised through the gathering of information from diverse cultures, contexts, and circumstances. Given the growing heterogeneity of the aging process, interdisciplinary research is essential. Such research must take account of both individual- and macro-level changes, must encompass the role of gender, race, and class, and must allow for the dynamic nature and meaning of the aging experience. We turn now to the social context and relationships addressed by many of the social theories of aging: the vital role of social supports in old age; how physical living arrangements can affect social interactions; the concept of productive aging which encompasses both paid and non-paid roles and activities; and coping with loss in dying, bereavement, and widowhood.

GLOSSARY

activity theory   a theory of aging based on the hypothesis that (1) active older people are more satisfied and better adjusted than those who are not active and (2) an older person's self-concept is validated through participation in roles characteristic of middle age, and older people should therefore replace lost roles with new ones to maintain their place in society

age stratification theory   a theoretical perspective based on the belief that the societal age structure affects roles, self-concept, and life satisfaction.

continuity theory   a theory based on the hypothesis that central personality characteristics become more pronounced with age or are retained through life with little change; people age successfully if they maintain their preferred roles and adaptation techniques throughout life

critical theory   the perspective that genuine knowledge is based on the involvement of the "objects" of study in its definition and results in a positive vision of how things might be better rather than an understanding of how things are

disengagement theory   a theory of aging based on the hypothesis that older people, because of inevitable decline with age, become decreasingly active with the outer world and increasingly preoccupied with their inner lives; disengagement is useful for society because it fosters an orderly transfer of power from older to younger people

feminist perspective   the view that the experiences of women are often ignored in understanding the human condition together with efforts to attend, critically, to those experiences

interactionist perspective   a perspective that emphasizes the reciprocal actions of persons and their social world in shaping perceptions, attitudes, behavior, etc., including person-environment, symbolic interaction, labeling, and social breakdown perspectives

labeling theory   a theoretical perspective derived from symbolic interactionism premised on the belief that people derive their self-concepts from interacting with others in their social milieu, in how others define us and react to us

life course perspective   the multidisciplinary view of human development that focuses on changes with age and life experiences

opportunity structures   social arrangements, formal and informal, that limit or advance options available to people based on such features as social class, age, ethnicity, and sex

political economy of aging   a theory based on the hypothesis that social class determines a person's access to resources and that dominant groups within society try to sustain their own interests by perpetuating class inequities

positivism   the perspective that knowledge is based solely upon observable facts and their relation to one another (cause and effect or correlation); the search for ultimate origins is rejected

postmodern theory   the critique of language, discourse, and research practices that constrict knowledge

productive roles   a concept central to activity theory; activities in volunteer associations, churches, employment, and politics

role exit   a process whereby individuals disengage from roles central to their identity

role theory   a theory based on the belief that roles define us and our self-concept and shape our behavior

social exchange theory   a theory based on the hypothesis that personal status is defined by the balance between people's contributions to society and the costs of supporting them

social phenomenology and constructionism   a point of view in studying social life that places an emphasis on the assumptions and meanings of experience rather than the "objective" facts, with a focus on understanding rather than explaining

structural lag   the inability of social structures (patterns of behavior, attitude, ideas, policies, etc.) to adapt to changes in population and individual lives

subculture theory   a theoretical perspective based on the belief that people maintain their self-concepts and social identities through their membership in a defined group (subculture)

symbolic interactionism   a theoretical perspective that is premised on the belief that the interactions of such factors as the environment, individuals, and their encounters in it can significantly affect one's behavior and thoughts, including the aging process

REFERENCES

Achenbaum, W. A., and Bengtson, V. C. Re-engaging the disengagement theory of aging: Or the history and assessment of theory development in gerontology. *The Gerontologist,* 1994, *34,* 756–763.

Arber, S., and Ginn, J. (Ed.). *Connecting gender and aging: A sociological approach.* Philadelphia, PA: Open University Press, 1995.

Arber, S., and Ginn, J. *Gender and later life: A sociological analysis of constraints.* Newbury Park, CA: Sage, 1991.

Atchley, R. C. Critical perspectives on retirement. In T. R. Cole, W. A. Achenbaum, P. L. Jakobi, and R. Kastenbaum (Eds.), *Voices and visions: Toward a critical gerontology.* New York: Springer, 1993.

Atchley, R. C. *The social forces in later life.* Belmont, CA: Wadsworth, 1972.

Baltes, P. B. Theoretical propositions of life-span developmental psychology: On the dynamics between growth and decline. Baltes, P. B. (Ed.). *Developmental Psychology,* 1987.

Bengtson, V. L. Cultural and occupational differences in level of present role activity in retirement. In R. J. Havinghurst, J. M. A. Munnicks, B. C. Neugarten, and H. Thomas (Eds.), *Adjustments to retirement: A cross-national study.* Assen, The Netherlands: Van Gorkum, 1969.

Bengtson, V. L., and Allen, K. R. The life course perspective applied to families over time. In P. G. Boss, W. J. Doherty, R. LaRossa, W. R. Schumm, and S. K. Steinmetz (Eds.), *Sourcebook of family theories and methods: A conceptual approach.* New York: Plenum Press, 1993.

Bengtson, V. L., Burgess, E. O., and Parrott, T. M. Theory, explanation and a third generation of theoretical development in social gerontology. *Journals of Gerontology,* 1997, *52B,* S72–S88.

Bleiszner, R. A socialist-feminist perspective on widowhood. *Journal of Aging Studies,* 1993, *7,* 171–182.

Bury, M. Aging, gender and sociological theory. In S. Arber, and J. Ginn (Eds.), *Connecting gender and aging: A sociological approach.* Philadelphia: Open University Press, 1995.

Calasanti, T. M. Bringing in diversity: Toward an inclusive theory of retirement. *Journal of Aging Studies,* 1993, *7,* 133–150.

Calasanti, T. M. Incorporating diversity: Meaning, levels of research, and implications for theory. *The Gerontologist,* 1996, *36,* 147–156.

Calasanti, T. M., and Zaijicek, J. M. A socialist-feminist approach to aging. *Journal of Aging Studies,* 1993, *7,* 117–131.

Cole, T. R., Achenbaum, W. A., Jacobi, P. L., and Kastenbaum, R. *Voices and visions of aging: Toward a critical gerontology.* New York: Springer, 1993.

Cottrell, L. The adjustment of the individual to his age and sex roles. *American Sociological Review,* 1942, *7,* 617–620.

Covey, H. A reconceptualization of continuity theory: Some preliminary thoughts. *The Gerontologist,* 1981, *21,* 628–633.

Cumming, E., and Henry, W. E. *Growing old.* New York: Basic Books, 1961.

Dannefer, W. D. *Reciprocal co-optation: Some reflections on the relationship of critical theory and social gerontology.* Revised version of paper presented at the International Sociological Association, Bieleveld, Germany, July, 1994.

Dannefer, W. D., and Perlmutter, M. Development as a multidimensional process: Individual and social constituents. *Human Development,* 1990, *33,* 108–137.

Diamond, T. *Making grey gold: Narratives of nursing home care.* Chicago: University of Chicago Press, 1992.

Dowd, J. J. *Stratification among the aged.* Monterey, CA: Brooks Cole, 1980.

Ekerdt, D. J., and DeViney, S. Evidence for a preretirement process among older male workers. *Journals of Gerontology,* 1993, *48,* S35–S43.

Elder, G. H., Jr. Models of the life course. *Contemporary Sociology: A Journal of Reviews,* 1992, *21,* 632–635.

Elder, G. H., Jr., George, L. K., and Shanahan, M. J. Psychosocial stress over the life course. In H. Kaplan, (Ed.), *Psychosocial stress: Perspectives on structure, theory, life-course, and methods.* San Diego: Academic Press, 1996.

Estes, C. L. *The aging enterprise.* San Francisco: Jossey Bass, 1979.

Estes, C. L., Gerard, L. E., Zones, J. S., and Swan, J. H. *Political economy, health, and aging.* Boston: Little Brown, 1984.

Estes, C. L., Linkins, K. W., and Binney, E. A. The political economy of aging. In R. H. Binstock and L. K. George, (Eds.), *Handbook of aging and the social sciences* (4th ed.). San Diego: Academic Press, 1996.

Garfinkle, H. *Studies in ethno-methodology.* Englewood Cliffs, NJ: Prentice-Hall, 1967.

George, L. K. Missing links: The case for a social psychology of the life course. *The Gerontologist,* 1996, *36,* 248–255.

George, L. K. Sociological perspectives on life transitions. *Annual Review of Sociology,* 1993, *19,* 353–373.

Ginn, J., and Arber, S. Only connect: Gender relations and aging. In S. Arber, and J. Ginn (Eds.), *Connecting gender and aging: A sociological approach.* Philadelphia: Open University Press, 1995.

Gubrium, J. F. *The myth of the golden years.* Springfield, IL: Charles C. Thomas, 1973.

Gubrium, J. F. *Speaking of life: Horizons of meaning for nursing home residents.* New York: Aldine de Gruyter, 1993a.

Gubrium, J. F. Voice and context in a new gerontology. In T. R. Cole, W. A. Achenbaum, P. C. Jakobi, and R. Kastenbaum (Eds.), *Voices and visions of aging: Toward a critical gerontology.* New York: Springer, 1993b.

Gubrium, J. F., and Lynott, R. J. Rethinking life satisfaction. *Human Organization,* 1983, *42,* 30–38.

Hagestad, G., and Neugarten, B. Age and the life course. In R. H. Binstock, and E. Shanas (Eds.), *Handbook of aging and the social sciences* (2nd ed.). New York: Van Nostrand, 1985.

Havinghurst, R. J. Personality and patterns of aging. *The Gerontologist,* 1968, *38,* 20–23.

Havinghurst, R. J. Successful aging. In R. Williams, C. Tibbits, and W. Donahue (Eds.), *Processes of aging,* Vol. 1. New York: Atherton Press, 1963.

Hendricks, J. Exchange theory in aging. In G. Maddox (Ed.), *The Encyclopedia of aging* (2nd ed.). New York: Springer, 1995.

Hendricks, J. Generations and the generation of theory in social gerontology. *International Journal of Aging and Human Development,* 1992, *38,* 31–47.

Herzog, A. R., Holden, K. C., and Seltzer, M. M. *Health and economic status of older women.* Amityville, NY: Baywood, 1989.

Herzog, A. R., and House, J. S. Productive activities and aging well. *Generations,* 1991, *15,* 49–54.

Herzog, A. R., Kahn, R., Morgan, J., Jackson, J., and Antonucci, T. Age differences in productive activities. *Journals of Gerontology,* 1989, *44,* S129–S138.

Hochschild, A. R. Disengagement theory: A critique and proposal. *American Sociological Review,* 1975, *40,* 553–569.

Hochschild, A. R. Disengagement theory: A logical, empirical, and phenomenological critique. In J. F. Gubrium (Ed.), *Time, roles and self in old age.* New York: Human Services Press, 1976.

Hooyman, N. R. Social policy and gender inequities in caregiving. In J. W. Dwyer and R. T. Coward (Eds.), *Gender, families, and eldercare.* Newbury Park, CA: Sage, 1992.

Hooyman, N. R., and Gonyea, J. *Feminist perspectives on family care: Policies for gender justice.* Thousand Oaks, CA: Sage, 1995.

Kaufman, S. R. The social construction of frailty: An anthropological perspective. *Journal of Aging Studies,* 1994, 8, 45–58.

Lynott, R. J., and Lynott, P. P. Tracing the course of theoretical development in the sociology of aging. *The Gerontologist,* 1996, *36,* 749–760.

Marshall, V. W. Sociology, psychology in the theoretical legacy of the Kansas City studies. *The Gerontologist,* 1994, *34,* 768–774.

Marshall, V. W. The state of theory in aging and the social sciences. In R. H. Binstock and L. K. George, (Eds.), *Handbook of aging and the social sciences,* pp. 12–30. (4th ed.). San Diego: Academic Press, 1996.

Meyer, M. H. Toward a structural, life course agenda for reducing insecurity among women as they age. Book Review. *The Gerontologist,* 1997, *37,* 833–834.

Minkler, M. Critical perspectives on aging: New challenges for gerontology. *Aging and Society,* 1996, *16,* 467–487.

Minkler, M., and Estes, C. *Readings in the political economy of aging.* Farmingdale, NY: Baywood, 1984.

Moody, H. R. Toward a critical gerontology: The contribution of the humanities to theories of aging. In J. E. Birren and V. L. Bengtson (Eds.), *Emergent theories of aging.* New York: Springer, 1988.

Neugarten, B., Havinghurst, R. J., and Tobin, S. S. Personality and patterns of aging. In B. L. Neugarten (Ed.), *Middle age and aging.* Chicago: University of Chicago Press, 1968.

Olson, L. K. *The political economy of aging.* New York: Columbia University Press, 1982.

O'Rand, A. M. The precious and the precocious: Understanding cumulative disadvantage and cumulative advantage over the life course. *The Gerontologist,* 1996, *36,* 230–238.

Overbo, B., and Minkler, M. The lives of older women: Perspectives from political economy and the humanities. In T. R. Cole, W. A. Achenbaum, P. L. Jakobi, and R. Kastenbaum (Eds.), *Voices and visions of aging: Toward a critical gerontology.* New York: Springer, 1993.

Phillipson, C. Interpretations of aging: Perspectives from humanistic gerontology. *Aging and Society,* 1996, 16, 359–369.

Ray, R. E. A post modern perspective on feminist gerontology. *The Gerontologist,* 1996, *36,* 674–680.

Riley, M. W. Social gerontology and the age stratification of society. *The Gerontologist,* 1971, *11,* 79–87.

Riley, M. W., Johnson, J., and Foner, A. *Aging and society: A sociology of age stratification,* vol. 3. New York: Russell Sage Foundation, 1972.

Riley, M. W., Kahn, R. L., and Foner, A. (Eds.). *Age and structural lag: Society's failure to provide meaningful opportunities in work, family and leisure.* New York: John Wiley, 1994.

Riley, M. W., and Loscocco, K. A. The changing structure of work opportunities: Toward an age-integrated society. In R. P. Abeles, H. C. Gift, and M. G. Ory (Eds.), *Aging and quality of life.* New York: Springer, 1994.

Riley, M. W., and Riley, J. W. Age integration and the lives of older people. *The Gerontologist,* 1994, *34,* 110–115.

Rose, A. M. A current theoretical issue in social gerontology. In A. M. Rose, and W. A. Peterson (Eds.), *Older people and their social worlds.* Philadelphia: F. A. Davis, 1965.

Rosow, J. Status and role change through the life cycle. In R. H. Binstock and E. Shanas (Eds.), *Handbook of aging and the social sciences* (2nd ed.). New York: Van Nostrand, 1985.

Stoller, E. P. Gender and the organization of lay health care: A socialist-feminist perspective. *Journal of Aging Studies,* 1993, *7,* 151–170.

Tornstam, L. Gerotranscendence: A theory about maturing in old age. *Journal of Aging and Identity,* 1996, *1,* 37–50.

Tornstam, L. The Quo Vadis of gerontology: On the scientific paradigm of gerontology. *The Gerontologist,* 1992, *32,* 318–326.

9

THE IMPORTANCE OF SOCIAL SUPPORTS: FAMILY, FRIENDS, AND NEIGHBORS

As people age, the nature of their social roles and relationships changes. Earlier chapters have noted and the introductory vignettes have illustrated that the way older people interact with others is affected by physiological, social, and psychological changes. For example, with children gone from the home and without daily contacts with co-workers, older people may lose a critical context for social involvement. At the same time, their need for social support may increase because of changes in health, cognitive, and emotional status. Such incongruence between needs and environmental opportunities can result in stress for some older people. Previous chapters have referred to formal support systems characteristic of the larger environment, such as the health care system. Consistent with the life course perspective and the person-environment model, this chapter focuses on informal social support systems. These systems of family, friends, neighbors, and acquaintances can profoundly influence an older person's well-being. They can also buffer some of the losses of aging and influence health and functioning. This chapter concludes with policy and

practice issues posed by the use of informal social networks to deliver services.

THE NATURE AND FUNCTION OF INFORMAL SUPPORTS

The importance of informal social supports in older people's lives has been extensively documented. The concept of social support includes the specific types of assistance exchanged (emotional or tangible support); frequency of contact with others; and how a person assesses the adequacy of the supportive exchange (Krause and Borawski-Clark, 1995). Informal reciprocal relationships are, in fact, a crucial concomitant of an older person's physical and mental well-being, feelings of personal control, morale, and autonomy (Krause and Borawski-Clark, 1995; Hansson and Carpenter, 1994; Hobfoll and Vaux, 1993). As noted in Chapter 6, there is also research evidence that strong social networks contribute to successful aging. A common myth is that older people are lonely and alienated from family and friends. Yet, even the most apparently isolated and vulnerable older person may be able to turn to an informal network for information, financial advice, emotional reassurance, or concrete services (Cantor, 1994). Consistent with social exchange theory discussed in Chapter 8, most older adults try to maintain reciprocity—being able to help others—in their interactions with each other and with younger people in their social networks. Older individuals first use informal social supports to meet their emotional needs, and move to more formal relationships only when necessary, typically when they live alone (Krause and Borawski-Clark, 1995). As suggested by the person-environment model, they draw upon these informal supports as a way to enhance their competence. In fact, too much support from others, creating inequality of exchange, can erode older adults' sense of competence; in addition, some interactions with informal networks can be negative if they are not consistent with the older person's needs and competence level (Silverstein, Chen, and Heller, 1996).

With cutbacks in formal services in the past decade, gerontologists have become more aware of the critical roles played by informal relationships. Families, friends, neighbors, and even acquaintances, such as grocery clerks and postal carriers, can be powerful antidotes to some of the negative consequences of the aging process, as in the description of Mr. Mansfield on p. 227. For example, informal networks have been found to reduce the adverse effects of stressful life events, such as bereavement and widowhood, although it is unclear whether an older person's social networks act as buffers against the negative impact of life events on health, or whether they have a more direct effect, independent of the presence or absence of major life events (Mor-Barak et al., 1991).

Alternatively, loss of social support, through divorce or death of a spouse, can contribute to health problems (Cohen and Syme, 1985; Asher, 1984). For example, for older people who live alone and are not tied into informal networks, the use of formal services and the likelihood of institutionalization are generally higher. Their self-reported

well-being tends to be lower; and their burdens of adjusting to widowhood are greater than for those with strong social supports (Kasper, 1988).

The family—the basic unit of social relationships—is the first topic considered here. We examine the rapid growth of the multigenerational family and how relationships with spouses, adult children, parents, grandparents, siblings, and gay and lesbian partners change with age.

THE CHANGING CONCEPT OF THE AGING FAMILY

There has been a "structural lag" in our tendency to think of families primarily in terms of young children and to overlook the important functions and roles played by older people in contemporary **extended families** (Riley and Riley, 1994). Contrary to the myth of alienation, the family is the primary source of social support for older people. In fact, persons in all stages of life are more likely to have kin relationships involving older people and thus be part of an extended family than in the past (Uhlenberg, 1996). Nearly 94 percent of people over age 65, similar to Mrs. Howard in the introductory vignette, have living family members—adult children, grandchildren, partners, and siblings, although this proportion decreases with age. While 67 percent live in a family setting (i.e., spouse, children, siblings), older men (82 percent) are more likely to do so than are older women (57 percent) (Hobbs and Damon, 1996). Older African American women, especially widows, are more likely to live in extended family households than are older white women (Choi, 1991).

Older people are not only likely to live in a family setting but also to receive assistance from them. Families provide 70 to 80 percent of the in-home care to older people with chronic illness, even when formal services are used selectively (National Alliance for Caregiving and AARP, 1997). The family not only helps directly, but also provides information and advocates for services for their older members. As an illustration of the importance of family support, it is estimated that 10 percent of older people would require nursing home placement if family members were not providing care in home settings (Hobbs and Damon, 1996). The assistance of family members is thus often a major determinant of whether an older person lives in a nursing home or in the community. Persons without family ties, primarily widowed women and the oldest-old who have outlived other family members, are most likely to be institutionalized.

The Multigenerational Family

As noted in Chapter 1, declining mortality has altered the structure of kinship relationships involving older adults. Along with the increase in life expectancy, patterns of earlier remarriage and child-bearing in some generations have resulted in the growth of **multigenerational families,** spanning four, and sometimes five, generations (Power, 1995). Among adult children, over 70 percent of married couples are part of a four-generation family (Juster, Soldo, Kington, and Mitchell, 1996). Accordingly, the "young-old," who may be facing their own declines in finances, energy, and health, increasingly have parents and grandparents who require some assistance. In 1900, 50-year-olds had only a 4 percent chance of having two parents still alive; by the year 2000, this probability will have increased to 27 percent (Uhlenberg, 1996). The changing multigenerational dynamics are reflected in the fact that 10 percent of people over age 65 have a child who is also over 65, so that they may be both a child and a grandparent at the same time (U.S. Senate Special Committee on Aging, 1992). Given continuing technological and medical advances, these trends will undoubtedly continue.

Another change is that the demographic structure of many family lineages has shifted from a pyramid to a narrow or elongated beanpole, with more relationships that cross generational lines, more time spent in intergenerational roles, and fewer siblings and other age peers within a single generation (Bengtson, Rosenthal, and Burton, 1990). Accordingly, the lines of demarcation be-

Family gatherings help maintain intergenerational ties.

tween generations are sharper. Only rarely nowadays do we hear of aunts and uncles the same age or younger than their nieces and nephews, which was a common phenomenon at the turn of the century (Cantor, 1991). However, as a result of remarriage, there may be some blended families in which an aunt-in-law or uncle-in-law or step-relatives are younger.

The multigenerational family is, in turn, influenced by a number of social trends that affect interactions of family members across generations. Women's labor force participation has increased. Rates of divorce and remarriage and the consequent number of **blended families** have escalated, with more grandparents responsible for raising grandchildren. New and diverse family structures, such as communal living, cohabitation by unmarried couples, and gay and lesbian partnerships, affect the frequency of interactions and the potential for conflicting relationships. How these various family structures affect obligation, commitment, or resources to meet the needs of older dependents is still largely unknown. It is clear that family relationships inevitably involve both solidarity and conflict. Cohesion or consensus appears to be based on sharing between generations along a variety of dimensions, including the extent to which they share activities, the degree of positive sentiment, and the exchange of assistance. Less is known about tensions, disagreements, or conflicts across generations over the life course (Bengtson, Rosenthal, and Burton, 1996; Bengtson and Roberts, 1991).

The Role of Culture

Norms of intergenerational contact and **filial responsibility** affect the meaning which a culture attaches to family and care responsibilities (Choi, 1995). American culture places a high value on the family's privacy and independence. What occurs within it is generally viewed as its private affair, not to be interfered with by government or other outside sources. Similarly, family members' independence from each other is emphasized. Offspring are expected to move away from childhood dependency and toward the independence of adulthood. As a result of this emphasis, family members' emotional interdependence tends to be overlooked. These values affect not only commonly held views of adult child-parent relationships, but also the right of the state to intervene in high-risk family situations, for example, cases of suspected elder abuse and/or neglect. They also partially underlie the relative infrequency of **intergenerational living** in our society. This contrasts with other countries, such as Japan and Mexico, where three- and four-generation families, although a small percentage of the total population, are more likely to live together under one roof. Generally, the extended family is stronger within ethnic minority groups in the United States (Markides and Black, 1996). Rapid growth of the multigenerational family, the Western cultural emphasis on family privacy, and the increasing demographic, cultural, and economic diversity within our society have all created a wider range of family relationships in old age. Consistent with the life course perspective, this chapter recognizes the wide variation in family and household structure as men's and women's primary roles change over the life cycle (Moen and Forest, 1995).

OLDER COUPLES

The marital relationship plays a crucial support function in most older people's lives, especially men's. Of all family members, spouses are most likely to serve as confidants, provide support, facilitate social interaction, foster emotional well-being, and guard against loneliness (Dykstra, 1995). Nearly 60 percent of the population aged 65 to 74 is married and lives with a spouse in independent households (Hobbs and Damon, 1996). Significant differences exist, however, in living arrangements by gender and age. Because of women's longer life expectancy and fewer options for remarriage, 41 percent of women aged 65 and older are married and living with a spouse, as compared to 76 percent of men (see Figure 9.1). Accordingly, women represent 80 percent of the older individuals who live alone. Among non-institutionalized older men, only about 16 percent are living without a partner, compared to 40 percent of their female counterparts. The percentages living with a spouse decline with age and among African Americans and Hispanics, as illustrated in Figure 9.2 (AOA, 1997). Those living alone typically have higher levels of depression, loneliness, social isolation, and use of formal social services (Mui and Burnette, 1994). Accordingly, married people typically benefit from three major health promoters: general social support, health monitoring, and stress reduction (Goldscheider, 1994).

Couples are faced with learning to adapt to changing roles and expectations throughout marriage. Family life is characterized by a continual tension between maintaining individual autonomy and negotiating issues of equitable exchange and dependence. Such tensions may be heightened in old age. As partners change roles through retirement, post-parenthood, or illness, they face the strain of relinquishing previous roles and adapting to new ones. Couples today experience a post-childrearing period of perhaps 30 to 40 years, ranging from late maturity to frailty, and must renegotiate their marital expectations and roles in light of their changed family structure. Failure to negotiate role expectations, such as the division of household tasks, can result in disagreements and divergent paths. For example, retirement can be a difficult transition, especially when partners do not retire at the same time. On the other hand, increased time together in shared activities and with friends

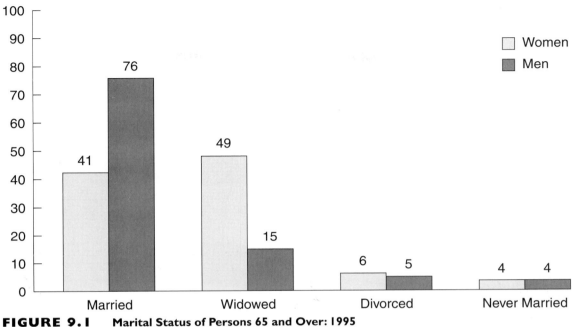

FIGURE 9.1   Marital Status of Persons 65 and Over: 1995

SOURCE: U.S. Bureau of the Census, unpublished data, 116th Edition, Statistical Abstract of the United States, 1996. Page 55, No. 59.

during retirement can have favorable effects (Whitbourne and Cassidy, 1995).

Strains may be heightened by the fact that long-lived relationships are a contemporary phenomenon. At the end of the nineteenth century, the average length of marriage at the time one's spouse died was about 28 years; now it is over 45 years. Never before in history have the lives of so many couples remained interwoven long enough to encounter the variety of life-changing events that later stages of marriage now bring. Yet most older couples are more likely than younger cohorts to view marriage as a lifetime commitment governed by obligation.

Marital Satisfaction

Despite the challenges inherent in long-lived relationships, most older partners appear satisfied, with men tending to be more satisfied with marriage and the degree to which their emo-

tional needs are fulfilled than are women (Bogard and Spilka, 1996; Adams and Blieszner, 1995). Marital satisfaction has been found to be high among those recently married, lower among those in the childrearing period—especially in middle age—and higher in the later stages (Robinson, 1990). More older spouses, especially men, report improvement in their marriages over time than do younger couples. They also report more positive interactions with less conflict and negative sentiment such as sarcasm, disagreement, and criticisms (Levenson, Cartensen, and Gottman, 1993).

Increases in marital satisfaction among the young-old may be partially due to children leaving home. Contrary to stereotypes, most women are not depressed when their children leave home, but rather view the **empty nest** as an opportunity for new activities, although both fathers and mothers may initially be unhappy and dissatisfied. As noted in Chapter 6, sex-role ex-

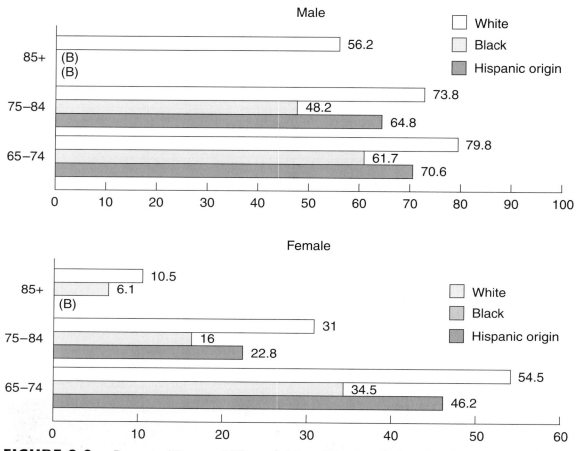

FIGURE 9.2   **Percent of Persons 65 Years and Over Who Are Married with Spouse Present by Age, Sex, Race, and Hispanic Origin: 1993 (Civilian noninstitutional population)**
NOTES: Base for minorities is less than 75,000. Hispanic origin may be of any race.

SOURCE: U.S. Bureau of the Census, Marital Status and Living Arrangements: March 1993, Current Population Reports, P20–478, U.S. Government Printing Office, Washington, DC, 1994, Table 1.

pectations and behaviors are often relaxed in old age. Men tend to become more affectionate and less career-oriented, and women more achievement-oriented. Both men and women share more sources of pleasure (Levenson et al., 1993). Successful negotiation of such role changes appears to be related to marital satisfaction. Happy marriages have been found to be characterized by more equality and joint decision-making through a gradual relaxation of boundaries between sex roles and a decreasing division of household labor according to traditional male/female sex roles (Bogard and Spilka, 1996). Nevertheless, some areas (e.g., dependent care and family finances) typically remain gender-differentiated (Miller and Cafasso, 1992). Freed from the demands of work and parental responsibilities and with more opportunities for companionship, partners may discover or develop common interests and interdependence. As a consequence, expressive aspects of the marriage—affection and companionship—may emerge more fully (House, Mero, and Webster, 1996).

Older partners' ability to negotiate these role transitions depends, in large part, on their prior adaptability and satisfaction in their relationship. Studies of marital longevity have found that couples celebrating golden anniversaries (who form approximately 3 percent of all marriages) are characterized by intimacy, autonomy, commitment, congruence of values, religious faith, communication, and an ability to accommodate one another (Robinson and Blanton, 1993). Overall, the perceived rewards from being married appear to strongly influence marital satisfaction (Reynolds, 1995). For happily married older couples, their relationship is central to a "good life." Married persons appear to be happier, healthier, experience higher levels of self-esteem, make fewer demands on the health care system, and live longer than widowed or divorced persons of the same age (Goldman, Korenman, and Weinstein, 1995). In fact, marital satisfaction may be more important than age, health, life expectancy, education, or retirement in predicting life satisfaction and quality of life. These positive effects appear to emanate from three major functions that marriage performs for older couples: intimacy, interdependence, and a sense of belonging. Not surprisingly, dissatisfied marriages tend to negatively affect health, especially for women (Levenson et al., 1993; Gilford, 1986; Atchley, 1985).

Although most older couples have been together since young adulthood, a small proportion remarry after widowhood or divorce later in life. Women have fewer options to remarry, since they generally outlive their male peers, and men tend to marry women younger than themselves. The likelihood that widowed men will remarry is seven times greater than for widowed women (Hobbs and Damon, 1996). Moreover, divorced people are more likely to remarry than are the widowed. Having sufficient economic resources is an important consideration in remarrying. The major reason for remarriage for both men and women, however, is a desire for companionship. A relationship with a partner appears to be of greater importance to men's well-being than to women's (Wright, 1994). Most older people who remarry choose someone they have previously known, with similar backgrounds and interests. Factors that appear to be related to successful late-life remarriages are long prior friendship, family and friends' approval, adequate pooled financial resources, and personal adaptability to life changes. Remarriage is an especially complex event since both partners have a long prior family history. Some older couples choose to live together but not to marry, generally for economic and inheritance reasons.

Spouses as Caregivers

With the increase in life expectancy, more older partners may end up caring for each other, frequently for long periods of time. In fact, over 12 percent of the people who care for older adults are themselves age 65 or older (National Alliance for Caregiving and AARP, 1997). Reflecting the fact that women outlive men by an average of seven years, more wives than husbands over age 65 provide care for disabled, often older husbands (Cantor, 1994). Nevertheless, husbands of wives with disabilities are more likely to provide care for their wives than are other family members. Older caregivers face not only the 24-hour responsibilities of care, but also may be coping with their own aging, physical illnesses, or financial and legal burdens. Stresses of isolation, loneliness, and role overload may be even greater for recently married older couples who cannot draw upon a lifetime of shared experiences. These are also high for spouses who are caring for partners with cognitive impairment and personality changes. The caregiver's health and quality of the marital relationship (e.g., high levels of spousal interaction and commitment) affect the continuation of the caregiving relationship (Wright, 1991). Most important, perhaps, is the extent to which caring for an ill or disabled spouse may be a normative experience—part of the marital contract and necessary for sustaining the quality of the marital relationship (Doty and Miller, 1993).

Divorce in Old Age

Even though most older marriages are reasonably happy, a small percentage are not, and an increasing proportion of older couples are choosing divorce rather than tolerate an unhappy marriage. Although only 5 to 6 percent of older persons are divorced, the numbers have increased four times as fast as the older population as a whole since 1990, and rates are even higher among ethnic minority older adults (AOA, 1997; Hobbs and Damon, 1996). Although late-life divorce is still relatively uncommon, 10 to 13 percent of persons aged 65 and over have experienced a divorce at some time, with the highest rates among African American older women (Choi, 1995). It appears that the frequency of divorce has changed for all ages, with more people of every age seeing divorce as an option.

The number of divorced older persons is predicted to increase in the future, from approximately 6 percent of older men and women currently to 9 percent of older men and 15 percent of older women in the year 2030 when baby boomers are over age 65 (Hobbs and Damon, 1996). There are more and more older adults who are either not married or are in their second or third marriage. This change may be partially explained by successive generations' acceptance of divorce as a solution to a bad marriage, and by an accompanying increase in remarriages. Across all groups, three out of four divorced persons remarry within 5 years. However, the risk of that marriage ending in divorce is ten times that of someone in his/her first marriage (Hammond and Muller, 1992). For older individuals, however, the likelihood of remarriage after widowhood or divorce is relatively small compared to other age groups (Brubaker, 1990). These trends clearly affect economic and social status. Being divorced in old age often means economic hardships for women, as well as diminished socioemotional support at a stage when other supports are also weakened

(Choi, 1996). Men in particular lose the "kin-keeping" function performed by their wives (Goldscheider, 1994). In general, divorced older persons are less satisfied with their lives than are married or widowed persons (Choi, 1995).

Lesbian and Gay Partners

As we have seen in Chapter 7, the concept of couples in old age needs to be broadened to include gay men and lesbians. Older gay men and lesbians share concerns similar to those of most older adults—loneliness, health, and income—but what is unique to them is that they have lived the majority of their lives through historical periods that have been actively hostile and oppressive toward homosexuality (Fullmer, 1995). Many older lesbians and gays have faced discrimination from family, friends, and professionals, so their later life development is not affected by sexual orientation per se, but rather by how they cope with the social stigma and low status attached to a gay identity (Adelman, 1990; Cruikshank, 1990).

Some older gay men and lesbians are concerned with "passing" or "being invisible" in a heterosexual society and only marginally accept some aspects of their homosexuality. For many gays and lesbians, they may be the only homosexual in their families of origin, which creates particular concerns because of the biased social context and unique social position in which they live. If they reveal their sexual orientation later in life, they must integrate their past lives into the coming-out process; they may need to give up part of their previously held identity, cope with their grief and that of family members, and be ostracized from children and family of origin at the stage when they most need support (Fullmer, 1995). Not all families are hostile, however, as illustrated by groups such as Parents and Friends of Lesbians and Gays, which support families in the process of accepting a family member's sexual orientation and aim to combat discrimination.

Nevertheless, the majority of older gays and lesbians, especially the young-old, emphasize positive aspects about being gay or lesbian and aging, experience self-acceptance and self-esteem, and

New family structures include gay and lesbian couples with children.

have satisfying long-term relationships (Fullmer, 1995; Quam and Whitford, 1992). Through the painful process of "coming out," they often become stronger and more competent in adjusting to changes associated with aging, thereby buffering losses, such as friends and family moving away or dying. Experiencing greater flexibility, freedom, and differentiation in gender-role definitions throughout their lives, gay men and lesbians tend to be more independent, non-traditional, and self-affirming, and to adapt more readily to the role changes associated with aging. Such role flexibility may ease an individual's adjustment when a partner dies or leaves (Quam and Whitford, 1992).

By having confronted real or imagined loss of family support earlier in life, gays and lesbians are less likely to assume that families will provide for them in old age and more likely to plan for their own future security. Accordingly, they tend to build a "surrogate family" through a strong network of friends, which either replaces or reinforces family supports. Some older gay men and lesbians share innovative housing arrangements and are a part of an empowering community that may include social and advocacy organizations, such as Senior Action in a Gay Environment (SAGE) based in New York City, the Lavender Panthers, and the National Association of Lesbian and Gay Gerontologists. Those who have the support of other gay men and lesbians as friends and confidants, in social organizations, and in housing alternatives tend to be characterized by high self-esteem and life satisfaction, less fear of aging,

and greater effectiveness in managing the societal aspects of aging, such as rejection (Quam and Whitford, 1992; Friend, 1991).

Despite the fact that most gay men and lesbians have acquired skills and attitudes that facilitate their adjustment to aging, they nevertheless face more structural and legal barriers than heterosexual couples do. The partners of those who are hospitalized or in a nursing home may be denied access to intensive care units and to medical records; staff may be insensitive to and ignore partners, even limiting their visits and discouraging expression of affection. Private space for conjugal visits for gay or lesbian couples in nursing homes is limited, and some institutions may admit only one member of a homosexual couple. Moreover, families may contest a gay or lesbian partner's right to an inheritance. Service barriers and research areas specific to older homosexual partners need to be better addressed.

SIBLING RELATIONSHIPS

Sibling relationships represent the one family bond with the potential to last a lifetime. Under contemporary mortality conditions, most persons will not experience the death of any particular sibling until they are past 70 years of age (Uhlenberg, 1996). Most older people, even those over age 80, have at least one sibling, and about 33 percent see a sibling monthly, although yearly visits are most typical. As with other kin-keeping responsibilities, sisters are more likely than brothers to maintain frequent contact with same-sex siblings, generally by phone or face-to-face interaction rather than by letter writing (Cicirelli, 1995, 1991).

The sibling relationship in old age is characterized by a shared history, egalitarianism, and increasing closeness, particularly among sisters (Scott, 1990; Brubaker, 1990). Studies based on the criterion of feelings of closeness and affection suggest that siblings often renew past ties as they age, forgive past conflict and rivalry, and become closer, frequently through shared reminiscence (Bengtson et al., 1996; Cicirelli, 1995; Adams and Blieszner, 1995). Siblings are particularly important sources of psychological support in the lives of never-married older persons and those without children, although their ability to provide support declines with age. Assistance generally increases after a spouse's death, at which time siblings, concerned about each other's welfare, may share households. In such instances, the widowed person's psychological well-being tends to be enhanced (Cicirelli, 1995). Siblings often come together around issues of caring for aging parents and report positive experiences in this regard (Bengtson et al., 1996).

Although siblings are less frequently caregivers to each other than are spouses and adult children, they do supplement the efforts of other family caregivers during times of crisis or special need. The very existence of siblings as a possible source of help may be important, even if such assistance is rarely used (Cicirelli, 1995; Connider, 1994). Siblings can also perform a socialization function in later life, acting as positive role models or as motivators to try new activities, thereby enhancing adaptations to late-life changes.

Current demographic trends will affect these relationships in future decades. As more couples remain childless or have only one or two children, their siblings will become even more important supports as they age. Greater longevity and better health among the current middle-aged cohort imply greater availability of living siblings in the future, with sibling relationships expected to strengthen. However, reduced fertility rates in the current period will mean that later cohorts will have fewer siblings on whom to rely and will need to be flexible in efforts to more equitably share caregiving tasks (Scott, 1990).

The steadily increasing rate of divorce and remarriage will undoubtedly affect sibling relationships. With the increase in blended families through remarriage, there will be more half-siblings and step-siblings. For divorced older people who do not remarry, sibling interaction may become more important than when they were married (Goldscheider, 1994). The degree of commitment to these new and varied relationships is unknown at this time.

NEVER-MARRIED OLDER PEOPLE

Approximately 4 percent of the older population has never married (Hobbs and Damon, 1996). Contrary to a commonly held image of lonely social isolates, the majority of never-married older persons have typically developed **reciprocal support** relationships with other kin, especially siblings, and with friends and neighbors (Baresi and Hunt, 1990). They may actually be more socially active and resourceful, with more diversity in their social networks, especially with younger persons, than their married counterparts (Stull and Scarisbrick-Hauser, 1989). Compared to widowed peers, they tend to be more satisfied with their lives, to be self-reliant, and to be oriented to the present. Accustomed to their independence, they are not necessarily lonely (Dykstra, 1995). Whites, Asians, and Hispanics who are young-old have higher rates of never-married than the middle and old-old among these ethnic minority groups; this pattern is reversed for African Americans and American Indians. Among Asian and American Indian populations, there are considerably more never-married males than females (Baresi and Hunt, 1990).

Increasing numbers of organizations specifically for single people have formed, although many of these are for younger singles. Alternative living arrangements, such as multigenerational share-a-home programs, may also appeal to some single older adults who choose not to live alone.

CHILDLESS OLDER ADULTS

Although the majority of older people have living children, approximately 20 percent are childless, and thus lack the natural support system of children and grandchildren (Hobbs and Damon, 1996). The adage that "children will take care of you in your old age" contains some degree of truth. Childless older people have been found to have fewer social contacts than their counterparts with living children, yet they are not necessarily unhappy and dissatisfied (Beckman, 1985; Houser, 1984). When faced with health problems, childless elders turn first to their spouses for support, then to siblings, then nieces and nephews. Childless older individuals also have a higher probability of illness and living alone. Given these factors, it is not surprising that unmarried childless elders utilize social services and nursing homes more than do married childless persons (Choi-Namkea, 1994).

On the other hand, some childless unmarried older people, particularly women, develop kin-like or "sisterly" non-kin relations and may be quite satisfied with their lives. Yet they do not want these relationships to be a source of care, fearing the change of voluntary mutuality into dependency (Rubenstein et al., 1991). The number of childless and unmarried older individuals is likely to grow, which may affect the proportion of older people who will need the assistance of service providers in the future.

OTHER KIN

Interaction with secondary kin—cousins, aunts, uncles, nieces, and nephews—appears to depend on geographic proximity, availability of closer relatives, and preference. Extended kin can replace or substitute for missing or lost relatives, especially during family rituals and holidays. For example, compared to their white counterparts, African American childless elders often turn to nieces and nephews when siblings are not available. Personal or historical connections that allow for remembering pleasurable events may be more important than closeness of kinship in determining interactions.

INTERGENERATIONAL RELATIONSHIPS: ADULT CHILDREN

After spouses, adult children are the most important source of informal support and social contact in old age. Over 80 percent of persons age 65 and over have surviving children, although the number of children in a family has decreased—a trend expected to continue. The majority of older adults live near at least one adult child, sharing a social life but not their homes (Juster et al., 1996). Most older people state that they prefer not to live with their children, generally for reasons of privacy and a sense of autonomy. Although less than 20 percent of older persons live in their children's households, this percentage increases with advancing age and for widowed, separated, and divorced older adults. Approximately 33 percent of all men, and 50 percent of all women, age 65 and over who are widowed, separated, or divorced share a home with their children or other family members. When older parents do live with their children, they usually live with a daughter (National Alliance for Caregiving and AARP, 1997). However, less than 14 percent of those aged 65 to 75 and 4 percent of those aged 85 and older live in multigenerational households composed of parents, children, and grandchildren (Hobbs and Damon, 1996). These percentages do increase, however, among some ethnic minority families, especially African Americans (Taylor and Chatters, 1991).

Although most older parents and adult children do not live together, they nevertheless see each other frequently. Studies over the past two decades have consistently found that approximately 50 percent of older people have daily contact with children, nearly 80 percent see an adult child at least once a week, and more than 75 percent talk on the phone at least weekly (AOA, 1997; Bengtson et al., 1996; Hobbs and Damon, 1996; Hansson and Carpenter, 1994). Older children, especially daughters, are more likely to maintain contact with their parents. However, these factors are less important than proximity and socioeconomic status, with more frequent contact among higher-income families (Greenwald and Bengtson, 1997). Less is known about the quality than about the frequency of interactions between older parents and their adult children across a geographic distance.

Geographic separation of family members is generally due to mobility of the adult children, not of the older relatives. Future cohorts of older persons may have an increasing proportion of distant children because of the growing trend toward greater residential separation between adult children and older parents. However, proximity does not appear to affect the quality of parent-child relationships. Instead, socioemotional distance seems more important than geographic distance. Most adult children feel "close" to their older parents despite geographic separation, creating what has been termed **intimacy at a distance** (Lee and Ellithorpe, 1982). Such emotional bonds tend to be strongest among female family members (Gallup, 1989).

In sum, studies have repeatedly found that most people over age 65 are integral members of family networks. They see their adult children frequently and interact regularly by telephone or letter with relatives who live at a geographic distance. Although most parents and children report positive feelings for each other, feelings of obligation and sense of duty often underlie intergenerational relationships (Finley, Roberts, and Banahan, 1988).

Patterns of Intergenerational Assistance

Generally, families establish a pattern of reciprocal support between older and younger members that continues throughout an individual's lifetime. Consistent with social exchange theory discussed in Chapter 8, those with more valued resources (e.g., money or good health) assist those with less. Not only concrete assistance is exchanged, but also emotional and **social support** (Rossi and Rossi, 1990). At various points, older parents provide substantial support, especially financial assistance, to their children and grandchildren, oftentimes at a geographic distance. Regardless of socioeconomic status, most **intergenerational transfers** of resources, especially of knowledge and financial support, go from parent to child (Juster et al., 1996; Bengtson et al., 1996).

In some instances, parents continue to provide care to adult children beyond normative ex-

pectations of "launching" one's adult children to be more independent. For example, parental care remains a central role late in life for parents of adult children who are developmentally disabled or chronically mentally ill. Yet many parental caregivers of adults with disabilities are facing their own age-related limits in functional ability, energy, and financial resources, which can affect their ability to provide care. The history of and the cumulative nature of care demands can make their situation particularly stressful (Kelly and Kropf, 1995; Smith, Tobin, and Fullmer, 1995). A major worry is how their child will be cared for after their own death or if they develop a debilitating illness. Despite their worry, most such caregiving parents do not make concrete long-term plans about where their children will eventually live (Freedman, Krauss, and Seltzer, 1997). As the population of adults with chronic illness or developmental disabilities grows, both the aging and developmentally disabled service networks need to develop new supports, such as respite care, more residential alternatives, and assistance with permanency planning (e.g., developing plans for permanent housing in the community) (Kelly and Kropf, 1995; Smith and Tobin, 1993).

Families as Caregivers

As parents age, exchange patterns shift. Adult children provide more assistance to their parents, particularly those who have chronic health problems and are widowed or divorced. Norms of filial responsibility—that adult children should help their parents—become operationalized in daily caregiving behavior (Walker and Pratt, 1991). As noted earlier, families provide 70 to 80 percent of the in-home care for older relatives with chronic impairments (National Alliance for Caregiving and AARP, 1997). Likewise, nearly 75 percent of people over age 65 with chronic disability rely exclusively on family and friends for help with everyday activities. Adult children are the primary caregivers for older widowed women and older unmarried men, and they are the secondary caregivers in situations where the spouse of an older person is still alive. Caregiving responsibilities are most likely to be experienced by those aged 45 to 54, with 17 percent of them caring for a disabled elder (Cantor, 1994, 1991). Parent care has thus become a predictable and nearly universal experience across the life course, yet most people are not adequately prepared for it.

The primary forms of assistance to older parents are emotional support, instrumental activities inside and outside the home (e.g., transportation, meal preparation, shopping, and housework), personal care (e.g., bathing, feeding, and dressing), and mediating with agencies to obtain services. In some cases, older parents also receive financial aid from their children. The type of familial assistance given is largely determined by the older member's functional level, intensity of care needed, co-residence, and the caregiver's gender, with personal care most often performed by wives, daughters, or daughters-in-law (National Alliance for Caregiving and AARP, 1997; Tennstedt, Crawford, and McKinley, 1993).

Given this pattern of care, it is perplexing that the myth persists that families do not care for their older members as well as they did in the "good old days." As we saw in Chapter 2, older relatives at the turn of the century were rare and valued because of their economic contributions to the family. Today, however, adult children provide more complex care to parents over much longer periods of time than they did when life expectancy was 47 years and elders comprised only 4 percent of the population. This is the first time in history that American couples have had more parents than children. In fact, today the average American woman can expect to spend 18 years caring for an older family member, compared to 17 years for her children. In 1900, the average woman spent an average of 8 years on elder care (Stone, Cafferata, and Sangl, 1987). These changes are due not only to increased longevity, but also to the fact that the current cohort of frail elders who raised children during the Great Depression had a low birth rate, which resulted in a smaller number of adult children as potential caregivers.

Another trend affecting intergenerational relationships is the longer economic dependence of young adults combined with parents who are living longer. As a result, many contemporary middle-aged individuals, described as the **sandwich generation** (illustrated in the box below), are faced with a dilemma that is relatively new historically—the competing responsibilities of

---

WOMEN IN THE MIDDLE

A woman in her mid-fifties with teenage children and a full-time job, Annette had cared for both her parents. Her mother, crippled with rheumatoid arthritis, lived with Annette's family for 5 years before she died. Within a year, Annette's father suffered a stroke and lived with the family for 3 years before his death. Annette's teenagers had resented the amount of time she gave to her parents, and her husband became impatient with how little time they had alone together. They had not had a vacation in 5 years. Since family and friends were not interested in helping her with the care of her parents, Annette and her husband rarely even had a night out alone together. As an employed caregiver, Annette frequently missed work and was distracted on the job whenever she had to consult doctors or take her parents for therapy during normal business hours. She felt alone, isolated, and overwhelmed by the stress. She was physically and mentally exhausted from trying to meet too many demands, not knowing that some support services were available in her community, and feeling that she had to be capable of handling these responsibilities on her own. When her mother-in-law became too frail to live alone, Annette knew her family and job would suffer once again if she tried to balance household duties, a full-time job, and the care of both older and younger relatives.

caring for parents and children, including young adult children. The "empty nest" is frequently filled by frail elders and by grown children who cannot afford to leave home, or who return home because of divorce, economic need, or substance-abuse problems (Cantor, 1994). This delayed departure—or return—of adult children has been referred to as the **cluttered nest** (Bengtson et al., 1996). In fact, the percentage of unmarried adults age 18 to 24 living at home has increased from 43 percent in 1960 to 55 percent in recent years (Saluter, 1994).

Another social trend that affects the adult child-parent relationship is the growth of "blended" or "reconstituted families" as a consequence of divorce and remarriage. An increasing number of older parents are experiencing the divorce of one or more of their adult children. It is estimated that over 50 percent of all marriages that occurred during the 1970s will end in divorce, and it is this cohort of individuals who are likely to be faced with caregiving responsibilities. Of the high proportion who will remarry, 44 percent are estimated to divorce again, creating the phenomenon of "serial monogamy" —persons having a series of divorces and remarriages throughout their lives (Hobbs and Damon, 1996). Adult children may thus be caring not only for their biological parents and for current parents-in-law, but, if previously divorced, may be emotionally tied to their former spouse's parents, especially through their children of the earlier marriage. Such ties may lead to caregiving responsibilities for former parents-in-law as well. Difficult definitions of family membership and loyalties may complicate the distribution of time, attention, and financial resources across generations.

Women as Caregivers

Women in the middle often face multiple cross-generational demands. Care responsibilities are usually differentiated by gender, such that women comprise over 70 percent of the family caregivers to chronically ill elders; over 50 percent of all women provide such care at some point in the life course (Pavalko and Artis, 1997). Although wives and husbands constitute the majority of the sole or primary caregivers, a hierarchy of preference exists within the female kin network, based on the centrality of the caregiver's relationship to the older person and on geographic proximity. Wives are favored over all others. If the older person who needs care is unmarried, widowed, or has an ill spouse, then an adult daughter or daughter-in-law is commonly the primary caregiver. Daughters are more likely than sons to be the primary caregivers who provide hands-on care. If a spouse or child is unavailable, then a sister is primarily responsible, and if none of these are available, a female member of the extended family— such as a niece or a granddaughter—assumes responsibility (Coward and Dwyer, 1990). Siblings, for example, tend to reduce their caregiving efforts in proportion to the number of sisters available (Wolf, Freedman, and Soldo, 1997). Even when siblings attempt to divide filial responsibilities, sisters have been found to be viewed by themselves and their brothers as being in charge. In some instances, brothers' and sons' services are seen as less important, ignored, or not acknowledged as genuine contributions (Matthews, 1995). Accordingly, daughters and daughters-in-law are more likely to assume care responsibilities than sons and sons-in-law. At the same time, they are more likely to experience the costs of caregiving without compensatory resources, in part because of lack of reciprocity in exchanges (Ingersoll-Dayton, Starrels, and Dowler, 1996). Even when older persons move in with the eldest son, as in East Indian, Korean, and Japanese cultures, the daughter-in-law is generally still the primary caregiver (Qureshi and Walker, 1989). The predominance of women as caregivers of older relatives seems to be a universal phenomenon in both industrialized and traditional cultures, as noted in Chapter 2.

The prominence of women in the caregiving role should not obscure the efforts of men who are primary caregivers, or what Brody (1985) calls the "unsung heroes." As noted earlier, hus-

FOR BETTER OR FOR WORSE/ *Lynn Johnston*

SOURCE: © 1991 Lynn Johnston Prod. Reprinted by permission of United Press Syndicate.

bands frequently provide care for wives with disabilities (Bengtson et al., 1996). But consistently, male adult children are less likely than women to provide the time-consuming and emotionally demanding primary personal care; rather, they tend to assist indirectly and intermittently, such as with financial management, home repair, and maintenance. Men generally become involved in personal care and instrumental tasks of cooking and cleaning only when no female relative is available. Similarly, sons are less likely than daughters to share their households with a dependent parent. Even when sons are involved in tasks similar to those performed by daughters, they experience less stress from caregiving. This results in part because men tend to maintain more emotional distance from the care receiver, focusing primarily on economic and concrete assistance. In general, they are less concerned with how caregiving affects the quality of the parental relationship. In addition, men are more likely to be part of a larger network of services and to perceive more supports. In contrast, women, who report higher levels of burden, frequently feel responsible for their older relative's psychological well-being, and perceive greater interference between caregiving and their personal and social lives. They also tend to be less likely to view resources as available to assist them with their care responsibilities (Ingersoll-Dayton et al., 1996; Kramer and Kipnis, 1995; Mui, 1995).

Women caregivers are more likely than their male counterparts to give up employment, modify their work schedules, or forgo promotions or career development opportunities to accommodate caregiving responsibilities. More women are employed than in the past: 75 percent between the ages of 45 and 54, and 49 percent between the ages of 55 and 64; for many, caregiving falls during the peak employment years of 35 to 64. Forty-three percent of the daughters and wives and 69 percent of the sons and husbands of the older population with disabilities are employed full-time (Pavalko and Artis, 1997; U.S. Bureau of the Census, 1996). However, being employed and having a college education do not preclude women from taking on care responsibilities (Robison, Moen, and Dempster-McClain, 1995). In fact, women employed full-time are four times more likely than working men to be the primary caregivers (Stone and Kemper, 1989). Moreover, employed daughters provide nearly equal amounts and types of care as non-employed daughters do, either directly or through purchased services (Kramer and Kipnis, 1995). Not surprisingly, work disruptions and economic strains are significant predictors of stress for female caregivers (Orodenker, 1990). Caregivers who frequently adjust their work schedules to accommodate parent care demands have been found to be less likely to sustain their caregiving commitment (Lechner, 1991).

In addition, 90 percent of today's middle-aged married women have children of their own to attend to—typically teenagers or young adults, compared to 66 percent of those born before the turn of the century (Cantor, 1991). These "women in the middle" (Brody, 1985), the traditional caregivers to older relatives, may thus be juggling extensive family responsibilities along with employment and their own age-related transitions. Given the increasing mobility of our society, they also may be providing care at a geographic distance. However, conflicts between caregiving and employment are more frequent than between care of young children and care of aging parents, in part because of the increases in life expectancy and the consequent likelihood that middle-aged, young-old grandmothers are caring for old-old parents (Stone and Kemper, 1989). Recent studies counter the concept of "women in the middle"; only about 33 percent of women in their early forties and 25 percent of women in their late forties were found to combine care of dependent children, elder care, and employment although, as noted above, teens or young adults may still be in the home (Bengtson et al., 1996). Regardless of their particular configuration of responsibilities, women generally do not reduce the amount of assistance given. Instead they manage their multiple responsibilities by maintaining rigid schedules, negotiating care tasks around their employment or children, and giving up their own free time or reducing hours worked, thereby affecting current income and future retirement benefits. Despite the amount of care provided, many female caregivers still feel guilty for not doing more (Pavalko and Artis, 1997).

Consistent with the life course perspective, many women experience caregiving as a "career" over the life course—caring first for children, then a partner, and then parents or parents-in-law. Women born in more recent cohorts are more likely than those born earlier to be caregivers and experience two or more different caregiving episodes, due to increases in life expectancy and chronic illness. The fact that women in young adulthood and middle age may assume caregiving

in the midst of numerous other roles, resources, and responsibilities can have long-term implications for their health and economic security in later life (Robison et al., 1995); these consequences are discussed more fully in Chapter 14.

Ethnic Minority Families as Caregivers

The extent to which race and culture rather than socioeconomic status influence intergenerational relationships is unclear. In contrast to Caucasian families, multigenerational households are more prevalent among African American, Latino, and Asian American families (Tennstedt, Crawford, and McKinley, 1993). The greater prevalence of co-residence in communities of color may underlie the higher levels of assistance to frail elders and the generally positive parent-adult child relationships reported by Hispanic American, African American, and Asian American families. Even when controlling for need, ethnic minorities have been found to be more likely to live in extended families, which provide both social support and instrumental assistance with finances and activities of daily living, especially for unmarried children and unmarried parents (Silverstein and Waite, 1993; Speare and Avery, 1993).

Others have argued that the role of the extended family is over-exaggerated or disintegrating in populations of color and that the strength of ties in ethnic minority families is more heterogeneous than has been noted in the historical literature on minority family life (Bengtson et al., 1996; Silverstein and Waite, 1993). It is generally acknowledged that some differences attributed to race may be due to socioeconomic status, education, cultural, historical, or other factors, and that it is important to examine differences within and between subgroups (Connell and Gibson, 1997). A growing body of research now suggests that race differences in the process of caregiving are minimal, although African Americans have been found to exhibit lower levels of stress. This may be due to the cultural meanings attached to caregiving and cultural differences in support resources (Bengtson et al., 1996; Miller et al., 1995; Miller, McFall, and Campbell, 1994; Mui, 1992). As described in Chapter 2, urbanization and modernization have weakened intergenerational ties among many ethnic minority families. In traditional Asian American families, the value system emphasizes the importance of the family unit rather than individual gain and independence. However, such values of family obligation are increasingly difficult to implement in a competitive, mobile society, particularly when adult children move into a higher social class than their parents. Many Latinos, for example, have developed strong intergenerational ties mandated by both their cultural heritage and economic realities. But urbanization and modernization have weakened patterns of intergenerational cohesion and support that characterized Latino families in the past. Although Latinos rely heavily on **informal** sources of **support,** they are increasingly dependent on non-kin caregivers (friends, neighbors and paid personal care workers) (Aranda and Knight, 1997). In some instances, the existence of extended family living arrangements and fictive kin may carry financial and emotional costs and divert policymakers' attention away from the need for **formal support** services. The effects of changing societal conditions and of socioeconomic class on ethnic minority families—and the wide variability within as well as among ethnic minority families—are explored further in Chapter 13.

THE STRESSES OF CAREGIVING

Demographic and social changes—more older adults with chronic disabilities, more employed women, and more complex family structures—underlie many of the stresses of caregiving. Caregiving demands or stresses can be conceptualized under the domain of environmental press. Consistent with the person-environment model, these demands have the potential to become stressful when there is an incongruence between the strength of the demand and the caregiver's competence (health, functional capabilities) to deal with the tasks of caregiving (Lawton and Nahemow, 1973).

Despite all the physical, financial, and emotional demands described above, most family members are willing to assume primary caregiving responsibility. For some, caregiving can be a rich and rewarding experience, characterized by greater closeness with family members (Cicirelli, 1990). In fact, the spillover effects of caregiving on other roles vary widely, with some caregivers expressing greater marital satisfaction, feelings of efficacy and self-worth, sense of the meaning of life, pride in their ability to meet challenges, and closeness in relationships than non-caregivers (Kramer, 1997a; Bengtson et al., 1996; Stephens and Franks, 1995). Multiple roles do not necessarily lead to overload and stress, because they may be associated with more extensive social support, greater access to resources (e.g., finances), and a heightened sense of personal competence (Bengtson et al., 1996; Spitze, Logan, Joseph, and Lee, 1994; Lopata, 1993). Caregivers tend to experience more gains than costs of care when they define the caregiving role as enriching, possess effective problem-solving coping strategies, have social support and assistance, and are in better physical health (Kramer, 1997a). Not surprisingly, satisfaction in the caregiving role is greater when there is some degree of reciprocity, often when the older person lives with the caregiver and is still able to provide some assistance with household tasks (Pruchno, Burant, and Peters, 1997). However, even when caring for relatives with dementia, where reciprocity is limited, caregivers may experience satisfaction based on norms of solidarity, deeply established attachments, and rich memories (Pearlin, Anashensel, Mullan, and Whitlatch, 1996).

For many, however, their health, employment, personal freedom, privacy, and social relationships are negatively affected by providing care. The literature on **caregiving** differentiates between *caring for* and *caring about*: the tangible tasks associated with personal assistance versus feelings of love, worry, and concern (Bengtson et al., 1996). *Objective* and *subjective*

caregiver burdens are also differentiated. Objective burden refers to the reality demands that confront the caregiver, such as symptomatic behaviors of the illness, disruptions in family relationships, income, and social life, and problems with service systems. Subjective stress refers to feelings aroused in caregivers as they fulfill their functions, such as worry, sadness, resentment, anger, or guilt (Braithwaite, 1992). This distinction recognizes that burden is a subjective phenomenon; what is difficult for one caregiver need not be difficult for another (Poulshock and Diemling, 1984). As an example of how caregiving is differentially evaluated, some ethnic minority caregivers have been found to endorse more strongly beliefs about filial support; turn to prayer, faith, and religion more readily; and consequently experience less stress, burden, and depression than Caucasian caregivers. The extent to which caregiving is experienced as stressful and burdensome and therefore negative is thus mediated by the extent of social support, coping mechanisms used, and cultural values and beliefs (Aranda and Knight, 1997; Connell and Gibson, 1997; Miller, Campbell, Farron, Kaufman, and Davis, 1995).

The physical demands of providing daily personal assistance, such as frequently changing the bedding of an incontinent elder, are experienced most frequently by caregivers who live with the care recipient and by caregivers of older relatives with dementia (Schulz, O'Brien, Bookwala, and Fleissner, 1995). Physical stress can manifest itself in health problems, including headaches, depression, anxiety, stomach disturbances, and weight changes (Vitaliano, Schulz, Kiecolt-Glaser, and Grant, 1997). As described in Chapter 6, caregivers of patients with dementia experience even greater levels of stress and have been found to use prescription drugs and medical services more than non-caregivers (Schulz et al., 1995). Not surprisingly, the physical and mental health consequences of caregiving tend to increase with the intensity of the level of care provided (National Alliance for Caregiving and AARP, 1997).

Financial burdens include not only the direct costs of medical care, adaptive equipment, or hired help, but also indirect opportunity costs of lost income or missed promotions. With 64 percent of caregivers either full- or part-time workers, it is not surprising that caregiving employees report greater job-family conflicts than non-caregiving employees (Scharlach and Boyd, 1989). In a recent national survey, more than 50 percent of caregiving employees had made changes at work to accommodate caregiving (National Alliance for Caregiving and AARP, 1997). As noted above, employed women tend not to limit the amount of care. Instead, they are more likely than their male counterparts to quit or modify their jobs, in part because women earn less than men and therefore their jobs are viewed by other family members as less important (Stone and Short, 1990; Anastas, Gibeau, and Larson, 1990). In the long term, this hurts the caregiving woman in her later years. As will be discussed in Chapter 14, those who interrupt employment to be caregivers generally receive lower retirement income than those who have a continuous work history (Kingston and O'Grady-LeShane, 1993).

The emotional burdens of feeling alone, isolated, worrying about the care recipient, and without time for oneself appear to be the greatest costs of caregiving. These feelings are experienced more frequently by women than men. Relationships with other family members and with friends are frequently disrupted. Most caregivers report that no one in their network of family or friends regularly assists them with hands-on care. Even when family and friends help, the timing and frequency of their well-intended actions may fail to be supportive (Pearlin et al., 1996). Rates of depression may increase, especially among long-term caregivers and those assisting relatives with dementia who evidence disruptive behaviors such as wandering and verbal outbursts (Vitaliano et al., 1997). The psychological effects of the older patient's decline and associated anticipatory bereavement are often more stressful than the tasks of providing care. Such psychological stress can itself result in health problems and may not necessarily be alleviated by services such as respite care (Pillemer and Suitor, 1996; Mittelman et al., 1995; Schulz et al., 1995). Although wide variability exists among caregivers, it appears that it is not necessarily the duration of caregiving, but rather the increasing amounts of care that wear down and isolate the caregiver and decrease caregiving satisfaction (Walker, Aacock, Bowman, and Li, 1996).

Although men are more likely than women to utilize formal caregiving services, most families do not use them, or do so selectively and for limited time periods (National Alliance for Caregiving and AARP, 1997). In fact, only about 5 to 10 percent of older adults depend solely on paid helpers, and those with only paid assistance tend to be institutionalized earlier (Juster et al., 1996). Home care is the most frequently used service, especially by caregivers who are providing higher levels of care, as for example for a relative with dementia (Miller et al., 1996; Short and Leon, 1995). In some instances, caregivers are unaware of services, do not think they need them, or are "too proud" to use them. In others, they may find that services, such as respite, may actually deplete their energy through the processes required to access them, or they may feel they are imposing on paid helpers (Worcester and Hedrick, 1997; National Alliance for Caregiving and AARP, 1997). Cultural differences in service utilization exist. African Americans, for example, are more likely to turn to informal supports and prayer and to use cognitive strategies to reframe the situation in positive terms than are whites. Whites are more likely to seek help from professionals and use problem-solving methods (Leutz et al., 1992; Wood and Parham, 1990). Despite these differences, only about 4 percent of African Americans and whites use only formal services for assistance (Miller et al., 1996).

Most informal care networks include secondary helpers, but such helpers are more likely to help with intermittent and predictable tasks than with the day-to-day personal care. The secondary helpers' limited role is illustrated by the fact that over 30 percent of primary caregivers report that no one is available to replace them if they become unable to continue this role (Penrod, Kane, Kane, and Finch, 1995). Lack of support resources can heighten caregivers' feelings of isolation, and, in turn, of stress. In fact, feelings of burden have been found to be related primarily to the availability of external helping resources and social support, not to the severity of the illness. Accordingly, positive informal networks and services such as personal care and assistance with household tasks can enhance the caregiver's well-being (Bass, Noelker, and Rechlin, 1996; Thompson et al., 1993). Formal support services thus are important to strengthening family care and preventing emotional, financial, and physical problems.

ELDER ABUSE

In some cases, caregiving stress may become severe enough to lead to family conflict, breakdown, neglect, abuse or financial exploitation of the older person. **Elder abuse** can be psychological (e.g., verbal aggression), financial, or involve physical violence. Financial exploitation is probably the most common form of abuse (Bengtson et al., 1996). It is estimated that 3 to 4 percent of older people—typically frail elders with limited incomes—are abused by someone with whom they share housing, often remaining invisible within the home (Kosberg and Garcia, 1995). Older adults with Alzheimer's disease or related dementia, who may display aggressive, unpredictable behavior and who are typically less able to report abuse or to access services, are most vulnerable. Warning signs of abuse include depression, fear, and anxiety in the older patient; illnesses that do not appear to be responding to treatment; and frequent trips to the emergency room. Husbands and middle-aged sons are most often the abusers (Hwalek, Neale, Goodrich, and Quinn, 1996). Spousal abuse may reflect lifelong patterns, with older women, often isolated, "falling between the cracks"—too old to go to shelters designed for younger women and invisible

---

WHAT IS ELDER ABUSE?

Physical or sexual abuse: Malnutrition or injuries such as bruises, welts, sprains, dislocations, abrasions, lacerations. Forced sexual contact.

Psychological abuse: Verbal assault, threat, fear, or isolation.

Material or financial exploitation: Theft or misuse of the person or the person's money or property for another person's profit or advantage.

Medical abuse: Withholding or improper administration of needed medications, or withholding of aids such as dentures, glasses, or hearing aids.

Passive or active neglect: Conduct by the abuser resulting in the deprivation of care necessary to maintain physical and mental health.

Violation of rights: Forcing an older person from home or into an institutional setting without their consent.

---

to community service providers (Bengtson et al., 1996). In some instances, elder abuse may be an inevitable outcome of stressful situations combined with inadequate caregiving skills. Substance abuse, most commonly addiction to alcohol, plays a role in many cases (Hwalek et al., 1996). Another factor associated with elder mistreatment is aggressive behavior by the older person toward the caregiver or other family members (Buckwalter, Campbell, Gerdner, and Garand, 1996). Legally competent but mentally or physically impaired elders may fall into the category of **elder** self-abuse or **neglect.** In many instances, failure to care for oneself and resisting services may be a lifestyle choice, often begun when younger (Simon et al., 1997). Instances of elder abuse illustrate that it is unrealistic to expect all families to assume care functions, especially when the caregivers themselves are vulnerable—over age 75, in fair or poor health, and low income (Wilson, 1990).

A growing number of states have passed laws requiring professionals to report familial abuse of older relatives, although only about 16 percent of elder abuse cases are reported (Hansson and Carpenter, 1994). A number of factors may explain this low rate, including the societal value placed on family privacy and health care providers' reluctance to report abuse. Adult Protective Services (APS) is the state or county service system that becomes involved in instances of abuse or neglect, including self-neglect. Since mandatory reporting laws require that APS

workers must accept all reports of abuse or neglect, their caseloads are often filled with the most troubled older adults with whom other agencies are unwilling or unable to work. An additional barrier faced by APS workers is that few community-based alternatives exist for older people who are removed from abusive situations. Although APS workers frequently deal with older people who are no longer competent to make decisions, they need to assess the individual's level of competence and therefore the older person's right to refuse professional assistance. This is especially critical in instances where families too readily seek guardianship or full decision-making authority over personal, financial, and estate affairs. Guardianships are often routinely approved by the courts, even though incompetence may not be demonstrated. Such family actions are motivated by interest in preserving the estate, and role conflict in guardians often occurs (Hansson and Carpenter, 1994).

INSTITUTIONALIZATION: A PAINFUL DECISION FOR FAMILY MEMBERS

The strain on caregivers, especially high levels of subjective burden, may cause them to seek relief through institutionalization of their older relatives (McFall and Miller, 1992). As noted above, most families first attempt to provide care on their own, without utilizing alternative community-based services, even though use of such services could perhaps prevent caregiver stress and burnout, avoiding nursing home admission. Although expensive, other alternatives such as respite care have been found to delay or decrease the likelihood of nursing home placement as well as to enhance caregivers' well-being and reduce subjective burden (Kosloski and Montgomery, 1995; Kammer, 1994; Collins, King, and Kokinakis, 1994).

Although older persons without families are more likely to be in nursing homes, 55 percent of those in institutions have children. In most cases, children and spouses resort to institutionalization only after exhausting their own resources, but caregiving husbands tend to turn to nursing home placement earlier than do wives. In approximately 25 percent of nursing home applications, the decision to seek institutionalization has been precipitated by the family caregiver's illness or death, or by severe family strain (Tennstedt et al., 1993). For example, the characteristics of the caregiver and of the caregiving context, especially perceived burden, are better predictors of whether an Alzheimer's patient will be institutionalized than are the illness characteristics or symptoms of the care receiver (Zarit, Todd, and Zarit, 1986; Poulshock and Diemling, 1984).

Most older people and their caregivers hold negative attitudes toward nursing homes and try to bring services into the home, even though the quality of care in many nursing homes is good. Placing an older relative in a nursing home is typically a stressful life event for the family, once referred to as the "nadir of life" for adult children (Johnson, 1990; Cath, 1972). Characterized by moral dilemmas, the placement decision may arouse feelings of grief, guilt, and fear, and renew past family conflicts. As a result of reduced burden, however, many families experience improvements in their relationship with institutionalized members; they continue to visit their older relatives and assist with their hands-on care, even though the level of their activities might decline (Pearlin et al., 1996). With the growth of the oldest-old, placement in a nursing home or other long-term care setting such as assisted living or an adult family home (as will be discussed in Chapter 10) may come to be viewed as a natural step in the life cycle. To ease the transition to the post-placement phase, many nursing homes have developed support and educational groups for families.

LEGAL AND POLICY QUESTIONS REGARDING CAREGIVING

The role of adult children in caring for older relatives is an increasingly important policy and practice issue, given the trends identified earlier. From a policy perspective, the issue of family responsibility has long been a topic of debate. Most states have had filial responsibility laws (rarely enforced) that require financially able children to contribute to their aging parents' support. Policies have been organized on the premise that the family has first responsibility for dependent older persons, and that the state should intervene only after the family's resources are exhausted. For example, ours is the only Western industrialized society without a caregiver allowance as part of the Social Security system. This is partially because policymakers fear that formal services would be overutilized and substitute for families. Yet, as noted above, most families provide care without formal assistance. This is particularly true for ethnic minority families. When they do use services, it is in addition to their own care, not to replace it, even though such services can serve to reduce caregiver stress and burnout (Noelker and Bass, 1994; Hendricks and Rosenthal, 1993; Tennstedt et al., 1993).

Since 1975, legislation has been introduced, and in some instances passed, in Congress that either requires adult children to financially support their older parents or, alternatively, supports family care through tax credits and limited cash benefits, oftentimes as a cost-effective way to reduce institutionalization (Stone and Keigher, 1994). There is growing recognition that the costs of caregiving are too great for either the family or the state to bear alone, and more policies and programs are being developed to complement the family's efforts. Social and health care providers need to assess the caregiver's status along with that of the older patient and consider caregivers' needs in the overall treatment plan. Programs have been structured either to improve the caregivers' abilities to manage the care situation, such as counseling, education, and support groups, or to relieve the caregiver's burden, such as through respite and adult day care (Kosloski and Montgomery, 1995). Broader policy changes to support caregivers, however, have been relatively limited in their impact. For example, after a lengthy political battle and compromise, the **Family and Medical Leave Act** was signed into law by President Clinton in 1993. This act offers job protection to workers requiring short-term leaves from their jobs for the care of a dependent parent or seriously ill newborn or adopted child. However, this legislation does not cover temporary or part-time workers or those in small firms, even though 50 percent of all employees in the private sector work for small businesses. In effect, it benefits only those who can afford to forgo income. In contrast, many Western European countries, particularly in Scandinavia, provide public social and health services to older people as well as pay relatives to stay home to provide care. Some also offer special pensions for those who have spent many years in a caregiving role (Chappell, 1990).

In the United States, some corporations have developed family leave policies, and over 34 states provide some type of economic supports through tax credits or direct payments, although these tax supports are underutilized by caregivers of older adults (Stone and Keigher, 1994). In addition, a growing number of localities have initiated services to support families, by decreasing the older person's needs for care (e.g., adult day care programs and in-home chore services) or by increasing the family's resources (e.g., educational programs, support groups, respite care, and clinical or direct service interventions). Local area agencies on aging are often the best place for families to access such services. Corporations are also beginning to provide elder care information, refer-

ral, and education, often through employee-assistance programs. Such services are often "good business," since caregiving carries costs in terms of absenteeism, shortened or interrupted workdays, and replacement of employees. Computer access to the Internet and Web sites can also provide caregivers with information on community resources and an opportunity to connect with other caregivers through 24-hour support (Hunt, 1997). More services, however, are needed for those with the greatest needs: low-income and those just above the poverty line, ethnic minority, and unmarried elders, and caregivers with multiple responsibilities.

Grandparenthood and Great-Grandparenthood

At the turn of the century, families with grandparents were rare. Now, with the increase in life expectancy, more older people are experiencing the role of grandparenthood and, increasingly, of great-grandparenthood, although they have proportionately fewer grandchildren. For women especially, the status of grandparenthood can engage 50 percent of their lives. Of the 80 percent of older people with children, 94 percent are grandparents and nearly 50 percent are great-grandparents. Another way of grasping the significance of this change is that by the year 2000, over 66 percent of adult children will have begun life with all grandparents living, and more than 75 percent will have at least one grandparent alive when they reach age 30 (Uhlenberg, 1996). In fact, the prevalence of grandparents who have adult grandchildren is historically unprecedented.

Approximately 75 percent of these grandparents see some of their grandchildren every week or two, and nearly 50 percent see a grandchild every day or so, although only about 5 percent of the households headed by older people include grandchildren (Giarrusso, Silverstein, and Bengtson, 1996). Geographic proximity appears to be more important than whether the grandparents get along with their own children in determining frequency of visits. On the other hand, geographic distance is not necessarily a barrier; grandparents who have close ties with their children may be emotionally tied to and important to their grandchildren, even when they do not see each other often, especially when a close relationship is established early in a child's life. Grandparent-grandchild relationships change over time, with generally less contact and expectation of closeness as grandchildren become older. However, some young adult grandchildren express strong affection toward their grandparents, especially their grandmothers, and initiate contacts with them, particularly when geographically near (Coony and Smith, 1996).

The meanings and functions of grandparenthood must be viewed within the societal context described previously: increases in geographic mobility, divorce, reconstituted families, and employed middle-aged women who are also grandmothers. There is wide diversity among grandparents, who range in age from late thirties to over 100 years, with grandchildren ranging from newborns to retirees. Accordingly, there are multiple grandparenting roles and meanings. Grandparenting styles are affected by the extent of bonds, solidarity, or connectedness in multigenerational relationships. A systems perspective, rather than a focus on grandparenthood as an individual attribute, better accounts for the complexity of the grandparent-grandchild relationship. This perspective takes account of the reciprocal and continually changing relationships that exist across generations, and recognizes that although nuclear families are becoming smaller, more members of more generations are alive at one time who share a greater part of each others' life spans. The grandparent-grandchild bond is initially mediated by parents, but this bond becomes more direct as time passes, and can be substantially altered by events such as divorce. The potential for direct voluntary interaction between young adult children and their grandparents contributes not only to the individuals involved, but also to the total kinship system.

Age, proximity, and parental influences all affect the extent of satisfaction that grandparents derive from the role (Roberto, 1990). Early studies typically found the role to be peripheral and not a primary source of identity, interaction, or satisfaction (Wood and Robertson, 1976). In a classic study by Neugarten and Weinstein (1964), older adults were categorized by the meaning given to the role and by the style of grandparenting. The prime significance of grandparenthood was reported to be (1) biological renewal and/or continuity (i.e., seeing oneself extended into the future); (2) emotional self-fulfillment, especially the opportunity to be a better grandparent than parent; and (3) distance from grandchildren, with little effect on the grandparents' lives. In terms of style, older grandparents were more apt to be formal or distant, whereas younger ones emphasized mutuality, informality, and playfulness.

Later research has found that grandparents, especially grandmothers, and those who are older, derive great emotional satisfaction from frequent interaction with their grandchildren and from relatively high levels of responsibilities for helping grandchildren (Strom, Buki, and Strom, 1997; Kivett, 1991; Roberto, 1990). In the absence of a family crisis, grandparents play a role that emphasizes emotional gratification from their grandchildren and serves as a symbol of continuity and stability in family rituals and values. Grandparenthood thus provides opportunities for older people to experience feelings of immortality, to relive their lives through grandchildren, to indulge grandchildren, and to develop an increased sense of well-being and morale (Adams and Blieszner, 1995; Cherlin and Furstenberg, 1986; Kivnick, 1986). Regardless of age, grandparents generally offer grandchildren unconditional love that their parents, because of other responsibilities, may be less able to offer.

The grandparenthood relationship appears to differ by gender; grandfathers are most closely linked to sons of sons, and grandmothers to daughters of daughters. Grandmothers tend to be more expressive, having more influence than grandfathers on how their grandchildren relate to family and friends, while grandfathers are more instrumental. However, both express strong affection and feelings of closeness toward their grandchildren (Kivett, 1991). This is a reflection of the increased acceptance of their nurturing side in men as they age, described in Chapter 6. It is unclear whether fathers who are more directly involved in parenting than only as providers will become more invested in the roles of grandfather and great-grandfather in the future.

Even less is known about how the grandparenthood role and its meaning vary by ethnic minority status. In an analysis of intergenerational family relations in Mexican American families, strong ties were observed between grandparents and grandchildren. Despite the majority of grandparents living in poverty, the flow of financial assistance in these families was generally from the older to the younger generations (Dietz, 1995). Some studies suggest greater interactions through an extended kin network and more grandparent responsibility for child-rearing among ethnic minorities. When the child's mother is a single parent,

the grandmother may have responsibilities essential to the child's care (Burnette, 1997; Chalfie, 1994), especially in urban African American families. Grandparent involvement in childrearing may be a consequence of teen pregnancy, substance abuse, AIDS, incarceration, emotional problems, and parental death combined with limited financial resources. In a growing number of instances, as illustrated by Mr. and Mrs. Smith (below), grandparents are the sole providers for their grandchildren.

Grandparents as Primary Caregivers of Grandchildren

Nearly 3.7 million children now live with grandparents, most often a grandmother, and in a third of these cases, neither parent is present. In fact, the incidence of **grandparents as** the sole **caregivers** of grandchildren has doubled in the last decade. Ten percent of grandparents assume grandchild care for at least 6 months and often longer, typically before the child turns 5 (Fuller-Thomson, Minkler, and Driver, 1997). Many older people who had looked forward to retire-

---

GRANDPARENTHOOD

Mr. and Mrs. Smith are both 69 years old. After successful careers as teachers, they retired 7 years ago with anticipation of a retirement of travel and continued learning through ElderHostel.

They have a daughter, 36, who lives about 50 miles away. After leaving home at 17, she lived a life of traveling from place to place and never settling down. She has one daughter who is now 10. Her husband left her when the baby was 6 months old and has not been heard from since. Four years ago, the daughter was taken from the custody of her mother by the courts because of severe problems with addiction and unwillingness to get treatment. It was felt that she could not care for the daughter's needs.

Mr. and Mrs. Smith could not bear the thought of their granddaughter being raised by strangers in the

foster care system, so they decided to bring her to live with them. Now their days have been filled with PTA meetings, Scouts, and helping with homework. Their daughter has only contacted them twice in the past 4 years, and the Smiths have begun proceedings to legally adopt their grandchild.

It has been a very difficult adjustment for the Smiths. Many of their friends from before have dropped away, as they have more freedom to "take off and do things." They also struggle with much guilt about their daughter and her situation. But they feel they would do it again if needed. A support group for grandparents raising grandchildren meets in their city, and they attend on a regular basis. They love their granddaughter and enjoy her company, so they also receive great emotional rewards from this relationship.

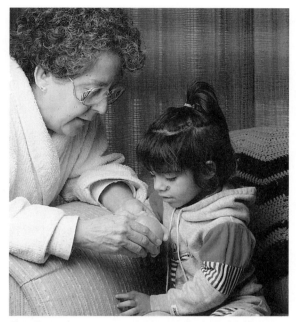

Grandparents as primary caregivers for grandchildren is a growing phenomenon.

ment and the "empty nest," and whose health and financial status may be declining, may instead be faced with the problems of sleepless nights, childhood illness, and locating child care. In addition, they may be responsible for their adult children who are coping with personal issues, such as substance abuse, incarceration, AIDS, or child abuse. Although custodial grandparenting cuts across gender, class, and ethnic lines, there is a disproportionate representation by single women, African Americans, and low-income persons. For example, 29 percent of caregiving grandparents are African American, and African Americans are nearly twice as likely to be grandparent caregivers as their white counterparts (Fuller-Thomson et al., 1997; Chalfie, 1994). For African American grandparents, this may reflect a long tradition of caring across generations that has its roots in West African culture. However, the experience of many of today's African American grandmothers may be very dif-

ferent from that of their foremothers, who took on caregiving under different historical circumstances. In fact, 25 percent of African American caregiving grandmothers live below the poverty line; caregiving grandparents are 60 percent more likely than non-custodial grandparents to report incomes below poverty and twice as likely to have major symptoms of depression as those not raising grandchildren (Minkler and Fuller-Thomson, 1997; Burton and Dilworth-Anderson, 1991). The increase in caregiving among grandparents thus often reflects differential opportunities of socioeconomic class, not cultural differences. The 1996 Welfare Reform Act, which limits the child welfare and Supplemental Security Income benefits that caregiving grandparents can receive, does not bode well for the economic health of many intergenerational households headed by grandparents.

Recognizing the need of grandparents for support and information, national organizations have formed and developed newsletters, support groups, technical assistance, and seed grants to initiate services. These include ROCKING (Raising Our Children's Kids: An Intergenerational Network of Grandparenting, Inc.), the National Coalition of Grandparents (NCOG), and the Relatives as Parents Program through the Brookdale Foundation in New York City. AARP has established a Grandparent Information Center, and the 1995 White House Conference on Aging was the first to include resolutions related to grandparenting. Unfortunately, the growing numbers of support groups for caregiving grandparents are often of short duration and fail to address the financial and health strain of such long-term responsibilities. Grandmothers have also identified the need for respite child care, legal counseling concerning foster care and guardianship, physical and mental health services for themselves, financial assistance, and training programs for coping with drug-dependent family members (Bengtson et al., 1996).

Despite the stress of caregiving, such intergenerational solidarity can benefit both the grandparent and the grandchild. Caregiving grandparents can ameliorate the negative impact of family disruption caused by divorce, drugs, and other social problems. Indirectly, they can influence the grandchild in symbolic ways (e.g., provide "roots") and act as "watchdogs." Children raised solely by grandparents have been found to fare well relative to children raised within other alternative family structures. They are healthier and have fewer behavioral problems in school than children living with only one biological parent, although they are more likely to have problems in academic performance (Fuller-Thomson et al., 1997; Solomon and Marx, 1995).

More recently, the role of great-grandparent has emerged with increasing frequency among the older population. There appear to be two predominant styles of performing this role. The most common, which tends to characterize generations separated by physical distance, is remote, involving only occasional and somewhat ritualistic contact on special occasions such as holidays and birthdays. Despite the remote nature of contacts, however, great-grandparents derive considerable emotional satisfaction and a sense of personal and familial renewal from seeing a fourth generation as representing family immortality. Living long enough to be a great-grandparent is viewed as a positive sign of successful aging or longevity (Roberto, 1990; Doka and Mentz, 1988). The other common great-grandparenting style occurs when great-grandparents are geographically close (within 25 miles) to the fourth generation, and thus have opportunities for emotional closeness to great-grandchildren as well. Even great-grandparents who are in their seventies and eighties may serve as babysitters, go shopping, and take trips with their great-grandchildren. These activities provide diversions in their lives and can lead to renewed zeal. Such positive interactions will undoubtedly be more common in the future, when great-grandparenthood is the norm and the oldest-old generations are healthier than current cohorts. Consistent with the reciprocal nature of most intergenerational relationships,

growing numbers of grandchildren care for great-grandparents (Roberto, 1990).

The Effects of Divorce

The growing divorce rate, discussed earlier, is a social trend that is affecting the meaning of grandparenthood. As noted above, at least 50 percent of all persons marrying today will face divorce. The consequences of this for younger generations—over 30 percent of children living in one-parent families or with neither parent—clearly influence the nature of the grandchild-grandparent relationship (U.S. Bureau of the Census, 1996). Since the tie between young grandchildren and their grandparents is mediated by the grandchildren's parents, divorce disrupts these links, changes the balance of resources within the extended family, and requires a renegotiation of existing bonds. Who is awarded custody primarily affects the frequency of interaction with grandchildren; the grandparents whose child, typically the mother's, is awarded custody have more contact (Cooney and Smith, 1996; Kruk, 1995). Controversies regarding **grandparents' rights** for visiting and proposed state legislation to ensure such rights highlight the issues faced by grandparents when the in-law is awarded custody and controls the amount of child-grandparent interactions. This loss of contact often has negative consequences for the grandparents (Kruk, 1995). Groups such as Grandparents Anonymous, the Foundation for Grandparenting, and Grandparents'-Children's Rights are pressing for grandparents' visitation rights legislation in several states.

During the past two decades, most states have passed laws granting grandparents the right to petition a court to legally obtain visitation privileges with their grandchildren. In 1983, a uniform nationwide statute was passed that ensures grandparents visitation rights even if parents object. These laws raise complex issues for the involved generations, however. For example, because of court-enforced visitation against the parents' wishes, a young child may unwittingly become involved in intergenerational conflicts. The long-term effects for grandchildren from visiting non-custodial grandparents over the objections of a parent are as yet unclear. What is apparent is that factors outside the family, such as the courts, are playing a larger role in how some families resolve conflicts and thus in children's development.

Conversely, complex issues have also emerged concerning the liability of grandparents and step-grandparents for support of grandchildren in the absence of responsible parents. When divorce in the parent generation occurs, the norm of noninterference by grandparents generally disappears. Instead, grandparents, especially those on the side of the custodial parent, provide substantial assistance to their grandchildren, function as surrogate parents, and mediate tensions. Grandparents have been referred to as "the family watchdogs," who are in the background during tranquil times, but are ready to step in during an emergency (Roberto, 1990).

Despite the fact that blended families constitute about 50 percent of all households with children (National Academy on Aging, 1994), little is known about step-grandparenting relationships. From a grandparent's perspective, the growing phenomenon of divorce-remarriage means sharing grandchildren with their newly acquired relatives under conditions in which grandchildren will be scarcer because of declining birthrates. Grandchildren, in turn, may find themselves with four or more sets of grandparents. Kinship systems are further complicated by the fact that with the increased divorce rate after 20+ years of marriage, grandparents may no longer be married to one another. It is difficult to predict the magnitude of the effects—positive and negative—of these trends on intergenerational relations because of the relatively limited research in this area.

In summary, the grandparent role is idiosyncratic and subject to negotiation. The role of valued grandparent is earned, and for some, it can bring considerable satisfaction. Furthermore, grandparents can play a major role within the extended family system during a family crisis such as divorce or other patterns facing adult children.

FRIENDS AND NEIGHBORS AS SOCIAL SUPPORTS

Although the majority of older people live with others, 30 percent of those over 65 and 46 percent of those over 85 live alone. In fact, the rate of older persons living alone increased by one-and-a-half times the growth rate for older people in general since 1970. Those living alone are most likely to be women, ethnic minorities, the oldest-old, and people of low socioeconomic status. They tend to rely on community services more than on support from friends and neighbors in their efforts to continue living independently in the community. They also report less satisfaction with the quality of their lives than married people (Hobbs and Damon, 1996).

As will be noted in Chapter 10, among those living alone, the most vulnerable are the homeless. While 27 percent of the homeless are estimated to be age 50 and over (including those who live in missions on skid row), their absolute numbers are increasing, especially among women (Kutza and Keigher, 1991). Characterized by higher rates of physical or mental disorders, economic deprivation, and alcohol misuse than the older population in general, homeless elders tend not to be tied into services and typically have fewer social supports (DeMallie, North, and Smith, 1997). Such experiences of chronic stress may function to produce social isolation rather than seeking social support (Hansson and Carpenter, 1994).

These individuals living alone and the estimated 5 percent of the older population who are without any family ties are dependent upon friends, neighbors, and acquaintances to create family-like relationships. Men, the widowed, and the childless are the most vulnerable to being without support in times of need, often experiencing exacerbated health problems and institutionalization as a result. A small percent of older persons living alone do not even have phone conversations with friends and neighbors (Administration on Aging, 1997).

However, most older adults who live alone, such as Mr. Valdres in our introductory vignette, have some friends and acquaintances to whom they can turn in emergencies. Although contact with friends tends to decline with age, the majority of older adults have at least one close friend with whom they are in frequent contact (Adams and Blieszner, 1995). Such non-kin informal helpers are especially common among the oldest-old in ethnic minority communities (Taylor and Chatters, 1991).

In fact, older persons who have kin may turn more to friends and neighbors for immediate assistance than to family, in part because friendship involves more voluntary and reciprocal exchanges between equals, consistent with social exchange theory described in Chapter 8 (Hatch and Bulcroft, 1992). Whether family, friends, or neighbors become involved appears to vary with the type of task to be performed, as well as the helper's characteristics, such as proximity, extent of long-term commitment, and degree of interaction. Friends and neighbors are well-suited to provide emotional support and to perform predictable tasks, such as transportation and running errands, while families are best equipped for personal care (Dykstra, 1995). Among ethnic minorities, friends often link older persons to needed community services. In fact, African American peers have been found more likely than whites to provide and receive both instrumental and emotional support (Silverstein and Waite, 1993). Friends also often link older people, particularly minority elders, to needed community services (Taylor, 1988). Even friends facing chronic health problems may still be able to provide assistance to others, such as listening and offering advice and support. Nevertheless, the percent of friends providing help declines after age 85, especially for assistance with personal care (Kincade et al., 1996). For the most part, friends and neighbors play smaller roles in the long-term helping network than family. Although they are important resources when children are absent or unavailable, their helping efforts usually do not approach those of family members in duration or intensity and do not fully compensate for the loss of spouse or children (DeMallie, North, and Smith, 1997; Dykstra, 1995). Friendships can also be characterized by negative interactions, such as unwanted advice or assistance, and may become strained by excessive demands for assistance (Hansson and Carpenter, 1994).

Although they may provide less long-term help, friends are often important sources of intimacy, especially when compared to relatives other than marital partners (MacRae, 1996; Wright, 1994). This is especially true after major role transitions such as widowhood or retirement; for example, an older widow generally prefers help from confidantes because relatives may reinforce her loss of identity as "wife" (Adams and Bleiszner, 1995). To the extent that friendships can satisfy social and material needs, and allow for reciprocity in relationships, they can compensate for the absence of a partner and can help mitigate loneliness (Adams and Blieszner, 1995; Dykstra, 1995). The role of friend can be maintained long after the role of worker, organization member, or spouse is lost. The extent of reciprocity and quality of interaction, not the quantity, appear to be the critical factors in the maintenance of friendship networks. For instance, an intimate friendship with a confidant has been found to be as effective as several less intimate ones in preventing the demoralization often produced by widowhood and retirement (Lowenthal and Haven, 1968). Friendship quality, including reciprocity among friends, has been found to be strongly related to psychological well-being and happiness (Adams and Blieszner, 1995).

Older people who refuse to leave their own homes and communities in order to live with or near their adult children may recognize that friends are important sources of companionship, and that replacing lost friends can be difficult in old age. Although mortality in the short run reduces the number of friends, most older people are steadily making new friends from acquaintances and neighbors, and close relationships generally get closer with age (Bleiszner and Adams, 1992; Adams, 1989).

Neighbors are an important source of assistance for older adults.

Types of social interaction vary by gender. Women in general, such as Mrs. Howard in the introductory vignette, have more intimate, diverse, and intensive friendships than men, who tend to have more acquaintances and who place a higher value on career-oriented activities (Bleiszner and Adams, 1992). For many men, their wives are their only confidants, a circumstance that may make widowhood devastating for them (Chappell, 1990). In contrast, women tend to satisfy their needs for intimacy throughout their lives by establishing close friendships with other women and therefore are less dependent emotionally on the marital relationship. When faced with widowhood, divorce, or separation, they can turn to these friends. Accordingly, widowed older women tend to receive more help and emotional support from friends than married older women. The resilience of some older women, in fact, may be rooted in their ability to form close reciprocal friendships (Riley and Riley, 1994; Litwak, 1985). On the other hand, some researchers suggest that as women respond to others for support, their caregiving networks may inadvertently increase

their exposure to stress, foster conflicts, and produce unhappiness (Antonucci, 1990).

Both men and women tend to select friends from among people they consider their social peers—those who are similar in age, sex, marital status, sexual orientation, and socioeconomic class. Most choose age peers as their friends, even though common sense would suggest that age-integrated friendship networks can reduce their vulnerability to losses as they age. A person's adult children are not likely to be chosen as confidants, primarily because of their being from different cohorts who are at different places in the life cycle and more likely to produce an inequality of exchange. Age homogeneity plays a strong role in facilitating friendships in later life, in part because of shared life transitions, reduced cross-generational ties with children and work associates, and possible parity of exchange. Age as a basis for friendship may be most pronounced at those stages where the individual's ties to other networks are loosened.

Type of living environment clearly affects the quality and quantity of informal exchanges, as will be discussed in Chapter 10. Although the results are mixed, some studies have found that age-segregated environments lead to more peer-group interaction, friendships, helping networks, and satisfaction with one's environment (Perkinson and Rockemann, 1996). Age segregation, however, may not always be by choice but may result when younger people leave an area. In such cases of "naturally occurring retirement communities," older people's length of residence rather than the homogeneity of the living situation may be more strongly related to extensive social ties and informal helping networks.

INTERVENTIONS TO STRENGTHEN OR BUILD SOCIAL SUPPORTS

Because of the importance of peer-group ties for well-being, there have been increased efforts to strengthen existing community ties or to create new ties if networks are nonexistent. Consistent with the person-environment model, such interventions are ways to alter the environment to be supportive of the older person. They can be categorized as personal network building, volunteer linking, mutual help networks, and neighborhood and community development. Such interventions aim to build upon the strengths and resources of local communities, including ethnic minority communities (Meyers and Souflee, 1990–91). Increasingly, these interventions include an intergenerational component.

Personal network building aims to strengthen existing ties, often through **"natural helpers"**— people turned to because of their concern, interest, and innate understanding. Such natural helpers can provide emotional support, assist with problem solving, offer concrete services, and act as advocates. Neighbors often perform natural helping roles, and may strengthen these activities through organized block programs and block watches. Even people in service positions, often referred to as **"gatekeepers,"** can fulfill natural helping functions, because of the visibility of their position and the regularity of their interactions with the older person. For example, postal alert systems, whereby postal carriers observe whether an older person is taking in the mail each day, build upon routine everyday interactions. Pharmacists, ministers, bus drivers, local merchants,

beauticians, and managers of housing for older people, as in the case of Mr. Valdres in the introductory vignette, are frequently in situations to provide companionship, advice, and referrals. In high-crime areas, local businesses, bars, and restaurants may have a "safehouse" decal in their windows, indicating where residents of all ages can go in times of danger or medical emergencies. These community-based supports are further described in Chapter 10.

Churches may also serve to strengthen and build personal networks, in some cases providing a surrogate family for older people. National initiatives affiliated with churches and synagogues emphasize empowering older people through caring for each other. Through intergenerational programs, church members can provide help with housework, home repair, transportation, and meal preparation, as well as psychological assurance. At the same time, older members may take on many leadership and teaching roles within the church, thereby enhancing their sense of belonging and self-worth, as in the example of Mr. Mansfield on p. 227. In many private and public programs, volunteers are commonly used to develop new or expand existing networks for older persons. For example, volunteers provide chore services in older people's homes, peer counseling and

---

GATEKEEPERS

Mrs. Jones, 80, shuffled down the sidewalk with the aid of a cane. A boy delivering newspapers from his bicycle zoomed past, nearly hitting her. Mrs. Jones was not fazed. She moved on, staring straight ahead, as if she hadn't seen the youngster. Other incidents could have alerted a trained observer that Mrs. Jones was having serious trouble. She had difficulty signing her name on the back of her Social Security check when she cashed it at the bank. She couldn't count out change to pay for a cup of coffee at a local diner. When Mrs. Jones picked up her prescription at the local drug store, she had difficulty conversing with the pharmacist she had known for many years.

The Gatekeeper Project tries to address the needs of people like Mrs. Jones. The program identifies and trains Gatekeepers, people who are in contact with the public during the course of their regular work activities. In Mrs. Jones' case, they could be the bank teller, the newspaper carrier, or the pharmacist. They are called Gatekeepers because they "open the gates" between isolated older people and sources of assistance, often times by turning to Senior Information and Assistance lines.

SOURCE: Washington State Aging and Adult Services Administration and Puget Sound Power and Light Company, 1986.

senior center outreach activities, and serve as Friendly Visitors. The Internet, e-mail, the Web, and interactive television also provide new opportunities for network building with peers and across generations for older people who have access to such information technology (Furlong, 1997).

Another approach aims to create or promote the supportive capacities of mutual help networks, especially through joint problem-solving and reciprocal exchange of resources. Mutual help efforts may occur spontaneously, as neighbors watch out for each other, or may be facilitated by professionals. They may also be formed on the basis of neighborhood ties or around shared problems, such as widow-to-widow programs, and support groups for caregivers of family members with Alzheimer's disease, stroke, or other types of chronic impairments. Interacting with peers who share experiences has been found to reduce stress and expand problem-solving capacities (Pillemer and Suitor, 1996). A growing number of mutual help efforts are **intergenerational programs,** linking seniors with school children, high-risk youth, and children with special needs. After-school telephone support, tutoring, and day-care programs have been initiated by Retired Senior Volunteer Programs around the country. The Foster Grandparents Program brings together low-income elders and disadvantaged youths. Both young and older participants frequently benefit from such interactions. The Internet is also providing new ways in which older adults can connect with peers and family, sharing resources, information, and peer support. For example, after the Los Angeles earthquake of 1993, members of the SeniorNet online community on America OnLine located all the members of the community and provided mutual assistance and support (Furlong, 1997).

Neighborhood and community development is another approach which attempts to strengthen a community's self-help and problem-solving capabilities and may involve social action through lobbying and legislative activities. The Tenderloin Project, in a low-income area of single-room occupants in San Francisco, is an example of neighborhood development. Nearby residents acted on the immediate problem of crime and victimization of older people and then moved on to deal with issues such as nutrition and health promotion. In the process, social networks were strengthened and weekly support groups were formed (Minkler, 1986). Neighborhood-based intergenerational helping networks have been used to connect the formal service system to provide personal care services to frail elders. More recently, Internet websites, such as Third Age, can also be used as a means to build community connections and reduce social isolation. Chat rooms, for example, are modeled upon community member's interests and needs and can be altered by the changing will of the community. As noted by Hagel and Armstrong (1997), "people are drawn to virtual communities because they provide an engaging environment in which to connect with other people" (p. 18). Creating an electronic community, however, is obviously limited to those older people who have the financial means to access computers and the Internet (Furlong, 1997).

RELATIONSHIPS WITH PETS

Pets are another source of affection and touch, and may offer a significant relationship in some older people's lives. The mere presence of a pet appears to have little effect on psychological well-being, but being attached to a pet can have emotional benefits (Tucker, Friedman, Tsai, and Martin, 1995). Many older adults talk to their pets as if they were people, confide in them, and believe that they are sensitive to their moods and feelings. Having a pet to feed, groom, or walk can provide structure and a sense of purpose to the day of an otherwise isolated older person, and caring for it can provide an anchor for those whose lives have undergone major change or loss. A pet may even serve as a family substitute, especially for residents in nursing homes (Zasloff and Kidd, 1994). Pet owners tend to score higher on measures of happiness, self-confidence, self-care, alertness, responsiveness, and dependability than non-pet owners (Dembicki and Anderson, 1996). These measures of well-being may be partially due to the fact that older people who care for pets, rather than being taken care of by others, can experience meaning, purpose, and a sense of control over their environment. On the other hand, the loss of a pet can result in grief as intense as that precipitated by the death of a family member or friend (Carmack, 1985).

The recognition that animals fulfill many human needs has led to an increase in pet-facilitated programs for older people living in senior housing and long-term care facilities, as well as in loan-a-pet programs for those individuals in their own homes. In fact, animals, even tropical fish and wild birds attracted to feeders, have been found to evoke responses such as care and stroking from persons who were previously non-responsive (Hendy, 1987). Older people participating in pet therapy programs have been found to become less depressed and more communicative, and to experience higher rates of survival than do controls who do not participate in such programs (National Institutes of Health, 1988). Although a pet should never be viewed as a substitute for human relationships, gerontologists are increasingly aware that pet ownership can enhance well-being and enrich the quality of older people's lives, particularly in institutional environments.

SUMMARY AND IMPLICATIONS

The importance of informal social relationships for older people's physical and mental well-being has been widely documented. Contrary to stereotypes, very few older people are socially isolated. The majority have family members with whom they are in contact, although they are unlikely to live with them. Their families serve as a critical source of support, especially when older members become impaired by chronic illness. The marital relationship is most important, with more than half of all persons age 65 and over married and living with a partner in independent households. Most older couples are satisfied with their marriages, which influences their life satisfaction generally. The older couple, freed from childrearing

demands, has more opportunities to pursue new roles and types of relationships.

Less is known about sibling, grandparent, and other types of family interactions in old age, although the importance of their support is likely to increase in the future. Also, comparatively little research has been conducted on lesbian and gay relationships in old age and on never-married older persons who may rely primarily on friendship networks to cope. Siblings can be crucial in providing emotional support, physical care, and a home. Interaction with secondary kin tends to depend on geographic proximity and whether or not more immediate family members are available.

Contrary to the myth that adult children are alienated from their parents, the majority of older persons are in frequent contact with their children, either face-to-face or by phone or letter. Filial relationships are characterized by patterns of reciprocal aid throughout the life course, until the older generation becomes physically or mentally disabled. At that point, adult children—generally women—are faced with providing financial, emotional, and physical assistance to older relatives, oftentimes with little support from others for their caregiving responsibilities. In ethnic minority and lower-income families, older relatives are most likely to receive daily care from younger relatives and to be involved themselves in caring for grandchildren.

Most families, regardless of socioeconomic class or ethnic minority status, attempt to provide care for their older members for as long as possible, and seek institutionalization only when they have exhausted other resources. Such caregiving responsibilities are affected by a number of social trends, most notable among them the increasing percentage of middle-aged women—traditionally the caregivers—who are more likely to be employed, and the number of reconstituted families resulting from divorce and remarriage. The needs of caregivers are clearly a growing concern for social and health care providers and policy makers.

With the growth of three- and four-generation families, more older persons are experiencing the status of grandparenthood and great-grandparenthood. Most grandparents are in relatively frequent contact with their grandchildren, and most derive considerable satisfaction from the grandparent role. The demands of grandparenthood are changing, however, as a result of divorce and remarriages. Perhaps the most dramatic change in the past decade has been the increase in the number of grandparents who are the primary caregivers to young grandchildren.

For many older persons, friends and neighbors can be even more critical than family members to maintaining morale and a quality of life. Generally, women have more interaction with friends than do men. Age-segregated settings appear to facilitate friendships rather than isolate older persons. In recognition of the importance of informal interaction to physical and mental well-being, an increasing number of neighborhood and community-based interventions have been developed to strengthen friendship and neighborhood ties. In recent years, many of these programs have attempted to foster intergenerational contacts and relationships. In sum, the majority of older persons continue to play a variety of social roles—partner, parent, grandparent, friend, and neighbor—and to derive feelings of satisfaction and self-worth from these interactions.

GLOSSARY

blended family   a family whose membership is comprised of blood and non-blood relationships through divorce, or remarriage

caregiving   the act of assisting people with personal care, household chores, transportation, and other tasks associated with daily living; by either family members without compensation or professionals

caregiver burden   the personal energy, time restrictions, financial strains, and/or psychological frustrations associated with assisting persons with long-term care needs

cluttered nest   delayed departure or return of adult children to parents' home

elder abuse   maltreatment of older adults, including physical, sexual, psychological, and financial exploitation

elder neglect   deprivation of care necessary to maintain the health by those trusted to provide the care (e.g., neglect by others) or by older persons (self-neglect)

empty nest   families whose adult children have left home

extended family   family members of two or more generations

Family and Medical Leave Act   federal legislation passed in 1993 that provides job protection to workers requiring short-term leaves from their jobs for the care of a dependent parent or seriously ill newborn or adopted child

filial responsibility   norms or expectations of what younger offspring owe older relatives

gatekeepers   people in formal (e.g., physician, nurses) or informal (e.g., friends and neighbors) service who, because of regular interactions with older adults, can watch for signs indicating a need for assistance and mobilize help accordingly

grandparents as caregivers   grandparents who are the primary caregivers for grandchildren, because adult children are unable to provide adequate care

grandparents' rights   legal rights of grandparents to interact with grandchildren following divorce of the grandchild's parents; liabilities of grandparent and step-grandparents as custodians of grandchildren in the absence of responsible parents

intergenerational living   families spanning two or more generations living in the same household

intergenerational programs   services that facilitate the interaction of people across generations, for example, the Foster Grandparent Program

intergenerational transfers   exchange of knowledge, finances, and other resources among family members of different generations

intimacy at a distance   strong emotional ties among family members even though they do not live near each other

multigenerational family   a family with three or more generations alive at the same time

natural helpers   people who assist others because of their concern, interest, and innate understanding

non-traditional families   new family structures derived through gay and lesbian partnerships, communal living, cohabitation, informal adoption, etc.

reciprocal support   sharing resources and assistance among individuals

sandwich generation middle-aged individuals most likely to have caregiving demands from more than one generation in addition to employment responsibilities

social support interactions among family, friends, neighbors, and programs which sustain and encourage them

social support, formal policies, programs, and services that impact and assist people

social support, informal friends, family, and neighbors who impact and assist persons

women in the middle women who have competing demands from older parents, spouses, children, and employment

REFERENCES

Adams, R. Conceptual and methodological issues in studying friendships of older adults. In R. Adams and R. Bleiszner (Eds.). *Older adult friendships*, Newbury Park, CA: Sage, 1989.

Adams, R., and Blieszner, R. Aging well with family and friends. *American Behavioral Scientist*, 1995, *39*, 209–224.

Adelman, M. Stigma, gay lifestyles and adjustment to aging: A study of later-life gay men and lesbians. In *Journal of Homosexuality*, 1990, *20*, 7–32.

Administration on Aging: *Aging into the 21st century*. Washington, DC: 1997.

Anastas, J., Gibeau, J., and Larson, P. Working families and eldercare: A national perspective in an aging America. *Social Work*, 1990, *35*, 405–411.

Antonucci, T. C. Social supports and social relationships. In R. H. Binstock and L. K. George (Eds.), *The handbook of aging and the social sciences* (3rd ed.). New York: Academic Press, 1990.

Aranda, M., and Knight, B. G. The influence of ethnicity and culture on the caregiver stress and coping process: A sociocultural review and analysis. *The Gerontologist*, 1997, *37*, 342–354.

Asher, C. C. The impact of social support networks on adult health. *Medical Care*, 1984, *22*, 349–359.

Atchley, R. *Social forces and aging* (4th ed.). Belmont, CA: Wadsworth, 1985.

Baresi, C., and Hunt, K. The unmarried elderly: Age, sex and ethnicity. In T. Brubaker, (Ed.), *Family relationships in later life* (2nd ed.). Newbury Park, CA: Sage, 1990.

Bass, D., Noelker, L. S., and Rechlin, L. The moderating influence of service use on negative caregiving

consequences. *Journals of Gerontology*, 1996, *51B*, S121–S131.

Beckman, L. *Childlessness, family composition and well-being of older men*. Presented at the Annual Convention of the American Psychological Association, Los Angeles, CA, August 1985.

Bengtson, V. C., and Roberts, R. E. Intergenerational solidarity and aging families: An example of formal theory construction. *Journal of Marriage and the Family*, 1991, *53*, 856–870.

Bengtson, V. C., Rosenthal, C. J., and Burton, C. Families and aging: Diversity and heterogeneity. In R. H. Binstock and L. K. George, (Eds.), *Handbook of aging and the social sciences* (3rd ed.). New York: Academic Press, 1990.

Bengtson, V. C., Rosenthal, C. J., and Burton, C. Paradoxes of families and aging. In R. H. Binstock and C. K. George (Eds.), *Handbook of aging and the social sciences* (4th ed.). San Diego: Academic Press, 1996.

Blieszner, R., and Adams, R. G. *Adult friendship*. Newbury Park, CA: Sage, 1992.

Bogard, R., and Spilka, B. Self-disclosure and marital satisfaction in mid-life and late-life remarriages. *International Journal of Aging and Human Development*, 1996, *42*, 161–172.

Braithwaite, V. Caregiver burden: Making the concept scientifically useful and policy relevant. *Research on Aging*, 1992, *14*, 3–27.

Brody, E. Parent care as a normative family stress. *The Gerontologist*, 1985, *25*, 19–30.

Brubaker, T. Family relationships in later life (2nd ed.). In T. Brubaker (Ed.), *An overview of family relationships in later life*. Newbury Park, CA: Sage, 1990.

Buckwalter, K. C., Campbell, J., Gerdner, L. A., and Garand, L. Elder mistreatment among rural family caregivers of persons with Alzheimer's disease and related disorders. *Journal of Family Nursing*, 1996, *2(3)*, 249–265.

Burnette, D. Grandparents raising grandchildren in the inner city. *Families in Society: The Journal of Contemporary Human Sciences*, 1997, 489–501.

Burton, L. M., and Dilworth-Anderson, P. The intergenerational roles of aged Black Americans. *Marriage and Family Review*, 1991, *16*, 311–330.

Cantor, M. Family and community: Changing roles in an aging society. *The Gerontologist*, 1991, *31*, 337–340.

Cantor, M. Family caregiving: Social care. In M. Cantor (Ed.), *Family caregiving: Agenda for the future*. San Francisco: American Society on Aging, 1994.

Carmack, B. J. The effects of family members and functioning after the death of a pet. In M. B. Sussman (Ed.), *Pets and the family*. New York: Haworth Press, 1985.

Cath, S. H. The institutionalization of a parent: A nadir of life. *Journal of Geriatric Psychiatry*, 1972, *5*, 25–46.

Chalfie, D. *Going it alone: A closer look at grandparents parenting grandchildren*. Washington, DC: American Association of Retired Persons, 1994.

Chappell, N. C. Aging and social care. In R. B. Binstock and L. K. George, (Eds.), *Handbook of aging and the social sciences* (3rd ed.). New York: Academic Press, 1990.

Cherlin, A. J., and Furstenberg, F. Grandparents and family crisis. *Generations*, 1986, *10*, 26–28.

Choi, N. Long-term elderly widows and divorcees: Similarities and differences. *Journal of Women and Aging*, 1995, *7*, 69–92.

Choi, N. G. The never-married and divorced elderly: Comparison of economic and health status, social support, and living arrangement. *Journal of Gerontological Social Work*, 1996, *26*, 3–25.

Choi, N. G. Racial differences in the determinants of living arrangements of widowed and divorced elderly women. *The Gerontologist*, 1991, *31*, 496–504.

Choi-Namkea, G. Patterns and determinants of social service utilization: Comparison of the childless elderly and elderly parents living with or apart from their children. *The Gerontologist*, 1994, *34*, 353.

Cicirelli, V. Family support in relation to health problems of the elderly. In T. Brubaker (Ed.), *Family relationships in later life* (2nd ed.). Newbury Park, CA: Sage, 1990.

Cicirelli, V. G. *Helping elderly parents: The role of adult children*. Boston: Auburn House, 1981.

Cicirelli, V. G. Siblings as caregivers in middle and old age. In J. Dwyer and R. Coward, (Eds.), *Gender, families and elder care*. Newbury Park, CA: Sage, 1991.

Cicirelli, V. G. Strengthening sibling relationships in the later years. In G. C. Smith, S. Tobin, E. A. Robertson-Tchabo, and P. Power (Eds.), *Strengthening aging families: Diversity in practice and policy*. Thousand Oaks, CA: Sage, 1995.

Cohen, S., and Syme, S. L. (Eds.) *Social support and health*. Orlando, FL: Academic Press, 1985.

Collins, C., King, S., and Kokinakis, C. Community service issues before nursing home placement of persons with dementia. *Western Journal of Nursing Research*, 1994, *16*, 40–52.

Connell, C. M., and Gibson, G. D. Racial, ethnic and cultural differences in dementia caregiving: Review and analysis. *The Gerontologist*, 1997, *37*, 355–364.

Connider, I. A. Sibling support in older age. *Journals of Gerontology*, 1994, *49*, S309–S317.

Cooney, T. M., and Smith, L. A. Young adults' relation with grandparents following recent parental divorce. *Journals of Gerontology*, 1996, *51B*, S91–S95.

Coward, R. T., and Dwyer, J. W. The association of gender, sibling network composition, and patterns of parent care of adult children, *Research on Aging*, 1990, *14*, 331–350.

Cruikshank, M. Lavender and gray: A brief survey of lesbian and gay aging studies. *Journal of Homosexuality*, 1990, *20*, 77–87.

DeMallie, D. A., North, C. S., and Smith, E. M. Psychiatric disorders among the homeless: A comparison of older and younger groups. *The Gerontologist*, 1997, *37*, 61–66.

Dembicki, D., and Anderson, J. Pet ownership may be a factor in improved health of the elderly. *Journal of Nutrition and the Elderly*, 1996, *15*, 15–31.

Dick-Muehlke, C., Yang, J., Yu, D. and Paul, D. Abuse of cognitively impaired elders: Recognition and intervention. In *silent suffering: Elder abuse in America*. Long Beach, CA: Archstone Foundation, 1997.

Dietz, T. L. Patterns of intergenerational assistance within the Mexican American family. *Journal of Family Issues*, 1995, *16*, 350–355.

Doka, K. J., and Mentz, M. E. The meaning and significance of great-grandparenthood. *The Gerontologist*, 1988, *28*, 192–197.

Doty, P., and Miller, B. Caregiving and productive aging. In S. Bass, F. Caro, and V-P Chen (Eds.), *Achieving a productive aging society*. Westport, CT: Auburn House, 1993.

Dykstra, P. Loneliness among the never and formerly married: The importance of supportive friendships and a desire for independence. *Journals of Gerontology*, 1995, *50B*, S321–S329.

Ehrenberg, P. Mortality decline in the twentieth century and supply of kin over the life course. *The Gerontologist*, 1996, *36*, 681–685.

Emick, M. A., and Hayslip, B. Custodial grandparenting: New roles for middle-aged and older adults. *International Journal of Aging and Human Development*, 1996, *43*, 135–154.

Finley, N., Roberts, D., and Banahan, B. Motivators and inhibitors of attitudes of filial obligation toward aging parents. *The Gerontologist,* 1988, *28,* 73–83.

Freedman, R. I., Krauss, M. W., and Seltzer, M. M. Aging parents' residential plans for adult children with mental retardation. *Mental Retardation,* 1997, *35,* 114–123.

Friend, R. A. Older lesbian and gay people: A theory of successful aging. *Journal of Homosexuality,* 1991, *20,* 99–118.

Fuller-Thomson, E., Minkler, M., and Driver, D. A profile of grandparents raising grandchildren in the United States. *The Gerontologist,* 1997, *37,* 406–411.

Fullmer, E. M. Challenging biases against families of older gays and lesbians. In G. C. Smith, S. Tobin, E. A. Robertson-Tchabo, and P. Power (Eds.), *Strengthening aging families: Diversity in practice and power.* Thousand Oaks, CA: Sage, 1995.

Furlong, M. Creating online communities for older adults. *Generations,* 1997, *21,* 33–35.

Gallup Poll News Service. *Mirror of America.* Los Angeles: Gallop Poll News Service, 1989.

Giarrusso, R., Silverstein, M., and Bengtson, V. L. Family complexity and the grandparent role. *Generations,* 1996, *20,* 17–23.

Gilford, R. Marriages in later life. *Generations,* 1986, *10,* 16–20.

Goldman, N., Korenman, S., and Weinstein, R. Marital status and health among the elderly. *Social Science and Medicine,* 1995, *40,* 1717–1730.

Goldscheider, F. K. Divorce and remarriage: Effects on the elderly population. *Reviews in Clinical Gerontology,* 1994, *4,* 258–259.

Greene, V. L., and Monahan, D. J. The effect of a support and education program on stress and burden among family caregivers to frail elderly persons. *The Gerontologist,* 1989, *4,* 472–477.

Greenwell, L., and Bengston, V. L. Geographic distance and contact between middle-aged children and their parents: The effects of social class over 20 years. *Journals of Gerontology,* 1995, *52B,* S13–S26.

Hagel, J. III, and Armstrong, A. G. *Net gain: Expanding markets through virtual communities.* Boston, MA: Harvard Business School Press, 1997.

Hammond, R. J., and Muller, G. O. The late-life divorced: Another look. *Journal of Divorce and Remarriage,* 1992, *17,* 135–150.

Hansson, R. O., and Carpenter, B. N. *Relationships in old age: Coping with the challenge of transition.* New York: The Guilford Press, 1994.

Hatch, L., and Bulcroft, K. Contact with friends in later life: Disentangling the effects of gender and marital status. *Journal of Marriage and the Family,* 1992, *54,* 222–232.

Hendricks, J., and Rosenthal, C. *The remainder of their days: Domestic policy in older families in the United States and Canada.* New York: Garland Publishing, 1993.

Hendy, H. M. Effects of pet and/or people visits on nursing home residents. *International Journal on Aging and Human Development,* 1987, *25,* 279–291.

Hobbs, F. B., and Damon, B. C. *65+ in the United States.* Washington, DC: U.S. Bureau of the Census, Current Population Reports, 1996.

Hobfoll, S. F., and Vaux, A. Social support: Resources and contact. In S. Cohen and S. L. Syme (Eds.), *Social support and health.* New York: Academic Press, 1993, 685–705.

Holahan, C. K., and Holahan, C. J. Self-efficacy, social support and depression in aging: A longitudinal analysis. *Journal of Gerontology,* 1987, *42,* 65–68.

House, J., Mero, R., and Webster, P. Marital quality over the life course. *Social Psychology Quarterly,* 1996, *59,* 162–171.

Houser, B. The relative rewards and costs of childlessness for older women. *Psychology of Women Quarterly,* 1984, *8,* 395–398.

Hunt, G. G. Cleveland free-net Alzheimer's forum. *Generations,* 1997, *21,* 37.

Hwalek, M. A., Neale, A. V., Goodrich, C. S., and Quinn, K. The association of elder abuse and substance abuse in the Illinois elder abuse system. *The Gerontologist,* 1996, *36,* 694–700.

Ingersoll-Dayton, Starrels, M., and Dowler, D. Caregiving for parents and parents-in-law: Is gender important? *The Gerontologist,* 1996, *36,* 483–491.

Johnson, M. A. Nursing home placement: The daughter's perspective. *Journal of Gerontological Nursing,* 1990, *16,* 6–11

Juster, F. T., Soldo, B., Kington, R. S., and Mitchell, O. *Aging well: Health, wealth, and retirement.* Washington, DC: Consortium of Social Science Association, 1996.

Kammer, C. Stress and coping of family members responsible for nursing home placement. *Research in Nursing and Health,* 1994, *17,* 89–98.

Kasper, J. *Aging alone: Profile and projections.* Baltimore, MD: Commonwealth Fund Commission, 1988.

Kelly, T., and Kropf, N. Stigmatized and perpetual parents: Older parents caring for adult children with lifelong disabilities. *Journal of Gerontological Social Work,* 1995.

Kincade, J. E., Rabiner, D. J., Bernard, S. L., Woomert, A., Konrad, T. R., DeFrisse, G. H., and Ory, M. G. Older adults as a community resource: Results from the National Survey of Self-Care and Aging. *The Gerontologist,* 1996, *36,* 474–482.

Kingston, E., and O'Grady-LeShane, R. The effects of caregiving on women's social security benefits. *The Gerontologist,* 1993, *33,* 230–239.

Kivett, V. R. Centrality of the grandfather role among older rural black and white men. *Journals of Gerontology,* 1991, *46,* S250–S258.

Kivnick, H. Grandparents and the life cycle. *Journal of Geriatric Psychiatry,* 1986, *19,* 39–55.

Kosberg, J. I., and Garcia, J. L. Confronting maltreatment of elders by their family. In G. C. Smith, S. Tobin, E. A. Robertson-Tchabo and P. Power (Eds.), *Strengthening aging families: Diversity in practice and policy.* Thousand Oaks, CA: Sage, 1995.

Kosloski, K., and Montgomery, R. The impact of respite use on nursing home placement. *The Gerontologist,* 1995, *35,* 67–74.

Kramer, B. J. Differential prediction of strain and gain among husbands caring for wives with dementia. *The Gerontologist,* 1997b, *37,* 239–249.

Kramer, B. J. Gain in the caregiving experience: Where are we? What next? *The Gerontologist,* 1997a, *37,* 218–232.

Kramer, B. J., and Kipnis. S. Eldercare and work-role conflict: Toward an understanding of gender differences in caregiver burden. *The Gerontologist,* 1995, *35,* 340–347.

Krause, N., and Borawski-Clark, S. Social class differences in social support among older adults. *The Gerontologist,* 1995, *35,* 498–505.

Kruk, E. Grandparent-grandchild contact loss: Findings from a study of "Grandparent Rights" members. *Canadian Journal on Aging,* 1995, *14,* 737–754.

Kutza, E. A., and Keigher, S. M. The elderly "new homeless": An emerging population at risk. *Social Work,* 1991, *36,* 288.

Lawton, M. P., and Nahemow, L. Ecology and the aging process. In C. Eisdorfer and M. P. Lawton (Eds.), *Psychology of adult development and aging.* Washington, DC: American Psychological Association, 1973.

Lechner, J. Predicting future commitment and care for frail parents among employed caregivers. *Journal of Gerontological Social Work,* 1991, *18,* 69–84.

Lee, G. R., and Ellithorpe, E. Intergenerational exchange and subjective well-being among the elderly. *Journal of Marriage and the Family,* 1982, *44,* 217–224.

Leutz, W. N., Capitman, J., Mac Adams, M. and Abrahams, R. *Care for frail elders: Developing community solutions.* Westport, CT: Auburn House, 1992.

Levenson, R., Cartensen, L., and Gottman, J. Long-term marriage: Age, gender and satisfaction. *Psychology and Aging,* 1993, *8,* 301–313.

Litwak, E. *Helping the elderly.* New York: The Guilford Press, 1985.

Litwak, E. *The modified extended family, social networks, and research continuities in aging.* New York: Center for Social Sciences at Columbia University, 1981.

Lopata, H. Z. The interweave of public and private: Women's challenge to American Society. *Journal of Marriage and the Family,* 1993, *55,* 176–190.

Lowenthal, M. F., and Haven, C. Interaction and adaptation. *American Sociological Review,* 1968, *33,* 20–30.

MacRae, H. Strong and enduring ties: Older women and their friends. *Canadian Journal on Aging,* 1996, *15,* 374–392.

Markides, K. S., and Black, S. A. Ethnicity and aging. In R. H. Binstock and C. K. George (Eds.), *Handbook of aging and the Social Sciences* (4th ed.). San Diego: Academic Press, 1996.

Matthews, S. H. Gender and the division of filial responsibility between lone sisters and their brothers. *Journals of Gerontology,* 1995, *50B,* S312–S320.

McFall, S., and Miller, B. H. Caregiver burden and nursing home admission of frail elderly persons. *Journals of Gerontology,* 1992, *47,* S73–679.

Meyers, R., and Souflee, F. Utilizing social support systems in the delivery of social services to the Mexican-American elderly. *Journal of Applied Social Sciences,* 1990–91, *15,* 31–50.

Miller, B., and Cafasso, L. Gender differences in caregiving: Fact or artifact? *The Gerontologist,* 1992, *32,* 498–507.

Miller, B., Campbell, R. T., Davis, L., Furner, S., Giachello, A., Prohaska, T., Kaufman, J. E., Li, M., and Perez, C. Minority use of community long-term care services: A comparative analysis. *Journals of Gerontology,* 1996, *51B,* S70–S81.

Miller, B., Campbell, R., Farron, C., Kaufman, J., and Davis, L. Race, control, mastery, and caregiver distress. *Journals of Gerontology,* 1995, *50B,* S376–S382.

Miller, B., McFall, S., and Campbell, T. Changes in sources of community long-term care among African American and white frail older persons. *Journals of Gerontology*, 1994, 49, S14–S24.

Minkler, M. Building support networks from social isolation. *Generations*, 1986, 10, 46–49.

Minkler, M., and Fuller-Thomson, E. Depression in grandparents raising grandchildren. *Archives of Family Medicine*, 1997, 445–52.

Mittelman, M., Ferris, S., Shalmon, E., Steinberg, G., Ambinder, A., Mackell, J., and Cohen, J. A comprehensive support program: Effect on depression in spouse caregiving of dementia patients. *The Gerontologist*, 1995, 35, 792–802.

Moen, P., and Forest, K. B. Family policies for an aging society: Moving to the twenty-first century. *The Gerontologist*, 1995, 35, 825–830.

Mor-Barak, M., Miller, L., and Syme, L. Social networks, life events and the health of the poor, frail elderly: A longitudinal study of the buffering versus the direct effect. *Family Community Health*, 1991, 14, 1–13.

Mui, A. C. Caregiver strain among black and white daughter caregivers: A role theory perspective. *The Gerontologist*, 1992, 32, 203–212.

Mui, A. C. Caring for frail elderly parents: A comparison of adult sons and daughters. *The Gerontologist*, 1995, 35, 86–93.

Mui, A. C., and Burnette, J. D. A comparative profile of frail elderly persons living alone and those living with others. *Journal of Gerontological Social Work*, 1994, 21, 5–26.

Mutran, E., and Skinner, G. Family support and the well-being of widowed: A black-white comparison. NIH Publ. No. 89–2247, Bethesda, MD: National Institutes of Health, 1989.

National Academy on Aging. *Old age in the 21st century*. Syracuse, NY: Syracuse University, The Maxwell School, 1994.

National Alliance for Caregiving and American Association of Retired Persons. *Family caregiving in the U.S.: Findings from a national survey*. Washington, DC: June 1997.

National Institutes of Health. *Health benefits of pets*. Washington, DC: U.S. Department of Health and Human Services, U. S. Government Printing Office, 1988.

Neugarten, B., and Weinstein, K. The changing American grandparent. *Journal of Marriage and the Family*, 1964, 26, 199–204.

Noelker, L., and Bass, D. Relationships between the frail elderly and informal and formal helpers. In E. Kahana, D. Biegel, and M. Wykle (Eds.), *Family caregiving across the lifespan*. Thousand Oaks, CA: Sage, 1994.

Orodenker, S. Family caregiving in a changing society: The effects of employment on caregiver stress. *Family and Community Health*, 1990, 12, 58–70.

Pavalko, E. K., and Artis, J. E. Women's caregiving and paid work: Causal relationships in late midlife. *Journals of Gerontology*, 1997, 52B, S170–S179.

Pearlin, L. I., Aneshensel, C. S., Mullon, J. T., and Whitlatch, C. J. Caregiving and its social support. In R. H. Binstock and L. K. George (Eds.), *Handbook of aging and the social sciences* (4th ed). San Diego: Academic Press, 1996.

Penrod, J. D., Kane, R. A., Kane, R. C., and Finch, M. D. Who cares? The size, scope, and composition of the caregiver support system. *The Gerontologist*, 1995, 35, 489–499.

Perkinson, M. A., and Rockemann, D. Older women living in a continuing care retirement community: Marital status and friendship formation. In K. Roberto (Ed.), *Relationships between women in later life*. New York: Haworth Press, 1996.

Pillemer, K., and Suitor, J. J. It takes one to help one: Effects of similar others on the well-being of caregivers. *Journals of Gerontology*, 1996, 51B, S250–S257.

Poulshock, S. W., and Diemling, G. T. Families caring for elders in residence: Issues in the measurement of burden. *The Gerontologist*, 1984, 24, 230–239.

Power, P. Understanding intergenerational issues in aging families. In G. C. Smith, S. Tobin, E. A. Robertson-Tchabo and P. Power (Eds.), *Strengthening aging families: Diversity in practice and policy*. Thousand Oaks, CA: Sage, 1995.

Pruchno, R. A., Burant, C. J., and Peters, N. Understanding the well-being of care receivers. *The Gerontologist*, 1997, 37, 102–109.

Quam, J. K., and Whitford, G. Adaptation and age-related expectations of older gay and lesbian adults. *The Gerontologist*, 1992, 32, 367–374.

Qureshi, H., and Walker, A. *The caring relationship: Elderly people and their families*. London: MacMillan, 1989.

Reynolds, W. Marital satisfaction in later life: An examination of equity, equality, and reward theories.

International Journal of Aging and Human Development, 1995, *40,* 155–173.

Riley, M. W., and Riley, J. W. Structural lag: Past and future. In M. W. Riley, R. L. Kahn, and A. Foner (Eds.), *Age and structural lag: Society's failure to provide meaningful opportunities in work, family and leisure.* New York: John Wiley & Sons, 1994.

Roberto, K. Grandparent and grandchild relationships. In T. Brubaker (Ed.), *Family relationships in later life.* Newbury Park, CA: Sage, 1990.

Robinson, L. *A qualitative study of marital strengths in enduring marriages.* Paper presented at the Annual Conference of the National Council on Family Relations, Seattle, WA: 1990.

Robinson, L., and Blanton, P. Marital strengths in enduring marriages. *Family Relations,* 1993, *42(1),* 38–45.

Robison, J., Moen P., and Dempster-McClain, D. Women's caregiving: Changing profiles and pathways. *Journals of Gerontology,* 1995, *50B,* S362–S373.

Rossi, A. S., and Rossi, P. M. *Of human bonding: Parent-child relations across the life course.* New York: Aldine, 1990.

Rubinstein, R. L., Alexander, B. B., Goodman, M. and Luborsky, M. Key relationships of never married, childless older women: A cultural analysis. *The Journals of Gerontology,* 1991, *46,* S270–277.

Saluter, A. *Marital status and living arrangements: March 1994.* Washington, DC: U.S. Bureau of the Census, Current Population Report. Population Characteristics, 1994.

Scharlach, A., and Boyd, S. C. Caregiving and employment: Results of an employee survey. *The Gerontologist,* 1989, *29,* 382–387.

Schulz, R., O'Brien, A., Bookwala, J. and Fleissner, K. Psychiatric and physical mobility effects of dementia caregiving: Prevalence, correlates, and causes. *The Gerontologist,* 1995, *35,* 771–791.

Scott, J. P. Sibling interaction in later life. In T. Brubaker (Ed.), *Family relationships in later life.* Newbury Park, CA: Sage, 1990.

Short, P., and Leon, J. *Use of home and community services by persons age 65 and older with functional difficulties. National Medical Expenditure Survey Research Findings 5.* Rockville, MD: Agency for Health Care Policy and Research, 1995.

Silverstein, M., Chen, X., and Heller, K. Too much of a good thing: Intergenerational social support and the psychological well-being of older parents.

Journal of Marriage and the Family, 1996, *58,* 970–982.

Silverstein, M., and Waite, L. Are blacks more likely than whites to receive and provide social support in middle and old age? Yes, no and maybe so. *Journals of Gerontology,* 1993, *48,* S212–S222.

Simon, M. L., Milligan, M., Guider, R., Puzan, L., Ellano, C., and Atkin, P. Self neglect: The revolving door. In *Silent suffering: Elder abuse in America.* Long Beach, CA: Archstone Foundation, 1997.

Smith, G. C., and Tobin, S. S. Case managers' perceptions of practice with older parents of adults with developmental disabilities. In K. A. Roberto (Ed.), *The elderly caregiver: Caring for adults with developmental disabilities.* Newbury Park, CA: Sage, 1993.

Smith, G. C., Tobin, S. S., and Fullmer, E. M. Assisting older families with lifelong disabilities. In G. C. Smith, S. Tobin, E. A. Robertson-Tchabo, and P. Power (Eds.), *Strengthening aging families: Diversity in practice and policy.* Thousand Oaks, CA: Sage, 1995.

Solomon, J. C., and Marx, J. "To grandmother's house we go": Health and school adjustment of children raised solely by grandparents. The *Gerontologist,* 1995, *35,* 386–394.

Speare, A., and Avery, R. Who helps whom in older parent-child families? *Journals of Gerontology,* 1993, *48,* S64–S73.

Spitze, G., Logan, J., Joseph, G., and Lee, E. Middle generation roles and the well-being of men and women. *Journals of Gerontology,* 1994, *49,* S107–S116.

Stephens, M. A., and Franks, M. Spillover between daughters' role as caregiver and wife: Interference or enhancement? *Journals of Gerontology,* 1995, *50B,* P9–P17.

Stone, R., Cafferata, G., and Sangl, J. *Caregivers of the frail elderly: A national profile.* Washington, DC: U.S. Department of Health and Human Services, 1987.

Stone, R., and Keigher, S. Toward equitable universal caregiver policy: The potential of financial supports for family caregivers. *Aging and Social Policy,* 1994, *6,* 57–76.

Stone, R., and Kemper, P. Spouses and children of disabled elderly: How large a constituency for long-term reform? *The Milbank Quarterly,* 1989, *67,* 485–506.

Stone, R., and Short, P. The competing demand of employment and informal caregiving to disabled elders. *Medical Care*, 1990, *28*, 513–526.

Strom, R. D., Buki, L. P., and Strom, S. K. Intergenerational perceptions of English-speaking and Spanish-speaking Mexican-American grandparents. *International Journal of Aging and Human Development*, 1997, 45, 1–21.

Stull, D., and Scarisbrick-Hauser, A. Never married elderly: A reassessment with implications for long-term care policy. *Research on Aging*, 1989, *11*, 124–139.

Taylor, R. *Aging and supportive relationships among Black Americans: Research on physical and psychosocial health*. New York: Springer, 1988.

Taylor, R., and Chatters, L. Extended family networks of older black adults. *Journals of Gerontology*, 1991, 46, S210–218.

Tennstedt, S. L., Crawford, S., and McKinley, J. Determining the pattern of community care: Is coresidence more important than caregiver relationship? *Journals of Gerontology*, 1993, 48, S74–S83.

Thompson, E., Futterman, A. Gallagher-Thompson, D., Rose, J., and Lovett, S. Social support and caregiving burden in family caregivers of frail elders. *Journals of Gerontology*, 1993, 48, S245–S254.

Thompson, R. A., Tinsley, B. R., Scalora, M. J., and Parke, R. D. Grandparents' visitation rights. *American Psychologist*, 1989, 44, 1217–1222.

Tucker, J. S., Friedman, H. S., Tsai, C. M., and Martin, L. R. Playing with pets and longevity among older people. *Psychology and Aging*, 1995, 10, 3–7.

Uhlenberg, P. The burden of aging: A theoretical framework for understanding the shifting balance of caregiving and care receiving vs. cohort ages. *The Gerontologist*, 1996, 36, 761–767.

U.S. Bureau of the Census. *Population projections of the United States by age, sex, race and Hispanic origin, 1992 to 2050*, Current Population Reports, P-25, No. 1092. Washington, DC: U.S. Government Printing Office, 1992.

U.S. Bureau of the Census. *Statistical Abstract of the United States, 116th Edition*. Washington, DC: U.S. Government Printing Office, 1996.

U.S. Senate Special Committee on Aging. *Aging America: Trends and projections*, Washington, DC: U.S. Government Printing Office, 1992.

Vitaliano, P. P., Schulz, R., Kiecolt-Glaser, J., and Grant, I. Research on physiological and physical concomitants of caregiving: Where do we go from here? *Annals of Behavioral Medicine*, 1997.

Walker, A., Aacock, A., Bowman, S., and Li, F. Amount of care given and caregiving satisfaction: A latent growth curve analysis. *Journals of Gerontology*, 1996, *51B*, P130–P142.

Walker, A. J., and Pratt, C. C. Daughters' help to mothers: Intergenerational aid versus caregiving. *Journal of Marriage and the Family*, 1991, *53*, 3–12.

Ward, R. Marital happiness and household equity in later life. *Sociological Abstracts*, 1992.

Whitbourne, S. K., and Cassidy, E. Achieving intimacy in late-life marriage. In G. C. Smith, S. Tobin, E. A. Robertson-Tchabo, and P. Power (Eds.), *Strengthening aging families: Diversity in practice and policy*. Thousand Oaks, CA: Sage, 1995.

Wilson, V. The consequences of elderly wives caring for disabled husbands. *Social Work*, 1990, *35*, 417–421.

Wolf, D. A., Freedman, V., and Soldo, B. The division of family labor: Care for elderly parents. *The Journals of Gerontology*, 1997, *52B (Special Issue)*, 102–109.

Wood, J., and Parham, I. Coping with perceived burden: Ethnic and cultural issues in Alzheimer's family caregiving. *Journal of Applied Gerontology*, 1990, *9(3)*, 325–339.

Wood, V., and Robertson, J. The significance of grandparenthood. In J. Gubruim (Ed.), *Time, roles and self in old age*. New York: Human Sciences Press, 1976.

Worcester, M., and Hedrick, S. Dilemmas in using respite for family caregivers of frail elders. *Family and Community Health*, 1997, *19*, 31–48.

Wright, L. K. Alzheimer's disease afflicted spouses who remain at home: Can human dialectics explain the findings? *Social Science and Medicare*, 1994, *38*, 1037–1046.

Wright, L. K. The impact of Alzheimer's disease on the marital relationship. *The Gerontologist*, 1991, *31*, 224–237.

Zarit, S., Todd, P., and Zarit, J. Subjective burden of husbands and wives as caregivers: A longitudinal study. *The Gerontologist*, 1986, *26*, 260–266.

Zasloff, R. C., and Kidd, A. H. Loneliness and pet ownership among single women. *Psychological Reports*, 1994, *75*, 747–752.

10

LIVING ARRANGEMENTS AND SOCIAL INTERACTIONS

As we have seen in previous chapters, successful aging depends on physical and functional health, cognitive and emotional well-being, and a level of activity that is congruent with an individual's abilities and needs. Another important element in the aging process is the environment, both social and physical, which serves as the context for activities as well as the stimulus that places demands on the individual, as suggested by the competence model. According to person-environment theories of aging, an individual is more likely to experience life satisfaction in an environment that is congruent with his or her physical, cognitive, and emotional needs and abilities.

Previous chapters have examined the relationships between older persons and their social environment. In this chapter, we focus on diverse *physical* environments and their social and psychological consequences. We examine the impact of the natural and built environment on older persons' social functioning, the influence of a grow-

ing older population on community planning and housing, and the interaction between older persons and their physical environments. Many of the age-related changes in physiological status, sensory function, and cognitive abilities, as well as the diseases and cognitive disorders associated with aging discussed in previous chapters, are affected in important ways by the physical environment. Age-related changes and disease conditions make the average older person more sensitive to characteristics of the setting that may have little effect on the typical younger person. They may impair the older person's ability to adapt to and interact with complex and novel environments. On the other hand, there are many older people who function as well as younger persons do in a wide range of physical surroundings. Observation of these differences in individual responses has led to the concept of *congruence* or *fit* between the environment and the individual. This concept is explored in other person-environment theories below.

PERSON-ENVIRONMENT THEORIES OF AGING

The impact of the environment on human behavior and well-being is widely recognized in diverse disciplines. It was in the early work of psychologist Kurt Lewin and his associates (Lewin, 1935; Lewin, Lippitt, and White, 1939) that the environment as a complex variable entered the realm of psychology. Lewin's field theory (1935, 1951) emphasizes that any event is the result of multiple factors, individual and environmental; or more simply stated, B = f(P,E) (i.e., behavior is a function of personal and environmental characteristics). A change in either the person or the environment produces a change in behavior.

Murray's theory of personality (1938), known as *personology*, provides the earliest framework for a person-environment congruence model. This theory depicts the individual in dynamic interaction with his or her setting, the type of interaction that we have portrayed throughout this book. Thus, the individual attempts to maintain equilibrium as the environment changes. Murray's concepts of *need* and *press* are relevant for theories of person-environment congruence. In Murray's theory of personology, need is viewed as a force in the individual that works to maintain equilibrium by attending and responding to, or avoiding, certain environmental demands (i.e., the concept of press in the P-E model).

According to Murray's and other theories of person-environment congruence, the individual experiences optimal well-being when his or her needs are in equilibrium with characteristics of the environment Thus, for example, an older woman who has spent most of her life on a farm will adjust more readily to a small nursing home in a rural area than to a large facility in an urban center. In contrast, an older couple who have always lived in a large city may be dissatisfied if they decide to spend their retirement years in a small home on a lake far from town; adaptation may be more difficult and perhaps never fully achieved. To the extent that individual needs are not satisfied because of existing environmental characteristics and level of "press," it is hypothesized that the individual will experience frustration and strain.

P-E Congruence Models in Gerontology

The environment plays a more dominant role for older than for younger people, because the older person's ability to control his or her surroundings (e.g., to leave an undesirable setting) is considerably reduced. The individual's range of adaptive behaviors to a stressful environment becomes constrained because of changes in physical, social, and psychological functioning. Therefore, this perspective may be even more useful for understanding older people's behavior than for understanding the behavior of other populations.

Kahana's theory of P-E fit (1975) is the first congruence model developed and empirically tested with older individuals. Kahana hypothesized that incongruence between specific individual needs and environmental press along parallel dimensions produces stress, which in turn requires adaptation, and ultimately affects the older person's well-being. For example, an older person who has a high need for privacy would experience discomfort in a nursing home that offered no opportunities for physical privacy or solitude. Adaptation may consist of modifying this environmental press or the individual's deciding to leave the setting, if circumstances permit. Further stress and discomfort result if the individual's response does not improve the situation. Such stress is compounded for older people whose cognitive and functional capacities are severely impaired, because they are less likely to be able to modify the environment or to leave the situation.

As noted in Chapter 1, a deficiency in environmental press relative to individual needs ("undersupply") has a negative effect, while an "oversupply" of press (i.e., more environmental demands than the individual prefers or is able to manage) can be beneficial if it slightly exceeds the individual's preferences or abilities, but it can create a feeling of stress or overload if it far exceeds one's comfort zone. Empirical tests of this model suggest that the relative effects of undersupply and oversupply depend on the specific aspects of environmental press that are examined. For example, moderate oversupply has been found to be as beneficial as congruence in the areas of privacy, organization, and order; in contrast, an undersupply of stimulation in the individual's immediate environment results in greater well-being than either congruence or an oversupply of stimulation (Kahana, Liang, and Felton, 1980). That is, older people who have as much privacy and order in their lives as they prefer, and those with more privacy and order than they prefer, are equally satisfied with their situation. In contrast, older people whose home environments are less physically stimulating (i.e., in terms of noise, lights, and colors) than they prefer tend to be more satisfied with their environments and with their lives than older people whose home environments are more stimulating than they prefer.

Examples of the differential benefits of oversupply, undersupply, and congruence abound in daily situations. An older woman who lives alone and keeps her home as tidy as she likes may be experiencing more privacy and order than she ordinarily prefers, but she is likely to be just as satisfied as she would be if she had as much privacy and order as she wished. If this level of homeostasis between her preference and the environment is disrupted in the direction of less privacy and order than she prefers (e.g., grandchildren visiting for several weeks, playing with their toys in all the rooms), a situation of undersupply in these two preferences is created. Similar to the older woman in the nursing home described previously, she is then likely to experience frustration, dissatisfaction, and a desire to leave the situation.

The advantage of an environment that provides less stimulation than an individual prefers is that the person can create a desired level of stimulation. In contrast, the overly stimulating environment does not permit an individual to manipulate the situation or to impose a chosen level of stimulation on it. An older man who lives with his daughter and teenage grandchildren in a small home may feel overwhelmed and unable to control the high level of activity (and choice of music!) by the younger family and their friends. In contrast, an older man who lives alone in a quiet neighborhood has greater control over the level of activity in his home, even though the house may seem too quiet and unstimulating at times.

The Competence Model

Another theory of person-environment transactions is the competence model that was described in Chapter 1. This model assumes that the impact of the environment is mediated by the individual's competence level. Competence is defined as "the theoretical upper limit of the individual to function in areas of biological health, sensation-perception, motives, behavior, and cognition" (Lawton, 1975, p. 7). This definition focuses on different aspects of the individual than does Kahana's model. The competence model is more concerned with cognitive and physical capacities; Kahana's model emphasizes the individual's perceived needs and preferences. Environment is also defined somewhat differently by these theorists. In the competence model, "environmental press" refers to the potential of a given environmental feature to influence behavior (for example, the level of stimulation, physical barriers, and lack of privacy).

As competence in cognition, physical strength and stamina, health, and sensory functioning decline with advanced age, the individual would be expected to experience increased problems with high environmental press. Thus, for example, grocery shopping in a large supermarket on a busy Saturday morning may become an overwhelming task for an older person who is having increasing difficulty with hearing and walking. To the extent that the aging person can reduce the level of environmental press, adaptation occurs, and the individual maintains his or her level of well-being. In this example, the older person might decide to shop in a smaller supermarket at nonpeak hours, or to avoid supermarkets altogether and use a neighborhood grocery store or order groceries by phone.

For the older person with Alzheimer's disease or other forms of dementia, it can be difficult to reestablish P-E congruence or to adapt to incongruence. Severe cognitive deterioration may result in an inability to recognize the incongruence experienced between one's needs and the external world. The dementia patient may become behaviorally disturbed unless others intervene to reestablish congruence. This may be accomplished by simplifying the environment in order to make it fit the individual's cognitive competence; for example, by providing cues and orienting devices in the home to help the individual find his or her way without becoming lost or disoriented. The ultimate goal of any modification should be to maximize the older person's ability to negotiate and control the situation, and to minimize the likelihood that the environment will overwhelm the person's competence.

GEOGRAPHIC DISTRIBUTION OF THE OLDER POPULATION

With the trend toward urbanization in the Western world, a smaller proportion of all population subgroups, including those aged 65 and over, currently reside in rural farm communities. The great majority of older persons (76 percent) lived in metropolitan areas (i.e., urban and suburban communities) in 1995, compared with only 5 percent in communities with fewer than 2500 residents. Ethnic minority differences are particularly pronounced in the proportion of older persons in urban centers. Thus, although only 29 percent of white elders live in central cities, 55 percent of all older African Americans and 53 percent of older persons with Spanish surnames reside in these settings. This distribution of older minorities in central cities places them at greater risk for victimization and poor-quality housing. Moreover, 24 percent of the white population, as opposed to only 11 percent of Hispanics, live in medium (2500—10,000) non-metropolitan communities (Administration on Aging, 1995).

There is also a "graying of the suburbs"; that is, a greater proportion of people who moved into suburban developments in the 1950s have now raised their children and have remained in these communities after retirement. Since 1977, increasing numbers of older people have lived in the suburbs than in central cities (see Figure 10.1). Compared to their urban counterparts, elders in suburban communities tend to have higher incomes, are less likely to live alone, and report themselves to be in better functional health. However, the lower density of housing, greater distance to social and health services, and lack of mass transit make it difficult for older suburban dwellers to continue living independently in these suburbs if they become frail or unable to drive. Many suburban communities are responding to their changing resident needs by developing community transit (e.g., vans or special buses) programs to take older and disabled persons to social and health services, senior centers, shopping, and restaurants that are not accessible to pedestrians (Golant and La Greca, 1994; Golant, 1992).

Older persons who live in non-metropolitan areas have lower incomes (near the poverty level)

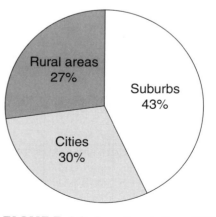

FIGURE 10.1   **Population of Older Americans Living in Urban, Suburban, and Rural Areas**
SOURCE: U.S. Bureau of the Census, Population Profile of the United States: 1993.

and poorer health than those in urban areas. A greater proportion rely on Social Security benefits for their primary source of income. This is particularly true for African Americans who reside in small towns and rural areas, where 41.5 percent have incomes near the poverty level, compared with 28 percent of black elders in metropolitan areas (McLaughlin and Jensen, 1993). Consistent with these findings, limitations in mobility and activity are greater among older people in rural communities and least among elders in suburbs. This may be a function of income and cohort differences. The greater availability of medical and social services (e.g., hospitals, clinics, senior centers, private physicians, transportation) in urban and suburban communities compared to rural settings may also explain these differences. Despite attempts to offset urban-rural differences in health and social services, significant gaps remain in terms of access and availability. Transportation remains a critical problem for older rural residents, both to transport them to medical and social services and to bring service providers to their homes.

Despite their lower income and poorer health, older persons in small communities have been found to interact more with neighbors and friends of the same and younger ages than do those in urban settings. Mr. and Mrs. Howard in the introductory vignette illustrate the positive aspects of smaller communities for older people. These include the greater proximity of neighbors, stability of residents, and shared values and lifestyles. Although proportionately few rural elders have been found to live near their children and generally do not receive financial and social support from them, friendship ties appear to be stronger and more numerous among rural older people. In sum, the data suggest that older persons in rural areas and small towns are more disadvantaged in terms of income, health, and service availability than are those in metropolitan areas. Based on the earlier discussion about the importance of P-E fit for older people, we would predict that those who have a high need for social interaction and have lived most of their lives in rural settings would be

most satisfied in such settings, and would experience severe adaptation problems in more anonymous urban environments.

RELOCATION

Relocation, or moving from one setting to another, represents a special case of P-E incongruence or discontinuity between the individual's competence and the demands of the environment. Anyone who has moved from one city to another, or even from one house to another, has experienced the problems of adjusting to new surroundings and to different orientations, floor plans, and design features in the home. A healthy person can usually adjust quite easily. An older person who has lived in his or her home for many years will require more time to adapt, even if the move is perceived as an improvement to a better, safer, more comfortable home. This is because the individual has adjusted to a particular configuration of P-E fit over a long period of time. The greater the change (e.g., moving from a private house in the suburbs to an assisted living facility in the city), the longer it will take to adapt. A relocation that entails extensive changes in lifestyle, such as a move to a retirement community or to a nursing home with its rules and policies governing the residents, requires even greater adjustments.

Older homeowners are far more likely than younger families to have lived in their current homes for at least 30 years (35 percent versus 4 percent). This difference also occurs among renters (16 percent versus one percent, respectively), and may explain why older people are less likely to relocate (Administration on Aging, 1997; Naifeh, 1993). A survey of AARP members revealed an overwhelming desire by people aged 55 and older to remain in their own homes; 86 percent preferred to remain in the same community. Among those who had moved in the past 10 years, most had moved within the same county (AARP, 1990). Older people who have resided in one place for many years are more likely to experience problems with deciding to move and adjusting to a new residence than those who have moved frequently throughout life and have not become attached to a particular residence. It may seem odd to family, friends, and service providers that an older person does not wish to leave a home that is too large and too difficult to negotiate physically, especially if he or she is frail and mobility-impaired. The problem is compounded if the home needs extensive repairs that an older person cannot afford. Despite such seemingly obvious needs for relocating, it is essential to consider older people's preferences before encouraging them to sell a home that appears to be incongruent with their needs. The emotional meaning of home, in terms of personal identity, history of family life (e.g., marriage, childrearing, and grandparenting), and associations with friends and neighbors, cannot be ignored. Older people who have lived in one place for many years will experience more problems adjusting to a new residence because they have adapted to a particular level of P-E fit over a long time.

In general, older people are less likely to move to a different community than are younger families, but are more likely to move to a different type of housing within the same community. Litwak and Longino (1994, 1987) suggest that older people generally relocate in response to changes in life conditions, such as retirement, or moderate and significant disabilities that make their existing home environments incongruent with their needs. As a result, the type of housing chosen varies according to the reasons for the move. They propose a three-stage model of migration. The first stage occurs most often among the young-old, generally to retirement communities in the sunbelt (this may include "snowbirds" who spend their winters in the warmer climate and the remaining months in their home states). The second stage is often precipitated by chronic illness that limits the older person's abilities to perform ADLs. These moves may be to retirement communities nearby that offer some amenities (e.g., meals, housekeeping), but the older person remains relatively independent. The third move is not experienced by most older adults, but occurs

Retirement communities offer opportunities for social interaction and support.

when severe or sudden disability (e.g., stroke) makes it impossible for the individual to live even semi-independently. In some cases the older person relocates from a sunbelt community to a nursing home near children or other family members. For many others, however, an intermediate stop may be the home of an adult child before the older person relocates to a long-term care facility. In one test of this model, older people in the National Longitudinal Study of Aging were most likely to move to retirement communities if they were moderately disabled. However, as their disabilities became more severe, they were less likely to move to such facilities and to remain in their own homes (receiving some home care) or to move to skilled care facilities (Silverstein and Zablotsky, 1996).

Those who move out of state, often to Florida, California, Arizona or Texas, are generally the young-old and are most likely recent retirees. This is part of a continuing trend that has resulted in a significant increase in the over age 65 population in sunbelt states. Older people may choose to move to communities, often located in sunbelt states, that were not planned for this population (unlike a Sun City or Leisure World, for example), but have become **naturally occurring retirement communities (NORCs)**. Such places have, over the years, attracted large numbers of older people who have "aged in place" there.

The problem of relocation is compounded for the person who is experiencing multiple or severe physical disabilities and dementia. As we have seen in Chapter 6, these individuals have more difficulty coping with stressful life events than healthy older people. Unfortunately, they are often the very people who must relocate to hospitals and skilled nursing facilities, environments that are most incongruent with the needs of many older people. Indeed, the oldest-old are most likely to relocate, often to their children's home or to a location near their children. Such moves are precipitated by widowhood, significant deterioration in health, or a disability.

Concern about adapting to a new setting is one reason that many frail older people who can no longer maintain their own homes are reluctant to move to congregate housing, even though they may recognize that they "should" move to a safer environment. As anyone who has searched for a new home can attest, it requires considerable stamina and determination to find housing and a neighborhood that best fits one's needs and preferences. To the extent that one is frail and unable to muster the energy to search for such housing, it becomes even more difficult to make the transition.

THE IMPACT OF THE NEIGHBORHOOD

All of us live in a neighborhood, whether a college campus, a nursing home, a retirement park, an apartment complex, or the several blocks surrounding our homes. Because of its smaller scale, the neighborhood represents a closer level of interaction and identification than does the community. Results of the American Housing Survey by the U.S. Bureau of the Census reveal that most older people (76 percent) are satisfied with their neighborhoods, even those in poorer neighborhoods (71 percent). Among those who reported problems, noise and traffic concerns topped the list, followed by complaints about

people and crime in the neighborhood (U.S. Bureau of the Census, 1993).

Satisfaction with one's neighborhood increases if amenities such as a grocery store, laundromat, or senior center are located nearby. These services also can provide a social network for an isolated older person. For many older people, however, special van services are necessary to access such services. Older people are willing to travel farther for physician services, entertainment, family visits (although friends need to be nearby for regular visiting to occur), and club meetings, probably because these activities occur less frequently than grocery shopping and laundry. Visits to family members may occur more often, but many older persons are less concerned with proximity in this case than with the chance to maintain family ties. Distance is less important if family members assume responsibility for driving older persons to various places, including their homes. In some cases, family members may prefer visits in the older person's home.

Proximity and frequent contact with families may not be as critical if neighbors and nearby friends can provide the necessary social support for older persons. As discussed in Chapter 9, neighbors play an important role in older people's social networks, especially for those who have lived in the same home for many years. Particularly for older people with children at a geographic distance, neighbors are more readily available to help in emergencies and on a short-term basis, such as contacting an ambulance when needed by the older person or for minor home repairs. It is often more convenient for neighbors than family to drive an older individual to stores and doctors' offices. In addition, neighbors can provide a "security net," as partners in a "Neighborhood Watch" crime-prevention program, or in informally arranged systems of signaling to each other (e.g., pulling open the living room drapes every day by 9:00 A.M. to signal that all is well). This does not mean that neighbors can or should replace family support systems because, as we have seen in previous chapters, families play a central role in assisting their older members, especially those with chronic illnesses or disabilities.

VICTIMIZATION AND FEAR OF CRIME

A commonly held stereotype is that crime affects the older population much more than other age groups. However, national surveys by the U.S. Department of Justice's Bureau of Justice Statistics have consistently revealed that people over age 65 have the lowest rates of all types of victimization than any age group over 12. As Table 10.1 illustrates, people aged 65 and older are 16 times less likely to be victims of violent crime (e.g., assault, robbery, rape, murder), 6 times less likely to experience a personal theft (e.g., purse snatching), and 4 times less likely to be victims of household crimes (e.g., burglary, larceny, motor vehicle theft) than people ages 12 to 24. In fact, these rates have steadily declined since 1974, when the rate of violent crime against older people was 9.0 per 1000.

Nevertheless, some segments of the older population are at greater risk for victimization. The young-old are more likely than those aged 75 and older to face all types of crime; African-American elders are twice as likely as whites to experience violent and household crime. Older Americans with incomes less than $7500 are most likely to become victims of violent crime (twice the rate for those with incomes over $25,000), and least likely to experience theft (half the rate of those with over

$25,000). Not surprisingly, older people living in urban centers are 2.5 times more likely than suburban or rural elders to experience violent crime and theft, and almost twice as likely to become victims of household crime. Contrary to common beliefs, white women aged 65 and older are at lowest risk for violent crimes (with a rate of 3 per 1000 versus 10 per 1000 for older black females and 113 per 1000 for teenage black males). Older African American women are at lowest risk for personal theft, with rates of 9 per 1000 in 1992, compared with 18 per 1000 for older white women, and 106 per 1000 for teenage white males (Bureau of Justice Statistics, 1993).

The conditions under which crimes are committed against older people differ from those of other age groups. For example, they tend to be victimized during the day, by strangers who more often attack alone, in or near their homes, and with less use of weapons (Bureau of Justice Statistics, 1993). This suggests that perpetrators of crimes feel they can easily overtake the older victim without a struggle. The sense of helplessness against an attacker may make many older persons more conscious of their need to protect themselves, and may produce levels of fear that are incongruent with the statistics about their relative vulnerability to violent crimes. It is true, however, that even a purse snatching can be traumatic for older women, because of the potential for injury and hip fractures during a struggle and because of the economic consequences for women on limited incomes. It can also disrupt the victim's sense of competence and subjective well-being. Older women are particularly vulnerable to a fear of crime, even though they are least likely to become victims as described above. While it may seem irrational, such fear of crime is an important determinant of older women's behavior that will require more societal efforts to empower and strengthen their environmental competence. For example, older women can benefit from education in self-defense and from support networks in their neighborhood. In sum, the significance of the fear of crime is not whether or not it is war-

TABLE 10.1 **Victimization Rates per 1000 Persons or Households, 1992**

AGE	VIOLENT CRIME	PERSONAL THEFT	HOUSEHOLD CRIME
12–24	64.6	112.7	309.3
25–49	27.2	71.2	200.2
50–64	8.5	38.3	133.0
65+	4.0	19.5	78.5

SOURCE: Bureau of Justice Statistics, 1993.

ranted, but the effect it has on older people's psychological well-being (Hollway and Jefferson, 1997; Bazargan, 1994).

In response to the problems of crime, "Neighborhood Watch" and other programs encourage neighbors to become acquainted and to look out for signs of crimes against neighbors and their homes. Such neighborhood crime prevention programs allow older people to have access to their neighbors; they break down the perception of neighbors as strangers and the fear of being isolated in a community, both of which foster fear of crime. Some large communities have established special police units to investigate and prevent crimes against older people; these units have helped to improve the satisfaction and confidence of older crime victims. Improvements in the built environment can also create a sense of security. For example, brighter and more uniform street lighting, especially above sidewalks and in alleys, can deter many would-be criminals.

Older people also have been found to be more susceptible to economically devastating crimes such as fraud and confidence games. Police departments in major cities have reported higher rates of victimization against older people by con-game artists and high-pressure salesmen. Medical quackery and insurance fraud are also more common, perhaps because many older people feel desperate for quick cures or are overwhelmed by medical care costs. They therefore become easy prey for unscrupulous people who exploit them by offering the "ultimate medical cure" or the "most comprehensive insurance coverage" at unbelievably cheap rates. Older people are also more vulnerable to commercial fraud by funeral homes, real estate brokers, and investment salespeople. Door-to-door salespeople of hearing aids have been investigated for fraud, often because the "hearing tests" they offer are inadequate and costly. Perhaps more important than the financial consequences of fraud, such salespeople prevent the older person from seeking appropriate professional services for hearing problems, medical conditions, investments, and other transactions.

HOUSING PATTERNS OF OLDER PEOPLE

In this section, we review the residential arrangements of older persons, including independent housing, planned housing and retirement communities, congregate housing, and nursing homes. We also discuss newer models of long-term care for older people who have physical and cognitive impairments. Policies that govern long-term care options are discussed in Chapter 16.

Independent Housing

Older people are more likely than any other age group to occupy housing that they own free and clear of a mortgage. Over 76 percent of all dwelling units in which older persons reside are owned by them. These include condominiums, mobile homes, and even congregate facilities that offer "life care" for retired persons; but by far the greatest proportion of owned units are single-family homes. As shown in Table 10.2, there is much variation in homeownership among the older population. Married couples, non-Hispanic whites, especially those with an annual income of $25,000 or more, and

TABLE 10.2 Characteristics of Older Homeowners

CHARACTERISTIC		PERCENT WHO OWN HOME
Age:	56–64	80
	all 65 +	77
	all 85 +	67
Marital Status:	Married	31
	Living Alone	64
Income:	≥ $25,000	91
	≤ $10,000	61
Community Type:	Rural	86
	Suburban	80
	Central Cities	65

SOURCE: Pynoos and Golant (1996); Golant and La Greca (1994).

those residing in rural communities are most likely to own their homes. However, the cost of utilities, taxes, insurance, and repair and maintenance can be prohibitive because their homes tend to be older and poorly constructed (Administration on Aging, 1997). In addition, the older person's current level of competence may be incongruent with the physical environment, and they may require a more appropriate housing situation.

One solution to this dilemma is the growing number of homesharing programs around the country (Danigelis and Fengler, 1991). These are community-based programs that are operated out of the Area Agency on Aging or other governmental or voluntary service agency. Their goal is to assist older persons who own their own homes and wish to rent rooms to others in exchange for rental income or services, such as housekeeping and assistance with other chores. The role of a homesharing agency is to serve as a "matchmaker," selecting appropriate homesharers for each older person with a home. These services have been especially popular near universities and colleges, where students can find low-cost or free living arrangements and can benefit from intergenerational contacts. The disadvantage of such programs is that, like any other living situation where dissimilar and unrelated persons share housing, differences in values and lifestyles may be too great to bridge. This is particularly true when a younger person moves into an older person's home. As a result, most intergenerational homesharing arrangements are short-lived. The success of such programs depends on appropriate matches between potential homesharers. Generally, there are more older people with homes to share than younger people wanting rooms. In some cases, a group of older people may choose to share a home.

Another implication of prolonged home ownership is that many of these houses are old, with inadequate weatherproofing and other energy-saving features, and with large indoor and outdoor spaces that are difficult to maintain. Exposed wiring, lack of sufficient outlets, and worn-out oil furnaces can be hazards. Older homeowners in

metropolitan areas, especially the oldest-old, Hispanics, and African Americans living below the poverty line, are more likely to live in housing with physical deficiencies, such as inadequate heating and cooling systems, and plumbing and structural problems. These differences are illustrated in Figure 10.2 (Gaberlavage and Citro, 1997; Golant and La Greca, 1995).

It is not unusual to hear news stories during winter months of fires starting in older homes due to faulty wiring, overloaded circuits, and the use of space heaters because of an inadequate furnace. The latter situation is particularly troublesome for older persons who have difficulties in maintaining body heat and prefer warmer ambient temperatures (see Chapter 3). Many communities have attempted to prevent these problems by providing free or low-cost home repairs for low-income elders and special assistance to all older clients to make their homes more energy efficient (e.g., providing no-interest loans for weatherproofing and installing storm windows). Major cities that have experienced sudden increases in their electricity and natural gas rates have also developed programs to aid low-income people of all ages. These services can be invaluable for helping older people to maintain their independence in their own homes.

Another way to help older people remain in their homes and pay for needed repairs and upkeep is through "home equity conversion mortgages," or "reverse mortgages." These first became available in the 1980s through mortgage banks, and some are backed by the federal government. It is a useful option for people aged 62 and older who are "house-rich but cash-poor." It has been estimated that 83 percent of older people have paid off their mortgages, and the average amount of equity exceeds $55,000 for these homes. This tends to be true for older persons of all income levels (Hobbs and Damon, 1996). In effect, such programs lend the older person money via a credit line on their mortgage. The title is retained by the lender, or the lender owns part of the home; the older person receives a monthly payment (or annuity) from the lender and still lives in

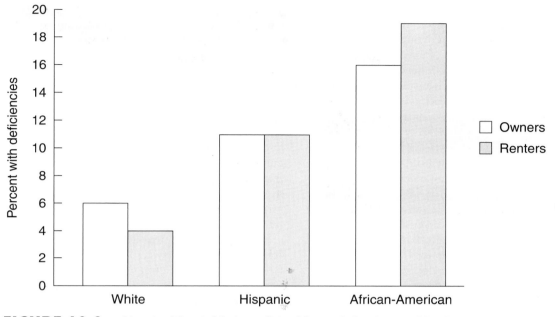

FIGURE 10.2   Housing That is Moderately and Severely Inadequate* by Owner and Ethnic/Racial Group (1993)

*"Inadequate" is defined as regular problems with plumbing, heating, leaks, signs of rodents, and non-functioning kitchen sink, refrigeration, or burners inside the structure for exclusive use of unit.

SOURCE: Gaberlavage and Citro, 1997.

the house. This can mean an additional $1000 or more each month for many older homeowners. When the older person dies or sells the house, the lender generally deducts the portion of the mortgage that has been paid, including interest, as well as a portion (usually about 10 percent) of the home's appreciated value or equity since the date of the reverse mortgage.

Since 1989, HUD has had the authority to offer insurance for reverse mortgages, available to homeowners age 62 and older with little or no mortgage debt remaining. With insurance from the FHA, numerous lenders across the country have been selected to provide reverse mortgages for older persons. There is some concern about the long-term risks of reverse mortgages for the lender; currently, there are no guidelines for the duration of such mortgage plans. For example,

what if the older homeowner outlives the home's equity? Lenders do not want to evict such a person, but at the same time they do not want to lose their investment. In addition, homeowners must consider the initial costs of such a mortgage. These include a 2 percent mandatory mortgage insurance fee, a loan origination fee, and standard closing costs. Together with interest, a borrower could pay an annualized credit-line rate of 13 to 17 percent for this loan. For older people with other assets to use as collateral, other types of loans may be more cost-effective than a reverse mortgage.

Planned Housing

During the past 40 years, federal and local government agencies and some private organizations (such as religious groups) have developed planned housing projects specifically for older persons; these have included subsidized housing for low-income elders and age-segregated housing for middle- and upper-income older persons. Gerontologists have attempted to understand the effects of the quality and type of housing on older persons' satisfaction level and behavior following relocation to such housing environments. It appears that planned housing can indeed improve the quality of life for low-income elders, but it is difficult to generalize to other older populations, particularly those of higher income status. The problem of where to locate planned housing projects for older persons has no simple solution. As stated earlier in the discussion of neighborhood characteristics, older people are most likely to use services such as a senior center or laundromat if they are on site. Public transportation should also be easily accessible in these settings. If a particular site is not already near a bus stop, this convenience should be arranged with the local public transportation authority. Alternatively, larger developments provide van services for their older residents to obtain medical and social services, as well as planned excursions to theaters, museums, parks, and shopping centers.

Developers of planned housing for older people must also take into account such factors as whether the area is zoned for residential, commercial, or industrial use. The topography of this site, crime rates, and security of the community are important considerations, as is the need to integrate the housing project into the neighborhood. The last item is especially crucial. In a housing project that is architecturally distinct from the rest of the neighborhood (e.g., a tall, multilevel structure in the midst of single-family homes, or a sprawling "retirement community" on the edge of an industrial area), residents are likely to experience a lack of fit with their environment and to feel isolated from the larger neighborhood. The lack of fit may also be felt by the residents of the larger neighborhood, who often reject the presence of an entire community of older people in their midst, even if the project is architecturally consistent with other neighborhood buildings. Both physical and psychological barriers are created by walls, vegetation, and architectural features that distinguish a housing project from its surroundings, adding to the older residents' sense of separation from the neighborhood.

Congregate Housing

Congregate housing differs from planned housing and single-family residences in its provision of communal services, a central kitchen, and a dining room for all residents. Some congregate facilities also provide housekeeping, social, and health services. Others may have space for such services, but do not have established services on site, including congregate meals, home health care, and transportation services. In 1970, when the first federally supported congregate housing act was passed, these services could not be paid through HUD programs that financed the construction, but space for such services was provided. Developers and planners assumed that tenants would be charged for these additional services, or that the services would be subsidized by local agencies. Recent evidence suggests that such services have indeed become necessary, as the residents of congregate housing have reached advanced old age. To the extent that a housing site has the space and resources to plan for such needs in the future, people are more likely to remain in such settings and to avoid or delay relocation to a skilled care facility, such as a nursing home. Congregate housing is a desirable option for many older persons who do not need skilled nursing care but prefer having meals and some personal care services. Probably the most important feature of congregate housing is the availability of prepared meals, which not only provide a balanced and nutritional diet but also offer regular opportunities for socializing. Residents may also eat some meals in their own units; many congregate buildings provide each unit with a small kitchen (often a refrigerator, a range, and a few kitchen cabinets). The opportunity to eat in a congregate dining facility *or* to cook in their own kitchen is an important choice for many older persons.

The growth of congregate housing is due in great part to the interest of private non-profit and profit-making corporations. However, despite their increased numbers, congregate sites are inadequate in many regions of the country and for specific segments of the aging population. Consistent with reductions in public funding generally, federal and local governments have significantly reduced their construction of new congregate facilities for low-income seniors since 1980. As a result, the number of congregate housing units for middle- and upper-income older persons has increased, but low-income elders who need housing subsidies have not benefited from this growth.

Continuous Care Retirement Communities

There has been a growth in the number of *multi-level facilities* or **continuous care retirement communities (CCRCs)** for older persons. These housing projects offer a range from independent to congregate living arrangements and intermediate to skilled care facilities. Such options are more widely available in housing that is purchased, less so for rental housing. As the number of oldest-old persons has increased, owners and administrators of facilities that do not provide extensive nursing services have become increasingly concerned. They realize that some of their residents will eventually need to move to other facilities; they are also more aware that potential buyers of units in these facilities would prefer to have a range of services and housing options on site. Such alternatives are often of particular concern for couples, who face the likelihood that one partner will require skilled nursing care eventually. When several levels of care are available at one site, older couples can feel assured that they will be able to remain near each other, even if one becomes institutionalized.

Many housing plans for older people that offer options in living arrangements have *lifecare contracts*, *life lease contracts*, or *founders' fees*. That is, the older person must pay an initial entry fee, often quite substantial, based on projections of life expectancy and on the size of his or her living quarters. In the case of a lifecare contract, the individual who eventually needs increased care is provided nursing home care without paying more for these services. This is a form of self-insurance for small groups of older adults that provides them with institutional and home-based care as needed. With a life lease contract or a founders' fee, the individual is guaranteed lifetime occupancy in the apartment. However, in the case of life lease contracts, if more expensive care is required, such services are generally not provided by the facility, and the older person must give up the apartment and find a nursing home. Lifecare, life lease, and founders' fees contracts also charge monthly fees, but the monthly costs are generally not as high as those in facilities that rely only on month-to-month payments. The advantage of lifecare contracts and founders' fees is that the individual is guaranteed lifetime care; this is important given the actuarial tables of life expectancy for those who reach age 65 (another 17 years) and those who reach 70 (another 13 years). The older person who pays month-to-month may use up all of his or her life savings long before dying if skilled care is needed. In contrast, the option of a lifecare contract may provide a sense of security for the older person who can pay a large lump sum. The individual is taking the chance that he or she will eventually need higher levels of care, so the costs are averaged out over a long period. For those who die soon after moving in, some facilities refund part of the entry fee to the family; in many cases, however, there is a policy of not refunding any portion of this fee. Obviously, the ability to purchase these contracts is limited to the small percentage of older people who have considerable cash assets. Indeed, older persons in these facilities are better educated and have greater financial resources than the general population of elders.

Considering the high cost of CCRCs with lifecare contracts or founders' fees, it is useful to understand the motivations of older people who enter into these contracts. The most frequently cited reasons for joining appear to be access to services that permit independent living and, for married respondents, the opportunity to continue to live together if one spouse needs institutionalization. A potential risk for older people who enter into a lifecare contract is that the facility will declare bankruptcy. In an attempt to avoid this, many states that license lifecare housing projects require providers to establish a trust fund for long-term care expenses.

NURSING HOMES

Many people who are unfamiliar with the residential patterns of older people mistakenly assume that the majority live in **nursing homes**; however, the actual proportion is far smaller. According to the U. S. Bureau of the Census (1993), 5.1 percent of the 65+ population occupied nursing homes, congregate care, assisted living, and board-and-care homes in 1990. The proportion in nursing homes is somewhat lower (4.2 percent) (Sirrocco, 1994). Estimates of an older person's risk of admission to a nursing home run as high as 50 percent and range from 30 percent for men to 50 percent for women. The rate of nursing-home use increases with age; from 1.4 percent of the young-old to 24.5 percent of the oldest-old. Almost 50 percent of those who are 95 and older live in nursing homes (U.S. Bureau of the Census, 1993). Each year more than 1 million older persons leave long-term care institutions, almost evenly divided among discharges to the community, transfers to other health facilities, and death. Therefore, the statistic of 4 to 5 percent is a cross-sectional snapshot of the institutional population that does not take account of movement into and out of long-term care facilities (Wiener, Illston, and Hanley, 1994; Manton, Corder, and Stallard,1993). However, with the increase in alternative long-term care options, such as assisted living and adult family homes, there is already a major change in the rates of nursing-home admissions. More older people, even those with multiple physical and cognitive impairments, are selecting or are placed in long-term care facilities other than nursing homes, while many others receive health care in their own homes. This has resulted in a decline in the number of nursing homes in the United States from 19,100 in 1985 to 16,700 in 1995. However, the total number of beds and average number of beds per home have both increased. This reflects a decline in the number of smaller nursing homes (NCHS, 1997).

The United States actually has lower rates of institutionalization than other developed countries have. The smallest proportion is in Germany and Japan (about 4 percent each); the highest rates are in Canada (8.7 percent), Sweden (9.6 percent), and Switzerland (9 percent) (Doty, 1988). In contrast, less-developed countries such as Greece, Turkey, and Argentina have fewer than 1 percent of their older elders in long-term care facilities. This may be because fewer facilities are available in these countries, the costs are too high for families and/or governments, or social attitudes deter potentially needed institutionalization. In some countries, such as Japan and Germany, hospitals provide both long-term and acute care, so the total number of institutionalized older persons is much higher.

THE PRIMARY FACTORS THAT DETERMINE INSTITUTIONALIZATION ARE:

- Age (85 or older)
- Being female
- A recent hospital admission
- Living in retirement housing rather than being a homeowner

- Not married or not living with a spouse
- Having no daughters or siblings nearby
- Having some degree of cognitive impairment
- One or more problems with instrumental activities of daily living

SOURCES: Freedman, 1996; Greene and Ondrich, 1990.

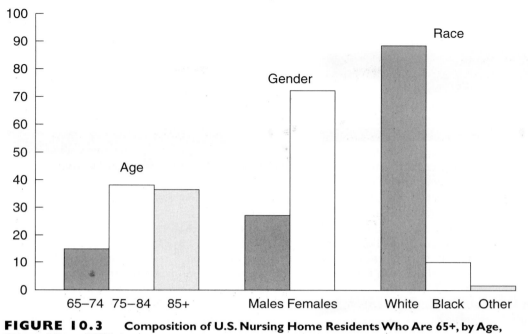

FIGURE 10.3 **Composition of U.S. Nursing Home Residents Who Are 65+, by Age, Sex, and Race: 1995.**

SOURCE: Strahan, 1997.

The lower rates of nursing-home admissions in the United States will probably continue into the twenty-first century, despite the significant growth in the oldest-old population. Nevertheless, nursing homes are often the best choice for the oldest, most frail, and most dependent segment of the population. As a result of more options prior to choosing a nursing home, typical nursing-home residents today are much sicker and require more intensive services than their counterparts 20 to 30 years ago (Vladeck and Feuerberg, 1995–1996). The average age of nursing home residents is 82, and, as illustrated by Figure 10.3, women are disproportionately represented. They make up 70 percent of this population; 66 percent are widowed or divorced, about 40 percent have a diagnosis of dementia, and 59 percent require assistance with four or more ADLs (Lair and Lefkowitz, 1990).

The gender differential in nursing homes is due to women's longer life expectancy, their greater

risk of multiple chronic illnesses, and their greater likelihood of being unmarried. The last factor is a critical one, since the absence of a spouse or other caregiver is a major predictor of institutionalization, and is discussed in greater detail in Chapter 13 (Freedman, 1996; Jette, Tennstedt, and Crawford, 1995).

In a 6-year follow-up of 634 persons aged 70 and over who had some disabilities at baseline, 41 percent had died and 23 percent had entered a nursing home for some time in those 6 years. Those whose primary caregiver was a male were more than twice as likely to enter a nursing home as elders with a female caregiver. Living with the primary caregiver reduced the risk of institutionalization by one-half. The use of formal services such as adult day care reduced the risk for cognitively impaired older persons, but increased the risk for physically frail persons by a factor of 2.5 when both formal and informal care were required. This apparent dichotomy may mean that formal services can relieve the burden of caregiving in cases of dementia (thereby postponing or preventing nursing-home placement). In contrast, physically disabled older people who need both formal and informal care may have too many impairments to live in the community, even when multiple services are brought into their homes. These elders represent the segment of the population that will continue to require nursing homes in the future, even with the growth of other, less restrictive and less costly long-term care alternatives (Jette, Tennstedt, and Crawford, 1995). The crucial role played by a live-in caregiver (most often a partner or adult child) in preventing or delaying institutionalization is supported by other studies that have found up to 25 percent of nursing-home placements were precipitated by the death or serious illness of the primary caregiver (Tennstedt, Crawford, and McKinley, 1993).

The typical resident has lived in a nursing home for more than a year. Nursing-home stays of 90 days or less account for only 15 percent of all nursing-home days nationally, whereas almost 45 percent of nursing-home days are represented by people who have stayed more than 2 years. Indeed, it has been estimated that 66 percent of all nursing-home expenditures are accounted for by people who stay more than 2 years (Pawlson, 1989). Nevertheless, daily costs for long-term care are considerably less than for acute care.

About 88 percent of nursing-home residents are white, compared to 9.7 percent who are African American, 3 percent who are Hispanic, American Indian, or Asian American (Strahan, 1997). This underrepresentation of ethnic minority groups appears to reflect cultural differences in the willingness to institutionalize older persons, greater availability of family supports, or discrimination in admission policies (generally unofficial) against ethnic minorities (Kart, 1993). It may also reflect the dearth of facilities that address the unique needs of these ethnic minorities, thereby forcing them to enter nursing homes that are incongruent with their cultural needs. In some communities with large ethnic minority populations, nursing homes have been built under the auspices of nonprofit organizations or religious groups. For example, in San Francisco and Seattle, Japanese and Chinese American elders can enter nursing homes operated and staffed by people who speak the same language as the older person and serve culturally specific foods. In most of the Chinese facilities, employees can communicate with residents in many dialects of Chinese.

Most nursing homes (about 66 percent) are *proprietary* or *for-profit,* and thus operate as a business that has a goal of making a profit for the owners. The number of nursing homes owned by large multifacility chains is increasing dramatically. Another 8 percent are owned by federal, state, or local governments. *Nonprofit* homes (26 percent of the total) are generally sponsored by religious or fraternal groups (Strahan, 1997). Although making a profit is not their goal, they must be self-supporting. These are governed by a board or advisory group, rather than owners or investors as in the case of proprietary homes. Although instances of reimbursement fraud by proprietary homes have been highly publicized, the terms *proprietary* and *nonprofit* do not designate type or quality of care, but rather how the home is governed and how its earnings are distributed. Although most studies have not found differences in the quality of care provided by different types of facilities, higher hospitalization rates have been found among residents of proprietary homes (Freiman and Murtaugh, 1993).

Nursing homes must follow federal guidelines to become certified by Medicare and to meet regulations that are imposed by each state. Such federal regulations have improved the quality of care in nursing homes. For example, after the 1987 legislation to reform nursing home care was passed, $2 billion was saved in 254 nursing homes nationwide because of fewer emergency hospitalizations and decreased use of catheters and of restraints (Hawes, et al., 1997). Most nursing homes are not certified for Medicare, however. This is because Medicare does not reimburse for long-term care or maintenance, but only for short-term care (i.e., up to 100 days of rehabilitation following hospitalization). As a result,

Medicaid is the primary payer of nursing-home care. Among those who enter a nursing home after age 65, 27 percent start and end their time in the facility as Medicaid recipients; another 14 percent who begin as private pay residents spend down their assets and become Medicaid users (Spillman and Kemper, 1995). Many older people with incomes below a specified level (varying across states) would not be able to afford nursing home care without Medicaid assistance. Under this program, nursing homes are reimbursed according to the level of care required by each resident. For example, residents who need more hands-on care by diverse staff are billed at a higher rate. Nursing personnel within the facility determine the level of care required on the basis of the older person's abilities to perform various ADLs and their mental status.

The decision to enter a nursing home is often a hurried one, in reaction to a crisis, such as the older person's imminent discharge from the hospital. Hospital staff who work with patients and families to plan the patient's discharge frequently pressure family members to make their decision after physicians and other hospital staff press them to "get those hospital beds open." This may mean that the discharge planner accepts the first available nursing-home bed rather than wait for the best possible placement. Unfortunately, this disruption in a frail older person's life may occur repeatedly; over half of those admitted to a nursing home are discharged within 3 months, and many of them are transferred to a hospital (just 33 percent return to the community), only to die there or return to the same or another nursing home (Kane and Kane, 1990). Increasingly, with the development of options such as home care, assisted living, and adult foster care (discussed below), the choice becomes more complicated and an older person who needs long-term care often needs more time to consider the "ideal" placement. Even when there is time to plan for placement, few older people willingly choose to live in a nursing home. Many enter after receiving informal care from family members, formal home care services, and, in some cases, after a stay in facilities such as assisted living or adult family homes. Nevertheless, it is important for older people and their relatives to realize that nursing home life offers some advantages over other types of long-term care. These include increased social contact, accessible social activities, intensive rehabilitation services that other long-term care options cannot provide, and relief from the stress of caregiving on family. Although the media tends to publicize instances of abuse and violation of regulations, there are many excellent nursing homes. Increased efforts to improve nursing homes and the development of innovative options, such as subacute care for post-hospital discharge residents, hospice care for terminally ill persons, and special care units (SCUs) for residents with cognitive or severe physical impairments, signal an important change in skilled nursing facilities (Mor, Banaszak-Holl, and Zinn, 1995–1996). Increasingly, residents of nursing homes and their families are having more influence over their lives, through resident councils, patients' bills of rights, nursing home ombudsmen, and the advocacy of groups such as the National Citizens Coalition for Nursing Home Reform (NCCNHR). In its resident surveys, this organization has found that a major concern of cognitively intact older people is to be involved in decisions about their daily lives in the facility. Through such efforts and through increased gerontological training, nursing home staff are also becoming more sensitive about ways to involve family, friends, and members from the larger community in their policies, procedures, and activities.

RECENT DEVELOPMENTS IN LONG-TERM CARE

Since the late 1980s, in response to perceived needs for more cost-effective long-term care options, there has been a dramatic growth in assisted living, adult foster home (or adult family homes), home care, respite care, and adult day care. One reason for this is the trend toward state licensure and Medicaid reimbursement, albeit at lower levels, for these alternatives. **Assisted living** is seen by its advocates as a new, more humane model of housing that is aimed at elders who need assistance with personal care (e.g., bathing and taking medications) and with some ADLs, but who are not so severely impaired physically or cognitively that they need 24-hour attention (Kane and Wilson, 1993). These facilities are generally smaller than the average nursing home. Most provide congregate meals in a common dining room, as well as housekeeping, laundry, and help with some activities of daily living. Staff often include at least one nurse, a social worker, and one or more people to provide case management services. Access to health care is provided for specific tenants as needed (often contracting the services of physicians, physical therapists, mental health specialists). As a result, staffing costs are lower than in nursing homes, thereby keeping the average cost of assisted living lower.

It is important not to place assisted living in a "continuum of care," since this type of facility can generally serve older people with a wide range of

Chore workers and other home and community-based services can help older people remain in their homes.

disabilities, many of whom are now in nursing homes. Many states are exploring the option of **Medicaid waivers** for assisted living, and some, such as Oregon and Washington, have implemented programs that encourage the use of assisted living and other long-term care options. However, most people in assisted living facilities today are private pay residents. Many who move out do so because they have run out of funds and must turn to nursing homes that are covered by Medicaid, even though they might benefit from the greater autonomy and self-care at assisted living facilities (Kane and Wilson, 1993). As more states provide Medicaid waivers, it is anticipated that greater congruence can be achieved between needs of specific elders and their housing needs.

Adult foster care (AFC) or adult family homes (AFH) are another alternative to nursing homes for older persons who do not need the 24-hour medical care provided by skilled care facilities. AFC is generally provided in a private home by the owners of the home who may have some health care training but are not required to be professionals in the field. These homes are licensed to house up to 5 or 6 clients. The owner and, in some cases auxiliary staff, provide housekeeping, personal care, and some delegated nursing functions, such as injecting medications and changing dressings on wounds if they have been trained and certified by a registered nurse. Medicaid reimbursement rates for AFC are one-half to two-thirds the rates paid to nursing homes. This works well for residents who do not require heavy care (e.g., bedridden or with severe behavioral problems due to dementia). However, for more frail older clients, or for those who have "aged in place" (i.e., have become more impaired while living in that AFC), the reimbursement rates do not reflect the time and effort required of caregivers in these facilities. For this reason, a recent survey of 290 AFH providers in Washington revealed high levels of dissatisfaction with reimbursement rates and complaints that case managers were not disclosing the severity of clients' needs when referring them to AFH (Kiyak, 1998).

This trend toward placing more impaired older persons in AFC or AFH is driven by states' efforts to control the costs of long-term care, as well as societal pressures toward a social rather than medical model of long-term care. Evidence of the problems inherent in such motivations, however, is provided by an analysis of 1032 nursing home residents and 279 AFC residents in Oregon. After one year, 79 percent of the former and 88 percent of the latter group were still alive. However, while 83 percent of the survivors in nursing homes still lived there at follow-up, only 53 percent of those in AFC were still there. The remainder had relocated to nursing homes (29 percent) or other living situations. By analyzing the 12-month change in ADL scores, the researchers concluded that almost all nursing home residents had been appropriately placed, compared with only 64 percent of AFC residents. That is, residents of AFCs who were frail at baseline generally declined more in their ADLs than did comparable residents of nursing homes. These individuals would have been more appropriately placed in nursing homes. Such differences may reflect the paucity of rehabilitation services and a greater emphasis on resident autonomy in AFC. Older clients in AFC can generally decide for themselves whether or not to take their medications and to exercise as much or as little as they want, unlike the more structured nursing home schedule. In sum, it appears that AFC works well for the less-severely impaired older person, but not for those with multiple ADL limitations (Stark, Kane, Kane, and Finch, 1995).

SERVICES TO AID OLDER PEOPLE IN THE COMMUNITY

In recent years, the term **long-term care** has evolved from an emphasis on purely institutional care to a broad range of services to help older adults in their own homes, in other community settings, and in nursing homes. Under this broader definition, homemaker services, nutrition programs, adult day care, and home health care are all part of long-term care. Indeed, for every person 65 and older residing in a nursing home, there are nearly four times as many living in the community who need some form of long-term care (U.S. Senate Special Committee, 1992).

Home Care

Over the last decades, there has been an increase in the number of federal, state, and local services to help older people maintain their independence for as long as possible and in the least restrictive environment feasible, thereby assisting the older person to maintain P-E congruence. Such support services include **home health care,** assistance with personal care, home maintenance, hot meals delivered to the home, and occasional or daily trips to an adult day health program. As the population of older people has increased, as newer cohorts of older adults have adopted the values of "aging in place," and as third-party payers (e.g., Medicare) have searched for alternatives to the escalating costs of hospitals and nursing homes, there has been a dramatic growth in home care services. Medicare reimburses "home health care" services, defined as skilled nursing or rehabilitation benefits that are provided in the patient's own home and prescribed by a physician. Since 1989, when a class-action lawsuit resulted in a more flexible interpretation of Medicare home care regulations, agencies that provide home care have been able to expand their visits and services to beneficiaries. For this reason, home care is now the fastest-growing component of personal health care expenditures, increasing by 20 percent per year since 1991. Not surprisingly, given the nature of health, personal, and household care provided, the average home health client is a woman aged 70 and has 1.7 ADL impairments. The oldest-old generally receive more visits on average than any other age group, about four times as many as for those aged 65–66 (Hughes, et al., 1997; Hughes, 1996).

Home health care is far less expensive than acute (hospital) care, about 40 percent less than nursing homes, and comparable to adult foster care or adult family homes. Recent studies have examined the costs and impact of home care on hospitalization rates among users. In one study, home health agencies that were Medicare-certified recorded the actual costs of providing an array of services (e.g., skilled nursing care, occupational therapy, physical therapy, home dialysis, durable medical equipment, hospice, homemaker). A U-shaped curve was found to be the best model of cost-efficiency; that is, a scope of 8 to 10 different services appears to be ideal for reducing the average cost of services provided by a home health agency. Those that provide fewer or more services do so at a higher cost per visit; this suggests that these agencies can function most economically if they provide an array of services, ideally between 8 and 10 (Gonzales, 1997). Another study examined hospital-use data among home health clients in a meta-analysis of 20 earlier studies. These studies provided a large number of home health programs and clients on which to test outcomes. When home health was defined strictly as the delivery of nursing, medical, and support services in the home of a terminally ill or chronically ill older person, a reduction of 2.5 to 6 hospital days was found among home health users, as compared to similar patient populations that did not use home health care. These results support the cost-effectiveness of home health care in curtailing the use of far more expensive acute care (Hughes, 1997).

As demand has increased, home care agencies have expanded their services beyond health care to include a broad array of "home and community-based services" (HCBS). Assistance such as chore services to maintain the home, personal care to help the person perform ADLs, home-delivered meals, and automatic safety response systems can help older people "age in place" in their own homes. Other HCBS options, such as adult day care and case management, are offered in community settings; they provide respite to family caregivers and opportunities for social interaction for isolated elders. These additional HCBS are not covered by Medicare, but by Title XX and Title III of the Older Americans Act. These funds (dis-cussed in greater detail in Chapter 15) make each state's unit on aging (SUA) responsible for their delivery. SUAs, in turn, designate Area Agencies on Aging (AAAs) to develop and administer these services at the local level, sometimes in the form of contracts to local providers.

Adult Day Care

Another long-term care option that allows the older person to remain at home and receive some health and social services is **Adult day care (ADC).** In this case, users attend a local ADC center one or more times per week, for several hours each day. ADC goes beyond senior centers in providing structured health and social services for older people with cognitive impairments such as dementia and those with functional impairments due to stroke and multiple chronic illnesses. Some ADCs are based on a health rehabilitative model of long-term care with individualized care ("Adult Day Health Care" or ADHC), while others fit into a social psychological model ("social day care"). Thus, although both may provide recreation, meals, transportation to and from the facility, and memory-retraining programs, ADHCs are more likely to offer nursing care, physical and speech therapy, and scheduled medication distribution (Tedesco, 1996). The greatest advantage of ADHCs over home health care is to bring together older people for social interaction. Equally important, they provide respite for family caregivers. Clearly, such services are not suitable for the most impaired or bedbound older person; nevertheless, they have been an invaluable resource for elders with moderate levels of dementia or with serious physical impairments and chronic illnesses who can still benefit from living in the community.

TECHNOLOGY TO HELP OLDER PERSONS REMAIN INDEPENDENT

There has been a dramatic growth in adaptive technology, stimulated not so much by large numbers of older people in the population, but by the increased numbers of younger people living with disabilities. The expansion and diversification of computer technology has been the greatest source of **assistive technology**. Older people and those with disabilities now have greater access to resources such as libraries, service providers, support groups, health care information, and even distant family members through e-mail and the World Wide Web. For people with sensory impairments, the computer itself can be adapted; for example, this can be done with software that enlarges text or that reads aloud text on the screen. Telephone equipment has become more user-friendly, with larger buttons, larger text, and automatic dialing capability. This growth in assistive technologies in telecommunications has been stimulated by the Telecommunications Act of 1996, which required manufacturers to make telephone equipment accessible to people with diverse disabilities. Voice-activated phones that can be dialed by voice commands and answered from across the room can help older people who have problems pressing buttons or rushing to answer the phone. Speaker and cellular phones can make it easier for older people to make calls from any part of the house, indoors and out, as well as from their car if an emergency arises. Caller ID features can also help the older person determine if a particular call is important enough to answer (Kaplan, 1997; Lubinski and Higginbotham, 1997).

Computers can also serve a useful function for older people who must take multiple medications throughout the day. They can be programmed to remind the older person when to take what specific drug and provide individualized information about drug interactions. Eventually these systems will allow the older person to report their symptoms and reactions to current medications to their doctors, who can then review the patient's medical history, symptoms, and drug reactions in order to change or discontinue prescriptions. This innovative technology could significantly reduce the number of visits made by older people to hospital emergency rooms due to adverse drug reactions (Deatrick, 1997). Another technological innovation that can help older persons who use multiple

medications is the "smart cap," a tiny computer chip embodied in a prescription bottle cap. The cap beeps to remind the older person to take the drug; it also counts how many pills were removed each day and when. The system is connected via modem to the company that manufactures the drug so that a phone reminder can be made if the user forgets a medication. Although the cost of such a system is currently prohibitive for most older people, it offers great promise for improving medication adherence by future cohorts of elders.

Some new trends in computer technology have been developed for industry, but will soon find their way into private homes. For example, computers that can detect and signal sudden changes in ambient temperature, noise, lighting levels, and air quality already exist for large workplaces. They can be a valuable resource in the homes of frail and cognitively impaired older people. Robotics is another field significantly altering many work environments. Robots are not yet cost-effective and practical for home use, but could play a major role in improving the quality of life for older people with sensory and physical disabilities. If these new technologies are adapted for home use, they can help reduce the concerns of many elders and their families about leaving an older person alone.

In recent years, several products and services that do not depend on "high tech" have come into the marketplace to assist older people in emergency situations, especially those who are living alone. Some of these are simply pullcords in the bathroom or bedroom that are connected to a hospital or to the local emergency medical service. Others, such as the Life Safety System and Lifeline Service, are more sophisticated communication systems that use a portable medical alert device or an alarm unit to transmit specific signals for a fire, a medical emergency, or "no activity" through telephone lines or computers. These systems have been found to be cost-effective in enhancing the older person's sense of security about living alone. Other "low tech" but helpful aids for independent living are the "Aladdin Personal Reader", which is a large electronic magnifying glass that looks like an overhead projector. It magnifies printed materials such as books, newspapers, and bottle labels up to 25 times their original size. Another simple device controls window shades and blinds without much physical force or manipulation by arthritic hands. This continuous-loop mechanism, marketed as a "Rollease", holds the window shade in position while the user pulls on one side of the loop to raise the shade or the other side to lower it. Unfortunately, while it is an option for many new shade and blind designs, currently it cannot be adapted to existing window covers (Harper, 1995).

Other products are being developed for home use that can significantly reduce the burden on family caregivers. For example, a battery-operated bathtub lift (marketed as "Libra" by Arjo, Inc.)

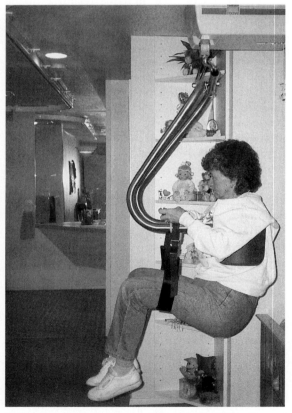

Technology can help older people with disabilities live more independently in their homes.

can help people get in and out of a bathtub without human assistance. It literally lifts the user from the floor, sets them into the tub, and removes them with the press of a button (Weiner, 1995). Another device helps bedbound people get out of bed and carries them to the bathroom or other parts of the house, using a harness attached to a track in the ceiling. Unfortunately, these are still costly and not covered by Medicare, and therefore must be paid out of pocket. This makes them accessible only to a small segment of the population with disabilities and functional impairments.

HOUSING POLICY AND GOVERNMENT PROGRAMS

Housing policy for older people has received less attention than has income security and health care. This is due, in part, to the influence of well-organized interest groups, such as builders and real estate developers.

The major housing programs that have benefited older people involve subsidies to suppliers of housing to enable them to sell or rent housing for less than the prevailing market price. The Section 202 Direct Loan program was originally designed as a direct loan for the construction of housing for older adults. It has provided housing for moderate-income older persons whose incomes are too high to qualify for public housing but too low to obtain housing in the private market. Under Section 202, low-interest loans are made to private nonprofit organizations or to nonprofit consumer cooperatives for the financing, construction, or rehabilitation of housing for older people. Currently 67 percent of nonprofit groups that provide supportive housing for this population use Section 202 funding; but this program has slowed as the federal government has withdrawn from supporting housing production (American Association of Homes and Services for the Aging, 1997; Pynoos and Golant, 1996).

Section 236 and Section 8 housing programs provide private enterprise with additional means of developing quality rental and cooperative housing for low- and moderate-income persons, regardless of age, by lowering their housing costs through interest-reduction payments (Section 236) and rent vouchers for qualifying older adults (Section 8). In the latter case, landlords receive from federal and state governments the difference between the rental cost of a housing unit and 30 percent of the tenants' income available for rent. Older people form an important segment of users of this rent supplement program. However, many of these 20-year contracts with owners of low-income housing began in the 1970s and are now expiring. There are fewer federal funds to renew the contracts, and many owners have lost interest in the low-income housing market, especially in urban centers now experiencing renewal. Some landlords have converted their buildings into higher rent apartments, hotels, or office spaces, or have sold the property outright to local developers. These changes in federal funding and local priorities have reduced the supply of section 8 housing which will continue to decline well into the twenty-first century.

Other policies that indirectly affect older homeowners are property tax relief, energy assistance, and home equity conversion or reverse mortgages, described earlier in this chapter. Energy assistance for low-income homeowners to offset air conditioning and heating costs is provided under the federal government's allocation of block grant money to cities and states. As noted previously, home equity conversions provide long-term homeowners with some additional income that converts their homes into more liquid assets.

As a result, less than 5 percent, or 1.5 million older people have benefited from federally funded housing assistance programs. The numbers are declining as HUD (Housing and Urban Development), the federal agency responsible for these programs, reduces its subsidies directly to older adults in the form of rent vouchers (Section 8) or indirectly through low-cost loans to builders of housing for older people (Section 202). In 1998, the budget for Section 202 housing is expected to be about half of its 1997 level, despite the fact that an average of eight people are waiting for each Section 202 apartment that becomes available (American Association of Homes and Services for the Aging, 1997). A major reason for the decline in housing subsidies is the growing public perception that older people have the financial adequacy to pay for their housing costs directly.

In summary, most recent federal activity in the housing arena has been to maintain what exists, modifying programs only incrementally to serve larger numbers of older people. The policy focus has been to make better use of existing housing resources through homesharing, accessory apartments, and home equity conversions, rather than to increase the overall housing supply for older adults. Another major need, especially for low-income and frail older persons, is for more congregate housing services. As described earlier, congregate housing is an important link in the long-term care continuum enabling older people to remain in the community and thereby maintain P-E congruence. The best way to achieve this may be innovations that modify existing communities and neighborhoods to meet the changing housing needs of the older population. This may include creating "granny flats" or accessory housing as part of existing homes to accommodate older people in smaller units near family or close friends.

ENVIRONMENTAL QUALITY

Regardless of the type of housing selected by older people, numerous elements of environmental quality need to be considered. These include security from crime, accessibility, and physical safety in and around the home. We have earlier reviewed security from crime in relation to specific housing types. In this section, housing characteristics that facilitate or hinder accessibility and physical safety are discussed.

Accessibility refers to the reduction of physical barriers that impede an individual's ability to enter a building and to move from one area of a building or site to another, as well as features that enable people with disabilities to manipulate the physical environment. We are all familiar with the international symbol of accessibility that denotes widened parking places, building entrances with ramps, and toilet stalls that are wider than average and include grab bars. These features are important for both younger and older persons who use wheelchairs, walkers, and canes. Regulations on accessible features in public buildings were established by the federal government in the early 1960s; specific standards for the slopes of ramps, width of doors, and other accessibility codes have been set by the American National Standards Institute (ANSI) and the Americans with Disabilities Act (ADA), passed in 1993.

These standards have made previously inaccessible facilities open to a much broader segment of the population, including older people. Unfortunately, however, many physical and sensory changes experienced by older persons (discussed in previous chapters) have not been considered in establishing federal or state accessibility codes. For example, older persons generally have more difficulty traversing long distances, but many congregate housing projects require long walks from individual units to the dining and recreational facilities. Older people who do not use wheelchairs may nevertheless have difficulty walking up and down stairs due to arthritis or stamina problems, but their homes may be built on multiple levels. Many such people "move" to the main level of their home, so that all their activities can take place on one floor. In an attempt to maximize the use of space, designers of independent housing and supportive housing often build cabinets and cupboards high above or below the reach of many older persons. This ignores the special problems of many older people with kyphosis or curvature of the spine, and of others whose upward reach has become limited by musculoskeletal changes. It also creates serious difficulties for those with arthritis and other motor disorders who cannot bend down to search in floor-level cabinets. Numerous other problems are created by designers who ignore age-related changes in vision, hearing, and tactile sensations. Other recommendations for

designing environments to counter these problems have been offered in Chapters 3 and 4.

Physical safety and age-related changes in mobility and sensory functioning are also important considerations in the design of facilities for older adults. Prosthetic aids such as handrails in bathtubs and showers, lift bars adjacent to the toilet, front door access, and reserved parking areas for persons with disabilities are essential for maintaining an adequate quality of life for older residents. Good lighting on stairs and at entrances, and non-skid surfaces on steps and bathroom floors are important for preventing accidents. Older persons and designers alike have noted these as the most important physical features of housing for the older population (Gunts, 1994).

SRO HOUSING

Single-room-occupancy (SRO) hotels in urban centers have traditionally served as minimal housing for the urban poor, particularly single older men, who make up the largest group of SRO residents. Indeed, the typical SRO resident is a white older man with 8.7 years of education and an income level 20 percent lower than that of his non-SRO peers, who reports multiple chronic conditions, and who has lived in his room (often with incomplete kitchens and with shared bathrooms) for at least 5 years. Increasing numbers of deinstitutionalized mental hospital patients have become SRO tenants as well (Rollinson, 1991). A survey in New York City found that because of their longer tenancy, older SRO residents paid less for their SRO unit than did younger tenants. However, because of lower income levels, they paid a higher *proportion* of their income (44 percent) than did younger tenants (25 percent) in the same buildings (Crystal and Beck, 1992). Although overall satisfaction with SRO housing was not high, older residents liked the opportunity to have their own room and the physical safety afforded by such a building in an otherwise hostile city core. The lack of services such as congregate meals and counseling was not considered a disadvantage by these elders.

Yet SRO housing is rapidly disappearing. For example, 89 percent of SRO units and other lower-price, substandard housing in New York City was lost to development between 1970 and 1983, while San Francisco (which still has proportionately more SRO hotel rooms than any other U.S. city) lost 40 percent of its SRO units between 1975 and 1982 (Ovrebo, Minkler, and Liljestrand, 1991). As the process of "gentrification" of urban cores becomes more popular across the country, and as more and more upper-income people discover the advantages of living downtown, the trend of demolishing SRO hotels and using this valuable land for upscale condominiums and office and retail space will continue. Already we are seeing the result of this—a dramatic increase in the number of homeless older people in urban centers. Many homeless elders have been displaced from low-cost housing and SRO hotels in central cities as these buildings have been demolished and replaced by expensive new housing and office developments, i.e., the "gentrification" of American cities (Singelakis, 1990).

THE PROBLEMS OF HOMELESSNESS

Although this chapter has focused on housing and community service options for older people, there is a growing segment of the older population who are homeless, often unable to afford basic housing or unaware of services to which they are entitled. **Homeless people** generally include those who, "for whatever reason, do not have a fixed, regular, and adequate night-time residence" (Stewart B. McKinney Homeless Assistance Act, 1987). In the mid 1960s, many homeless elders had recently been released from long-term psychiatric facilities as a result of the 1963 Community Mental Health Act. Today's homeless elders are largely the chronic homeless who have lived on the streets for many years and have lost any contact with their families. People

over age 50 comprise between 10 and 20 percent of the homeless population, which includes an increasing number of women. Many suffer from psychiatric disorders, alcoholism, or dementia, and lack strong social support systems. Those who become redomiciled (i.e., find permanent housing) tend to be mostly older homeless women with some social support, who attend community facilities (presumably becoming more familiar to service providers), and who do not display psychotic symptoms (Cohen et al., 1997; Sokolovsky, 1997; Crane, 1996; Wallsten, 1994). One epidemiological study interviewed 900 homeless persons using standard diagnostic criteria for psychiatric disorders. Although the rates for other psychiatric diagnoses did not differ by age or gender, alcohol abuse was significantly more prevalent among men aged 50 and older than among younger men (81 percent versus 60 percent); the

Many older homeless men have no social support systems.

reverse was true for drug abuse (16 percent versus 43.5 percent). No differences emerged in rates of substance abuse or other psychiatric diagnoses between younger and older homelesss women (Demallie, North, and Smith, 1997).

Not only do homeless people have no place to live, but they also lack food, clothing, medical care, and a social support system. Such a disorganized lifestyle can magnify the usual age-related declines in biological and psychological processes described in earlier chapters. A life at the edge, in which the individual is constantly trying to fulfill basic human needs (food, shelter, safety from predators), does not leave much energy for these elders to maintain even a modicum of health and well-being; their problems are compounded by chronic psychiatric disorders, alcoholism, drug abuse, and cognitive impairment (often a result of long-term alcohol abuse). Homeless older persons with chronic health problems often do not have the physical, social, or psychological resources to seek regular medical care for these conditions, or even to follow the necessary medication schedules and dietary restrictions. In a study of 281 men residing in the Bowery, New York's skid row, physical illness was much higher than among men in the general community. The most common health problems were respiratory disorders, high blood pressure, dizziness or weakness, edema, and gastrointestinal complaints. The primary source of medical care for these men was local hospitals (73 percent) or clinics (26 percent). Although 26 percent reported being hospitalized for psychiatric disorders, only 3 percent were currently using medications for these conditions. Although the majority had annual incomes far below poverty levels—which should have qualified them for some social service assistance—only 45 percent of the men living on the street and 33 percent living in flophouses or apartments received some form of social service aid (Cohen, Teresi, and Holmes, 1988; Cohen, Teresi, Holmes, and Roth, 1988).

These findings provide a disturbing portrait of the plight of homeless elders. The prevalence of chronic diseases in this group is higher than for other segments of the older population, yet their access to health services is inadequate and sporadic at best. Their ability to maintain their health and their medication regimens are limited by the unstable nature of their lifestyles and frequent disruptions in psychological well-being. They obtain most of their health care through the emergency rooms of public hospitals, and even necessary clinical appointments and follow-up visits are not kept. Thus, they often die because of diseases that are neglected and as a result of accidents and victimization on the streets. The needs of this population for housing, health care, and social services may increase in the next few decades, given growing poverty, chronic mental illness, and homelessness among younger cohorts in urban centers.

SUMMARY AND IMPLICATIONS

This chapter presented ways in which environmental factors affect the physical and psychological well-being of older people. Perhaps the most important lesson to be gained from this discussion is that a given environment is not inherently good or bad. Some environments are more conducive to the optimal functioning of *some* older people, while other older people need an entirely different set of features. For example, the older person who has a high need for activity and stimulation, and who has always lived in an urban setting, will be more satisfied with a large nursing home in a metropolitan center than will the individual from a rural community who has always lived in a single-family dwelling. Most person-environment models point to the necessity of examining each older person's specific needs, preferences, and abilities, and of designing environments that can both meet the needs of this broad cross-section and, more important, flexibly respond to individual differences. To the degree that environmental press can be reduced to accommodate personal abilities and needs, the aging person can function more effectively and maintain his or her level of well-being. Relocation represents a special case of P-E incongruence that can disturb the well-being of an impaired older person by raising the level of environmental press.

There has been some concern with differences in housing quality and services for rural older residents. Current cohorts are much less likely than previous cohorts to live in farm and nonfarm rural communities. However, those who do, particularly African Americans, tend to have lower incomes and poorer health, with more limitations in activities of daily living. The recognition of these disparities has led to the growth of state and federally funded services for rural elders, but more are needed. Older persons in rural communities appear to have more frequent social interactions with neighbors and friends than do urban elders, but at the same time they need more formal health and social services.

The neighborhood and neighbors play a significant role in the well-being of older people. With retirement and declining health, the older person's physical lifespace becomes more constricted. The neighborhood takes on greater significance as a source of social interactions, health and social services, grocery shopping, banking, and postal services. Neighbors represent an important component of older people's social and emotional network, especially where family members are not available.

Fear of crime among older persons is widespread but is inconsistent with actual victimization rates. Older people experience far lower rates than younger people for violent crimes, and somewhat lower for other types of crime. The potential danger of injury and long-term disability, as well as the fear of economic loss, may contribute to this incongruence between actual victimization rates and older people's fear of crime.

The high rate of home ownership and long-term residence in their homes make it difficult for older people to relocate to new housing, even when the new situation represents a significant improvement over the old. The poor condition of many older people's homes and the high costs of renovating and maintaining them sometimes makes relocation necessary, even when the older homeowner is reluctant. Better living conditions

and a safer neighborhood in which several other elders reside have been found to improve older people's morale and sense of well-being, especially following a move to a planned housing project from substandard housing. The growth of planned and congregate housing and of assisted living programs for older people has raised the issue of site selection and service provision. It is especially important when designing housing that public transportation be located nearby and that facilities such as medical and social services, banks, and groceries be within easy access of the housing facility. As people live longer and healthier lives beyond retirement, the need for multilevel housing (providing a range of care options) will continue to grow. Several alternative methods of purchasing such housing are available—some guarantee lifetime care, others do not provide personal and health services. Considering the high likelihood of using a nursing home facility at some time in old age, many retirees prefer to select the more comprehensive options.

The proportion of older people in a nursing home at any one time is very low, but up to 50 percent will need some type of long-term care before they die. Because of the greater likelihood of physical and cognitive impairments among residents of nursing homes, it is critical to enhance the environmental quality of these facilities at the design stage. If the facility has already been built, features can be added that increase privacy and control and allow for the expression of territoriality and other personal needs. Aging and institutionalization do not reduce the individual's needs for identity and self-expression.

Assisted living and adult foster care or adult family homes are rapidly becoming a cost-effective option for many older people who need help with ADLs but do not necessarily need 24-hour care. Many of these facilities provide greater autonomy, more options for privacy, and less direct supervision for their older tenants. Funding for assisted living is not covered by Medicaid in the great majority of states, making it a viable option only for those elders with adequate personal financial resources. However, more states are offering Medicaid waivers for AFCs and, to some extent, for assisted living. Home care is now the fastest-growing component of personal health care expenditures. It is reimbursed by Medicare and Medicaid to offer more services than other long-term care options. It allows older people to "age in place" while bringing services such as skilled nursing care, rehabilitation, and personal and household care to the person's home. Adult day care, both as a rehabilitative model and as a social model, provides opportunities for social integration of frail older people who are living at home alone or with a family caregiver. The older person can attend adult day care for several hours each day and receive some nursing and rehabilitation services, while the caregiver obtains some respite from caregiving tasks. Many ADCs also offer counseling and support groups for caregivers.

Single-room-occupancy hotels have traditionally been a low-cost housing option for older people, especially for older men living alone. However, as these buildings have been demolished or remodeled in many cities, SRO residents have become displaced; some have become homeless. Many older homeless people have chronic medical, psychiatric, and cognitive disorders that often go unattended because of lack of access to health services. As a result, these homeless elders grow physiologically older more rapidly than do their more stable peers.

GLOSSARY

adult day care (ADC)   a community facility where frail older people living at home can attend several hours each day; when based on a health rehabilitation model, it provides individualized therapy plans; those based on a social model focus on structured social and psychotherapeutic activities

adult foster care (AFC)   a private home facility licensed by the state in which the owner of the home provides housekeeping, personal care, and some delegated nursing functions for the residents

assisted living   a housing model aimed at elders who need assistance with personal care, e.g., bathing and taking medication, but who are not so physically or cognitively impaired as to need 24-hour attention

assistive technology   a range of electronic and computer technologies whose goal is to assist people with disabilities to remain independent and perform as many ADLs as possible without assistance from other people

congregate housing   a form of group housing which provides communal services, the minimum of which is a central kitchen and dining room for residents; some facilities also provide housekeeping, social, and health services

continuous care retirement community (CCRC)   a multilevel facility offering a range from independent to congregate living arrangements

home health care   a variety of nursing, rehabilitation, and other therapy services, as well as assistance with personal care and household maintenance, that are provided to people who are homebound and have difficulty performing multiple ADLs

homeless people   those living without a fixed, regular, and adequate night-time residence

long-term care   a broad range of services geared to helping frail older adults in their own home and community settings; can include nursing homes, nutritional programs, adult day care, and visiting nurse services

Medicaid waivers   exceptions to state Medicaid rules that allow use of Medicaid funds for services that are traditionally not covered by Medicaid, such as chore services and adult family homes

naturally occurring retirement community (NORC)   a neighborhood or larger area occupied mostly by older people, but without being planned specifically for this population

nursing homes   facilities with three or more beds staffed 24 hours per day by health professionals who provide nursing and personal care services to residents who cannot remain in their own homes due to physical health problems, functional disabilities, and/or significant cognitive impairments

single-room-occupancy (SRO) hotels   older buildings in urban centers that have been converted to low-cost apartments; often these are single rooms with no kitchen, minimal cooking and refrigeration facilities, and bathrooms shared with other units

REFERENCES

Administration on Aging. *A profile of older Americans: 1996*. Washington, DC, 1997.

American Association of Homes and Services for the Aging (AAHSA), 1997. *Senior housing*, Web page: http://www.aahsa.org/members/backgrd2/htm

American Association of Retired Persons (AARP). *The gadget book: Ingenious devices for easier living.* Washington, DC: AARP, 1987.

American Association of Retired Persons (AARP). *Understanding senior housing.* Washington, DC: AARP, 1990.

Ashley, M. J., Olin, J. S., Le Riche, W. H., Kornaczewski, A., and Rankin, J. G. Skid row alcoholism: A distinct sociomedical entity. *Archives of Internal Medicine,* 1976, *136,* 272—278.

Atchley, R. C. *Social forces and aging: An introduction to social gerontology.* Belmont, CA: Wadsworth, 1985.

Auerbach, A. J. The elderly in rural areas. In L. H Ginsberg (Ed.), *Social work in rural communities.* New York: Council on Social Work Education, 1976.

Barker, R. G., Dembo, T., and Lewin, K. Frustration and regression: An experiment with young children. *University of Iowa Studies in Child Welfare,* 1941, *18.*

Bazargan, M. The effects of health, environmental, and socio-psychological variables on fear of crime and its consequences among urban black elderly individuals. *International Journal of Aging and Human Development,* 1994, *38,* 99–115.

Bureau of Justice Statistics. *BJS highlights from 20 years of surveying crime victims: The National Crime Victimization Survey,* NCJ-144525, 1993.

Cohen, C. I., Ramirez, M., Teresi, J., Gallagher, M., and Sokolovsky, J. Predictors of becoming redomiciled among older homeless women. *The Gerontologist,* 1997, *37,* 67–74.

Cohen, C. I., Teresi, J. A, and Holmes, D. The physical well-being of old homeless men. *Journals of Gerontology,* 1988, *43,* S121–S128.

Cohen, C. I., Teresi, J. A., Holmes, D., and Roth, E. Survival strategies of older homeless men. *The Gerontologist,* 1988, *28,* 58–65.

Crane, M. The situation of older homeless people. *Reviews in Clinical Gerontology,* 1996, *6,* 389–398.

Crystal, S., and Beck, P. A room of one's own: The SRO and the single elderly. *The Gerontologist,* 1992, *32,* 684–692.

Danigelis, N. L., and Fengler, A. P. *No place like home: Intergenerational homesharing through social exchange.* New York: Columbia University Press, 1991.

Deatrick, D. Senior-Med: Creating a network to help manage medications. *Generations,* 1997, *21,* 59–60.

Demallie, D. A., North, C. S., and Smith, E. M. Psychiatric disorders among the homeless: A comparison of older and younger groups. *The Gerontologist,* 1997, *37,* 61–66.

Dibner, A. S., Lowry, L., and Morris, J. N. Usage and acceptance of an emergency alarm system by the frail elderly. *The Gerontologist,* 1982, *22,* 538–539.

Doty, P. Long-term care in international perspective. *Health Care Financing Review,* 1988, Annual supplement, 145–155.

Freedman, V. A. Family structure and the risk of nursing home admission. *Journals of Gerontology,* 1996, *51B,* S61–S69.

Freiman, M. P., and Murtaugh, C. M. Determinants of the hospitalization of nursing home residents. *Journal of Health Economics,* 1993, *12,* 349–359.

Gaberlavage, G., and Citro, J. *Progress in the housing of older persons.* Public Policy Institute, American Association of Retired Persons, Washington, DC: 1997.

Goffman, E. *Asylums.* Garden City, NY: Anchor Books, 1961.

Golant, S. M. The suburbanization of the American elderly. In A. Rogers (Ed.), *Elderly migration and population distribution.* New York: John Wiley and Sons, 1992.

Golant, S. M., and La Greca, A. J. City-suburban, metro-nonmetro, and regional differences in the housing quality of U.S. elderly households. *Research on Aging,* 1994, 16, 322–346.

Golant, S. M., and La Greca, A. J. The relative deprivation of U.S. elderly households as judged by their housing problems. *Journals of Gerontology,* 1995, *50B,* S13–S23.

Gonzales, T. I. An empirical study of economies of scope in home healthcare. *Health Services Research,* 1997, 32, 313–324.

Greene, V. L., and Ondrich, J. I. Risk factors for nursing home admissions and exits. *Journals of Gerontology,* 1990, 45, S250–S258.

Gunts, E. Housing the elderly. *Architecture,* 1994, *83,* 82–87.

Harper, D. Ease and independence without stigma: Three products that work. *Generations,* 1995, *19,* 58–60.

Hawes, C., Mor, V., Phillips, C. D., Fries, B. E., Morris, J. N., Steele-Friedlob, E., Greene, A. M., and Nennstiel, M. The OBRA-87 nursing home regulations and implementation of the Resident

Assessment Instrument: Effects on process quality. *Journal of the American Geriatric Society,* 1997, *45(8),* 977–985.

Henretta, J. C. Retirement and residential moves by elderly households. *Research on Aging,* 1986, *8,* 23–37.

Hobbs, F., and Damon, B. L. *65+ in the United States.* Washington, DC: U.S. Department of Commerce, Bureau of the Census, Current Population Reports, 1996.

Hollway, W., and Jefferson, T. The risk society in an age of anxiety: Situating fear of crime. *British Journal of Sociology,* 1997, *48,* 255–266.

Hughes, S. L. Home health. In C. J. Evashwick (Ed.), *The continuum of long-term care.* Albany, NY: Delmar, 1996.

Hughes, S. L., Ulasevich, A., Weaver, F. M., Henderson, W., Manheim, L., Kubal, J. D., and Bonarigo, F. Impact of home care of hospital days: A meta-analysis. *Health Services Research,* 1997, *32,* 415–432.

Jette, A. M., Tennstedt, S., and Crawford, S. How does formal and informal community care affect nursing home use? *Journals of Gerontology,* 1995, *50B,* S4–S12.

Kahana, E. F. A congruence model of person-environment interaction. In M. P. Lawton (Ed.), *Theory development in environments and aging.* New York: Wiley, 1975.

Kahana, E. F., Liang, J., and Felton, B. Alternative models of P-E fit: Prediction of morale in three homes for the aged. *Journal of Gerontology,* 1980, *35,* 584–595.

Kane, R., and Kane, R. Health care for older people: Organizational and policy issues. In R. Binstock and L. George (Eds.), *Handbook of aging and the social sciences* (3rd ed.). New York: Academic Press, 1990.

Kane, R. A., and Wilson, K. B. *Assisted living in the United States: A new paradigm for residential care for frail older persons?* Washington, DC: AARP, 1993.

Kaplan, D. Access to technology: Unique challenges for people with disabilities. *Generations,* 1997, *21,* 24–27.

Kart, C. S. Community-based, noninstitutional long-term care service utilization by aged blacks: Facts and issues. In C. M Barresi and D. E Stull (Eds.), *Ethnic elderly and long-term care.* New York: Springer, 1993.

Kiyak, H. A. *A survey of adult family homes and assisted living in Washington.* Final report submitted to the Aging and Adult Services Administration, Department of Social and Health Services, Olympia, Washington, 1998.

Lair, T., and Lefkowitz, D. *Mental health and functional status of residents of nursing and personal care homes.* DHHS Publication No. 90–3470. Rockville, MD: AHCPR, 1990.

Lawton, M. P. Competence, environmental press, and the adaptation of older people. In P. G Windley and G. Ernst (Eds.), *Theory development in environment and aging.* Washington, DC: Gerontological Society, 1975.

Lewin, K. *Dynamic theory of personality.* New York: McGraw-Hill, 1935.

Lewin, K. *Field theory in social science.* New York: Harper and Row, 1951.

Lewin, K., Lippitt, R., and White, R. Patterns of aggressive behavior in experimentally created social climates. *Journal of Social Psychology,* 1939, *10,* 271–299.

Litwak, E., and Longino, C. F. Migration patterns among the elderly: A developmental perspective. In R. B. Enright (Ed.), *Perspectives in social gerontology.* Boston: Allyn and Bacon, 1994.

Litwak, E., and Longino, C. F. Migration patterns among the elderly: A developmental perspective. *The Gerontologist,* 1987, 27, 266–272.

Lubinski, E., and Higginbotham, D. J. *Communication technologies for the elderly: Vision, hearing and speech.* San Diego: Singular Publishing Group, 1997.

Manton, K. G., Corder, L. S., and Stallard, E. Estimates of change in chronic disability and institutional incidence and prevalence rates in the U.S. elderly population from the 1982, 1984, and 1989 National Long-Term Care Survey. *Journals of Gerontology,* 1993, *48,* S153–S166.

McLaughlin, D. K., and Jensen, L. Poverty among older Americans: The plight of nonmetropolitan elders. *Journals of Gerontology,* 1993, *48,* S44–S54.

Mor, V., Banaszak-Holl, J., and Zinn, J. The trend toward specialization in nursing care facilities. *Generations,* 1995–1996, *19,* 24–29.

Murray, H. A. *Explorations in personality.* New York: Oxford University Press, 1938.

Naifeh, M. L. *Housing of the elderly: 1991.* Current Housing Reports, Series H123/93–1, 1993.

National Center for Health Statistics (NCHS). *Advance Data,* No. 28, Jan. 23, 1997.

National Center for Health Statistics (NCHS). Use of nursing homes by the elderly: Preliminary data from the 1985 National Nursing Home Survey. *Vital and Health Statistics,* No. 134, 1987.

National Low Income Housing Information Service. *The fiscal year 1991 budget and low income housing* (SM-290). Washington, DC: National Low-Income Housing Information Service, 1990.

Ovrebo, B., Minkler, M., and Liljestrand, P. No room in the inn: The disappearance of SRO housing in the United States. In S. Keigher (Ed.), *Housing risks and homelessness among the urban elderly.* Chicago: Haworth Press, 1991.

Pawlson, L. G. Financing long-term care: The growing dilemma. *Journal of the American Geriatrics Society,* 1989, *37,* 631–638.

Pynoos, J., and Golant, S. M. Housing and living arrangements for the elderly. In R. H. Binstock and L. K. George (Eds.), *Handbook of aging and the social sciences* (4th ed.). San Diego: Academic Press, 1996.

Redfoot, D., and Gaberlavage, G. Housing for older Americans: Sustaining the dream. *Generations,* 1991, *15,* 35–38.

Rollinson, P. A. Elderly single room occupancy (SRO) hotel tenants: Still alone. *Social Work,* 1991, *36,* 303–308.

Silverstein, M., and Zablotsky, D. L. Health and social precursors of later life retirement-community migration. *Journals of Gerontology,* 1996, *51B,* S150–S156.

Singelakis, A. T. Real estate market trends and the displacement of the aged. *The Gerontologist,* 1990, *30,* 658–667.

Sirrocco, A. *Nursing homes and board and care homes.* Advance Data, No. 244. Hyattsville, MD: NCHS, 1994.

Sokolovsky, J. One thousand points of blight: Old, female and homeless in New York City. In J. Sokolovsky (Ed.), *The cultural context of aging.* Westport, CT: Bergin and Garvey, 1997.

Spillman, B. C., and Kemper, P. Lifetime patterns of payment for nursing home care. *Medical Care,* 1995, *33,* 280–296.

Stark, A. J., Kane, R. L., Kane, R. A., and Finch, M. Effect on physical functioning of care in adult foster homes and nursing homes. *The Gerontologist,* 1995, *35,* 648–655.

Stewart B. McKinney Homeless Assistance Act, P. L. 100–77 (1987).

Strahan, G. An Overview of nursing homes and their current residents: Data from the 1995 National Nursing Home Survey. *Vital and Health Statistics.* No. 280. Hyattsville, MD: National Center for Health Statistics, 1997.

Tedesco, J. Adult day care. In C. J. Evashwick (Ed.), *The continuum of long-term care.* Albany, NY: Delmar, 1996.

Tennstedt, S. L., Crawford, S., and McKinley, J. Determining the pattern of community care: Is coresidence more important than caregiver relationship? *Journals of Gerontology,* 1993, *48,* S74–S83.

U.S. Bureau of the Census. *American Housing Survey for the United States in 1991.* Current Housing Reports, Series H150/91, 1993.

Vladeck, B. C., and Feuerberg, M. Unloving care revisited. *Generations,* 1995–1996, *19,* 9–13.

Wallsten, S. M. Geriatric mental health: A portrait of homelessness. *Journal of Psychosocial Nursing and Mental Health Sciences,* 1994, *30,* 20–24.

Weiner, M. D. Bringing an award-winning product to the marketplace. *Generations,* 1995, *19,* 56–57.

Wiener, J. M., Illston, L. H., and Hanley, R. J. *Sharing the burden: Strategies for public and private long-term care insurance.* Washington, DC: Brookings Institute, 1994.

11

PRODUCTIVE AGING: PAID AND NONPAID ROLES AND ACTIVITIES

Typically, we think of productivity in terms of paid work. In fact, disengagement and role theory focused on the losses associated with withdrawal from the work role. However, there are a variety of ways in which older people can be active and productive without being employed or engaged in obligatory activities. *Productivity* is broader than paid work; it includes any activity that produces goods and services such as housework, child care, volunteer work, help to family and friends, and acquiring training and skills to enhance the capacity to perform such tasks (Danigelis and McIntosh, 1993; Caro, Bass, and Chen, 1993; Herzog and Morgan, 1992). Recent research has found that if there is a good fit between societal and individual expectations about roles in old age, then the activity—formal or informal, paid or nonpaid—can have a positive influence on the older person's mental and physical well-being (McIntosh and Danigelis, 1995). Consistent with the person-environment framework that undergirds this book, productive older people appear to choose and adjust their behavior and aspirations in order

to maintain a sense of competence in a changing environment (Herzog and House, 1991).

As described in Chapter 8, there are widely different perspectives on participation in old age—from activity theory, which stresses the beneficial effects of continued involvement, to disengagement theory, which argues the appropriateness of withdrawal. These and other theoretical perspectives have addressed the questions: Does age bring a desire for increased social autonomy? Is daily activity essential to successful adjustment to aging? How is use of time related to life satisfaction and to feelings of competence toward the larger environment? Are late-life activities consistent with those earlier in life? These questions have long been topics of research and debate.

The living arrangements, neighborhoods, and socioeconomic status of adults, as well as their physical capacities, attitudes, skills, and values, all influence their activity patterns. People's use of time and arenas of involvement vary with the opportunities provided by the environment and with each developmental phase in the life cycle.

319

Some older people work part-time for social and financial reasons.

Young and middle-aged adults may feel that there is not enough time for all they want to do. Their days are crowded with task-oriented activities—employment, child care, and household maintenance. During middle age, people may idealize the free time of retirement, postponing travel or classes until they are retired and have "time for things like that." With retirement, the departure of children, and other role changes, most older adults experience discretion over their use of time, perhaps more than at any other point in their adult lives. The reality of non-work time for retirees, however, may be quite different from their middle-age fantasies of "if only we had the time." Many retirees overestimate the extent and variety of activities they will pursue upon retirement. Poor health, reduced income, transportation difficulties, isolated living arrangements, and role changes all may disrupt and reduce these anticipated activities in old age.

Although time is less fragmented upon retirement than it is at earlier life stages, there still are constraints on how people choose to become involved in different social arenas. As identified in earlier chapters, the normal physical and psychological changes of aging, and any diseases that affect older persons, may limit their capacities to engage in certain activities and to maintain competence in relation to environmental demands. Co-

hort experiences and socialization to certain activities and values, gender and ethnic minority group memberships, and type of living arrangements (e.g., a retirement community or nursing home) may interact and result in certain activities being stratified by age. Some older individuals may not undertake particular activities because they feel they lack the skills, physical strength, or knowledge to do them, or that they are too old for them. Past activity patterns and personality dynamics do shape the use of time. There appears to be continuity between leisure pursuits enjoyed at earlier and later stages of life, consistent with continuity theory. Adults have been found to have a core of leisure activities that persists across the life course, although the specific means of carrying out such patterns may alter with age (Kelly, Steinkamp, and Kelly, 1986). As people's interests crystallize over the life span, they generally become more selective about how they invest their time and energy. On the other hand, there are many instances of individuals' successfully pursuing new activities, such as art, music, running, or skiing, for the first time in old age.

This chapter begins by discussing retirement as a status and a social process that affects both economic status and roles and activities in old age. However, not all older people are retired from the paid workforce. After reviewing the employment status of older people, we examine their **socioeconomic status,** including their income and extent of poverty and near-poverty. Contrary to common images, old age is not necessarily a life phase of idleness or nonproductivity. Instead, many older people are engaged in a wide range of nonpaid roles that are contributing to their families, their communities, and the larger society. We focus on the activity patterns most common among older adults: leisure pursuits, membership in community and voluntary associations, education, volunteering, religious participation and spirituality, and political involvement. Even with changes in their competence in physical health and physiological functioning, as described in earlier chapters, older people can stay active and maintain optimal quality of life by modifying their involvement in community and organizational activities, thereby re-establishing congruence between their needs and abilities and the demands of the social environment.

RETIREMENT

With increased longevity and changing work patterns, **retirement** has become as much an expected part of the life course as having a family, completing school, or working. Men in particular, but increasingly women among younger cohorts, develop age-related expectations about the rhythm of their careers—when to start working, when to be at the peak of their careers, and when to retire; and they assess whether they are "on time" according to these socially defined schedules.

In U.S. society, the value placed on work and productivity shapes how individuals approach employment and retirement. Those over age 65 in particular were socialized to a traditional view of hard work, job loyalty, and occupational stability. Current demographic trends and social policies mean that values and expectations about work and retirement are changing, as many of the young-old exit and re-enter the work force through partial employment or new careers. Changing work patterns and increased longevity mean that both men and women are spending more years in retirement. Nearly all adults are aware that they will encounter the question of their retirement, with most people in their 50's actively involved in anticipating it (Ekerdt, DeViney, and Kosloski, 1996). As individuals live longer, a smaller proportion of their lifetime is devoted to paid employment, even though the number of years they work is longer. For example, a man born in 1900 could expect to live about 47 years. He would work for 32 years (70 percent of his lifetime) and be retired for about one year (2 percent of his lifetime). In contrast, a man born today can anticipate living about 75 years, working for about 55 percent of his life, and being retired for over 26 percent. Women, too, are living longer past the age of retirement and are devoting a

smaller portion of their lives to childbearing and rearing. A woman born in 1900 could expect that 6 years of her 48-year life span (or 12 percent) would be spent in the labor force, whereas the comparable figure for a woman born in 1987 is nearly 40 percent of her 78-year lifespan (U.S. Senate Special Committee on Aging, 1992).

The institutionalization of retirement is a relatively recent phenomenon in Western society. Retirement developed as a twentieth-century social institution, along with industrialization, surplus labor, and a rising standard of living. **Social Security** legislation, passed in 1935, established the right to financial protection in old age and thus served to institutionalize retirement. Based on income deferred during the worker's years of employment, Social Security was viewed as a reward for past economic contributions to society and a way to support people physically unable to maintain their jobs. At the same time, Social Security served to create jobs by removing people from the labor market when they reached age 65.

From the perspective of critical gerontology, discussed in Chapter 8, retirement serves a variety of institutional functions in our society. It can stimulate and reward worker loyalty. In addition, it is a way to remove older, presumably more expensive, workers and replace them with younger employees, assumed to be more productive. There are also negative societal and individual consequences. For example, earlier retirement combined with longer life expectancies has created prolonged dependency on Social Security and other retirement benefits as well as a loss of older workers' skills. This shift from "near-universal" work to near-universal retirement has raised concerns about Social Security for future generations. A negative consequence for older individuals is that since retirement has become associated in the public mind with the chronological age of 65 (the current age of eligibility for full Social Security benefits), it also carries the connotation of being old, physically disabled, and no longer capable of full-time employment (Atchley, 1993). In fact, society has come to associate aging with decreased work and training capacity, with little or no regard for the heterogeneity of the older population and limited knowledge of new work arrangements and retraining techniques (Mor-Barak and Tynan, 1993).

The Timing of Retirement

The arbitrary nature of any particular age for retirement is shown by the fact that most people retire between the ages of 60 and 64, and very few continue to work past age 70. In fact, it can hardly be said that age 65 is the "normal" retirement age. Instead, 60.6 years is the median age for retirement. Three-quarters of all new Social Security beneficiaries each year retire before their sixty-fifth birthday, and most begin collecting reduced benefits at age 62.5. The average retirement age in heavy industries, such as steel and auto manufacturing, is even lower than age 62, because of private pension inducements. Those who retire from the military in their early forties after the minimum required 20 years often move on to other careers that enable them to draw two pensions after age 65. Even though the 1983 amendments to the Social Security Act delayed the age of eligibility for full benefits and increased the financial penalty for retiring at age 62, this has not altered the overall trend toward early retirement. In fact, it is generally agreed that further delays in Social Security benefits and reductions in the early retirement benefits of private pensions would have little effect on significantly delaying the retirement age (Juster, Soldo, Kington, Mitchell, 1996; National Academy of Aging, 1994).

Retirement policies, labor market conditions, and individual characteristics all converge on the decision to retire and affect the timing of retirement. Prior to 1986, mandatory retirement may have influenced the retirement age. Even so, this factor was not as salient as financial incentives, since less than 10 percent of employees were forced to retire because of such requirements (Quinn and Burkhauser, 1993). The limited effect of mandatory retirement is also shown by the fact that federal workers retire at the average age of 62, even though there was never a mandatory retirement age for federal employees (U.S. Department of Labor, 1989).

A major factor affecting retirement timing is having an adequate income, through Social Security or a private pension. Despite our society's work-oriented values and the importance of income derived from work, employment and retirement policies and pensions since the 1900s have been directed toward encouraging early retirement. Nine out of ten U.S. pension plans, particularly for white-collar workers, provide financial incentives for early retirement. Even employees who were not planning on retirement often feel they cannot turn down attractive retirement benefits. Economic factors are thus central in influencing attitudes toward retirement, inasmuch as they directly affect decisions about the feasibility of retirement and indirectly contribute to worker health and job satisfaction. When given a choice and assuming financial security and adequate health insurance, most people elect to retire as soon as they can (Taylor and Shore, 1995; Clark, Ghent, and Heeden, 1994).

In addition to income, the timing of retirement may be determined by health, families' preferences, informal norms of the work situation, and long-range plans. Recent research has suggested that functional limitations and health impairments may be more important than economic status in the retirement decision (Ozawa, 1996; Taylor and Shore, 1995). Two categories of people who retire early have been identified: those with good health and adequate financial resources who desire additional leisure time, and those with health problems that make their work burdensome. Poor health, when combined with an adequate retirement income, usually results in early retirement. In contrast, poor health and an inadequate income generally delay retirement by reason of necessity. Health problems are a greater motivation for retirement from physically demanding and stressful jobs and for ethnic minority elders (Colsher et al., 1988). Self-reports of poor health as the motivation for retirement need to be interpreted cautiously, however. Retirees may report poor health as the reason, despite their actual health status, because they perceive this to be a socially acceptable response.

The nature of one's job, including job satisfaction and organizational commitment, also influences the timing of retirement. Some workers retire to escape boring, repetitive jobs such as assembly line and office work. Workers who have a positive attitude toward retirement and leisure but a negative view of their jobs, often because of undesirable and stressful working conditions, are likely to retire early. Employees with a high school education or less tend to retire earlier than well-educated employees, as illustrated by Mr. and Mrs. Howard in the introductory vignette (Taylor and Shore, 1995; Quinn and Burkhauser, 1993).

The effects of gender and ethnic minority status on the decision to retire are not clear-cut. Although both men and women overall are choosing early retirement, women of retirement age are less likely to be fully retired than men in their age group, and their retirement decisions may be determined by different variables (Quadagno and Hardy, 1996; Taylor and Shore, 1995). Nevertheless, current income and receipt of a pension other than Social Security are primary factors in women's retirement decisions (Szinovacz, 1989; Belgrave, 1989). Women who entered the labor force in middle age or later, after performing family caregiving roles, may need to continue to work for economic reasons. In contrast, career women, particularly those who never married, are more likely to retire early than re-entry women (Moen, 1996; Feuerbach and Erdwins, 1994).

The timing of retirement for ethnic minorities, particularly African Americans and Mexican Americans, tends to be very different from the traditional pattern for white males. Their lifetime work patterns often yield an unclear line between work and non-work; they tend to have lengthy periods of non-work at an early age and lack access to pensions (Zsembik and Singer, 1990; Gibson, 1987). Studies comparing African American and Caucasian men and women found that white men were the most likely to be retired and African American and white women least likely, even if they were in poor health (Belgrave, 1988; Belgrave, Haug, and Gomez, 1987).

In sum, the most important factors for the timing of retirement appear to be financial security and health status. For most U.S. workers, retirement is desired, and their decision is not *whether* to retire but *when*. Not surprisingly, many of these same factors influence the degree of satisfaction with retirement.

Satisfaction with Retirement

The importance of factors other than policies that set retirement age and benefits suggests the value of examining retirement as a *process* or transition that affects people's lives in multiple ways. This concept encompasses not only the timing and type of retirement situation as a life stage, but also the phases after the event of retirement (Bossé et al., 1991). Similarly, an individual's degree of satisfaction with the outcome depends to some extent on how the retirement process is experienced, especially the degree of choice and the amount of preparation and planning (Hardy and Quadagno, 1995). In describing a "typical progression of processes," Atchley (1983) has suggested that an initial euphoric, busy honeymoon phase is followed by a letdown or disenchantment phase due to loss of status, income, or purpose, which, in turn, is followed by a reorientation to the realities of retired life. This sequence leads to a subsequent stable phase, when the retiree has settled into a predictable routine (Jacobs, 1990). Of course, not every individual will experience all the phases or in the order described. Another conceptualization of retirement as a process of role-exit found that as individuals approach retirement, they express increasing discontent and fatigue with the job as a way of withdrawing from their current role commitments (Ekerdt and DeViney, 1993).

Early gerontological studies emphasized the negative impacts of retirement as a life crisis due to loss (Atchley, 1976; Streib and Schneider, 1971). Later research has identified the positive effects of retirement on life satisfaction, health, and stress, especially during the first year post-retirement.

While there may be some decline in measures of physical and psychological health after 6 to 7 years of retirement, most retirees still report good health and overall life satisfaction (Gall, Evans, and Howard, 1995). Although retirement is a major transition, it is often blurred, with the majority of retirees experiencing minimal stress and being relatively satisfied with their life circumstances (Midanik, Soghikian, Ransom, and Tekawa 1995; Bossé, Aldwin, Levenson, and Workman-Daniels, 1991). In fact, for some, retirement appears to be a benign event, with no apparent impact on the individual's well-being. Inconsistency in findings regarding retirement satisfaction may be due more to the length of time in retirement than to the retirement process per se (Gall et al., 1995).

In general, financial security and health appear to be the major determinants of retirees' satisfaction with life, rather than retirement status per se. Not surprisingly, retirees with higher incomes or at least adequate finances report being more satisfied in retirement than those with lower incomes (Reitzes, Mutran, and Fernandez, 1996; Gall et al., 1995). Higher economic status is also associated with more positive health status in old age (Juster et al., 1996; Mor-Barak, Scharloch, Birba, and Sokolov, 1992; Bossé et al., 1991). Retirement does not *cause* poor health, as is commonly assumed. Although some people's functional health does deteriorate after retirement, other people's functional health improves after retirement because they are no longer subject to stressful, unhealthy, or dangerous work conditions. Contrary to stereotypes about the negative health effects of retirement, people who die shortly after retirement were probably in poor health before they retired. In fact, deterioration in health is more likely to cause the retirement than vice versa. Accordingly, retirement has not been found to increase the incidence of mental health problems, and in some instances has improved mental health (Bossé, Aldwin, Levinson, and Ekerdt, 1987; Howard, 1986; Palmore et al., 1985). The misconception that people become ill and die as a consequence of retirement undoubtedly persists on the basis of findings from cross-sectional data, as well

as reports of isolated instances of such deaths. In addition, the traditional American ideology that life's meaning is derived from paid work may reinforce the stereotype that retirement has negative consequences. Another factor is that retirees may be motivated to exaggerate their health limitations in order to justify their retirement.

Personal and social characteristics—perceptions of daily activities as useful, internal locus of control, a sense of having chosen the timing of retirement, living in a suitable environment, and access to an adequate social support system—all contribute to satisfaction in retirement (Gall et al., 1995; Hardy and Quadagno, 1995; Bossé, Aldwin, Levenson, Spiro, and Mroczek, 1993). Consistent with continuity theory, pre-retirement self-esteem and identity factors continue to influence post-retirement self-esteem (Reitzes, Mutran, and Fernandez, 1996). Individuals for whom employment was not their primary source of meaning and who have weaker traditional work values adjust to a satisfying routine more readily than do those with strong work values who did not develop leisure activities during their employment. Conversely, retirees who do not adjust well have been found to have poor health, inadequate family finances, marital problems, and difficulties making transitions throughout the life span. Those who retire early because of poor health or lack of job opportunities or who are experiencing other stressful events in their life are less satisfied with being retired, but they are also dissatisfied with other aspects of their lives, such as their housing, standard of living, and leisure (Bossé et al., 1991).

Occupational status, which is frequently associated with educational level, is also an important predictor of retirement satisfaction; lower-status workers have more health and financial problems and therefore less satisfaction than higher-level white-collar workers. The more meaningful work characteristics of higher-status occupations may "spill over" to a greater variety of satisfying non-work pursuits throughout life, which are conducive to more social contacts and more structured opportunities during retirement (Calasanti, 1988). For example, a college professor may have a work and social routine that is more readily transferable to retirement than that of a construction worker. Differences between retirees in upper- and lower-status occupations do not develop with retirement, but rather reflect variations in social and personal resources throughout the life course. This view of retirement as a long-term process that presents continual challenges as retirees adapt is consistent with continuity theory.

Less is known about how gender or ethnic minority status influences retirement satisfaction. Women's retirement plans and satisfaction, like men's, appear to be strongly influenced by their health and their own pension and Social Security eligibility, not by their husbands'. The slightly lower levels of retirement satisfaction found among women seem to be due primarily to their lower retirement incomes, typically because of the lack of a private pension (Hayward, Grady, and McLaughlin, 1988; Johnson and Williamson, 1987). In addition, adjusting to a full-time housewife role during retirement can be difficult for women accustomed to the routine, rewards, and sociability of paid employment. In such instances, women's role transition may not be in synchrony with their husband's (Ekerdt and Vinick, 1991; Szinovacz, 1989).

Some African Americans who have had a lifetime of discontinuous work patterns and continue to experience economic need are unlikely to define themselves as retired. As "unretired-retired," they spend a greater percentage of their lives both working and disabled, employed intermittently beyond retirement because of their low wage base. In addition, African American males tend to have higher rates of disability and mortality across the life span, which result in inequities in retirement (Hayward, Friedman, and Chen, 1996; Gibson, 1991).

More recent literature portrays retirement not as a single transition in a person's life course but as a dynamic process with several stages where the retired/nonretired roles may overlap, and individuals move in and out of the work force through **serial retirement.** Instead of a "crisp" or unidirectional one-step movement from work to retirement, transitions are "blurred," involving complex patterns such as returning to employment, "unretirements," and later, second or third partial or full retirements. The exit and then re-entry into the work force reflect the increasing numbers of older people who want to return to employment, typically on a part-time or part-year basis, because they lack pension and nonwage resources of other kinds. The propensity to work part-time for economic reasons appears to be generalized, not specific to a particular job. Those who change jobs shortly before retirement are the most likely to work afterward, suggesting that "unretirement" is part of a repertoire of adaptive behavior in the later years. In sum, consistent with the life-course perspective discussed in Chapter 8, there is growing diversity regarding the timing of retirement, with changing norms about the timing and sequencing of paid and nonpaid roles or repeated work exits and re-entry (Henretta, 1997; Mutchler et al., 1997; Quadagno and Hardy, 1996; Treas and Torrecilka, 1995).

The Importance of Planning

Since retirement is a process, preparation and planning for a range of productive roles in old age are important in facilitating a successful transition to retirement. In fact, preparation and a belief in one's ability to make the transition to retirement have been found to be associated with a more positive retirement experience (Taylor and Shore, 1995). Retirement affects identity, self-esteem, and feelings of competence to the extent that it influences opportunities for new nonpaid roles and activities. Community involvement, for example, is an important predictor of well-being in retirement. People who have focused only on paid work all their lives cannot expect suddenly to develop new interests and skills upon their retirement. If nonwork interests are not developed prior to retirement, it is difficult to cultivate them after retirement (Kunkel, 1989).

Comprehensive retirement planning programs that address social activities, health promotion, and family relationships are one way of encouraging this development. Unfortunately, such programs are not widespread. Older men with more years of education, higher occupational status, and private pensions have greater access to these programs, as do government employees. Accordingly, older workers who might benefit the most from retirement preparation—single people, women, and those facing the probability of lower retirement incomes—are the least likely to have access to or utilize such services (Perkins, 1992).

Another approach to preparation is to restructure work patterns, gradually allowing longer vacations, shorter work days, job-sharing, and more opportunities for community involvement during the pre-retirement working years, thereby easing the transition to more leisure time. Most retirees seem not to want the constraints inherent in full-time employment. Instead, 75 percent of workers would prefer to retire gradually, phasing down from full-time to part-time work, if their employers were willing to retrain them for a new job, to continue making pension contributions after age 65, or to transfer them to jobs with less responsibility, fewer hours, and less pay as a transition to full retirement (Juster et al., 1996). In the Labor Force 2000 Survey, only 35 percent of participating firms offer opportunities to transfer

to jobs with reduced pay and responsibility, and only 21 percent offer a program of phased retirement through a gradual decrease in hours worked (The Commonwealth Fund, 1993). Fortunately, more companies are beginning to recognize that older workers are eager for new career directions or for part-time and other flexible work to meet their economic and social needs.

In sum, most people do not experience retirement as a difficult transition, provided they have sufficient preparation for it and an adequate income, enjoy good health, were not forced to retire, and were not wedded to their work. When people are unhappy in retirement, it is more often because of health or income problems than because of the loss of the worker role per se.

EMPLOYMENT STATUS

As noted above, some older adults never fully retire, and employment remains the primary means by which they are productive. Among those over age 65, approximately 16 percent of men and 9 percent of women are in the labor force (Hobbs and Damon, 1996). As illustrated in Figure 11.1, these percentages represent a decline from 1950, when nearly 46 percent of older men and 10 percent of older women were employed. In fact, the

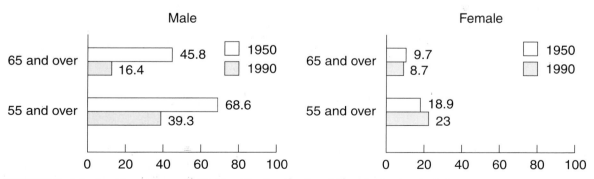

FIGURE 11.1 **Percentage of Civilian Noninstitutional Population in the Labor Force, by Age and Sex: 1950 and 1990**
SOURCE: U.S. Bureau of Labor Statistics. Data for 1990, Employment and Earnings, Vol. 38. No. 1, January 1991, Table 3; data for 1950, unpublished tabulations from 1950 Current Population Survey, available from the Bureau of Labor Statistics.

pattern of more men retiring early and more middle-aged and young-old women entering the labor force has meant that the labor-force activity of older Americans is becoming similar for men and women. This pattern of declining labor-force participation, especially among men, will continue through 2005. Older workers, who comprise less than 3 percent of the total labor force, are concentrated in jobs that initially require considerable education and a long training process (e.g., managerial and professional positions or self-employment), or those with flexible retirement policies (Quadagno and Hardy, 1996; Hobbs and Damon, 1996). Compared with their younger counterparts, older workers are less likely to be in jobs that are physically demanding, low or entry level, or high-technology.

While full-time employment has declined, part-time work among older women has expanded to 60 percent of those age 65 and over, but declined among their male counterparts, as illustrated in Figure 11.2. As noted above, part-time work is perceived by the working public of all ages as a desirable alternative, especially when a flexible work schedule is combined with the ability to draw partial pensions and therefore allows gradual retirement. Although the number of older people working part-time is smaller than the number who report they would like to do so, the proportion of workers on part-time schedules increases with age. Similarly, more older workers (25 per-

cent) are self-employed compared to younger workers (8 percent) (Hayward, Hardy, and Liu, 1994; AARP, 1991). Depending upon one's definition of career, 25 to 50 percent of all Americans, especially those who are self-employed, remain in the labor force in some capacity after they leave their primary career job. What is unclear is the extent to which part-time work represents underemployment of individuals whose hours of work have been reduced because of slack work or who cannot find full-time employment (Quadagno and Hardy, 1996).

Unemployment among Older People

Unfortunately, approximately 3 percent of older adults who seek employment are unable to find a job, with this rate increasing for older minorities (Hobbs and Damon, 1996). Several factors partially explain why more older people, especially among the young-old, are seeking employment, despite the trend toward early retirement. A primary factor is that many people choose to retire and then find it harder to live on their retirement income than they had anticipated (Calasanti and Bonardo, 1993). In fact, some studies have found that over 52 percent of retired workers return to work within 4 years, largely for economic reasons, moving back and forth from full or partial retirement into non-retirement, accepting jobs in the service sector and in smaller firms at substantially

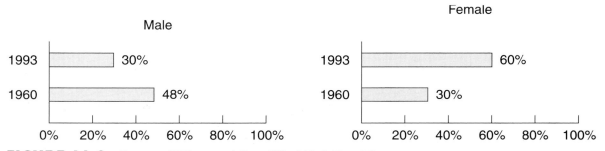

FIGURE 11.2 **Persons 65 Years and Over Who Work Part-Time**
SOURCE: Bureau of Labor Statistics, 1950, from 1950 Current Population Survey, unpublished tabulations; 1993 from Reprint of 1993, Annual Average Tables from the January 1994 Issue of Employment and Earnings.

lower pay in order to get by financially (Quadagno and Hardy, 1996).

Although financial need is the most important reason for seeking employment, others want to continue working after retirement in order to feel productive, to share expertise, and to reduce boredom. In such instances, retirees are often more willing to work in lower-status positions (Quadagno and Hardy, 1996; Achenbaum and Morrison, 1993). Continued employment into old age has been found to be associated with higher morale, happiness, adjustment, and longevity, in part because of the friendship networks with coworkers (Mor-Barak and Tynan, 1993). For some older people, a job can be a new career, a continuation of earlier work, or a way to learn new skills and form friendships.

Another major factor for older workers seeking to re-enter the work force is that they are more likely than younger workers to be forced out of work because of company closures, technological change, downsizing, mergers or reorganization. Many older workers who retire early may feel forced out of their jobs by workplace changes. In such instances, retirement is generally not "voluntary" (Quadagno and Hardy, 1996). In the past decade, more employers have tried to reduce costs and increase productivity by creating labor-force structures that can be readily altered at management discretion. This has resulted in the growth of a contingent or temporary work force, even for highly skilled professional positions, which does not provide security and benefits based on workers' seniority or skills (National Academy on Aging, 1994). Workers displaced by these market changes may be too old to have good job prospects, but nevertheless need to work to make ends meet. Those who do find jobs often experience downward mobility to low wages, temporary, or part-time work in smaller firms with fewer benefits (Quadagno and Hardy, 1996).

Even though the unemployment rate is lower among older workers compared to younger workers, they stay out of work longer than younger workers, suffer a greater loss of earnings in subsequent jobs, and are more likely to become dis-couraged and stop looking for work. For those needing to work for economic reasons or wanting to stay active, unemployment has been found to be associated with dissatisfaction with their lives (Commonwealth Fund, 1993; Quinn and Burkhauser, 1993).

Barriers to Employment

Unemployed older workers have a difficult time with their job search for a number of reasons. They may have been in one occupation for many years and therefore lack experience in job-hunting techniques. In addition, they are more vulnerable to skill obsolescence with changes in the economy, including the shift away from product manufacturing and medium-wage jobs in manufacturing toward low-wage positions in the service industries and high-wage positions in high-tech fields (National Academy on Aging, 1994; Hall and Mirvis, 1993; Mor-Barak and Tynan, 1993). Most businesses have not made changes in the work environment to prepare older workers for the rapidly changing workplace. Only about 4 percent of U.S. corporations provide retraining programs as incentives for older workers to return to active labor-force participation; in contrast, 62 percent encourage early retirement through inducement programs (Ramirez, 1989). Only a few programs, such as the federal **Senior Community Service Employment Program,** specifically target low-income older adults through retraining and subsidized employment.

The extent to which age-based employment discrimination is a barrier to employment is a topic of considerable debate. The U.S. public has been nearly unanimous in opposing mandatory retirement policies as discriminatory. The **Age Discrimination in Employment Act (ADEA)** was passed in 1967 to protect workers age 45 and over from denial of employment strictly because of age. This act was amended in 1978 to prohibit the use of pension plans as justification for not hiring older workers and to raise the mandatory retirement age to 70. In 1986, mandatory retirement was eliminated, and in 1990, the Older Workers

Benefit Protection Act prohibited employers from treating older workers differently from younger workers during a reduction in work force. The Americans with Disabilities Act, passed in 1990, also offers protection to older adults. Employers are expected to make work-related adjustments and redesign jobs for workers with disabilities, including impairments in sensory, manual, or speaking skills. Despite such legislation, age discrimination alleged as the basis for loss of employment is the fastest-growing form of unfair dismissal litigation, and the ADEA has been ineffectual in promoting the hiring of older workers (Quadagno and Hardy, 1996). Perceptions that most employers discriminate against older people remain widespread and can make it difficult for older people to find employment. Although the most blatant forms of age discrimination, such as newspaper ads restricting jobs to younger people, have declined since the passage of the ADEA, more subtle forms persist, such as norms of attractiveness in dress and hairstyle. Employers can make a job situation undesirable to older workers by stopping raises and promotions and removing responsibilities to downgrade workers' jobs.

One reason that discrimination persists is the pervasiveness of negative stereotypes about aging and productivity. Many employers still assume that older workers will not perform as well as younger workers because of poor health, declining energy, diminished intellectual ability, or different work styles. Employers express concerns about older workers in terms of cost effectiveness, given their proximity to retirement; their flexibility with the changing workplace; their comfort with new technology; and their suitability for and costs of training. These attitudes endure despite the growth of research findings that older workers have lower rates of turnover, voluntary absenteeism, and injuries (Quadagno and Hardy, 1996; Sterns and McDaniel, 1994). In fact, despite their concerns, most employers rate older workers highly on loyalty, dependability, emotional stability, and ability to get along with coworkers (Barth et al., 1993).

In addition to these general barriers to employment, numerous obstacles exist to part-time employment. Even when an older person indicates an interest in working part-time, he or she may not be able to find such employment at the same wage level that full-time work offers. There are employer policies against part-time workers drawing partial pensions (e.g., defined-benefit pension plans do not permit a worker to stay on the job and collect a pension) and Social Security limits on the amount that can be earned at a given age before full benefits are reduced (until after age 70). Employers may resist the additional administrative work and higher health insurance costs entailed in hiring part-time or temporary older workers, (e.g., it is more costly to insure older than

---

BARRIERS TO EMPLOYMENT

Mr. Lewis is a 60-year-old with no car, no savings, and no relatives nearby. He works two part-time jobs and finds it difficult to make ends meet. One of his jobs is under a government program with a local agency that signed an agreement to hire him full-time when an opening arose. That was over 2 years ago. In that time, they have hired 15 to 20 people without experience or training in the field to do the job he would like. They are all people under age 40. Mr. Lewis has a background of 20 years in large organizations, so he assumes that he has the appropriate experience.

At first, Mr. Lewis was told he had to "go through the system" to be hired full-time. Much later, after he had been through the system time and time again, it became obvious he would never be hired full-time. Eventually, he was told that "the agency wants to give younger employees a chance to come up the career ladder." He is resentful at seeing these younger workers move ahead so quickly. He is beginning to wonder if he is a victim of age discrimination, but he does not know what he can do about his situation.

younger workers); those costs, however, may be tempered by the advantage of fewer employer-paid benefits for dependents among older workers (Quadagno and Hardy, 1996).

Creating New Opportunities for Work

Advocacy organizations for older people maintain that judging a person's job qualifications solely on the basis of age, without regard to suitability for a job, is inequitable, and that chronological age alone is a poor predictor of job performance. Not hiring older workers deprives society of their skills and capacities. To address potential labor shortages in the future, changes in government and corporate policies and pensions are needed both to extend employment opportunities for older workers and to modify the financial incentives for work. In most cases, work environments may be modified and technical training provided to compensate for any drawbacks associated with older workers, if employers are willing to do so.

However, relatively few companies have implemented skills training programs or educated managers about ways to involve older workers. This pattern of not fully utilizing the resources and expertise of older workers will need to change early in the twenty-first century when a majority

of the older population is likely to seek employment. New opportunities for older workers will be needed for the following reasons: a decreasing pool of younger workers, a healthier and better educated cohort of older persons who are oriented toward lifelong careers, economic expectations to continue a similar lifestyle, and increasingly expensive health and long-term care (Parnes and Sommers, 1994; Mor-Barak et al., 1992). Already, older people are moving into jobs traditionally filled by youth (e.g., providing service at fast food restaurants), in part because of the decline among young people willing to work in such positions.

ECONOMIC STATUS: SOURCES OF INCOME IN RETIREMENT

We turn now to economic status in old age, which is largely influenced by environmental conditions, especially past and current employment patterns and resultant retirement income and benefits. These patterns are major components of the larger environment that shapes older people's daily opportunities and competence in numerous ways. Although economic resources in themselves do not guarantee satisfaction, they do affect many of the options available to older people to lead satisfying lives—their health, social relationships,

WAYS TO RESTRUCTURE WORK TO ENABLE OLDER PEOPLE TO HAVE THE OPTION OF LONGER WORK LIVES INCLUDE:

1. Changes in federal policy, such as modifying Social Security and pension restrictions against earnings, and giving tax incentives to employers who hire older workers.
2. Job referral, training, and counseling programs to link older adults and potential employees. For example, the Experience Plus Program which provides training in computer processing, the Retired Senior Executives Program, and counseling services through the American Association of Retired Persons.
3. Programs to accommodate older workers' needs in the job environment, such as part-time work, job sharing, flex time, and incremental retirement though reduced work weeks or "gliding out" plans of staged retirement that permit a gradual shift to a part-time schedule (Mor-Barak and Tynan, 1993). Examples of innovative use of retirees are the Travelers Insurance Company's hiring of temporary workers and Days Inn's employment of older workers in national reservation centers.

living arrangements, community activities, and political participation. For many people, economic status is consistent across the life course. For example, ethnic minorities in low-paying jobs in young and middle adulthood generally face a continuation of poverty in old age. Other older people, including widowed or divorced women who depended on their husbands' income, or retirees with only Social Security as income, may face poverty or near-poverty for the first time in their lives. Alternatively, those in higher-paying careers with private pensions and assets continue to enjoy economic advantages in old age, reflecting a pattern of cumulative advantage across the life course (Crystal, 1996).

The median income for older men in 1995 was $16,484; for older women, $9355 (Administration on Aging, 1997). It is estimated that older individuals need 65 to 80 percent of their preretirement income in order to maintain their living standard in retirement (Juster et al., 1996). Since retirement can reduce individual incomes by one-third to one-half, most retirees must adjust their standard of living downward—at the same time that their out-of-pocket spending for items such as health care needs may increase. Sources of income for the older population include savings, assets, and as illustrated in Figure 11.3, investments, Social Security, private pensions, and for a small percentage, a salary. The distribution of income sources varies widely, however, with women, ethnic minorities, and the oldest-old most likely to rely on Social Security. Mr. Valdres and Mrs.

Howard in the introductory vignettes demonstrate the diversity among older people in their reliance on these various income sources.

Social Security

Older people depend more heavily on Social Security for their retirement income than on any other source. In 1995, 42 percent of all income received by older units (i.e., a married couple with one or both members aged 65 or older and living together, or a person aged 65 or older not living with a spouse) was from Social Security (see Figure 11.3). Social Security is received by approximately 95 percent of older people. Of those aged 65 and over, 66 percent received at least half of their income and 16 percent all their income from Social Security; this rate increases to 85 percent among low-income households and those elders over age 85 (see Figure 11.4). The average monthly benefit for retired workers in 1995 was $720, with Social Security replacing, on average, only 44 percent of preretirement earnings (Atchley, 1997; Social Security Administration, 1996).

Yet Social Security was never intended to provide an adequate retirement income, but rather a floor of protection or the first tier of support. It was assumed that pensions and individual savings would also help support people in their later years. This assumption has not been borne out, as reflected in the proportionately lower income received by retirees from savings and private pensions. It has been estimated that without Social

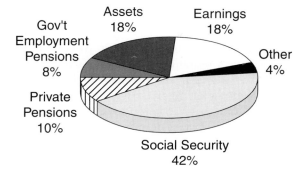

FIGURE 11.3 **Percent of Aggregate Income of the Population 65+ from Various Sources, 1994**
SOURCE: Social Security Administration.
Fast Facts and Figures about Social Security. Washington, DC: U.S. Government Printing Office, 1996.

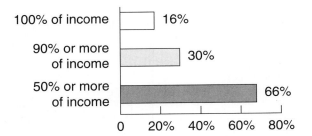

FIGURE 11.4 **Percent of Beneficiary Units with Social Security Benefits as a Major Source of Income, 1994**
SOURCE: Social Security Administration.
Fast Facts and Figures about Social Security. Washington, DC: U.S. Government Printing Office, 1996.

Security, poverty rates among the older population would increase from 11 percent to 55 percent (Devlin and Arye, 1997). Not surprisingly, older individuals with the lowest total income have Social Security as their sole income source.

The Social Security system is a public trust into which all pay and all are guaranteed an income floor in old age or disability. In order to be insured, a worker retiring now must be age 62.5 or more and must have been employed at least 10 years in covered employment. The level of benefits received is based on a percentage of the retired worker's average monthly earnings that were subject to Social Security tax. Insured persons are eligible for full benefits at age 65; if they choose to retire at age 62.5, their monthly benefits are permanently reduced and are not increased when they reach age 65. Approximately 60 percent of all recipients currently receive such reduced benefits because they have retired before the age of 62 (Hobbs and Damon, 1996). Social Security benefits may also be reduced for those who work after age 65. This "earnings test" has been strongly criticized as an unfair deterrent to older people's labor-force participation. Limited exceptions to this rule now exist, and workers over age 70 are exempt from the earnings test (Quadagno and Hardy, 1996). Since 1975, Social Security benefits have been automatically increased annually whenever the Consumer Price Index increases by 3 percent or more. This is known as the *cost of living adjustment,* or COLA. They have thus been protected from inflation. Since benefits are related to a worker's wage and employment history, women and ethnic minorities, with their pattern of inter-

mittent or part-time work, tend to receive less than the average monthly benefit. Some of the oldest-old persons never qualify for Social Security benefits because they were employed in occupations such as domestic work not covered by the system.

Women's Social Security payments may also be sharply reduced by widowhood or divorce. A widow may start to collect surviving dependents' benefits when she reaches age 60; however, she will lose about 28 percent of what she would have received if she had waited until age 65. But for each additional year after age 60, a widow receives a larger percentage of Social Security benefits. And after age 65, she receives full benefits even if she has been getting only 72 percent for the past 4 years. Widows and divorcees under age 60 who are not disabled and who do not have children under age 18 entitled to Social Security, or who are not responsible for disabled persons, cannot receive Social Security benefits. This group of women, who generally do not have a paid work history and do not qualify for any public benefits, are often referred to as **displaced homemakers.** Since the average age at widowhood is 66 years, many women face this "widow's gap" (Martin-Matthews, 1996). A woman who is divorced after at least 10 years of marriage and who reaches retirement age may collect up to 50 percent of her ex-husband's retirement benefits, but only when he turns 62 and if she remains single. Because many widows or divorced women do not meet these criteria, a large percentage of single older women live in poverty or near-poverty conditions. These gender inequities are discussed further in Chapter 14.

DISPLACED HOMEMAKER

Mrs. Kelly lost her husband over a year ago at the age of 56. Her daughter was 15 years old at the time. When the daughter turned 16 and was no longer considered a legal dependent, Mrs. Kelly's Social Security check stopped. Mrs. Kelly has no health insurance; she cannot work because she is caring for her 90-year-old mother. Nevertheless, she is too young for Social Security and Medicare benefits.

As described in Chapter 15, the Social Security payroll tax is a regressive tax (i.e., requiring the same rate for both the rich and the poor). This means that low-income workers, many of whom are women and minorities, pay a larger proportion of their monthly salary for the Social Security tax compared to higher-income workers. On the other hand, proportionately, lower-income workers benefit more from Social Security when they retire, receiving benefits equal to 90 percent of their working wages, while high-income workers' benefits are only 19 percent of their prior salary. In addition, they must now pay income tax on 50 percent of their Social Security benefits (Beedon, 1994). Most people do not plan sufficiently for their retirement income, presuming that Social Security will be adequate and failing to assess the impact of inflation and reduced income levels. Some are able to supplement their Social Security income with assets, pensions, or part-time employment.

Assets

Income from **assets** (e.g., savings, home equity, and personal property) comprised 18 percent of all income received by older people in 1994, and was the second most important income source. The median income of those with asset income is more than twice the median income of those without asset income ($19,996 compared to $8590; Social Security Administration, 1996). However, asset income is unevenly distributed, with larger income disparities intensified by race and gender. Nearly 33 percent of the older units—typically the oldest-old, women, and ethnic minorities—report no asset income, and 26 percent of those with asset income report less than $500 a year. Only 33 percent of those with asset income—typically married-couple households—received more than $5,000 a year from this source. Older people's assets consist primarily of home equity, representing 40 to 50 percent of their net worth. Currently 76 percent of older people own their homes, although this percentage declines among ethnic minority elders. Yet 50 percent of older homeowners spend at least 45 percent of their incomes on property taxes, utilities, and maintenance (Smith 1997a; Hobbs and Damon, 1996; Quinn and Smeeding, 1994). Home equity therefore does not represent liquid wealth or cash and cannot be relied on to cover daily expenses. Even though most older people with fixed incomes cannot depend on assets to meet current expenses, it is nevertheless true that their net worth tends to be greater than those under age 35 (National Academy on Aging, 1994).

Earnings

Earnings are an important income source to the young-old and to those with the highest income from assets and pensions, but decline in importance with age. Thus, individuals age 65 to 69 receive 30 percent of their income from earnings, compared with only 4 percent for those 80 years and older. Overall, current job earnings form approximately 18 percent of the income of older units (Hobbs and Damon, 1996). This low percentage is consistent with the declining labor-force participation among people age 65 and over.

Pensions

While most jobholders are covered by Social Security, which is a *general public pension,* some employees are covered by *job-specific pensions*. These are available only through a specific position of employment and are administered by a work organization, union, or private insurance company. Job-specific pensions include *public employee pensions* (for those who work for federal, state, or local governments) and *private pensions*. Since 1950, pension plans have increased from 25 to 50 percent among private sector workers and from 60 to 90 percent among civilian government workers. However, only half of those eligible for benefits have had enough years of service to be fully vested in a plan and thus entitled to future benefits. Relatively few workers are enrolled in private pension programs that provide the replacement rate of income necessary for retirement. Employee pensions provide approximately 18 percent of the older population's aggregate income. Overall, 66 percent of older units receive some income from public and/or private pension benefits. In recent years, employee pension coverage, especially among ethnic minorities, has declined (Hardy and Kruso, 1998; Atchley, 1997; Villa, Wallace, and Markides, 1997). Most private pensions are intended to supplement Social Security, not to be the sole source of income. In addition, economic recessions, escalating health care costs, and inflation during the past two decades have reduced pension assets.

Pension benefits are generally based on earnings or a combination of earnings and years of service. Eligibility age is usually between ages 60 and 65, although it ranges from ages 50 to 70. Only about 3 percent of pension plans provide for cost-of-living increases. Yet an annual inflation rate of 5 percent for 15 years can erode the real value of benefits by about one-half, making inflation the greatest threat to those dependent on private pensions. Federal policies support private pension programs by postponing taxation of pension benefits, allowing benefits to be invested and to generate earnings that are not taxed. Only when the pension is drawn is tax paid, after the money has produced many years of earnings.

Private pensions go to workers with long, continuous service in jobs that have such coverage. In general these are higher-income, relatively skilled positions of 30 or more years concentrated among large, unionized settings or service and financial sectors. As a result, retirees who benefit from private pensions tend to be in the middle and upper income brackets, with the lowest-income older persons receiving, on average, only 3 percent of their income from pensions (Villa et al., 1997). Pension coverage varies dramatically by class, race, gender, and age, being relatively low for women, ethnic minorities, and lower-income workers in small nonunion plants and low-wage industries such as retail sales and services, and for retirees currently over age 65. In particular, African Americans and whites with the lowest wages are ten times less likely to have a pension compared to those with the highest wages (Juster et al., 1996). Inequities are compounded for women, who are more likely than men to be "in and out" of the labor force and therefore less likely to achieve the required length of service for vesting. Nonemployed women face an additional problem: most pension plans reduce benefits for those who elect to protect their spouses through survivors' benefits. In the past, many men have chosen higher monthly benefits rather than survivors' benefits; when they died, their wives were left without adequate financial protection.

The **Employment Retirement Income Security Act (ERISA)**, enacted in 1974 to strengthen private pension systems, was the first comprehensive effort to regulate them. As a result, private pension plans must **vest benefits** (vesting refers to the amount of time a person must work on a job in order to acquire rights to the pension) in such a way that all covered workers are guaranteed a full pension upon retirement after 10 or 15 years with the company, regardless of whether or not they remain with that organization until retirement. This means that a person could work for one firm for 12 years, move to a second company until retirement at age 65, and then receive pensions from both based on years of service. Although vesting options increased under ERISA, portability (whereby pension contributions and rights with one organization can be transferred to another) remains low. This has been criticized for penalizing worker mobility and career changes. For example, an individual who serves 40 years with one company will receive a higher pension than one who spent 20 years with one firm and 20 with another.

ERISA also strengthened standards for financing, administering, and protecting pension plans, although during the recession of the 1990s some major pension plans were discontinued. Tax-exempt individual retirement accounts (IRAs) were made available to all workers in 1981, in an effort to increase personal savings for retirement. Under the 1986 tax reform plan, employees with other private pensions are no longer able to use an IRA as a tax deduction. Yet IRAs are not an option for most workers; they are used primarily by those earning $50,000 or more who have disposable income. Lower-income workers generally cannot spare the money, and the tax benefit is considerably less for them. Ironically, the people who need retirement income the most generally cannot take advantage of IRAs. As with employer pension plans, the tax deferral of IRAs provides the equivalent of a long-term interest-free loan (e.g., tax shelter) to the predominantly high-income taxpayers who use IRAs. In sum, the equity goals of Social Security are outweighed by private pensions, asset income, IRAs, and other preferential tax treatment for a small percentage of wealthy older adults, which has resulted in greater economic inequality among the older population over time.

POVERTY AMONG OLD AND YOUNG

The economic status of older people has improved since the 1960s. In 1959, 35.2 percent of the population aged 65 and over fell below the official poverty line compared to 10.5 percent in 1995. In contrast, the poverty figure was 14.7 percent for all those under age 65, and 22 percent of children under age 18. Nearly 66 percent of white married couple households with an older person, and 48 percent of such African American households, had incomes of at least $20,000 (Hobbs and Damon, 1996). (See Figure 11.5 for median income in 1994.) At the same time, there has been an accumulation of wealth among a small percent of older adults, with the older population increasingly dichotomized into rich and poor. Between 1979 to

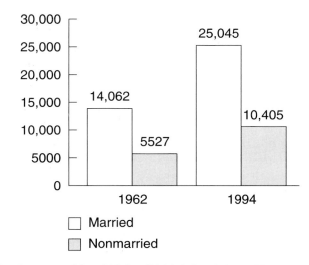

FIGURE 11.5   Median Income of Aged Units (1994 dollars) Ages 65+

SOURCE: Social Security Administration. *Fast Facts and Figures about Social Security.* Washington, DC: U.S. Government Printing Office, 1996.

1990, 20 percent of older families with lowest incomes experienced a decline in real income, while older families in the top fifth experienced increases in real income. As a result, the top 5 percent of older people with financial means possess 27 percent of all the wealth among Americans over age 70 (Smith, 1997b; Villa et al., 1997). These high-income elders depend primarily upon assets, earnings, private pensions, and savings for their retirement income, not on Social Security.

The primary reasons for the older population's improved economic status are that today's older cohort has benefited economically from the strong performance of the economy in the 1950s and 1960s, accumulation of home equity, and expansion of Social Security and other pension protection. The major factors underlying these gains are improved and longer coverage by pensions, the 1972 increases in Social Security benefits, the 1975 automatic annual cost of living adjustments (COLAs) in Social Security, and implementation of the Supplemental Security Income program.

As a result of these changes, a widely held public perception is that all older persons are better off financially than other age groups. This perception is also fueled by the increase of poverty among children under age 18, making them the poorest age group. It is important to recognize, however, that this decline in the income status of children is largely structural, caused by economic and demographic forces, not by the older population itself (Ozawa, 1996).

It is true that when all sources of income are considered (including tax and in-kind benefits), fewer older families have subpoverty resources than younger families. But this overlooks the fact that many older people are not financially comfortable, despite the overall improved income status. A larger proportion (7.5 percent) of older people than younger (4.5 percent) fall just above the poverty line and thus are "near poor" and at risk for poverty. This means that approximately 18 percent of older people are poor or near poor (Administration on Aging, 1997). These "tweeners" are a group caught between upper-income and poor older people—not well enough off to be financially secure but not poor enough to qualify for the means-tested safety net of Medicaid and Supplemental Security Income. Paradoxically, the only way that they can improve their economic well-being and qualify for Medicaid and Supplemental Security Income is to spend down. In fact, without Social Security, the poverty rate for the older population would be nearly 55 percent (Social Security Administration, 1996). The percent of subgroups who are poor even with Social Security and the percent kept out of poverty by Social Security is illustrated in Figure 11.6.

These figures also do not reflect the fact that the federal poverty standard for a single adult younger than age 65 is higher than for an older individual. The U.S. Bureau of the Census has assumed that the costs of food and other necessities are lower for older people, even though they spend proportionately more on housing, transportation, and health care than do younger groups. If the same standard were applied to the older population as to the other age groups, the poverty rate for older people would increase to over 15 percent (Crystal, 1996; Quinn and Smeeding, 1994). In addition, older people spend a greater share of their income than younger adults do on the basic necessities of food, utilities, and health care—areas particularly hard hit by inflation. Older adults are also less likely to have reserve funds to cover emergencies such as catastrophic medical expenses. As a result, low-income elders are at risk of malnutrition, poorly heated and inadequate housing, and neglect of medical needs.

The stereotype of the static nature of poverty, suggested by cross-sectional information, must be altered to take account of the fact that many older people move in and out of poverty over time. When such individual movements are identified, the risk of falling below the poverty line *at some time* during a specified period is more than double the highest average risk for older couples, and is raised by almost 30 percent for widows. For example, many women become poor for the first time in their lives after depleting their assets while

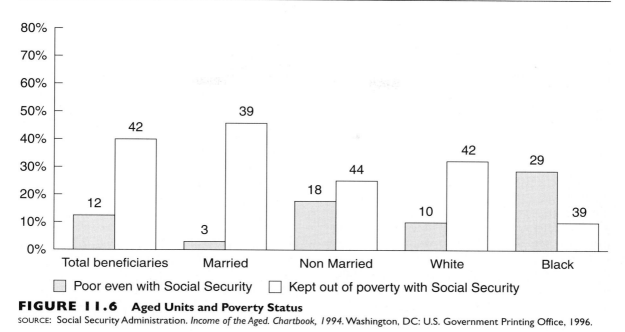

FIGURE 11.6   **Aged Units and Poverty Status**
SOURCE: Social Security Administration. *Income of the Aged. Chartbook, 1994.* Washington, DC: U.S. Government Printing Office, 1996.

caring for a dying partner. Once an older person moves into poverty, she or he is less likely to exit than younger age groups. There are also many "hidden poor" among the older population who are either institutionalized or living with relatives and thus not counted in official census statistics. In sum, more older people are at marginal levels of income and at greater risk of poverty than younger people; they are also more likely to be trapped in long-term poverty (Hobbs and Damon, 1996; Crystal, 1996). In addition, there is wide socio-economic diversity within the older population, with economic marginality more pronounced among older women, those who live alone, those outside metropolitan areas, ethnic minorities, and the oldest-old.

As discussed in detail in Chapter 14, older women are among the poorest group in our society. The risk of poverty among couples and single men has sharply fallen, leaving poverty in old age a characteristic primarily of single frail women over age 85 who have outlived their husbands. Although women account for approxi-

mately half of the older population, they comprise nearly 75 percent of the older poor. Nearly 16 percent of older women are poor compared to approximately 9 percent of older men; this rate increases to 19.7 percent among women age 85 and over living in metropolitan areas, to 21 percent among widowed women, and to approximately 23 percent among women living alone and 26 percent of those divorced or separated (Simon-Rusinowitz, Wilson, Marks, Krach, and Welch, 1998; Hobbs and Damon, 1996). Widows account for nearly 50 percent of all older poor, reflecting the loss of pension income and earnings often associated with the death of a wage-earner spouse. The median income of widowed women is four-fifths that of widowed men, since men are more likely to have retained pensions or earned income after a spouse's death (U.S. Senate Special Committee on Aging, 1992). The primary reasons for their lower retirement incomes are women's interrupted work histories related to family responsibilities; lower wages and their resultant lower

Social Security benefits; and less likelihood of private pensions to supplement Social Security. These factors that lead to higher proportions of poor older women are referred to as the **feminization of poverty.**

African American and Hispanic elders of both sexes have substantially lower incomes than their white counterparts, as shown in Figure 11.7. The median income of older African American and Hispanic men living alone is about one-third lower than older white men living alone. Although the differences are less pronounced among women, the median incomes of older African American and Hispanic women are generally two-thirds to three-quarters those of white women. Minority women's slight economic advantage relative to that of their male peers stems from the higher rates of unemployment and unsteady work histories among ethnic minority men. Not only are median incomes lower but the average black or Hispanic

households have no financial or liquid assets at all (Smith, 1997b). Not surprisingly, the poverty rates among ethnic minority elders are higher than among whites. In 1993, nearly 30 percent of older African Americans and over 21 percent of older Hispanics were poor compared to 10.7 percent of older whites (Hobbs and Damon, 1996). Poverty rates are the highest among minority women living alone. Fifty to sixty percent of older African American women not living with family have incomes below the poverty line; and almost 70 percent of rural African American women live in poverty, making them the most economically deprived group in our society; this contrasts with 6 percent for persons in families headed by a male. Within each ethnic minority population, poverty is more common for women than for men (Administration on Aging, 1997).

The poverty rates among the young-old are lower, in part due to continued employment or to

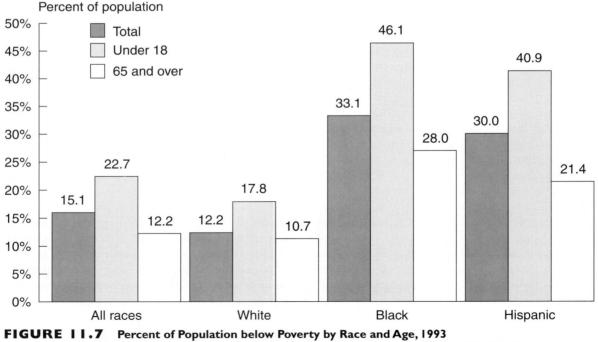

FIGURE 11.7   **Percent of Population below Poverty by Race and Age, 1993**
SOURCE: Income, Poverty, and Valuation of Noncash Benefits: 1993. U.S. Bureau of the Census, February, 1995, Table 8.

the greater likelihood of retirement with good pension plans. In contrast, older cohorts continue to experience income loss as they age, and therefore economic deprivation relative to younger cohorts. The poverty rate for those 65 to 74 years is 10.7 percent; for those over age 85, 19.8 percent. The fact that median income declines with age is due in part to the disproportionate number of non-married women in older age groups (Hobbs and Damon, 1996; Social Security Administration, 1996). The economic hardships of older cohorts are often compounded by a lifetime of discrimination, by historical factors such as working at jobs with no pension or inadequate health insurance, and by recent stressful events such as loss of spouse or declining health. Accordingly, older cohorts are more likely to live alone, which is associated with poverty. Of all older people living alone, 24 percent are poor, compared to 14 percent of those living with others. When the poor and the near-poor are grouped together, 45 percent of older people living alone fall into this category. This increases with age, with nearly 50 percent of those age 85 and over either poor or near-poor (U.S. Senate Special Committee on Aging, 1992). Mr. Valdres and Mrs. Clark in the introductory vignettes illustrate such older adults. Mr. Valdres worked as a migrant farm laborer and therefore relies on the minimum Social Security level for his income. Mrs. Clark, on the other hand, thought her savings would be adequate for her old age, but the cost of caring for her ill husband for 18 years left her penniless.

In sum, despite the improved financial situation of the older population generally, large pockets of poverty and near-poverty exist, particularly among women, ethnic minorities, those over age 75, those who live alone, and those who live in rural areas. As a result, economic inequality is actually greater among older people than among other age groups. Aging advocates maintain that any strategies to alleviate poverty among today's older Americans cannot rely on an improving labor market and must be immediate, such as increasing levels of Social Security for those with low lifetime earnings and insuring that women and men have full access to benefits accrued by their spouses (Smith, 1997b; McLaughlin and Jensen, 1993).

Public Assistance

Of the older population, approximately 12 percent receive some type of public assistance, primarily in the form of **Supplemental Security Income (SSI)** (Hobbs and Damon, 1996). This percentage increases among ethnic minorities and women. SSI was established in 1974 to provide a minimum income for elders living on the margin of poverty. In contrast to Social Security, SSI does not require a history of covered employment contributions. Instead, eligibility is determined by a categorical requirement that the recipient be 65 years of age, blind, or disabled, with limits on amount of monthly income and assets determining eligibility. In 1995, SSI provided a subsistence income to over 6.5 million needy persons, 75 percent of whom are women age 65 and over. Yet only about 50 percent of the eligible older poor participate in SSI, and the percent of older recipients has actually declined since 1974. For those who do so, the federal SSI benefits fall substantially below the poverty line. Even when states supplement federal benefits, levels remain low, so that SSI supplies only 14 percent of the income of poor older people (Social Security Administration, 1996). Those who receive SSI may also qualify for food stamps, but only a minority of older recipients receive the minimum food-stamp benefit. An additional limitation of SSI is that gifts or contributions from family members for food, clothing, or housing may be counted as income and may result in the older person's benefit being cut. Becoming eligible for SSI is a time-consuming and often demeaning process, requiring extensive documentation and the ability to deal with the complexity of conflicting criteria for benefits from SSI, Medicaid, and food stamps. Despite these barriers and public perceptions that older people are not needy, increasing numbers of "poor" or "near-poor" rely on public assistance, either through SSI or food stamps.

As noted earlier, economic status, along with health, living arrangements, and marital status, influence the nonpaid roles and activities in old age—particularly voluntary association membership, voluntarism, religious participation, and political involvement. We turn now to discuss these other forms of productive aging.

PATTERNS AND FUNCTIONS OF NONPAID ROLES AND ACTIVITIES

Leisure

The term **leisure** evokes different reactions in people. For some, it signifies wasting time. For others, it is only the frenzied pursuit of "leisure activities" on the weekends that sustains them through the work week. Leisure can be defined as any activity characterized by the absence of obligation that is inherently satisfying and has intrinsic meaning. Free time alone is not necessarily leisure. Instead, the critical variable is how a person defines tasks and situations to bring intrinsic pleasure. Accordingly, leisure implies feelings of freedom and pleasure. People who engage in sports, travel, or visits to museums and do not experience such feelings may still be at "work" rather than at "leisure" (Kelly, 1982; Kleiber and Kelly, 1980). People's reactions to the concept of leisure are clearly influenced by cultural values attached to work and a mistrust of non-work time. Because of American cultural values of productivity and hard work—values that are particularly strong for the current generation of older persons—many older people lack experience in satisfying non-work activities at earlier phases in their lives. Societal values regarding leisure are changing, however, with more legitimacy given to non-work activities throughout the life cycle, as evidenced by the growing number of classes and businesses that specialize in leisure. For low-income or ethnic minority elders or for older people in developing countries, however, leisure may be a meaningless concept if they have had to continue working or lack the resources for satisfying recreational time.

Disagreement regarding the value of leisure pursuits for older people is reflected in the gerontological literature. Most definitions of productive aging do not include activities of a personal enrichment nature, which would exclude leisure activities such as watching television, attending a concert, and travel (Caro, Bass, and Chen, 1993; Herzog and Morgan, 1993, 1992; Danigelis and McIntosh, 1993). An early perspective was that leisure roles cannot substitute for work roles because they are not legitimated by societal norms. Since work is a dominant value in U.S. society, it was argued that individuals cannot derive self-respect from leisure. It was also observed that older individuals, fearing the embarrassment of failing in a leisure activity, avoid leisure pursuits that are common to younger people (Miller, 1965).

A closely related perspective is that retirement is legitimated in our society by an ethic that esteems leisure that is earnest, occupied, and filled with activity—a "busy" ethic, which is consistent with the activity theory of aging (Ekerdt, 1986). For those with strong work values, work-like activities are probably important for achieving satisfaction in retirement (Hooker and Ventes, 1984). The prevalence of the "busy" ethic is reflected in the question commonly asked of retirees: What do you do to keep busy? "Keeping busy" and engaging in productive activities analogous to work are presumed to ease the adjustment to retirement by adapting retired life to prevailing societal norms, although the "busy" ethic is contrary to the definition of leisure as intrinsically satisfying. A counter argument is that leisure can replace the work role and provide personal satisfaction in later life, especially when the retired person has good health and an adequate income, and when retirement activities build upon preretirement skills and interests.

Although there are wide variations, patterns of meaningful nonpaid activity among older individuals have been identified. Most activity changes are gradual, reflecting a consistency and a narrowing of the repertoire of activities as individuals age. Compared to younger people, older people are more likely to engage in solitary and sedentary pursuits, such as watching television, visiting with family and friends, and reading. The time spent on personal care, sleep and rest, and hobbies and shopping is greater for older adults than younger and middle-aged individuals, comprising a larger fraction of older adults' days (Verbrugge, Gruber-Baldini, and Fozard, 1996). When judged by younger persons or by middle-class standards, these essential and universal activities may be viewed as "boring and nonproductive." Yet, the ability to perform these more mundane activities—personal care, cooking, puttering around the house, or sitting in quiet reflection—can be critical to maintaining older people's competence, self-esteem, and life satisfaction. Furthermore, these routines may represent realistic adjustments to de-

Leisure activities for many older people include maintaining their gardens.

clining energy levels and incomes. Such routine leisure pursuits, consistent with the broader concept of productive aging, may thus reflect rational choices to develop ways of coping congruent with environmental changes and may also enhance quality of life.

Leisure activities also vary by gender and socioeconomic status. Older men tend to do more household and yard maintenance and paid work outside the home, while older women perform more housework, child care, volunteer work, and participate in more voluntary associations. Not surprisingly, higher-income older people, especially those living in planned retirement communities, tend to be more active in leisure pursuits than low-income elders (Verbrugge et al., 1996; Riddick and Stewart, 1994; Danigelis and McIntosh, 1993). Such differences in activities are attributable primarily to the costs of pursuing them, not necessarily to inherent differences in people of low and high socioeconomic status. Several benefit programs are designed to reduce financial barriers to leisure. For instance, Golden Passports give older people reduced admission fees to national parks. Similar programs at the local or state level provide free admission to parks, museums, and cultural activities, and reduced prices from businesses and transportation. Not surprisingly, a wide range of leisure-oriented businesses, including group travel programs, are marketing services to higher income older adults.

The psychological benefits of leisure perceived by older participants include: companionship (e.g., playing cards or going dancing); compensation for past activities (e.g., picnicking instead of hiking); temporary disengagement (e.g., watching TV); comfortable solitude (e.g., reading); expressive solitude (e.g., knitting and crocheting); and expressive service (e.g., volunteer service, attending meetings of social groups) (Tinsley, Colbs, Teaff, and Kaufman, 1985). Nonpaid activities also serve to help maintain ties with others and to provide new sources of personal meaning and competence to replace earlier sources that have been lost. An association has been found between leisure activities and a positive identity and self-concept among older people. Accordingly, activities that result in a sense of being valued and contributing to society have been found to be positively related to life satisfaction and mental well-being in retirement (Riddick and Stewart, 1994). This relationship does not mean, however, that leisure activity itself creates well-being, since older people who are active also tend to be healthier and of higher socioeconomic status. In fact, it appears that the quality of interactions with others in non-work may be more salient than the number or frequency of interactions for life satisfaction and morale (Kelly, Steinkamp, and Kelly, 1986; Cutler and Hendricks, 1990).

Membership in Voluntary Associations

Given the emphasis in our society on being active, productive, and a participant, voluntary association membership is often assumed to be "good" leisure activity for older people. Based on such assumptions, well-meaning professionals may go to considerable lengths to try to recruit older people to such associations, oftentimes without success. Overall, older people are less likely to belong to organizations than are younger people, but their reduced membership does not necessarily indicate a slackening of interest with age. Rather, membership is most closely tied to social class and varies among cultures. When socioeconomic status is taken into account, older people show considerable stability in their general level of voluntary association participation from middle age until their sixties (Cutler and Hendricks, 1990).

The kinds of organizations in which older people participate vary by gender and ethnic minority status. Older women appear to be more active participants in voluntary associations than older men. Women's multiple roles at earlier phases of the life span, such as volunteer work, have been found to be positively related to health and occupying multiple roles in old age (Danigelis and McIntosh, 1993; Moen, Dempster-McClain, and Williams, 1992). Older African Americans have higher rates of organizational membership than do older whites or members of other ethnic

minority groups; although for both blacks and whites, membership is most frequent among those with better health and higher income and education levels. Black and white elders differ in the types of associations they join. Older blacks are especially likely to belong to church-related groups and social and recreational clubs; older whites frequently belong to nationality organizations and senior citizen clubs (Walls and Zarit, 1991; Krout, Cutler, and Coward, 1990). Hispanics participate in fraternal and service-oriented organizations, mutual aid societies, and "hometown" clubs.

Senior centers are a common mechanism for voluntary association activities. These vary greatly in the type of services offered, ranging from purely recreational events to social action, or the delivery of social and health services, including health screening and health promotion. In fact, the Older Americans Act identifies senior centers as preferred focal points for comprehensive, coordinated service delivery. Despite the range of activities, only about 15 percent of older persons participate in senior centers. There are several reasons for this: individuals may be uninterested in the center's activities, in poor health, or without the necessary transportation. Also, some older people refuse to participate because they "don't want to be with only old people," and the low proportion of men in many centers may deter other men from taking part. Furthermore, centers typically draw from a relatively narrow population, reaching primarily healthy, lower- to middle-class individuals under age 85 with a "lifetime of joining clubs" (Krout et al., 1990). Nationwide, individuals who are generally less advantaged, but not the least advantaged, are most likely to participate in senior center activities. Those who participate tend to do so out of a desire for social interaction and have been invited by friends (Wagner, 1995; Bazargan, Barbre, and Torres-Gil, 1992).

Senior centers face a number of programmatic challenges. One is that they have gotten "older" as their users have "aged in place," and the young-old have been less inclined to attend. However, participation declines after age 85 (Krout, 1989). Centers have been criticized for not doing more to reach older ethnic minorities and older people who are frail, low-income, or disabled. Although African American elders are slightly more likely than whites to attend centers, critics maintain that programs must change to be multicultural. Many communities with ethnic minority neighborhoods have established senior centers in these areas and have successfully attracted diverse elders who would not otherwise participate. In contrast, some observers contend that targeting services to ethnic minorities, the disabled, and the poor runs counter to the universal nature of services under the Older Americans Act and could reduce the participation of those relatively more-advantaged older people who currently attend centers (Ralston, 1991).

Older persons who are active in community and interest organizations such as senior centers derive a variety of benefits. Socializing appears to be the primary reward, especially for people like Mrs. Howard in the introductory vignette. Because many organizations are age-graded, people interact with others similar in age and interests. These interactions often result in friendships, support, mutual exchanges of resources, and collective activity. Consistent with the broader concept of productivity, voluntary associations can also serve to maintain the social integration of older people, countering losses in roles and in interactions with others (Cutler and Hendricks, 1990). Older people in voluntary organizations have been found to have higher morale, although this may be attributed to their higher levels of health, income, and education. When these other characteristics are taken into account, organizational membership is apparently unrelated to overall life satisfaction. The most satisfied members of organizations are those who become involved in order to have new experiences, achieve something, be creative, and help others. Such members in turn participate actively through planning and leadership. Opportunities for more active participation are found in senior advocacy groups or in organizations such as advisory boards to Area Agencies on Aging where older people must, by charter, be in leadership roles. Thus, voluntary association membership appears to be more satisfying when it

provides opportunities for active, intense involvement, and significant leadership roles.

Volunteer Work

With cutbacks in public funding, non-profit, service, educational, and religious organizations increasingly rely upon volunteers to accomplish their missions. Because Americans are retiring at younger ages and are in better health and better educated than earlier cohorts, they are likely to have the time, energy, and skills to contribute to society through volunteer work. Such activity is consistent with the concept of productive aging, whereby older people produce valued goods and services even though they are not paid. Similar to participation in voluntary associations, volunteering is more characteristic of U.S. society than others.

It is estimated that 40 percent of older people volunteer. Even among those over age 75, nearly 30 percent are still active as volunteers—rates of involvement that are higher than other age groups. Among the older population, rates of volunteering are highest among those with higher income and education, better health, a history of volunteering throughout their lives, and a broad range of interests along with a belief that they can make valuable contributions (Chambre, 1993; Herzog and Morgan, 1993; The Commonwealth Fund, 1993). The most frequent type of volunteer work is through religious organizations, followed by direct service such as tutoring, handiwork, raising money, serving on a board or committee, or assisting in an office; about 40 percent of volunteers serve more than one organization. The average amount of time volunteered per week is 6.5 hours, but for some, volunteer work is equivalent to a full-time job (Caro et al., 1993; The Commonwealth Fund, 1993; Taylor and Bass, 1992).

As is the case generally in voluntary activities, women (especially widows) are more likely to volunteer than men, 27 percent versus 25 percent, respectively (The Commonwealth Fund, 1993). These rates may decline, however, as more women enter the paid work force. Although women generally view volunteering as a way to help others, men more frequently define it as a substitute for the worker role. Differences have also been noted among ethnic minorities. Volunteering as a way to help others through informal networks is frequent in minority communities, primarily through African American churches, and may represent a history of self-reliance and incorporating a lifetime of hard work into leisure experiences and services to others (Allen and Chin-Sang, 1990). Mutual aid (e.g., providing food and lodging to older persons) is common in American Indian communities. Volunteer activities among Pacific Asian elders reinforce the continuation of their value systems. Older Chinese, for example, often work through family associations or benevolent societies. Some Japanese elders participate in clubs which are an extension of the "family helping itself" concept that is rooted in traditional Japanese culture. The Hispanic community has been found to emphasize self-help, mutual aid, neighborhood assistance, and advocacy for their older members.

Within the past 20 years, a number of public and private initiatives have been designed to expand community service by older persons. One of the best-known of the government-sponsored initiatives is the **Foster Grandparent Program,** which pairs seniors with children with disabilities; it has been found to be beneficial to both. This mutual aid concept was extended to the **Senior Companion Program,** in which able-bodied seniors serve older adults with disabilities. The Peace Corps has also increased its recruitment of older volunteers, who form over 4 percent of its volunteers. The **Older American Volunteer Program** of ACTION recruits older people to work with disadvantaged groups within the United States. One of the largest of the volunteer networks is the **Retired Senior Volunteer Program (RSVP),** which has projects in schools, hospitals, adult and child day centers, and nursing homes.

Within the private sector, programs sponsored by the **American Association of Retired Persons (AARP)** involve 8 percent of older volunteers, who are matched with jobs through a nationwide Volunteer Talent Bank (Chambré, 1993). Other private-sector programs are the Na-

Older adults often tutor children in the classroom.

tional and International Executive **Services Corps of Retired Executives (SCORE),** where retired executives use their technical and financial expertise to consult with companies in the United States and abroad; and the Citizen Democracy Corps, where retirees provide assistance to formerly Communist countries.

Volunteer programs serve two major social benefits: they provide individuals with meaningful social roles, and they furnish organizations with experienced, reliable workers at minimal cost. In a national survey, 90 percent of older volunteers believe that their work contributes to their organization, and 71 percent are very satisfied with their lives compared to 58 percent of those who do not volunteer. Volunteers have been found to rank higher in life satisfaction, physical and mental well-being, and a sense of accomplishment and feelings of usefulness. Contrary to the assumptions of activity theory, the desire to replace lost roles such as the role of employee or spouse is not a primary motivator for volunteers. In fact, older people are more likely to volunteer if they are married, involved in other organizations, and employed part-time, while nonemployed older people tend to volunteer less. For most retirees, volunteering is apparently not a work substitute (The Common-

---

VOLUNTEERING AS A SUBSTITUTION FOR PAST ROLES

Ted was a teacher of sixth-grade science in an inner-city public school for 35 years. When he retired at age 57, he began a successful second career selling real estate. Now at age 72, he continues to work on average 2 days per week. He enjoys the contact with people and finds his work very different from teaching. Because he believes it is important to give back to his community, he also volunteers as a tutor in an after-school program run by his church for neighborhood "latchkey" children.

---

wealth Fund, 1993; Chambré, 1993; Herzog and Morgan, 1993). Consistent with the continuity theory of aging, most older volunteers have volunteered earlier in their lives and have a sense of obligation to be productive. Volunteerism is part of an overall active lifestyle that unfolds in the formal arenas of work and organized activities, with their long-standing involvement either remaining constant or expanding as they age. Nevertheless, it is still possible to recruit new volunteers in old age, especially if volunteer assignments are perceived as meaningful and challenging (Chambré, 1993; Caro et al., 1993). From the perspective of social exchange theory, volunteering may ensure valued social resources as a basis of exchange, primarily by assisting others rather than by being perceived as dependent.

The first vignette above illustrates how some older adults achieve life satisfaction by substituting volunteering for previous professions as teachers and mentors. The second vignette below illustrates how volunteering can support older people in helping roles.

A number of trends will influence the meaning and functions of volunteerism for older persons. Changing economic conditions may mean that fewer individuals can afford the additional costs of transportation, meals, and out-of-pocket expenses. With the increasing emphasis nationally on self-help and mutual aid, people may choose instead to become more active in neighborhood and community advocacy organizations that seek to empower individuals through solving problems. In the future, older people may be likely to be more involved in advisory councils and commissions; in lobbying efforts as legislative aides and interns; and in national senior organizations such as those described later in this chapter. These volunteer and advocacy efforts will continue to face the challenge of developing ways to involve older people who are low-income, ethnic minorities, living alone, frail and disabled, or from areas without adequate public transportation.

Educational Programs

Many educational programs have been oriented toward enrichment or practical personal assistance in such areas as health and finances, and therefore have not necessarily supported older people moving

---

VOLUNTEERING AS A SOURCE OF SUPPORT

Mary, a homemaker and mother of four children, spent her early years being involved with Scouts, PTA, and teaching Sunday School. Her last child left home when she was 52, and she felt "lost" because there was no one to "need" her in the same ways the children had. At 53, she began volunteering, answering the phone for a community center that served children and elders, and found a new role. When she was widowed at age 70, she increased the hours of volunteering to fill the lonely hours when she missed her husband. Since she has never driven, she takes the bus one day a week to the community center. Now at age 80, she was recently honored by the city at a special reception for her 8000 hours of volunteer service.

into new productive roles (Caro et al., 1993). A primary reason for the limited role of education for productive aging is that higher education institutions have not viewed older learners as a priority. Even though 80 percent of state universities have tuition-free, space-available policies for older people, state legislators typically have provided little funding to support older adult programs. In addition, in times of fiscal constraint, older adult programs are often the first to be cut (Moody, 1993).

Fortunately, some creative late-life learning initiatives have been developed in higher education that are constructed around images of productive aging, not of decline or need. One of the best known is **Elderhostel,** where older learners attend special seminars or institutes on campuses throughout the country. An example of effective marketing of higher education to older residents within a geographic area is Saddleback College's Emeritus Institute near the Leisure World retirement community in California. As a sign of its success, nearly 20 percent of the 21,000 student body are retired persons. Some gerontology certificate programs, such as the University of Massachusetts at Boston, are committed to preparing significant numbers of older people for roles as advocates and service providers. Community colleges, because of their accessibility, are ideal settings in which to develop educational programs that offer older adults a variety of ways to be productive. A few states are beginning to fund a range of programs, including liberal arts education, peer learning groups, health promotion, training of older volunteers, intergenerational programming, and seniors' mentoring of younger undergraduates for career guidance. **Senior Net** is a national educational program that aims to teach computer skills and opportunities for older people to communicate with one another through on-line computer networks (Middleton, 1991).

These programs are illustrative of the social investment model of adult education, in which older people are viewed as both productive active teachers and as learners (Moody, 1993). They are also characterized by strong links with the practice community that serves older adults, intergen-

erational opportunities, and models of peer learning. As suggested in Chapter 5, educational programs need to take account of older learners' particular needs, such as, flexibility, avoiding time pressures, promoting self-paced learning, and being sensitive to hearing and vision problems. **Senior learning programs** represent an area in need of further development and funding, especially with the increase in healthy, active older people who seek new opportunities to contribute to society after retirement.

Religious Participation, Religiousness, and Spirituality

Of the various options for organizational participation, the most common choice for older persons is religious affiliation. After family and government, religious groups are an important source of instrumental and emotional support for older people (Blazer, 1991). Across the life span, church and synagogue attendance is lowest among those in their thirties, peaks in the late fifties to early sixties (with approximately 60 percent of this age group attending), and begins to decline in the late sixties or early seventies. Despite this slight decline, the level of organizational religious involvement for older people exceeds that of other age groups, with 50 percent of persons over age 65 attending church or synagogue in an average week, and many more attending less frequently. Furthermore, people age 65 and over are the most likely of any age group to belong to church-affiliated groups and fraternal associations. In contrast to other types of voluntary organizations, leadership positions in churches and synagogues tend to be concentrated among older people. Such formalized religious involvement has been found to be related to general measures of personal adjustment and subjective health and life satisfaction (Levin, Chatters, and Taylor, 1995; Levin, 1994; Worthington, 1989).

Rates of church attendance in themselves do not indicate the extent of religiosity among older persons, however (Levin, Chatters, and Taylor, 1995; Kaye and Robinson, 1994). Religiosity can be examined in terms of three factors: (1) participation in religious organizations, (2) the personal meaning of religion and private devotional activities within the home, and (3) the contribution of religion to individuals' adjustment to the aging process and their confrontation with death and dying. Slight declines in rates of religious participation after age 70 may reflect health and transportation difficulties more than lack of religiousness and spirituality per se. In fact, while attendance at formal services declines slightly with age, older individuals apparently compensate by an increase in internal religious practices through reading the Bible, listening to religious broadcasts, praying, or studying religion. Older adults pray more often than other age groups, and the emotions of hope and forgiveness may represent significant components by which prayer exerts a salutary influence on mental health. For many elders, spirituality—defined broadly as encompassing trust and faith in a power greater than oneself, prayer, and strength from a greater being—is an effective way to cope with loss (Levin and Taylor, 1997; Kaye and Robinson, 1994). Religious *beliefs,* as contrasted with church attendance, appear to be relatively stable from the late teens until age 60 and to *increase* thereafter. Thus, some older people who appear to be disengaged from religious organizations may be fully engaged non-organizationally, experiencing a sense of spirituality and strong and meaningful subjective ties to religion (McFadden and Gerl, 1990; Stuckey, 1990). Although religion appears to be very important to many older people, they probably also valued it when they were young. That is, contrary to popular stereotypes, we do not necessarily become more religious as we age.

Most surveys on religiousness share the limitations of cross-sectional research, as discussed in Chapter 1. That is, they do not attempt to measure the individual's past religious values and behaviors. The few longitudinal studies available suggest that cohort differences may be more important than the effects of age, although one 16-year study found increased participation in religious services as people entered their sixties

and early seventies, then declined by age 75 (Atchley, 1995). Thus, although religious convictions appear to become more salient over the years, this may be a generational phenomenon captured by the cross-sectional nature of most of the research. The current cohort of older persons, raised during a time of more widespread religious involvement, had their peak rates of attendance in the 1950s, when this country experienced a church revival. All cohorts, not only older people, have shown a decline in church or synagogue attendance since 1965, although this may be changing in the 1990s.

Studies of religious activity have found both gender and ethnic minority differences. Consistent with patterns of involvement in other organizations, women, particularly African American women, have higher rates of religious involvement than men (Levin, Taylor, and Chatters, 1994). Religion appears to be central to the lives of most older African Americans of both sexes and to be related to their life satisfaction, feelings of self-worth, personal well-being, and sense of integration in the larger community (Levin and Taylor, 1997; Chatters and Taylor, 1994). The high esteem afforded African American elders in the church may partially underlie these positive associations. Historically, African Americans have had more autonomy in their religious lives than in their economic and political lives. The negative effects of life stress for older African Americans have been found to be offset by increased religious involvement through prayer, other private religious activities, and a cognitive reframing of the situation in positive terms (e.g., "I have been through a lot before and I'll get through this too") as effective coping mechanisms. For some African American caregivers, for example, the church and God are considered part of their informal system of support and respite (Wood and Wan, 1993). The church has also provided social services such as in-home visitation, counseling, and transportation for African American elders. Such instrumental support reflects the fact that the African American church has historically been responsible for improving the socioeconomic and political conditions of its parishioners (Walls and Zarit, 1991; Taylor and Chatters, 1991; Gurin, Hatchett, and Jackson, 1989).

Although the relationship between religious involvement and life satisfaction is not clear-cut, religious attitudes, beliefs, and participation have generally been found to be positively associated with well-being, happiness, a sense of usefulness, and morale. The strength of these relationships increases over time. In fact, for some individuals age 75 and over, religion is second to health in its relationship to morale, especially for women (Mickley, Carson, and Soeken, 1995). Across all religions, the more religiously devout are usually less afraid of death, more effective at coping with chronic illness, and less prone to depression and loneliness than the less devout (Leifer, 1996; Koenig et al., 1992). Accordingly, individuals for whom faith provides meaning experience greater feelings of internal control and a more positive self-concept (Mickley et al., 1995). Findings regarding the relationships between religiosity and self-esteem are mixed, however. Self-esteem has been found to be highest among older persons with the greatest and the least religious commitment and lowest among older adults with only modest levels of religiosity. Therefore, it is unclear if the changes in religiosity precede changes in self-worth, or whether those with initially positive self-evaluations are more capable of mustering the effort needed for mature faith (Krause, 1995). It is also not clear whether religiousness itself is beneficial, or if the organizational aspects of the sense of belonging and social support are the determinants, since religious participation is associated with other types of group involvement. Satisfaction, serenity, or acceptance of death may result not from faith or spirituality per se, but rather from participation in social networks and reference groups that offer support and security. Older people themselves list among the benefits of religion both the meaning it gives to life and the social interaction it affords (Walls and Zarit, 1991; Stuckey, 1990). Therefore, it is important to consider

how social support through churches and synagogues complements and interacts with religious beliefs and activities.

The Value of Spiritual Well-Being

Spirituality or spiritual well-being can be differentiated from organized religion and is defined as follows:

1. Self-determined wisdom in which the individual tries to achieve stability in his or her environment.
2. Self-transcendence or crossing a boundary beyond the self in which the individual adjusts to losses and rejects material security.
3. Achievement of meaning and purpose for one's continued existence.
4. Acceptance of the wholeness of life (Blazer, 1991).

According to this perspective, people can be spiritual, believing in one's relationship with a higher power, without being religious in the sense of organized religion (Mickley et al., 1995). In fact, the dimensions of spirituality are applicable to older adults who are nonreligious or even anti-religious (Forbes, 1994). Listening to music, viewing a sunset or a painting, loving and being loved can all be profound spiritual activities. Accordingly, spirituality can be expressed in trying to find the meaning and purpose of life, in looking at the significance of past events, and in wondering what will happen after death. High levels of spirituality have been found to be associated with mental health indicators such as purpose in life, self-esteem, and social skills (Kavanaugh, 1997; Paloutzian and Ellison, 1982). Spirituality has also been identified as an important factor in an individual's perception of quality of life (irrespective of age or socioeconomic status) and in maintaining a healthy lifestyle. Spiritual well-being is related not only to the quality of life but also to the will to live. Some gerontologists and theologians maintain that the person who aims to enhance spiritual well-being and to find meaning in life will have a reason to live despite losses associated with aging (Levine, 1983; Thorson, 1983). Mr. Mansfield, in the introduction to this section, illustrates the role of spirituality in helping older persons cope with tragic losses in their lives.

Aging has been characterized as a spiritual journey in which the person aims to achieve integration across a number of areas of life—biological, psychological, social, and spiritual. An ageless self, that is, a person who is not preoccupied or discouraged by his or her aging, has an identity that maintains continuity and is on a spiritual journey in time, despite age-related physical and social changes. For such an individual, being old per se is neither a central feature of the self nor the source of its meaning (Kaufman, 1986). Confronting negative images of aging, loss, and death is believed to be essential for psychological-spiritual growth and successful aging. In fact, dealing with loss has been viewed as one of aging's greatest spiritual challenges (Fischer, 1985). Autobiographical storytelling, journal keeping, and empathic interactions with others have been found to be useful in supporting older persons' spiritual integration (McFadden and Gerl, 1990).

There is growing attention to the spiritual dimensions of health care, since good health is seen as an indication that one's life is in harmony (Wood and Wan, 1993). Practitioners who view spiritual well-being as important to older people's physical and mental health have attempted to develop instruments to measure an individual's spiritual interests and resources, such as personal values, philosophy, and sense of purpose. Some health-promotion screening tools include questions on the individual's spiritual or philosophic values, life goal-setting, and approach to answering questions, such as: What is the meaning of my life? How can I increase the quality of my life? Similarly, spiritual beliefs influence definitions of health, prevention of illness, health promotion and coping with illness, and give meaning in life beyond coping with chronic health problems (Koenig, 1995; Forbes, 1994). Increasingly, health care providers are encouraged to be sensitive to,

and to ask questions about, spiritual well-being that may guide health care choices.

Political Participation

Another major arena of participation in U.S. society is political life. Political acts range from voting, to participation in a political party or a political action group (e.g., organizations seeking to advance the interests of older persons), to running for or holding elective office. In an examination of older people's political behavior, three factors make any interpretation of the relationship between age and political behavior complex. These factors are *stages in the life cycle, cohort effects,* and *historical* or *period effects,* as discussed in Chapter 1.

Historical effects have influenced interpretations of older people's political behavior, particularly analyses of the extent of conservatism. Some early studies of political participation found older people to be more conservative than younger people, as measured by preference for the Republican party and voting behavior (Dobson, 1983; Campbell, 1962). Older people's apparent conservatism partially reflects the fact that people born and raised in different historical periods tend to have perspectives reflecting those times—in this instance, the historical effect of party realignments in the late 1920s and 1930s. Before the New Deal of the 1930s and 1940s, people entering the electorate identified with the Republican party to a disproportionate extent; they have voted Republican ever since, and form the majority of the population over age 65. This apparent association of Republicanism with age thus reflects generational differences, not the effects of aging per se (Hudson and Strate, 1985). Conclusions about older people's political behavior and attitudes are thus limited by the cross-sectional nature of most research on these variables, which has not taken account of historical and cohort effects. In short, how a person thinks and acts politically can be traced largely to environmental and historical factors, not to that person's age (Binstock and Day, 1996).

Age differences in conservatism/liberalism are less a matter of people becoming more conservative than of their maintaining these values throughout life (Binstock and Day, 1996). Successive generations entering the electorate since World War II have become comparatively more liberal, with more older people identifying with the Democratic party since the mid-1980s, as illustrated in Figure 11.8. For example, in the 1992 Presidential election, more older people voted Democrat than Republican; recent polling data show higher rates of Democratic party identification among older than among younger age groups (Statistical Abstracts of the United States, 1994). This shift may be due in part to more low-income and retired blue-collar people opposed to the fiscal conservatism of the Republican party, especially on issues such as pensions and health care. In fact, older persons are more likely to favor major health care reforms than are younger people, in part because of the escalating costs of care. At the same time, increasing numbers of young people, including many among the

baby boom generation, have identified with the conservative element of the Republican party since the 1980s (Alwin, 1998).

Overall, individuals of all ages are not ideologically consistent in their issue-specific preferences. For example, exit poll data from the 1996 Presidential election found that older voters were not influenced by age-related policy issues such as Medicare any more than younger voters. While such issues at the state level may have influenced older voters, this was not a consistent pattern (Binstock, 1997). Furthermore, both older and younger people may hold beliefs on specific issues that contradict their views on more general principles. Within a heterogeneous group such as the older population, differences of opinion on any political issue are likely to equal or exceed variations between age groups and are more likely to be due to economic status and partisanship than age. In fact, most studies have revealed little evidence of intergenerational conflict over policy issues (Binstock and Day, 1996).

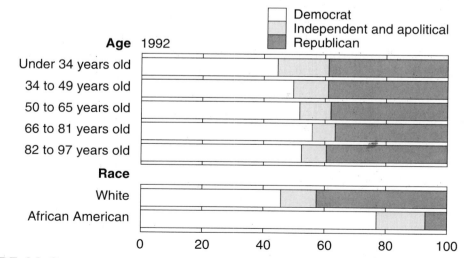

FIGURE 11.8 1992 Political Party Identification of the Adult Population
SOURCE: Chart prepared by U.S. Bureau of the Census.

Voting Behavior

Older Americans are somewhat more likely than younger adults to vote, although rates of electoral participation are low for all age groups in our society. Older people currently comprise 20 percent of the general electorate; nearly 70 percent of older people vote in presidential elections and 60 percent in Congressional election years (Statistical Abstracts of the United States, 1994). The participation rate of older people in elections from 1980 through 1996 has been almost three times the rate of 18-to-20 year olds. Although voting participation declines for those age 75 and older, the 75-plus group was still more likely to vote in the last six presidential elections than people younger than age 35 (Alwin, 1998; Hobbs and Damon, 1996; Binstock and Day, 1996).

In instances where voter turnout is lower among older people, factors other than aging are probably the cause, including gender, ethnic minority, education, partisanship, and generational factors. For example, the voter turnout of ethnic minority groups is lower than that of whites, with Hispanics the least likely to vote (Hobbs and Damon, 1996). The political acculturation of ethnic minority groups appears to influence their participation. As an illustration, Mexican American elders, historically fearful of deportation, have a more cautious, conservative approach to political involvement (Torres-Gil, 1976). On the other hand, a more recent study found that older African Americans who were active in their communities, had a strong sense of citizen duty, identified themselves as Democrats, and had higher levels of education, were more likely to vote (Bazargan et al., 1992). These and earlier findings suggest that differences in the rates of political participation among older people of color do not reflect age or ethnic minority identity per se, but rather lower educational levels, feelings of powerlessness, cohort experiences, and real or perceived barriers to voting and other political activities. In sum, when education, gender, and ethnic minority status are taken into account, political interest, awareness, and activity actually increase with age (Binstock and Day, 1996). The older electorate therefore has the potential to exert political influence substantially beyond what their numbers might suggest.

Senior Power

Research on "senior power" reflects an ongoing debate about whether age can serve as a catalyst for a viable political movement. It is contended that older people can be a powerful political constituency in the policymaking process because legislators and appointed officials are influenced by public opinion, especially by those who vote and are political party leaders, as is the case with older people (Torres-Gil, 1993). Since the 1980s, older Americans have been portrayed by the media and by some policymakers as an organized group of "greedy geezers," acting as a monolithic bloc to achieve their interests (Binstock, 1993). Those who believe that older adults have benefited economically at the expense of younger age groups define the "tyranny of America's old," united to maintain old age benefits at the expense of the young, as "one of the most crucial issues facing U.S. society" (Smith, 1992; Preston, 1984).

This perspective of senior power is consistent with the subculture theory of aging, discussed in Chapter 8. This theory suggests that older people, because of common values and experiences, develop a shared political consciousness which is translated into collective action on old-age related issues (Thomson, 1993). Since future cohorts of older adults will be better educated and healthier and may retire earlier with higher incomes, it is argued that they will have more resources essential to political power. It also assumes that older people in the future will experience increasing pride, dignity, and shared consciousness about old age and thus define problems collectively. From this perspective, age is viewed as becoming a more salient aspect of politics, even if all older persons and their organizations do not speak (or vote) with a unified political voice. It is argued that heterogeneity among the older population does not preclude age—as with gender and ethnic minority status—from exerting political influence (Binstock and Day, 1996).

Admittedly, old-age advocacy groups enjoy a number of advantages in the political arena, including large active memberships, policy information and expertise, and widespread public support and legitimacy as public benefit recipients (Day, 1993a). "Senior citizens" have traditionally been one of the prime targets of campaign efforts focused on critical states with large blocs of electoral votes; this is because of their aggregate numerical importance and the relative ease with which they can be accessed through age-segregated housing and existing programs such as senior centers, AARP chapters, and congregate meal sites (Binstock, 1993).

The alternative argument is that older people do not constitute a significant age-based political force (Torres-Gil, 1992, 1993; Hudson and Strate, 1985; Binstock, 1983). Early critics of the subculture theory argue that the diversity of the older population precludes their having shared interests around which to coalesce. Most older people, especially the young-old, do not identify themselves as "aged," nor do they perceive their problems as stemming from their age. Nor are they captives of any single political philosophy, party, or mass organization. Therefore, according to this position, age alone cannot predict political behavior or age-group consciousness based on differential access to resources (Day, 1993b; Binstock and Murray, 1991). Lacking age-based consciousness, older people are unlikely to be swayed by politicians' appeals to the age vote, nor can they substantially influence social policy development.

Even though older adults can be mobilized for meetings with legislators or political rallies, it cannot be assumed that they necessarily act in a unified manner with regard to social policies. There are increasing differences by socioeconomic class, race, gender, and religion among older people that affect political interests. For example, contrary to widely held perceptions, older people are rarely unified toward issues affecting the young, such as school levies, and do not vote as a bloc against increasing property taxes to support public schools

(Binstock and Day, 1996). This example suggests that old-age related issues are not necessarily more important to them than other issues, partisan attachments, or the characteristics of specific candidates. In fact, recent studies indicate that older and younger people are more likely to form alliances along economic, racial, ethnic, and ideological lines than to unite horizontally on the basis of age (Binstock and Day, 1996; Torres-Gil, 1993). The national organization **Generations United** represents one such vertical alliance across age groups.

As an example of a cross-age, cross-class alliance, poor older people may work with younger welfare beneficiaries for better health insurance for all ages, while upper-income older adults may be more interested in long-term care (Achenbaum, 1993; Torres-Gil, 1993). In the face of budget deficits, future subgroups of older people may become more politically organized, with political agendas different from most of today's senior organizations, especially around issues of means-testing and higher eligibility ages for benefits such as Social Security (Torres-Gil, 1993). For example, lower-income older people have a much greater stake in the maintenance and enhancement of Social Security, since it accounts for a much larger proportion of their income (Binstock, 1993). Accordingly, the failure of the 1988 Medicare Catastrophic Coverage Act illustrates the fragility of interest-group politics when upper-middle-class older adults were asked to sustain a program that benefited primarily low-income older people.

At first glance, the number, variety, and strength of age-based national organizations appear to support the viewpoint that older people are a powerful political force. Age-based organizations are viewed as able to build memberships, conduct policy analyses, marshal grass-roots support, and utilize direct mail and political action. Conscious organizing of older individuals is not without historical precedent in this country. The first age-based politically oriented interest group grew out of the social and economic dislocations of the Depression. The Townsend Movement proposed a tax on all business transactions to finance a $200/month pension for every pensioner over age 60. However, passage of the Social Security Act, in which groups of older people played a supporting but not a leading role, took away the Townsend Movement's momentum, and the organization died out in the 1940s. Most political divisions during the turbulent period of the Depression were class- and labor-based rather than age-based. The Townsend Movement did demonstrate, however, that old age could be a short-term basis for organizing (Binstock and Day, 1996). The McClain Movement, another early age-based organization, aimed to establish financial benefits for older persons through a referendum in the 1938 California elections, but lost followers after economic conditions improved in the 1940s. These early groups did furnish older people with a collective voice and identity, however (Torres-Gil, 1993).

Organized interest groups representing older people did not re-emerge until the 1950s and 1960s. Currently, over 1000 separately organized groups for older adults exist at the local, state, and national levels, with at least 100 major national organizations involved in political action on behalf of older persons (Binstock and Day, 1996). In many ways, the diversity of the older population is reflected in the variety of organizations themselves, ranging from mass membership groups to non-membership staff organizations and associations of professionals or service providers. Yet the very diversity of these groups reduces their potential to act together as a unified bloc. For example, the National Caucus for the Black Aged, the National Hispanic Council on Aging, and the National Indian Council on Aging have been created to address political inequities facing ethnic minority elders and may not act in concert with organizations such as the American Association of Retired Persons (AARP) that represent primarily a white, middle-class constituency.

Three of the largest mass-membership organizations are the **National Council of Senior Citizens (NCSC),** the **National Association of Retired Federal Employees (NARFE),** and the American Association of Retired Persons (AARP) together with the National Retired Teachers' Association (NRTA). Their combined membership represents a significant political force. The National Council of Senior Citizens (NCSC) was developed by organized labor in the early 1960s with the objective of passing Medicare. Although anyone may join, most members of NCSC are former blue-collar workers who receive insurance and other tangible membership benefits. The National Association of Retired Federal Employees (NARFE) was also formed for a specific political purpose—the passage of the Federal Employees Pension Act in the 1920s. It has since concentrated on bread-and-butter issues for federal employees, such as labor/management relations, rather than broader political issues affecting older persons generally.

The best known and largest of these organizations is the American Association of Retired Persons (AARP), with a membership of approximately 35 million which includes 50 percent of the nation's population over age 55, and 13 percent of the population generally. With a modest annual fee, members are attracted by the benefits of lower-cost health insurance, credit cards, travel discounts, and mail-order drugs, and by a myriad of programs related to retirement planning, crime prevention, housing, and widowhood. AARP's magazine, *Modern Maturity,* is the most widely circulated membership periodical in the world. In recent years, AARP has become increasingly active politically, particularly in terms of expanding public financing of long-term care. It was instrumental in helping to end mandatory retirement based on age and in the initial passage of catastrophic health care legislation (Binstock and Day, 1996).

A wide range of trade associations, professional societies, and coalitions concerned with aging issues also exist. Trade associations include the American Association of Homes and Services for the Aged, the American Nursing Home Association, the National Council of Health Care Services (consisting of commercial enterprises in the long-term care business, such as the nursing home subsidiary of Holiday Inns), and the National Association of State Units in Aging (NASUA), which is composed of administrators of state area agencies on aging. The emphasis of these associations

Many older people advocate for their rights.

is on obtaining federal funds and influencing the development of regulations for long-term care facilities and the delivery of public services. Two professional associations active in aging policy issues, the **Gerontological Society of America (GSA)** and the **American Society on Aging (ASA)**, are composed primarily of gerontological professionals from many disciplines. The major confederation of social welfare agencies concerned with aging is the **National Council on the Aging (NCOA)** which encompasses over 2000 organized affiliates, including public and private health, so-

cial work, and community action agencies. The Leadership Council of Aging is a coalition of 41 age-related organizations. Another coalition, Generations United, encompasses 120 organizations composed of different age groups.

Political momentum is also building in several organizations that began at the grass-roots level and now have a nationwide membership and enjoy national recognition. The **Older Women's League (OWL)**, founded in 1981, brings together people concerned about issues affecting older women, especially health care and health insurance, Social Security, pensions, and caregiving. It has advocated for older women both in the federal policymaking process and within the programs of national associations such as the Gerontological Society of America. Women activists within OWL may represent a trend away from the comparatively lower rates of past political participation among older women. Nearly half the states have a **Silver-haired Legislature** which, through the state legislative process, promotes the concerns and rights of older people and participates in the National Silver-haired Congress to influence federal legislation. The **Gray Panthers,** founded by the late Maggie Kuhn, aimed to form grass-roots intergenerational alliances around issues affecting all ages. Since Maggie Kuhn's death, the Gray Panthers' social change efforts have declined.

On certain issues such as health care reform, the influence of organizations of older people has been shown to be limited relative to powerful in-

POLITICAL ACTIVISM AND OLDER WOMEN

Tish Sommers is an example of the increasing political activism of older women. Sommers, a long-time homemaker, learned about the vulnerability of older women when she was divorced at age 57. She found that newly single homemakers her age had a hard time getting benefits that people who have been employed take for granted. She coined the term *displaced homemaker* and built a force of women. They successfully lobbied for centers where displaced homemakers had

job training during the late 1970s. In 1980, she and Laurie Shields founded the Older Women's League, a national organization that has grown to over 14,000 members and over 100 chapters. Her maxim always was "Don't agonize, organize." During the 6 years of organizing OWL, Sommers also fought a battle with cancer. Even at her death in 1986, she was still fighting, organizing groups nationally around the right to maintain control over the conditions of one's death.

terest groups like the insurance, medical, and pharmaceutical industries (Day, 1993a). Nevertheless, until recently, most politicians did not want to offend age-based organizations and constituencies of older people. After higher-income older people organized to influence Congress to repeal the 1988 Medicare Catastrophic Coverage Act, no proposals concerning seniors got out of committees in the next Congressional election year. Whether or not older people act as a unified bloc, many policymakers act as if there were a "politics of age" founded on cohort-based interest groups. Even if older people cannot effect the passage of legislation, they can at least block changes in existing policies, especially when programs such as Social Security and Medicare are threatened. Perceptions of such influence then affect whether major changes in policies on aging are viewed as feasible (Binstock and Day, 1996; Binstock, 1993; Torres-Gil, 1993; Day, 1990).

National age-based organizations have been subject to the criticism that they are biased toward the interests of middle- and upper-working-class older people. AARP, for example, has been criticized for advancing only the interests of its primarily middle-class membership and for recruiting members largely on the basis of selective incentives and direct member services (e.g., insurance, drug discounts, travel, etc.), not by appeals to change existing policies to benefit lower-income older people. However, in recent years, age-based organizations have made more effort not only to reach out to lower-income older persons, but also to collaborate with other groups; this is reflected by the cross-age coalitions that have formed around health care reform and long-term care. In addition to national associations, a wide range of organizations at the local and state level have mobilized around intergenerational and cross-class issues such as affordable public transportation, safe streets, and low-cost health care (Binstock and Day, 1996; Reitzes and Reitzes, 1991).

In sum, national organizations of older adults have influenced a wide range of policies, even though they have not functioned consistently to deliver a unified bloc of votes, nor to change sig-

nificantly the social and economic conditions faced by the most disadvantaged segments of older people. Age-based groups that will have the greatest influence in the future will be characterized by effective use of direct mail, fund-raising, ability to act on "red flag" issues such as Social Security and Medicare benefits, direct services to members, use of the media, and lobbying at the federal and state levels (Torres-Gil, 1993). However, given limited public resources, such groups must also form alliances with other populations and age groups that crosscut socioeconomic and partisan lines. For example, advocates for older people and persons with disabilities worked together in the planning process for President Clinton's 1993 initiative on long-term care, although this temporary unity has eroded since national health care reform failed (Binstock and Day, 1996). Such intergenerational collaboration is further discussed in Chapter 15 with regard to influencing social policies.

SUMMARY AND IMPLICATIONS

Paid employment is typically associated with productivity in our society. Increasingly, however, Americans are retiring in their early sixties and looking forward to two to three decades of leisure time in relatively good health. Health status, income, and attitudes toward the job influence the decision about when to retire. Most retirees adjust well to this important transition and are satisfied with the quality of their lives. Those with good health, higher status jobs, adequate income, and previously developed social networks and leisure interests are most likely to be satisfied. Not all retirement is desired, however; many older people would prefer the opportunity for part-time work, but are unable to find suitable and flexible work options. Preparation for the retirement transition is beneficial, but planning assistance is generally not available to those who need it most—workers who have less education, lower job status, and lower retirement incomes. Retirement by itself does not cause poor health or loss of identity and self-esteem. Dissatisfaction in this stage of life is more often due to poor health and low income.

Although a smaller percentage of older people have incomes below the poverty line than they did in the past, more older than younger people live at marginal economic levels. Social Security is the major source of retirement income for a large proportion of the older population; those who depend on Social Security alone are the poorest older group. Private pensions tend to be small in relation to previous earnings, to be subject to attrition through inflation, and to go primarily to workers in large, unionized, or industrialized settings. Income from assets is distributed unequally among the older population, with a small number of older persons receiving sizable amounts from savings and investments, whereas the most common asset of older people is their home, which provides no immediate income. In addition to those older adults who are officially counted as living below the poverty line, many others live near this level, and many are "hidden" poor who live in nursing homes or with their families. Frail, unmarried women—ethnic minority women especially—are the most likely to live in or near poverty. Public assistance programs such as SSI have not removed the very serious financial problems of the older poor.

The trends toward greater longevity, early retirement, low rates of labor-force participation, and pockets of poverty among older women, ethnic minorities, and the old-old suggest that a growing problem for the United States is the increase in the relative size of an older population encouraged not to work. The increased segmentation of life into a period of full-time work and one of total or partial retirement is, to a great extent, a product of our present pension systems. Changes that are needed include greater flexibility in the workplace, opportunities for part-time work, and a gradual transition from full-time productive work to leisure activities and retirement.

As earlier chapters have documented, changes in employment and parenting roles, income, and physical and sensory capacities often have detrimental social consequences for older adults. Nev-

ertheless, there are arenas in which older people may still experience meaningful involvement and develop new opportunities and skills, consistent with the broader definition of productive aging that includes nonpaid contributions to society. This chapter has considered six of these arenas: leisure pursuits, voluntary association membership, volunteering, education, religious involvement, and political activity. The meaning and functions of participation in these arenas are obviously highly individualized. Participation may be a means to strengthen and build informal social networks, influence wider social policies, serve other persons, and substitute for role changes. The extent of involvement is influenced not by age alone, but also by a variety of other salient factors including gender, ethnic minority status, health, socioeconomic status, and educational level.

Because of the number of interacting variables, age-related patterns in participation are not clearly defined. There are some general age-related differences in types of leisure pursuits: with increasing age, people tend to engage in more sedentary, inner-directed, and routine pursuits in their homes than social activities or obligations outside the home. Changes in organizational participation and volunteering are less clearly age-related. Participation in voluntary associations stabilizes or declines only slightly with old age; declines that do occur are likely to be associated with poor health, inadequate income, and transportation problems. Volunteering, which is higher among the older population than other age groups, tends to represent a lifelong pattern of community service.

Past research on religious and political participation has pointed inaccurately to declines in old age. Although formal religious participation such as church or synagogue attendance appears to diminish slightly, other activities such as reading religious texts or listening to religious broadcasts increase. Religiosity has been found to be an effective way of coping, particularly among ethnic minority elders. Spirituality has been differentiated from religion as a positive factor in older people's physical and mental well-being and their quality of life.

Voting by older people has increased since the 1980s. Declines in voting and political participation in the past may have been a function of low educational status or physical limitations, not of age per se. In fact, older persons' skills and experiences may be more valued in the political arena than in other spheres. The extent to which older people form a unified political bloc that can influence politicians and public policy is debatable. Some argue that older adults form a subculture with a strong collective consciousness; others point to their increasing diversity and political inequity, as apparent with the Medicare Catastrophic Health Care legislation.

Most forms of organizational involvement appear to represent stability across the life course; the knowledge and skills necessary for a varied set of activities in old age are generally developed in early or middle adulthood and maintained into later life. On the other hand, preretirement patterns of productivity are not fixed; individuals can develop new interests and activities in later life, often with the assistance of senior centers, continuing education programs, or community or special interest organizations.

GLOSSARY

Age Discrimination in Employment Act (ADEA) federal law that protects workers age 45 and over from denial of employment strictly because of age

American Association of Retired Persons (AARP) national organization open to all adults age 50 and over, offering a wide range of informational materials, discounted services and products, and a powerful lobby

American Society on Aging (ASA) association of practitioners and researchers interested in gerontology

assets an individual's savings, home equity, and personal property

displaced homemakers widowed or divorced women under age 60 who do not yet qualify for Social Security benefits but may lack the skills for employment

Elderhostel program in which older adults can take inexpensive, short-term academic programs at colleges and universities around the world

Employment Retirement Income Security Act (ERISA) 1974 legislation to regulate pensions

feminization of poverty variety of factors that lead to higher proportions of poverty among women than men

Foster Grandparent Program volunteer program pairing seniors with children with special needs

Generations United a national intergenerational coalition

Gerontological Society of America (GSA) an association of researchers, educators, and practitioners interested in gerontology and geriatrics.

Gray Panthers a national organization, founded by Maggie Kuhn, which encourages intergenerational alliances around social issues

leisure time (not devoted to "work") when one has options in selecting activities

National Association of Retired Federal Employees (NARFE) national organization of adults retired from the federal government, primarily involved in political and social issues

National Council of Senior Citizens (NCSC) mass-membership organization involved in political action for older adults

National Council on the Aging (NCOA) national organization of over 2000 social welfare agencies concerned with aging that provides technical consultation and is involved in federal legislative activities

Older American Volunteer Program federally sponsored volunteer program which recruits older people to work with disadvantaged groups

Older Women's League (OWL) a national organization, formed by Tish Sommers and Laurie Shields, concerned about issues affecting older women

Retired Senior Volunteer Program (RSVP) federally sponsored program in which older adults volunteer in schools, hospitals, and other social agencies

retirement the period of life, usually starting between age 60 and 65, during which an individual stops working in the paid labor force

socioeconomic status a measure of one's position in society, based on education, income, or occupation

Senior Community Services Employment Program (SCSEP) programs sponsored by government or business that encourage the employment of older workers

Senior Companion Program a volunteer program in which seniors assist other seniors

senior learning programs academic programs specially designed for older adults, or programs of tuition waivers that allow older adults to take college courses at no cost

Senior Net   national educational program that teaches computer skills and provides opportunities for on-line communication

serial retirement   term to describe individuals who move in and out of the work force

Service Corps of Retired Executives (SCORE)   a program that links executives as technical and financial consultants with companies in the United States and abroad asking for assistance

Silver-haired Legislature   organizations modeled after state legislatures in which seniors are elected to "office" and learn lobbying and policymaking skills

Social Security   federal program into which workers contribute a portion of their income during adulthood and then, beginning sometime between age 62 and 65, receive a monthly check based on the amount they have earned/contributed

spirituality   believing in one's relationship with a higher power without being religious in the sense of organized religion

Supplemental Security Income (SSI)   federal program to provide a minimal income for low-income older people (and other age groups with disabilities)

vesting of pension benefits   amount of time a person must work on a job in order to acquire rights to a pension

REFERENCES

Achenbaum, W. A. Generational relations in historical context. In V. L. Bengtson and W. A. Achenbaum (Eds.), *The changing contract across generations.* New York: Aldine De Gruyter, 1993.

Achenbaum, W. A., and Morrison, M. H. Is unretirement unprecedented? In S. A. Bass, F. G. Caro, and Y-P Chen (Eds.), *Achieving a productive aging society.* Westport, CT: Auburn House, 1993.

Administration on Aging. *Aging into the 21st century.* Washington, DC: Administration on Aging, 1997.

Allen, K., and Chin-Sang, V. A lifetime of work: The context and meaning of leisure for aging black women. *The Gerontologist,* 1990, 30, 734–740.

Alwin, D. The political impact on the baby boom: Are there persistent generational differences in political beliefs and behaviors? *Generations,* Spring 1998, 22, 46–54.

American Association of Retired Persons (AARP). *A profile of older Americans, 1990.* Washington, DC: AARP, 1991.

Atchley, R. C. *Aging: Continuity or change.* Belmont, CA: Wadsworth, 1983.

Atchley, R. C. Continuity of the spiritual self. In M. A. Kimble (Ed.), *Aging, spirituality, and religion: A handbook.* Minneapolis, MN: Fortress Press, 1995.

Atchley, R. C. Critical perspective on retirement. In T. Cole, W. A. Achenbaum, P. L. Jakobi, and R. Kastenbaum (Eds.), *Voices and visions of aging: Toward a critical gerontology.* New York: Springer Publishing, 1993.

Atchley, R. C. Retirement and leisure participation: Continuity or crisis? *The Gerontologist,* 1971, 11, 13–17.

Atchley, R. C. Retirement income security: Past, present and future. *Generations,* 1997, (21), 9–12.

Atchley, R. C. *The sociology of retirement.* New York: Wiley/Schenkman, 1976.

Bammel, L. L. B., and Bammel, G. Leisure and recreation. In J. E. Birren and K. W. Schaie (Eds.), *Handbook of the psychology of aging* (2nd ed.). New York: Van Nostrand Reinhold, 1985.

Barth, M., McNaught, W., and Rizzi, P. Corporations and the aging workforce. In P. H. Mirvis (Ed.), *Building the competitive workforce.* NY: John Wiley and Sons, 1993.

Bazargan, M., Barbre, A., and Torres-Gil, F. Voting behavior among low-income black elderly: A multi-election perspective. *The Gerontologist,* 1992, 12, 584–591.

Beedon, L. *Administering Social Security.* Washington, DC: American Association of Retired Persons, 1994.

Belgrave, L. L. The effects of race differences in work history, work attitudes, economic resources and health on women's retirement. *Research on Aging,* 1988, 10, 383–398.

Belgrave, L. L. Understanding women's retirement. *Generations,* Spring 1989, (13), 99–152.

Belgrave, L., Haug, M. R., and Gomez, B. Gender and race differences in effects of health and pension and retirement before 65. *Comparative Gerontology,* 1987, 1, 109–117.

Binstock, R. H. The aged as scapegoat. *The Gerontologist,* 1983, 23, 136–143.

Binstock, R. H. *The implications of population aging for American politics.* Paper delivered at the annual meeting of the American Political Science Association, Chicago, September 1987.

Binstock, R. H. Older voters and the 1992 Presidential election. *The Gerontologist,* 1993, 32, 601–606.

Binstock, R. H. Reframing the agenda of policies on aging. In M. Minkler and C. Estes (Eds.), *Readings in the political economy of aging.* Farmingdale, NY: Baywood, 1984.

Binstock, R. The 1996 election: Older voters and implications for policies on aging. *The Gerontologist,* 1997, 37, 15–19.

Binstock, R. H., and Day, C. L. Aging and politics. In R. H. Binstock and L. K. George (Eds.), *Handbook of aging and the social sciences.* San Diego, CA: Academic Press, 1996.

Binstock, R. H., Levin, M. A., and Weatherley, R. The political dilemmas of social intervention. In R. H. Binstock and E. Shanas (Eds.), *Handbook of aging and the social sciences* (2nd ed.). New York: Van-Nostrand Reinhold, 1985.

Binstock, R. H., and Murray, T. The politics of developing appropriate care for dementia. In R. H. Binstock, S. G. Post, and P. Whitehouse (Eds.), *Dementia and aging: Ethics, values and policy choices.* Baltimore, MD: Johns Hopkins University Press, 1991.

Blazer, D. Spirituality and aging well. *Generations,* Winter 1991, *15,* 61–65.

Bossé, R., Aldwin, C. M., Levenson, M. R., and Ekerdt, D. J. Mental health differences among retirees and workers: Findings from the normative aging study. *Psychology and Aging,* 1987, *2,* 383–389.

Bossé, R., Aldwin, C. M., Levenson, M. R., Spiro, A., and Mroczek, D. Changes in social support after retirement: Longitudinal findings from the Normative Aging Study. *Journals of Gerontology,* 1993, *48,* S210–217.

Bossé, R., Aldwin, C. M., Levenson, M. R., and Workman-Daniel, K. How stressful is retirement? Findings from the normative aging study. *Journals of Gerontology,* 1991, *46,* 9–15.

Button, J. W., and Rosenbaum, W. A. Seeing gray: School bond issues and the aging in Florida. *Research on Aging,* 1989, *11,* 158–173.

Calasanti, T. M. Participation in a dual economy and adjustment to retirement. *International Journal of Aging and Human Development,* 1988, *26,* 13–27.

Calasanti, T., and Bonardo, A. Working "over-time": Economic restructuring and retirement of a class. *Sociological Quarterly,* 1993, *33,* 135.

Campbell, A. Social and psychological determinants of voting behavior. In W. Donohue and C. Tibbits (Eds.), *Politics of age.* Ann Arbor: University of Michigan, 1962.

Caro, F. G., Bass, S. A., and Chen, Y-P. Introduction: Achieving a productive aging society. In S. A. Bass, F. G. Caro, and Y-P Chen (Eds.), *Achieving a productive aging society.* Westport, CT: Auburn House, 1993.

Chambré, S. M. Is volunteering a substitute for role loss in old age? An empirical test of activity theory. *The Gerontologist,* 1984, *23,* 292–299.

Chambré, S. M. Volunteerism by elders: Past trends and future prospects. *The Gerontologist,* 1993, *33,* 221–228.

Chatters, L. M., and Taylor, L. J. Religious involvement among older African-Americans. In J. S. Levin (Ed.), *Religion in aging and health: Theoretical foundations and methodological frontiers.* Thousand Oaks, CA: Sage, 1994.

Clark, R. L., Ghent, L., and Heeden, A. Retiree health insurance and pension coverage: Variations by firm characteristics. *Journals of Gerontology,* 1994, *49,* 553–561.

Colsher, P., Dorfman, L., and Wallace, R. Specific health conditions and work: Retirement among the elderly. *Journal of Applied Gerontology,* 1988, *7,* 485–503.

Commonwealth Fund. *The untapped resource: The final report of the Americans over 55 at work program.* New York: The Commonwealth Fund, 1993.

Crystal, S. Economic status of the elderly. In R. H. Binstock and L. K. George (Eds.), *Handbook of aging and the social sciences.* San Diego, CA: Academic Press, 1996.

Cutler, N. E. Introduction: Financial dimensions of aging—and middle aging. *Generations,* 1997, *21,* 5–8.

Cutler, S. J., and Hendricks, J. Leisure and time use across the lifecourse. In R. Binstock and L. K. George (Eds.), *Aging and the social sciences* (3rd ed.). New York: Academic Press, 1990.

Danigelis, N. C., and McIntosh, B. R. Resources and the productive activity of elders: Race and gender as contexts. *Journals of Gerontology,* 1993, *48,* S192-S203.

Day, C. L. Older Americans' attitudes toward the Medicare Catastrophic Coverage Act of 1988. *Journal of Politics,* 1993b, *55,* 167–177.

Day, C. L. The organized elderly: Perilous, powerless, or progressive. *The Gerontologist,* 1993a, *33,* 426–427.

Day, C. L. *What older Americans think: Interest groups and aging policy.* NJ: Princeton University Press, 1990.

Devlin, S., and Arye, L. The Social Security debate: A financial crisis or a new retirement paradigm. *Generations,* Summer 1997, *21,* 27–34.

Dobson, D. The elderly as a political force. In W. Browne and L. K. Olson (Eds.), *Aging and public policy.* Westport, CT: Greenwood Press, 1983.

Ekerdt, D. J. The busy ethic: Moral continuity between work and retirement. *The Gerontologist,* 1986, *26,* 239–244.

Ekerdt, D. J., and DeViney, S. Evidence for a pre-retirement process among older male workers. *Journals of Gerontology,* 1993, *48,* S35–S43.

Ekerdt, D. J., DeViney, S. S. and Kosloski, K. Profiling plans for retirement. *Journals of Gerontology,* 1996, 51B, S140–S149.

Ekerdt, D. J., and Vinick, B. H. Marital complaints in husband working vs. husband retired couples. *Research on Aging,* 1991, *13,* 364–382.

Feuerbach, E., and Erdwins, C. Women's retirement: The influence of work history. *Journal of Women and Aging,* 1994, *6,* 69.

Fischer, K. *Winter grace. Spirituality for the later years.* New York: Paulist Press, 1985.

Forbes, L. Spirituality, aging and the community-dwelling caregivers and care recipients. *Geriatric Nursing,* 1994, *15,* 297–302.

Gall, T. L., Evans, D. R., and Howard, J. The retirement adjustment process: Changes in the well-being of male retirees across time. *Journals of Gerontology,* 1995, *52B,* P110–P117.

Gallup, G. J., and Jones, J. *One hundred questions and answers: Religion in America.* Princeton, NJ: Princeton Research Center, 1989.

Gibson, R. C. Reconceptualizing retirement for black Americans. *The Gerontologist,* 1987, *27,* 691–698.

Gibson, R. C. The subjective retirement of black Americans. *Journals of Gerontology,* 1991, *46,* S204–209.

Gurin, P., Hatchett, S., and Jackson, J. S. Hope and independence: *Blacks' response to electoral and party politics.* New York: Russell Sage Foundation, 1989.

Hall, P. T., and Mirvis, H. *The new workplace and older workers.* Paper presented at a symposium of the National Planning Association/National Council on the Aging Joint Project on U.S. Competitiveness and the Aging American Workforce. Washington, DC: 1993.

Hardy, M. and Kruse, K. Realigning retirement income: The politics of growth. *Generations,* Spring 1998, *22,* 22–28

Hardy, M., and Quadagno, J. Satisfaction with early retirement: Making choices in the auto industry. *Journals of Gerontology: Social Sciences,* 1995, 50B, S217–S228.

Hayward, M. D., Friedman, S., and Chen, H. Race inequities in men's retirement. *Journals of Gerontology,* 1996, *51B,* S1–S10.

Hayward, M., Grady, W., and McLaughlin, S. The retirement process among older women in the United States: Changes in the 1970s. *Research on Aging,* 1988, *10,* 358–382.

Hayward, M., Hardy, M., and Liu, M. Work after retirement: The experience of older men in the United States. *Social Science Research,* 1994, *23,* 82–107.

Henretta, J. C. Changing perspectives on retirement. *Journals of Gerontology,* 1997, *52B,* S1–S3.

Herzog, A. R., and House, J. S. Productive activities and aging well. *Generations,* Winter 1991, 49–54.

Herzog, A. R., and Morgan, J. Age and gender differences in the value of productive activities. *Research on Aging,* 1992, *12,* 169–198.

Herzog, A. R., and Morgan, J. N. Formal volunteer work among older Americans. In S. A. Bass, F. G. Caro, and Y-P. Chen (Eds.), *Achieving a productive aging society.* Westport, CT: Auburn House, 1993, 119–142.

Hobbs, F., and Damon, B. L. *65+ in the United States.* Washington, DC: U.S. Department of Commerce, Bureau of the Census, Current Population Reports, 1996.

Hooker, K., and Ventes, D. Work ethic, daily activities and retirement satisfaction. *Journal of Gerontology,* 1984, *39,* 478–484.

Howard, M. I. Employment of retired-worker women. *Social Security Bulletin,* 1986, *49,* 4–18.

Hudson, R. B., and Binstock, R. Political systems and aging. In R. Binstock and E. Shanas (Eds.), *Handbook of aging and the social sciences.* New York: Van Nostrand, 1976.

Hudson, R. B., and Strate, J. Aging and political systems. In R. Binstock and E. Shanas (Eds.), *Handbook of aging and the social sciences* (2nd ed.). New York: Van Nostrand, 1985.

Hyer, L., Jacob, M. R., and Pattison, E. M. Later life struggles: Psychological/spiritual convergence. *Journal of Pastoral Care,* 1987, *41,* 141–149.

Jacobs, B. The elderly: How do they fare? In D. Besharov (Ed.), *Measuring poverty: Scientific controversy and political implications.* New York: Free Press, 1990.

Johnson, E., and Williamson, J. Retirement in the United States. In K. Markides and C. Cooper (Eds.), *Retirement in industrialized societies.* New York: John Wiley & Sons, 1987.

Juster, F. T., Soldo, B., Kington, R. S., and Mitchell, O. *Aging well: Health, wealth and retirement.* Washington, DC: Consortium of Social Science Associations, 1996.

Kasper, J. *Aging alone: Profiles and projections.* Baltimore, MD: Commonwealth Fund, 1988.

Kaufman, S. R. *The ageless self.* New York: New American Library, 1986.

Kavanaugh, K. M. The importance of spirituality. *Journal of Long-Term Care Administration,* 1997, 24, 29–31.

Kaye, J., and Robinson, K. M. Spirituality among caregivers. *Image Journal Nursing Scholarship,* 1994, 26, 218–221.

Kelly, J. R. *Leisure.* Englewood Cliffs, NJ: Prentice-Hall, 1982.

Kelly, J. R., Steinkamp, M., and Kelly, J. Later life leisure: How they play in Peoria. *The Gerontologist,* 1986, 26, 531–537.

Kleiber, D., and Kelly, J. R. Leisure, socialization and the life cycle. In Seppo Iso-Ahola (Ed.), *Social psychological perspectives on leisure and recreation.* Springfield, IL: Charles C. Thomas, 1980.

Koenig, H. G. *Aging and God: Spiritual pathways to mental health in midlife and later years.* New York: Haworth Pastoral Press, 1995.

Koenig, H. G., Cohen, H. J., Blazer, D. G., Pieper, D., Meador, K. G., Shelp, F., Goli, V., Veeraindor, G., and DiPasquale, B. Religious coping and depression among elderly, hospitalized medically ill men. *American Journal of Psychiatry,* 1992, 149, 1693–1700.

Koenig, H. G., Kvale, H., and Ferrel, C. Religion and well-being in later life. *The Gerontologist,* 1988, 28, 18–28.

Krause, N. Religiosity and self-esteem among older adults. *Journals of Gerontology,* 1995, 50B, P236–P246.

Krout, J. *Senior centers in America.* Westport, CT: Greenwood,1989.

Krout, J., Cutler, S. J., and Coward, R. T. Correlates of senior center participation: A national analysis. *The Gerontologist,* 1990, 30, 72–79.

Kunkel, S. An extra eight hours a day. *Generations,* 1989, 13, 57–60.

Lawton, M. P., Moss, M., and Fulcomer, M. Objective and subjective uses of time by older people. *International Journal of Aging and Human Development,* 1986–87, 24, 171–188.

Leifer, R. Psychological and spiritual factors in chronic illness. *American Behavioral Scientist,* 1996, 39, 752–66.

Levin, J. S. *Religion in aging and health: Theoretical foundations and methodological frontiers.* Thousand Oaks, CA: Sage Publications, 1994.

Levin, J. S., Chatters, L. M., and Taylor, R. J. Religious effects on health status and life satisfaction among Black Americans. *Journals of Gerontology,* 1995, 50B, S154–S169

Levin, J. S., and Taylor, R. J. Age differences in patterns and correlates of the frequency of prayer. *The Gerontologist,* 1997, 37, 75–88.

Levin, J. S., Taylor, R. J., and Chatters, L. M. Race and gender differences in religiosity among older adults: Findings from four national surveys. *Journals of Gerontology,* 1994, 49, S137-S145.

Levine, S. The hidden health care system. *Medical Care,* 1983, *21,* 378.

Martin-Matthews, A. Widowhood and widerhood. *Encyclopedia of Gerontology,* 1996, 2, 621–625.

McFadden, S., and Gerl, R. Approaches to understanding spirituality in the second half of life. *Generations,* Fall 1990, 14, 35–38.

McKenzie, R. The retreat of the elderly welfare state. *Wall Street Journal,* 1991, March 12, 29.

McIntosh, B. R., and Danegelis, N. C. Race, gender and the relevance of productive activity for elders' affect. *Journals of Gerontology,* 1995, 50B, S229-S239.

McLaughlin, D., and Jensen, C. Poverty among older Americans: The plight of non-metropolitan elders. *Journals of Gerontology,* 1993, 48, S44–S54.

Mickley, J. R., Carson, V., and Soeken, K. Religion and adult mental health: *Issues in Mental Health and Nursing,* 1995, 16, 345–360.

Midanik, L. T., Soghikian, K., Ransom, L. J., and Tekawa, I. S. The effect of retirement on mental health and health behaviors: The Kaiser Permanent Retirement Study. *Journals of Gerontology,* 1995, 50B, S59–S61.

Middleton, F. Computers for seniors. In R. Harootyan (Ed.), *Resourceful aging: Today and tomorrow,* Vol. V (pp. 75–78). Lifelong Education, Washington, DC: American Association of Retired Persons, 1991.

Miller, S. The social dilemmas of the aging leisure participant. In A. Rose and W. Peterson (Eds.), *Older people and their social world.* Philadelphia: F. A. Davis, 1965.

Moen, P. Gender, age and the life course. In R. H. Binstock and L. K. George (Eds.), *Handbook of aging and the social sciences.* San Diego, CA: Academic Press, 1996.

Moen, P., Dempster-McClain, D., and Williams, R. M. Jr. Successful aging: A life course perspective on women's multiple roles and health. *American Journal of Sociology,* 1992, 97, 1613.

Moody, H. R. A strategy for productive aging: Education in later life. In S. A. Bass, F. G. Caro, and Y-P Chen (Eds.), *Achieving a productive aging society.* Westport, CT: Auburn House, 1993.

Mor-Barak, M. E., Scharloch, A. E., Birba, L., and Sokolov, J. Employment, social networks, and health in the retirement years. *International Journal of Aging and Human Development,* 1992, 352, 143–157.

Mor-Barak, M., and Tynan, M. Older workers and the workplace: A new challenge for occupational social work. *Social Work,* 1993, 38, 45–55.

Mutchler, J. E., Burr, J. A., Planta, A. M., and Massagil, M. P. Pathways to labor force exit: Work transitions and work instability. *Journals of Gerontology,* 1997, 52B, S4–S12.

National Academy of Aging. *Facts on Social Security: The old age and survivors trust fund.* Washington, DC, July 1996.

National Academy of Aging. *Old age in the 21st century.* Syracuse, NY: Syracuse University, The Maxwell School, 1994.

Ozawa, M. N. *The economic well-being of the elderly in a changing society.* The Seventeenth Annual Leon and Josephine Winkelman Lecture, Ann Arbor: University of Michigan, School of Social Work, December 2, 1996.

Palmore, E. B., Barchett, B. M., Fillenbaum, G. G., George, L. K., and Wallman, L. M. *Retirement causes and consequences.* New York: Springer, 1985.

Paloutzian, R. F., and Ellison, C. W. Loneliness and quality of life measures: Measuring loneliness, spiritual well-being and their social and emotional correlates. In L. A. Peplau and D. Perlman (Eds.), *Loneliness: A sourcebook of current theory, research and therapy.* New York: Wiley InterScience, 1982.

Parnes, H. S., and Sommers, D. G. Shunning retirement: Work experience of men in their seventies and early eighties. *Journals of Gerontology,* 1994, 49, S117–S124.

Perkins, K. Psychosocial implications of women and retirement. *Social Work,* 1992, 37, 526–527.

Pratt, H. J. *Gray agendas: Interest groups and public pensions in Canada, Britain and the United States.* Ann Arbor, MI: University of Michigan Press, 1993.

Preston, S. H. Children and the elderly in the United States. *Scientific American,* 1984, 251, 44–49.

Quadagno, J. and Hardy, M. Work and retirement. In R. H. Binstock and L. K. George (Eds.), *Handbook of aging and the social sciences.* San Diego, CA: Academic Press, 1996.

Quinn, J. F., and Burkhauser, R. V. Labor market obstacles to aging productively. In S. A. Bass, F. G. Caro, and Y-P Chen (Eds.), *Achieving a productive aging society.* Westport, CT: Auburn House, 1993.

Quinn, J. F., and Smeeding, T. M. Defying the averages: Poverty and well-being among older Americans. *Aging Today,* September/October 1994, 9.

Ralston, P. Senior centers and minority elders: A critical review. *The Gerontologist,* 1991, 31, 325–331.

Ramirez, A. Making better use of older workers. *Fortune,* January 1989, 179–182.

Reitzes, D. C., and Reitzes, D. C. Metro services in action: A case study of a citywide senior organization. *The Gerontologist,* 1991, 31, 256–266.

Reitzes, D.C., Mutran, E., and Fernandez, E. Preretirement influences on post-retirement self-esteem. *Journals of Gerontology,* 1996, 51B, S242-S249.

Riddick, C., and Stewart, D. An examination of the life satisfaction and importance of leisure in the lives of older female retirees: A comparison of blacks to whites. *Journal of Leisure Research,* 1994, 26, 75–87.

Simon-Riesinowitz, L., Wilson, L. Marks, L., Kroch, C., and Welch, C. Future work and retirement needs: Policy experts and baby boomers express their views. *Generations,* Spring 1998, 22, 34–40.

Smith, J. *The changing economic circumstances of the elderly: Income wealth and Social Security.* Maxwell School Center for Policy Research, Syracuse, NY, 1997b.

Smith, J. Wealth inequality among older Americans. *Journals of Gerontology, Special Issue,* 1997a, 52B, S74–81.

Smith, L. The tyranny of America's old. *Fortune,* 1992, 125, 68–72.

Social Security Administration. *Fast facts and figures about Social Security.* Washington, DC: U.S. Government Printing Office, 1996.

Social Security Administration. *Income of the Aged, Chartbook, 1994.* Washington, DC: U.S. Government Printing Office, 1996.

Social Security Administration. *Social Security: Understanding the benefits.* Washington, DC: U.S. Government Printing Office, 1996.

Statistical Abstract of the United States, 114th Edition. U.S. Department of Commerce, Bureau of the Census, Washington, DC, 1994.

Sterns, H., and McDaniel, M. Job performance and the older worker. In S. Rix (Ed.), *Older workers: How do they measure up?* Washington, DC: AARP, 1994.

Streib, G., and Schneider, C. J. *Retirement in American society. Impact and process.* Ithaca, NY: Cornell University Press, 1971.

Stuckey, J. D. *The Sunday school class: The meaning of older women's participation in church.* Presented at the Annual Scientific Meeting of the Gerontological Society, Boston, MA, November 1990.

Szinovacz, M. Retirement, couples and household work. In S. J. Bahi and E. T. Peterson (Eds.), *Aging and the family.* Lexington, MA: Lexington Press, 1989.

Taylor, H., and Bass, R. *Productive aging: A survey of Americans age 55 and over.* New York: Louis Harris & Associates, 1992.

Taylor, M., and Shore, L. M. Predictors of planned retirement age: An application of Baehr's Model. *Psychology and Aging,* 1995, 10, 76–83.

Taylor, R. J., and Chatters, L. M. Nonorganizational religious participation among elderly black adults. *Journals of Gerontology,* 1991, 46, S103–110.

Thomson, D. Generations, justice and the future of collective action. In P. Laslett and J. Fishkin (Eds.), *Philosophy, politics and society, Vol. VI: Relations between age groups and generations.* New Haven, CT: Yale University Press, 1993.

Thorson, J. Spiritual well-being in the secular society. *Generations,* 1983, 8, 10–11.

Tinsley, H., Teaff, J., Colbs, S., and Kaufman, N. A system of classifying leisure activities in terms of the psychological benefits of participation reported by older persons. *Journal of Gerontology,* 1985, 40, 172–178.

Torres-Gil, F. M. Interest group politics: Generational changes in the politics of aging. In V. L. Bengtson and W. A. Achenbaum (Eds.), *The changing contract across generations.* New York: Aldine de Gruyter, 1993.

Torres-Gil, F. M. *The new aging: Politics and change in America.* Westport, CT: Auburn House, 1992.

Torres-Gil, F. M. *Political behavior: A study of political attitudes and political participation among older Mexican Americans.* Unpublished dissertation, Heller School, Brandeis University, 1976.

Treas, J., and Torrecilke, R. The older population. In R. Farley (Ed.), *State of the Union: America in the 1990s, Vol. 2: Social trends.* New York: Russell Sage, 1995.

U.S. Department of Labor, Bureau of Labor Statistics. *Employment and earnings, 37.* Washington, DC: U.S. Department of Labor, 1989.

U.S. Senate Special Committee on Aging. *Aging America: Trends and projections.* Washington, DC: U.S. Department of Health and Human Services, 1992.

Verbregge, L., Gruber-Baldini, A. C., and Fozard, J. L. Age differences and age changes in activities: Baltimore Longitudinal Study of Aging. *Journals of Gerontology,* 1996, 51B, S30–S41.

Villa, V. M., Wallace, S. P., and Markides, K. Economic diversity and an aging population: The impact of public policy and economic trends. *Generations,* 1997, *21,* 13–18.

Wagner, D. L. Senior center research in America: An overview of what we know. In D. Shollenberger, *Senior centers in America.* Washington, DC: The National Council on the Aging, 1995.

Walls, C. T., and Zarit, S. Informal support from black churches and the well-being of elderly blacks. *The Gerontologist,* 1991, *31,* 490–495.

Wood, J. B., and Wan, T. Ethnicity and minority issues in family caregiving to rural black elders. In C. Barresi and D. Stull (Eds.), *Ethnic elderly and long-term care.* New York: Springer, 1993.

Worthington, E. L. Religious faith across the life span: Implications for counseling and research. *Counseling Psychology,* 1989, *17,* 555–612.

Zsembik, B., and Singer, A. The problem of defining retirement among minorities: The Mexican Americans. *The Gerontologist,* 1990, 30, 749–757.

12

DEATH, DYING, BEREAVEMENT, AND WIDOWHOOD

You have probably heard of people who "lost their will to live" or "died when they were ready." Such ideas are not simply superstitions. Similar to other topics addressed throughout this book, death involves an interaction of physiological, social, and psychological factors. The social context is illustrated by the fact that all cultures develop beliefs and practices regarding death in order to minimize its disruptive effects on the social structure. These cultural practices influence how members of society react to their own death and that of others. Although measures of death are physical, such as the absence of heartbeat or brain waves, psychosocial factors, such as the will to live, can influence the biological event. For instance, terminally ill people have been found to die shortly after an important engagement, such as a child's wedding, a family reunion, or holiday, suggesting that their social support systems, their enthusiasm for life, and their "will to live" prolonged life to that point (McCue, 1995). How people approach their own death and that of others is closely related to personality styles, sense of competence, coping skills, and social supports, as discussed in Chapter 6.

This chapter examines age-related attitudes toward death in our culture; the dying process and its meaning to the dying person; the conditions for care of the dying; the concept of the right to die; the increasing ethical, medical, and legal issues raised by whether to continue life-sustaining technologies; the legal options of advance directives available to individuals; the rituals of bereavement, grief, and mourning; and the experience of widowhood. Research on death and dying and professional interventions to support dying persons and their families are relatively recent and are a significant and growing area for gerontological research and practice; these interventions are discussed briefly here.

THE CHANGING CONTEXT OF DYING

In our culture, dying is associated primarily with old age. Although, as we have seen, aging does not cause death, and younger people also die, there are a number of reasons for this association. The major factors are medical advances and the increase in life expectancy. In pre-industrial societies, death rates were high in childhood and youth, and parents could expect that one-third to one-half of their children would die before the age of ten. Now it is increasingly the old who die, making death predictable as a function of age. Death has thus come to be viewed as a timely event, the completion of the life cycle in old age.

Others view death not only as the province of the old, but also as an unnatural event that is to be fought off as long as medically possible. In this sense, death has become medicalized, distorted from a natural event into the end point of untreatable or inadequately treated disease or injury. Prior to the 1900s, the period of time spent dying was relatively short due to infectious diseases and catastrophic events. With improved diagnostic techniques and early detection, individuals are living for longer periods of time with terminal illnesses. At the end of a prolonged chronic illness, when medicine may care for but not cure the patient, dying may seem more unnatural than if the person had been allowed to die earlier in the progression of the illness. With expanded technological mastery over the conditions of dying, chronically ill people have often been kept alive long past the point at which they might have died naturally in the past. As noted by Callahan (1993), achieving a peaceful death is difficult because of the complexity in drawing a clear line between living and dying, which is partially a result of technology, and partly due to societal and professional ambivalence about whether to fight or accept death.

The surroundings in which death occurs have also changed with increased medical interventions. In pre-industrial society, most people died at home, with the entire community often involved in rituals surrounding the death. Now over 80 percent of all deaths occur in institutions, generally in hospitals and nursing homes, with only small groups of relatives and friends present. This is the case even though most people express a preference to die at home surrounded by friends and family (McCue, 1995).

Attitudes toward Death

More insulated from death than in the past, most people are uncomfortable with talking about it, especially the prospect of their own death. This discomfort is shown even in the euphemisms people use—"sleep, pass away, rest"—instead of the word "death" itself. Freud, in fact, recognized that although death was natural, undeniable, and unavoidable, people behaved as though it would occur only to others; that is, "they" will die, but not "me." Fear and denial are natural and comforting responses to being unable to comprehend our own death and nonexistence. Such fear has tended to make death a taboo topic in our society. Although in recent years death has become a more legitimate topic for scientific and social discussion, most people are more likely to talk about it on a rational, intellectual level than to discuss their own deaths.

Whether people's fear of death is natural or learned is unclear. When asked what they fear most about death, respondents mention suffering and pain, loss of their body, punishment, loss of self-control, concern over an afterlife and the unknown, loneliness, the effect on survivors, and the destruction of the personality. In general, people fear the inability to predict what the future might bring and the process of dying, particularly the prospect of dying slowly and in pain, more than death itself (Maro, 1996). Yet, when questioned directly, people typically are more concerned with the death of close friends and family than with their own, and generally express an acceptance of their own death. Although the validity of responses to questions about one's own death is difficult to ascertain, it appears that most people both deny and accept the reality of dying. These ambivalent views reflect the basic paradox surrounding death, in which we recognize its universality, but cannot comprehend or imagine our own dying.

Variation by Age and Gender

Multiple factors, particularly age and gender, influence socioemotional responses to death, although more research is needed regarding such differences. Attitudes toward death and dying do appear to differ by sex and age. Women more often report a fear of death, although this may reflect gender differences in socialization and emotional expressiveness (Dattel and Neimeyer, 1990). In research utilizing metaphors for death, women fear pain and bodily decomposition, but are also more accepting of their own death, viewing it as peaceful, like a "compassionate mother" or an "understanding doctor." Men tend to perceive death as antagonistic, a "grinning butcher" or a "hangman with bloody hands" (Thorson and Powell, 1988). In general, older people think and talk more about death and appear to be less afraid of their own death than are younger people; however, when they face "unfinished business," they tend to be more likely to fear death (Rasmussen and Brems, 1996).

A number of factors may explain this apparent paradox of a lessened fear of death in the face of its proximity. Having internalized society's views, older people may see their lives as having ever-decreasing social value, thereby lowering their own positive expectation of the future. If they have lived past the age they expected to, they may view themselves as living on "borrowed time" (Henderson, 1990). A painless death tends to be viewed as preferable to deteriorating physically and mentally, and being socially useless or a burden on family. In addition, dealing with their friends' deaths, especially in age-segregated retirement communities or nursing homes, can help socialize older people toward an acceptance of their own. Experiencing deaths and other losses more frequently, they are more likely to think and talk about death on a regular basis than are younger people and to develop effective means of coping (Lester and Templer, 1993; Lund, 1993). On the other hand, sustained family contacts tend to create a greater desire to prolong life (Mutran et al., 1997). If they achieve the developmental stage of ego integrity, as described in our discussion of Erikson in Chapter 6, and engage in life review, they are able to resolve conflicts and relieve anxiety, becoming more accepting of death as fair.

Older adults also have been found to react differently to perceptions of limited remaining time, and thus to death as an "organizer of time."

Spirituality can assist older people in facing their own mortality.

Compared to youth, older people confronting death may conclude that little of meaning can be accomplished, because all activities will be short-lived and unfinished. Accordingly, many older people whose death is imminent make less effort than younger people to alter their way of life or to attempt to complete projects. Instead, they are more likely to turn inward to contemplation, reminiscence, reading, or spiritual activities (Kalish, 1985).

The awareness of one's mortality can stimulate a need for the "legitimization of biography," to find meaning in one's life and death. People who successfully achieve such legitimization experience a new freedom and relaxation about the future and tend to hold favorable attitudes toward death. Many older people consider a sudden death to be more tragic than a slow one, desiring time to see loved ones, settle their affairs, and reminisce. Older people generally can accept the inevitability of their own death, even though they tend to be concerned about the death of relatives. Many older people are already experiencing "**bereavement overload**" through the increased frequency of family and friends' deaths, and thus are more aware of the reduced impact of their death on others (Kastenbaum, 1991; Marshall, 1986; Keller, Sherry, and Piotrowski, 1984).

It is unclear whether variability in the acceptance of death is due to age or to cohort differences. For example, the current cohort of older people has fewer years of formal schooling than younger generations have, a factor that affects attitudes toward death. The interactive effects of other variables with age need to be further probed. For instance, in all age groups the most religious persons who have the greatest belief in an afterlife have less anxiety about dying. For the religious, death is the doorway to a better state of being. Similarly, people who are most confirmed in their lack of religious belief also express less fear about death. Those most fearful about death are the irregular church-goers, or those intermediate in their religiosity whose belief systems may be confused and uncertain (Kalish, 1985). Religion apparently can either comfort or create anxiety about an afterlife, but it provides some individuals with one way to try to make sense of death. Age is also a factor in how survivors react to death. Because the death of older people is often anticipated, it may be viewed as a "blessing" for someone whose "time has come" rather than as a tragic experience.

Death as Loss

Researchers have also defined death as loss—loss of self, of all forms of sensory awareness, and of loved ones. Seven values lost through death have been identified (Marshall and Levy, 1990):

1. Loss of ability to have experiences
2. Loss of control and the ability to predict subsequent events
3. Loss of body (and fear of what will happen to the body)
4. Loss of ability to care for dependents
5. Loss suffered by friends and family (e.g., causing grief to others)
6. Loss of opportunity to continue and plan projects
7. Loss of being in a relatively painless state

Loss of the ability to retain control over one's life can be especially poignant for an older dying person, particularly since concern with being in control tends to increase with age. It is important to recognize that to an older person, the meaning of threats to identity and the loss of the physical body may be very different from the meaning of a loss of self-control over how they die.

THE DYING PROCESS

One of the most widely known frameworks for understanding the stages of the **dying process** has been advanced by Kübler-Ross (1969, 1981).

According to Kübler-Ross, dying persons experience five stages in reaction to their death: (1) denial and isolation, (2) anger and resentment, (3) bargaining and an attempt to postpone, (4) depression and sense of loss, and (5) acceptance. Each of these stages represents a form of coping with the process of death.

Denial is initially a healthy buffer, but it can prevent dying persons from moving to subsequent stages if others are unwilling to talk with them about their concerns. In the second stage, anger ("Why me?") may be displaced on family or medical staff and can lead to withdrawal and avoidance. This stage may be the most difficult for caregivers to tolerate. In the bargaining stage, the dying person may try to make a deal with God to live long enough to attain some goal or to postpone death as a reward for good behavior. The fourth stage is depression, which represents a natural grieving process over the final separation of death. The dying person may withdraw from loved ones as a way to prepare for this separation. The final stage, acceptance, is achieved only if the dying person is able or allowed to express and deal with earlier feelings, such as anger and depression. The dying person thereby achieves a sense that personal tasks have been accomplished and the struggle is over. Rather than a happy stage, the acceptance phase is almost devoid of feelings, and should not be confused with wishing to die. Although Kübler-Ross cautioned that these stages were not invariant, immutable, or universal, she nevertheless implied that progression from one to the other is normal and adaptive. She encouraged health care providers to help their patients to advance through them; and she depicted the final stage as consummate. Kübler-Ross (1975) emphasized that dying can be a time of growth. By accepting death's inevitability, dying persons can use life meaningfully and productively and come to terms with who they really are. Since the dying are "our best teachers," those who work with them can learn from them and emerge from such experiences with fewer anxieties about their own dying (Kübler-Ross, 1969).

The religious assumptions and allegations about life after death that are embedded in Kübler-Ross's writings have evoked scientific and theological criticism, and have often detracted from the importance of her work with dying patients. The empirical usefulness and generalizability of these stages continue to be debated. Although her work is controversial, Kübler-Ross has been a pioneering catalyst, increasing public awareness of death and the needs of the dying and their caregivers. Her framework should be viewed as a helpful cognitive grid or guideline of possible modes and ways of coping with death and loss, not as a fixed sequence that determines a "good death." Apathy, apprehension, and anticipation have been found as well as acceptance of death. Moreover, any of these feelings and behaviors may occur at any time during the dying process, and the person may move back and forth between them, displaying several of the feelings simultaneously. Many patients remain at one of the first stages (denial or anger) and never pass through all five stages.

Family members and health care providers must be cautious about implying that the dying person must follow Kübler-Ross's stages, and thus creating the illusion of control by naming phases. Instead, they should be open to the dying person's choice of whether and how to move through these stages. In sum, subsequent studies have found that there is no "typical," unidirectional way to die through progressive stages. Instead, there may be an alternation between acceptance and denial, between understanding what is happening and magically disbelieving its reality (Kastenbaum, 1991, 1985). Consistent with the framework of dynamic interactions discussed throughout this book, the dying process is shaped by an individual's own personality and philosophy of life, by the specific illness, and by the social context (e.g., whether at home surrounded by family who encourage the expression of feelings, or isolated in a hospital).

THE DYING TRAJECTORY FRAMEWORK

An alternative to the framework of stage theories is the concept of "**dying trajectory,**" or the perceived course of dying and expected time of death (Glaser and Strauss, 1968). The pace of a dying trajectory can be sudden or slow, regular or erratic; it is usually shaped by the condition causing death (e.g., dying from lung cancer versus a heart attack) and by how much information is disclosed to the dying person (Marshall and Levy, 1990). Most people with terminal conditions have an idea of how much longer they will live and plan their lives within that interval. A **death crisis** in the dying trajectory is an unanticipated change in the amount of time remaining to live. The **living-dying interval,** which occurs between the death crisis and the actual time of death, is characterized by three phases. During the acute phase, the dying person expresses maximum anxiety or fear. At the chronic phase of dying, anxiety declines as the person faces death's reality, confronts questions about the dying process and the future, and enacts necessary rituals and preparations. The terminal phase is characterized by the dying person's withdrawal. Just as Kübler-Ross's stages are not fixed or invariant for all people, not every individual goes through the trajectory of these three phases.

CARE OF THE DYING

Both frameworks just discussed—stages and trajectories—highlight the importance of giving attention to the ways in which care is provided to the dying. Although most dying people prefer to die at home, the common practice has been to hospitalize them, with most deaths occurring in hospitals or nursing homes.

In recent years, more training has been provided to health care providers who work with the dying. For example, the American Medical Association is planning a nationwide effort to teach physicians better end-of-life care, which contrasts with an emphasis on technological interventions to prolong life. Medical professionals have become more open in talking about death with their patients as well as among themselves. Most now believe that dying persons have the right to know their condition and prognosis and to have some control over their death (American Medical Association, 1996). Increasingly, the pursuit of a peaceful death is viewed as the proper end of medicine, although less agreement exists on how this is to be achieved, largely because of advances in medical technology. This breaking of "professional silence" is in part a reaction to external pressures, including patients who insist on being informed about their illnesses, and current public affirmations about the "right to know" and the "right to die."

The **Dying Person's Bill of Rights,** developed over 20 years ago, states that individuals have the right to personal dignity and privacy; informed participation, including to have their end-of-life choices respected by health care professionals; and considerate, respectful service and competent care. As highlighted below, the **right to die,** rather than to endure prolonged suffering through life extension, is currently emphasized more than it was at the time the Dying Person's Bill of Rights was articulated. Although controversy surrounds the use of life-sustaining technology, both sides would agree that the dying person's self-determination and right to be free from physical pain are essential to humane care. As articulated by the Ethics Committee of the American Geriatrics Society (1995) in its position paper on the care of dying patients, dying persons should be provided with opportunities to make the circumstances of their dying consistent with their preferences and lifestyle. **Palliative** care to comfort, not to cure, dying patients should focus on both the relief of symptoms and of pain, and can be addressed by both pharmacological and non-pharmacological means. It is critical to establish conditions in which

dying persons can be open about their concerns and reassured by others for expressing feelings, without necessarily being forced to be expressive. Individual needs and preferences for privacy, making decisions, and saying good-byes should be supported. The social support of friends and family, perhaps more than other interventions, can be a major source of strength and can enhance the quality of their remaining days for older dying people (Kavanaugh, 1996–97).

Hospice Care

Another trend toward being more responsive to dying patients and their families has been the expansion of the **hospice** model of caring for the terminally ill. Hospice is a philosophy of caring and an array of services that can best be implemented

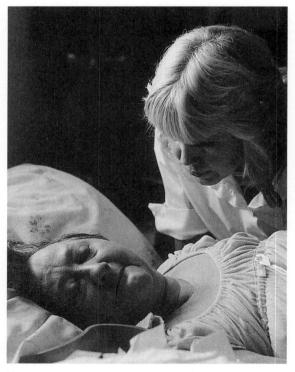

Hospice care can enhance quality of life for the dying person.

through the home, although its principles can also be enacted as inpatient services for the terminally ill. As palliative care, hospice is dedicated to helping individuals who are beyond the curative power of medicine to remain in familiar environments that minimize pain and to maintain personal dignity and control over the dying process. Maintaining the patient's quality of life, and assessment and coordination of the physical, psychosocial, and spiritual needs of patient and family, are fundamental to the hospice approach. St. Christopher's Hospice, started by Dr. Cecily Saunders in Great Britain in 1967, was the first hospice in the world.

The first hospice in the United States was developed in 1974 in New Haven, Connecticut, and now nearly 2000 hospices exist in the United States (Miller, 1996). The majority of these provide in-home services for cancer patients. In 1986, Congress passed legislation making hospice a permanent Medicare benefit and granting a modest increase in reimbursement rates, although strict guidelines have been established by Medicare. Some private insurance plans may cover hospice, and some states provide hospice benefits under Medicaid. Most hospices, however, are small, not-for-profit community-based organizations. Even though older people have been both providers and recipients of hospice care, there is some evidence that hospices have underserved the population 75 years of age and older compared to other age groups with terminal illnesses. Ethnic minorities also appear to be underserved (Miller, 1996; Levy, 1994).

Both professional and lay providers contribute as an interdisciplinary team to hospice goals. Hospice workers advocate for giving dying persons full and accurate information about their condition. Another important function is to develop supportive environments in which people can tell their life stories and find meaning in their deaths. Listening, touching the dying person, family involvement, and ritual celebration of special events such as birthdays and weddings are all emphasized by the staff (Miller, 1996). In addition, hospice staff work directly with family and friends to help them resolve their feelings, clarify expectations, and relate most effectively to the dying patient. Hospice workers also recognize the importance of bereavement counseling after the death, generally following up with support to grieving family members. In addition, hospice programs provide counseling and support to staff members to help prevent "burnout." There is some evidence that hospice provides better quality of life for both patients and caregivers, although the difficulties in scientifically evaluating quality of life are recognized. Several studies have found savings to Medicare associated with hospice care relative to conventional care (Miller, 1996). Unfortunately, hospice models of care are still unavailable to many terminally ill persons, because of restrictive Medicare reimbursement mechanisms for in-patient care. Despite its 30-year history internationally, hospice remains essentially outside the mainstream of American medicine. With a separate philosophy, it therefore is limited in its overall impact on quality of care of dying persons (Sachs, 1994).

Although it has many benefits, hospice is not always the best approach for all terminally ill patients, since caring for a dying person at home can severely strain the resources of family and friends. Such burdens on families, discussed further in Chapter 16, have intensified with restrictions in public funding for home health care. A danger is that cost-containment objectives may take priority over the goals of quality care for the dying and their families. If the preference of most people to die at home is to be realized, more publicly funded, community-based programs to ease the strain on family caregivers must be developed.

Psychotherapeutic Approaches

Due largely to Kübler-Ross's work, increased recognition has been given to the value of psychotherapy with dying persons. Until recently, psychotherapists have generally preferred to work with people presumed able to return to productive life, as discussed in Chapter 6. The focus of most psychotherapy with dying persons is to support the process of working through their denial and despair, thereby enabling them to live out their remaining months as fully as their disease allows. Even in the first interview, a therapist should strive to open the door for the dying person to communicate without fear and anxiety. The process and satisfaction of personal growth, not a sense of accomplishment, are believed to be of therapeutic value in themselves. Caring relationships with health care providers may also have therapeutic effects, even though formal psychotherapy is not involved.

THE RIGHT TO DIE

Along with increased attention to the ways in which people choose to die and the meanings they assign to their deaths, the right-to-die movement has grown in recent years, and has given rise to new ethical and legal debates regarding **euthanasia,** which, literally translated, means a "good death." Whether others have a right to help people die, and under what conditions, has been discussed throughout history, but recent debates about the complex ethical, social, and legal issues raised by euthanasia have intensified with increased medical advances used to prolong life. These issues revolve around three different types of patients: the terminally ill who are conscious, the irreversibly comatose, and the brain-damaged or severely debilitated who have good chances for survival but are at a low level of existence (e.g., Alzheimer's patients). Central to these debates is the doctrine of informed consent, which establishes a competent patient's right to accept or refuse medical treatment based on his or her understanding of the benefits and harms of that treatment. Standard informed-consent procedures work best in the acute-care setting, where they involve treatment choices that lead to cure, significant improvement, or death. Decision-making for older people with chronic illness, often in long-term care settings, is much more ambiguous than in acute-care environments (Cole and Holstein, 1996).

Passive Euthanasia
(Voluntary Elective Death)

Euthanasia can be passive (allowing death) or active (causing death). In **passive euthanasia,** treatment is withdrawn, and nothing is done to prolong the patient's life artificially, such as use of a feeding tube or ventilator. Suspension of medical interventions allows the natural dying process to occur, but no active steps are taken to bring about death. In order to relieve pain, medications are sometimes given which may hasten death, but the object is to relieve suffering, not to bring about death. Withholding or withdrawing useless or unwanted medical treatments, or providing adequate pain relief, even if it hastens death, has been determined to be neither illegal nor unethical (Choice in Dying, 1994). The legal context for this is the 1990 U.S. Supreme Court case of *Cruzan v. Director, Missouri Department of Health,* which recognized the right of a competent patient to refuse unwanted medical care, including artificial nutrition and hydration, as a "liberty" interest, and therefore as constitutionally protected. Although the Cruzan decision recognized this, the Supreme Court delegated regulation of this constitutional right to the states. Another indicator of the changing legal interpretations was the position of the American Medical Association (AMA). Their 1984 statement on euthanasia presented two fundamental guidelines: the patient's role in decision-making is paramount, and a decrease in aggressive treatment of the hopelessly ill patient is advisable when treatment would only prolong a difficult and uncomfortable process of dying (Wanzer et al., 1984). A 1988 American Medical Association poll found that 80 to 90 percent of physicians agree that withholding and withdrawing nutrition and hydration are permissible in certain circumstances and that it is the physician's duty to initiate discussion of these issues with patients and their families (New York Times, 1988). In fact, in 1989, the American Medical Association adopted the position that, with informed consent, physicians could withhold or withdraw treatment from patients who are close to death. Consistent with this changing medical position is that over 57 percent of the

American public support the option of doctor-assisted suicide for patients with incurable disease (Seattle Times, June 26, 1997, A23). Nevertheless, the official position of the American Medical Association is to oppose physicians directly assisting their patients in committing suicide; this position is based on the historical role of physicians as advocates for healing (AMA, 1996).

In contrast to passive euthanasia where deliberate decisions are made about withholding or withdrawing treatment, there is also a form of euthanasia whereby older people may voluntarily make decisions that are equivalent to choosing to die by refusing extra help at home or by insisting on hospital discharge directly to their home, in spite of their need for skilled nursing care. When an older person commits suicide through the process of **self-neglect,** the effects of their decisions are subtle and gradual. If older people neglect their care needs or choose an inappropriate living situation because of impaired judgment, involuntary treatment laws can sometimes be used to move them to protected settings. If their "failure to care," however, is not immediately life-threatening, they usually have to be allowed to deteriorate to that point before being legally compelled to comply with treatment.

Active Euthanasia

Active euthanasia refers to positive steps taken to bring about someone else's death, by administering a lethal injection or by some other means. Sometimes called mercy killing, active euthanasia is not legal in any state at this time, but its legality has been tested by several highly controversial court cases, voter initiatives, and state legislation. As noted above, a subject of intense controversy is physician-assisted suicide or assisted suicide; this occurs when someone else provides the means by which an individual ends his or her life. For example, a physician may prescribe medication knowing that the individual intends to use it to commit suicide, but it is the individual who decides when and whether or not to take it (Choice in Dying, 1994). One of the states in which the legality of assisted suicide has been the focus of public attention is Michigan, where Dr. Jack Kevorkian, as of 1997, had assisted nearly 100 people to commit suicide (Reibstein, 1997). In the first case involving a woman with Alzheimer's disease, the court dismissed the murder charges on the grounds that no law in Michigan prohibited assisting in a suicide. Subsequently, the legislature passed legislation in an effort to stop Dr. Kevorkian's activities. Some cases have been dismissed on the grounds that the law is unconstitutional, and many others are pending. Although controversial, Kevorkian's crusade to legalize active euthanasia has been functional in pushing the debate on physician-assisted suicide to the forefront of the American political scene. Those who argue against the legalization of assisted suicide view that a "right to die" could become a "duty to

ISSUES RAISED BY THE RIGHT TO DIE

Consider the case of a California couple, both home-bound and under the care of round-the-clock nurses. The wife had emphysema and was unable to walk, talk, or stand up straight without severe breathing difficulties. She was attached 24 hours a day to a machine that delivered oxygen to her through two nasal prongs. The husband, in the final stages of congestive heart disease, was subject to hallucinations and could not walk, read, hear clearly, get dressed, bathe himself, or control his bladder. If they had waited 4 months, they could have celebrated their fiftieth wedding anniversary, but instead they chose, as they put it in their letters to their children, to "terminate their terminal illnesses." During the last year of their lives, they had discussed their plans with their children and grandchildren, written detailed letters describing their intentions and philosophies, and carefully studied manuals published by *right to die* societies. Their adult children believed that their parents, perceiving a painful and narrowed future, had availed themselves of their right to choose the dignity of death over the sanctity of life (Fadiman, 1984).

die" and be inappropriately applied to older adults and other dependent members of society. They fear that a law made to convey permission could become seen as prescriptive, with assisted suicide viewed as a solution no longer requiring careful scrutiny.

Citizen initiatives and recent state legislation have reflected increasing public support for physician-assisted suicide. *Compassion et al. v. Washington State* was the first case to challenge in a federal court the constitutionality of a state law on assisted suicide insofar as it applies to mentally competent, terminally ill patients seeking prescribed medications with which to hasten death. An initiative in Washington State to permit physician aid-in-dying was only narrowly defeated in 1992. Patients could request such assistance in writing at the time they wanted to die, as long as two witnesses would certify that the request is voluntary and two doctors would state that the patient would die within 6 months. However, 4 months after the initiative was defeated at the polls, the legislature passed a bill giving comatose and dying people the right to have food and water withdrawn (*Seattle Times*, 1992). In 1994, the federal district court ruled that the Washington State ban on physician-assisted suicide violates the patient's constitutional right to liberty, but this ruling did not protect physicians from prosecution if they assisted in a terminally ill patient's suicide (Hudson, 1994).

Measure 16, passed by Oregon voters in 1994, allows doctors to write a prescription of lethal drug doses for an aware, terminally ill adult who asks for it, both orally and in writing, although doctors are not compelled to comply with this request. A 15-day waiting period is required for the first oral request, and two witnesses are necessary for the written request along with agreement of a second doctor. The doctor must inform the patient about options, including pain control, and make sure that the request really is voluntary. At the end of this elaborate process, only the patient can decide whether and when to take fatal drugs and must do so him- or herself. However, in response to a lawsuit that argued that the law does

not provide adequate safeguards against undue influence, particularly in instances of depression, a federal judge blocked implementation of this citizen initiative that would have made Oregon the second entity (after the Netherlands) to legalize physician-assisted suicide (Egar, 1994). In 1996, a federal appeals court struck down both Washington and New York statutes banning physician-assisted suicide. The plaintiffs (near-death patients and physicians) argued that there is no public interest served by prolonging pain in truly hopeless situations and that to do so is to subject patients to potential abuse. The courts linked the right to facilitate death with the right to refuse medical treatment.

These conflicting state rulings and pressure from advocacy organizations such as Compassion in Dying brought the issue of assisted suicide to the U.S. Supreme Court. In June 1997, the U.S. Supreme Court ruled that there is no constitutional or fundamental "right to die." They thus upheld the Washington and New York laws that make it a crime for doctors to help patients kill themselves, although several justices indicated that they are willing to revisit the issue in specific cases. This ruling by the Supreme Court, however, does not preclude states from deciding on their own to pass laws allowing doctor-assisted suicide. By returning the debate to the states, the justices apparently opened the way for other jurisdictions to follow Oregon, whose citizens voted in 1994 and again in 1997 to be the only state to legalize the physician-assisted suicide choice for patients who are diagnosed by two doctors as having less than 6 months to live. The Oregon law also provides for a 15-day waiting period and prohibits lethal injection. It is being challenged legally by opponents of assisted suicide, such as National Right to Life.

Nor will the Supreme Court ruling stop patients from seeking physicians to prescribe lethal medications or stop doctors from providing them illegally. The court ruled that prescribing medication with the intent to relieve suffering is legal and acceptable, but presenting drugs with the intent to cause death is not. Since "intent" is difficult to determine, the Court does give significant discretion and latitude to physicians to use adequate pain medication and explicitly endorses "terminal sedation." A dying patient who is suffering and is in pain, wrote Justice Sandra Day O'Connor, "has no legal barriers to obtaining medication from qualified physicians to alleviate that suffering, even to the point of causing unconsciousness and hastening death" (Ostrom, 1998). In many ways, this solution, known as the "double effect," is an old one. In the Supreme Court's definition, this occurs when a physician, intending to relieve pain or suffering, gives a terminally ill patient medication that has the unintended—but foreseeable—side effect of hastening death. Often, this medication is morphine. It has been estimated that about 25 percent of doctors have had patients ask for assistance with suicide, and of these, about 25 percent actually provided the help, through prescribing pain medication, despite the possibility of legal penalties (Ostrom and Westnext, 1997). In spite of individual physicians' assistance with suicide, the American Medical Association continues to oppose such actions. Instead, they advocate compassion and high-quality palliative care.

Although there is growing support for physicians to provide aggressive pain control, most physicians are not always well informed about how to minimize suffering and help patients **die with dignity.** Some physicians view use of aggressive pain relief as an admission of failure in an effort to cure. Increasing numbers of medical organizations, such as the American Medical Association and the American College of Physicians, have released recommendations on standards for end-of-life care, quality pain-management technologies, or created expert panels to make recommendations. A 1997 report by the Institute of Medicine criticizes physicians and other providers for failing to provide competent palliative and supportive care (Institute of Medicine, 1997). The American Geriatrics Society has issued a statement of principles to measure quality of life at the end of life, including physical and emotional symptoms, advance care planning, aggressive care near death, and global quality of life. Last Acts is a coalition of 72 organizations that seeks reforms to improve communication and decision-making among physicians and other health care providers, payers, hospitals, nursing homes, and consumers regarding end-of-life issues. Many of these initiatives are based on the assumption that if individuals can be assured that pain is not an inevitable part of the dying process, they are less likely to request physician-assisted suicide. The American Civil Liberties Union is putting forth the "End of Life Care Act of 1998"; this would remove legal liability from physicians who offer patients a full range of end-of-life care choices, including palliative sedation. They argue that if a patient is not comfortable, then it is appropriate to give more palliative care through stronger pain medication. Overall, there is growing recognition of the need for more training and research related to aggressive end-of-life care to ensure the patient's comfort.

LEGAL OPTIONS REGARDING END-OF-LIFE CARE

While active euthanasia continues to be debated in courtrooms and the ballot box, all 50 states have laws authorizing the use of some type of **advance directive**; this refers to a patient's oral and written instructions about future medical care in the event of their inability to speak for themselves. Both federal and state laws govern the use of advance directives. The federal law, the **Patient Self-Determination Act**, requires health care facilities that receive Medicaid and Medicare funds to inform patients of their rights to execute advance directives regarding how they want to live or die; state regulations vary widely.

The most frequently used type of advance directive is a **Living Will**, in which an individual's wishes about medical treatment are put in writing should he or she be unable to communicate at the end of life (see the example of Florida State Health Care Directive or Living Will on page 377). Living Wills can direct physicians at hospitals to withhold life-sustaining procedures in the event of an irreversible terminal condition and can assist family members in making decisions when they are unable to consult a comatose or mentally incompetent relative. Such stipulations only apply to care in hospitals, although some states have drafted laws that would exempt emergency medical technicians from liability for not resuscitating patients who have legal do-not-resuscitate (DNR) medical directives (Gianelli, 1994). The majority of Americans appear to approve of Living Wills; yet only about 20 percent of older people have such advance directives on file. Most seem to trust their families to know what to do (Cole and Holstein, 1996). There are limitations to Living Wills. Even when there is a Living Will, this does not mean that health care providers, oftentimes with conflicting beliefs, will always follow it, especially if there is no one to advocate for the dying individual. Or family members may later change their minds about adhering to a Living Will. In addition, forms differ from state to state; patients and their families can access these through national organizations, such as **Choice in Dying** and **Compassion in Dying,** local hospitals, state attorney general's offices, or the Internet through web sites of organizations such as Compassion in Dying.

In situations where there is no Living Will, the family of an incompetent patient must go to court to obtain legal authority if they wish to refuse life support on the patient's behalf. This expensive and time-consuming process has been viewed as necessary where doctors and health care facilities are unwilling to make decisions to remove life-sustaining treatment because of the perceived risk of liability. To obviate this court process, 24 states and the District of Columbia have passed statutes governing **surrogate decision-making.** The surrogate has a duty to act according to the known wishes of the patient; if those wishes are not known, the surrogate must act according to the "best interest" of the patient. Such laws support the concept that the people closest to the patient are in the best position to know their wishes or to act in their best interest. Each state's law includes a prioritized list of peo-

ple connected to the patient who are potential surrogates. The doctor must approach these individuals, in order of priority, to find someone who is willing to make decisions about life support (Choice in Dying, 1994).

Durable Power of Attorney is another type of advance directive, usually in addition to a Living Will. This authorizes someone to act on an individual's behalf with regard to property and financial matters. The individual does not relinquish control with a power of attorney since it is granted only for the financial matters specifically set forth in the relevant document.

A *Medical Power of Attorney* (or Durable Power of Attorney for Healthcare) specifically allows for a health care surrogate to make decisions about medical care if the patient is unable to make them him- or herself. Many people use a Durable Power of Attorney for Healthcare instead of, or in addition to, a Living Will because it is more broadly applicable to nearly any type of health care during periods of incapacitation. **Durable** means that the arrangement continues even when the person is incapacitated and unable to make his or her own medical decisions. A durable power of attorney agreement may be written either to go into effect upon its signing or only when the disability occurs. When the disability does occur, bills can continue to be paid and revenues can continue to be collected while other more permanent arrangements are being made, such as the appointment of a conservator or guardian.

Conservatorship generally relates to control of financial matters. In this instance, probate court appoints a person as a **conservator** to care for an individual's property and finances because that person is unable to do so due to advanced age, mental weakness, or physical incapacity. Such a condition must be attested to by a physician. Once appointed, the conservator will be required to file an inventory of all the assets and to report annually all income and expenses. The old or disabled individual, however, loses control over his or her property and finances.

FLORIDA DESIGNATION OF HEALTH CARE SURROGATE

INSTRUCTIONS

PRINT YOUR NAME

Name: _____
          (Last)   *(First)*   *(Middle Initial)*

In the event that I have been determined to be incapacitated to provide informed consent for medical treatment and surgical and diagnostic procedures, I wish to designate as my surrogate for health care decisions:

PRINT THE NAME, HOME ADDRESS AND TELEPHONE NUMBER OF YOUR SURROGATE

Name: _____

Address: _____

_____ Zip Code: _____

Phone: _____

If my surrogate is unwilling or unable to perform his duties, I wish to designate as my alternate surrogate:

PRINT THE NAME, HOME ADDRESS AND TELEPHONE NUMBER OF YOUR ALTERNATE SURROGATE

Name: _____

Address: _____

_____ Zip Code: _____

Phone: _____

I fully understand that this designation will permit my designee to make health care decisions and to provide, withhold, or withdraw consent on my behalf; to apply for public benefits to defray the cost of health care; and to authorize my admission to or transfer from a health care facility.

ADD PERSONAL INSTRUCTIONS (IF ANY)

Additional instructions (optional):

© 1996
CHOICE IN DYING, INC.

FLORIDA DESIGNATION OF HEALTH CARE SURROGATE—PAGE 2 OF 2

I further affirm that this designation is not being made as a condition of treatment or admission to a health care facility. I will notify and send a copy of this document to the following persons other than my surrogate, so they may know who my surrogate is:

PRINT THE NAMES AND ADDRESSES OF THOSE WHO YOU WANT TO KEEP COPIES OF THIS DOCUMENT

Name: _____

Address: _____

Name: _____

Address: _____

SIGN AND DATE THE DOCUMENT

Signed: _____

Date: _____

WITNESSING

Signed: _____

Address: _____

TWO WITNESSES MUST SIGN AND PRINT THEIR ADDRESSES

Witness 2:

Signed: _____

Address: _____

© 1996
CHOICE IN DYING, INC.

Courtesy of **Choice In Dying, Inc.** 6/96
1035 30th Street, NW Washington, DC 10007 800-989-9455

Guardianship is a legal tool that establishes control over a person's body as well as financial affairs. In a guardianship, a probate court appoints someone to care for the individual's person, property, and finances because of the individual's mental inability to care for him- or herself. The **guardian** has a responsibility for directing the individual's medical treatment, housing, personal needs, finances, and property. To establish guardianship, a medical certificate from a physician must state that the individual is incapable of caring for him- or herself because of mental illness. As with conservatorships, the medical certificate required by the physician must be made not more than 10 days before the probate court hearing, so in this sense, guardianship cannot be arranged in advance of need. However, through a durable power of attorney for health care decisions, an individual may nominate someone he or she would like to act as guardian in the event that such a need develops. Since the guardian manages all the affairs of the individual, guardianship is generally considered a last resort. This is because the process essentially eliminates an individual's legal rights since consent is not required, and it is costly and rarely reversible.

Family members who are concerned about finances may move too quickly through these options. However, families and service providers should try, as long as possible, to respect the wishes of the older person with regard to living arrangements, legal will, and other financial decisions. In other words, the older person should be encouraged to exercise as much control as possible, to the extent that his or her cognitive status allows. In general, less restrictive approaches than guardianship are needed which balance the need for protection with self-determination (Wilber and Reynolds, 1995).

A wide range of organizations have been developed to educate the public, health care providers, and lawmakers regarding right-to-die issues and advance directive options. The largest of these is **Choice in Dying**, Inc., a national not-for-profit organization that was created in 1991 by a merger of the nation's two oldest organizations advocating the rights of dying patients, Concern for Dying and Society for the Right to Die. These two organizations pioneered patients' rights to refuse unwanted life support and developed the first Living Will document in 1967. Choice in Dying has provided national leadership on Living Wills, guided the enactment of advance directives in all states, and lobbied for the passage of the Patient Self-Determination Act. Their goal is to achieve full societal and legal support for the right of all individuals to make decisions regarding the nature and extent of life-sustaining measures, as well as the conditions under which dying occurs, and to have those decisions recognized and honored (Choice in Dying, 1994). Another national patient advocacy organization that promotes legal strategies for death with dignity is the Compassion in Dying Federation. They also established a Center for End-of-Life Law and Policy that will assist in the development of challenges to state laws that bar patients from requesting aid in dying from their physicians.

An organization that has actively attempted to change the law in order to legalize assisted suicide for the terminally ill is the **Hemlock Society.** Their popular publication, *Final Exit,* by their founder, Derek Humphry, is a manual on nonviolent methods to commit suicide with prescription barbiturates to assure a gentle, peaceful death. The Hemlock Society distinguishes between "rational or responsible suicide" (i.e., the option of ending one's life for good and valid reasons) and suicide that is caused by a rejection of life because of emotional disturbance. Public opinion polls also reflect a growing acceptance of the idea of assisted suicide, especially among those who believe that to force people to endure prolonged pain is inhumane and cruel. Advocates of physician-assisted suicide view the right to request assistance in dying as merely an extension of the individual's right to control the kind of treatment he or she receives when dying. Rejecting remote chances of recovery as a basis to justify prolonging life, they also discard the notion of any ethical difference between stopping treatment and assisting someone to die.

Societal cost-benefit criteria inevitably come into play in discussions of active and passive euthanasia. As society seeks to contain rising health and long-term care costs, physicians are subject to demands for financial restraint. Admittedly, a significant proportion of the money spent on medical care in a person's lifetime goes to services received during the last years and months of life. In spite of that, even if such end-of-life care were eliminated, the nation's health care expenditures would be reduced by only one-half of one percent (Alliance for Aging Research, 1997). Nevertheless, given limited resources on a societal level, the public often perceives the costs to keep alive a comparatively small number of people prohibitively high (Cole and Holstein, 1996; Callahan, 1993).

Rapid improvements in medical technology have not been matched by refinements in the law and the ethics of using those therapies, although the field of **bioethics** *or medical ethics,* which focuses on procedural approaches to questions about death, dying, and medical decision-making, has grown in the past 20 years. Euthanasia raises not only complex ethical and legal dilemmas, but also resource-allocation issues that cannot be ignored. On a personal level, many dying people find that the medical technology that prolongs their lives may financially ruin their families. It is important that families discuss in advance issues such as who should assume medical care decision-making on their own behalf, if necessary, or under what circumstances one would prefer or not prefer life support. However, most families find it emotionally difficult to do such planning, especially if the older adult is experiencing advanced dementia and cannot make a rational decision at this later stage of the disease.

BEREAVEMENT, GRIEF, AND MOURNING RITUALS

Death affects the social structure through the dying person's survivors, who have social and emotional needs resulting from that death. Some early studies found that the intensity of these needs is reflected in the higher rates of suicide, hospitalization for psychiatric disorders, visits to physicians, and somatic complaints among survivors (Kalish, 1982; Marshall, 1980). As a whole, however, the research on the relationship between widowhood and morbidity and mortality is fraught with contradictory findings. Despite early research findings of high mortality rates among widowers, more current epidemiological studies have found no significant relationships between bereavement and mortality. Although there is evidence of short-term decreases in health status and perceived health following widowhood, long-term health appears largely unaffected (Martin-Matthews, 1996). In fact, some studies suggest that the resiliency and ability of the grieving spouse to cope effectively are often underestimated (Lund, 1993; Caserta and Lund, 1992).

Findings of the long-term impact of widowhood on mental health are also equivocal, although the early bereavement period is generally associated with depression, mood alterations, disruptive sleep patterns, obsessive thoughts of the deceased, and disorientation (Martin-Matthews, 1996). Accordingly, the relationship between bereavement and suicide in the older population requires further investigation. Although findings are inconsistent, the first 6 months of widowhood appear to be the most stressful, especially for older men who are more at risk of poor health, death, and suicide. To minimize these disruptive effects, older survivors, who frequently face multiple losses, need help from both formal and informal networks in dealing with their grief. Such efforts to be supportive must take account of cultural values and belief.

Bereavement refers to both the situation and the long-term process of adjusting to the death of someone with whom the person felt close (Lund, 1993). **Grief** is the complex emotional response to bereavement. *Bereavement* refers to the state of being deprived of a loved one by death. **Mourning** signifies culturally patterned expectations about the expression of grief. Grief reactions can include shock and disbelief, guilt, psychological numbness, depression, loneliness, fatigue, loss of appetite, sleeplessness, and anxiety about one's ability to reorganize and carry on with life (Martin-Matthews, 1996).

Although there appear to be clusters or phases of grief reactions, the progression is more like a roller coaster—with overlapping responses and wide individual variability—rather than orderly stages or a fixed or universal sequence. To expect grieving individuals to progress in some specified fashion is inappropriate, and can be potentially harmful to them. The highs and lows within broad phases can occur within minutes, days, months, or years, with grieving individuals moving back and forth among them. Even within the individual, there can be mixed reactions, with a person simultaneously experiencing anger, guilt, helplessness, and loneliness along with personal strength and pride in their coping. Emotions change rapidly, beginning with shock, numbness, and disbelief, followed by an all-encompassing sorrow. Early months following the loss are the most difficult, with early indicators serving as predictors of longer-term adjustment (Lund, 1993; Lund, Caserta, and Dimond, 1993).

An intermediate phase of grief often involves an idealization and searching for the presence of the deceased person, as well as an obsessive review in an attempt to find meaning for the death. Anger toward the deceased, toward God, and toward caregivers may also be experienced, as well as guilt and regrets for what survivors did not do or say. When the permanence of the loss is acknowledged and yearning ceases, anguish, disorganization, and despair often result. The grieving person tends to experience a sense of confusion; a feeling of aimlessness; a loss of motivation, confidence, and interest; and an inability to make decisions. These feelings may be exacerbated if the grieving person tries to live according to the expectations of others, including those of the deceased. Instead, successful adjustments require active rather than passive coping strategies in which the individual finds his or her own best way to live with grief (Lund, 1993).

The final phase—reorganization—is marked by a resumption of routine activities and social relationships, while still remembering and identifying with the deceased. The ability to effectively communicate one's thoughts and feelings to others and to experience a reciprocal relationship be-

tween one's self-esteem and learning new skills and competencies enhances the adjustment process (Lund, 1993). Adaptation or accommodation might be more appropriate terms to describe changes in the person's identity and emotional reorganization than recovery. The end point of bereavement may best be understood as the return of ordinary levels of functioning (Weiss, 1993).

Estimates of the duration of time for the completion of grief among the bereaved range from 2 to 4 years. On the other hand, some people never fully resolve their loss nor cease grieving, but learn to live with it (Martin-Matthews, 1996; Lund, 1993). Unresolved grief may be misdiagnosed as illness, and may lead to depression, as described in Chapter 6. For most people, some of the pain of loss remains for a lifetime. Older adults' experiences with grief may be even more complex than other age groups' for several reasons. As noted in Chapter 6, they are more likely to experience unrelated, multiple losses over relatively brief periods, at a time when their coping capacities and environmental resources are often diminished. The cumulative effects of losses may be greater, especially if the older person has not resolved earlier losses, or interprets current losses as evidence of an inevitable continuing decline. Health care providers must be careful not to misdiagnose grief symptoms as physical illness, dementia, or hypochondria. Not surprisingly, loneliness has been found to be the greatest difficulty for older bereaved spouses and cannot be managed simply by surrounding oneself with others (Lund et al., 1993).

Research findings are mixed regarding whether adjustment to bereavement is more difficult when death is sudden or unexpected. In comparison to the young, older people may be less affected by a sudden death because they have rehearsed and planned for widowhood as a life stage task. As noted in Chapter 6, in the discussion of anticipatory coping, an expected death can allow survivors to prepare for the changes through **anticipatory grief,** but it does not necessarily minimize the grief and emotional strain following the death. However, some studies indicate that a longer period of anticipatory grief, through caring for an individual during a long period of chronic or terminal illness, can actually create barriers to successful adaptation, increasing the risk of post-mortem depression. Family members who experience the death as a relief from long-term demands of care may experience premature detachment, ambivalent and hostile feelings, guilt, depression, and a reduced ability to mourn publicly. Others have concluded that the adjustment process is similar whether the loss is expected or unexpected, although suddenness may make a difference early in the process of bereavement (Lund et al., 1993).

Factors that have been found to help minimize grief are whether the death is viewed as natural, the degree to which relationships seem complete, and the presence of surviving confidants to provide emotional support. To work through grief successfully requires facing the pain and fully expressing the related feelings. Health care providers increasingly recognize the importance of grief work, and view grieving as a natural healing process. Because of the cumulative impact of multiple losses, older adults especially may need assistance in grief resolution, perhaps through life review and encouragement of new risk-taking. Unfortunately, most studies of bereavement have been based on case studies or retrospective studies during the early phase of grief. There are few well-controlled longitudinal studies of the bereavement process. An additional limitation is that few researchers have controlled for the effects of variables such as gender, ethnic minority status, age, social class, and education. Our understanding of the emotional components of bereavement is based largely on middle-aged, middle-class Caucasians, thereby limiting the cultural relevance of interventions to address the emotional aspects of grieving.

Mourning involves cultural assumptions about appropriate behavior during bereavement. Mourning rituals develop in every culture as a way to channel the normal expression of grief, to define the appropriate timing of bereavement, and to encourage support for the bereaved among family and friends. Professionals need to be sensitive to cultural and ethnic differences regarding the form and meaning of death and the burial of the dead. Grief rituals, such as sorting and disposing of personal effects and visiting the grave site, are important in working through the grief process (Bolton and Delpha, 1989).

The funeral, for example, serves as a rite of passage for the deceased and a focal point for the expression of the survivors' grief. Funerals also allow the family to demonstrate cohesion through sharing ritual, food, and drink, and thus minimize the disruptive effects of the death. Funerals and associated customs are more important in societies with a high mortality throughout the life cycle than in societies where death is predominantly confined to the old. Money donations instead of flowers, memorial services and celebrations of the deceased person's life instead of funeral services, and cremations instead of land burial signal the development of new kinds of death rituals today. Traditional funeral ceremonies have been criticized for being costly, for exploiting people at a time when they are vulnerable, and for elaborate cosmetic restorations of the body. Legislation has been enacted to control some of the excesses of the funeral industry. Despite such criticisms, however, most people approve of some type of ceremony to make the death more real to the survivors and to offer a meaningful way to cope with the initial grief.

WIDOWHOOD

A spouse's death (or that of a partner, in the case of gay and lesbian couples or unmarried heterosexual couples) may be the most stressful event that an older person will experience, altering one's self-concept to an "uncoupled identity" (Lund, 1993). Among women age 65 and over, it has been estimated that 50 to 70 percent are widowed, compared to 12 to 22 percent among their male peers. The average age of widowhood is 66 years for women and 69 for men; when combined with women's greater life expectancy, this means that the average duration of widowhood for women is 15 years compared with 6 years for men (Martin-

Matthews, 1996; Arbuckle and deVries, 1995). Widows outnumber widowers 5 to 1; among non-whites, the proportion of widows is twice that among whites; non-white women are also widowed earlier (Angel and Hogan, 1994). This is a reflection of the shorter life expectancy of non-white men in our society, as discussed in Chapter 13.

Despite the stress, the course of spousal bereavement is often characterized by resiliency and effective coping which allows depression, loneliness, and sadness to be followed by feelings of self-confidence, self-efficacy, and personal growth. In fact, only 15 to 25 percent of bereaved spouses have long-term difficulties in coping, and as noted earlier, the stress of bereavement does not necessarily have a negative impact on health (Lund, 1993; Caserta and Lund, 1992). One exception is that the bereaved tend to experience loneliness more than the non-bereaved (Arbuckle and deVries, 1995).

It appears that the impact of widowhood can be attenuated through a number of complex social-psychological variables. These include the adequacy of the social support network, including closeness to children and having intimate friends; the individual's characteristic ways of coping with

Older widows generally have more extensive peer support than widowers.

stress; and religious commitment. Although family plays an important role following widowhood, 20 percent of widowed persons report not having a single living relative to whom they feel particularly close. Older widows are more likely to use social supports as a coping strategy when their social networks are characterized by reciprocity and reliability. At the same time, friendships developed on the basis of marital relationships may not survive widowhood. In fact, the ability to make new friends may be an important indicator of how an individual is coping with the loss of a spouse (Ducharme and Corin, 1997; Martin-Matthews, 1996). Other variables that appear to affect the degree of stress of widowhood are age, gender, and health status of the widowed person. Age by itself, however, has been found to have little effect on bereavement outcomes. Differences between younger and older widows can be explained by the relationship of age to employment status and income. Age is associated, however, with a greater need to learn new life skills, such as older women's mastering of financial-management tasks. Gender has been found to have fairly consistent effects on personal functioning; women tend to exhibit lower levels of completing plans, lower self-efficacy, and higher levels of depression, and to express greater fatalism and more vulnerability than their male counterparts (Arbuckle and deVries, 1995).

It is unclear whether the stress of bereavement is greater for the young than for the old. Psychological distress tends to be greater for younger widows than older ones, since the death of one's spouse is more likely to be unanticipated and few of their peers are experiencing similar loss. Although younger spouses have been found initially to manifest more intense grief, a reverse trend has been noted after 18 months, with older spouses showing exacerbated grief reactions. As noted earlier, older people are more likely to experience other losses simultaneously, or "bereavement overload" (Kastenbaum, 1991), which may intensify and prolong their grief. On the other hand, spousal bereavement in later life is an "on-time" event, and older adults have had more opportunities to manage a variety of losses and to develop a variety of coping strategies. In such instances, widowhood may be less stressful, even among the oldest-old, and different death circumstances do not appear to have a significant impact on long-term adjustment (Lund, 1993).

Gender Differences in Widowhood

Whether widowhood is more difficult for women or men is unclear. Certainly, coping or adaptation to widowhood is related to income. Adequate financial resources are necessary to maintain a sense of self-sufficiency and to continue participation in meaningful activities. Older widows are generally worse off than widowers in terms of finances, years of education, legal problems, and prospects for remarriage. Women who have been economically dependent on their husbands often find their incomes drastically reduced, especially if they do not yet qualify for Social Security or if their husbands had not chosen survivors' pension benefits. Financial hardships may be especially great for women who have been caring for a spouse during a long chronic illness or who have depleted their joint resources during the spouse's institutionalization. Furthermore, many older widows have few opportunities to augment their income through paid employment. Insurance benefits, when they exist, tend to be exhausted within 2 years of the husband's death. Not surprisingly, higher income has been found to be associated with better bereavement outcomes (Sanders, 1993). Accordingly, more years of schooling are related to higher levels of personal functioning, since education tends to provide the ability to clarify problems, identify resources, and take action toward solutions (Lopata, 1993).

Some women, however, do not depend on a man for economic or social support. Because women generally have more diverse, extensive friendship networks than men do, and because widowhood is prevalent in later life, older women form strong support networks with other widows. These friendship groups can compensate for the loss of a husband's companionship and ease the

adjustment to living alone. Friends are of greatest support, in some instances more so than children. This is especially true when friends accept the widow's emotional ambivalence, do not offer advice, and respond to what she defines as her needs. Among women over age 70, two-thirds of whom are widowed, the married person is the unusual case, and she may have fewer friends than does the widow in the same age group (Martin-Matthews, 1996).

Many widows have no interest in remarriage. Even among Lopata's (1973) classic study of widows with happy prior marriages, 36 percent said they would not marry again. Although many persons feel great loss with a spouse's death, for some who have been restricted in their marriage or who faced long-term caregiving responsibilities, widowhood can bring relief and opportunities to develop new interests. In fact, for those in unhappy marriages who feel they cannot divorce, death may be the only acceptable separation.

Adjusting to the loss of a spouse is likely to be most difficult for women who are in poor health, have had few economic and social resources throughout their lives, and perceive themselves as dependent. It is also difficult for women whose identity as a wife is lost without the substitution of other viable roles and lifestyles (O'Bryant and Morgan, 1991). However, as the example below illustrates, older widows can learn to become more independent. The importance of economic and social supports has been identified in societies throughout the Middle East, Asia, and the Pacific, as well as in various cultures within Canada and the United States. A closely related factor appears to be whether a gap exists between how a woman was socialized to be dependent upon a man and how she must now live more independently as a widow (Lopata, 1987). For example, in a classic study, Lopata (1973) found that widows who did not have their own friends or who had only couple-based friendships before their husband's death generally had difficulty forming new friendships and were left without satisfying roles. They also tended not to access social services. In our couples-oriented society, such women were lonely and isolated, and turned primarily to their children for emotional support. Friendships were thus the least frequent and the least deeply involving among the most disadvantaged and uneducated of the urban widows studied by Lopata. (Because more women have entered the work force in the past 30 years, future cohorts of older women may be better prepared to live independently than the women in Lopata's early studies.) Whether widows have strong friendship networks appears to vary with socioeconomic class and ethnic minority status, with whether they had a social network and satisfying roles before their husbands' deaths, and with the prevalence of widowhood among a person's own age, sex, and class peers. Hispanic and Asian American widows are more likely to live with others and thus to have more active support systems than do Caucasian widows or those from other ethnic minority groups (Moen, 1996).

A woman's change in status inevitably affects her relationship with her children and other relatives. Most widows move in with their children only as a "last resort," although their children may view them as "helpless" and urge them to make the move. Older widows tend to grow closer to their daughters through patterns of mutual assistance, but sons may provide instrumental support for mothers in their own homes. Nevertheless, although children provide both socioeconomic support and assistance with tasks, this may not necessarily reduce their widowed parents' loneliness. For example, interactions with an adult child are less reciprocal, while friends and neighbors are

better suited for sharing leisure activities and providing companionship; such reciprocity tends to be associated with higher morale. What is clear is the importance of diverse social networks that include age-generational peers, whether family or non-family (McCandless and Conner, 1997; Bengtson et al., 1990).

Most research on widowhood has focused on women, since there are five widows to every widower in our society. Less is known about the effects of widowhood on older men. Men more often complain of loneliness and appear to make slower emotional recoveries than do women. They may have more difficulty expressing their grief and adjusting to the loss than women do; this is because of their lower degree of involvement in family and friendship roles throughout life, their life-long patterns of restraining emotions, their limited prior housekeeping and cooking, and the greater likelihood of a double role loss of worker and spouse (Patterson, 1996; Martin-Matthews, 1988). On the other hand, some men experience pride and enhanced self-esteem from mastering new housekeeping skills (Lund et al., 1993). Many older men have depended on their wives for emotional support, household maintenance, and social planning. Given these factors, men appear to "need" remarriage more than women do, and perhaps have been socialized to move more quickly into restructuring their lives through remarriage. Other studies have concluded that the impact of bereavement on older people's mental health is comparable for both men and women, and that

DEVELOPING NEW ROLES IN WIDOWHOOD

Martha had always seen her role as wife and mother and left the paying of the bills and "business" aspects of family life to her husband. Her "job" was to keep the home a comfortable place for him and their daughter. When he died 5 years ago, she was 63. She felt ill-prepared to take on paying the bills and managing other financial matters. She sought the advice of

her banker on the best way to set up a bookkeeping system. After paying the bills, ordering some appliances for the house, and taking care of the Medicare paperwork for the past few years, she now sees herself as being in the role of "manager" for herself, and is pleased with what she has learned.

with advancing age and increasing functional limitations, the similarities between widows and widowers become more striking than the differences (Lund et al., 1993; Bengtson et al., 1990). Men, however, have been found to experience more medical problems (as measured by increased physicians' visits and use of medications) and to be at greater risk of mortality during the 6 months following their wife's death. Higher rates of illness may result from hormonal responses to the stress of loss, which can lead to depression of the body's immune system. Although widowhood may significantly impair older men's emotional and medical well-being, it is less likely to place men at an economic disadvantage. More research is needed on how men cope with the loss of their wives. Even less is known about how older men's experience of widowhood varies by social class or ethnic minority status.

Generally, widowhood increases social isolation for both men and women, with loneliness perceived as a major problem. In order to provide such support for persons coping with loneliness and isolation, mutual help groups and bereavement centers have been developed by both mental health professionals and lay organizations. Women are the most frequent participants. These widow-to-widow groups are based on the principle of bringing together people who have the common experience of widowhood and who can help each other identify solutions to shared concerns. They recognize that a widowed person generally accepts help from other widowed people more readily than from professionals or family members. Support groups thus can provide widows with effective role models and can help integrate them into a social network and enhance their sense of competence toward their environment. Similar groups also need to be developed for gay men and lesbian women who are coping with the loss of a partner. Recent studies have suggested that a widowed person's sense of self-esteem, competence, and life satisfaction may be as or more important resources than the self-help intervention. One implication is that interventions should focus upon ways for the bereaved to draw

upon and enhance their internal resources and to experience growth and development, not just serve as a forum to address the disruptive effects of the loss (Caserta and Lund, 1993). Clearly, more research is needed on group objectives and how support-group dynamics and structure relate to specific adjustment outcomes.

SUMMARY AND IMPLICATIONS

Although death and dying have been taboo topics for many people in our society, they have become more legitimate issues for scientific and social discussion in recent years. At the same time, there has been a growing emphasis on how professionals should work with the dying and their families, as well as a movement to permit death with dignity. Two major frameworks have been advanced for understanding the dying process: the concept of stages of dying and the formulation of a dying trajectory. Both frameworks are only an inventory of possible sequences, not fixed steps.

Most people appear both to deny and to accept death, being better able to discuss others' deaths than their own, and fearing a painful dying process more than the event of death itself. Different attitudes toward dying have been noted among the old and the young. Older people are less fearful and anxious about their death than younger people and would prefer a slow death that allows them time to prepare. Likewise, survivors tend to view an older person's death as less tragic than a younger individual's.

Professionals and family members can address the dying person's fears, minimize the pain of the dying process, and help the individual to attain a "good death." One of the major developments in this regard has been hospice care, a philosophy of caring that can be implemented in both home and institutional settings, and that provides people with more control over how they die and over the quality of their remaining days.

The movement for a right to a dignified death has prompted new debates about euthanasia. Both passive and active euthanasia raise complex moral and legal questions that have been only partially addressed by the passage of Living Will legislation and a growing number of judicial decisions, including the June 1997 Supreme Court decision which ruled that there is no constitutional "right to die." Economic issues are also at stake; as resources for health care become more scarce, questions about how much public money should be spent on maintaining chronically ill people are likely to intensify. Bioethics, with its emphasis on informed consent, patient rights, and autonomy, addresses the moral issues raised by the health care of older people.

Regardless of how individuals die, their survivors experience grief and mourning. The intensity and duration of grief appear to vary by age and sex, although more research is needed regarding gender differences in reaction to loss of spouse and adjustment to widowhood.

By age 70, the majority of older women are widows. A much smaller number of older men become widowers, generally not until after age 85. The status of widowhood has negative consequences for many women in terms of increased legal difficulties, reduced finances, and few remarriage prospects. Although men are less economically disadvantaged by widowhood, they may be lonelier and have more difficulty adjusting than women do. For both men and women, social supports, particularly close friends or confidants, are important to physical and mental well-being during widowhood. In addition to mourning rituals to help widows and widowers cope with their grief, support services, such as widows' support groups, are also needed. Comprehensive and diverse service formats are essential, given the variety of grief responses, and interventions should be available early in the bereavement process and continue over relatively long periods of time to ensure maximum effectiveness. Health and social service professionals can play a crucial role in developing services for the dying and their survivors that are sensitive to cultural, ethnic minority, sexual orientation, and gender differences.

GLOSSARY

active euthanasia positive steps to hasten someone else's death, such as administering a lethal injection; assisted suicide, perhaps by a physician

advance directive documents such as Living Wills, wills, and durable power of attorney for health care decisions that outline actions to be taken when an individual is no longer able to do so, often because of irreversible terminal illness

anticipatory grief grief for a loved one prior to his or her death, usually occurring during the time that the loved one has a terminal illness that may allow survivors to prepare *or* may be a barrier to adaptation

bereavement state of being deprived of a loved one by death.

bereavement overload an experience of older adults who are exposed to the increased frequency of family and friends' deaths and become desensitized to the impact of death

bioethics addresses procedural approaches to questions about death, dying, and medical decision-making

Choice in Dying national organization supporting passive euthanasia and providing information on advance directives

Compassion in Dying national organization supporting the right to die and working to educate health care providers about aggressive pain management

conservator person designated by a court to manage the affairs, either personal or fiscal or both, of persons unable to do so for themselves

death crisis an unanticipated change in the amount of time remaining to live

death with dignity dying when one still has some independence and control over decisions about life

Durable Power of Attorney legal document that conveys to another person designated by the person signing the document the right to make decisions regarding either health and personal care or assets and income or both of the person giving the power; it is a durable power that does not expire, as a power of attorney normally does, when a person becomes incompetent

Dying Person's Bill of Rights affirms dying person's right to dignity, privacy, informed participation, and competent care

dying process as advanced by Kübler-Ross, five stages experienced by the dying person are (1) denial and isolation, (2) anger and resentment, (3) bargaining and an attempt to postpone, (4) depression and sense of loss, and (5) acceptance

dying trajectory   the pace of dying, sudden or slow, regular or erratic, usually shaped by the cause of death and by how much information is disclosed to the dying person

euthanasia   the act or practice of killing (active euthanasia) or permitting the death of (passive euthanasia) hopelessly sick or injured individuals in a relatively painless way; mercy killing

grief process   intense emotional suffering caused by loss, disaster, misfortune, etc.; acute sorrow; deep sadness; grief reaction; a state of shock, disbelief, and depression experienced following the death of a loved one

guardian   person who establishes legal control over another person's body as well as finances.

Hemlock Society   national organization that promotes the right to die for terminally ill persons, calls for legalizing assistance for those who decide to take their own lives, and publishes information on nonviolent painless methods to commit suicide

hospice   a place or a program of care for dying persons which gives emphasis to personal dignity of the dying person, reducing pain, sources of anxiety, and family reconciliation when indicated

living-dying interval   the time that occurs between the death crisis and the actual time of death, characterized by three phases: acute, provoking anxiety; chronic, characterized by decline of anxiety and facing death's reality; and terminal, eliciting withdrawal

Living Will   legal document in which an individual's wishes about medical treatment are put in writing should he or she be unable to communicate at the end of life, directing physicians and hospitals to withhold life-sustaining procedures, take all measures to sustain life, or whatever seems appropriate to the person executing the document

mourning   culturally patterned expressions of grief at someone's death

palliative treatment   treatment designed to relieve pain provided to a person with a terminal illness for whom death is imminent

passive euthanasia   voluntary elective death through the withdrawal of life-sustaining treatments or failure to treat life-threatening conditions

Patient Self-Determination Act   federal law requiring that health care facilities inform their patients about their rights to decide how they want to live or die; for

example, by providing them information on refusing treatment and on filing advance directives

right to die   the belief that persons have a right to take their own lives, especially if they experience untreatable pain, often accompanied by the belief that persons have a right to physician assistance in the dying process

self-neglect   a process by which a person voluntarily makes decisions that are equivalent to choosing to die (e.g., refusing help, not eating)

surrogate decision-maker   person legally designated to act according to patient's known wishes or "best interest"

REFERENCES

Alliance for Aging Research. *Seven deadly myths: Uncovering the facts about the high cost of the last year of life.* Washington, DC: 1997.

American Geriatrics Society. The care of dying patients: A position paper from the American Geriatrics Society. *Journal of the American Geriatrics Society,* 1995, 43, 577–578.

American Medical Association, Report 59(A-96). Physician-assisted suicide. Reference Committee on Amendments to Constitution and Bylaws. *Journal of the Oklahoma State Medical Association,* 1996, 89, 281–293.

Angel, J. L., and Hogan, D. P. The demography of minority aging population. In *Minority elders: Five goals toward building a public policy base* (2nd ed.) Washington, DC: The Gerontological Society of American, 1994.

Arbuckle, N. W., and deVries, B. The long-term effects of later life spousal and parental bereavement on personal functioning. *The Gerontologist,* 1995, 35, 637–645.

Bengtson, V., Rosenthal, C., and Burton, L. Families and aging: Diversity and heterogeneity. In R. Binstock and L. K. George (Eds.), *Handbook of aging and the social sciences* (3rd ed.). New York: Academic Press, 1990.

Bengtson, V., Rosenthal, C., and Burton, L. Families and aging: Diversity and heterogeneity. In R. H. Binstock and L. K. George (Eds.), *Handbook of aging and the social sciences* (4th ed.). San Diego, CA: Academic Press, 1996.

Bolton, C., and Delpha, C. J. The post-funeral ritual in bereavement counseling and grief work. *Journal of Gerontological Social Work,* 1989, 13, 49–57.

Callahan, D. *The troubled dream of life: Living with mortality.* New York: Simon and Schuster, 1993.

Caserta, M. S., and Lund, D. A. Bereavement, stress and coping among older adults: Expectations versus the actual experience. *Omega*, 1992, *25*, 33–45.

Caserta, M. S. and Lund, D. A. Intrapersonal resources and the effectiveness of self-help groups to bereaved older adults. *The Gerontologist*, 1993, *33*, 619–629.

Choice in Dying, *Fact Sheets: National Advance Directive Campaign.* New York: Choice in Dying, 1994.

Cole, T. R., and Holstein, M. Ethics and aging. In R. H. Binstock and L. K. George (Eds.), *Handbook of aging and the social sciences (4th ed.).* San Diego, CA: Academic Press, 1996.

Dattel, A. R., and Neimeyer, R. A. Sex differences in death anxiety: Testing the emotional expressiveness hypothesis. *Death Studies*, 1990, *28*, 1–11.

Ducharme, F., and Corin, E. Widowed men and women—An exploratory study of the significance of widowhood and coping strategies. *Canadian Journal on Aging*, 1997, *16*, 112–141.

Egar, T. Suicide law placing Oregon on several uncharted paths. *The New York Times*, December 25, 1994, A1, A13.

Fadiman, A. The liberation of Lolly and Gronky. *Life Magazine*, 1984, 71–94.

Fox, R. The sting of death in American society. *Social Science Review*, 1981, *49*, 42–59.

Gianelli, D. Right-to-die debate turns to out-of-hospital DNR order. *American Medical News*, November 7, 1994, *37*, 3.

Glaser, B., and Strauss, A. *Time for dying.* Chicago: Aldine, 1968.

Henderson, M. Beyond the Living Will. *The Gerontologist*, 1990, *30*, 480–485.

Hudson, T. Court strikes down assisted suicide ban in Washington State. *Hospitals and Health Networks*, August 5, 1994, *68*, 180.

Institute of Medicine. *Approaching death: Improving care at the end of life.* Washington, DC: National Academy Press, June 1997.

Kalish, R. Death and survivorship: The final transition. *Annals of the American Academy of Political and Social Sciences*, 1982, *464*, 163–173.

Kalish, R. The social context of death and dying. In R. Binstock and E. Shanas (Eds.), *Handbook of aging and the social sciences* (2nd ed.). New York: Van Nostrand Reinhold, 1985.

Kastenbaum, R. *Death, society and human experience* (4th ed.). New York: Macmillan/Merrill, 1991.

Kastenbaum, R. Dying and death: A life-span approach. In J. Birren and K. W. Schaie (Eds.), *Handbook of the psychology of aging.* New York: Van Nostrand Reinhold, 1985.

Kavanaugh, KI.M. The importance of spirituality. *Journal of Long-Term Care Administration*, 1996–97, *24*, 29–31.

KCR Communications Research. Survey conducted for the *Boston Globe* and the Harvard School of Public Health by Richard Knox, October 18–20, 1991.

Keller, J. W., Sherry, D., and Piotrowski, C. Perspectives on death: A developmental study. *Journal of Psychology, 116*, 1984, 137–142.

Kübler-Ross, E. *On death and dying.* New York: Macmillan, 1969.

Kübler-Ross, E. (Ed.). *Death: The final stage of growth.* Englewood Cliffs, N.J.: Prentice-Hall, 1975.

Kübler-Ross, E. *Living with dying.* New York: Macmillan, 1981.

Lester, D., and Templer, D. Death anxiety scales: A dialogue. *Omega*, 1993, *26*, 239–253.

Levy, J. A. The hospice in the context of an aging society. In R. Enright (Ed.), *Perspectives in Social Gerontology.* Boston: Allyn and Bacon, 1994.

Lopata, H. Z. The support systems of American urban widows. In M. Stroebe, W. Stroebe, and R. Hanson (Eds.), *Handbook of bereavement: Theory, research and intervention.* NY: Cambridge University Press, 1993.

Lopata, H. Z. *Widowhood in an American city.* Cambridge, MA: Schenkman, 1973.

Lopata, H. Z. *Widows.* Durham, NC: Duke University Press, 1987.

Lund, D. A. Widowhood: The coping response. In R. Kastenbaum (Ed.), *Encyclopedia of adult development.* Phoenix, AZ: Onyx Press, 1993.

Lund, D. A., Caserta, M., and Dimond, M. The course of spousal bereavement in later life. In M. Stroebe, W. Stroebe, and R. Hanson (Eds.), *Handbook of bereavement: Theory, research and intervention.* NY: Cambridge University Press, 1993.

Maro, R. Victory through the courts. *Compassion in Dying*, Spring 1996, 1.

Marshall, V. A sociological perspective on aging and dying. In V. Marshall, (Ed.), *Later life: The social psychology of aging.* Beverly Hills, CA: Sage, 1986.

Marshall, V. *Last chapters: A sociology of aging and dying.* Monterey, CA: Brooks Cole, 1980.

Marshall, V., and Levy, J. Aging and dying. In R. Binstock and L. George (Eds.), *Handbook of aging and the social sciences* (3rd ed.). New York: Academic Press, 1990.

Martin-Matthews, A. Widowhood and widowerhood. *Encyclopedia of Gerontology*, 1996, *2*, 621–625.

Martin-Matthews, A. Widowhood as an expectable life event. In V. Marshall (Ed.), *Aging in Canada: Social perspectives* (2nd ed.). Markham, ON: Fitzhenry and Whiteside, 1988.

McCandless, N. J., and Conner, F. P. Older women and grief: A new direction for research. *Journal of Women and Aging*, 1997, *9*, 85–91.

McCue, J. D. The naturalness of dying. *Journal of the American Medical Association*, 1995, *273*, 1039–43.

Miller, G. Hospice. In C. Evashwick (Ed.), *The continuum of long-term care: An integrated systems approach*. Albany, NY: Delmar Publishers, 1996.

Moen, P. Gender, age and the life course. In R. H. Binstock and L. K. George, *Handbook of aging and the social sciences* (4th ed.). San Diego, CA: Academic Press, 1996.

Mutran, E. J., Danis, M., Bratton, K., Sudha, S., and Hanson, L. Attitudes of the critically ill toward prolonging life: The role of social support. *The Gerontologist*, 1997, *37*, 192–199.

New York Times, Doctors polled on life support. Sunday, June 5, 1988.

O'Bryant, S., and Morgan, C. Recent widows' kin support and orientation to self-sufficiency. *The Gerontologist*, 1991, *30*, 391–398.

Ostrom, C. New focus on debate on assisted suicide. *The Seattle Times*, January 1998, 1, A18.

Ostrom, C., and Westnext, D. Next target of assisted suicide efforts: State laws. *The Seattle Times*, June 27, 1997, A2.

Patterson, J. Participation in leisure activities by older adults after a stressful life event: The loss of a spouse. *International Journal of Aging and Human Development*, 1996, *42*, 123–142.

Rasmussen, C. A., and Brems, C. The relationship of death anxiety with age and psychosocial maturity. *The Journal of Psychology*, 1996, *130*, 141–144.

Reibstein, L. Matters of life and death. *Newsweek*, July 7, 1997, *18*, 30.

Sachs, G. A. Improving care of the dying. *Generations*, Winter 1994, 3.

Sanders, C. M. Risk factors in bereavement outcome. In M. Stroebe, W. Stroebe, and R. O. Hanson (Eds.), *Handbook of bereavement: Theory, research and intervention*. NY: Cambridge University Press, 1993.

Seattle Times, "Death with dignity" bill approved by Senate, March 6, 1992, 1-B2.

Seattle Times. "No right to die, say justices." June 26, 1997, 1, 23A.

Thorson, J. A., and Powell, F. C. Elements of death anxiety and meanings of death. *Journal of Clinical Psychology*, 1988, *44*, 691–701.

Wanzer, S., Adelstein, J., Cranford, R., Federman, D., Hook, E., Moertel, C., Sofar, P., Stone, A., Taussig, H., and Vey Eys, J. The physician's responsibility toward hopelessly ill patients. *New England Journal of Medicine*, 1984, *310*, 955–959.

Weiss, R. S. Loss and recovery. In M. Stroebe, W. Stroebe, and R. O. Hanson (Eds.), *Handbook of bereavement: Theory, research and intervention*. NY: Cambridge University Press, 1993.

Wilber, K. H., and Reynolds, S. C. Rethinking alternatives to guardianship. *The Gerontologist*, 1995, *35*, 248–256.

13

THE RESILIENCY OF OLDER ETHNIC MINORITIES

When discussing the physiological, psychological, and social changes experienced by older people, there is a tendency to speak about them as if they were a homogeneous group. Yet, as illustrated throughout this book, the older population is more heterogeneous than any other. Two primary variables in this differentiation are gender and ethnic minority status; both influence an individual's position in the social structure and typical lifetime experiences (Angel and Hogan, 1994). To be an older ethnic minority, or an older woman, is to experience environments substantially different from those of a white male across the life span. For example, both older women and African American elders are more likely to live alone, which places them at greater risk of economic insecurity, poorer health status, and social isolation. Other examples of the interaction of gender, ethnicity, living arrangements, and socioeconomic status are:

- The poverty rate for women who live alone is five times greater than that for their peers who live with a spouse

- The mean income of older African American households is about 51 percent that of older white households
- Older minority women who live alone form the poorest group in our society (Hobbs and Damon, 1996; Quinn and Smeeding, 1994)

Consistent with the *life course perspective* outlined in Chapter 8, such economic and health disparities in old age are typically related not only to current living arrangements, but also to early life mortality and to earlier patterns in education, labor-force participation, health status and access to health care, and to cultural beliefs and practices (Wykle and Kaskel, 1994).

Whereas relevant differences among older people arising from their gender and their ethnic minority status have been noted throughout this text, the next two chapters focus specifically on these factors because of their interactive effects with age and the resulting higher incidence of social problems, such as poverty, poor health, and inadequate living arrangements. In this sense, both older women and ethnic minorities are affected by changes in the environment that are not always congruent with their needs as they age. Throughout, the role of socioeconomic status, along with race and gender, in creating health differences across the life course is recognized. In addition, the need to examine how socioeconomic status influences variation within groups, not only between groups, is acknowledged. Despite the greater problems facing both women and ethnic minorities, their strengths and resiliency in old age are also emphasized.

DEFINING ETHNICITY

Ethnicity as discussed here involves three components: (1) culture, values, and beliefs, and an internalized common heritage which are not fully understood or shared by outsiders; (2) social status; and (3) support systems (Barresi and Stull, 1993). These components influence the way people feel about themselves and how they interact with their environments, resulting in particular patterns of adjustment to the experience of aging.

Ethnicity can serve several functions. These include:

1. An integrating force in passing through significant life changes;
2. A buffer to stresses of old age, especially when the environment encourages the expression of ethnicity; and
3. A filter to the aging process, influencing beliefs, behaviors, and interactions with professionals

Given these various functions, social and health care providers need to understand ethnicity and how it influences help-seeking behaviors and beliefs, for example (Hopper, 1993; Markides, Liang, and Jackson, 1990).

By identifying culturally conditioned beliefs and values in an older person's heritage, we can gain a better understanding of that person's attitudes and behaviors in the face of aging. For example, many Japanese American elders emigrated from small farming villages where ancestor worship was practiced, reflecting the respect traditionally accorded older people. They have grown old in a country where youth is more highly valued than age, and thus may experience conflicts between the views they hold and those of their children. Based on its unique history, each ethnic minority population has developed its own methods of coping with the inevitable conflicts between traditional and adopted ways of life, leading to both vulnerabilities and strengths.

Ethnicity may or may not encompass minority status, since there are older people in the United States who belong to white ethnic groups that are not necessarily social and cultural "minorities," as defined by the U.S. Congress as federally protected groups. Gutmann's (1979) work on immigrants from eastern, central, and southern Europe demonstrates that white ethnics may preserve the traditional practices of their culture, religion, or nationality, and remain homogeneous and segregated within their own ethnic communities, but not necessarily experience prejudice, discrimination, or oppression characteristic of populations of color. These ethnic groups of European origin in the United States (Irish, Germans, Italians, etc.), who at some point have been sociological minorities, today are generally considered part of the dominant group (Markides et al., 1990). Although our focus is on people of color who have experienced economic and racial discrimination, we also consider how ethnicity or cultural homogeneity influences the aging process.

Who Are Ethnic Minority Older People?

For purposes of this chapter, ethnic minority elders include older people belonging to groups whose language and/or physical and cultural characteristics make them visible and identifiable, who have experienced differential and unequal treatment, who share a distinctive history and bonds of attachment among group members, and who regard themselves as objects of collective discrimination and oppression by reason of their social class or race (Markides et al., 1990). Specifically, this chapter examines the life conditions and adaptation to aging among people of color who are defined by the federal government as protected groups—African Americans, Hispanic Americans (including Mexican Americans/Chicanos, Puerto Ricans, Cubans, and Latin Americans), American Indians, and Asian Americans and Pacific Islanders.

Two distinct issues should be kept in mind in this discussion of ethnic minority elders: (1) the unique historical calendar of life events and culture and their impact on lifestyles, many of which are positive, and (2) the consequences of racism, ageism, discrimination, and prolonged poverty, most of which are negative. For ethnic minorities, race is a social status that shapes an individual's values, behaviors, and distribution of resources in society. In fact, race may interact with individual conditions (e.g., functional impairment) and social structural factors (e.g., socioeconomic status) to influence the receipt of help, including the use of informal and formal care (Norgard and Rodgers, 1997). It is not only their ethnic and cultural traditions that influence their socialization process, but also their experience of being a minority within a majority culture (Wykle and Kaskel, 1994). Accordingly, their aging process

and quality of life are inevitably affected by the experiences of a lifetime of racial discrimination.

There are some recurring themes in analyses of ethnic minority status and older people, such as family structure and behavior and values about independence. Nevertheless, variations within as well as among these groups must be kept in mind. Differences in immigration patterns, birthrates, region, social class, rural or urban location, gender, and acculturation level add to the intragroup variations. Hispanics, for example, who are defined by the U.S. Bureau of the Census as Spanish-speaking persons, include people from many different cultures and a high percentage of immigrants. American Indian refers to the indigenous peoples of North America, including Indians, Eskimos, and Aleuts and over 500 recognized tribes, bands, or Alaskan Native villages. African Americans differ from one another in terms of cultural background, socioeconomic status, and geographic location. Recent immigrants from Laos, Cambodia, and Vietnam have a higher proportion of older persons than do other Asian American/Pacific Islander groups.

Today, ethnic minorities comprise 15 percent of the population over age 65. Their distribution is reflected in Table 13.1. They include a smaller

TABLE 13.1   Ethnic Minority Distribution of the Older Population

	% OF TOTAL POPULATION, 65+	% OF THE ETHNIC MINORITY POPULATION, 65+	MEDIAN AGE
Whites	89.8	—	34.6
African Americans	8.0	8.0	29.5
Asian Americans/Pacific Islanders	1.5	6.0	28.7
American Indians	0.4	5.0	27
Hispanic Americans	4.0*	4.9	26.4

*The sum of the specific percentages reported here will never round off to approximately 100 percent if a Hispanic percentage is included. The reason for this anomaly is that the U.S. Bureau of the Census does not treat the Hispanic category (which includes Mexicans, Venezuelans, and Latinos who self-designate themselves as being white) as one that is mutually exclusive from the racial categories. Thus, the Hispanic data are also included within each of the racial categories. Persons of Hispanic origins may be of any race, and represent 3 percent of the older population.

SOURCE: U.S. Bureau of the Census, 1995 Selected Population Tables.

proportion of older adults and a larger proportion of younger adults than the white population. This differential results primarily from higher rates of fertility and higher mortality rates, as well as patterns of immigration, among the nonwhite population under age 65 than among the white population under age 65. Although small in size, ethnic minority populations are of increasing concern to gerontologists because of the disproportionately greater number of social problems which they face, relative to whites.

Another reason for concern is that in the early part of the twenty-first century, the proportion of older persons is expected to increase at a higher rate for the non-white population than for the white population. As noted in Chapter 1, this will occur partially because of the large proportion of children in these groups, who, unlike their parents and especially their grandparents, are expected to reach old age. The greatest growth is expected to occur in the percent 85 and over. Currently, less than one in ten ethnic minority elders are among the oldest-old; this percent will increase to one in five by the year 2050 (Angel and Hogan, 1994). Although immigrants are generally younger persons, many have brought or sent for their older parents and relatives, especially from countries experiencing political oppression (Barresi and Stull, 1993). Accordingly, it has been predicted that the immigrant groups of the twentieth century—Hispanics, Asian Americans, and Pacific Islanders—will redefine American culture in the twenty-first century (Angel and Hogan, 1994).

RESEARCH HISTORY

Ethnogerontology is a new and relatively underdeveloped field of social gerontology. It is the study of the causes, processes, and consequences of race, national origin, and culture on individual and population aging. From 1940 to 1970, when both scholarly and political concern with older adults grew, little was written about the special circumstances of ethnic minority elders; this was, in part, because of their relatively small size compared to Caucasian older adults (Markides and Black, 1996). In 1956, Tally and Kaplan first raised the **double jeopardy hypothesis:** Are the African American aged doubly jeopardized relative to their white counterparts? That is, do lifetime factors of economic and racial discrimination make adjusting to old age more difficult for African Americans (and other minorities) than for whites? As a result of such double jeopardy, do ethnic minorities experience lower life satisfaction (Cuellar and Weeks, 1980)? Debates about double jeopardy—whether it exists and is related to socioeconomic status or to race per se—have been central in research and policy discussions in ethnogerontology.

A second but related position asserts that patterns of racial inequality are changing, and that minorities' opportunities throughout their lives are related more to their economic class position rather than to their minority group status. It is social class, not minority membership, that jeopardizes them. The **multiple hierarchy stratification** perspective encompasses both views, defining ethnic minority status as one source of inequality along with class, gender, and age itself (Bengtson, 1979). Ethnogerontologists now argue that double jeopardy should not be a central concept because cross-sectional studies have rarely produced useful information about age changes as opposed to age differences (Gibson, 1989; Markides et al., 1990). They suggest that double jeopardy may be time-bound, resulting largely from major social and political changes in the status of minorities, not from racial differences. They also point to the lack of empirical support for widening differentials in health and socioeconomic status with age (Markides and Black, 1996). Since cross-sectional studies have rarely produced useful information about age changes as opposed to age differences, more longitudinal studies are required to determine the effects of ethnic minority group status on age changes in the later years.

A counter-argument to the double jeopardy hypothesis is that age is a leveler of differences in life expectancy. This **crossover effect** refers to the fact that ethnic minorities experience poorer health and higher death rates, especially from homicides, than whites at all ages until very old age. After age 75, the death rates for African Americans, Asian Americans, and American Indians are actually lower than for whites. Accordingly, life expectancy for these survivors is greater, due to a combination of biological vigor, psychological strength, and resources for coping with stress, such as religious practices that link individuals to the community. Thus, the oldest-old segment of the ethnic minority population may represent successful or robust aging, as described in Chapter 6. In fact, although ethnic minorities may experience increasing income and health disadvantages with age, they nevertheless display considerable strengths and may experience higher levels of psychological well-being and emotional support than do white non-minority elders. This may result from selective survival and adaptation factors that cause those who survive to be more hardy (Wykle and Kaskel, 1994; Markides et al., 1990). It is unclear, however, if the apparent racial crossover and selective survival are due to enumerative errors and reliance on cross-sectional data to make comparisons between advantaged and disadvantaged populations, not to health differences. The apparent racial crossover effect also raises questions about the usefulness of chronological age as a measure of aging. Given these issues, the relative status and mortality risks of whites and non-whites are still debated. What is clear is that tremendous variation occurs both across and within ethnic minority categories (Markides and Black, 1996).

The year 1971 marked a turning point in the recognition of ethnic minority elders as a special area of study within the field of gerontology. In that year, the National Caucus on the Black Aged was formed (later becoming the National Center and Caucus on the Black Aged), and a session on "Aging and the Aged Black" was held at the White House Conference on Aging. This conference was especially important from a policy perspective, because it highlighted the need for income and health care supports. Since 1971, the National Association for Spanish-speaking Elderly, the National In-

Oldest-old African American men are remarkable survivors.

dian Council on Aging, and the National Asian Pacific Center on Aging have been established. These associations function as advocacy groups for ethnic minority elders and as research and academic centers.

The Census has been the primary source of information for these organizations involved in planning services for ethnic minority elders. Census data, however, are criticized for undercounting minority subgroups, misclassifying individuals, or merging data about various non-white groups. For example, the Census Bureau has often grouped people by race as "white," "black," or "other." Similarly, there are growing debates about how mixed race or biracial individuals should be classified in the Census. In addition, research on ethnic minorities generally does not provide a breakdown of data by gender, and studies on older women do not cross-classify data by minority status. From the feminist perspective discussed in Chapter 8, there is no way to determine how racism and sexism interact to produce "gender-specific race effects and race-specific gender effects" (Gould, 1989). Another limitation is that studies in the 1970s and 1980s were based on small, nonrepresentative samples. Fortunately, positive methodological developments have been made in recent years, especially in the areas of cross-cultural measurement and sampling (Markides and Black, 1996; Markides et al., 1990).

Because of the limitations of Census data and the wide diversity of cultural patterns among ethnic minority older populations, few generalizations are valid for this population as a whole. Using race per se as a variable will rarely lead to straightforward interpretations, because cultural values (e.g., the meaning attached to caregiving) and socioeconomic status are interdependent and difficult to separate (Miller et al., 1994). Within the overall context of the limitations of the data, we turn next to a brief review of the life conditions of each of the four major ethnic minority groups in the United States.

OLDER AFRICAN AMERICANS

Although African Americans are the largest ethnic minority population in the United States, the percentage of older persons among the African American population is still smaller than among its non-minority counterpart. That is, about 8 percent of the African American population is over 65 years of age, compared to 14 percent of the white population. The young outnumber the old in the African American population, due primarily to the higher fertility of African American women and blacks' higher mortality in their younger years. The median age of African Americans, 29.5 years, is 5 years younger than the median age for whites (34.6). The life expectancy for African American men and women is 65 and 74.5 years, respectively, compared with the life expectancy of 73.5 years for white men and 80 years for white women (Administration on Aging, 1997). Although disparities in life expectancy between African Americans and whites reflect differences in childhood and youth mortality rates, differences in life expectancy after age 75 are less dramatic. African American men who live to age 65 can expect to live another 14 years; African American women, 18 years. This is only slightly less than for their white counterparts (15.5 and 19 years, respectively). This narrowing

of difference in life expectancy after age 75 (the crossover effect discussed earlier) may be accounted for by the fact that most African Americans who survive to this age are the most robust of their cohort.

Although a relatively small percent of the total African American population, adults over age 65 form the fastest-growing segment of that population. While the overall African American population is expected to increase by 45.6 percent by 2020, the proportion of older people is expected to increase by 90 percent, from 8 percent to 15.3 percent in the year 2020, and to 21.3 percent by 2050. It is also noteworthy that the growth among the 85 and older African American population has been greater since 1980 than in the white population (Angel and Hogan, 1994).

The ratio of men to women among African Americans aged 65 and over is slightly lower than among whites, 62 males for every 100 females, compared to 67 males for every 100 females among the white population. However, in the population age 85 and over, there are 42 African American men for 100 women, compared to 38 among their white counterparts (Administration on Aging, 1997). Women age 80 and over are the most rapidly growing group of African American elders, and they have the longest average remaining life span.

Nearly three times the proportion of African Americans age 65 and over live below the poverty line compared to older whites. The poverty rate across ethnic minority groups is shown in Figure 13.1. The incidence of poverty increases dramatically among households composed of unrelated African American individuals, especially females age 65 and over. The median income of African American males over 65 is approximately 60 percent of white men; that of African American women about 66 percent that of white women, with the proportion of older African American female-headed families in poverty increasing in the past decade (Miller et al., 1996). Differences in education do not explain this gap in income between white and African American older people, which has not changed

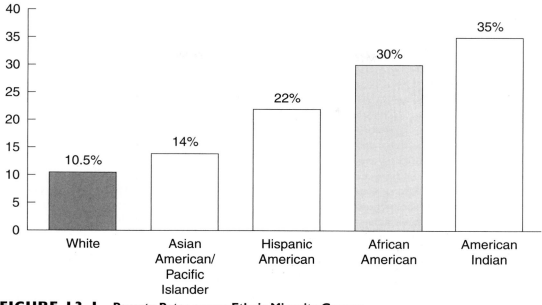

FIGURE 13.1 **Poverty Rates across Ethnic Minority Groups**
SOURCE: Hobbs, F. and Damon, B. L. *65+ in the United States.* Washington, DC.: US Department of Commerce, Bureau of the Census, 1996.

substantially since 1985. In fact, the gap is increasing, due to general economic conditions from the 1970s to the 1990s, such as the lack of growth in real wages, income inequities, decline in pension coverage, and reductions in public supports such as Supplemental Security Income (SSI).

As noted in Chapter 11, the primary reason for the lower socioeconomic status of older African Americans is their pattern of limited employment opportunities and periods of unemployment throughout their lives, as well as their concentration in low-paying, sporadic service jobs with few benefits that were not covered by Social Security prior to the 1950s. Not only do African Americans accumulate less employment experience, but they also are more likely to leave the work force earlier, frequently because of health problems. Out of economic necessity, however, they often return to work after retirement, creating the phenomenon of the "unretired/retired." In effect, they spend a greater proportion of their lives both working and disabled, thus reducing

their years in retirement (Hayward, Friedman, and Chen, 1996; Harper and Alexander, 1990; Gibson, 1989). This pattern reduces not only their lifetime earnings, but also their Social Security and pension benefits. As a result, they are more likely to receive only the minimum Social Security benefits and less likely to receive pension income than are whites. Accordingly, more African Americans than white older persons rely on SSI.

By most measures, the health of African American adults is worse than their white counterparts, oftentimes a continuation from middle age. Declines in functional ability are more rapid for African Americans compared to whites between the ages of 45 and 64 (Markides and Black, 1996; Gibson, 1994). The socioeconomic disadvantages experienced by African Americans explain much of the variance in their lower utilization of health services, their reduced access to health care, their poorer health status, and higher rates of mortality. Gaps in mortality are reduced when socioeconomic class is controlled for. In fact, marginal increases in socioeconomic status and education generally have larger positive effects on the health of African Americans than on whites (Schoenbaum and Waidman, 1997; Guralnik et al., 1993).

The prevalence of chronic diseases has been estimated to be twice as high among African Americans as among whites, and the former more often perceive themselves as being in poor health than do their white counterparts (Barresi and Stull, 1993; Harper and Alexander, 1990). For example, in national health surveys, 16.4 percent of African Americans have reported poor health, compared with 8.7 percent of whites. Older African Americans experience hypertension, heart disease, stroke, and diabetes more frequently than do their white peers, although these differences are greatest at age 45 and decline with age, especially after age 85 (Markides and Black, 1996). Obesity is also a frequent health problem among African American women, which can lead to complications of hypertension and diabetes. The rate of diabetes mellitus among Black women is almost twice that among white women. Kidney failure, which may result from hypertension and diabetes, is more common in older African Americans. They also experience more days of functional disability (i.e., substantially reduced daily activities) and bed disability (i.e., being confined to bed for at least half of the day), and at earlier ages than whites. Proportionately more African American older people are completely incapacitated and unable to carry on any major activity (e.g., paid employment, keeping house), although still residing in community-based households (Belgrave, Wykle, and Choi, 1993).

African American elders also appear to have less access to health care than their white counterparts, although they are more likely than whites to use hospital emergency rooms as a way to enter the health care system. An important predictor of health service utilization is the availability of health insurance. Older African Americans are more likely to depend on Medicaid and less likely to have private supplemental health insurance than their white counterparts, and therefore less

likely to receive adequate care at hospitals than other acutely ill older patients (Kahn, Pearson, and Harrison, 1994). At the same time, they are more likely to use self-care health practices, such as home remedies, lay consultations, and folk medicine that diverge from mainstream Western scientific medical concepts (Davis and McGadney, 1993; Hopper, 1993).

Black-white differences in mortality rates are notable for the three leading causes of death. Thus, while heart disease, strokes, and cancer are the leading causes of death for both races at age 65 and older, rates for African Americans are 5 percent, 17 percent, and 24 percent higher, respectively, for each of these conditions (NCHS, 1992). African Americans have higher death rates for cancers of the lungs, prostate, and cervix than do other ethnic groups. Similarly, their 5-year survival rate for cancer of the cervix, uterus, and esophagus is lower than for any other segment of the population. They have many of the risk factors for cancer, higher occupational and residential exposure to cancer-causing substances, higher rates of obesity (e.g., 60 percent of black women over age 45 are obese), higher prevalence of smoking, and less knowledge about cancer and its prevention (Baquet, 1988). This greater vulnerability is compounded by their lower access to health care, so that many cancers are not detected early enough to prevent metastasis. However, due to the crossover phenomenon, the higher likelihood of death for blacks from these conditions occurs only until about age 75, when both black men and women begin to have a lower incidence of death (Gibson, 1994). Deaths in late life due to lifestyle and environmental hazards, including accidents and homicides among men, are also much higher in blacks than in whites, except for those who survive into their eighties.

The proportion of African Americans who are married is lower than that of any other population because of lower life expectancy for black men in particular. Among African Americans over age 65, 54 percent of men and 25 percent of women are married. This compares with 80 percent and 41 percent, respectively, among whites

(Rawlings, 1993). Almost 50 percent of African American women live alone, a higher proportion than that of their white counterparts or older black males. Those who live alone are more likely to be poor. In addition, rates of remarriage are lower than in other groups. One reason for these differences is that widowhood, separation, or divorce are more prevalent among older African Americans and are more likely to have occurred at an earlier age (Angel and Hogan, 1994).

Although most older African Americans do not live in extended families, approximately 20 percent of them, compared to 12 percent of their white counterparts, live with some family member other than their spouse. Comparative studies depict older African Americans as having larger, more extended families than do whites, a higher frequency of family-based households, and higher levels of social support from their extended families, including friends, neighbors, and co-workers. Accordingly, older African American women are more likely than white women to have family living with them in their homes. Most often, these are three-generation households, with older women at the top of the family's power hierarchy, playing an active role in the management of the family. For example, they often provide financial assistance and care for grandchildren as well as children of other family members and friends. Indeed, an increasing number of older blacks are affected by stressors influencing members of their social networks, particularly children and grandchildren, and face caregiving responsibilities as a result. As noted in Chapter 9, a growing number of African American women have primary responsibility for the care of grandchildren because of their adult children's substance abuse and financial problems (Johnson, 1995; Minkler and Roe, 1993).

Similar to whites, adult children remain a primary source of assistance and support for older African Americans (Harper and Alexander, 1990). For childless older adults, siblings are the most important kin tie. The creation of **fictive kin,** including foster parents or children who function in the absence of blood relatives or when family relationships are unsatisfactory, is another source of loving support. In some instances, African American women active in church are more likely to turn to non-relatives in times of need than to their children, but these non-relatives may be considered part of an extended family network. Similarly, they are more likely than whites to have larger, looser social networks that include non-immediate family members among their pool of unpaid caregivers (Burton et al., 1995).

Although African Americans are more likely to receive help from children and grandchildren, and to take children into their homes, giving such intergenerational assistance is a function not just of race, but of age, marital and socioeconomic status, and level of functional disability. In some instances, such multigenerational households may be an adaptation to poverty rather than an indicator of a supportive extended family. Such adaptation should not be viewed as a weakness associated with low income and joblessness; instead, intergenerational households that develop out of financial necessity illustrate the resourcefulness of black families whose domestic networks expand and contract according to economic resources. Even though socioeconomic factors are important in helping to explain race differences in intergenerational exchanges, there is strong adherence to norms of filial support and attitudes of respect toward elders among African Americans across social classes (Burton et al., 1995; Barresi and Stull, 1993; Silverstein and Waite, 1993).

In sum, African American elders appear to have a broader range—not just a larger number—of informal instrumental and emotional supports than is characteristic of Caucasian older people. Norms of reciprocity are strong and have evolved from a cooperative lifestyle that served as a survival mechanism in earlier times and that continues to be a source of support (Burton et al., 1995; Wood and Wan, 1993).

Studies of psychological and general well-being among African American elders have illustrated the benefits of social integration. Despite significant economic hardships, the majority of older blacks report high life satisfaction and happiness compared to their white counterparts, regardless of living conditions. The fact that this is most likely for those age 75 and over may reflect the decreasing demands of family and employment responsibilities in this oldest group, and the associated perception of few significant stressors affecting them. At the same time, however, older African Americans are more likely to report high levels of life satisfaction and happiness if they perceive their physical health to be good, which is consistent with other evidence of the link between physical and psychological health generally among the older population. Thus, it appears that black elders who survive to age 75, are in good health, and are relieved of the burdens of family caregiving are most likely to experience life satisfaction.

Older African Americans' life satisfaction has also been explained in terms of their spiritual orientation and the support of their extended families and of the church. As noted in Chapter 11, religion, which is important in the lives of many black elders for adaptation and support, is related to feelings of well-being, self-esteem, and personal control. The church also provides a support network of spiritual help, companionship, advice, encouragement, and financial aid. Older African Americans tend to draw from a more varied pool of friends, fellow church members, and other associated contacts, and are more likely to use them interchangeably than are their white counterparts (Wood and Wan, 1993).

African Americans are less likely to enter a nursing home than whites; institutional care is considered a last resort. As a result, only 3 percent of all African Americans age 65 and older and only 12 percent of those over age 85 are institutionalized, compared to 5 percent and 23 percent of their white counterparts, respectively (Miller et al., 1994). African American nursing-home residents have been found to be more limited in their ability to carry out activities of daily living and less often receiving the appropriate level of care than are whites. Once admitted to a nursing home, older African Americans are less likely to be discharged, in large part because informal resources have been exhausted. Low rates of nursing-home

placement may reflect (1) the lack of nursing homes in African American communities, (2) inadequate income to pay for private nursing home care, (3) the greater probability that an African American elder, dependent upon Medicaid, has fewer institutional options, (4) current or historical racist practices among medical providers and nursing home staff, and (5) the practice of some elders turning to traditional folk medicine (Belgrave et al., 1993; Wood and Wan, 1993; Greene and Ondrich, 1990).

OLDER HISPANIC AMERICANS

Hispanic Americans are the largest ethnic minority population following African Americans. They are also the fastest-growing population group in the United States. In fact, the percentage of older people among the Hispanic population will double from 5.6 percent in 1995 to 13 percent in 2030 (Administration on Aging, 1997; US Bureau of the Census, 1996). Hispanics are a highly diverse population that includes many groups, each with its own distinct national/cultural heritage: Mexicans, Puerto Ricans, Cubans, Central or South Americans, and the native Mexican American, or Chi-

Grandparents in the Hispanic community often play vital intergenerational roles.

cano population, whose history in the United States predates settlement by English-speaking groups. They thus encompass native-born, legal, and undocumented immigrants with varying lengths of residence in the United States. The greatest proportion of Hispanics (47.6 percent)—and also the poorest—are Mexican Americans, or Chicanos, who are concentrated in five, primarily rural southwestern states. Cubans form 18 percent of the Hispanic population, and represent the wealthiest and most educated; they also have the largest proportion of foreign-born older adults among the Hispanic population. Puerto Ricans form 10.9 percent of the Hispanic population (Angel and Hogan, 1994). Although bonded by a common language, each group within the Hispanic population differs substantially in terms of geographic concentration, income, education, length of residence in the United States, cultural heritage, history, and dialect.

The needs of Hispanic elders may be underestimated, since many studies have not considered Hispanics as a separate group; they are often included in either black or white ethnic categories. In addition, studies that include a Hispanic ethnic classification often fail to differentiate among the diverse Hispanic subgroups. The Hispanic older population is projected to grow much faster than the white or black counterparts. Compared to white and other ethnic minorities, the Spanish-speaking population is a youthful group, with a median age of 26.4 years, 8 years younger than the norm in the United States. A number of factors underlie the relative youthfulness of the Hispanic American population. One variable is its lower average life expectancy, which may be partially explained by poor economic and health status among the two largest subgroups of Hispanics, Mexican Americans and Puerto Ricans. The most important contributing factor, however, is the generally high fertility rate among many Hispanic groups. The number of children born and the average family size exceed the national average. High levels of net immigration and repatriation patterns are secondary factors, with the youngest (and often poorest) people most likely to move to a new

country, and some middle-aged and older Mexican Americans moving back to Mexico. Despite its current relative youthfulness, the Hispanic population has experienced the greatest increase in median age of all ethnic groups from 1960 to 1990 (Hobbs and Damon, 1996). As noted above, this suggests that the percentage of older Hispanic Americans will rise steeply in the future, as younger cohorts reach old age.

Within the overall Hispanic population, there are variations in the sex ratio because of the gender imbalance in previous immigration streams and women's survival rates. There are proportionately more Hispanic men to women over age 65 than among the white older population, but this is due to the higher mortality rate of Hispanic women than white women at earlier ages, not to increases in longevity among Hispanic men. Nevertheless, the overall gender patterns of Hispanic Americans are similar to those of other groups of older people. Women live longer and outnumber men, more often remaining widowed and living alone than men do. Older Hispanic men marry or remarry more often than men in other ethnic minority groups: 83 percent of older Hispanic males are married, but only 33 percent of older Hispanic women live with a spouse (Angel and Hogan, 1994).

Sociocultural factors underlie the poor economic and health status of Hispanics. More than any other group, they have retained their native language, partially because of geographic proximity to their home countries, combined with the availability of mass communication. In fact, it has been estimated that 40 percent of older Hispanics speak only Spanish. Although serving to preserve their cultural identity, their inability to speak English is a major barrier to their education, employment, and utilization of social and health services. Mexican Americans and Puerto Ricans are also the most educationally deprived group in our society, with 31 percent of men and 31.5 percent of women having less than a fourth-grade education. Another barrier has been encountered by those who entered the country illegally and thus have been unable to apply for Social Security, Medicare, or Medicaid. All these factors may partly explain why such large numbers of Mexican American and Puerto Rican elders have minimal education and work in unskilled, low-paying jobs with few benefits, particularly retirement pension benefits and income from annuities, or are unemployed. Although Social Security and Supplemental Security Income are their primary sources of retirement income, 19 percent receive neither Social Security nor pension income, and 8 percent have no public or private medical insurance (Lacayo, 1993). Such patterns are likely to be intensified by the 1996 Welfare Reform Act which restricted benefits for immigrants.

These employment and educational conditions contribute to the high rate of poverty among older Hispanic Americans. In 1990, approximately 22 percent lived below the poverty level, compared to 10.7 percent of older whites. Another 33 percent, compared to 18 percent of older whites, hover just above the "near poverty" threshold at incomes below 125 percent of the poverty line. The median personal income of Hispanic men age 65 and over is about 65 percent of white males; for Hispanic women age 65 and over, the median income is 68 percent of white females (Chen, 1994).

The poverty of Hispanic Americans is undoubtedly a major factor in their generally poor health across the life span, which reduces their opportunities for work and education and lowers their chances of a lifetime accumulation of income. Given the high proportion of Hispanics who have been migrant farm workers, exposure to potentially harmful pesticides may put them at further risk of health problems. Eighty-five percent of older Hispanics report at least one chronic condition and 45 percent indicate some limitation in their activities of daily living (Espino, 1993). Physiological aging tends to precede chronological aging, with those in their late forties experiencing health disabilities typical of 65-year-old whites. Because of aging "faster" than whites, 66 percent of a sample of older Mexican Americans viewed themselves as old beginning at or below 60 years of age (Espino, 1993). Such earlier func-

tional aging can be attributed to harder working conditions, poor nutrition, and inadequate health care (Lacayo, 1993). Arthritis, high blood pressure, circulatory disorders, diabetes, cataracts, glaucoma, kidney disease, and heart disease are the most common health problems. Women are more likely than men to suffer multiple illnesses. Hispanic women have higher mortality rates from cervical cancer and cancer of the uterus than do white women (Chen, 1994; Wykle and Kaskel, 1994). As with African Americans, this may be due to lower access to health care and preventive services, resulting in cancer detection occurring too late for successful treatment. Some studies, however, suggest that immigrants among the Hispanic population are healthier than native-born regardless of age, due to protective cultural factors and selective immigration (e.g., those who immigrate tend to be healthier than those who remain at home) (Stephen, Foots, Hendershot, and Schoenbaum, 1994).

For various reasons, Hispanics are the least likely among all groups of older adults to have a regular physician, to use hospitals, to have private insurance coverage, to seek preventive care, or to access dental care. Factors that may partially underlie their underutilization of health care services and their greater negative perceptions of their health than whites include: social and cultural barriers to health care, such as mistrust of white medical providers; stigmas associated with receiving mental health services; reliance on folk medicine and religious healing; and structural factors such as less health insurance coverage and greater dissatisfaction with services (Miranda, 1990). Difficulty in comprehending English is another important barrier, highlighting the need for bilingual and bicultural health care providers. Only about 3 percent are in nursing homes, with 10 percent of those over age 85 institutionalized, compared to 23 percent of oldest-old whites. Since families attempt to provide support as long as possible, when older Hispanics do enter nursing homes, they tend to be more physically and functionally impaired than their non-Hispanic white counterparts (Espino, 1993; Cuellar, 1990).

Historically, the extended family has been a major source of emotional support to older Hispanics, especially in rural areas. Older Hispanics are more likely than whites to believe that older persons should be cared for in the community; they are more than four times as likely as Anglos between the ages of 65 and 74, and more than two times as likely as those 74 years of age and older, to live with their adult children. Widowed women over 75 are the most likely to live in extended family households (Cuellar, 1990). Those who live alone are generally inadequately housed, with the incidence of substandard housing substantially greater among Hispanics than among whites.

As a culture, Hispanics place a high value on family relations, believing that the needs of the family as a whole or of individual family members should take precedence over one's own needs. Although patterns of intergenerational assistance are strong compared to Caucasian populations, the percentage of Hispanics living in multigenerational households has declined in recent years. With their urbanization and greater acculturation, younger Hispanics are increasingly unable to meet their older parents' expectations to support an extended family in one location. More older Mexican Americans, for example, are reporting unfulfilled expectations of filial responsibility by their adult children. Not surprisingly, how older parents evaluate their care from their adult children may differ from the objective reality (Markides et al., 1990).

Nevertheless, even when families are living apart, elders often still perform parental roles; assist with child care, advising, and decision-making; and serve as role models (Johnson, 1995). Socioemotional help and advice are typically sought from elders by the young and vice versa. Although families remain the most important system of support for their older members, it does appear that a division of labor is emerging between the family, which provides support and personal care, and public agencies, which give financial assistance and medical care, along with churches and mutual aid, fraternal, and self-help groups in the Hispanic community. These community-based groups provide outreach, advocacy, and information about resources, socialization opportunities, financial credit for services, and folk medicine. The supportive social and cultural context of neighborhood and community is congruent with the Hispanics' strong sense of cultural identity. Being part of "La Raza" encompasses a shared experience, history, and sense of one's place in the world (Espino, 1993).

OLDER AMERICAN INDIANS

American Indian refers to indigenous people of the current United States, including Eskimos and Aleuts (Kramer, 1992). The median age of the American Indian population is 27 years; this means that approximately half of all Indians are under the age of 27 years, compared to approximately 34 years for the general population. Only 5 percent of this population is 65 years of age and older. Their current life expectancy at birth is 65 years for both men and women, approximately 8 years less than for the white population. Life expectancy tends to be even lower in non-reservation areas. With a sex ratio of approximately 64.5 men to every 100 women age 65 and over, more than 75 percent of American Indian men, but less than 50 percent of their female counterparts, are married. Although only 13 percent of the American Indian population will enter the 65-plus age category, compared to 19.5 percent of the U.S. population as a whole, by the end of this century the number of American Indians who are age 75 and over will at least double. In fact, between 1940 and 1980, life expectancy for American Indians at birth increased by 20 years, from 50 to 71.1 years, compared to a 10-year increase for whites to 74.4 years (Administration on Aging, 1997; John, 1994). This increase is due, in large part, to efforts of the Indian Health Service to eliminate infectious diseases and meet acute-care needs. The greatest reductions have occurred in death rates due to acute and infectious diseases such as tuberculosis, gastrointestinal disease, and maternal and infant mortality, but mortality rates for the major killers of older people—heart disease, cancer, and stroke—have not been reduced in the American Indian population.

Except for very general trends, less systematic data are available for American Indians than for the other ethnic minority groups discussed thus far. The two federal agencies responsible for collecting data, the Bureau of Indian Affairs (BIA) and the Census Bureau, frequently have different estimates, making it difficult to generalize about American Indian older people. An additional complication in generalizing findings is that there are nearly 500 federally recognized tribes, an estimated 100 non-recognized tribes, and approximately 278 federally recognized reservations. Also, many urban Indians do not live on reservations, and therefore their conditions and needs are less visible. A further complication is that approximately 20 percent of American Indian elders who live in federally recognized areas are nevertheless not enrolled in a tribe, and thus would not be seen by social and medical providers within the Bureau of Indian Affairs or the Indian Health Services (John, 1994). Among this highly diverse population, nearly 200 native languages are spoken, and cultural traditions vary widely. More American Indian elders live in rural areas than do other minority older populations, with nearly 25 percent on reservations or in Alaskan Native villages. The older American Indian population is characterized by relatively high levels of residential stability; over 50 percent are concentrated in Southwestern states, with the remainder mostly in states along the Canadian border.

To understand American Indian elders, a life course perspective is necessary that takes into consideration the experience of American Indians in this century. The urbanization of the American Indian population during and after World War II has created two worlds of aging. For American Indian elders who are dispersed among the general urban population, there is no tribal community or governments concerned with their welfare; nor do they have special government institutions, such as the Indian Health Service or the Bureau of Indian Affairs responsi-ble for the well-being of American Indians on reservations.

It has been estimated that over 35 percent of older American Indians are poor, with per capita incomes that are 40 to 59 percent less than those of whites. The median income is barely above the poverty threshold. Although about 50 percent of older urban American Indians live with family members, their families are also more likely to be poor than their white counterparts (Manson, 1993). As in other ethnic minority populations, the poverty of older American Indians tends to reflect lifelong patterns of unemployment, employment in jobs not covered by Social Security, especially on reservations, and poor working conditions. Of all populations, American Indian elders are the most likely to have never worked. By age 45, incomes have usually peaked among men in this group, and decline thereafter. An additional factor is that historical circumstances and federal policies toward tribes have intensified the pattern of economic underdevelopment and impoverishment in "Indian country," which has led to a steady net migration to urban areas (John, 1994).

American Indian women are generally less educated than the men and seldom earn even half the income of the men, putting them in a severely disadvantaged position. Another factor negatively affecting the socioeconomic and living conditions of American Indian women is that more than 50 percent of those age 60 and over are widowed. High unemployment and low income levels tend to necessitate intergenerational living arrangements, with the elder often the sole provider of the family through their Social Security or Supplemental Security Income. Yet only about 50 percent of American Indian elders receive Social Security and Medicare benefits, and less than 40 percent receive Medicaid, even though such public supports appear to be essential to the survival of many older American Indians (John, 1994).

American Indians may have the poorest health of all Americans, due in part to inadequate housing conditions and the isolation of many American Indian communities. Older American Indians have a higher incidence than their white counterparts of diabetes, hypertension, accidents, tuberculosis, heart disease, liver and kidney disease, strokes, influenza, pneumonia, hearing and visual impairments, and problems stemming from obesity, gall bladder, or arthritic ailments. In fact, nearly 75 percent suffer limitations in their ability to perform activities of daily living. The primary risk factors for disease are smoking and diet, especially consumption of alcohol. The death rate from alcoholism among American Indians is seven times higher than that of the United States generally; alcoholism, however, usually takes its toll before old age. Alcohol-related deaths drop sharply among American Indians who have reached age 55. Automobile accidents also take a disproportionately heavy toll on American Indian males (Manson, 1993; John, 1994; Barresi and Stull, 1993; Rhoades, 1990).

Given these health problems, it is not surprising that people on reservations appear to be physiologically old by 45 years of age, and in urban areas, by age 55. American Indians are less likely than non-Indians to define aging chronologically. Social functioning and decline in physical activities are generally used to identify an elder. As a result, a significant barrier to using publicly funded health services is that eligibility is typically based on chronological, not functional, age.

Because of the importance of tribal sovereignty, many American Indians believe that health and social services are owed to them as a result of the transfer of land and derive from solemn agreements between sovereign nations. Despite this attitude, the majority of American Indian elders rarely see a physician, often because of living in isolated areas, lacking transportation, and not trusting non-Indian health professionals. In addition, many prefer traditional health care from their tribal medicine people and resist using non-Indian medical resources. For traditional American Indians, medicine is holistic and wellness-oriented. It focuses on behaviors and lifestyles through which harmony can be achieved in the physical, mental, spiritual, and personal aspects of one's role in the family, community, and environment (Manson, 1993; Kramer, 1992).

The **Indian Health Service** (IHS) provides health care to those on reservations and has developed health clinics for urban Indians. As noted earlier, the IHS has been successful in controlling infectious diseases and providing acute care earlier in life, thereby extending life expectancy (Markides and Black, 1996). The IHS, however, tends to emphasize services to youth and families and acute care, rather than long-term care such as skilled- and intermediate-care facilities. As a result, the majority of American Indian elders receive social and medical services from the BIA and IHS on only a periodic basis. For example, the IHS operates only 10 nursing-homes on reservations as compared to 49 hospitals. This means that older American Indians who need nursing-home care frequently have to go to facilities that are at a geographic distance and not oriented to Indian peoples. Such cultural and geographic barriers have resulted in a pattern of repeated short-term hospitalizations or revolving-door admissions for chronic conditions. Accordingly, among those over 85 years of age, only 13 percent are in nursing homes, compared to 24.5 percent of whites (Manson, 1993). Other barriers to care include transportation difficulties and professionals' lack of sensitivity to Indians' ritual folk healing or cultural definitions of disease.

American Indians perceive their physical and mental health to be poorer than do white older adults. Research findings regarding the mental health of older American Indians are mixed, with some studies documenting a higher incidence of suicide. Depression appears to be a major mental health problem but is difficult to diagnose because of cultural factors. American Indians' low utilization of mental health services is not necessarily a reflection of fewer mental health problems, but may represent barriers to treatment and lack of information about psychological services from their health care providers (Markides and Black, 1996; John, 1994; Kramer, 1992). Maintaining a tribal identity may serve to buffer various stresses; as American Indians grow older, they appear to shift to a more passive relationship with their world, accepting age-related changes as a natural part of life and utilizing passive forbearance as a coping strategy. This movement from active mastery to passive accommodative styles is consistent with Gutmann's findings for diverse cultures, described in Chapter 6. It is also an adaptation to the decreasing P-E congruence experienced by many ethnic minorities as they age.

A factor that often creates adjustment problems is the degree to which older American Indians' lives are dictated by government bureaucratic policies. Unlike any other group in the United States, various tribes are sovereign nations that have a distinct and special relationship with the U.S. government, based largely, but not exclusively, on treaties agreed to by the two parties. Congress and the Bureau of Indian Affairs, not the individual states, largely determine daily practices on the reservations. Although the bureau's regulations are intended to ensure basic support, it has been criticized for its inflexibility. American Indian advocates have accused the bureau of expending the majority of its budget on maintaining and supporting the bureaucracy, with only a small percent actually going to services for Indian people (Cook, 1990). It has also been criticized for denying traditional cultural values. As an example, land-grazing privileges were historically extended to all tribal members for as long as they desired. Today, older American Indians must transfer their grazing rights to their heirs before they qualify for supplemental financial assistance. Although extra income may be welcome, the program serves to deprive the old of their traditional position within the tribal structure. The history of older American Indians and their relationship with the federal bureaucracy must be considered in any efforts to develop culturally appropriate social and health services.

Historical and cultural factors also strongly influence the family relationships of American Indians. For them, family is the central institution; "honoring" and giving respect to elders and sharing family resources are an integral part of their ethos. American Indians' deep reverence for nature and belief in a supreme force, the importance of the clan, and a sense of individual autonomy as

Congregate meal sites offer an important source of social support and cultural continuity.

a key to group cohesiveness and lack of competition all underlie their practices toward their elders. Historically, as described in Chapter 2, the old were accorded respect and fulfilled specified useful tribal roles, including that of the "wise elder" who instructs the young and assists with child care, especially for foster children and grandchildren. They also maintained responsibility for remembering and relating tribal philosophies, myths, and traditions, and served as religious and political advisors to tribal leaders. These relationships have changed, however, with the restructuring of American Indian life by the BIA and by the increasing urbanization of native populations.

Despite these changes, many American Indian older people, particularly in rural settings, continue to live with, often as head of, an extended family. Approximately 66 percent of all American Indian elders live with family members (e.g., spouse, children, grandchildren, and foster children), and over 40 percent of American Indian households are headed by an older women. Some 25 percent of Indian older people, typically the grandmother, care for at least one grandchild, and 67 percent live within 5 miles of relatives. Given the cultural values and norms of intergenerational assistance, family caregivers may feel less anger and guilt toward relatives for whom they provide care, accepting such care as the reality of aging relatives. This pattern of helping family members, combined with mistrust of government programs, may partially underlie American Indians' comparatively low utilization of social and health services. These factors may combine to put undue pressure on families to keep their elders at home, even though they may lack sufficient resources to do so (John, 1994; Kramer, 1992; Manson and Callaway, 1990).

ASIAN AMERICANS AND PACIFIC ISLANDERS

Asian American and Pacific Islander elders consist of two main groups, composed of at least 30 distinct cultural groups: (1) Asian Americans include Burmese, Cambodian, Chinese, East Indian, Indonesian, Japanese, Korean, Laotian, Malaysian, Filipino, Thai, and Vietnamese, and (2) Pacific Islanders encompass Fijian, Guamanian, Hawaiian, Micronesian, Samoan, and Tongan populations. Each of these groups represents a culture with its own history, religion, language, values, socioeconomic status, lifestyle, and patterns of immigration and adaptation. Adding to this diversity is the timing of immigration. Some Asian American and Pacific Islanders have lived in the United States since the 1850s; others have immigrated here only in the past 20 years. The Asian American elders who were born in this country around the turn of the century or who came to the United States during the early 1900s share the experience of discrimination and isolation. Laws discriminating against Asians are numerous, ranging from the Chinese Exclusion Act of 1882, the Japanese Alien Land Law of 1913, denial of citizenship to first-generation Asians in 1922, the anti-miscegenation statute of 1935, the Executive Order of 1942 for the internment of 110,000 persons of Japanese ancestry during World War II, and more recently, Public Law 95–507 excluding Asians as a protected minority under the definition of "socially

and economically disadvantaged." Such legislation, combined with a history of prejudice and discrimination, has contributed to feelings of mistrust, injustice, powerlessness, and fear of government among many Asian American/Pacific Islander elders, and thus to a reluctance to utilize services. In 1965, immigration quotas based on race and nationality were repealed. These changes resulted in a rapid growth of immigrants, especially those from Vietnam, Cambodia, and Laos. In addition, there has been an increase in the direct immigration of older Asian Americans, often as parents or grandparents of younger immigrants from the Philippines, China, Korea, and Vietnam. These four countries are the source of 30 percent of all older immigrants from countries to the United States (Tanjasiri, Wallace, and Shibeta, 1995). The 1996 welfare legislation poses new barriers, however, since legal alien and immigrant older persons are restricted from getting government assistance for 5 years.

Approximately 6 percent of the Asian Americans/Pacific Islander population is 65 years of age and over. They are the fastest-growing racial group age 65 and over in the United States, due mostly to immigration rates. In fact, they increased in size by 115 percent from 1980 to 1990 and are expected to form 7.4 percent of the older population by the year 2000. As the largely young immigrant population of Asian Americans ages over the next 50 years, the number who are old is expected to increase by 1000 percent (Tanjasiri et al., 1995). Within the Asian American/Pacific Islander population, there is considerable variability in the percentage of foreign-born. For example, of all older immigrant groups, Filipino older adults have the highest percent of foreign-born (95.9 percent), compared with Chinese (80.9 percent) and Japanese (43.1 percent). Among new immigrants (Koreans, Thais) or refugees (Vietnamese, Laotians, and Cambodians), the percentage of foreign-born is even higher (Tanjasiri et al., 1995; Yee, Kim, Liu, and Wong, 1993).

Although there is a widely held perception that Asian Americans and Pacific Islanders are a "successful" minority, there is a bifurcation in income and educational attainment among the older population. The older Asians, especially Japanese and Chinese who immigrated prior to 1924, generally differ substantially in their occupational and educational background from those who came later. As a result of denial of property rights and discrimination against them for public jobs, most older Asians who immigrated in the early part of the century are less educated and more economically deprived than many of their white counterparts. At the same time, there are subgroups of poverty among recent immigrants; for example, the Vietnamese tend to have incomes below the poverty level and high rates of no education. Older Asian Americans/Pacific Islanders have, on average, 6 years of school, with the exception of the Japanese, who average 8.5 years. Many still speak only their native language. In fact, 30 percent of all Asian Americans and Pacific Islanders who are age 65 and over live in households where no adults speak English. This reduces their ability to interact with most public services (Tanjasiri et al., 1995). Their social worlds, therefore, have been limited to ethnic enclaves, such as Chinatown and Korea-town in communities large enough to have such enclaves, where they have developed small retail and service businesses, mutual aid or benevolent societies, and recreational clubs. Although representing segregation from the general society, these ethnic enclaves are a center for leisure activities and for the delivery of services to Asian American/Pacific Islander older people. These functions served by the closely knit community, however, will probably not exist for future generations of Asian American/Pacific Islanders, who will be more geographically and socially mobile.

Although U.S.-born Chinese American and Japanese American older people tend to be economically better off than other ethnic minority groups, approximately 14 percent of Asian American and Pacific Islander elders live below the poverty level (Young and Gu, 1995; Nishi, 1995). The poverty rate may be even higher than that reflected in official statistics, since the number of employed adults, often self-employed as farmers or in small businesses, is greater than in other groups, thereby inflating "family" income. The poverty figures are highest among recent immigrants, particularly the Chinese and Vietnamese (Rumbaut, 1995). Many older Chinese and Filipinos have experienced a lifetime of low-paying jobs, often in self-employment, garment factories, and service or farming work not covered by Social Security or other pensions. Filipino males, in particular, were concentrated in live-in domestic, migrant agricultural, or other unsettled work, often living in homogeneous male camps. This prevents them from gaining an insured work history and developing close ties with family and neighborhood.

As is the case with older Hispanics, many older Asian Americans/Pacific Islanders qualify for public financial supports, such as Supplemental Security Income, but do not apply. After years of living under discrimination and fear of deportation, they resist seeking help from a government bureaucracy which they distrust. Their reluctance to seek non-familial assistance is also influenced by cultural and linguistic traditions emphasizing hierarchical relationships, personal social status, and self-restraint. When unsure of others' social status, some older Asian Americans and Pacific Islanders avoid interaction with them. In the past, they turned to the benevolent societies and clubs in their tightly knit communities, as well as to their families. Yet many are caught between their cultural traditions of group and familial honor and the values of their adopted culture that stress independence and self-sufficiency, making them loath to turn to others for support (Braun and Browne, 1998).

The cultural values of Asian-American/Pacific Islanders can create reluctance to utilize services. Filipino-Americans, for example, are guided by values of both respect and shame. Respect includes listening to others, self-imposed restraints, loyalty to family, and unquestioning obedience to authority; shame involves fear of being left exposed, unprotected, and unaccepted. Filipino Americans are also very concerned with good relations or the avoidance of disagreement or conflict. Their high value on personal relationships may impede their accepting formal assistance, especially institutional care. For first-generation Japanese, or Issei, a value that transcends that of family is group conscience, characterized by cohesiveness, strong pride, and identity through a devotion to and sense of mutuality among peer-group members. This value has been preserved through the residential and occupational isolation of older Japanese American cohorts from mainstream American culture. Even among the second generation (Nissei), the Japanese vision of Buddhism endures in the cherishing of filial devotion and the loving indulgence of the old toward young children. The interdependence on the aged and respect for elders who have greater life experience, knowledge, and wisdom are widely accepted values. Accordingly, Japanese American older people tend to value social interaction, hierarchical relationships, interdependency, and empathy—all characteristics that may not be present in the delivery of formal services. These situations illustrate the problem of lack of person-environment fit between the cultural values of ethnic minority groups and the insensitivity to cultural differences of the service system that is generally established by the larger society (Browne, Fong, and Mokuau, 1994; Kim, 1990).

Compared to the national average, Asian American/Pacific Islander groups show higher proportions of extended family arrangements, although the majority of older adults live by themselves or with a spouse, not with children. In contrast to other ethnic minorities and to white older persons, men living alone constitute a larger percent of the older Asian American/Pacific Islander population. This reflects the continuing influence of disproportionate male immigration in the early part of the century and past restrictions on female immigration rather than a higher life expectancy for men. In contrast to other subgroups of older adults, the ratio of men to women in the Asian American/Pacific Islander population increases with age, controlling for gender, social class, and levels of functional ability. On the other hand, Asian American/Pacific Islander women are much more likely to be married than their white counterparts, with a smaller proportion remaining single in their later years (Angel and Hogan, 1994).

Advancing age increases the probability of living alone (Manson, 1993). Some 2 percent of Asian Americans/Pacific Islanders over age 65, and 10 percent over age 85, are in nursing homes, compared to 23 percent of whites. One of the major reasons for a relative decline in intergenerational living arrangements is acculturation of younger generations of Asians into the larger society. For example, many Chinese older people prefer to remain in their ethnic communities rather than live with children who have moved to the suburbs or across the country. Despite their strong commitment to family and filial responsibility, Chinese American elders generally live with their children only in cases of extreme poverty or poor health. Living with adult children may also be a function of their dependency on them for translation. As another example, Korean American older persons accept separation from their children as a way to promote the children's happiness and success.

Although Asian Americans/Pacific Islanders represent tremendous diversity in terms of country of origin, degree of acculturation, and transcending values and religion, they all share the erosion of the **law of primogeniture,** or the relationship between aged parents and oldest son who provides care for them and, in turn, inherits their wealth. This is a value that is still prevalent in most Asian countries today, as discussed in Chapter 2, although it is eroding there as well. A strain faced by many families is the duality of cultures and the inevitable clashes when different generations have different languages, values, and ethos. As a result, traditional cultural values regarding care of elders by adult children are weakening (Antonucci and Cantor, 1994). Nevertheless, compared with the majority culture, Asian American/Pacific Islanders place a higher value on reciprocal exchanges between young and old and the prestige of being old, and seek outside help only in desperate circumstances. Any discussion of family caregiving should take account of differences in culture, economic circumstances, and generations among Asian American/Pacific Islanders.

Information on the health of this ethnic minority group is limited. Less comparative research has been conducted on the health status and behaviors of other Asian American/Pacific Islander groups due in part to the difficulties in collecting epidemiological data on the relatively small Asian groups. Given the wide variability within population groupings, their overall health status compared to the general population is unclear, although immigrants appear to be healthier than native-born Americans (Markides and Black, 1996). As noted earlier, in terms of socioeconomic and health status, there appears to be a bimodal distribution, with some Asian American/Pacific Islanders (e.g., Japanese and Chinese-Americans) doing quite well, while others have very low income and poor health status (e.g., Vietnamese and Hawaiians) (Chen and Hawks, 1995; Min, 1995; Tanjasiri et al., 1995). What is known about their health status is that they face problems of hypertension and higher rates of cancer, especially among low-income subgroupings. The incidence of strokes in Chinese and Japanese living in the United States is lower than in China and Japan. The relatively better health status of these two Pacific Asian groups may be due to their diet, with lower fat and higher carbohydrate intakes compared with whites, and lower obesity rates compared with other ethnic minority groups. On the other hand, the rates of digestive system cancer, diabetes, and suicide are higher in Japanese Americans than their white counterparts (Wright and Mindel, 1993; Wykle and Kaskel, 1994).

There is even less research on the mental health of Asian Americans/Pacific Islanders. The average level of depression is slightly higher than that for whites, with the highest rate among Koreans. This is attributed to their recent immigration status and difficulties adjusting to American society (Markides and Black, 1996). Suicides are often explained by perceived incongruities between the elder's values and the reality of their lives in an alien culture (Kim, 1990). Older Japanese males in California have been found to be hospitalized for schizophrenia more frequently than their white counterparts, for example. However,

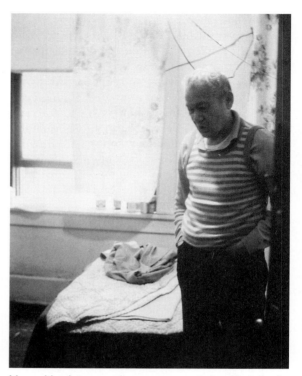

Many older Asian men have never married and lack family ties.

since cultural factors influence the diagnosis of mental health problems, these findings may not necessarily reflect the mental health status of this highly diverse population.

Asian American/Pacific Islanders tend to underutilize Medicare and Medicaid, relying on non-Western medicine or family and friends to assist them with their health problems. It has been estimated that 33 percent of Asian American/Pacific Islander elders have never seen a Western doctor or a dentist, and only about 2 percent are in nursing homes (Braun and Browne, 1998; Kim, 1990). This low utilization of traditional health services is probably due to a combination of their having fewer chronic diseases than do their majority group peers; to structural barriers to health care; and to elders' reluctance to use formal Western health services. For example, among Chinese American elders who value traditional healing practices, hospitals are seen as places to die, not to get well (Baker, 1990). Southeast Asian refugees' belief in the supernatural powers of ancestral and natural spirits is the cause of their low utilization of health care services. For some Japanese American older adults, the use of public services may be perceived as shameful and as an indicator of dependency and inability to care for oneself. Accordingly, Japanese American elders' low utilization of mental health services is due in large part to their definition of mental illness as stigma. Korean Americans tend to hold themselves and their families responsible for their problems rather than turn to others for assistance. Such reluctance to use services may reinforce the myth held by some service providers that Asian American/Pacific Islander older persons do not have problems and "take care of their own."

This chapter has been able to highlight only a few characteristics of Asian American/Pacific Islander elders, because of the large inter- and intragroup differences that exist. Because of population and political pressures in Asia, the high rate of immigration is likely to continue, and the diversity under the label of Asian American/Pacific Islanders to increase. A major challenge for researchers and service providers is to take account of this diversity in terms of history and cultural values in developing culturally sensitive research and practice models (Braun and Browne, 1998).

IMPLICATIONS FOR SERVICE DELIVERY

Because it is important that gerontologists develop services responsive to ethnic minority older adults, we briefly consider the implications of sociocultural factors for the delivery of social and health services. Findings are mixed regarding whether ethnic minority elders underutilize social and health care services (Miller et al., 1996; Markides and Black, 1996; Mui and Burnette, 1994). On the one hand, Medicaid is not fully used by potentially eligible minority elders, even when they are aware of it. Underutilization of Medicaid has been attributed to lack of knowledge about the program,

difficulties in applying, and an aversion to accepting publicly funded benefits (Wykle and Kaskel, 1994). On the other hand, a recent analysis of three national data sets on service use found that living arrangements, health status, number of functional limitations, region and insurance/income status affect use of services more than race or ethnicity (Markides and Black, 1996). It is acknowledged, however, that service use by ethnic minority elders may vary more in the cultural contexts of local and regional levels than at the national level.

Although some service providers have rationalized that ethnic minority older adults do not utilize formal services because they have their families' assistance, patterns of underutilization cannot fully be explained in terms of strong family support. Underutilization of in-home services, for example, may result more from services not being presented to ethnic minorities as a viable, culturally appropriate alternative to long-term care than to the existence of family supports. In fact, medical and psychosocial interventions that are culturally sensitive have been found to increase ethnic minority service utilization (Miller et al., 1996).

Barriers to service utilization can be conceptualized as (1) cultural and economic factors within the ethnic minority groupings and as (2) structural factors within the service delivery system, as follows:

Cultural and economic barriers:

- Cultural isolation, including language differences.
- Perceived stigma of utilizing services, especially mental health, and embarrassment and fear in attempting to describe symptoms.
- Confusion, anger at, and fear of health care providers and hospitals, which may be related to present or historical acts of racism by medical providers.
- Lack of trust and faith in the efficacy of service professionals within a Western biomedical health care system, which may be intensified by cohorts' experiences. For ex-

ample, segregated health care and explicit policies, such as the Tuskegee experiment with African Americans and the internment of Japanese Americans on the West Coast, underlie a distrust of the health care system.

• Lack of knowledge of services, including how to make appointments and how to negotiate a clinic visit.

Structural barriers within the service system:

• Lack of services that are specifically oriented toward and operated by members of respective ethnic minority groups.
• Real or perceived discrimination by service providers.
• Assessment instruments whose meaning is altered in translation.
• Geographic distance of services from ethnic minority neighborhoods.
• Lack of transportation to services.
• Non-minority staff who are not bilingual, who are insensitive to ethnic and cultural differences, and who serve meals that conflict with customary dietary preferences.

Within the field of gerontology, there is overall agreement that services need to be designed to take account of inter- and intra-cultural and geographic differences within and across groups. From this perspective, preferential consideration is needed to reduce social inequities between the elders of dominant and minority groups, along with consideration of the diversity of needs, and to increase the participation of various ethnic minority groups. Accordingly, service providers need to be trained to be culturally competent. Increasingly, the importance of cross-cultural care or **ethnogeriatrics** is being recognized (Yeo, 1996–97).

Service providers should recognize and respect that many older ethnic minorities may adhere to traditional paradigms of health and illness and associated folk beliefs and behaviors that diverge from mainstream Western scientific medical concepts, or they may combine these with orthodox or scientific treatments. As noted earlier, such folk

Shared cultural backgrounds can enhance communication between health care providers and older patients.

treatments are often important in terms of psychological well-being (Hopper, 1993). Accordingly, current health promotion efforts aimed at older whites may not be appropriate for ethnic minorities. For example, social entities that play a key role in older African Americans' lives, such as the church and group leaders from the community, are more likely to change health beliefs and behaviors than traditional approaches to health promotion. The involvement of health-promotion experts from the same culture may also help bridge the gap between cultural values and scientific knowledge about the causes and treatment of disease. This is particularly true for American Indian and Asian American/Pacific Asian cultures, where traditional ways of treating disease are still widely practiced among older cohorts. Health-promotion efforts that ignore traditional beliefs about harmony between the individual, nature, and the universe are more likely to fail in these cultures. For example, the Chinese believe that health represents a balance between Yin and Yang energy forces; certain foods are believed to bring about this balance. Because they also believe that the aging process predisposes people to Yin (or cold forces), older people avoid eating many cold foods such as leafy green vegetables (Yee and Weaver, 1994). Health-promotion facilitators must recognize the basis for such avoidance if they are to encourage healthier diets among older Asians.

In general, services are most likely to be used by ethnic minority older people under the following conditions:

1. Services should be located in the ethnic minority community, easily accessible, and near complementary supports; transportation should be provided.
2. Services should adhere to the cultural integrity of the ethnic minority group's lifestyle; for example, nutrition programs should include appropriate ethnic foods, and nursing homes should offer culturally appropriate recreation.
3. The organizational climate should be informal and personalized.
4. Staff should include bilingual, bicultural, and/or indigenous workers, or translators who are culturally sensitive, who convey respect, and who use personalized outreach methods to establish trust and rapport. Medical and insurance forms, newsletters, and descriptions of services should be bilingual.
5. Ethnic minorities should be involved in both the planning and the delivery of services, so that programs are accountable to the community served.
6. Services should be advertised in ways to reach ethnic minorities, such as through minority-oriented television and radio programs and newspapers, and announcements made through churches, neighborhood organizations, civic and social clubs, other natural support systems, and influential persons as advocates. For example, black churches can be used to recruit more African American elders to participate in the formal delivery of services as well as to coordinate and link with other agencies (Walls and Zarit, 1991).
7. Given major differences in the epidemiology and risk factors of certain diseases (for example, all ethnic minority groups are at greater risk of diabetes than are their white counterparts), screening, prevention, and education are essential.

In sum, rather than a deficits model, in which interventions are developed to ameliorate personal or social problems, service providers should look for community strengths and use them to supplement and augment existing services. This also suggests the value of utilizing existing organizational structures, such as churches, to provide services and to link informal and formal sources of help (Wood and Wan, 1993; Mayers and Souflee, 1990–91).

Underlying such strategies are assumptions that the needs of ethnic minority elders are best understood by members of their own groups, that these elders should be treated as distinct populations, and that ethnic minorities should concentrate on the welfare of their own older members, rather than on the well-being of older people in general. These assumptions have led to demands by advocates for the minority aged that separate indigenous services be developed, that research and training programs give special attention to ethnic minorities, that ethnic minority practitioners be employed as service providers, and that federal regulations for aging programs include minority-specific statutes. These demands have been met in many communities, such as in Seattle with a special Asian Health Program that has both community-based and nursing-home care, and in San Francisco with the On Lok program that provides comprehensive care for older Chinese and has been replicated in other ethnic communities. However, it may not be feasible to provide separate services for all ethnic minorities in all communities.

Likewise, the premises and strategies used by these minority advocates have been challenged. The extent to which ethnic minority professionals reflect the needs of their older members has been questioned, as well as whether ethnic minority issues are overemphasized. Critics of separate strategies advocate that ethnic minorities should become involved in larger issues that affect all older persons, and that programs should be developed on the basis of need, regardless of ethnic minority status. For example, if socioeconomic status is more important than race in explaining health differences, then research and policy should begin by addressing deficits in income, education, and other socioeconomic measures (Schoenbaum and Waidman, 1997). As younger members of ethnic minority groups advance economically and move out of formerly insulated ethnic communities and into the mainstream culture, the need for preferential services may decrease.

Others would argue, however, that even greater attention needs to be given to ethnic minorities in a period of growing competition for scarce public resources. Two policy directions, the devolution of federal responsibility to the state level and the targeting of services to the oldest-old, may, in fact, serve to exclude older members of ethnic minority groups who are less able to influence decentralized decision-making and less likely to reach advanced age. The persistently high unemployment rates among non-whites across the life span, which will perpetuate major gaps in earnings, Social Security, and pension coverage in old age, suggest that strategies targeted to ethnic minority elders will continue to be necessary in the near future. During the current period of cutbacks in public funds, advocacy efforts are required to sustain the economic and social position of both minority and non-minority older people; this suggests the importance of collaborative efforts to ensure that low-income white and ethnic minority elders do not fall below the presumed "safety net" of services. In addition, more consideration needs to be given to improving the circumstances under which younger ethnic minorities will age, especially employment conditions, so that they will be better off when old. Such a perspective recognizes the need for cross-generational approaches to addressing long-term inequities.

SUMMARY AND IMPLICATIONS

Although age is sometimes called the great equalizer, today's elders are a highly diverse group. As we have seen throughout this book, differences in income, health, and social supports significantly affect older adults' quality of life. An important source of this diversity is ethnic minority status. Ethnogerontology is the study of the causes, processes, and consequences of race, national origin, and culture on individual and population aging. One of the earliest debates in that field continues: whether ethnic minorities experience double jeopardy because of their race or whether age is a leveler of differences in income and life expectancy. Recent studies indicate a narrowing of differences in health status and life expectancy after age 75 or a crossover effect.

This chapter has reviewed the social, demographic, economic, and health status of African Americans, Hispanic Americans, American Indians, and Asian American/Pacific Islander older people. Although there are variations among these groups, several common themes also emerge. For most ethnic minority older persons, their resources and status reflect social, economic, and educational discrimination experienced earlier in life. Many, especially those who immigrated to the United States from other countries, experience cultural and language differences as well. As a whole, they face shorter life expectancy and increased risks of poverty, malnutrition, substandard housing, and poor health, although there are wide variations within each group. Nevertheless, many ethnic minority elders, especially among the oldest-old, display considerable strengths and resiliency. Social and health care assistance is of particular concern to ethnic minority elders. Cultural and language difficulties, physical isolation, and lower income, along with structural barriers to service accessibility, affect their underutilization of health and social services. Efforts must continue to modify services to be more responsive to the particular needs of ethnic minority older adults.

In recent years, the older population has been growing faster among ethnic minorities than among whites—a trend that is expected to continue. Still, white elders outnumber their ethnic minority peers. The status of ethnic minority older people is not likely to improve greatly in the immediate future. The factors that largely determine the older population's quality of life—education, employment, income, and health—will not vary considerably among the ethnic minority population now approaching retirement age. This trend suggests the importance of targeting services to meet the needs of ethnic minority elders. On the other hand, some minority aging advocates maintain that policies and programs should increase opportunities for education and employment among younger minorities in order to assure that the next generation will enjoy a higher quality of life than that of their predecessors.

GLOSSARY

crossover effect   refers to the lower death rates among African Americans, Asian Americans, and American Indians after age 75

double jeopardy hypothesis   the hypothesis that aging ethnic minorities are in jeopardy in our society due to both growing old and being part of an ethnic minority

ethnogeriatrics   cross-cultural geriatric care

ethnogerontology   study of causes, processes, and consequences of race, national origin, and culture on individual and population aging

fictive kin   foster parents of children, close friends, or neighbors who function in the absence of blood relatives or when family relationships are unsatisfactory

Indian Health Service   federal program that provides health care for Native Americans and Alaskans of all ages through hospitals and community clinics

multiple hierarchy stratification   maintains that social class, in addition to ethnic minority status, can jeopardize older minorities

primogeniture, law of   the exclusive right of the eldest son to inherit his father's estate

REFERENCES

Administration on Aging. *Aging into the 21st century.* Washington, DC: Administration on Aging, 1997

Angel, J. L., and Hogan, D. P. The demography of minority aging populations. In *Minority elders: Five goals toward building a public policy base* (2nd ed.). Washington, DC: The Gerontological Society of America, 1994.

Antonucci, T. C., and Cantor, M. H. Strengthening the family support system for older minority persons.

In *Minority elders: Five goals toward building a public policy base* (2nd ed.). Washington, DC: The Gerontological Society of America, 1994.

Baker, F. M. Ethnic minority issues: Differential diagnosis, medication, treatment and outcomes. In M. S. Harper (Ed.), *Minority aging.* DHHS Publication #HRS (P-DV-90–4), Washington, DC: U.S. Government Printing Office, 1990.

Baquet, C. R. Cancer prevention and control in the black population. In J. S. Jackson (Ed.), *The black American elderly.* New York: Springer, 1988.

Barresi, C., and Stull, D. Ethnicity and long-term care: An overview. In C. Barresi and D. Stull (Eds.), *Ethnic elderly and long-term care.* New York: Springer, 1993.

Belgrave, L. L., Wykle, M. L., and Choi, J. M. Health, double jeopardy, and culture: The use of institutionalization by African-Americans. *The Gerontologist,* 1993, *33,* 379–385.

Bengtson, V. L. Ethnicity and aging: Problems and issues in current social science inquiry. In D. E. Gelfand and A. J. Kutzik (Eds.), *Ethnicity and aging: Theory, research and policy.* New York: Springer, 1979.

Braun, K. L. and Browne, C. Cultural values and caregiving patterns among Asian and Pacific Islander Americans. In D. E. Redburn and L. P. McNamara (Eds.), *Social Gerontology.* Westport, CT: Greenwood Press, 1998.

Browne, C., Fong, R., and Mokuau, N. The mental health of Asian and Pacific Island elders: Implications for research and mental health administration. *Journal of Mental Health Administration,* 1994, *21,* 52–59.

Burton, L., Kasper, J., Shore, A., Cagney, K., LeVeist, T., Cubbins, C., and German, P. The structure of informal care: Are there differences by race? *The Gerontologist,* 1995, *35,* 744–752.

Chen, M. S., and Hawks, B. L. A debunking of the myth of healthy Asian Americans and Pacific Islanders. *American Journal of Health Promotion,* 1995, *9,* 261–268.

Chen, Y. P. Improving the economic security of minority persons as they enter old age. In *Minority elders: Five goals toward building a public policy base* (2nd ed.). Washington, DC: The Gerontological Society of America, 1994.

Cook, C. D. American Indian elderly and public policy issues. In M. S. Harper (Ed.), *Minority aging.* DHHS Publication #HRS (P-DV-90–4), Washington DC: U.S. Government Printing Office, 1990.

Cuellar, J. Hispanic American aging: Geriatric educational curriculum development for selected health professions. In M. S. Harper (Ed.), *Minority aging*. DHHS Publication #HRS (P-DV-90-4), Washington, DC: U.S. Government Printing Office, 1990.

Cuellar, J., and Weeks, J. Minority elderly Americans: The assessment of needs and equitable receipt of public benefits as a prototype in area agencies on aging. Final report. San Diego: Allied Home Health Association, Grant AOA/DHHS 90-A-1667(01), 1980.

Davis, L., and McGadney, B. Self-care practices of black elders. In C. Barresi and D. Stull (Eds.), *Ethnic elderly and long-term care*. New York: Springer, 1993.

Espino, D. Hispanic elderly and long-term care: Implications for ethnically sensitive services. In C. Barresi and D. Stull (Eds.), *Ethnic elderly and long-term care*. New York: Springer, 1993.

Ferraro, K. F., and Farmer, M. M. Double jeopardy, aging as leveler or persistent health inequality? A longitudinal analysis of white and Black Americans. *Journals of Gerontology*, 1996, *51B*, S319–S328.

Gallagher-Thompson, D. Service delivery and recommendations for working with Mexican American family caregivers. In G. Yeo and D. Gallagher-Thompson (Eds.), *Ethnicity and the dementias*. Washington, DC: Taylor Frances, 1996.

Gibson, R. C. The age-by-race gap in health and mortality in the older population: A social science research agenda. *The Gerontologist*, 1994, *34*, 454–462.

Gibson, R. Minority aging research: Opportunity and challenge. *Journals of Gerontology*, 1989, *44*, S52–53.

Gould, K. H. A minority-feminist perspective on women and aging. *Journal of Women and Aging*, 1989, *1*, 195–216.

Greene, V. L., and Ondrich, J. I. Risk factors for nursing home admissions and exits: A discrete-time hazard function approach. *Journal of Gerontology*, 1990, *45*, S250–S258.

Guralnik, J. M., Land, K. C., Blazer, D. G., Fillerbaum, G. G., and Branch, L. G. Educational status and active life expectancy among older blacks and whites. *New England Journal of Medicine*, 1993, *329*, 110–116.

Gutmann, D. Use of informal and formal supports by white ethnic aged. In D. E. Gelfand and A. J. Kutzik (Eds.), *Ethnicity and aging: Theory, research and policy*. New York: Springer, 1979.

Harper, M., and Alexander, C. Profile of the black elderly. In M. S. Harper (Ed.), *Minority aging*. DHHS Publication #HRS (P-DV-90-4), Washington, DC: U.S. Government Printing Office, 1990.

Hayward, M. D., Friedman, S., and Chen, H. Race inequities in men's retirement. *Journals of Gerontology*, 1996, *51B*, S1–S10.

Hobbs, F., and Damon, B. L. *65+ in the United States*. Washington, DC: U.S. Department of Commerce, Bureau of the Census, 1996.

Hopper, S. V. The influence of ethnicity on the health of older women. *Clinics in Geriatric Medicine*, 1993, *9*(1), 231–259.

John, R. The state of research on American Indian elders' health, income security, and social support networks. In *Minority elders: Five goals toward building a public policy base* (2nd ed.). Washington, DC: The Gerontological Society of America, 1994.

Johnson, T. Utilizing culture in work with aging families. In G. Smith, S. Tobin, E. A. Robertson-Tchabo, and P. Power (Eds.), *Strengthening aging families: Diversity in practice and policy*. Thousand Oaks, CA: Sage, 1995.

Kahn, K., Pearson, M. L., and Harrison, E. R. Health care for black and poor hospitalized Medicare patients. *Journal of the American Medical Association*, 1994, *271*, 1169–1174.

Kim, P. Asian-American families and the elderly. In M. S. Harper (Ed.), *Minority aging*. DHHS Publication #HRS (P-DV-90-4), Washington, DC: U.S. Government Printing Office, 1990.

Kramer, B. J. Cross-cultural medicine a decade later: Health and aging of urban American Indians. *Western Journal of Medicine*, 1992, *157*, 281–285.

Lacayo, C. G. Hispanic elderly: Policy issues in long-term care. In C. Barresi and D. Stull (Eds.), *Ethnic elderly and long-term care*. New York: Springer, 1993.

Manson, J. Long-term care of older American Indians: Challenges in the development of institutional services. In C. Barresi and D. Stull (Eds.), *Ethnic elderly and long-term care*. New York: Springer, 1993.

Manson, S. M., and Callaway, D. G. Health and aging among American Indians. In M. S. Harper (Ed.), *Minority aging*. DHHS Publication #HRS (P-DV-90-4), Washington, DC: U.S. Government Printing Office, 1990.

Markides, K. S. and Black S. A. Race, ethnicity and aging. In R. H. Binstock and L. K. George (Eds.), *Handbook of aging and the social sciences* (4th ed.). San Diego, CA: Academic Press, 1996.

Markides, K., Liang, J., and Jackson, J. Race, ethnicity and aging: Conceptual and methodological issues. In R. Binstock and L. K. George (Eds.), *Handbook of aging and the social sciences* (3rd ed.). New York: Academic Press, 1990.

Mayers, R. S., and Souflee, L. Utilizing social support systems in the delivery of social services to the Mexican-American elderly. *Journal of Applied Social Sciences*, Fall/Winter 1990–91, *15*, 31–50.

Miller, B., Campbell, R. T., Davis, L., Turner, S., Giachello, A., Prohaska, T., Kaufman, J. E., Li, M., and Perez, C. Minority use of community long-term care: A comparative analysis. *Journals of Gerontology*, 1996, *51B*, S70–S81.

Miller, B., McFall, S., and Campbell, R. T. Changes in sources of community long-term care among African American and white frail older persons. *Journals of Gerontology*, 1994, 49, S14–S24.

Min, P. G. *Asian Americans: Contemporary trends and issues.* Thousand Oaks, CA: Sage Publications, 1995.

Minkler, M., and Roe, K. *Grandmothers as caregivers.* Newbury Park, CA: Sage, 1993.

Miranda, M. Hispanic aging: An overview of issues and policy implications. In M. S. Harper (Ed.), *Minority aging.* DHHS Publication #HRS (P-DV-90–4), Washington, DC: U.S. Government Printing Office, 1990.

Mui, A. C., and Burnette, D. Long-term care service use by frail elders: Is ethnicity a factor? *The Gerontologist*, 1994, *34*, 190–198.

National Center for Health Statistics, *Health: United States, 1990.* Hyattsville, MD: NCHS, 1992.

Nishi, S. M. Japanese Americans. In P. G. Min (Ed.), *Asian Americans: Contemporary issues and trends.* Newbury Park, CA: Sage Publications, 1995.

Norgard, T. M., and Rodgers, W. C. Patterns of in-home care among elderly black and white Americans. *Journals of Gerontology: Social Sciences*, 1997, *52B*, S93–S101.

Quinn, J. F., and Smeeding, T. M. Defying the averages: Poverty and well-being among older Americans. *Aging Today*, September/October 1994, *XV*, 9.

Rawlings, S. Household and family characteristics: March 1992. *Current Population Reports*, Series P-20, No. 463. Washington, DC: U.S. Bureau of the Census, 1993.

Rhoades, E. Profile of American Indians and Alaska natives. In M. S. Harper (Ed.), *Minority aging.* DHHS Publication #HRS (P-DV-90–4), Washington, DC: U.S. Government Printing Office, 1990.

Rumbaut, R. G. Vietnamese, Laotian, and Cambodian Americans. In P. G. Min (Ed.), *Asian Americans: Contemporary issues and trends.* Newbury Park, CA: Sage Publications, 1995.

Schoenbaum, M., and Waidman, T. Race, socioeconomic states and health: Accounting for race differences in health. *Journals of Gerontology, Series B* (Special Issue), 1997, *52B*, 61–73.

Silverstein, M., and Waite, C. J. Are blacks more likely than whites to receive and provide social support in middle and old age? Yes, no and maybe so. *Journals of Gerontology*, 1993, *48*, S212–S222.

Stephen, E. H., Foote, K., Hendershot, G. E., and Schoenbaum, C. A. Health of the foreign born population: United States 1989–90. *Advance data from vital and health statistics;* No. 241. Hyattsville, MD: National Center for Health Statistics, 1994.

Tanjasiri, S. P., Wallace, S. P., and Shibata, K. Picture imperfect: Hidden problems among Asian Pacific Islander elderly. *The Gerontologist*, 1995, *35*, 753–760.

U.S. Bureau of the Census. *Statistical Abstract of the United States*, 116th edition. Washington, DC: Current Population Reports, 1996.

U.S. Senate Special Committee on Aging. *Aging America: Trends and projections. 1990–91.* Washington, DC: U.S. Department of Health and Human Services, 1992.

Walls, C., and Zarit, S. Informal support from black churches and the well-being of elderly blacks. *The Gerontologist*, 1991, *31*, 490–495.

Wood, J. B., and Wan, T. Ethnicity and minority issues in family caregiving to rural black elders. In C. Barresi and D. Stull (Eds.), *Ethnic elderly and long-term care.* New York: Springer, 1993.

Wright, R., and Mindel, C. Economics, health and service use policies: Implications for long-term care of ethnic elderly. In C. Barresi and D. Stull (Eds.), *Ethnic elderly and long-term care.* New York: Springer, 1993.

Wykle, M., and Kaskel, B. Increasing the longevity of minority older adults through improved health status. In *Minority elders: Five goals toward building a public policy base* (2nd ed.). The Gerontological Society of America, 1994.

Yee, B. W. K., and Weaver, G. D. Ethnic minorities and health promotion. *Generations*, 1994, *18*, 39–44.

Yee, E., Kim, K., Liu, W., and Wong, S-C. Functional abilities of Chinese and Korean elders in congregate housing. In C. Barresi and D. Stull (Eds.), *Ethnic elderly and long-term care*. New York: Springer, 1993.

Yeo, G. Ethnogenetics: Cross-cultural care of older adults. *Generations*, Winter 1996–97, *20*, 72–77.

Young, J. J., and Gu, N. *Demographic and socio-economic characteristics of elderly Asian and Pacific Island Americans*. Seattle: National Asian Pacific Center on Aging, 1995.

THE CHALLENGES FACING OLDER WOMEN

Previous chapters have illustrated numerous areas in which women's experiences with aging differ from men's: in patterns of health and life expectancy, marital opportunities, social supports, employment, and retirement. We have devoted a separate chapter to elaborate on these gender differences, with attention to how personal and environmental factors interact vis-à-vis the particular problems facing women in old age. The impact of social factors, particularly economic ones, on physiological and psychological variables is vividly illustrated in terms of women's daily lives. This chapter first reviews the economic conditions faced by older women, then their health and social status, and how these factors interact. The strengths and resiliency of older women are acknowledged. The chapter concludes with a brief discussion of program and policy options to reduce older women's vulnerability to poverty, poor health, and social isolation, primarily through modifying socioeconomic conditions.

RATIONALE FOR A FOCUS ON OLDER WOMEN'S NEEDS

A major reason for gerontological research and practice to take account of older women's special needs is that they form the fastest-growing segment of our population (Diczfalusy and Bengiano, 1997). As noted in Chapter 1, the aging society is primarily a female one. Women represent 56 percent of the population aged 65 to 74 and 72 percent of those over age 85; also, they outnumber men age 65 and over by three to two, men age 85 and over by five to two; and centenarians by three to one. These ratios differ among ethnic minorities, as described in Chapter 13. Chapter 1 noted that these disproportionate ratios result from a nearly 7-year difference in life expectancy between women and men; this is due to a combination of biological factors, such as the genetic theory that the female's two X chromosomes make her physiologically more robust, and to lifestyle factors,

Many older women have overcome a wide range of obstacles and are remarkable survivors.

such as women's greater likelihood of consulting doctors and their lower rates of smoking, problem drinking, and other high-risk behaviors. At age 65, women can expect to live about 19 more years compared to 15.5 more years for men at the same age (Costello and Krimgold, 1996). At age 75, the comparable figures are 12 more years for women and 9 more years for men. Even at age 85, the life expectancy for females is 1.5 years more than that for males (U.S. Bureau of the Census, 1996). However, men who survive beyond age 85 are likely to be in better health and to have similar or even more remaining years of independent life than women (Moen, 1996).

Another reason to examine the status of older women separate from that of older men is that gender structures opportunities across the

life course so that the processes of aging and the quality of life in old age are often very different for men and women (Moen, 1996; Holstein, 1993). Consistent with the feminist perspective described in Chapter 8, research on women and aging increasingly recognizes that gender and age interact to affect the distribution of power, privilege, and social well-being of both men and women. This means that the interaction of age and gender produces distinctive patterns for men and women at all stages of the life course (Moen, 1996). As noted by feminist writers, as more women reach old age, age compounds a woman's already devalued status (Gottlieb, 1989; Holstein, 1993). Since gender and age are powerful systems for patterning inequities, neither can be understood fully without reference to the other (Hess, 1994). Given this interaction, it is not surprising that the problems of aging are increasingly women's problems. Older women are more likely than older men to be poor; to have inadequate retirement income; to be widowed, divorced, and alone; and to be caregivers to other relatives. Women are viewed as experiencing double jeopardy—they are discriminated against both for being old and for being female. In addition, the emphasis on youth and beauty in our society, which traditionally values women for their sex appeal and ability to bear children, is particularly difficult for older women.

Despite their greater problems, many older women display resilience and innovation in the face of adversity. In terms of measures of subjective well-being, they do not inevitably experience double jeopardy. For example, women who live alone are not necessarily unhappy but often draw upon prior social networks or create new relationships (Moen, 1996; Barer, 1994). These networks can buffer many of the losses with age. Many older women are remarkable survivors, having developed skills to cope with discontinuities and losses through their lives. Women who successfully manage multiple roles over their life course and whose life pathways reflect choice and autonomy seem to benefit in terms of increased confidence and self-esteem later in life (Moen,

Dempster-McClain, and Williams, 1995). There is growing awareness of middle-aged and older women's capacity to move in new directions—to advance their education, to enter new occupations, and to combine marriage and care for dependents with employment and volunteer roles. The impact of advocacy groups, such as the Older Women's League, on federal legislation clearly illustrates older women's power as activists. It is predicted that today's middle-aged women, who are enacting more diverse roles than past cohorts, will reach old age with even greater role flexibility and skills in coping with complex, changing life experiences (Moen, 1996).

Given the predominance of older women, it might be supposed that they, rather than men, would be the major focus of social gerontology. Yet, older women were nearly invisible in social gerontological research until the mid-1970s. For example, they were not added to the Baltimore Longitudinal Study (one of the major studies of aging described in Chapter 1) until 1978, because it was assumed that women's hormonal cycles would affect the data (Leonard, 1991)! It was not until 1975 that the first older women's caucus met at the annual meetings of the Gerontological Society of America. The 1981 White House Conference on Aging was the first to sponsor a special committee on older women's concerns. Research on issues specific to women, such as menopause, breast cancer, hormone replacement therapy, and osteoporosis, has been relatively limited until the 1980s. In 1991, Congress directed the National Institutes of Health to establish an Office of Research on Women's Health to redress the insufficient attention that had been paid to women's health issues in the biomedical and behavioral research community. This directive is intended to stop the practice of excluding women from major research studies and help to increase the research on diseases that primarily afflict women, such as breast cancer. One positive outcome is the Women's Health Initiative, the first randomized controlled study of **postmenopausal** women and the impact of fat intake and hormone replacement therapy on breast can-

cer and heart disease, which is to be completed by the year 2008. Similarly, the Women's Health and Aging Study, funded in 1994 by the National Institutes of Health, is focusing on the causes, prevention, management, and rehabilitation of disability among older women. Research on aging has thus moved from (1) ignoring gender, (2) merely "controlling" for gender, (3) simply describing contrasts, to (4) efforts at understanding the sources of gender variations as well as (5) their implications for individual lives (Moen, 1996).

In recent years older women's resilience as well as their vulnerability to social, economic, and health problems have been increasingly recognized, primarily as the result of the educational and advocacy efforts of such interest groups as the Older Women's League (OWL). Although the women's movement of the 1970s tended to focus on issues specific to young women, younger feminists are aligning themselves with efforts to influence older women's economic and social situations. Women of all ages have become more aware of their interdependence as both the primary recipients and providers of long-term care, and of the potential power of age-integrated women's organizations. Young and old women are beginning to unite around issues of caregiving, for example, pressing for unpaid, job-guaranteed leave for the care of both dependent parents and newborn children through the Family and Medical Leave Act that was passed in 1992. Women are typically caregivers throughout their lives, whether as daughters, daughters-in-law, wives, mothers, or staff members within public social service agencies, nursing homes, and hospitals. Consistent with the feminist perspective described in Chapter 8, which emphasizes the interrelationships between women's public and private lives, women's roles as unpaid caregivers and as underpaid employees are interconnected and influence all aspects of their lives. Feminist and postmodern researchers have emphasized how women's unpaid and undervalued work as family caregivers, along with their employment in low-status, low-paid jobs, result in economic insecurity in old age, with consequent negative effects on their health status and health and long-term care options.

OLDER WOMEN'S ECONOMIC STATUS

As described in Chapter 11, women age 65 and over account for nearly 75 percent of the older poor population. They thus form one of the poorest groups in our society, with nearly 16 percent of them living in poverty compared to 9 percent of men, representing the feminization of poverty across the life span and into old age. With less than one in ten women over age 65 currently in the labor force, the median annual income of older women is approximately 58 percent that of older men (Hobbs and Damon, 1996). Furthermore, older men are three times as likely as older women to be financially well off, with incomes of $20,000 or more, and this difference persists even among employed women (Costello and Krimgold, 1996; U.S. Bureau of the Census, 1996). While, on average, women's wages peak at age 44 before beginning to decline, men's median earnings continue to climb until age 55. Although older women have less education and employment experience than both men and younger women, these differences do not completely account for gender-based inequities in wages, which persist even among those with educational levels similar to their male peers (Ovrebo and Minkler, 1993).

Women currently and continuously married to the same man receive more retirement income than women who have experienced widowhood or divorce (DeViney and Solomon, 1995). Accordingly, unmarried women living alone, ethnic minority women, and those aged 75 and over are especially likely to be poor. The poverty rate among unmarried older women living alone, for example, is about 25 percent compared to less than 6 percent of older married women or men, and seven out of ten poor older women live alone. Over 66 percent of older African American women not living with family and 61 percent of older Hispanic women living alone have incomes below the poverty level (Smith, 1997; National Policy and Resource Center on Women and Aging, 1996). Figure 14.1 reflects the disparities of median income by gender and race. The greater likelihood that old women will be poor compared to their male counterparts tends to be true of most other industrialized societies. In addition, the poverty rate increases with age for all women age 75 and over, to nearly 52 percent of white women, 42 percent of Indian, Eskimo, and Aleut women, over 50 percent of African American women, 37 percent of Mexican American and Puerto Rican women, and 37 percent of Asian and Pacific Islander women (Hobbs and Damon, 1996). These

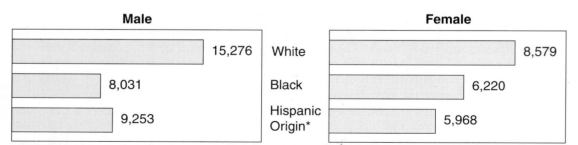

FIGURE 14.1 Median Income of Persons 65 Years and Over by Sex and Race: 1992

*Hispanic Origin may be of any race

SOURCE: U.S. Bureau of the Census, *Money Income of Households, Families, and Persons in the United States: 1992*, Current Population Reports, P60–184, U.S. Government Printing Office, Washington, DC, 1993, Table 26.

figures may not reveal the extent of poverty among single older women, primarily widows, who are not counted as poor, despite their low income, because they may live in a household headed by a younger person whose income is above the poverty line. When these hidden poor are taken into account, over 55 percent of older women are estimated to be poor. In addition, old women are more likely than old men to be "near poor" or slightly above the official poverty line (National Policy and Resource Center on Women and Aging, 1996).

As noted above, gender differences in employment history, career interruptions, types of occupations, earnings, and retirement circumstances all contribute to older women's higher rates of poverty and near-poverty (Moen, 1996). A primary reason for their economic vulnerability is that most women of this current cohort aged 65 and over did not work consistently for pay, largely because they were socialized to marry, have children, and depend on their husbands for economic support. Their labor-force participation rate was 9.7 percent in 1950, rose slightly in the 1950s, and then dropped to 7.8 percent in 1983. When they were employed, women tended to be concentrated in low-paying clerical or service positions without adequate pensions. Currently those who try to enter the labor market after age 40 are likely to encounter discrimination and a growing earnings gap from their male counterparts. Although older African American women are more likely to have been employed during their youth than their white counterparts, their rates of labor-force participation throughout their lives are not significantly higher; and they are most likely to have worked in low-paying jobs (U.S. Bureau of the Census, 1996). Generally dependent on men for both their income and their retirement benefits, most women of previous generations, especially those caring for children and other relatives, lacked the means to build up their economic security for old age.

A deleterious consequence of such dependency is that when women become widowed or divorced, they frequently lose their primary source of income. With over 60 percent of older women living without a spouse, many women face old age

without pension income, particularly if their husbands retired before the 1984 Retirement Eligibility Act and did not select survivors' benefits (Costello and Krimgold, 1996). In fact, the economic gap between married and widowed older women is increasing, especially among the oldest-old. The median income of widowed women is approximately 76 percent that of widowed men, since men are more likely to retain pension incomes through current earnings after their wives die (U.S. Senate Special Committee on Aging, 1992). Of those eligible for pension benefits, less than 60 percent of widows receive them in full, oftentimes because of misinformation about how to access these funds.

At age 65, widows can receive full Social Security benefits based on their husband's earnings or their own, whichever is larger. However, because most women aged 60 and over are unemployed, the majority opt for reduced benefits at age 62, an amount about 28.5 percent lower than what she would have received if her husband had lived to retire at age 65. Widowed women receive an average of 60 percent of their income from Social Security (Costello and Krimgold, 1996). This monthly income is barely adequate, even for women who support only themselves and their homes. Widowhood has been found to reduce living standards by 18 percent, on average, and to push 10 percent of women into poverty whose incomes were above the poverty line prior to widowhood (Bound, Duncan, Laren, and Oleinick, 1991).

Older women are also not immune to the growing divorce rate. Sixteen percent of divorces occur among women age 45 and over, and 1.3 percent occur among those age 65 and above; these rates continue to increase (AARP, 1991). Older divorced women may experience a lower standard of living than do widows, with the majority lacking alimony payments and less than 50 percent receiving property settlements (Uhlenberg, Cooney, and Boyd, 1990). Further compounding the problem for divorced women is the Social Security regulation that a marriage of less than 9 years' duration does not allow for the payment of a divorced spouse's Social Security benefits. Upon retirement, divorced wives married for at least 10 years are entitled to a benefit amount of 50 percent of their ex-husbands' benefits. However, they are not eligible until the former husband reaches age 62, regardless of whether he has retired. Divorced and separated women are more likely to be employed out of economic necessity than are married women. Remarriage tends to be the most effective route out of post-divorce poverty, but with increasing age and number of children, the rate of remarriage declines (MacLean, 1991).

Although not all old women are poor, those who rely primarily on their own resources are likely to have fewer assets such as savings, to have lower lifetime earnings, to depend on Social Security as their sole source of income, and to receive low benefits as retirees or disabled workers. While 95 percent of women receive Social Security, only 38 percent have income from interest or dividends, 28 percent from pensions or annuities, and 13 percent from earnings (Schwenk, 1992). This pattern holds true across widowed, divorced, and never-married women, as illustrated in Table 14.1. Even though they form 60 percent of Social Security beneficiaries, older women are three times more likely than their male peers to receive only the minimum benefits. Yet, a person who receives only So-

cial Security income is seven times more likely to be poor than one who also has wage and salary income (Older Women's League, 1990).

A number of political, social, and economic factors underlie these low Social Security benefit levels. One factor that affects both men and women age 70 and over is that the Social Security program was not established until 1935; thus, there are relatively fewer years upon which to base benefits for the cohort of older people today. An additional handicap for women is that they are more likely than men to have interrupted their employment for marriage and childrearing. Women of the current older cohort generally worked until marriage or the birth of children and then withdrew from the paid labor force, either permanently or until their children were grown. They often assumed their first full-time job on the average of 5 years later than male workers. Even after becoming employed, they are more likely than their male counterparts to leave jobs to assume caregiving responsibilities, either for older generations or for a spouse, and usually not by choice (Kingson and O'Grady-LeShane, 1993). As noted by the late Tish Sommers, the first president of the Older Women's League, "Motherhood and apple pie may be sacred, but neither guarantees economic security in old age"(1975).

TABLE 14.1 Sources and Distribution of Income among Older Women

INCOME SOURCE	AVERAGE INCOME[1]			PERCENT RECEIVING INCOME		
	WIDOWED	DIVORCED	NEVER MARRIED	WIDOWED	DIVORCED	NEVER MARRIED
Before-tax income	$9,777	$11,077	$12,415	100	100	100
Social Security and Railroad Retirement	5,855	5,354	5,658	96	93	85
Pensions and annuities	1,272	2,033	3,429	26	33	45
Interest and dividends	1,648	629	2,340	37	35	51
Earnings	754	2,251	935	12	24	10
Other	248	810	53	19	32	6

[1]Calculated for all women 65 years or older living alone, with and without the income source.

The average woman now spends nearly one-half of her life fulfilling the role of family care-giver to dependents, leaving the paid labor force to provide care for 11.5 years compared to 1.3 years for her male counterparts (Older Women's League, 1990). For many women, such discontinuities carry severe economic costs that are cumulative, since years of lower or no earnings reduce their Social Security benefits. Homemakers have no individual eligibility and no credits to add to their employment credits, and cannot receive disability supports on their own, despite the economic value of their household labor to their families. If they left the work force to care for a husband during his final illness, this amounts to early retirement, especially given the low probability of re-employment among older workers. They have lost not only wages but also the opportunity to develop higher earnings profiles and subsequently greater retirement benefits (Moen, 1996).

Another factor affecting Social Security benefits for women is that those who are employed tend to have worked fewer years and to be concentrated in part-time, short-term, or irregular and poorly paid jobs (Moen, 1996). Even when they have been employed throughout their lives, most women have received inadequate salaries, generally in low-status service, clerical, and retail-sales jobs. As a result, they frequently find that their husbands' Social Security benefits are higher than benefits based on their own employment records. In such instances, women who have been employed all their lives in low-paying jobs are not much better off at retirement than women who have never worked for pay outside the home. As an example, in 1970, women's total average retirement benefits were 70 percent that of their male counterparts; in 1990, despite more women in the paid work force, the figure increased to only 73 percent (Older Women's League, 1990). Because of fewer years of employment and consequent lower retirement benefits compared to men, older women may find themselves forced to continue working well beyond the age at which they would choose to re-tire (Herz, 1988). Women who in their youth cared for children and parents thus frequently find themselves alone and with less than subsistence income in old age. These dire economic conditions have prompted a number of proposals to ensure homemakers' economic security in old age, such as paying them Social Security or some other form of income, but none of these proposals has received widespread Congressional support. The likelihood of such endorsement in the future is small, considering current legislative efforts to reduce federal spending.

Women are also less likely to have private pensions than men, both because of their concentration in low-paying positions and their shorter work careers, and because mandatory pension laws were not in effect when many women of this cohort were employed (i.e., in the 1920's and 1930's). As discussed in Chapter 11, pension plans reward the long-term steady worker with high earnings and job stability, a pattern that tends to be more characteristic of men than of women who have interrupted their careers to marry, rear children, and perhaps care for older relatives. This continues to be the trend even among the current cohort of women. Over 40 percent of men are covered by private pensions, compared with fewer than 20 percent of women who have been employed. Women with pensions receive approximately half the benefit income of men because of salary differentials during their working years (Older Women's League, 1995). A woman whose family role resulted in economic dependence on her husband can benefit from his private pension only if he is covered by one, does not die before retirement age, stays married to her, and is willing to reduce his monthly benefits in order to provide her with a survivor's annuity. Given the economic vicissitudes of aging, most older men choose higher monthly benefits rather than survivors' benefits. Such a choice can be detrimental to older women, since, as noted earlier, most wives outlive their husbands by an average of 8 years. Fortunately, pension provisions enacted by Congress in 1980 will benefit older women by shortening the time it takes to earn a pension and improving coverage for lower income workers, for those who begin work after age 60, and for those who continue to work after age 65. However, most of these provisions are effective for pension plans that began in January 1989, and thus do not affect the current cohort of older women. In addition, federal laws designed to provide protection to spouses of private pension plans do not apply to state government pension plans. As a result, 26 states do not have a **"spousal consent" requirement** before a plan participant can waive survivor benefits. Thus, a wife may discover only after the death of her husband that she will no longer be entitled to pension benefits which were paid prior to her husband's death (AARP, 1994). Another limitation is that most policies to address women's special vulnerability as non-employed or late-entry workers have focused on improving the financial well-being of older women in danger of being impoverished, not those who have been poor throughout life.

Older women who have never married may be in better financial condition than their divorced or widowed counterparts. They tend to have a higher average annual income than widowed and divorced women. They are also far more likely to derive their income from pensions and annuities, as well as from interest and dividends. In addition, never-married women spend less on housing and health care than do widowed women, in spite of their comparable ages (Schwenk, 1992).

The economic outlook for women in the future remains bleak. One reason for this is that when middle-aged and older women are employed, they are more likely to hold part-time and poorly paid jobs in the service sector. In fact, more than 66 percent of working women aged 55 and over were employed in three traditionally female jobs: sales; administrative support, including clerical; and services (Quadagno and Hardy, 1996). It is predicted that by the year 2020, poverty will remain widespread among older women living alone—those who are divorced, widowed, or never married—while Social Security and pension systems will have practically eroded poverty among older men and couples (Older Women's League, 1990). Older women without private pensions and whose Social Security income falls below the poverty line must rely on Supplemental Security Income (SSI). In fact, women comprise nearly 75 percent of older SSI recipients (Older Women's League, 1995). For women who value economic self-sufficiency, dependency on the government for such support can be stigmatizing.

In summary, traditional family caregiving roles of women tend to result in discontinuous employment work histories. This pattern, combined with limited pension opportunities and lower Social Security benefits, produces a double jeopardy for women's economic status in old age. Unfortunately, most changes in Social Security and pension laws have improved the benefits of women as dependents rather than as employees. As discussed in the following section, the disadvantaged economic position of old women also increases their health risks.

OLDER WOMEN'S HEALTH STATUS

As noted in Chapter 4, women may live longer than men, but they have higher rates of illness, physician visits, and drug-prescription use as a result of more acute illnesses and non-fatal chronic conditions (Moen, 1996). As described in Chapter 4, older people who are poor, represented primarily by women and minorities, tend to be less healthy than higher-income older adults. Their living conditions are not conducive to good health. Compared to their wealthier peers, low-income elders are more likely to be living alone, to have inadequate diets, to have less access to information about how to maintain their health, and to have fewer dental visits and physician contacts per year (Barer, 1994). Since older women, especially the divorced and widowed, predominate among the older poor, women's health status is more frequently harmed by the adverse conditions associated with poverty than is men's. In turn, the cost of poor health can deplete the limited resources of the low-income poor.

Less Access to Health Insurance

Previous family and work patterns affect older women's access to adequate health care and health maintenance information. Specifically, the work place determines such access through opportunities to enroll in group insurance plans. Most insurance systems exclude the occupation of homemaker, except as a dependent. More women than men lack health insurance. This is often because women have never been or have sporadically been employed. Low-income divorced and/or widowed women, unable to rely on their husbands' insurance, are especially disadvantaged. Divorced women are about twice as likely to lack health insurance as married women, and are more likely than widows to be uninsured (Costello and Krimgold, 1996). Some uninsured women gamble on staying healthy until qualifying for Medicare coverage at age 65. Since the incidence of chronic diseases is higher among older women than among men, many women do not win this gamble. Yet they may not qualify for Medicaid at an earlier age. The late Tish Sommers, founder of the Older Women's League, represented this group of women. When she was diagnosed with cancer in her late fifties, she was too young to qualify for Medicare, too sick to obtain private insurance, yet fell just above the income limits for Medicaid, and, as a divorcee, unable to turn to her former husband's insurance. Groups such as the Older Women's League have succeeded in advocating for **conversion laws** that require insurance companies to allow widowed and divorced women to remain in their spouse's group insurance for up to 3 years. Even with adequate health insurance, older women spend more of their annual income for out-of-pocket health care costs.

Because of their lower socioeconomic status, older women are more likely than men to depend on Medicaid (Costello and Krimgold, 1996). An insidious negative effect of this dependency is that health care providers, fearing financial losses, are often unwilling to accept Medicaid patients, making it difficult for older women to obtain adequate care. Male-female differences in longevity, marital status, and income are central in assessing the impact of recent increases in Medicaid co-payments and deductibles. Women outnumber men two to one among frail elders, for whom health and long-term care use and costs are greatest. This means that, as Medicaid costs are shifted to the patient, more low-income frail women will be unable to afford health care. For example, co-payment provisions in Medicaid may force some women to choose between prescriptions and groceries, or between clinic visits and the bus fare to get there.

Higher Incidence of Chronic Health Problems

Limited insurance options and greater dependence on Medicaid are especially problematic because 85 percent of older women have some kind of chronic disease or disability. Although men tend to experience fewer daily aches and pains than do women, when they do become ill, they are more likely to face life-threatening acute conditions and to require hospitalization. In contrast, women are more likely to experience the disabling effects of chronic conditions. These differences in types of chronic health problems may be one reason why women live longer than men, even though they are less healthy (Costello and Krimgold, 1996). As discussed in Chapter 4, older women experience arthritis, hypertension, strokes, diabetes, most digestive and urinary problems (except ulcer and hernia), incontinence, most types of orthopedic problems, cataracts, and depression more frequently than do older men.

Contrary to common perceptions that men are at higher risk of heart attacks than are women, cardiovascular disease is the number-one killer for both men and women, although men experience the symptoms of coronary heart disease at younger ages. The rate of heart disease triples for women age 65 and over, while remaining nearly equal for men and women between the ages of 45 and 64. Coronary heart disease kills five times as many women as breast cancer does. This is because, as noted in Chapter 4, women lose the advantage of estrogen's protection against heart disease after menopause and have a longer life expectancy than do men after ages 45 to 55.

Women also face health problems specifically associated with their reproductive functions, such as breast, cervical, and uterine cancers—all of which have increased in recent years—as well as high-risk complications from hysterectomies. Of women with breast cancer, 75 percent are over age 50 (National Policy and Resource Center on Women and Aging, 1997). In the past 25 years, the chances of a woman developing breast cancer have grown from 1 in 16 to 1 in 9, while prevention, diagnosis, and treatment have lagged. One fortunate change, taken by Congress in 1990, was to include **mammography** screening as a biennial Medicare benefit; in addition, the 1997 changes in Medicare provided for fuller reimbursement for mammograms. Yet, physicians frequently do not refer older women for mammography even though both the American Cancer Society and the National Cancer Institute recommend yearly mammograms after age 50 (Leonard, 1991). In fact, in 1995, only 50 percent of women were getting regular mammography checkups in accordance with established medical guidelines. One reason for this low compliance rate is that many older women think that they will not get breast cancer because of their age. In reality, the longer a woman lives, the more likely she is to develop breast cancer. A similar pattern can be seen where women over age 60 who are most at risk of cancers of the reproductive system are least likely to have annual pap smears (National Policy and Resource Center on Women and Aging, 1997).

As noted above, although women suffer from more chronic health conditions, most of these are not life-threatening; they do, however, interfere with daily functioning and require frequent physician contacts. For example, over 50 percent of women age 70 to 74 find it difficult or impossible to lift or carry 25 pounds, and 60 percent of women over age 65 have been screened out of random public physical fitness testing for reasons of

health risk. This lack of basic strength increases the likelihood of falls (O'Brien and Vertinsky, 1991). On the other hand, the NIH Women's Health and Aging Study found that the majority of women respondents, despite high levels of disability, engage in some form of physical activity, typically related to household chores (Simonsick, Phillip, Skinner, Davis, and Kasper, 1995). Furthermore, women who begin an exercise program even in their 70s and 80s can improve their fitness and strength.

Compared to their male counterparts, older women also experience more injuries and more days of restricted activity and bed disability. These measures are generally indicators of chronic disorders, such as high blood pressure and arthritis, although it may be that they reflect women's greater readiness to take curative action and spend more time in bed recuperating when they are ill. Among people aged 85 and over, gender differences in patterns of illness become even more striking, with 65 percent of women age 85 and over likely to enter a nursing home compared to 50 percent of men (National Policy and Resource Center on Women and Aging, 1997; Hobbs and Damon, 1996). There are, of course, several factors besides health status that may account for such differences. As discussed in Chapter 9, old men are more likely to be married, with wives to care for them at home instead of being placed in a nursing home. Women over age 75, on the other hand, have few available resources for home-based care, and are often unable to afford private home health services. In addition, as noted earlier, men who survive to age 75 and older are the healthiest and hardiest of their cohort.

Osteoporosis

As noted in Chapter 4, the majority of older people with osteoporosis are women. In fact, 20 percent of women age 50 have osteoporosis in both their hips and spine (Speroff et al, 1996; Bush et al., 1996). Women begin losing bone mass between 30 and 35 years of age, resulting in a 35 percent reduction in their bone mineral content by

65 years of age and 50 percent by age 75, with a consequent increase in the risk of bone fracture. The higher incidence of wrist, spinal, and hip fractures related to postmenopausal osteoporosis is one reason for the greater number of injuries and days of restricted activity among older women. Spinal fractures frequent and severe enough to cause dowager's hump (loss of up to 8 inches in height) occur in 5 to 7 percent of women. It is estimated that 75 percent of postmenopausal women will fracture a hip and 25 to 40 percent will suffer spine shortening and often painful vertebral fractures (Speroff, Rowan, Symons, Genant, and Wilburn, 1996). The incidence of hip fractures in older women doubles every 5 years after the age of 60, and is higher for white women than African American women (National Policy and Resource Center on Women and Aging, 1996). The threat of hip fractures can create numerous fears among older women—of additional falls, further fractures, hospitalization, institutionalization, loss of independence, and death. As a result, an older woman's social world may become increasingly circumscribed, with accompanying feelings of isolation and loneliness. Strategies that prevent falls and minimize injuries have been found to be effective, as noted in Chapter 4.

The case for and against hormone replacement therapy was discussed in Chapter 4. To briefly recap, HRT has been found to actually increase bone mass in the spine and hip, even among women who start using it in their sixties. However, women with the greatest bone density in their hips, spines, and wrists also have been found to have the highest incidence of breast cancer, illustrating the ongoing controversy about the risks of estrogen replacement therapy (Speroff et al., 1996). Although women who take estrogen for at least 7 years between menopause and age 75 have been found to reduce their risk of fracture by half during that time, recent studies indicate little difference after age 75, the period when women are most at risk. Fortunately, increasing attention has been given to the prevention and treatment of osteoporosis in recent years, including changes in diet and exercise. However, some of this focus is fostered by the me-

dia and sponsored by drug companies, which may inflate warnings about who is at risk in order to encourage bone-density screening technology and use of new non-hormonal therapies (National Policy and Resource Center, 1996).

Menopause

The physiological changes associated with menopause were discussed in Chapters 3 and 7. Social and cultural attitudes can make menopause troublesome as well, given that many of its associated discomforts result from society's tendency to view menopause as a disease, rather than as a normal biological process. Hence, many women anticipate that depression, loss of sexual desire and sexual attractiveness, and such signs of aging as wrinkled skin and weight gain are inevitable. Contrary to such expectations, menopause is not an illness or a deficiency, and 30 to 50 percent of women have no symptoms as they pass into menopause. It can, however, be a major transition for many women (Barer, 1994). Menopausal symptoms thus provide another example of the interaction of normal physiological changes with psychological conditions and societal expectations.

The culturally prevalent model of menopause as a disease attributes changes to loss of estrogen. When thus defined as a "deficiency disease," a treatment implication is that estrogen must be replaced. Accordingly, the primary medical response to treating symptoms such as hot flashes has been hormone replacement therapy. When menopause is viewed as a normal life transition, however, lower estrogen levels among postmenopausal women can then be considered normal. Recently, many women have been using non-medical approaches to minimize uncomfortable symptoms. These include hypnosis, biofeedback, acupuncture, paced respiration, muscle relaxation techniques, exercise, support groups, herbal remedies, Vitamin E, and diets low in fats and preservatives and high in fiber and calcium.

Although the disease model of menopause links depression with the endocrine changes that occur, depression among postmenopausal women appears to be more closely associated with psychosocial variables, particularly changes in women's roles and relationships, than with physiological factors. Women who have had prior episodes of depression, especially during other periods of hormonal fluctuation (e.g. postpartum depression), those with poor social supports, and those who experience menopause at a younger age are at higher risk, but menopause alone is **not** a risk factor for depression. Health care providers have often treated the symptoms of depression with drugs, including estrogen replacement therapy, or have assumed that middle-aged and older women were "too old" to benefit from therapeutic interventions. More recently, efforts have been made to provide women with ways of exerting control over their lives, such as assertiveness training, and to develop women's counseling and social support interventions as a means of combating depression. Such social support groups have been found to reduce women's feelings of isolation and to enhance their self-esteem and self-control. Increasingly, women find that menopause can bring a renewed sense of living and time for oneself, or what the anthropologist Margaret Mead termed **"postmenopausal zest."**

OLDER WOMEN'S SOCIAL STATUS

Older women's physical and mental health problems are frequently intensified by the greater likelihood of their living alone. For example, old women who live alone are more likely to be diagnosed as malnourished. This is not surprising when the social functions of eating are considered. The older person living alone may derive no pleasure from eating and may skip meals, subsisting instead on such snacks as tea and cookies. The high poverty rates among older women who live alone, as we have seen earlier in this chapter, may also account for their poor eating habits. Even mild nutritional deficiencies may produce

disorientation, confusion, depression, and reduced ability to respond to stress. One result is that a person with few immediate social supports may be less likely to resist infections and viral diseases. Her ability to live in the community may thus be sharply curtailed.

Approximately 42 percent of older women (compared to 17 percent of older men) live alone for nearly one-third of their adult lives, primarily because of widowhood or divorce. Among widowed, divorced, and never-married older women, the percentage living alone increases to 68 percent. At the turn of the century, widows lived alone for 5 to 10 years; now the average is 24 years alone, at the same time that fewer adult children are available to provide care (Huckle, 1991). In fact, only 41 percent of all women aged 65 and over live with their husbands, compared to 77 percent of men, and only 16 percent live with other family members, generally a daughter. Among women aged 75 and over, the percentage living with their husbands drops to less than 25 percent compared to 70 percent of men; and the proportion living alone increases to over 54 percent, a rate at least twice that of their male counterparts (Moen, 1996). However, older ethnic minority divorced and widowed women are more likely to live in extended family households. For example, African American and Mexican American women often extend their households to include children and grandchildren, assuming child care and housekeeping responsibilities into old age (Choi, 1991).

Widowhood

As discussed in Chapter 12, the average age of widowhood for women is 66 years. Because women generally marry men older than themselves, live longer than men, and, in their later years, seldom remarry after the deaths of their husbands, 85 percent of all wives outlive their husbands. Some 52 percent of women aged 65 and over are widowed, in contrast to 14 percent of men in this age group; this gap increases dramatically with age. The expected years of widowhood are far more than the 4-year difference in life expectancy between women and men at these ages. At age 65 a widow can anticipate living another 18 years; at age 70, 11 years; and at age 85, another 9 years. Not surprisingly, after age 85, 66 percent of women live alone (National Policy and Resource Center, 1996). Moreover, this increased time living alone is accompanied by shrinking family size, with fewer children as potential caregivers (Moen, 1996).

As noted previously, the primary negative consequence of widowhood is low socioeconomic status, with nearly 30 percent of older widows living in poverty (Smith, 1997). These economic conditions have numerous social implications: low-income women have fewer options to interact with others, fewer affordable and safe accommodations, and fewer resources to purchase in-home support services. The most negative consequence may be that older women's economic situation precludes continued independent living when health problems arise. Despite these objective disadvantages of widowhood, the "lonely widow" may be a stereotype, and widowhood may not necessarily produce the major, enduring negative emotional effects that typically have been reported (Moen, 1996; Hatch and Bulcroft, 1992).

Divorce

Divorced women are even more vulnerable to social and economic problems. Compared to both their married and widowed peers, divorced women aged 65 and over have been found to have poorer health, lower income and rates of home ownership, higher mortality rates, and lower levels of life satisfaction. Many of the assets that middle-aged and older women have accumulated over the years of marriage are lost in late-life divorce. If divorced earlier in life, the disadvantages of having no financial support and often being employed in low-paying positions may have resulted in a lifetime of marginal economic security (Uhlenberg et al., 1990).

Limited Opportunities to Remarry

Although remarriage may be viewed as a way to ensure economic security, older widowed and divorced women have fewer remarriage options than do their male peers. The primary obstacles to remarriage are the disproportionate number of women to men age 65 and over and the cultural stigma against women marrying younger men. At age 65 and over, remarriage rates are 2 per 1000 for unmarried women compared to 17 per 1000 for unmarried men. The remarriage rate of divorced women age 45 to 60 is less than 3 out of 100 (Uhlenberg et al., 1990). As noted earlier, with the ratio of 80-year-old women to men being three to one, the chances for remarriage decline drastically with age. These differences lead to differential needs for support in the face of failing health; most older men are cared for by their wives, whereas most older women rely on their children, usually daughters, for help and may turn later to paid assistance. As discussed in Chapter 9, women are the primary caregivers of older relatives. Increasingly, adult daughters who assist their widowed mothers are themselves in their sixties and seventies, and are faced with their own physical limitations. One consequence of this pattern is that older women may have to depend more on public support services. They are thus the primary informal providers of care as well as the major users of public services. As invisible laborers, women's work is essential to the health care system and to their relatives' long-term care, but it is not well supported by public policies.

In addition to having high rates of widowhood and increasing rates of divorce, the current cohort of older women have relatively high rates of remaining unmarried throughout their lives (approximately 5 percent for women now in their seventies and eighties). Therefore, a cohort effect also may explain the large numbers of older women living without spouses. Another factor that increases the probability of being alone among this current cohort of older women is that approximately one in five has either been childless throughout her life or has survived her offspring (Saluter, 1994).

The absence of children and spouse also increases the chance of being placed in a nursing home. This suggests that women are more likely to be institutionalized for social rather than medical reasons, and may be inappropriately placed in a nursing home when alternative community supports might have permitted more independent lifestyles. For this reason, as noted in Chapter 10, women form over 70 percent of nursing-home residents, with the majority of them widowed or single, often dependent on Medicaid and lacking family members to assist them either socially or financially. After age 85, 1 in 4 women, especially never-married and widowed women, are in nursing homes (Wiener and Illston, 1996).

In general, older women have fewer economic but more social resources and richer, more intimate relationships than do older men. Men tend to have larger non-kin networks, perhaps as a result of employment, but are less resourceful in planning social get-togethers and building social networks that substitute for the sociability in marriage (Moen, 1996; Barer, 1994). Widowed women, in particular, tend to have more frequent and intimate contacts with friends (Hatch and Bulcroft, 1992). Even when their friends die, women generally establish new relationships, exchanging affection and material assistance outside their families, although they may not feel that such relationships should be called upon to provide them with secure care. Instead, they value the mutuality of their friendships and do not want to become dependent for personal care upon friends (Roberto, 1996; Rubenstein, Alexander, Goodman, and Lubovsky, 1991). Support groups for widows and family caregivers build on such reciprocal exchange relations among peers. With age, some women first be-

Group exercise offers physical and social benefits.

come comfortable with being open about their lesbianism and their strong emotional bonds with other women, though they may face rejection from their adult children when they do so (Fullmer, 1995). One function of the affirmation of women's competencies by the women's movement has been to encourage them to support each other rather than depend on men, as evidenced by the growth of shared households, older women's support and advocacy groups, and intergenerational alliances.

FUTURE DIRECTIONS

Since women's socioeconomic status compounds most of the problems they face in old age, fundamental changes are needed to remove inequities in the workplace, Social Security, and pension systems. Most such changes, however, will benefit future generations of older women, rather than the current cohort, which was socialized for work and family roles that no longer prevail. For example, recent efforts in some states to assure that women and men earn equal pay for jobs of comparable economic worth and to remove other salary inequities may mean that future generations of older women will have retirement benefits based on a lifetime of more adequate earnings, and will have more experience in handling finances. Some businesses and government agencies have initiated more flexible work arrangements with full benefits, which will allow men and women to share employment and family responsibilities more equitably. When such options exist, women may have fewer years of zero earnings to be calculated into their Social Security benefits, and will be more likely to hold jobs covered by private pensions. Even so, it is predicted that 60 percent of women in the year 2030 will still have had 5 or more years of zero earnings averaged into the calculation of their Social Security benefits, widening the current gap between older women living alone and all other groups (Crystal, 1996). This is in large part due to the fact that despite three decades of legislation, women have not achieved equality in the work force. Women remain disproportionately in the secondary labor market, marked by low wages, few benefits, part-time employment, and little job security (Holstein, 1993). Even the entrance of more women into previously male-dominated positions has not resulted in a significant restructuring of the distribution of responsibilities within families, with women still responsible for the majority of child care and housework (Moen, 1996).

Changes in Social Security that would benefit women workers have been proposed by a number of federal studies and commissions. The current Social Security system is based on an outmoded model of lifelong marriage, in which one spouse is the paid worker and the other is the homemaker. As the prior discussion of divorce and changing work patterns suggests, this model no longer accommodates the emerging diversity of employment and family roles. Nor, for that matter, has this model really represented the diversity of American families. The most commonly discussed remedy is **earnings sharing**, whereby each partner in marriage is entitled to a separate Social Security account, regardless of which spouse is employed in the paid labor force. Covered earnings would be divided between two spouses, with one-half credited to each spouse's account. Credits for homemaking, benefits for

widows under age 62, full benefits for widows after age 65, and the option of collecting benefits as both worker and wife have also been discussed by senior-citizen advocacy groups and by some legislators. Given the Congressional intent to reduce federal spending, the likelihood of any such changes being instituted in the next few years is small. Pension reforms have also been passed on the federal level that would increase by more than 20 percent the number of women covered by private pensions, through a reduction of the amount of time required for vesting. In the long run, changes are needed in society's view of work throughout the life cycle, so that men and women may share more equitably in caregiving and employment responsibilities. At the same time, employers must recognize that skills gained through homemaking and voluntary activity are legitimate and transferable to the marketplace. As discussed in Chapters 9 and 11, the ways in which women contribute to society through their volunteerism, caregiving, housekeeping responsibilities, and informal helping of others also need to be recognized under a broad concept of productivity, rather than equating productivity with only paid work (Holstein, 1993).

An important improvement in the quality of older women's lives is that more women of all ages are increasingly supporting one another, as illustrated by the intergenerational advocacy efforts of the Older Women's League. Another promising change is the growth of social support groups among old women. Groups of older widows and women caregivers have been found to be effective in reducing women's isolation. They have encouraged group members to meet their own needs and have expanded women's awareness of public services to which they are entitled. This function of educating and politicizing older women has also helped many to see the societal causes of the difficulties that they have experienced as individuals. Awareness of external causes of their problems may also serve to bring together for common action women of diverse ages, ethnic minority backgrounds, socioeconomic classes, and sexual orientation. As women unite to work for change, they can make further progress in reducing the disadvantages of their economic and social position.

Summary and implications

Older women are the fastest growing segment of our population, making the aging society primarily female. In addition, the problems of aging are increasingly the problems of women. Threats to Social Security, inadequate health and long-term care, and insufficient pensions are issues for women of all ages. Increasingly, older women are not only the recipients of social and health services, but also are cared for by other women, who are unpaid daughters and daughters-in-law, or staff within public social services, nursing homes, and hospitals.

Women's family caregiving roles are interconnected with their economic, social, and health status. Women who devoted their lives to attending to the needs of children, spouses, or older relatives often face years of living alone on low or poverty-level incomes, with inadequate health care, in substandard housing, and with little chance for employment to supplement their limited resources. Women face more problems in old age, not only because they live longer than their male peers, but also because, as unpaid or underpaid caregivers with discontinuous employment histories, they have not accrued adequate retirement or health care benefits. If they have depended on their husbands for economic security, divorce or widowhood increases their risks of poverty. As one of the poorest groups in our society, women account for nearly three-fourths of the older poor. The incidence of problems associated with poverty increases dramatically for older women living alone, for ethnic minority women, and for those age 75 and over. Frequently outliving their children and husbands, they have no one to care for them and are more likely than their male counterparts to be in nursing homes.

On the other hand, many women show remarkable resilience in the face of adversity. Fortunately, the number of exceptions to patterns of economic deprivation and social isolation is growing. With their lifelong experiences of caring for others, for example, women tend to be skilled at forming and sustaining friendships with each other, which provide them with social support and intimacy. Recently, increasing attention has been paid to older women's capacity for change and to their strengths, largely because of efforts of national advocacy groups such as the Older Women's League. Current efforts to improve the employment and educational opportunities available to younger women will undoubtedly mean improved economic, social, and health status for future generations of women.

Glossary

conversion laws these require insurance companies to allow widowed and divorced women to remain on their spouses' group insurance for up to 3 years

earnings sharing proposed change in Social Security whereby each partner in a marriage is entitled to a separate Social Security account, regardless of employment status

mammography an X ray technique for the detection of breast tumors before they can be seen or felt

postmenopausal zest renewed sense of life and time for oneself that many women experience at menopause

postmenopause in women, referring to the period of life after menopause

pousal consent requirement federal law requires that a spouse must consent to or agree to waiving survivor's benefits; not true of state government pension plans

References

American Association of Retired Persons (AARP). *A profile of older Americans, 1990.* Washington, DC: AARP, 1991.

American Association of Retired Persons (AARP). *Falling short: A 50-state survey of spousal rights under state pension plans.* Washington, DC: AARP, 1994.

Barer, B. M. Men and women aging differently. *International Journal on Aging and Human Development*, 1994, *38,* 29–40.

Bound, J., Duncan, G., Laren, D. S., and Oleinick, L. Poverty dynamics in widowhood. *Journals of Gerontology,* 1991, *46,* S115–124.

Bush, T. L., Wells, H. B., James, M. K., Barrett-Connor, E., Marcus, R., Greendale, G., Hunsberger, S., and McGowan, J. Effects of hormone replacement therapy on endometrial histology in post-menopausal women: The postmenopausal estrogen/progestin interventions (PEPI) trial. *Journal of the American Medical Association,* 1996, *275,* 370–375.

Choi, N. Racial differences in the determinants of living arrangements of widowed and divorced elderly women. *The Gerontologist,* 1991, *31,* 496–504.

Costello, C., & Krimgold, B. K. (Eds.). *The American woman 1996–97: Women and work.* New York: W. W. Norton & Company, 1996.

Crystal, S. Economic status of the elderly. In R. H. Binstock and L. K. George (Eds.), *Handbook of aging and the social sciences,* (4th ed.). San Diego, CA: Academic Press, 1996.

DeViney, S., and Solomon, J. C. Gender differences in retirement income: A comparison of theoretical explanations. *Journal of Women and Aging,* 1995, *7,* 83–100.

Diczfalusy, E., and Bengiano, G. Women and the third and fourth age. *International Journal of Gynecology and Obstetrics,* 1997, *56,* 177–188.

Fullmer, E. M. Challenging biases against families of older gays and lesbians. In G. C. Smith, S. Tobin, E. A. Robertson-Tchabo, and P. Power (Eds.), *Strengthening aging families: Diversity in practice and policy.* Thousand Oaks, CA: Sage, 1995.

Gottlieb, N. Families, work, and the lives of older women. In J. D. Garner and S. Mercer (Eds.), *Women as they age: Challenge, opportunity, and triumph.* New York: Haworth Press, 1989.

Guralnik, J. M., Fried, L. P., Simonsick, E. M., Kasper, J. D., and Lafferty, M. E. (Eds.). *The women's health and aging study: Health and social characteristics of older women with disabilities.* Bethesda, MD: National Institute on Aging, 1995.

Hatch, L., and Bulcroft, K. Contact with friends in later life: Disentangling the effects of gender and mental status. *Journal of Marriage and the Family,* 1992, *54,* 222–232.

Herz, D. Bureau of Labor Statistics. Employment characteristics of older women, 1987. *Monthly Labor Review* (September, 1988), 3.

Hess, B. Gender and aging: The demographic parameters. In Robert Enright (Ed.), *Perspectives in Social Gerontology.* Boston: Allyn and Bacon, 1994.

Hess, B., and Waring, J. Family relationships of older women: A women's issue. In E. Markson (Ed.), *Older women.* Lexington, MA.: Lexington Books, 1983.

Hobbs, F. and Damon, B. L. *65+ in the United States,* Washington, DC: U.S. Department of Commerce, Bureau of the Census, Current Population Reports, 1996.

Holstein, M. Women's lives, women's work: Productivity, gender, and aging. In S. A. Bass, F. G. Caro, and Y-P Chen (Eds.), *Achieving a productive aging society.* Westport, CT: Auburn House, 1993.

Huckle, P. *Tish Sommers, activist and the founder of the Older Women's League.* Knoxville: The University of Tennessee Press, 1991.

Kingson, E. R., and O'Grady-LeShane, R. The effects of caregiving on women's Social Security benefits. *The Gerontologist,* 1993, *33,* 230–239.

Leonard, F. The curse. *The Owl Observer,* September/October, 1991, 7.

MacLean, M. *Surviving divorce: Women's resources after separation.* New York: MacMillan, 1991.

Moen, P. Gender, age and the life course. In R. H. Binstock and L. K. George (Eds.), *Handbook of aging and the social sciences,* (4th ed.). San Diego, CA: Academic Press, 1996.

Moen, P., Dempster-McClain, D., and Williams, Jr. R. M. *Pathways to women's well-being in later adulthood: A life course perspective.* Unpublished manuscript, 1995.

National Policy and Resource Center on Women and Aging. Osteoporosis. *The Women and Aging Letter,* March 1996, 1, 8.

National Policy and Resource Center on Women and Aging. Half of America's women are not getting the mammograms they should. *The Women and Aging Letter,* May 1997, 1, 8.

National Policy and Resource Center on Women and Aging. *Planning for retirement security.* Waltham, MA: Brandeis University, May 1996, 1, 1–6.

O'Brien, S., and Vertinsky, P. Unfit survivors: Exercise as a resource for aging women. *The Gerontologist,* 1991, *31,* 347–348.

Older Women's League. *Heading for hardship: Retirement income for American women in the next century.* Washington, DC: Older Women's League, 1990.

Older Women's League. *The path to poverty: An analysis of women's retirement income.* Washington, DC: Older Women's League, 1995.

Ovrebo, B., and Minkler, M. The lives of older women: Perspectives for political economy and the humanities. In T. R. Cole, W. A. Achenbaum, P. L. Jakobi, and R. Kastenbaum (Eds.), *Voices and visions of aging: Toward a critical gerontology.* NY: Springer, 1993.

Quadagno, J., and Hardy, M. Work and retirement. In R. H. Binstock and L. K. George (Eds.), *Handbook of aging and the social sciences,* (4th ed.). San Diego, CA: Academic Press, 1996.

Roberto, K. A. Friendships between older women: Interactions and reactions. *Relationships between women in later life.* New York: The Haworth Press, 1996, 55–69.

Rubenstein, R., Alexander, B., Goodman, M., and Lubovsky, M. Key relationships of never-married, childless older women: A cultural analysis. *Journals of Gerontology,* 1991, 46, S270–277.

Saluter, A. *Marital status and living arrangements:* March 1994. Washington, DC: U.S. Bureau of the Census, Current Population Reports, Population Characteristics, 1994.

Schwenk, F. N. Income and expenditures of older, widowed, divorced, and never-married women who live alone. *Family Economics Review,* 1992, 5, 2–8.

Simonsick, E. M., Phillip, C. L., Skinner, E. A., Davis, D., and Kasper, J. D. The daily lives of disabled older women. In J. Guralnik, L. P. Fried, and E. M. Simonsick (Eds.), *The women's health and aging study: Characteristics of older women with disability.* Bethesda, MD: National Institute on Aging, NIH Publication No. 95–4009, 1995.

Smith, J. *The changing economic circumstances of the elderly: Income, wealth and Social Security.* Maxwell Center for Policy Research, Syracuse, NY, 1997.

Speroff, L., Rowan, J., Symons, J., Genant, H., and Wilborn, W. The comparative effect on bone density, endometrium, and lipids of continuous hormones as replacement therapy (CHART Study): A randomized controlled trial. *Journal of the American Medical Association,* 1996, 276, 1397–1403.

Uhlenberg, P., Cooney, T., and Boyd, R. Divorce for women after midlife. *Journals of Gerontology,* 1990, 45, S3–11.

U.S. Bureau of the Census *Statistical abstract of the United States, 116th edition.* 1996. Washington, DC: U.S. Department of Commerce, 1996.

U.S. Senate Special Committee on Aging. *Aging America: Trends and projections, 1991 edition.* Washington, DC: U.S. Department of Health and Human Services, 1992.

Wiener, J. M., and Illston, L. H. Financing and organization of health care. In R. H. Binstock and L. K. George (Eds.), *Handbook of aging and the social sciences* (4th ed.). San Diego, CA: Academic Press, 1996.

THE SOCIETAL CONTEXT OF AGING

The final section of this book examines aging and older people from the broader context of society. The values and beliefs that policy makers and voters hold toward a particular group or topic are often the basis on which policies are made. To the extent that these policies also are grounded in knowledge, they can aid the status of that group. On the other hand, policies that are based solely on stereotypes or generalizations about a segment of society may be inadequate and even harmful.

Throughout this book, we have reviewed the current state of knowledge about the physiological, psychological, and social aspects of aging. We have examined variations among older ethnic minority groups, between older men and women, and among other segments of the older population. The diversity in processes of aging has been emphasized. Differences in lifestyle, work patterns, and family and social experiences in earlier periods of life can have a significant impact on health and social functioning in old age. As a result, there are greater variations among the older population than among members of any other segment of society. As Chapter 15 points out, increasingly, this

diversity is a factor affecting the development of social policies and programs.

Some age-based programs such as Medicare are directed toward all people who fulfill age criteria, whereas others such as Supplemental Security Income (SSI) and food stamps are based on financial need. The eligibility criteria and services provided through these programs and policies are often determined by the prevailing social values and by those of the political party and presidential administration in power. These values, in turn, reflect society's attitudes toward older people, their contributions, and their responsibilities to society. For example, attitudes and values regarding older people's rights and needs, whether chronological age is an appropriate basis for services, and whether care of the aging population is a societal or individual responsibility, all influence the development of social, health, and long-term care policies. The historical development of aging policy in the United States and changes in existing programs such as Social Security are also reviewed within the context of societal changes that influence such values. One societal change examined in this section is the growing economic security of a proportion of the older population that, in turn, has fueled an attitude that they are financially better off than other age groups. As noted in Chapter 11, such an attitude also stereotypes older adults as being "all alike"; it overlooks both the economic and racial diversity among older people and that younger and older generations engage in reciprocal exchanges and share interests throughout life.

Health and long-term care policies toward older people also have evolved in response to society's values and expectations of responsibility and need. Chapter 16 describes these policies; the impact of demographic changes, especially the increased number of the oldest-old with multiple chronic illnesses; the growing need for long-term care for older persons, especially home and community-based long-term care; the rising costs of health and long-term care; and current attempts at cost containment through changes in Medicare and Medicaid. Innovative community-based services have emerged in response to the escalating costs of hospital and nursing home care, but public funding for these programs is relatively limited. The need for and obstacles to major change in funding long-term care are also discussed.

Finally, we examine in the Epilogue the implications of a changing older population upon future social, health, and long-term care policy and programming. As noted throughout this book, society is undergoing major transitions regarding the role and perceptions of older people. Changes such as the termination of mandatory retirement, the growing numbers of older people desiring part-time work, and the increased proportions of workers covered by employer pension plans suggest that the cohort entering old age in the next few decades will be far different from previous ones. These changes will have a dramatic impact on society as a whole. Conversely, the tremendous technological advances in medicine raise hopes of a longer life but also questions about the quality of such extended years. Moreover, computers have revolutionized society and will play an increasing role in older people's social and physical well-being. The

following vignettes illustrate the impact of changing societal attitudes and policies regarding the older population upon individuals who have been raised in different eras.

An Older Person Born at the Turn of the Century

Mr. O'Brien was born in 1910 in New York City. His parents had migrated to the United States from Ireland ten years earlier, in search of better employment opportunities for themselves and a better life for their children. One of Mr. O'Brien's brothers died during a flu epidemic while still in Ireland; a sister and brother who were born in New York died of measles. Mr. O'Brien and his three surviving siblings worked from the age of 12 in their parents' small grocery store. He could not continue his education beyond high school because his father's death of tuberculosis at age 45 left him in charge of the family store. Mr. O'Brien thought of signing up for the newly created Social Security program in 1940, but he was confident that he would not need any help from the government in his old age. The family grocery was supporting him and his wife quite well; he planned to work until the day he died, and besides, his family had all died in their forties and fifties anyway. He has been a heavy smoker all his life, just as his father had been. As he approaches his eighty-third birthday, however, Mr. O'Brien has been having second thoughts about old age. His emphysema and arthritis make it difficult for him to manage the store. He has had two heart attacks in the past ten years, both of which could have been fatal if it had not been for the skills of the emergency medical team and their sophisticated equipment in his local hospital. Mr. O'Brien's savings, which had seemed substantial a few years ago, now are dwindling as he pays for his wife's care in a nursing home and for his medications and doctor's care for his heart condition, emphysema, and arthritis. Despite these struggles, Mr. O'Brien is reluctant to seek assistance from the government or from his children and grandchildren. They, in turn, assume that Mr. O'Brien is financially independent because he still works part-time, and never seems to require help from anybody.

An Individual Born in the Post-War Baby Boom

Ms. Smith was born in 1949, soon after WWII ended and her father returned from his military duty. Her father took advantage of the GI bill to complete his college education and purchase a home in one of the newly emerging suburbs around Chicago. As Ms. Smith grew up, her parents gave her all the advantages they had missed as children of the Depression: regular medical and dental check-ups, education in a private school, a weekly allowance, and a college trust fund. She completed college, obtained a Master's degree in business, and now holds a middle-level management position in a bank. She has already begun planning a "second career" by starting work on a Master's degree in systems analysis. Recognizing the value of health promotion at all ages, she has been a member of a health club for several years, participating in aerobic exercise classes and jogging every day. She has also encouraged her parents, now in their mid-seventies, to participate in health promotion activities in their local senior center. Her parents both receive pensions, are enrolled in Medicare Parts A and B, and have planned for the possibility of catastrophic illness by enrolling in a supplemental health insurance program. Ms. Smith has encouraged her parents to get on the waiting list of an excellent retirement community nearby, which includes a life contract for residential and nursing home care, should they ever need it. She is also considering some long-term investments that will support her if she needs long-term care or costly medical care as she herself reaches old age. In this way, both Ms. Smith and her parents are planning for an independent and, to the extent they can control it through prevention, a healthy old age.

These vignettes illustrate the changing social and economic status of older people today and in the future. The implications of these changes for the development of social, health, and long-term care policy, as well as on individuals' planning for their own aging, are discussed in the remainder of this book. We conclude with a brief discussion of career opportunities for those who want to work with older people.

15

SOCIAL POLICIES TO ADDRESS SOCIAL PROBLEMS

A wide range of policies has been established within the past 60 years to improve the social, physical, and economic environments of older people. Approximately 50 major programs are directed specifically toward older persons, with another 200 affecting them indirectly. Prior to the 1960s, however, the United States lagged behind most European countries in its development of public policy for its older citizens. For example, Social Security benefits were not awarded to retirees in the United States until 1935, whereas alternative Social Security systems were instituted in the nineteenth century in most Western European countries. The United States has slowly and cautiously accepted the concept of public responsibility for older persons.

Since the 1960s, however, federal spending for programs for older adults has rapidly expanded, resulting in the "graying of the federal budget." Although the overall size of the federal government has remained relatively stable in the past several decades, the composition of expenditures has changed dramatically. In particular, defense expenditures have been reallocated to health and re-

tirement benefits. The growth in federal support for these services is vividly shown through budgetary figures (see Figure 15.1). In 1960, only 13 percent of federal expenditures went to general health, retirement, and disability programs, compared to over 50 percent in 1995 (Quinn, 1996).

Raising even greater public concern is that approximately 66 percent of federal spending goes toward **entitlement programs**—those for which spending is determined by ongoing eligibility requirements and benefit levels rather than by annual Congressional appropriations—and toward the interest on the federal debt. These programs—Social Security, Medicare, Medicaid, and civil service and military pensions—are growing so fast that it is predicted they will consume nearly all the federal tax revenues by 2012 (see Figure 15.2). Already Social Security represents 22 percent of the federal budget, and Medicare 12 percent. In fact, Medicare is the fastest-growing entitlement program (Bryce and Friedland, 1997). The long-term increase in the share of the budget spent on the older population has occurred primarily because of legislative improvements in income protection, health insurance, and services enacted in the late 1960s and early 1970s to reduce poverty among older adults. Since Social Security and Medicare were passed, the growth of the older population has raised concern about the long-term financial viability of these programs. Such concern is reflected in the reports of the 1995 Bipartisan Commission on Entitlement and Tax Reform, the 1996 Advisory Council on Social Security, and contemporary debates in Congress about new retirement and Medicare options to reduce expenditures on programs for older people.

It is important to recognize, however, that when Social Security and Medicare are excluded from these allocations, only about 4 percent of the total federal budget is devoted to programs that benefit older individuals. The growing percentage of expenditures for older adults also masks the fact that funded services are often fragmented, duplicated, and do not reach those with the greatest need. Despite growing allocations to age-based programs, the United States lacks an integrated, comprehensive, and effective public policy toward older persons, and is increasingly faced with complex unresolved policy dilemmas.

This and the next chapter describe the social, health, and long-term care programs associated with the "graying of America," along with perceptions that older people have benefited at the expense of younger age groups. First, policy is briefly defined, types of policies are differentiated, and factors that affect policy development are identified. The relatively slow development of policies for older persons prior to the 1960s is contrasted with the rapid expansion of programs in the 1970s and the federal budget cuts of the 1980s and 1990s. The policy impact of the White House Conferences on Aging and of public perceptions about the "deservingness" of older persons are then reviewed. The two major programs that comprise the bulk of federal expenditures and thus shape public policy in old age are discussed in depth: first, Social Security, and then in Chapter 16, Medicare and Medicaid. The development and coordination of direct social services, comprising less than 1 percent of federal expenditures for older people, are also described. Each chapter

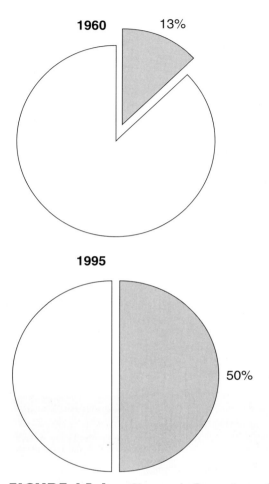

FIGURE 15.1   **Changes in Percentage of Federal Budget for Health, Retirement, and Disability Programs**
SOURCE: Quinn, J. *Entitlement and the Federal Budget: Securing Our Future*, Washington, DC: National Academy on Aging, 1996.

concludes with highlighted policy dilemmas, which have numerous implications for future directions discussed in the Epilogue.

VARIATIONS AMONG POLICIES AND PROGRAMS

Policy refers generally to the principles that govern action directed toward specific ends. It is within

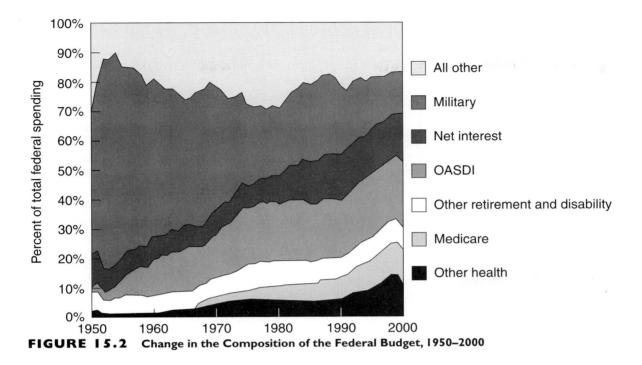

FIGURE 15.2   **Change in the Composition of the Federal Budget, 1950–2000**

the purview of social policy not only to identify problems, but also to take action to ameliorate them. The development of policy thus implies a change in situations, systems, practices, beliefs, or behaviors. The procedures that governments develop for making such changes encompass planned interventions, bureaucratic structures for implementing interventions, and regulations governing the distribution of public funds. Policy for the older population thus reflects society's definition of what choices to make in meeting their needs and how to share such responsibilities between the public and private sectors. Each policy development serves to determine which older persons should receive what benefits, from which sources, and on what basis.

Social programs are the visible manifestations of policies. The implementation of the 1965 Older Americans Act, for example, resulted in numerous programs—senior centers, nutrition sites, meals-on-wheels, homemaker and home health services, and adult day care. Some programs are designed

specifically for older people, whereas others benefit them indirectly. Programs can be differentiated from each other in many ways; these dimensions are presented in Table 15.1 and described next.

1. *Eligibility Criteria:* In some programs, **eligibility** for benefits depends on age alone (i.e., a person is entitled to Medicare benefits at age 65), whereas in other programs, eligibility depends on financial need (i.e., a person's financial need entitles him or her to benefits, such as Medicaid, food stamps, and public housing). Although **"age entitlement" programs** are categorical and specifically for older persons, **"need entitlement"** programs affect all age populations that meet particular income criteria, such as Supplemental Security Income, a means-tested program for low-income older and disabled persons. Most programs for older adults are age entitlements, with the government automatically paying benefits to anyone who qualifies on the basis of age and is thereby "entitled" to the benefits. In contrast, many programs for children are discretionary and **means-based,** which limits participation. This difference fuels ongoing debates about generational equity.

   2. *Form of Benefits:* Another variation is the form in which benefits are given, either as **direct benefits** or as **indirect benefits** through a cash transfer or a cash substitute. Social Security benefits are a direct **cash transfer,** whereas tax policies that affect selected groups (e.g., personal income tax exemptions for older persons) are indirect cash transfers of funds from one segment of the population to another. An example of a direct **cash substitute** is vouchers for the purchase of goods, such as food stamps and rent supplements. Medicare payments to health care providers, rather than directly to beneficiaries, are indirect cash substitutes.

   3. *Method of Financing:* Programs also vary in how they are financed. Social Security and Medicare are **contributory programs;** benefit entitlement is tied to a person's contributions to the

system through his or her prior status as a paid worker across the life span. In contrast, Supplemental Security Income (SSI) is a **non-contributory program** available to older persons who meet financial need criteria, regardless of their prior contributions through payroll taxes.

   4. *Universal or Selective Benefits:* Programs differ according to whether they benefit populations on a universal or selective basis. **Universal benefits** are available on the basis of social right to all persons belonging to a designated group. Eligibility for Medicare, the Old Age Survivors Insurance of Social Security, and the Older Americans Act is established by virtue of belonging to the older population. In contrast, **selective benefits** are determined individually. These include Supplementary Security Income, Medicaid, food stamps, and housing subsidies, which use economic need as a criterion. Whether or not aging services should be targeted to low-income elders and subsidized by higher-income older individu-

TABLE 15.1   **Dimensions along Which Programs and Policies Vary**

	EXAMPLES
Eligibility	
On basis of age	Medicare
On basis of financial need	Supplemental Security Income
	Medicare
Form of benefits	
Cash	
Direct cash transfers	Social Security
Indirect cash transfers	Income tax exemption
Cash substitute	
Direct cash substitutes	Vouchers
Indirect cash substitutes	Medicare payments to service providers
Method of financing	
Contributory (earned rights)	Social Security
Noncontributory	Supplemental Security Income
Universal or selective benefits	
Universal—for all persons who belong to a particular category	Older Americans Act
Selective—determined on an individual basis	Food stamps

als is an ongoing debate. There is no public consensus on which approach to service delivery is best, as reflected in the following discussion of the factors that influence social policy.

FACTORS AFFECTING THE DEVELOPMENT OF POLICIES

Despite the orderliness of these dimensions, the policy-development process is not necessarily rational nor part of an overall plan. Approaches to the financing and delivery of aging services evolved in a very different time period when life expectancy was shorter and there was less concern about the federal deficit. A major characteristic of our public policy process is its shortsightedness— its general inability, because of annual budgetary cycles and the frequency of national elections, to deal with long-term economic, demographic, and social trends, or to anticipate future consequences of policies established to meet today's needs or political imperatives. In an aging society, shortsightedness in policy development has resulted in a diversity of programs, with separate entitlements and eligibility requirements added to a fragmented array of services. In fact, this can be so complex and confusing to older people and their families that it has spawned the growth of private case managers to coordinate services for them.

The complexity of the process of public policy formation for the older population is also magnified by the variety of societal factors influencing it. These factors include values and beliefs; economic, social, and governmental structures; the configuration of domestic and international problems; and powerful interest groups.

Two different sets of values have been played out in American social policies. In one, individual welfare is held to be essentially the person's responsibility within a free-market economy unfettered by government control. This belief in individual freedom and rights, self-determination, and privacy is deeply rooted in our history and culture, widely embraced by many segments of our society, and underlies many public policies. The second set of values assumes individual welfare to be the responsibility both of the individual and the community at large. Government intervention is necessary to compensate for the free market's failure to distribute goods and opportunities more equitably, although given the belief in individual productivity and competitiveness, some degree of income inequality is accepted as desirable. Our society's emphasis on individual and family responsibility has resulted in a "public burden" model of welfare, whereby older persons are often viewed as a burden on the taxpayers rather than being entitled to services as a matter of right. Accordingly, government performs a **residual** or "back-up" role to informal support systems. In other words, programs are developed to respond **incrementally** to crises, not to prevent problems nor to attack their underlying causes. This contrasts with many other countries where national health and welfare polices represent a consensus that citizens are universally entitled to have certain needs met. Even when our government intervenes, it is justified because of the failure of the market economy, the family, or the individual to provide for themselves or their relatives (Gill and Ingman, 1994). Accordingly, solutions tend to be patterned after private-sector initiatives, as illustrated by many of the proposed changes in both Social Security and Medicare that are discussed later in these two chapters.

Since the New Deal of the 1930s, policy has oscillated between these two value orientations as public mood and national administrations have shifted. American cultural values of productivity, independence, and youthfulness, public attitudes toward government programs and toward older citizens, and public perceptions of older people as "deserving" have converged to create universal **categorical** programs that are limited to older persons, but available to all elders, regardless of their income. In contrast, policies that use income (e.g., means-testing) to determine if a person is "deserving" of services reflect our cultural bias toward productivity and independence. Although Social Security was the first federal initiative to address the income needs of older adults, it succeeded largely because it is perceived as an insurance plan for "deserving" elders who have contributed through their prior employment, not a means-tested income maintenance policy for all vulnerable citizens. The increasingly frequent debate about the nature and extent of public provisions versus the responsibility of individuals, families, and private philanthropy often has moral overtones. Judgments about the relative worth of vulnerable populations that compete for a share of limited resources, and about the proper divisions between public and private responsibilities, are ultimately based on values (or preferences) held by individuals or groups. Therefore, a major policy issue revolves around the question of whose values shape policy.

In the past, the American public tended to perceive older people as more deserving of assistance than other populations. Accordingly, Social Security and Medicare have generally been viewed as inviolate and not to be cut drastically. The passage of such otherwise unpopular programs as a national health insurance for older people (i.e., Medicare) and guaranteed income (i.e., Supplemental Security Income) can be partially explained by the fact that older persons have aroused public support. In addition, older people were viewed as a powerful and organized constituency. As a result, they were more likely than children and low-income or homeless families to arouse a favorable response from politicians in the past. As noted in Chapter 11, such catering to the senior vote also reflects a model of interest-group politics to advance one's agenda in our political system, although older people are now less likely to act as a unified bloc to influence legislation than in the past.

Society's technical and financial resources and current economic conditions (e.g., unemployment, inflation, and the deficit) also significantly influence policy development. Adverse economic conditions can create a climate conducive to the passage of income-maintenance policies. For instance, Social Security was enacted in part because the Great Depression dislodged the middle class from financial security and from their belief that

older people who needed financial assistance were undeserving of aid. A strategy to increase the number of persons retiring at age 65 was also congruent with economic pressures to reduce widespread unemployment in the 1930s. With economic constraints, program cost factors were salient. For example, Social Security as a public pension was assumed to cost less than reliance on local poorhouses, as had been the practice prior to the 1920s. Thus, a variety of economic and resource factors converged to create the necessary public and legislative support for a system of social insurance in the 1930s. In contrast, periods of economic growth can be conducive to new programs. Both Medicare and the Older Americans Act were passed during the 1960s and early 1970s. This was a period of economic growth and optimism; government resources expanded under the so-called War on Poverty on behalf of both the younger poor and older people.

The influence of both economic resources and cultural values is also evident in the current public emphasis on fiscal austerity and deficit reduction, private responsibility for the care of older persons, program **cost effectiveness** and **cost containment,** and targeting services to those most in need. Particularly under the fiscal conservatism of a Republican Congress in the 1990s, the concept of states' rights and prerogatives has been emphasized. States have assumed a stronger role in the development and financing of social programs. Unfortunately, this has resulted in increased variability among the states of eligibility criteria and benefits such as SSI and Medicaid. Periods of scarcity tend to produce limited and often punitive legislative responses, as occurred in the 1980s and early 1990s. As illustrations of the erosion of public support for universal age-based benefits, Medicare co-payments, deductibles, and Part B premiums have been increased; Social Security benefits for higher-income older people are taxed; and many legislators propose cutting Medicare, Medicaid, and Social Security in order to reduce the federal deficit. The growing preoccupation with ways to reduce public expenditures has meant that the priority is to find the most efficient and least expensive solutions, rather than emphasizing equity and the common good.

In sum, these cultural values, economic conditions, and the consequent resource capability underlie the fact that American policy for older adults tends to be categorical, residual, and incremental. One of the most vocal critics of this approach, Estes (1979, 1984, 1989, 1993; Estes, Linkins, and Binney, 1996) maintains that our conceptions of aging have socially constructed the major problems faced by older people and thereby have adversely influenced U.S. age-based policies. These conceptions, discussed briefly as the political economy perspective in Chapter 8, are shown in the box below.

According to Estes, our societal failure to develop a comprehensive, coordinated policy framework has served to reinforce older persons' marginality and to segregate them. For example, Social Security and employer-sponsored pensions have ensured that most older people leave the labor force (Estes, Linkins, and Binney, 1996).

In contrast, others maintain that the older population has benefited at the expense of other age groups and is "busting the budget." Expenditures for older persons are viewed as a primary reason for the growing federal budget deficit and for the declining economic status of many younger people (Marmor, Cook, and Scher, 1997; Quinn, 1996; Concord Coalition, 1993). In reality, however, what Social Security and Medicare actually contribute to the federal deficit has been nearly the same since 1980. There is widespread disagreement about the extent to which the deficit is due to excessive spending for entitlement programs which "mortgage the future" of succeeding generations of Americans, or to spiraling interest rates, high unemployment, and shrinking real incomes. Within this context of the factors affecting policy development, we turn now to the development of public policy for older persons in the United States.

THE DEVELOPMENT OF POLICIES FOR OLDER PEOPLE

1930 to 1950

Prior to 1930, the United States had few social programs for older people. Family, community, charity organizations, and local government (e.g., county work farms) were expected to respond. Factors such as the lower percentage of older persons in the population in the past, a strong belief in individual responsibility, and the free-market economy partially explain why our government was slow to respond. Table 15.2 traces the historical development of policy for older adults. The Social Security Act of 1935 was the first truly national public benefits program and established the federal government as a major player in the area of social welfare (Bryce and Friedland, 1997). The

---

POLITICAL ECONOMY OF AGING

1. Older individuals, not economic or social structural conditions, are defined as a "social problem."
2. Older people are seen as special and different, requiring separate programs.
3. Through categorical and age-segregated services, public policy has promoted an "aging enterprise" of bureaucracies and providers to serve older people.
4. There is a growing perception that problems of older adults cannot be solved by national programs, but rather by initiatives of state and local governments, the private sector, or the individual.
5. The problems of older people are individually generated and best treated through medical services to individuals. This has resulted in the medicalization of aging and limited public funding for home- and community-based social services.
6. The use of costly medical services is justified by characterizing old age as a period of inevitable physical decline and deficiency.

TABLE 15.2   Major Historical Developments of Policies That Benefit Older People

1935	Social Security Act
1950	Amendments to assist states with health care costs
1959	Section 202 Direct Loan Program of the Housing Act
1960	Extension of Social Security benefits
1960	Advisory commissions on aging
1961	Senate Special Committee on Aging
1961	First White House Conference on Aging
1965	Medicare and Medicaid, Older Americans Act, establishment of Administration on Aging
1971	Second White House Conference on Aging
1972 & 1977	Social Security amendments
1974	Supplemental Security Income
1974	Title XX
1974	House Select Committee on Aging
1974	Change in mandatory retirement age
1974	Establishment of the National Institute on Aging
1980	Federal measures to control health care expenditures
1981	Third White House Conference on Aging
1981	Social Services Block Grant Program
1986	Elimination of mandatory retirement
1987	Nursing Home Reform Act
1989–90	Medicare Catastrophic Health Care Legislation passed, then repealed
1995	Fourth White House Conference on Aging

act is based on an implicit guarantee of social insurance—that the succeeding generation will provide for its older members through their Social Security contributions as employees. The original provisions of the act were intended to be only the beginning of a universal program covering all "major hazards" in life. However, this broader concept of the program, including a nationwide program for preventing sickness and ensuring security for children, was never realized.

After the passage of Social Security, national interest in policies to benefit older persons subsided. One exception was President Truman's advocacy to expand Social Security benefits to include farmers, self-employed persons, and some state and local government employees. He also attempted to launch a national health insurance plan, but was opposed by organizations such as the American Medical Association. President Truman did succeed, however, in his push for a Social Security amendment in 1950 to provide financial

help to states that choose to pay partial health care costs for needy older persons. This amendment then became the basis for the establishment of Medicare in 1965.

Program Expansion in the 1960s and 1970s

Since the 1960s, programs for older people have rapidly evolved, including Medicare, Medicaid, the Older Americans Act, Supplemental Security Income (SSI), the Social Security Amendments of 1972 and 1977, Section 202 Housing, and Title XX social services legislation. The pervasiveness of "compassionate stereotypes," which assumed most older people to be deserving poor, frail, ill-housed, unable to keep up with inflation, and therefore in need of government assistance, served to create a "permissive consensus" for government action on age-based services in the 1960s and 1970s. A negative consequence of "compassionate ageism," however, was a tendency to develop programs that obscured individual and sub-group differences among the older population. A large constituency—including older people who are not poor, frail, or inadequately housed—has benefited from the policy consensus built upon the "compassionate stereotype" in the 1960s and 1970s (Binstock and Day, 1996). Since old-age constituencies have been viewed as relatively homogeneous (white, English-speaking, and male), many older people with the greatest needs—women, ethnic minorities, and those living alone—have not always benefited from program improvements. These inequities were described in Chapters 13 and 14.

The first White House Conference on Aging and the establishment of the Senate Special Committee on Aging in 1961 were significant in highlighting older people's needs. Four years later, Medicare and the Older Americans Act were passed for which eligibility is determined by age, not by need. Although the Older Americans Act established the Administration on Aging at the federal level, as well as statewide area agencies and advisory boards to provide aging services, funding to implement these provisions was low. Therefore, one of the primary objectives of the 1971 White House Conference on Aging was to strengthen the Older Americans Act. In 1972, Social Security benefits were expanded 20 percent, and the system of **indexing** benefits to take ac-count of inflation ("**cost of living adjustments**" or **COLA**) was established. Additional funding was provided for the Older Americans Act in 1973.

The 1970s witnessed more developments to improve older people's economic status:

- The creation of the Supplemental Security Income (SSI) program.
- Protection of private pensions through the Employee Retirement Income Security Act (ERISA).
- Formation of the House Select Committee on Aging; increases in Social Security benefit levels and taxes.
- The change in mandatory retirement from age 65 to age 70. (As noted in Chapter 11, mandatory retirement was later abolished for most jobs in 1986.)

During this period of federal government expansion, more than 40 different national committees and subcommittees were involved in legislative efforts affecting older people. As a result of the expansion of age-related programs, agencies, and benefits, along with more interest groups representing older people, individuals grew to expect that they would be entitled to receive certain benefits, such as Social Security and Medicare, based on age rather than on income or need.

Program Reductions in the 1980s and 1990s

Although compassionate stereotypes about older people and a "permissive consensus" underlay the growth of age-entitlement programs in the 1960s and 1970s, the fiscal pressures and increasing concern about the younger age groups in the 1980s and 1990s brought into question the size and structure of these programs. In those years, a new stereotype of older people as relatively well-off resulted in their being a scapegoat and blamed as "greedy geezers." Older people were seen as being responsible for the increasing poverty rates among younger age groups (Bengtson, 1993; Torres-Gil, 1992).

National debates on social policy draw older citizens and key political leaders.

The impact of tax cuts, reductions in federal programs, the huge federal deficit, and an overemphasis on economic growth prevented consideration of any large or bold programs for domestic spending in social and health care services during the Reagan Administration (1980–1988). At the same time, public perceptions of and support for aging programs varied widely. Senior advocates urged more funding, particularly for social services, and watched closely that Social Security not be cut. Concern over the future of Social Security was fueled by the near-term deficit facing the Social Security trust fund. As a result, Social Security was amended in 1983 to address short-term financing problems. As public scrutiny of the costs of Social Security, Medicare, and Medicaid grew, **cost-efficiency** measures were implemented, such as taxation on Social Security benefits and less generous cost of living increases.

During the 1980s, the political reality of the economic and social diversity of the aging population—that chronological age is not an accurate marker of economic status—became more apparent. The variability in distribution of income is reflected among three different groupings of older people: (1) those not eligible for Social Security, including both the lifelong underclass and the working poor who have interrupted employment histories, hourly wages without benefits, and few personal assets; (2) those who depend heavily on Social Security, with small or no private pensions and few assets except for their own home; and (3) those with generous private pensions, personal savings, and Social Security benefits. A number of policies passed in the 1980s recognized that the older population has differential capabilities for helping to finance public programs, so that both age and economic status are considered as eligibility criteria for old-age benefit programs (Binstock, 1994). For example, the Social Security Reform Act of 1983 taxed Social Security benefits for higher-income recipients. The Tax Reform Act of 1986 provided tax credits on a sliding scale to very low-income older people and eliminated a second or third exemption on federal tax income previously available to older people. Meanwhile,

programs funded under the Older Americans Act have been gradually targeted toward low-income people. These policy changes, combined with public perceptions that older people are better off than younger populations, reflect a transition from the legacy of a modern aging period (1930–1990) to a new period in which old age alone is not sufficient grounds for public benefits (Torres-Gil and Puccinelli, 1994).

The Politics of Diversity and Deficit Spending in the 1990s

The growing federal deficit profoundly affected public policy development in the 1990s. To reduce the deficit, there were two major options—reductions in spending through program cutbacks, or revenue enhancement through higher taxes. National groups that cut across the political spectrum, such as the Bipartisan Commission on Entitlement and Tax Reform, and the Concord Coalition, maintained that entitlement programs for older people were growing so fast that they will consume nearly all the federal tax revenues by the year 2012, leaving government with little money for anything else. Increasingly such groups argued that programs such as Social Security, Medicare, and Medicaid must be drastically curtailed to balance the federal budget by the year 2000. Such a perspective, for example, is reflected in the Balanced Budget Act of 1997 where cuts were made in Medicare and Medicaid but not Social Security. On the other hand, in the 1996 Personal Responsibility Act, President Clinton signed welfare legislation, but vetoed the bill containing changes that would have altered the nature of entitlements to Medicare and Medicaid. Social Security remained basically untouched. Resistance against dramatically changing these entitlement programs for older people remains strong in the Clinton Administration.

The fact that such entitlement programs are "under attack" (although not yet dramatically altered) reflects that older people are now less often perceived as a "politically sympathetic" and powerful group (Binstock, 1993, 1994; Peterson,

1993). At the same time, differences within the older population are becoming more evident, with subgroups of poor, ethnic minorities, women, and persons living alone likely to join political alliances that may compete with groups of more affluent elders. The "politics of diversity" may thus fragment the political influence of established aging organizations, further eroding support for universal programs. In fact, incremental changes in Social Security, the Older Americans Act, and Medicare to target benefits toward relatively poor older people reflect recognition of this diversity (Binstock, 1995; Torres-Gil, 1992).

Such diversity among the older population, combined with the growing federal deficit, has resulted in a greater emphasis on private sector initiatives that can be supported by higher-income older adults. With more older people able to self-finance or privately insure against the social and health costs of later life, the base of support for high-quality government programs may erode. This could result in more limited services available to elders without retirement plans and health insurance and thus lead to increasing inequality among the older population. A policy challenge in the 1990s has been to target policy responses to those who risk seriously declining income and who have never had economic stability, while maintaining public support for the financing of quality universal programs. These complex issues set the framework for the 1995 White House Conference on Aging. Delegates at the 1995 conference voted to maintain Social Security, the Older Americans Act, the basic features of Medicaid and Medicare, and the advocacy functions under the Older Americans Act—all directions that conflicted with the Republican Congress of the 1990s' emphasis on cutting entitlement programs as a way to reduce the federal deficit.

Social Security and SSI

We next review the programs that account for the majority of federal expenditures related to older people: Social Security (OASDI) and Supplemental Security Income (SSI); tax provisions and private pensions that provide indirect benefits; and social services through Title XX **block grants** and the "**Aging Network**" of the Older Americans Act. In Chapter 16 we will address Medicare and Medicaid. As noted earlier, Social Security (OASDI), federal employee retirement, and Medicare and Medicaid combined represent the largest and most rapidly growing federal entitlements expended on behalf of older persons, as illustrated in Figure 15.2. However, as will be noted in this chapter and in Chapter 16, many younger people also benefit from OASDI and Medicaid.

INCOME SECURITY PROGRAMS: SOCIAL SECURITY AND SUPPLEMENTAL SECURITY INCOME

Social Security

As indicated earlier, the primary objective of the 1935 Social Security Act was to establish a system of income maintenance for older persons through individual insurance. A secondary purpose was to provide a basic level of protection for the most needy of the older population, initially through state plans for Old Age and Survivors Insurance (OASI) and, since 1974, through the federally funded Supplemental Security Income (SSI) program. A more recent objective has been to provide compensatory income to persons, regardless of age, who experience a sudden loss of income, such as widows, surviving children, and persons with disabilities.

To meet these objectives, Social Security has four separate "trust funds":

1. Old Age and Survivors Insurance (OASI)
2. Disability Insurance (DI)
3. Hospital Insurance (HI), which is funded through Medicare
4. Revenues for the supplemental insurance portion of Medicare

Out of every tax dollar from **payroll taxes** that a worker pays into Social Security and Medicare, 69 cents goes to a trust fund that pays monthly benefits to retirees and their families and to widows, widowers, and children of workers who have died; another 19 cents goes to a trust fund that pays some of the cost of hospital and related care of Medicare beneficiaries; and the remaining 12 cents goes to a trust fund that pays benefits to people with disabilities and their families (Social Security Administration, 1996a, b) (see Figure 15.3). This discussion focuses on the combined OASDI fund, of which programs for persons with disabilities are only 7 percent of the combined obligation. Funding for Medicare is discussed in Chapter 16.

As described in Chapter 11, the Social Security system was based first on the concept of earned rights, rather than universal eligibility for all older persons. In fact, only 60 percent of the labor force was initially eligible to earn future benefits on the basis of the 1935 law. Coverage has since been expanded so that approximately 95 percent of the labor force is insured, reflecting nearly universal protection across socioeconomic classes (Bryce and Friedland, 1997). Beneficiaries must have worked at least 10 years in covered employment to qualify, and full benefits are calculated based on retirement at age 65 (this increases to age 67 in the year 2003). Social Security is thus distin-

guished by nearly universal coverage and wage-price indexing that protect recipients against economic changes over which they have no control. Although Social Security provides a mechanism to pool resources and share the risk, no one is excluded no matter how "bad" a risk they may be. Therefore, it is unlike a private insurance or a welfare program (Kingson and Schulz, 1997).

Contrary to public perceptions, Social Security was never intended to be the sole source of retirement income, but rather a minimum floor of protection. The reality, however, is that Social Security is the major source of income (providing for at least 50 percent of total income) for 66 percent of total beneficiary units, and the only source of income for 16 percent. Social Security's average older recipients are paid 42 percent of their income at retirement, a figure that is projected to remain stable through the year 2040 (Social Security Administration, 1996a). This percent varies with income, however. Social Security provides 75 percent of the aggregate income of older households with annual incomes of less than $10,000, and 31 percent of the aggregate income for those with incomes above $30,000 (Villa, Wallace, and Markides, 1997). While higher-income workers receive higher benefits, lower-income workers are assured a greater rate of return for what they have paid into the system (e.g., the proportion of earnings that is replaced after retirement is higher for lower-paid workers). Social Security therefore is most helpful to those at the lowest end of the income scale—oldest-old, ethnic minorities, and women. In fact, without Social Security, it is estimated that 55 percent of older people would be in poverty (Devlin and Arye, 1997).

This distribution of benefits reflects Social Security's dual goals of social adequacy and individual equity. **Social adequacy** refers to shared societal responsibility to provide a basic standard of living for all potential beneficiaries, or a "safety net," regardless of the size of their economic contributions. **Individual equity** refers to an individual's receiving benefits that reflect that person's actual monetary contributions proportionate to what workers have paid into the system. In short,

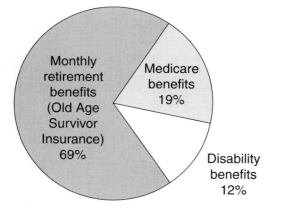

FIGURE 15.3   **Where Our Social Security Tax Dollars Go**

SOURCE: Social Security Administration, Secondary Benefits. Washington, DC: U.S. Government Printing Office, 1996.

consistent with the conclusion of the National Commission on Social Security Reform, Social Security's nearly universal coverage and predictability of income make it the foundation of economic security for most retirees.

Social Security is financed through separate trust funds, revenues raised equally from the taxing of employees and employers, and income based on current tax revenues. It is a myth that Social Security is a funded pension system in which retirees are merely paid back, with interest, the "contributions" which they made during their working years. Instead, it is a system whereby current workers support former workers. This "pay-as-you-go" system is like a pipeline: payroll taxes from today's workers flow in, are invested in special U.S. government bonds, and then flow out to current beneficiaries (Hardy and Hardy, 1991).

However, payroll taxes have risen enormously, from a combined 3 percent on employers and employees in 1950 to 15.3 percent today (including Medicare). But the average return that a worker can expect has declined dramatically: an average earner born in 1915 could expect to get back at age 65 approximately $60,000 more than he or she paid into the system (adjusted for inflation and interest) while someone born in 1936 and retiring in the year 2001 will just about break even (Miller, 1998).

This pay-as-you-go method of financing partially underlay the fiscal crisis faced by the system in the early 1980s, when the reserves were inadequate for projected benefits. A primary factor behind threats of bankruptcy was the economic recession; high unemployment and low productivity resulted in fewer taxes collected, so that less money was available in the Social Security trust funds. Another structural factor was increased longevity and more retired workers in proportion to younger employees, with fewer workers paying into Social Security. This changing **dependency ratio,** discussed in Chapter 1, means that the ratio of taxpayers to older retired persons is projected to drop to fewer than 4 to 1 by 2020. When Social Security was enacted, life expectancy was 61 years and the average recipient collected for 12 years, compared to 78 years and 19 years, respectively, today. Social Security was never intended to support individuals for up to a third of their lives (Devlin and Arye, 1997; Mathews, 1995).

Pessimistic interpretations of these shifts argue that "apocalyptic demography" will make it difficult for our nation to sustain all age-related benefits through the first half of the twenty-first century; the "graying of the welfare state" is likely to have catastrophic consequences for the after-tax living standards of most working-age Americans (Quinn, 1996; Howe, 1995). This view, fostered by the media, is put forth by groups such as the Third Millennium, which point to a survey where people under age 35 stated they were more likely to believe in UFOs than they are in the future of Social Security (Conte, 1997; Lukefar, 1994). It appears, however, that these data have been misrepresented as public support for "radical reform"; many polls consistently show that people overwhelmingly support Social Security even though they have little confidence in its future (Quinn, 1996). An alternative and more optimistic view is that projected shortfalls—25 to 30 years in the future—are a warning which can be addressed with relatively minor adjustments in the program, not a crisis requiring major structural changes (Conte, 1997; Kingson and Quadagno, 1995). One minor change, for example, is a 0.7 percent reduction in annual cost of living adjustments that will, over time, result in enormous reductions in the program. Accordingly, future benefits to older populations will not depend solely on the proportion of workers to retirees, but also on whether the economy generates sufficient resources to be transferred and whether the political will to transfer them to older persons will be present (Binstock, 1994).

As noted above, the short-term danger of bankruptcy was averted through remedial legislation passed in 1983, which resulted in benefit reductions and increased the age of full Social Security eligibility from 65 years to age 67 by the year 2003. These reforms allowed the system to accumulate reserves which currently exceed the benefits paid. Despite such solvency, there is a long-range concern that the federal government debt is turning the surplus into paper savings. This concern stems from the fact that the Treasury Department borrows and then spends the Social Security reserves by investing them in Treasury bonds. In effect, it gives Social Security an IOU so that the reserves accumulated now may be consumed by deficits in later years.

Beginning in 2012, Social Security expenditures (or the "outgo") will exceed funds collected through current taxes, largely because of the aging of the baby-boom generation. At that point, Social Security will be funded through a combination of payroll taxes and interest generated by the trust fund. In 2019, the benefit payouts are projected to exceed taxes and interest, which means a drawing down on the reserves in the trust fund. The exhaustion of the trust fund, however, does not mean that Social Security will stop paying benefits; this would happen only if Congress passed legislation ending Social Security payroll taxes. In fact, even by 2029, the benefits will not end, but the financial security of a trust fund will be lost and benefits will be lower. Congress will be able to pay only 75 percent of its obligations promised to future retirees (e.g., 75 cents for every dollar of benefits). Most proposals for change suggest that the only way to repay the reserves in the future within the current system is for the federal government to raise payroll taxes, increase the age of eligibility, use means-testing, increase borrowing, reduce benefits, or rely on economic growth (Wheeler and Kearney, 1996).

There are widely varying points of view regarding the magnitude of the Social Security crisis, and numerous proposed solutions. The differences in Social Security reform proposals can be attributed to different perspectives regarding Social Security's goals. As noted above, the primary goals are **social insurance** (e.g., provide benefits upon disability or death) and **income redistribution** (transfer resources from the wealthier to those with fewer resources, both within and between generations). Those who focus on the traditional social insurance and income-adequacy goals tend to favor addressing the fiscal imbalance within the

current structure. For example, the 1997 Social Security Advisory Council suggested a range of changes which would lower Social Security benefits within the current system: taxing Social Security benefits as ordinary income; calculating benefits based on a 38-year average instead of 35 years (this would further reduce benefits to women, however, who tend to have shorter work histories than men); raising the age for full benefits to age 69; and cutting spousal benefits from 50 percent to 33 percent (Ball, 1997; Atchley, 1997).

Currently, workers pay 6.2 percent on earnings up to $65,400 in taxes to support OASDI, with employers paying a matching 6.2 percent for a combined tax rate of 12.4 percent. Even if taxes had to be raised to pay benefits for the next 75 years, the combined tax would only have to be raised to 14.6 percent of earnings, which is defined as a "problem" but not a "crisis" (Moon, 1997; Stern, 1997). Others argue that there should be an income or means test for Social Security, which would exclude or sharply lower benefits to the well-off and target resources to those in greatest need. However, this approach undermines the universal nature of Social Security and the basic principles that workers at all income levels will receive some reasonable return in exchange for making payroll tax contributions during their working years (Kingson and Schulz, 1997).

In recent years, there has been growing interest by critics of Social Security in conceptualizing it as a savings program which maximizes the "rate of return" to beneficiaries and fosters economic growth by encouraging savings. Advocates of Social Security as a savings instrument argue for major structural changes that privatize Social Security by greater reliance on individual savings and higher rates of return on individual contributions through investments in the stock market. One proposal is to allow workers to invest half of their Social Security retirement money in the stock market and set aside the remainder in individual retirement accounts. Such proposals have been criticized as putting workers at risk of failing investments and losing disability and survivor insurance, especially since historical experience indicates that many workers are unable to deal with the complexities of retirement planning (Wheeler and Kearney, 1996). Another proposal is a "double decker" system. The lower deck would provide a flat benefit for those meeting eligibility requirements, equal to 47 percent of benefits paid to an average worker, and therefore would address the goals of social adequacy. The upper deck would require payment into a government-supervised retirement plan that would offer some choices about where money was invested. This proposal would not include a redistribution component but would address individual equity concerns by providing a benefit proportionate to contributions (Devlin and Arye, 1997). Table 15.3 highlights some of the current proposals to reform Social Security.

Proposals that privatize or individualize Social Security and reduce government control tend to be supported by groups such as the Investment Company Institute, a trade association for the mutual funds industry that would benefit if workers must invest in private accounts, and the CATO In-

TABLE 15.3 An Overview of Proposals to Reform Social Security

Changes within the current system:

- Diversify the trust funds to invest a larger portion in the stock market
- Lower benefits
- Tax Social Security benefits as ordinary income
- Raise the payroll tax
- Compute benefits on 38-year work history instead of 35 years
- Raise the age for full benefits to age 70
- Raise the early retirement age to 65
- Cut spousal benefits from 50 percent to 33 percent
- Establish income or means test

Changing the underlying principles of the system:

- Savings programs and individual investment in the stock market
- "Double decker system": flat benefit as first tier; government supervised retirement plan as second tier

stitute, a conservative Washington, DC-based think tank (Deets, 1997; Dentzer, 1997; Stern, 1997). It is important to recognize that such changes toward privatization are counter to the basic philosophy of a social insurance plan with universal eligibility. This philosophy represents societal willingness to compensate those whose income has been destroyed or lowered by economic forces of the marketplace, regardless of the individual's actual contribution (Quadagno, 1990). As such, these proposed changes challenge the notion that governments subsidize programs that are deemed to be in the common good (Binstock, 1993). Although there are a growing number of proposals to reform Social Security, some policymakers view it as a "sacred entitlement," not to be altered, even at the expense of other groups.

Despite the rhetoric of some national leaders to alter Social Security, the majority of the public, in national opinion polls, do not perceive that older people receive an inequitable amount of government benefits, nor that the programs provide benefits that are too costly. In fact, Social Security is supported by over 80 percent of the U.S. population in most national polls (National Academy on Aging, 1997). This support may reflect recognition of how Social Security can also benefit younger family members by reducing their financial responsibility to their older relatives. There may be greater support for intergenerational transfer programs than the media and politicians typically portray, an issue discussed below vis-à-vis the intergenerational-equity framework.

Supplemental Security Income

Supplemental Security Income (SSI) is the central income transfer for older people who are living on the margin of poverty. About 6 percent of Social Security recipients also receive SSI. SSI is financed fully by the federal government under the Social Security Administration, although states may supplement the federal payment; this has resulted in variability in benefits among states. As noted in Chapter 11, SSI is intended to be a protective system or "safety net" for the least economically fortunate, but it has not eliminated poverty among older people and reaches only 50 percent of the older poor. A primary reason for this is that SSI only brings needy individuals up to 75 percent of the poverty level and couples up to 90 percent, even in those states that supplement the federal payment. About 17 percent of low-income older persons receive food stamps; of these, 20 percent will lose their benefits due to the Personal Responsibility and Work Opportunity Reconciliation Act, also known as the Welfare Reform Act of 1996 (Kassner, 1996).

PRIVATE PENSIONS AND INCOME TAX PROVISIONS

Private Pensions

Some older persons receive a combination of government-supported public and/or private pensions in addition to their Social Security checks. As described in Chapter 11, approximately 50 percent of the current labor force, primarily middle- and high-income workers, is covered by an employer-sponsored pension plan, which supplements Social Security. This translates into nearly 40 percent of older adults receiving some income from public or private pensions. However, only about 10 percent of these receive in private pensions an amount equivalent to that of Social Security. It is expected that about 55 percent of retirees early in the next century will have private pension income, only a small increase from the current situation (Bryce and Friedland, 1997). Overall, the rate of pension growth has slowed due to the changing nature of the work force, with a decrease in manufacturing jobs which historically provided pensions, and growth in service sector and part-time, temporary contingent employment.

The pension system tends to perpetuate systematic inequities across the life span by income and ethnic minority status as well as gender. Lower-income workers, often women and ethnic minorities, are least likely to be in jobs that are covered by pensions and least likely to have at-

Older people who have multiple sources of income are generally financially secure.

tained the vesting requirements (e.g., 10 years on the same job). Another inequity is that retired military veterans, civil service, and railroad employees also receive cash benefits in addition to Social Security. This means that cash benefits from government-supported private savings plans and favorable tax policies accrue to those who are already relatively well off, intensifying economic inequities over time (Wheeler and Kearney, 1996). Private pensions help many upper- or middle-income workers to replace more of their income when they retire, but they do not meet the value of adequacy inherent in Social Security, since lower-income workers are generally non-participants (Wheeler and Kearney, 1996).

As described in Chapter 11, the Employee Retirement Income Security Act of 1974 (ERISA) established standards for participation, vesting, and minimum funding to protect workers. Since then, corporate contributions to pension plans have declined, and many businesses have instead used pension funds to pay for employee health care expenses and to increase their own profitability. Defined benefit plans beneficial to employees have been terminated and replaced by contribution plans, such as 401Ks, which are more uncertain for the employee. This has represented a shift in pension responsibility away from the company and toward the individual (Bryce and Friedland, 1997; Woods, 1994).

Income Tax Provisions

Pension plans are not the only "tax expenditures" related to aging. Some older individuals also benefit from extra tax deductions and pay on average a smaller percent of their income in taxes. Many older people who file tax returns benefit from not paying a tax on Railroad Retirement and other government pensions, for example. Higher-income older persons also benefit from property-tax reductions and preferential treatment of the sale of a home (e.g., exemption from capital gains taxation for sale of a home after age 55). The 1997 Tax Reform Act also benefits wealthy older persons who own stocks and bonds. Capital gains realized from the sale of stocks and mutual funds now are taxed at lower rates than ever before, 20 percent in 1998 for those in the highest income brackets. Tax provisions thus highlight the inequitable distribution of public benefits to older people. Tax benefits go to the majority of the older population who have an annual income of over $20,000, and only a small percent goes to persons with incomes less than $5000 (Hudson, 1995).

SOCIAL SERVICES

Social service programs for older people have developed in response to needs unmet by income maintenance, health, and housing programs. Despite these developments, federal and state expenditures are primarily oriented toward medical care. Less than 1 percent of the older population's share of the federal budget is spent on social service programs. From a political economy perspective, as discussed in Chapter 8, social services are underfunded because they do not fit within the dominant medical model (Estes et al., 1996).

Funding for social services for older people derives from four federal sources: Medicare, Medi-caid, amendments to the Social Security Act (Title XX), and the Older Americans Act of 1965. This section will focus on Title XX (of the Social Services Block Grants) and the Older Americans Act as the primary basis of social service funding.

Title XX was established in 1974 to provide social services to all age groups. Entitlements are means-tested, with most services to older persons going to those who receive SSI. In terms of the program classification system discussed earlier, Title XX is a universal program aimed at redressing needs. Because income is an eligibility criterion, older people compete with a diverse group of Title XX recipients—primarily families with dependent children and persons who are blind or mentally and/or physically disabled. Title XX encompasses basic life-sustaining, self-care services to compensate for losses in health and the capacity for self-maintenance: homemaker and chore services, home-delivered meals, adult protective services, adult day care, foster care, and institutional or residential care services. These have generally assured a minimum level of support for vulnerable older people.

Under the federal Omnibus Budget Reconciliation Act of 1981, Title XX was converted to the Social Services Block Grant program at the same time that federal funds allocated to the states were reduced on the average by 30 percent (Estes et al., 1996). The Social Services Block Grant program was one of the initial decentralization efforts emerging from the new federalism of the 1980s. Block grant funding increased the states' discretion in determining clients' needs and allocating Title XX funds among the diverse eligible groups. For example, national income-eligibility guidelines aimed at targeting programs to needy persons were eliminated. Accordingly, the competition for funds increased, along with variability in services between and within states. As a result, most states have allocated a greater percentage of block grant funds to children than to older persons. Limits to federal funding under decentralization, along with fiscal crises in most cities and states, have served to decrease revenues for social services under Title XX for older people at the same time that the demand for services has increased. Competition for limited funds has intensified, sometimes pitting the poor and their allied service providers against older groups.

The **Older Americans Act (OAA)** seeks to alter state and local priorities to ensure that older people receive a proportionate share of social services allocations. Title III of the Older Americans Act is the single federal social service statute designed specifically for older people. Entitlements to services are universal for all people over age 60, regardless of income or need. The OAA was to create a national network for the comprehensive planning, coordination, and delivery of aging services. At the federal level, the act charges the Administration on Aging (AOA), through the Assistant Secretary on Aging, to oversee the activities of the Aging Network (i.e., the system of social services for older people) and to advocate for them nationally. The Federal Council on Aging is appointed by the President, and advises the President and the Commissioner on Aging.

The Older Americans Act also established State Units on Aging (SUAs). Each of these has a state advisory council to engage in statewide planning and advocacy on behalf of older persons' service needs. State Units on Aging designate local **Area Agencies on Aging** (AAAs) to develop and administer service plans within local areas. Approximately 700 Area Agencies on Aging operate at regional and local levels, and have advisory boards that must include older persons. In addition to federal, state, and local agencies that are responsible for planning and coordination, a fourth tier is composed of direct service providers in local communities (see Table 15.4). As described in Chapter 10, these include information and referral, case management, transportation, **outreach,** homemaker services, day care, nutrition education and congregate meals (both hot meals at senior centers and home-delivered meals), legal services, **respite care,** senior centers, and part-time community service jobs. These services under OAA overlap with the goals and provisions of the Social Services Block Grants. Given the range of programs, the relatively low level of funding

TABLE 15.4 Services Provided under the Older Americans Act

Access Services: Information and referral; care management

In-Home Services: Homemaker assistance, respite care; emergency response systems; home health care, friendly visiting, and telephone reassurance

Senior Center Programs: Social, physical, educational, recreational, and cultural programs

Nutrition Programs: Meals at senior centers or nutrition sites; in-home meals (Meals on Wheels)

Legal Assistance Advocacy: For individual seniors and on behalf of programs and legislation. The Older Americans Act is the only major federal legislation that mandates advocacy on behalf of a constituency.

Additional services provided based on local community needs and resources.

available for the OAA requires it to target services to low-income, ethnic minority, rural or frail older adults at risk of institutionalization, even though it retains its original goal of universality (National Academy on Aging, 1995).

Since participation rates in many OAA services have been highest among middle-income older individuals, proposals have been introduced for cost-sharing of services. This raises fears among OAA program staff that cost-sharing would introduce means-testing and stigmatize OAA programs as "welfare," thereby discouraging their use. However, by targeting services to low-income older people, an implicit means test is already being employed. Another concern is to increase minority participation in OAA programs through targeted outreach and increased recruitment of ethnic minority staff and board members of local agencies receiving OAA funds. Proponents of the political economy perspective fear that the current focus on indirect services (care assessment and management) rather than direct service delivery may impede the achievement of improved quality of life as a goal (Estes et al., 1996).

POLICY DILEMMAS

Age-Based versus Needs-Based Programs

Ongoing debates about the need for age-based programs underlie most policy developments in the aging field. These debates highlight choices about whom to serve and how to restrict eligibility for program benefits. The major argument for age-based programs is that they are an efficient way to set a minimum floor of protection for beneficiaries, are less stigmatizing than means-tested services, and support the values of individual dignity and interdependence. According to proponents of age-based programs, efficiency is enhanced by the fact that certain policies, such as Social Security, exclusively or predominantly affect older people. Similarly, it is argued that age-based programs involve fewer eligibility disputes and are less administratively intrusive into applicants' lives (Holstein, 1995).

Neugarten (1982; Neugarten and Neugarten, 1986), in particular, has argued strongly against age-based services. She maintains that they reinforce the perception of "the old" as a problem, thereby stigmatizing older people and adding to age segregation. The Older Americans Act, for example, implicitly views anyone over age 60 as vulnerable and therefore needing services. Yet, as we have seen, growing numbers of people over age 60 are in good health, have an adequate income, and therefore do not need services. The use of age as a criterion for benefits assumes that older people are homogeneous and different from other age groups; but Neugarten maintains that old age in itself does not constitute a basis for treatment different from that of other ages. As noted in Chapter 1, chronological age has become a poor predictor of the timing of life events and of health, income, and family status; and therefore of people's interests and needs. Since age is not a useful indicator of changes within a person, it is an arbitrary criterion for service delivery. Instead, many universal age-based programs have benefited the young-old who are relatively healthy and in the top third of the income distribution. In fact, Torres-Gil (1992) argues that with up to 25 percent of the population qualifying for age-related benefits, a purely age-based approach has become politically and economically unfeasible.

An alternative view is that economic and health needs, rather than age, should be the basis for selectively targeting services. For example, the need for services increases after age 75, when an individual's health and income also tend to decline. Proposals to take account of older people's socioeconomic status as a basis for eligibility for Social Security and Medicare are congruent with a needs-based approach. Some advocates for targeting services to older persons at greatest risk favor a combination of categorical and group eligibility mechanisms. For example, a portion of Older Americans Act service funds could be restricted for allocation to SSI and older Medicaid recipients, thereby reaching individuals with the lowest incomes and presumably the most service needs. Given the increasing economic inequality within the older population, it can be argued that means-testing programs that comprise the "safety net" for the least well-off older adults, such as Supplemental Security Income and Medicaid, should be priorities for improvement.

Meals-on-Wheels is an age-based program that can help older people remain independent.

The Politics of Productivity versus the Politics of Entitlement

Closely related to the ongoing debate about age-based versus needs-based programs is a more recent debate on the politics of productivity versus entitlement (Moody, 1990). The **politics of entitlement** is characterized as follows:

1. In a "failure model of old age," older people, solely because of their age, are defined as needy, worthy, and deserving of public support.
2. Issues are defined in terms of needs and rights.
3. The emphasis is on what older people deserve to receive as their right rather than what they can give.
4. Resources are transferred to the older population as a categorical group.
5. Other groups must pay for the benefits due the older population.

The **politics of productivity,** as discussed in Chapters 8 and 11, is characterized this way:

1. The older population is increasingly diverse.
2. The implementation of new policies will require an expanding economy toward which older adults can contribute.
3. Older people are defined as a resource in an interdependent society and can contribute to younger populations. Old age is a time for giving assistance and advice to the young.
4. "Investing in human resources" across the life span is essential to future economic growth to benefit all ages.

As we noted earlier, a growing number of national groups as well as members of Congress, particularly among the "New Right," are questioning entitlement programs for all age groups. While they point to the increased socioeconomic diversity of the older population, especially the growing middle class, as a rationale for means-testing, there is no agreement on how much to target resources in order to benefit those most at-risk, such

as women and ethnic minorities. In other words, most advocates for changing entitlement programs appear to be motivated by fiscal goals, not by considerations of reducing status inequities within the older population.

Intergenerational Inequity Framework

Closely related to the debate about both age-based entitlement programs and a politics of productivity is the argument that older persons are benefiting at the expense of younger age groups, who lack the political clout represented by senior organizations. The **intergenerational inequity** debate began in 1984 with Samuel Preston's analysis of poverty rates among the young and old and public expenditures on behalf of older people. The old were perceived to be thriving, at the expense of children, as a result of expanded Social Security benefits and inflationary increases in real estate and home equity (Preston, 1984). This generated a rather simplistic picture of generational conflict, expounded in a growing number of newspaper and magazine editorials. It also resulted in the formation of groups such as **Americans for Generational Equity** (AGE), which later merged with the American Association of Boomers (AAB) and the National Taxpayers Union. These organizations maintain that the baby-boom generation (i.e., those born between 1946 and 1964) will collectively face a disastrous retirement, and its children will, in turn, be much more heavily burdened with the support of their parents than any other generation has been in our nation's history. More recently, advocates for the baby boomers have been joined by the Third Millennium and PAC 20/20, groups that are concerned about the future of **Generation X,** young adults in their 20s.

Underlying their arguments is the assumption that our country faces significant distribution choices, especially related to Social Security and other retirement incentives, about how to pay the costs of an aging society (Moody, 1990). Policy questions then become framed in terms of competition and conflict between generations. This cre-

---

THE THEMES OF THE BACKLASH ARGUMENT ARE:

- America's older citizens, now better off financially than is the population as a whole, are selfish and concerned only with personal pension and income benefits and their share of the federal budget.
- Programs for older people are a major cause of current budget deficits, economic problems, and increases in poverty among mothers and children.

- Children are the most impoverished age group.
- Younger people will not receive fair returns for their Social Security and Medicare investments.
- The future of younger generations is also threatened by declining expenditures for national defense.

---

ates a backlash against the gains experienced by the older population and polarizes younger and older generations.

Admittedly, high inflation, lack of real wage growth, and runaway housing costs hurt young adults struggling to start jobs and families and to buy a home. Similarly, the growing divorce rate has thrown millions of children into one-parent households and poverty. At the same time, older people are perceived as benefiting from generous entitlement programs which policymakers have been loath to cut. As described in Chapter 11, the average older person today is financially better off than in the past. In many ways, their improved economic status actually represents a success story of government interventions rather than a basis for criticism. Yet, beneath the appearance of a dramatic decline in poverty among the older population is the reality that many of those who "moved out" of poverty have shifted from a few hundred dollars below the poverty line to a few hundred above it, forming the "near poor" and "hidden poor." In addition, the distribution of income among the older population is extremely diverse, and the level of inequality among them is extraordinarily high.

Critique of the Intergenerational Inequity Framework

The intergenerational inequity framework that attempts to measure the relative hard times of one

generation against the relative prosperity of another has been widely criticized by advocates for older people. The major criticisms of this framework are as follows: Contrary to the pessimistic argument that society will not be able to provide for future generations of older people, the economy of the future, barring unforeseen disasters, will be able to support a mix of programs for all age groups. In fact, in 1994, 50.5 percent of all American families received at least one benefit from entitlements or other safety-net programs, and 23 percent received at least one need-related benefit. These figures show that the distribution of benefits extends far beyond the older population (Wu, 1995). Evidence of significant intergenerational conflict is limited. Instead, younger and older generations appear to recognize their interdependence and to support benefits to each other across the life span (Adams and Dominick, 1995). For example, the Children's Defense Fund argues that funding for programs for the young should be increased at the cost of military spending, not at the expense of programs for the old. The American Association of Retired Persons concurs, and maintains that older people's well-being contributes to the welfare of all other generations.

The definition of fairness put forth by groups such as Americans for Generational Equity is narrow and misleading. When fairness is equated with numerical equality, this assumes that the relative needs of children and older people for public funds are identical, and that equal expenditures are the equivalent of social justice. Even if needs and expenditures for each group were equal, this would not result in equal outcomes or social justice. By framing policy issues in terms of competition and conflict between generations, the intergenerational inequity perspective implies that public benefits to older individuals are a one-way flow from young to old, and that reciprocity between generations does not exist. It is true that younger generations are facing increased economic pressures. However, as noted earlier, rather than blame older adults, the role of federal deficits, economic conditions, and increasing housing costs also needs to be recognized. In some instances, the intergenerational debate has become a convenient mechanism to justify shifting responsibility for all vulnerable groups to individuals, the private sector, and local governments (Quadagno, 1990). Accordingly, it overlooks other ways of increasing public resources through economic growth, increased tax revenues, or reduced defense spending, and that the economic well-being of future generations will ultimately depend on growth rates of real wages (Quinn, 1996).

Nevertheless, some advocates for older adults are beginning to acknowledge that it is no longer realistic to proceed on the assumption that all benefits are sacrosanct. They recognize that it is counterproductive to oppose all measures imposed on financially better off older persons, such as treating part of Social Security as taxable income or subjecting Social Security and Medicare to means-testing. Yet the negative reaction of higher-income elders to paying the surtax for Catastrophic Health Care Insurance in 1988 suggests that there are still many older adults who believe that services should be provided on the basis of age, not need.

The Interdependence of Generations Framework

Consistent with social exchange theory (as discussed in Chapter 8), a continuing human dilemma is the "contract between generations." Typically, this has been defined between parents to children

and children to aging parents. What is different today is the focus on relationships between age groups in society rather than individuals within the family. This shift from generations to age groups has increased the magnitude and complexity of the issues involved, so that it is no longer youth versus elders, but rather elders versus middle-aged and youth. Never before have so many individuals lived so long, and never have there been so relatively few members of the younger generation to support them (Bengtson, 1993).

The **"interdependence of generations" framework,** advocated by the Gerontological Society of America, recognizes the changing societal and political context. Along with the increase in life expectancy and decreases in fertility, there are increased policy concerns about welfare costs and public expenditures that are targeted to various age groups (Bengtson, 1993). Within this larger context, public and private intergenerational transfers are viewed as central to social progress. A major way in which generations assist one another is through the family; for example, through care for children and dependent adults, financial support, gifts to children and grandchildren, and inheritances. Private intergenerational transfers are essential to meeting families' needs at various points over the life course and to transmitting legacies of the past (e.g., culture, values, and knowledge) (Adams and Dominick, 1995).

Transfers based on public policy (e.g., education, Social Security, and health care programs) also serve intergenerational goals. For example, Social Security benefits are distributed widely across all generations and protect against risks to families' economic well-being over the course of their lives. It is erroneous to think of Social Security as a one-way flow of resources from young to old. Instead, younger generations have at least two important stakes in Social Security: they will be served by it when they become old, and, as stated earlier, programs that support their older relatives' autonomy currently relieve them from financial responsibilities. Similarly, when it is recognized that long-term care can affect all age groups, particularly the growing number of younger adults with

A major way in which older generations provide assistance is through child care.

AIDS or who are developmentally disabled or chronically mentally ill, then long-term care services can benefit all generations. Likewise, it is erroneous to think of education as a one-way flow to children, resisted by the older population. Instead, older people have contributed to public education throughout their working careers. As noted in Chapter 11, the extent of support among them for school levies is higher than commonly assumed. Such support reflects their recognition that older generations benefit from education programs that increase work-force productivity.

Within the framework of interdependence, other paradigms have been proposed as a way to conceptualize how the burdens and opportunities within our society can be fairly shared among generations. One paradigm is the concept of **generational investment,** in which age-based services and other social programs, such as public education, play an integral part in the system of reciprocal contributions that generations in any society make to one another. Programs such as Social Security and Medicare are mechanisms through which generations invest in one another and publicly administer returns to older cohorts for the investments made in the human capital of younger groups. As such, old-age benefits represent claims based on merit and social contributions and should not be subject to means testing (National Academy on Aging, 1994).

Similarly, it has been argued that older people can be the vanguard of renewed efforts to ensure a decent standard of living for all Americans, perhaps through measures such as a universal family-allowance program and paid parental leaves that recognize the contributions of child rearing to society (Adams and Dominick, 1995). This assumes that intergenerational competition can be reduced by enhancing people's opportunities earlier in their lives. A broadened welfare consensus also could be fostered through an understanding of the life-course experiences that lead to problems in old age. This perspective of our common human vulnerability across the life course is not a new one. In fact, President Lyndon B. Johnson's charge to the 1968 Task Force Report on Older Americans was to determine the most important things to be done for the well-being of most older Americans. Since vulnerability in old age is the product of a lifetime of experiences, the Task Force concluded that the priority is to provide social and economic opportunities for young and middle-aged persons (Jacobs, 1991; Binstock, 1990).

Similar to the "politics of productivity" and the interdependence framework, Torres-Gil (1994, 1992) argues for a paradigm of "New Aging" in the post-1990s. The politics of the New Aging aims to identify how all generations can contribute to a new society, in contrast to a focus on serving the older population that has characterized the period from 1930 to 1990. He argues that our society must alter both our view of older adults to take account of their growing diversity, and the manner in which we provide for them. With the increased heterogeneity of the older population, intergenerational conflict of old versus young cannot be assumed. While some tensions between young and old will remain, a more likely outcome is the politics of diversity in which some older people may have more in common with younger age groups than with their peers. There will be greater differences of political opinions among older people and between age cohorts, with more linkages based on political priorities, not age per se (Torres-Gil, 1992).

In the politics of the New Aging, advocacy and lobbying should be rechanneled from special-interest issues toward politics to benefit all future generations. Groups of older people should shift from the horizontal alliances that characterize interest-group politics to new vertical alliances, representing common needs between aging and non-aging groups (Binstock, 1995; Torres-Gil and Kmet, 1990). Previously underrepresented groups of older persons—ethnic minorities, women, rural residents—must establish alliances with non-aging groups. In fact, this has already started to occur. For example, Generations United has established a coalition of consumer, labor, children, and senior groups, and AARP is forming networks with minority populations. Not only should older adults be viewed as a resource able to contribute to the economy and their own income security, but the young should also be educated to prepare for their own aging.

To address the problems of the disadvantaged under the interdependence framework of the New Aging requires an ideological consensus that government should help people in need, regardless of age. As we have seen in our earlier analysis of factors that affect policy development, such a consensus does not exist. Given this lack of consensus, some policy analysts argue that the real issue for the 1990s is not intergenerational conflict or interdependence but rather the role of the public sector in caring for its vulnerable citizens and the relationship between the public and private sectors (Estes, Swan, and Associates, 1993).

WHO IS RESPONSIBLE?

As noted, many of these policy debates revolve around the division of responsibility between the public sectors of federal and state governments, and the private realms of family and business. The current public–private debate is not new, but long-standing, reflected even in the passage of Social Security. Until recently, Social Security benefits, Medicare, Medicaid, SSI, and services under the Older Americans Act settled the question of responsibility for older citizens: It was to be a collective responsibility of the entire population, exercised through the national government, and a protection to which every older citizen was entitled, simply by virtue of age.

A growing view held by public officials since the 1980s is that the problems of older people and other disadvantaged groups cannot be solved with federal policies and programs alone. Instead, solutions must come from state and local governments, and from private sector and individual initiatives, such as advocacy, self-help, family caregiving, and personal retirement planning and private investments. Individuals are assumed to be responsible for their own problems, and federal government interventions are considered to be too costly and to threaten national economic well-being by increasing the deficit. An anti-tax mentality, combined with growing public concern about the federal deficit, have resulted in legislative changes to reduce federal funds and to rely upon the states through block grants. These cuts are also justified by the assumption that the states can most efficiently and innovatively respond to local needs. A limitation of this decentralized approach, however, is that states have the fewest resources for supporting community services. Therefore, they are generally the least likely to respond to the needs of the most disadvantaged. As noted previously, with decentralization, there is little assurance of policy uniformity and of equity for powerless groups across different states. National initiatives that establish stable, uniformly administered federal policies are usually necessary to bring the states with the lowest expenditures up to a minimum standard.

Reductions in Government Support

What is more important than federal–state relations, however, is the level of public spending. Although public spending has increased in terms of total dollars, it has declined when measured as a percentage of the gross national product or as government expenditures per capita, corrected for inflation. Economically disadvantaged older persons have been hurt the most by the budget cuts of the past 20 years, especially under the Republican "Contract with America" and the 1996 "Personal Responsibility and Work Opportunity Legislation" (welfare reform).

Public spending levels are being reduced at the same time that private and local spheres are being expected to be more responsible for older people with chronic disabilities. Policymakers often assume that public programs reduce family involvement and that families could do more for their older relatives. However, as discussed in Chapter 9, the family has consistently played a major role in caring for older relatives. Family members may be providing all the support that they are able or willing to do, although such assistance is not necessarily financial. When resources become scarce, the family tends to be viewed as a cost-effective alternative to nursing-home placement and to publicly funded social services.

Not only are families unable to carry expanded responsibilities on their own, but the private non-profit service sector cannot fill the gaps created by federal cuts. In fact, federal tax laws have reduced incentives for corporate giving. In addition, private contributions traditionally have not been concentrated on social services, so that increased private giving would not automatically flow into areas most severely cut. Instead, both public and private funds are decreasing as the older population and their need for services increase.

SUMMARY AND IMPLICATIONS

Rapid demographic and social changes mean that U.S. society is faced with complex, difficult policy choices. It is increasingly apparent that the older population is not one constituency but several, in which race, gender, and socioeconomic class may be greater unifiers than age. A political agenda must be drafted that can unite different older constituencies—low-income, middle-class, and wealthy—as well as different ethnic minority and age groupings with common needs. Lack of

public resources in itself is not the primary barrier to action, however. For example, the cost of eliminating poverty among both older people and children is well within our societal resources. The greater challenge is in framing the political consensus to ensure a minimal level of economic security and health for all Americans. Progress could be made in both areas largely by improving the basic income support of SSI and expanding Medicaid eligibility—changes that are possible within current budgetary restraints. Unfortunately, such gains are unlikely to occur without major changes in our political structures and belief systems of democratic pluralism, states' rights, and individual freedom. Until then, Americans will continue to be personally generous but reluctant to support income-maintenance programs for an entire class of needy persons or a national health care system that is perceived to threaten individual choice.

This chapter has reviewed federal programs that benefit older persons. Since 1960, age-specific spending has increased significantly, mostly through Medicare and Old Age and Survivors and Disability Insurance of Social Security. In the past, such age-entitlement programs have been based on cultural values and public attitudes that older people are deserving. However, the rapid expansion of these programs combined with the improved economic status of the majority of older people have created a growing public and political sentiment that such age-based entitlement programs must be reduced, perhaps through means-testing to minimize the benefits received by higher-income older adults.

The United States developed policies aimed at older populations more slowly than European countries. The Social Security Act of 1935 was the first major policy aimed at older people. Social Security was expanded slightly in 1950 to support partial health care costs through individual states. These changes led to the enactment of Medicare in 1965. Since then, there has been a significant growth in the number of programs aimed at improving the welfare of older people: the Older Americans Act, Supplemental Security Income, the Social Security Amendments of 1972 and 1977, and Title XX social services legislation. These programs have been strengthened by national forums such as the 1961 and 1971 White House Conferences on Aging. During the 1980s, however, there was a decline in social services. Allocations for homemaker, nutrition, chore services, adult day care, low-income energy assistance, respite, and volunteer programs such as Retired Senior Volunteer Programs all diminished. These cost-efficiency measures were based on a national perception that the older population has greater financial security than younger age groups. The fiscal crisis faced by the Social Security system in the early 1980s fueled this stereotype through speculations that the growing number of older persons would drain the system before future generations could benefit from it. However, numerous structural factors were responsible for the problems. Changes that have subsequently been made in this system assure its future viability until approximately 2029.

The debate over age-based versus needs-based programs has also led to the emergence of organizations that have expounded arguments about older people benefiting at the expense of younger age groups. Yet, evidence for such inequities is weak; numerous other organizations such as the Children's Defense Fund and Generations United recognize generational interdependence and the importance of seeking increased public support for all ages through other sources. This framework, known as the interdependence of generations, assumes that assistance from young to old and old to young benefits all ages and supports the role of families across the life span.

The policy agenda for older Americans for the remainder of the twentieth century is full and complex. The current federal emphasis on fiscal austerity underlies all policy debates about how much the government should be expected to provide and for whom. Increasing public perceptions of older people as well off, combined with decreased government resources, will undoubtedly affect the types of future programs and policies developed to meet older adults' income, housing, and social service needs. Older people are less likely to act as a unified bloc in support of age-based programs.

Instead, the increased diversity of the older population suggests that there will be alliances formed between at-risk elders and other age groups. Consistent with the frameworks of interdependence and generational investment, such alliances may be able to develop policies that benefit both older people and future generations. Threatening such cross-age efforts, however, is the anti-tax mood of the public and the fiscal conservatism of the "New Right." These pressures suggest that advocates for older people will need to find new ways to address the complex needs created by increased life expectancy and diversity among the older population. A major challenge is the development and funding of health care, especially home- and community-based forms of long-term care. This topic is addressed in Chapter 16.

GLOSSARY

age-entitlement (age-based) programs   programs only available to people of a certain age

Aging Network   the system of social services for older adults funded by the Older Americans Act

Americans for Generational Equity   a group that questions age-entitlement programs for older people, since such programs are perceived as reducing the resources available to other age groups

Area Agencies on Aging   offices on aging at the regional and local level that plan and administer services to meet the needs of older adults within that area; established and partially funded through the Older Americans Act

block grants   funds provided by one level of government (federal or state) to a lower level (state or local) for purposes of supporting a substantial range of benefits or services, generally at the discretion of the lower level

cash substitute   a benefit given in a form other than cash, such as a voucher, which may be exchanged for food, rent, medical care, etc.

cash transfer   a benefit paid by cash or its equivalent

categorical   in this context, a manner of dealing with public problems by addressing the problems of specific groups of persons rather than attempting solutions that are comprehensive or dealing with problems as they affect the entire population

contributory programs   programs providing benefits that require the beneficiary to contribute something toward the cost of the benefit

cost containment   the effort to minimize cost, usually expressed in financial terms, without damaging effectiveness of product

cost effectiveness   the assessment of benefit or effect against cost; used in reaching decisions about the value of programs

cost efficiency   the assessment of a benefit or program based on the ratio of costs of inputs to value of outputs; the most efficient program produces the greatest benefit or output for the least cost of input

cost of living adjustments (COLA)   changes in benefits designed to maintain steady purchasing power of such benefits

dependency ratio   the number of people who are "dependent" compared to the number who are employed; the ratio is calculated by dividing the number of people under age 18 plus people over age 65 by the number of workers (i.e., people between age 18 and 65)

direct benefit   a benefit given directly, either in the form of a cash payment or of some commodity such as food or housing

eligibility criteria   factors that determine the ability of programs to deliver benefits to people

entitlement programs   government programs organized in such a way that appropriations from a legislative body are not required; rather, eligibility on the part of applicants triggers receipt of benefits regardless of the total cost of the program

Generation X   those who are, at present, between 20 and 29 years of age

generational investment   investments made by one generation for the benefit of another, such as the payment of Social Security taxes by the working population for the benefit of retirees, the services provided by older persons for the care of children, and the payment of property taxes that benefit school children

income redistribution   transfer of income from people with greater to those with less income

incrementally   in this context, a manner of dealing with public problems by making small changes in policy rather than attempting comprehensive or major changes

index   in this context, steps taken to maintain the value of a benefit as changes in the value of currency decrease

or increase by increasing or decreasing the benefit in accord with changes in the cost of living

indirect benefit   a benefit given indirectly, such as a tax deduction or exemption

individual equity   an individual receiving benefits that reflect that person's actual monetary contributions

interdependence of generations framework   recognizes intergenerational transfers that occur across the life span

intergenerational inequity   the view that one generation or age group receives benefits that are disproportional to those received by another

means- or need-based entitlements   social programs delivered to persons who meet defined criteria of eligibility based on need or ability to pay for the benefits

non-contributory programs   programs providing benefits that do not require the beneficiary to contribute toward the cost of the benefit

Older Americans Act   federal legislation for a network of social services specifically for older people

outreach   a strategy of service that endeavors to locate those in need of services, explains possible benefits to them, and facilitates their delivery

payroll taxes   taxes calculated as a percentage of an entity's payroll or of an individual's income

policy   principles that govern action directed toward specific ends, designed to identify and ameliorate problems and implying changes in situations, systems, practices, beliefs, or behaviors

politics of entitlement   political preferences, especially as applied to the aged, for the allocation of resources based on notions of older persons as needy, worthy, and deserving of public support

politics of productivity   political preferences, especially as applied to the aged, for the allocation of resources based on a recognition of the diversity of the aging population (some are well-off, others are poor; some are capable of continued productive work, while others are ill or disabled)

residual role of government   based on values commonly held by Americans of individual freedom and rights, self-determination and privacy, and personal responsibility; the belief that government should serve only a backup role in providing benefits, responding to crises rather than attempting to prevent problems or attack underlying causes

respite care   a service designed to relieve, for relatively brief periods, persons assuming responsibility for the care of ill or disabled persons

selective benefits benefits available on an individually determined need or means basis

social adequacy shared societal responsibility to provide a basic standard of living for all potential beneficiaries—a "safety net"—regardless of the amount of their economic contributions

social insurance benefits paid to persons based upon contingencies to which all people are exposed, including such factors as age, disability, sickness, and unemployment

social programs the visible manifestations of policies (see policy)

Title XX or the Social Services Block Grant funding for social services (e.g., homemaking chores, adult day care) based on need, not age

universal benefits benefits available on the basis of social right to all persons belonging to a designated group

References

Adams, P., and Dominick, G. The old, the young and the welfare state. *Generations,* Fall 1995, 19, 38–42.

Atchley, R. Retirement income security: Past, present and future. *Generations,* Summer 1997, 21, 9–12.

Ball, R. The case for maintaining benefits plan for Social Security. In D. Salisbury, *Assessing Social Security reform alternatives.* Washington, DC: Employee Benefits Research Institute, 1997.

Bengtson, V. L. Is the contract across generations changing? Effects of population aging on obligations and expectations across age groups. In V. L. Bengtson and W. A. Auchenbaum (Eds.), *The changing contract across generations.* New York: Aldine de Gruyter, 1993.

Binstock, R. H. A new era in the politics of aging: How will the old-age interest groups respond? *Generations,* Fall 1995, 19, 68–74.

Binstock, R. H. Changing criteria in old-age programs: The introduction of economic status and need for services. *The Gerontologist,* 1994, 34, 726–730.

Binstock, R. H. The deficit entitlements and policies on aging. *Gerontology News,* Washington, DC: Gerontological Society of America, February, 1993, 2.

Binstock, R. H. The politics and economics of aging and diversity. In S. Bass, E. Kutza, and F. M. Torres-Gil (Eds.), *Diversity in aging.* Glenview, IL: Scott, Foresman and Co., 1990.

Binstock, R. H., and Day, C. L. Aging and politics. In R. H. Binstock and L. K. George (Eds.), *Handbook of aging and the social sciences* (4th ed.). San Diego, CA: Academic Press, 1996.

Bryce, D. V., and Friedland, R. B. *Economic and health security: An overview of the origins of federal legislation.* Washington, DC: The National Academy on Aging, January 16, 1997.

Concord Coalition. *The zero deficit plan: A plan for eliminating the federal budget deficit by the year 2000.* Washington, DC: The Concord Coalition, 1993.

Conte, C. Executive Summary: Assessing Social Security reform alternatives. In D. Salisbury, *Assessing Social Security reform alternatives.* Washington, DC: Employee Benefit Research Institute, 1997.

Deets, H. B. Social Security reform? Just follow the money. *AARP Bulletin,* May 1997, 3.

Dentzer, S. Social Security reform: Gaps in perception. In D. Salisbury, *Assessing Social Security reform alternatives.* Washington, DC: Employee Benefits Research Institute, 1997.

Devlin, S., and Arye, L. The Social Security debate: A financial crisis or a new retirement paradigm. *Generations,* Summer 1997, 21, 27–34.

Estes, C. L. *The aging enterprise.* San Francisco: Jossey-Bass, 1979.

Estes, C. L. Aging, health and social policy: Crisis and crossroads. *Journal of Aging and Social Policy,* 1989, 1, 17–32.

Estes, C. L. Austerity and aging: 1980 and beyond. In M. Minkler and C. L. Estes (Eds.), *Readings in the political economy of aging.* Farmingdale, NY: Baywood, 1984.

Estes, C. L., Linkins, K. W., and Binney, E. A. The political economy of aging. In R. H. Binstock and L. K. George (Eds.), *Handbook of aging and the social sciences* (4th ed.). San Diego, CA: Academic Press, 1996.

Estes, C. L., Swan, J. H., and Associates. *The long-term care crisis.* Newbury Park, CA: Sage, 1993.

Gill, D., and Ingman, S. *Eldercare, distributive justice, and the welfare state: Retrenchment or expansion.* Albany, NY: State University of New York, 1994.

Hardy, D., and Hardy, C. *Social insecurity.* New York: Villard Books, 1991.

Holstein, M. The normative case: Chronological age and public policy. *Generations,* Fall 1995, 19, 11–14.

Howe, N. Why the graying of the welfare state threatens to flatten the American dream—or worse. *Generations,* Fall 1995, 19, 15–20.

Hudson, R. The history and place of age-based public policy. *Generations,* Fall 1995, 19, 5–10.

Jacobs, B. Public policy and poverty among the oldest old: Looking to 2040. *Journal of Aging and Social Policy,* 1991, *2,* 85–99.

Kassner, E. *The impact of food stamp cuts in the welfare reform bill on older persons.* Washington, DC: AARP, Public Policy Institute, 1996.

Kingson, E. R. Testing the boundaries of universality: What's mean? What's not? *The Gerontologist,* 1994, *34,* 736–742.

Kingson, E. R., and Quadagno, J. Social Security: Marketing radical reform. *Generations,* Fall 1995, 19, 43–47.

Kingson, E. R., and Schulz, J. H. Should Social Security be means-tested? In E. R. Kingson, and J. H Schulz. (Eds.), *Social Security in the 21st century.* New York: Oxford Press, 1997.

Lukefar, R. Testimony before the Bipartisan Commission on Entitlement and Tax Reform. Washington, DC: September 23, 1994.

Marmor, T. R., Cook, F. L., and Scher, S. Social Security politics and the conflict between generations. Are we asking the right questions? In E. R. Kingson, and J. H. Schulz, *Social Security in the 21st century.* New York: Oxford University Press, 1997.

Mathews, J. The retirement crisis. *The Seattle Times,* Friday, January 6, 1995, B5 (Special to *The Washington Post*).

Miller, M. Rebuilding retirement. *US News and World Report,* April 20, 1998, 20–26.

Moody, H. R. The politics of entitlement and the politics of productivity. In S. Bass, E. Kutza, and F. M. Torres-Gil (Eds.), *Diversity in aging.* Glenview, IL: Scott, Foresman and Co., 1990.

Moon, M. Are Social Security benefits too high or too low? In E. R. Kingson, and J. H. Schulz (Eds.), *Social Security in the 21st century.* NY: Oxford Press, 1997.

Moon, M. Social Security: Critics get it wrong. *AARP Bulletin,* October 1997, *38,* 14.

National Academy on Aging. *Facts on the Older Americans Act.* Washington, DC: The National Academy on Aging, 1995.

National Academy on Aging. *Facts on Social Security: The Old Age and Survivors Trust Fund, 1996.*

Washington, DC: The National Academy on Aging, 1997.

National Academy on Aging. *Old age in the 21st century.* A report to the Assistant Secretary for Aging, U.S. Department of Health and Human Services. Syracuse University, Maxwell School of Public Affairs and the U.S. Administration on Aging, June 1994.

Neugarten, B. Policy in the 1980s: Age or need entitlement. In B. Neugarten (Ed.), *Age or need: Public policies for older people.* Beverly Hills, CA: Sage, 1982.

Neugarten, B., and Neugarten, D. Changing meanings of age in the aging society. In A. Pifer and L. Bronte (Eds.), *Our aging society: Paradox and promise.* New York: W. W. Norton, 1986.

Peterson, P. G. *Facing up: How to rescue the economy from crushing debt and restore the American Dream.* New York: Simon & Schuster, 1993.

Preston, S. H. Children and the elderly in the United States. *Scientific American,* 1984, *251,* 44–49.

Quadagno, J. Generational equity and the politics of the welfare state. *International Journal of Health Services,* 1990, *20,* 631–649.

Quinn, J. *Entitlements and the federal budget: Securing our future.* Washington, DC: National Academy on Aging, 1996.

Social Security Administration. *Fast facts and figures about Social Security.* Washington, DC: U.S. Government Printing Office, 1996a.

Social Security Administration. *Social Security: Understanding the benefits.* Washington, DC: U.S. Government Printing Office, 1996b.

Stern, L. Can we save Social Security? *Modern Maturity,* Jan-Feb. 1997, 28–36.

Torres-Gil, F. M. *The new aging: Politics and change in America.* New York: Auburn House, 1992.

Torres-Gil, F. M., and Kmet, M. Elder leadership for a diverse America. In S. Bass, E. Kutza, and F. M. Torres-Gil (Eds.), *Diversity in aging.* Glenview, IL: Scott, Foresman and Co., 1990.

Torres-Gil, F. M., and Puccinelli, M. Mainstreaming gerontology in the policy arena. *The Gerontologist,* 1994, *34,* 749–752.

Villa, V. M., Wallace, S. P., and Markides, K. Economic diversity and an aging population: The impact of public policy and economic trends. *Generations,* Summer 1997, 21, 13–17.

Wheeler, P. M., and Kearney, J. R. Income protection for the aged in the 21st century: A framework to help inform the debate. *Social Security Bulletin,* 1996, *59,* 3–19.

Woods, J. Pension coverage among the baby boomers: Initial findings for the 1995 Survey. *Social Security Bulletin,* Fall 1994, *57,* 12–25.

Wu, K. B. *Recipiency of Entitlement and other safety-net program benefits among families in 1993.* Washington, DC: AARP Public Policy Institute, 1995.

16

HEALTH AND LONG-TERM CARE POLICY AND PROGRAMS

Throughout this book, we have examined the interplay of social, physiological, and psychological factors in how older people relate to their environments, and how health status affects this interaction. Technological advances oriented toward cure have created the paradox that while people are now living longer, they face serious, often debilitating or life-threatening disabilities that create the need for ongoing custodial care. Although we have noted in Chapter 4 that disability per se in old age does not create dependency, growing numbers of older people, especially among the oldest-old, have multiple problems that result in physical and mental frailty, and they depend on the assistance of others as well as medical and non-medical services. This dependence is often intensified because of the interaction of age, race, gender, and poverty, and because of changes in family structure described in Chapter 9. And, as we have seen, the oldest-old, ethnic minorities, women, and those who are low-income are more likely to have chronic disabilities that affect their ability to function.

As described in Chapter 10, *long-term care* (LTC) refers to a wide range of supportive services and assistance provided to persons who, as a result of chronic illness or frailty, are unable to function independently on a daily basis. It is *not* limited to special housing such as nursing homes for older people but includes assistance to people living in their own homes. The need for LTC does not necessarily correspond to medical conditions, but rather problems with performing activities of daily living (ADLs)—bathing, dressing, toileting, eating, and transferring—and **instrumental activities of daily living (IADLs)**—shopping, cooking, and cleaning. In addition to help with specific daily life tasks, people with cognitive impairments such as Alzheimer's disease may need nearly constant supervision. The need for long-term care services is growing; in 1995, 10.5 percent of persons age 65 to 74 and 51 percent of those over 85 years of age required assistance with activities of daily living.

Overall, 57 percent of those who report using long-term care are age 65 or older (Moon, 1996; Coleman, 1996). Although the LTC system also encompasses younger adults with AIDS, serious and chronic mental illness, and developmental disabilities, the focus of our discussion is on the structural and regulatory aspects of LTC that affect older people. Because the current health care system emphasizes primary and acute care, long-term care is often perceived as a residual function to be undertaken when medical care has failed, rather than an essential and ongoing element of health care. Given the high incidence of chronic health needs in old age and the increasing numbers of older adults projected for the future, it is not surprising that the costs of health care, including long-term care, are one of the most critical and controversial policy issues facing our nation.

Most people associate long-term care services with an institutional setting, such as nursing homes or assisted-living sites. But such services are also delivered at community-based settings, such as nutrition programs, senior centers, adult daycare, respite, hospice, and transportation, and in a person's home, such as visiting nurses or social work services, chore services, home-delivered meals, homemaker/home health aides, in-home respite, friendly visiting, and telephone reassurance. Of all persons age 65 and over, 25 to 33 percent are likely to be admitted to a nursing home during their lifetimes, and the numbers needing long-term care over the next 30 years have been projected to increase threefold. Of those admitted, 33 percent are discharged within 3 months to community settings but still require some degree of home health care or personal assistance (Coleman, 1996; Gerety, 1994). In fact, two to three times as many older persons with disabilities are likely to receive long-term care at home as in nursing homes (National Academy on Aging, 1994). Although such home-based services are available in nearly all communities, family and friends most frequently provide long-term care. As many as 80 percent of older adults in need of long-term care live in their own homes or community settings. Of those who reside in the community, about 54 percent with severe disabilities rely exclusively on help from family and friends (Graves, 1997; Moon, 1996). The burdens faced by caregiving relatives are illustrated by the case of Kay Ruggles and her daughter described in the vignette below.

We begin by examining the rising costs of health and long-term care and the factors that underlie these. Next, the public programs that fund long-term care—Medicare, Medicaid, Title XX, and the Older Americans Act—along with private insurance are described. This review highlights the need for publicly funded home- and community-based care more than institutional care. Although major health care reform initiatives have failed at both the federal and state levels, the marketplace has begun to change dramatically the way in which health and long-term care services are delivered.

Health and Long-term Care Expenditures

Policymakers, service providers, and the general public are all concerned about the "crisis in health care." This refers mostly to the costs of care, the growing numbers of uninsured individ-

---

Kay Ruggles, age 87, suffers from severe osteoporosis and arthritis. Although she worries about falling, she wants to stay in her home as long as possible. Since she is not eligible for any publicly funded home care program, she must pay out of pocket for daily assistance with bathing, walking, and cooking. Her daughter is employed and has a family to care for, but tries to stay with her mother on weekends and assist her with the household chores. Because the cost of home care is so much greater than her income, Mrs. Ruggles' savings are dwindling. She and her daughter worry that she will have to go into a nursing home as a Medicaid patient as the only way to fund her care.

uals, and the status and future of health care systems (Zis, Jacobs, and Shapiro, 1996). From 1980 to 1990, all consumer prices grew by 58.6 percent, while the consumer price index for health care grew by 117.4 percent (Moon, 1996). People over 65 account for approximately 30 percent of the nation's annual federal health care expenditures (Wiener and Illston, 1996). In fact, the average expenditure for health services for persons age 65 and over is nearly four times the cost for those under age 65 and increases even more among the oldest-old. This is largely attributable to older people's greater chronic disease needs and use of hospital and nursing-home services, as described in Chapters 4 and 10. Of long-term care expenditures (e.g., nursing home, home health care), 73 percent is for people age 65 and over (Evashwick, 1996).

Although cost-containment changes in the private health care marketplace, especially through managed care, appear to have slowed the rate of increase of medical costs, expenses are still rising faster than the national income. Medicare and Medicaid are expanding at several times the economic growth rate, adding to the pressure to make changes in them in order to cut spending and the federal deficit. Based on current trends, it is projected that spending on Medicare and Medicaid will consume 26.4 percent of the federal budget in the year 2003, up from 16.5 percent in 1994 (Driscoll, 1996). While public expenditures for health and long-term care are rising, older individuals and their families are also paying more for care. Only 67 percent of total personal health care costs of older people are covered by government funding (Medicare, Medicaid, and other sources such as Veterans Administration), as illustrated in Figure 16.1. As mentioned in Chapter 11, older Americans now spend a higher proportion (and more in actual dollars) of their incomes on acute health care services than they did before Medicare and Medicaid were established three decades ago (23 percent versus 11 percent, respectively). They also spend more out-of-pocket than younger

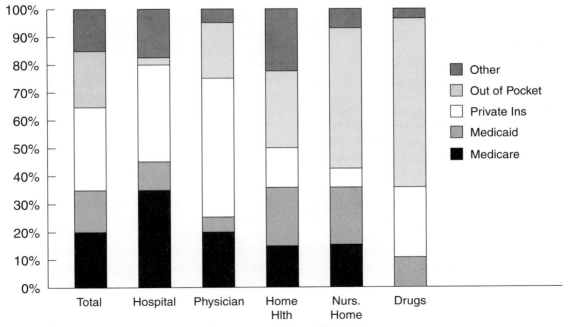

FIGURE 16.1   **Personal Health Care Expenditures, 1995**

REASONS FOR OLDER PEOPLE'S HIGHER OUT-OF-POCKET HEALTH CARE COSTS

- Their greater need for diverse health services (physician, hospital, home health care, dental and vision services, prescription drugs, and durable medical equipment, typically through the for-profit sector)

- The fact that Medicare benefits are often more limited than private insurance benefits
- The higher premiums and cost-sharing required by Medicare

Americans (National Academy on Aging, 1997). Over the same period that the median income of the older population rose 18 percent, real out-of-pocket spending on health care more than doubled (Moon, 1996). On average, a person age 65 and older who lives in the community paid an estimated $2750 out-of-pocket for health care costs in 1995, with over 56 percent of these expenditures going toward prescription drugs (Wiener and Illston, 1996).

The burdens of health care are expected to expand faster than the older population's ability to pay for the foreseeable future (Moon, 1996). At the same time, private health insurance costs have actually grown more annually, on average, than Medicare spending and increases have been greatest for home health and skilled nursing facility care (Driscoll, 1996).

Factors Underlying Growing Costs

A number of structural factors underlie escalating health care costs. One is the success of modern medical care. Costs have grown not so much in terms of the overall number of visits to health care providers, but in the type and complexity of health care services. While advances in medical science produce some cost-saving breakthroughs, they also make possible more sophisticated and expensive medical treatments that are in addition to services consumed rather than as replacements for old technologies or procedures. For example, an older patient now may receive X rays, CAT scans, and MRIs to diagnose a problem, whereas before only X rays would have been used. Closely related to the success of

medical technology in prolonging life is the conflict between the curative goals of medicine and the chronic care needs of older adults. As a result, there is a poor fit between the medical and related social service needs of the older population (e.g., long-term care needs) and the funding mechanisms, regulations, and fragmented services of the health care system.

Because of the rapid growth of the older population along with the public funding of a large portion of their care through Medicare and Medicaid, older people have often been "blamed" for escalating costs. Yet, contrary to media portrayals that medical costs in the last year of life escalate for the oldest-old, hospital and physician costs actually *decline* for those age 80 and over, although "custodial" or personal-care costs are high (Blanchette, 1996–97). This is because, as noted in Chapter 1, the very old are generally survivors and strongest of their cohort. Rather than population aging as the cause, escalating expenditures result, in large part, from: (1) the system of public financing, which is biased toward acute care, (2) and the lack of comprehensive, coordinated health and long-term care policy and programs that integrate acute and chronic care.

As we have seen in Chapter 15, underlying all these factors is a growing distrust of government and its ability to tackle health care reform, and a strong belief in the private sector; this is resulting in an approach to providing services that is determined by the market (who can provide the best services at lowest cost) (Moon, 1996). The shape of health care in the United States is largely influenced by its method of payment.

Funding mechanisms are shifting with the growth of **managed care,** which aims to control the level of resources devoted to health care. Nevertheless, the emphasis is on the private provision of health services, without effective market control or uniform governmental regulation of expenditures. Instead, most health services are provided privately and are financed by a mix of public programs, private insurance, and direct patient payments. Patients have been largely free to choose the health care providers they prefer. In turn, physicians have been able to charge patients whatever they choose. These patterns are even more pronounced with regard to the "non-system" of long-term care, which begins with the assumption that individuals are financially responsible for costs until their assets and income have been exhausted. At that point, welfare in the form of Medicaid takes over.

Acute and long-term care are, for the most part, two separate fragmented systems, with distinct caregivers, treatment settings, financing structures, and goals. Physicians are the primary care providers in hospitals and outpatient settings, and Medicare covers most of the costs. Nursing staff and family members are the principal caregivers in nursing homes and private home settings. Medicaid pays for a large percentage of institutional care (Evashwick, 1996). In the acute-care

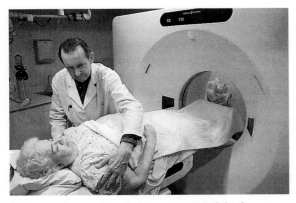

Expensive diagnostic techniques are one of the factors influencing growing health care costs.

setting, intensity of services determines costs, compared to duration of treatment in long-term care. As noted by Vladeck (1994), the "irony with long-term care is that the better the care, the longer the individual lives and remains in the system accruing costs." The different purposes between Medicaid and Medicare for health and long-term care for older people—the primary sources of funding and regulation—are the greatest barrier to the integration of the two systems of care.

MEDICARE

As a social insurance system, **Medicare,** or Title XVIII of the Social Security Act of 1965, is intended to provide financial protection against the cost of hospital and physician care for people age 65 and over. A value underlying Medicare is that older people are entitled to access to *acute medical care,* and society has an obligation to cover the costs associated with inpatient hospital care. Medicare's focus on the older population grew out of a compromise with the medical profession, which successfully opposed comprehensive health insurance for the general public. Yet Medicare was also viewed as the "first step" toward increasing access to health care for all age groups (Moon, 1996). Despite Medicare's goal of financial protection, it covers less than 50 percent of the total health expenditures of older adults, since it explicitly does not pay for long-term care (Driscoll, 1996; Aaronson, 1996). As noted above and illustrated in Figure 16.1, the remainder is paid by older people out-of-pocket, by private supplemental insurance, by Medicaid, and other public payers such as the Veterans Administration.

Contrary to many older persons' assumptions that Medicare will cover their health care costs, it pays only 80 percent of the allowable charges, not the actual amount charged by health providers (see Table 16.1). The patient must pay the difference between "allowable" and "actual" charges, unless the physician accepts "assignment" and agrees to charge only what Medicare pays. Beneficiaries whose doctors do not accept Medicare assign-

TABLE 16.1   Components of Medicare

HOSPITAL INSURANCE (PART A)

- Covers 99 percent of the older population.
- Financed through the Social Security payroll tax.
- Available for all older persons who are eligible for Social Security.
- Pays for up to 90 days of hospital care and for a restricted amount of skilled nursing care, rehabilitation, home health services (if skilled care is needed), and hospice care.
- Recipients are responsible for their first day's hospital stay and for co-payments for hospital stays exceeding 60 days.
- When the 90 days of hospital care are used up, a patient has a "lifetime" reserve of 60 days.

SUPPLEMENTAL MEDICAL INSURANCE (PART B)

- Covers 97 percent of the older population.
- Paid voluntarily through a monthly premium.
- Annual $100 deductible.
- Generally pays 80 percent of physician and hospital outpatient services, home health care limited to certain types of health conditions and specific time periods, diagnostic laboratory and x-ray services, and a variety of miscellaneous services, including 50 percent of the approved amount for outpatient mental health care.

ment are responsible for the amount that their doctor charges above the Medicare-approved rate, as illustrated by Mr. Fox.

Individuals with both Parts A and B must also pay an annual deductible and, in recent years, increasing co-payments. Although 75 to 85 percent of Medicare beneficiaries, such as Mr. Fox, now have supplemental insurance ("medigap") coverage to help pay for additional health care costs, the purchase of such private coverage is not a solution to health costs. Instead, it means the average spending on health care is increased. Since the majority of older people pay fully for this insurance, they effectively still bear the burden of health care costs (Moon, 1996).

Medicare's major limitation is its focus on acute care (e.g., inpatient hospital and physicians) as illustrated in Figure 16.2. As described above, it either excludes or gives little coverage to significant long-term care expenses, such as nursing homes, preventive health measures, outpatient costs of prescriptions, mental health services, and custodial or non-medical services. Instead, the majority of Medicare dollars pay for hospital care,

Mr. Fox went to his physician for a sigmoidoscopy, a procedure to examine the large colon for polyps or cancer. His physician charges $100 for this procedure. Medicare determined that the going rate for the procedures in Mr. Fox's community is $80. This means that Medicare pays the physician 80 percent of that amount, or $64.00. If Mr. Fox's physician accepts the assignment, then Mr. Fox owes his doctor the difference between $80 and $64, or $16. Fortunately, Mr. Fox has private "medigap" insurance that covers this difference. If Mr. Fox's physician had not accepted assignment, then Mr. Fox would have been responsible for paying $100 less the amount paid by Medicare ($64) or a total of $36.

typically for catastrophic illness. Nursing-home care is restricted to 100 days of skilled nursing care or skilled rehabilitation services, with eligibility contingent on acute illness or injury after hospi-

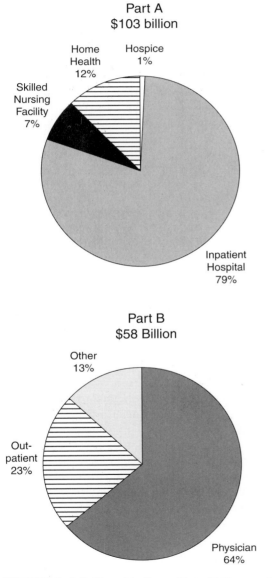

Part A
$103 billion

Home
Health
12%

Hospice
1%

Skilled
Nursing
Facility
7%

Inpatient
Hospital
79%

Part B
$58 Billion

Other
13%

Out-
patient
23%

Physician
64%

FIGURE 16.2   Medicare Benefit Payments, 1994
SOURCE: HCFA, Office of the Actuary.

talization, and requiring co-payments. As a result, Medicare covers 45 percent of health care spending for older people overall, but less for the oldest-old who require more nursing-home care. In fact, less than 29 percent of the total Medicare budget covers nursing-home expenditures. Accordingly, the health care expenses of only 3 to 5 percent of the institutionalized older population are covered by Medicare (National Academy on Aging, 1997; Burwell, Crown, O'Shaugnessy, and Price, 1996). Believing that it pays for long-term care, some older people only become aware of Medicare's lack of protection upon their first hospitalization or admission to a nursing home.

Another gap in Medicare funding has been home- and community-based care, although this now is the most rapidly growing Medicare benefit. With over 20 percent of nursing-home placements estimated to be incongruent with older persons' needs, home care is widely advocated as the lower-cost preferred alternative to inappropriate institutionalization. Even those in nursing-homes or hospitals may require home care at some point, since 25 to 45 percent of nursing home stays are less than 3 months, and 50 percent of these "short stayers" are able to return to live in the community (Kane and Kane, 1990; The Pepper Commission, 1990). As described in Chapter 10, home care has been found to permit earlier discharge, reduce the number of days of hospital care, and thus to cut costs (Hughes et al., 1997). Not only do most older people require home care, but they also prefer and tend to recover faster at home, when there is continuity of care.

Despite the need for home care and its impact on reducing hospital use, Medicare has some limitations on home care utilization. An older person must be homebound and in need of intermittent skilled nursing, physical therapy, or speech therapy; in addition, a doctor must prescribe the care as necessary to rehabilitate from an acute illness. The number of hours of care a day is limited as is the total number of days. Despite these limits, since 1989 to 1994, Medicare spending on home health care increased fivefold and now accounts for 14 percent of all Medicare Part A expenditures (although these expenditures are still dwarfed by hospital payments) (Wiener and Illston, 1996). This increase is due to a number of factors. One is earlier hospital discharges as a result of the 1983 Prospective Payment Systems which meant that patients required more technical care at home, such as intravenous therapy and ventilation therapy. Home care has served as the "safety net" for patients being discharged from acute and rehabilitation institutional settings after shorter lengths of stay (Schlenker, 1996). Another factor is a 1989 class action lawsuit that created a more flexible interpretation of Medicare home care regulations (for example, it could cover part time or intermittent care, and skilled nursing judgment, not just skilled nursing care). During that 5-year period, the percentage of beneficiaries receiving home health services nearly doubled, and the average number of visits per user almost tripled. In effect, with many recipients receiving 100 or more home visits, Medicare has begun to approximate a system of long-term care. Many of these long-term users of home health are getting home health aide visits, which are less-skilled services. Such visits are also likely to be lucrative for home health agencies, because they do not require the same skill levels in providing care but are still highly compensated. Nevertheless, some home health care remains a brief recovery "subacute" service, usually after a hospital stay. Medicare-funded home health benefits thus serve a dual purpose, caring for both the short- and long-term needs of beneficiaries (Hughes, 1996; Moon, 1996).

Another factor underlying increasing home care costs has been a dramatic growth in the number of **proprietary** or for-profit home health agencies that are reimbursed under Medicare. In the past, home care was dominated by non-profit agencies such as the Visiting Nurses Association. The growth of for-profit chains occurred in response to the 1980 and 1981 Omnibus Budget Reconciliation Acts. These eliminated the requirement for state licensing as a basis for reimbursing proprietary agencies. These regulatory changes served to stimulate competition for the provision and contracting out of services to new proprietary agencies. Such agencies, however, are less likely to

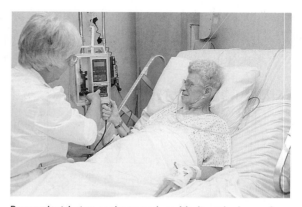

Recent legislation seeks to reduce Medicare's share of hospital costs.

concentrate on the ambulatory care of older people after hospital discharge. Recent allegations that Medicare-home health agencies are not complying with federal health and safety standards, are overcharging, and are providing substandard care are of concern to consumers and policymakers (Pear, 1997). These concerns have resulted in a 1997 decision by the **Health Care Financing Adminstration** (HCFA), the federal agency that manages Medicare, to put a freeze on licensing new home health agencies. In recognition of growing costs of home care, the 1997 Congress, under the balanced budget agreement, voted to impose a new payment system for home health care. Instead of separate payments for each visit, Medicare will adopt a new **prospective-payment system (PPS)**, with fixed, limited payments in advance for a general course of treatment. This is similar to the programs' current hospital reimbursement system that is described below under diagnostic-related groups (DRGs). Such limits may have the effect that Medicare enrollees and their families will need to purchase private paid care through out-of-pocket expenditures (Schlenker, 1996).

THE CRISIS IN MEDICARE

Despite the gaps in Medicare coverage and the current policy focus on cost containment, Medicare expenditures have spiraled. The problem is due primarily to significant increases in hospital costs into the early 1990s. Medicare currently forms 12 percent of the federal budget, and is predicted to be 18 percent of total federal outlays by 2005 (Bryce and Friedland, 1997). This increase is due to the projected increase in numbers of people reaching age 65 by 2005, and because of the rapid increase in hospital costs. Total Medicare spending is projected to grow by 8 to 10 percent per year over the next decade, just to maintain the same level of Medicare services for a growing Medicare population that is living longer (Driscoll, 1996). Medicare Part A (the Hospital Insurance Trust Fund) faces insolvency as early as mid-2001 (Smolka, 1997). For the past several years, the Trustees of the Hospital Insurance Trust Fund have warned Congress of the need to restore the balance between income and spending in order to reduce insolvency. The threats to the Trust Fund are due, in part, to the fact that the number of workers paying taxes relative to the number of beneficiaries is decreasing as the population continues to age (e.g., the age-dependency ratio discussed in Chapters 1 and 15). In contrast, the Supplementary Medicare Insurance Trust Fund, because it is financed on a yearly basis, remains adequately financed. As one of the fastest growing programs in the federal budget, Medicare became a target for budget cuts in the 1997 Balanced Budget Act. It is predicted that even greater spending reductions are needed because any legislative cuts have been outweighed by spending growth, so that Medicare has continued to expand (Moon, 1996). Medicare cuts of even billions of dollars do not mean declines in spending, just a slower rate of increase. These Medicare expenditure problems are due, in part, to the much larger and more intractable problem of rising health care costs generally in the United States.

Efforts to Reduce Medicare Costs

A number of measures have been taken to reduce costs under Medicare. As noted above in our discussion of home care, a **prospective-payment system** (PPS) was instituted in 1983 to reduce incentives for physicians to provide more hospi-

tal-bed services under fee-for-service payment plans. Instead of reimbursing providers for each service for each patient, the Health Care Financing Administration determines payment by the diagnostic category in which each patient is placed. These categories, which are used to classify patients by medical condition and thus establish Medicare payments prior to the patient's admission, are called "diagnostic related groupings," or DRGs. Under the prior cost-based reimbursement system, hospitals were paid more if they provided more and longer services, resulting in higher subsequent costs. With DRGs, a hospital is paid a fixed amount per admission, according to the diagnostic category. The rates for DRGs are, in turn, based on an expected length of stay for each condition. A hospital that keeps patients longer than needed, orders unnecessary tests, or provides care inefficiently must absorb the differential in cost between the care provided and the amount reimbursed by Medicare. Alternatively, hospitals that provide care at a cost below the established DRG can keep the financial difference. This serves as an incentive for hospitals to release patients as soon as possible.

Congress passed the Medicare Catastrophic Health Care Act (MCHCA) in 1988 in an effort to reduce costs associated with physician services, hospitalizations, and after-care for acute illness. Expanded benefits were to be financed by a mandatory supplemental premium. This surtax, ranging from $4 to $800 a year based on income, affected approximately 40 percent of the older population, specifically individuals with incomes over $30,000 or couples with incomes over $50,000 a year. Although the American Association of Retired Persons actively supported this legislation, none of its supporters anticipated the negative grassroots reaction among older persons nationwide. Many reacted against changes in the basic premise of Medicare financing: that higher-income older adults would pay a surtax for benefits serving primarily low-income older people, and that financing was entirely through a transfer of funds within older and disabled populations, not shared across populations. In addition, the legislation failed to address what most older people want—protection from the bankrupting expenses of long-term care. In 1989, Congress voted to repeal the legislation, leaving many legislators wary of making changes in Medicare.

In 1992, attempts were made to limit Medicare spending on physician care through implementation of a physician payment reform. This established a physician fee schedule and a system of limiting payment increases when the total cost of physician services billed in a year exceeds estimated levels. The physician payment reform program also limits the amount doctors can charge beneficiaries above the approved Medicare rate. Nevertheless, preliminary data suggest that Medicare expenditures are continuing to grow, albeit at a slower rate than might have occurred otherwise (National Academy on Aging, 1997).

Although findings are mixed, it appears that both lengths of stay per admission and number of admissions have fallen under PPS and DRGs. The total number of inpatient hospital days under Medicare has declined since 1991, even though hospital admissions have been on the rise (Moon, 1996). This is partially explained by the trend toward performing simple surgical and diagnostic procedures more frequently on an outpatient basis. What is less clear is how PPS and DRGs have affected utilization of nursing homes, home care by families, and home health care. Initially, it appeared that these groups faced increased pressures to provide care for patients discharged from the hospital on average 2 days earlier and sicker. Since families and home health agencies often cannot provide these more complex and intensive levels of care, some early studies found that premature discharges resulted in a "revolving door" pattern of more patients in and out of hospitals (Gaumer et al., 1989; Hing, 1989; Sager et al., 1989). On the other hand, findings of greater need for care and higher rates of mortality may be due, in part, to differences in risk factors (e.g., the inpatient population is now older and sicker than before the prospective payment system), not because of shorter stays or declining quality of care. Nevertheless, quality of care as a whole appears to be affected by earlier hospital discharge and restrictions on physician payment levels (Moon, 1996), as illustrated by Mr. Jones below. This is partly because DRGs discourage the extra time required to make appropriate discharge plans and the use of ancillary personnel such as social workers, except to expedite discharges from hospitals.

Ironically, Medicare costs across the health care system as a whole have not declined substantially since the passage of DRGs. This is because the prospective payment system has not altered Medicare's basic approach nor the structural arrangements that depend upon fee-for-service financing. Nor have DRGs reduced all the incentives for applying costly technologically oriented care. In fact, there has been an *increase* in the use of specialists and improved procedures such as hip replacement and cataract surgery that result in higher utilization rates. Costs have also grown because of increased federal oversight and regulatory control through hospital rate setting and the regulation of physician behavior. Other Medicare costs have increased, for example, by shifting medical proce-

Mr. Jones underwent major surgery for a radical prostatectomy for prostate cancer. Despite the pain that he was still experiencing, he was discharged after 3 days in the hospital and had to return home with a catheter in place that requires careful monitoring by a physician or nurse. His wife was in her late 80s and unable to provide the skilled care that a catheter requires. He was extremely fatigued. With only his frail wife to care for him, he required the services of a visiting nurse. He continued to experience considerable pain for which his medication was inadequate; if he could have remained in the hospital, his pain could have been relieved by an anesthesiologist. Perhaps the most difficult issue was his uncertainty and anxiety about a variety of symptoms, such as loss of appetite, which could have been resolved with a somewhat longer hospital stay.

dures to ambulatory settings and doctors' offices, which thus far have not been restricted by the prospective payment system (Moon, 1996).

The New Medicare

The changes now being discussed in Medicare have more to do with downsizing government than with focusing on Medicare per se. Medicare's future as a public program is viewed as tied to the larger financial problems facing the federal government during a period of fiscal restraint. As long as the federal budget deficits continue, changes in Medicare will be caught up in the pressure to limit all types of federal spending. This perspective is shown in the types of changes made in Medicare under the 1997 Federal Balanced Budget Agreement. These included an increase in Part B premiums and cuts in Medicare payments to doctors, hospitals, and HMOs. These cuts of $115 billion dollars are the largest reduction in the program's history. All of these changes are predicted to postpone the financial crisis of the Medicare Trust Fund until 2007. However, after 2010 when the baby boomers begin receiving benefits, the financial outlook is extremely unfavorable (Rosenblatt, 1997). As a result, Congress also established the National Bipartisan Commission on the Future of Medicare to study how Medicare can accommodate baby boomers in the twenty-first century.

The Federal Balanced Budget Agreement also established "**Medicare Choice**" to give beneficiaries choices in the way that their health care is delivered. It also allows Medicare to pay for a wider range of preventive services, including fuller payment for mammograms, PAP smears, cervical exams, prostate screening, bone density measurement procedures to diagnose osteoporosis, diabetes screening and self-care, and enhancement of the vaccination program. The array of choices available to beneficiaries include:

1. **Health Maintenance Organizations/Preferred Provider Organizations (HMOs/PPOs):** networks of independent hospitals, physicians, and other health care providers who contract with an insurance entity to provide care at discount rates. Members are given incentives to use the HMO/PPO physicians, but also allowed to use providers outside the network at higher out-of-pocket costs.
2. Purchase of private insurance plans.
3. Establishment of **Medical Savings Accounts,** which allow beneficiaries to put Medicare dollars into a tax-exempt account to pay for qualified medical expenses.

The Medical Savings Account is combined with a high-deductible insurance policy to cover catastrophic injuries or illness. Advocates of these accounts believe that they will make older adults more cost-conscious and allow them, rather than insurers, to decide where to seek care. Critics fear that only the wealthier and healthier older adults can afford such a plan. With all the options under Medicare Choice, Medicare begins to look more like a private health care system than a publicly funded base of services for all older persons. What is unclear is how many adults age 65 and over will migrate to these new forms of care rather than rely upon the past Medicare model of reimbursement.

Other strategies to reduce Medicare costs continue to be debated at the national level, as illustrated in Table 16.2. Contrary to these proposed changes, 83 percent of 1000 respondents in a 1997

TABLE 16.2 Strategies to Reduce Medicare Costs

- Limit eligibility for the next cohort of Medicare recipients by increasing the age of eligibility to 67.
- Bill enrollees $5 for home health visits.
- Ration services by age.
- Use an income test as a basis for eligibility.
- Increase coinsurance and deductible to shift more financial risk onto the beneficiaries.
- Increase Supplemental Medical Insurance premiums (Part B) for higher-income beneficiaries.
- Reduce the coverage of services and the reimbursement given to providers.

SOURCE: Meyer, Silow-Carroll, and Regenstein, 1996.

national poll agreed that the federal government has a basic responsibility to guarantee that older people have adequate health care. Of these respondents, 58 percent favored adding dollars to Medicare from new taxes or general government funds and opposed all the options noted above (Bernstein, 1997). It is also noteworthy that while Medicare is the current focus of many cost-cutting debates and expenditures have continued to grow, costs remain below those of private insurers on a per capita basis. One major reason for this is that Medicare is administratively more efficient than most private insurers (Moon, 1996).

MEDICAID

In contrast to Medicare, **Medicaid** is not a health insurance program for older people, but rather a federal and state means-tested welfare program of medical assistance for the categorically needy, regardless of age (e.g., to recipients of Aid to Families with Dependent Children and Supplemental Security Income). Providing assistance to more than 10 percent of people over age 65, Medicaid plays three essential roles for older adults: (1) It makes Medicare affordable for low-income beneficiaries by paying Medicare's premiums, deductibles, and other cost-sharing requirements; (2) it provides coverage of medical benefits that Medicare does not cover, such as prescription drugs; and (3) it stands alone as the only public source of financial assistance for long-term care in both institutional and community settings (Lyons, Rowland, and Hanson, 1996).

Medicaid also differs from Medicare in that federal funds are administered by each state through local welfare departments. For some older

---

OLDER PEOPLE MAY QUALIFY FOR MEDICAID IN THE FOLLOWING WAYS:

1. Participation in Supplemental Security Income, a federal-state program of public assistance to older people and persons with disabilities, automatically triggers Medicaid eligibility. Although Medicaid is the principal health care insurance provided for the poor and is viewed as a "safety net" program, only 33 percent of poor older persons meet the stringent categorical eligibility requirements. Most of these are older people who reside in nursing homes (Lyons et al., 1996). Those who do qualify for cash assistance are provided the broadest coverage under Medicaid, including payment of Medicare premiums, cost-sharing, and payment for additional services, such as prescription-drug, vision-care, and dental-care coverage under state Medicaid programs.

2. Having incomes above welfare cash assistance levels, but having such high medical or long-term care expenditures that they "**spend down**" to Medicaid eligibility requirements. These income levels are established by each state and therefore differ. However, before Medicaid will pay for services, an older person must deplete almost all personal assets and apply all monthly income, except for a small personal allowance, toward the cost of nursing home care.

3. Being eligible for both Medicare and Medicaid, typically those whose income falls 100 percent below the federal poverty guidelines and yet have limited financial assists, who are often very ill, less likely to have a spouse or any living children, and more likely to live in a nursing home. Known as Qualified Medicaid Beneficiaries (QMB) or Specified Low Income Medicaid Beneficiaries (SLMB), they get help from Medicaid to cover Medicare's co-payments and deductibles (e.g., out-of-pocket expenses) and their monthly premiums of physician and outpatient coverage. In other words, even though they have too many financial resources to be eligible for Medicaid full benefits, Medicaid does pay for what Medicare does not cover (National Academy on Aging, 1997).

people, this method of funding carries a stigma of welfare. Federal regulations require that all state Medicaid programs provide hospital inpatient care, physician services, skilled nursing facility care, laboratory and x-ray services, home health services, hospital outpatient care, family planning, rural health clinics, and early and periodic screening. In contrast to Medicare, home health care services are a mandatory area of coverage for Medicaid, while personal-care services and home and community-based services are optional. Nevertheless, states vary widely in the services they include and the groups eligible to receive them. For example, states may elect to provide coverage for personal care services but are not required to do so. States differ greatly in terms of providing "optional" services, such as intermediate care, prescription drugs outside the hospital, dental services, eyeglasses, and physical therapy. Similar to Medicare, coverage for mental health and social services is limited. Because of such limitations, Medicaid, like Medicare, provides only 60 to 80 percent of daily health care charges, even though Medicaid public expenditures have grown more rapidly than inflation (Burwell et al., 1996). As with Medicare, the growth in federal and state expenditures is due primarily to price increases by health providers, not population growth or expansion of care.

Older persons constitute a minority (approximately 12 percent) of the total users of Medicaid, yet they account for about 30 percent of the total Medicaid expenditures (Lyons et al., 1996). The predominant cause of this disproportionate rate of expenditures is that Medicaid is the primary public source for funding nursing home care. Sixty-four percent of persons age 90 and over use nursing homes at some point, as do 30 percent of those age 75 to 79 and 12 percent of those age 65 to 69 (Coleman, 1997). Accordingly, Medicaid is the primary source of publicly funded long-term care (in addition to nursing homes). (See Figure 16.3.) In most states, Medicaid spending on long-term care services comprises 30 to 50 percent of total Medicaid spending. Nursing home costs account for approximately 80 percent of these total Medicaid expenditures, as illustrated in Figure

16.4 (National Academy on Aging, 1997; Coleman, 1996; Evashwick, 1996; Temkin-Greener and Meiners, 1995). While Medicare covers only skilled nursing care for patients with rehabilitative potential, Medicaid can cover both skilled care for rehabilitation and intermediate care of a more custodial nature. However, to qualify for Medicaid-reimbursed nursing home care, the older person must first spend down their income to a certain level (determined by each state) and must contribute almost all personal income to the cost of nursing home care coverage. This means that Medicaid-reimbursed nursing home care is generally available only to those who have less than approximately $2000 in financial assets. This figure may vary slightly depending on the state, and community-dwelling spouses of nursing home residents may have incomes and assets higher than $2000.

Approximately 33 percent of nursing home costs are still paid by individuals out-of-pocket. Nursing home expenditures are increasing at an

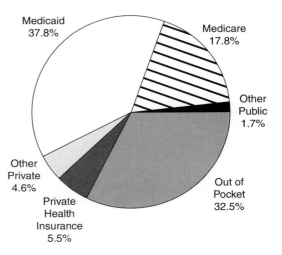

FIGURE 16.3   **Sources of Long-Term Care Financing,* 1995 $106.5 billion**
*Total of national health expenditures for nursing homes and home health services by source of funds.
SOURCE: G. Spencer, Health Care Financing Administration, 1996.

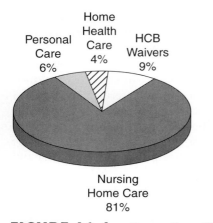

FIGURE 16.4 **Proportion of Medicaid Long-Term Care Spending by Service,* 1995**
*Personal care refers to services to assist a person with activities of daily living such as bathing and dressing; home health care generally refers to skilled nursing care and care provided by home health aides; and home and community-based (HCB) waivers refers to services that a state provides to persons at risk of needing nursing home care.
SOURCE: Brian Burwell, The MEDSTAT Group, 1996.

average annual rate of 10 percent (in 1995, the average cost of nursing home care was $127 a day or $46,000 a year) and form the fastest growing category of Medicaid costs (Graves, 1997). States are attempting to limit nursing home expenditures through certificate of need requirements and moratoria on construction of new beds or facilities. Some states also limit the number of people entering nursing homes under Medicaid coverage by tightening the medical and functional eligibility requirements for nursing home admission. Efforts to control Medicaid spending for nursing home care are difficult because the number of oldest-old continues to increase and because of resistance by nursing home lobbyists. An additional concern is that when nursing home care is restricted, some older consumers may have fewer choices and lower quality of care (Coleman, 1997).

In contrast, only a small percent of Medicaid expenditures go to community-based home health services, even though the average cost of home health care is significantly less (approxi-

mately $78 a visit) (Moon, 1996). In 1995, 19 percent of Medicaid long-term care expenditures were for home and community-based care, compared with 81 percent for institutional care (Graves, 1997). The financing of home care services under Medicaid occurs under three different coverage options:

1. Home health services, which are skilled services typically provided by a Medicaid certified home health agency.
2. Personal care services, which are semiskilled or non-skilled services provided to Medicaid beneficiaries who need assistance with basic activities of daily living in their own home (typically provided by non-licensed individuals; these constitute the majority of total spending of home care services under Medicaid).
3. Home- and community-based waiver services.

The home- and community-based waiver services were first authorized under the 1981 Omnibus Budget Reconciliation Act. This permits the

Medicaid is the primary source of public funding for nursing home care.

waiver of Medicaid statutory requirements so that states can provide community-based alternatives to institutionalization. The waiver program specifies seven core services that have not been traditionally considered "medical," but which are necessary to keep people at home: case management, homemaker, home health aide, personal care, adult day care, rehabilitation, respite care, and other services approved by the federal government as "cost-effective." The primary criterion is that states must demonstrate that the costs of such home- and community-based services are less than care in institutions, and also that they serve to divert at-risk individuals from nursing home placement. Since the Medicaid waiver program assumes that home care is less expensive than placement in a nursing home or intermediate care facility, the target for benefits must meet the "but for" criterion; that is, the person has a level of care need required for nursing home coverage and would be in a Medicaid-financed nursing home, *but for* the services provided by the community-based program (Coleman, 1996). Although nearly all the states have an array of waivers, the program's cost-containment goals mean that most states restrict the scope of services and the number of persons who can receive them (Lyons et al., 1996).

Medicaid has become a highly visible target for federal and state cost-cutting, because it forms a growing proportion of state budgets at the same time that federal funds allocated to states for Medicaid have declined to less than 50 percent of the total expenditures (Wiener and Illston, 1996). In 33 states, spending on older people accounts for 25 percent or more of the overall Medicaid budget (Lyons et al., 1996). Many states are unlinking Medicaid from welfare benefits and using managed-care models with **capitated payments** to control Medicaid expenditures; however, most states have focused on enrolling children and non-disabled adults in Medicaid managed care programs. They have not actively attempted to enroll older people (Wiener, 1996). States have also tried to cut costs through reducing Medicaid benefits (for example, elimi-

nating coverage of prescription drugs), restricting eligibility and utilization, and increasing co-payments. Such benefit reductions, however, fail to address the rising hospital and nursing home costs caused by health providers' price increases. Rather, Medicaid cuts have created a growing number of older adults who lack access to care and who are at risk of declining health status and increased mortality. The major issue facing Medicaid is thus how to provide coverage for acute and long-term care for low-income and vulnerable populations in the face of intense pressure to limit public spending.

SOCIAL SERVICES BLOCK GRANTS AND THE OLDER AMERICANS ACT

In addition to the limited allocations of Medicare and Medicaid for community-based services, Title XX Amendments to the Social Security Act (Social Services Block Grants) and Title III of the Older Americans Act provide some funding for non-medical, custodial services for older people with disabilities.

As noted in Chapter 15, most services to older persons under Title XX go to those who receive Supplemental Security Income. Title XX services are viewed as necessary to carry out basic ADLs, and include homemaker and chore services, home-delivered meals, adult protective services, adult day care, foster care, and institutional or residential care. With federal reductions in block grant funding to the states, competition for decreasing funds at the local level has increased. Long-term care services funded under Title III of the Older Americans Act include information and referral, case management, transportation, homemaker, day care, nutrition education and congregate meals, respite care, and senior centers. In-home services are designed as a priority service for states. Since the primary eligibility criterion is age 60, OAA services may be provided without the restrictions of Medicare and the means test of Medicaid. However, services must be targeted to persons with the greatest social or economic need and to frail older individuals. With Medicaid cuts, some states are targeting their resources on those persons with the greatest financial and functional needs and thus serve only the most severely disabled.

Both Title XX and Title III are limited in their impact by the relatively small allocation of federal resources. Moreover, the Omnibus Budget Reconciliation Act, which intensified the tilt toward medical care, reduced federal funds, removed state matching funds, and increased state reporting requirements for these programs (Bergthold, Estes, and Villanueva, 1990). Community agencies that relied heavily on Title XX funds tried to recover their losses by restructuring their programs toward the medical services reimbursed under Medicare. The programs most likely to be eliminated or reduced were homemaker, chore, and personal care services. These changes in the Social Services Block Grant and the Older Americans Act, along with those in Medicare and Medicaid, have reduced older adults' access to long-term care. This is particularly the case for low-income elders; therefore gender and racial inequities in accessing services have increased. The general approach under both programs has been to give a few services to as many people as possible, which does not necessarily reach the most vulnerable older persons.

Private insurance

Although the U.S. health and long-term care system is based on the assumption that individuals are first responsible for paying for their care, 40 million Americans lack insurance for hospital and physician costs. A substantially greater number—over 200 million—have no insurance for long-term care. Therefore, as noted earlier, 33 percent of all long term care expenditures are paid on an out-of-pocket basis (National Academy on Aging, 1997).

Among the older population, wide disparities exist in terms of their ability to purchase private supplemental and **long-term care insurance.** For older adults who can afford more extensive coverage than Medicare provides, private "medigap"

insurance is available. About 75 percent of the older population has purchased some type of private supplemental insurance. Of these, about 50 percent were able to obtain coverage through their former place of employment. This translates into unequal access to private health insurance to higher-income elders or those who have access through employment/unions. Eleven percent of Medicare's recipients have neither assistance from Medicaid nor supplemental health coverage to help pay for Medicare's coinsurance, deductibles, and uncovered services. Not surprisingly, this group is more likely to have low incomes and/or to be in poor health (Driscoll, 1996). Of poor or near-poor older persons, who suffer from more chronic illnesses and disability than do their higher-income peers, only 47 percent have private insurance, compared to 87 percent of high-income older adults. Less than 18 percent of older ethnic minorities have private coverage, compared to 48 percent of poor older whites. Furthermore, older women are less likely to have had access to group health insurance through employment than men are (Moon, 1996).

Even those who carry supplemental coverage can suffer burdensome medical expenses if they are seriously ill, since Medicare does not cover the full costs of care. Few "medigap" policies pick up physician charges in excess of Medicare's allowable fees, nor do they ordinarily cover prescriptions, dental care, or nursing-home care—all services essential to the long-term maintenance of the older population. In fact, less than 6 percent of the expenditures for nursing-home care and home- and community-based services are paid by private insurance. Instead, nearly 37 percent of such expenditures are out-of-pocket. As a result, 36 percent of all older people admitted to nursing homes in 1995 incurred catastrophic financial expenses (National Academy on Aging, 1997).

As older adults have become more aware of the limits of public funding for long-term care, an increasing number of insurance companies are selling private long-term care insurance plans. Most policies are written to exclude people with certain conditions or illnesses and contain benefit restrictions that limit access to covered care. The period of coverage is usually only 4 or 5 years. The majority of policies cover nursing-home care (at a range of $40 to $120 a day), with home health and adult day-care services usually reimbursed at 50 to 80 percent of the selected nursing-home benefit. The high premiums and co-payments mean that most policies are out of the financial reach of up to 20 percent of Americans age 55 to 79. Indeed, high-quality policies cost as much as $2500 annually when purchased at age 67 and $7700 for those age 79. The policies are expensive for two reasons: 9 out of 10 are sold individually and therefore carry high administrative costs, and most are bought by older people whose risk of needing long-term care is great. Given these costs, only 10 to 20 percent of older people can afford private long-term care insurance. Among those who purchase a policy, it is estimated that 50 percent of them lapse due to high premiums (Wiener and Illston, 1996; Driscoll, 1996). Not surprisingly, women are less likely than men to be able to afford long-term care insurance, and they spend a higher proportion of their income when they do, reflecting both gaps in coverage and their lower median income (Allen, 1993). People who are most likely to purchase and benefit from long-term care insurance are those with assets and a spouse to protect. Those who are covered by private insurance form about 1 percent of older individuals with disabilities. Even if private policies were to become more affordable, questions have been raised about their adequacy and standards (Wiener and Illston, 1996; Burwell et al., 1996).

Resultant Inequities

Health and long-term care for older adults have been based on public funding that is biased toward institutional and acute care, and private policies that are beyond the financial reach of low-income older Americans. This has created a **two-tier system of health care delivery:** one level for those with private health insurance or the means to pay for expensive medical treatment, and another for those forced to rely on Medicaid, Veterans' Assis-

tance, or to do without health care altogether. Even with Medicare recipients, there are disparities. Older people who have Medicare only, many of whom may be near-poor, tend to have fewer doctor visits and hospital stays, and buy fewer prescription medications than those who can afford cost-sharing provisions and other private insurance. People between the ages of 60 and 65, who are too "young" for Medicare and are often no longer covered by job-related or other health insurance, also fall between the cracks. Not surprisingly, the proportion of income spent on health care increases as income decreases.

Medicaid, in particular, has been criticized for perpetuating class inequities. About 25 percent of physicians refuse to take Medicaid patients, especially those with a high level of need. This is because the reimbursement rates are generally below prevailing cost levels. Physicians who accept Medicaid patients typically limit them to 20 percent of their patient load. Since the number of Medicaid beds in nursing homes is limited, Medicaid patients must often wait longer for placement than do private-pay patients. The homes available to them are frequently of lower quality. These burdens disproportionately fall on older women and ethnic minorities. Individuals must spend down their assets to be eligible for Medicaid. Older persons who have been private-pay patients in a nursing home may find that the facility will no longer accept them after they have "spent down." Moreover, some 40 percent of the older population have incomes that are too high to be eligible for Medicaid, yet they typically lack the resources to pay out-of-pocket for long-term care. Those who fall in this "Medicaid gap" frequently receive inadequate medical care or must depend on families to provide care (Wiener, Illston, and Hanley, 1994).

HEALTH AND LONG-TERM CARE REFORMS

Given these gaps, national reform in health and long-term care has been widely debated in recent years. Such debates are often polarized between those advocating private-sector strategies and those who look to the public sector or some combination of public and private coverage. In some respects, the debates are not new, but rather more visible. In fact, since 1912, there have been efforts to create a program of access to health care for all Americans. In 1986, Wilbur Cohen, Assistant Secretary of Health, Education, and Welfare, noted that major social legislation occurs in 30-year intervals, with Social Security (1935) followed by Medicare and Medicaid (1965) and national health care reform embracing universal coverage and continuity of care in 1995 (Brody, 1994). Yet the United States, along with South Africa, remain the only industrialized nations that do not provide some form of universal health coverage, regardless of ability to pay. Since the 1992 federal elections, health care reform moved from academic debates to the legislative process, but one which ended in gridlock. In spite of escalating costs, growing numbers of uninsured citizens, and restrictive insurance policies, attempts to change the health care system created a clash between the goals of cost containment versus guaranteeing access to all. These debates ended without even modest changes in insurance industry practices. Although the majority of Americans support health care reform in the abstract and believe that government should guarantee adequate health care, they are generally satisfied with their own care. Their ambivalence is expressed further by their unwillingness to accept government interference and any restriction of their choice of doctors or hospitals, even if doing so would reduce health care costs or make universal coverage possible (Zis et al., 1996).

We turn now to a brief review of the history and status of long-term care legislation at the national level. The first comprehensive long-term care legislation was introduced by the late Florida Representative Claude Pepper, who linked an initiative to fund long-term care in the home to the ill-fated catastrophic health care legislation in 1988. In 1990, the Pepper Commission recommended public funding of home, community, and nursing-home care for seriously disabled Americans. In 1992, the Democratic leadership in the House and the Senate introduced bills for long-term care known as the Long Term Care Family Security Act. During the 1992 campaign, Bill Clinton was the first Presidential candidate to call for expanded public funding for home care services provided on a non-means-tested basis. Major national organizations concerned about long-term care, such as the National Committee to Preserve Social Security and Medicare, and the Leadership Council of Aging Organizations, favored universal and comprehensive long-term care plans for all people with disabilities. They proposed services encompassing institutional, home- and community-based care, and personal assistance. In fact, this alliance between senior organizations, such as AARP, and groups serving other populations has been a positive development in the long-term care arena, despite the present lack of a successful outcome. Of the major proposals that have been extensively debated by Congress, President Clinton's National Health Security Act of 1993 was one of the few to offer new long-term care benefits and set forth the principles of universal access, comprehensive health care benefits, and high-quality care.

What ultimately killed national health care reform, however, was the disproportionate influence of powerful special-interest lobbies, particularly insurance companies and many small businesses. These groups spent at least $100 million in the 1994 Congressional debates on health care reform to protect their financial interests and ways of doing business. Resistance to large-scale change in the health care system has grown since the Republican sweep in the November 1994 federal elections. Today, for all intents and purposes, fundamental health care reform at the national level is a "dead" issue.

While major changes in long-term care have been stalled at the national level, most states have moved to plan, finance, and implement their own long-term care packages. They often did so to overcome the bias in federal funding toward institutional care, to contain costs, and to address the growing numbers of individuals who lack access to adequate care. In addition, some states such as

Washington and Oregon are involved in efforts to dramatically restructure their long-term care delivery system, usually through consolidation of financing and delivery systems into more streamlined, coordinated, and efficient administrative structures (Burwell et al., 1996). The primary goals of most states has been to improve access to private health insurance and to assure universal access for people who are uninsured (Mollica, Riley, and Rydell, 1994). At the same time, the market has moved more quickly to achieve the goals of competitiveness and reduced costs, largely through managed health care (HMOs or PPOs) which provides an established package of services for enrollees for a single monthly capitated (limited) rate.

Health Maintenance Organizations (HMOs)

HMOs are health plans that combine coverage of health care costs and delivery of health care for a prepaid premium. Members typically receive services from personnel employed by or under contract to the HMO. HMOs generally require patients to select a primary care physician (PCP) who coordinates the patient's care. PPOs are networks of independent physicians, hospitals, and other health care providers who contract with an insurance entity to provide care at discount rates. Members may use providers outside the PPO, but must pay higher out-of-pocket costs.

In the past, HMOs have served primarily younger, healthier populations because of the presumed higher costs associated with older patients (Moon, 1996). Although older adults are still less likely to be in managed care systems than the rest of the population, approximately 15 percent of Medicare recipients today are enrolled in HMOs or a similar type of managed care plan. This percentage will increase as more managed care plans become available and as future cohorts have experience with HMOs in their working years. Many offer broader coverage than Medicare, including some preventive services and prescription drug coverage. Such HMOs thus take on the risk of providing the full range of Medicare-covered services in return for a fixed payment that approximates 95 percent of the costs for similar enrollees in fee-for-service systems. Because the HMOs charge a fixed payment per beneficiary, costs to Medicare are presumed to be more predictable. Whether enrollment in an HMO for a fixed cost has generated savings for the older patient or a reduction in overall expenditures is yet unclear (Meyer et al., 1996). Such enrollment has been associated with reduced health care utilization (e.g., hospital length of stay), but this may result from HMO beneficiaries being healthier than the average older population. After controlling for factors such as health status, it has been found that the costs to Medicare associated with HMO enrollment are actually *higher* than through Medicare per se. This is because Medicare only "saves" 5 percent on each HMO participant, since the capitated rate is set at 95 percent of the expected expenditure level (Moon, 1996; Driscoll, 1996). These savings may not, in fact, be real. If HMOs selectively attract enrollees who are healthier than average, or have less propensity to use health services, they may be skimming off enrollees who would never have cost Medicare the estimated expenditure level even if they had remained in the regular fee-for-service part of Medicare. If that is the case, then Medicare would not actually be saving under the HMO program.

Of greater concern are some recent studies that suggest that health outcomes after 4 years are worse on average for chronically ill older people and for poor patients treated in HMOs (Newcomer, Harrington, Manton, and Lynch, 1995). Consumers in HMOs have also been found to be less satisfied with their care than those utilizing the fee-for-service system. But these same people are more satisfied with their out-of-pocket expenses being reduced by their HMO membership. AARP and other consumer advocacy groups are working to ensure through disclosure requirements and ratings of HMO services that older adults are accurately informed about the benefits and the quality of care they will obtain through HMOs.

The ability of HMOs or other managed care systems to control health costs is limited by the development of medical technology that continues to drive cost and by consumers' expectations for immediate access to any and all care with the slightest potential to help (Meyer et al., 1996). At this point, it is unclear whether the majority of Medicare beneficiaries who are not enrolled in such managed care plans will choose to do so. Although it is clear that managed care can make a contribution to addressing Medicare's financial problems, managed care, per se, is unlikely to obviate the need for other strong policy measures to solve the long-term costs of health care (Meyer et al., 1996).

Social Health Maintenance Organizations (SHMOs) and Other Model Innovative Programs

Because of growing awareness of the inadequacies of the current system, there is increasing policy interest in finding ways to bring the acute-care and long-term care sectors together into a single integrated system. Some of the best known of these initiatives are Social Health Maintenance Organizations (SHMOs), On Lok, and The Program for All-inclusive Care for the Elderly (PACE). **SHMOs** are prepaid health plans that provide both acute and long-term care to voluntarily enrolled Medicare beneficiaries. They offer all Medicare benefits, as well as home- and community-based care, prescription drugs, and case management to prevent nursing-home placement. SHMOs are testing whether comprehensive health services, linking acute and chronic care under an integrated financing scheme within a managed care setting, can be provided at a cost that does not exceed the public costs of Medicare and Medicaid, and can reduce nursing-home placement (Aaronson, 1996). Some concerns have been raised about the quality of care of SHMOs, and whether mortality rates are higher among SHMO patients (Wiener, 1996).

Another model that is being tested in a wide range of communities is San Francisco's On Lok model of social care. **On Lok** aims to integrate a full continuum of acute and chronic care into one agency and thus to prevent institutionalization of frail older people who are certified as needing a nursing-home level of care. As a capitated system, On Lok is paid a flat amount for each person served, similar to the way that HMOs are paid. A comprehensive day health program is integrated with home care, including nursing, social work, meals, transportation, personal care, homemaker, and respite care.

The Program for the All-inclusive Care for the Elderly (**PACE**) is a 15-site federal demonstration project that aims to replicate the On Lok model. It provides "one-door access" to a comprehensive care package of preventive, acute, and long-term care services to allow frail elders to live as independently as possible. Physicians, nurses, social workers, aides, and therapists coordinate their care through adult day health centers and case management at predetermined reimbursement rates. To date, evaluations of both On Lok and PACE reveal cost savings to Medicare and Medicaid but difficulties in integrating the delivery of acute and long-term care, even when the financing systems are the same (National Academy on Aging, 1997; Eng, Pedullo, Eleazer, McCann, and Fox, 1997). Because all these programs rely upon voluntary enrollment, there have also been some difficulties in reaching persons with the most limitations in ADLs (Weiner, 1996). Nevertheless, such model programs that aim to control costs and integrate services are likely to expand.

The rapid changes in the health care arena make predictions about future directions difficult. It is clear that health care has shifted from a system oriented toward acute care, independent providers, and fee-for-service insurance to one oriented toward chronic care, disability prevention, and managed care. Because of market changes and the growth of managed care, these patterns of consolidation and cost saving in the delivery of health care will continue at the local level. This will take place even without the passage of national legislation to insure health care as a right, regardless of income or age. As noted earlier, the current dichotomy between long-term care and acute care is not functional for either older persons or care providers, since long-term care is a health crisis for which virtually every American is uninsured. Because acute and chronic disease are frequently experienced concurrently, a health care system is needed that combines acute and long-term care over the course of each individual's lifetime (Riley and Mollica, 1994). From the perspective of older people with chronic disabilities, an ideal is a national health plan that integrates preventive, acute, hospital, ambulatory, community-based, and home care to ensure continuity of care across the life span. In the short run, however, legislation at the federal level will be focused on ways to reduce Medicare and Medicaid expenditures, on delegating more financing responsibility to the state level, and on funding demonstrations that attempt to integrate acute and long-term care.

SUMMARY AND IMPLICATIONS

The growing health and long-term care expenditures by both federal and state governments and by older people and their families are a source of concern for most Americans. Escalating hospital and physician costs have placed enormous pressures on Medicare—the financing mechanism through which almost half of the funds for the older population's acute care flows. The government's primary response to these Medicare costs has been cost-containment, especially through diagnostic-related groupings (DRGs), financial incentives for shortening the hospital stays of Medicare patients, greater deductibles and co-payments, and most recently, cuts in Medicare funding. Efforts have also been made to provide more choices for Medicare recipients, including managed care options. For most older adults, Medicare fails to provide adequate protection against the costs of home and community-based care. In fact, changes in Medicare funding have reduced the availability of non-profit home care agencies. They have also meant that more older persons and their families have either had to pay privately for home

care or do without. As the fastest-growing portion of the federal budget, Medicare is under intense scrutiny, especially with the federal emphasis upon "balancing the budget."

Medicare is the major payment source of hospital and physician care for older adults, but is almost absent from nursing home financing. The reverse applies to Medicaid, however. The largest portion of the Medicaid dollar goes to services needed by older persons, but not covered by Medicare—nursing-home, home, and personal care, and prescription drugs. However, as Medicaid has been increasingly subject to cost-cutting measures at the state level, benefits have been reduced. For example, co-payments for health care services have increased as a way to reduce Medicaid spending, but this cost is borne disproportionately by low-income elders. Another disadvantage for Medicaid recipients is that most nursing homes and doctors limit the number of Medicaid recipients they will accept. Although waivers by the federal government have allowed state funding of some community-based alternatives to institutionalization, Medicaid remains biased toward nursing home care. Other federal programs that fund community-based services are relatively limited in terms of the numbers of older people reached. Given the gaps in public funding for long-term care, private insurers are offering long-term care insurance options, but these are beyond the financial reach of most older adults and fail to provide comprehensive home-care benefits.

While there is widespread concern about the costs and gaps in public funding, there is little agreement about potential solutions. Since 1992, there has been increased visibility and legislative debate about health care reform, although most proposals have been oriented to acute care and not toward the greatest need of the older population for long-term care. Currently, the prospects for a comprehensive health care reform bill that guarantees universal access along with cost containment are dim. Instead, many states, hospitals, and agencies have moved ahead with reforms that seek to integrate acute and chronic care and to reduce costs through managed care models. At the federal level, the emphasis in the near future will be on cutting Medicare and Medicaid to reduce the federal deficit and on incremental insurance reforms. However, as illustrated in earlier chapters, long-term care reform in the next decade will become an issue that Congress and the President cannot ignore because of the aging of the baby boomers and the continued growth of other vulnerable populations, such as older adults with developmental disabilities and chronic mental illness. Given the magnitude of both the need and the potential changes, it is not surprising that no other part of the health care system generates as much passionate debate as does long-term care (Wiener and Illston, 1994). How to meet the needs of growing populations with chronic disabilities will require creative solutions that integrate acute and long-term care. What is less clear is the balance that will be achieved between public and private financing for future solutions.

Glossary

capitated payments   payments for services based on amount per person per day rather than fees for services

Health Care Financing Administration   the federal agency that administers the Medicare and Medicaid programs

Health Maintenance Organizations (HMOs)   health plans that combine coverage of health care costs and delivery of health care for a prepaid premium, with members typically receiving services from personnel employed by or under contract to the HMO

instrumental activities of daily living (IADL)   shopping, cooking, and cleaning

long-term care insurance   private insurance designed to cover the costs of institutional and sometimes home-based service for people with chronic disabilities

managed care   policies under which patients are provided health care services under the supervision of a single professional, usually a physician

Medicaid   a U.S. federal and state means-tested welfare program of medical assistance for the categorically needy, regardless of age

Medical Savings Accounts   proposed Medicare program that will allow beneficiaries to carry private "catastrophic" insurance for serious illness and pay routine costs from a special account

Medicare   the social insurance program, part of the Social Security Act of 1965, intended to provide financial protection against the cost of hospital and physician care for people age 65 and over

Medicare Choice   starting in 2002, Medicare beneficiaries would choose between traditional Medicare and a Choice Plan that includes HMOs

On Lok   a comprehensive program of health and social services provided to very frail older adults, first started in San Francisco, with the goal of preventing or delaying institutionalization by maintaining these adults in their homes

PACE   federal demonstration program that replicated On Lok's integrated services to attempt to prevent institutionalization

Preferred Provider Organizations (PPOs)   networks of independent physicians, hospitals, and other health care providers who contract with an insurance entity to provide care at discount rates

proprietary   privately owned and operated, in contrast to government ownership

prospective-payment system (PPS)   a system of reimbursing hospitals and physicians based on the diagnostic category of the patient rather than fees for each service provided, as applied to inpatient services

Social Health Maintenance Organizations (SHMOs)   prepaid health plans that provide both acute and long-term care to voluntarily enrolled Medicare beneficiaries

spend down   to use up assets for personal needs, especially health care, in order to become qualified for Medicaid

two-tier system of health care delivery   two levels of health care, depending upon ability to pay; for example, some health providers will not accept Medicaid patients because the reimbursement is too low

References

Aaronson, W. Financing the continuum of care: A disintegrating past and an integrating future. In C. J. Evashwick (Ed.), *The continuum of long-term care:*

An integrated systems approach. Albany, NY: Delmar Publishers, 1996.

Allen, J. Caring, work and gender: Equity in an aging society. In J. Allen and A. Pifer (Eds.), *Women on the front lines: Meeting the challenge of an aging America*. Washington, DC: The Urban Institute Press, 1993.

Bergthold, L., Estes, C., and Villanueva, A. Public light and private dark: The privatization of home health services for the elderly in the U.S. *Home Health Care Services Quarterly*, 1990, *11*, 7–33.

Bernstein, J. *Restructuring Medicare: Values and policy options*. Washington, DC: National Academy of Social Insurance, 1997.

Blanchette, P. L. Age-based rationing of health care. *Generations*, Winter 1996–97, *20*, 60–65.

Brody, S. A responsible geezer's analysis of the Clinton health proposal. *The Gerontologist*, 1994, *34*, 586–589.

Bryce, D. V., and Friedland, R. B. *Economic and health security: An overview of the origins of federal legislation*. Washington, DC: The National Academy on Aging, January 16, 1997.

Burwell, B., Crown, W. H., O'Shaugnessy, C., and Price, R. Financing long-term care. In C. J. Evashwick (Ed.), *The continuum of long-term care: An integrated systems approach*. Albany, NY: Delmar Publishers, 1996.

Coleman, B. *New directions for state long-term care systems. Volume I: Overview*. Washington, DC: AARP, Public Policy Institute, 1996.

Coleman, B. *New directions for state long-term care systems. Volume IV: Limiting state Medicaid spending on nursing home care*. Washington, DC: AARP, Public Policy Institute, April 1997.

Driscoll, L. *The Medicare program*. Washington, DC: AARP, Public Policy Institute, 1996.

Eng, C., Pedullo, J., Eleazer, G. P., McCann, R., and Fox, N. Program of all-inclusive care for the elderly (PACE): An innovative model of integrated geriatric care and financing. *Journal of the American Geriatrics Society*, 1997, *45*, 223–232.

Evashwick, C. J. (Ed.), *The continuum of long-term care: An integrated systems approach*. Albany, NY: Delmar Publishers, 1996.

Gaumer, G. L., Poggio, E. L., Coelen, C. G., Sennett, C. S., and Schmitz, R. J. Effects of state prospective reimbursement programs on hospital mortality. *Medical Care*, 1989, *27*, 724–736.

Gerety, M. B. Health care reform from the view of a geriatrician. *The Gerontologist*, 1994, *34*, 590–597.

Graves, N. R. *Long-term care*. Washington, DC: AARP, Public Policy Institute, 1997.

Hing, E. Effects of the prospective payment systems on nursing homes. *Vital health statistics*. Hyattsville, MD: National Center for Health Statistics, 1989.

Hughes, S. Home health. In C. J. Evashwick (Ed.), *The Continuum of long-term care. An integrated systems approach*. Albany, NY: Delmar Publishers, 1996.

Hughes, S. C., Ulasevich, A., Weaver, F., Henderson, W., Manheim, L., Kubal, J., and Bonango, F. Impact of home care on hospital days: A meta analysis. *Health Services Research*, 1997, *32*, 416–431.

Kane, R. C., and Kane, R. A. Health care for older people: Organizational and policy issues. In R. Binstock and L. K. George (Eds.), *Aging and the social sciences* (3rd ed.). New York: Academic Press, 1990.

Lyons, B., Rowland, D., and Hanson, K. Another look at Medicare. *Generations*, Summer 1996, *20*, 24–30.

Meyer, J. A., Silow-Carroll, S., and Regenstein, M. *Managed care and Medicare*. Washington, DC: AARP, Public Policy Institute, 1996.

Miller, G. Hospice. In C. J. Evashwick (Ed.), *The continuum of long-term care: An integrated systems approach*. Albany, NY: Delmar Publishers, 1996.

Mollica, R. L., Riley, T., and Rydell, C. *The impact of health reform on vulnerable adults: Volume I*. Waltham, MA: Brandeis University, Center for Vulnerable Populations, 1994.

Moon, M. *Medicare now and in the future*. (2nd ed.). Washington, DC: The Urban Institute Press, 1996

National Academy on Aging. *Facts on long-term care*. Washington, DC: The National Academy on Aging, 1997.

National Academy on Aging. *Facts on Medicare: Hospital insurance and supplementary medical insurance*. Washington, DC: The National Academy on Aging, 1997.

National Academy on Aging. *Old age in the 21st century*. Syracuse University and the Administration on Aging, 1994.

Newcomer, R. J., Harrington, C., Manton, K. G., and Lynch, M. A response to representatives from Social HMOs regarding program evaluation. *The Gerontologist,* 1995, *35,* 292–294.

Pear, R. Medicare-paid home health care rife with fraud, investigation finds. *The Seattle Times,* July 27, 1997, 1, A18.

The Pepper Commission (U.S. Bipartisan Commission on Comprehensive Health Care). *A call for action.* Washington, DC: U.S. Government Printing Office, 1990.

Riley, T., and Mollica, R. L. *The impact of health reform on vulnerable adults: Volume II. An analysis of national health reform proposals.* Waltham, MA: Brandeis University, Center for Vulnerable Populations, 1994.

Rosenblatt, R. A. Medicare: 'Savings,' 'Choices,' and worries. *Aging Today,* Sept/Oct 1997, *XVIII,* 1–2.

Sager, M. A., Easterling, D. U., Kindig, D. A., and Anderson, O. W. Changes in the location of death after passage of Medicare's prospective payment system. *New England Journal of Medicine,* 1989, *320,* 433–439.

Schlenker, R. *Home health payment legislation: Review and recommendations.* Washington, DC; AARP, Public Policy Institute, 1996.

Smolka, G. *Medicare Hospital Insurance (HI) Trust Fund: The trustees' 1997 annual report.* Washington, DC: AARP, Public Policy Institute, 1997.

Temkin-Greener, H., and Meiners, M. Transitions in long-term care. *The Gerontologist,* 1995, *35,* 196–206.

Vladeck, B. Overview: The case for integration. Conference Proceedings, *Integrating acute and long-term care: Advancing the health care reform agenda.* Washington, DC: AARP, Public Policy Institute, 1994.

Wiener, J. M. Managed care and long-term care: The integration of financing and services. *Generations,* Summer 1996, *20,* 47–51.

Wiener, J. M., and Illston, L. H. Financing and organization of health care. In R. H. Binstock and L. K. George (Eds.), *Handbook of aging and the social sciences.* (4th ed.). San Diego, CA: Academic Press, 1996.

Wiener, J. M., and Illston, L. H. Health care reform in the 1990s: Where does long-term care fit in? *The Gerontologist,* 1994, *34*(3), 402–408.

Wiener, J. M., Illston, L. H., and Hanley, R. *Sharing the burdens: Strategies for public and private long-term care insurance.* Washington, DC: The Brookings Institute, 1994.

Zis, M., Jacobs, L. R., and Shapiro, R. Y. The elusive common ground: The politics of public opinion and health care reform. *Generations,* Summer 1996, 7–12.

EPILOGUE

In this final section, we turn toward the twenty-first century to study how future cohorts will differ from the current population of older adults. We also attempt to anticipate how societal conditions and social and health policies will influence the quality of life of older adults in the next century. Central to any predictions are the concepts of successful aging, productive aging, and extending the quality of life that have been presented in earlier chapters. The major changes examined are demographics, particularly the growth of the "senior boomers"; health status and the delivery of health care; alternative family relationships; work and productivity; innovative design and living arrangements; and ethical dilemmas posed by the increased ability to extend life. A common thread throughout all these areas is the impact of technology upon the ways in which older people live and how services will be delivered. We close with a brief discussion of career opportunities in gerontology.

DEMOGRAPHICS

As noted throughout, the growth of the population over age 65, and the increased numbers who will survive to age 85 and beyond, provide a major challenge to society and to individuals themselves. The greatest increase in the aging population will occur around 2010 as the "baby boom" generation (those individuals born between 1946 and 1964) begins to reach old age and creates the "senior boom." The oldest among this cohort will reach age 65 in 2011 and age 85 in 2031, and the younger members will reach age 65 in 2029 and 85 in 2049. Since this population is already alive, we can predict with considerable accuracy that 54 million people, or approximately 20.2 percent of the U.S. population, will be 65 and older in 2020. Baby boomers will represent about 60 million of the projected 69 million people age 65 and over in 2030. In that same period, the proportion of the oldest-old will increase dramatically. Currently,

Senator John Glenn is charting new frontiers for older people.

3.8 million people in the United States are age 85 or older; it is estimated that these numbers will more than double by the year 2020. By the year 2050, when the baby boomers are age 85 and over, they are expected to number 19 million. An even more dramatic increase is expected among centenarians, with 1 in 26 of the baby boomers living to be over 100 (U.S. Bureau of the Census, 1996).

Even without this demographic bulge due to the baby boomers, the number and proportion of people living longer would have continued to increase, as they have since the turn of the twentieth century. It is the unprecedented rapid jump in the number of older people through the first half of the next century which has created the sense of a demographic or aging crisis. As noted in Chapter 1, these changes mean an increasing rectangularization of the age pyramid, with more older people becoming self-sufficient, and proportionately fewer young persons available to care for frail elders. Although these demographic changes are dramatic, it is the economy, not demography, that holds the key to the United States' ability to "afford" the aging society and which sets the parameters for discussions about how to prepare for the aging boomers. Demographic changes must be

viewed within the context of recent budget cuts in federal and state programs, including Medicare and Medicaid, despite a booming economy; increasing competition for limited public dollars with more emphasis on accountability; growing expectations that the private sector will meet the gaps in responding to the needs of vulnerable populations; and increasing income inequities across American households, with the top fifth of families benefiting disproportionately from the economic growth of the late 1990s.

These demographics, along with increases in longevity and the tremendous variability in the aging process, are changing the definition of "old age," with 65 no longer considered old. As noted in Chapter 1, biological age is more important than chronological age in determining an individual's health status. In turn, functional age (i.e., the ability to carry out activities of daily living) is more critical in terms of developing services for older people than chronological age. Accordingly, it has been argued that the study of aging should not be restricted to persons 65 and over but rather should cover the entire life course, since the nature of old age is substantially influenced by one's lifestyle and circumstances earlier in life (Cornman and Kingson, 1996).

A central question confronting individual citizens as well as policymakers is: what will life be like for the baby boomers when they become the senior boomers? Unfortunately, we do not have a crystal ball to predict the future with certainty. Some factors are well beyond the control of social gerontologists, including economic conditions, international conflicts, globalization of markets, fatal diseases such as AIDS, and natural disasters. While acknowledging the complexity of making predictions about the aging of baby boomers, there is, however, adequate knowledge about the baby-boom generation to begin to speculate about the future (Morgan, 1998).

The future cohort of older people will differ from current cohorts in ways other than living longer. Some baby boomers are likely to enter old age in a better economic position than pre-boom cohorts (e.g., their parents and grandparents) because of deferred marriage, reduced childbearing, greater pension coverage, and increased labor-force participation of women (Cutler, 1997). Nevertheless, there will be tremendous disparity in income and education among the senior boomers, especially between "early" (e.g., those who remember John F. Kennedy's death) and "late" baby boomers (e.g., those whose youth was influenced by Watergate and the energy crisis of the early 1970s). The "older baby boomers" are likely to be better off economically and in terms of home ownership than younger boomers. They entered a growing economy, benefited from lower housing costs, and were more likely to have private pensions and higher net earnings than the "younger" boomers who followed them (Cornman and Kingson, 1996). Those likely to have lower retirement income than their parents are boomers who are poorly educated, single parents, or unable to buy a house. Because of longer life expectancy, rising out-of-pocket health care costs, and the probability of high college costs for their children at a time when they should be preparing for retirement, all baby boomers face the possibility that they will need more retirement income for longer periods of time than their parents did (Manchester, 1997).

Another difference from prior generations will be the growing number—at least 18 million—of ethnic minorities among the boomers. Ethnic minorities are expected to comprise nearly half of the United States population by the year 2050, growth fueled in part by increased immigrant and refugee populations. The number of older Hispanics and Asians will increase by factors of more than 5 from 1990 to 2050, compared to a doubling of whites and a tripling of African Americans (Morgan, 1997). Accordingly, in many sections of the country, a "minority" population will be a majority, raising questions about the identity and meaning of "minority" and community. There will be proportionately more ethnic minorities in the younger, employed population than today, supporting an older population that will remain predominantly white. Ethnic minorities among the baby-boom cohort are, on average, poorer than their Euro-American counterparts and therefore likely to bring fewer financial resources and often poorer health to old age (Cornman and Kingson, 1996; Day, 1992).

Women will predominate among senior boomers, with more than 50 percent of them living alone. Although the status of women and ethnic minorities in the early part of the twenty-first century is likely to represent an improvement over current cohorts, gains in education and employment have not necessarily been widely distributed. Women, for example, are still paid only about 70 cents for every dollar earned by their male counterparts, and they remain concentrated in secondary sector industries and traditionally female-oriented, lower-paying occupations. In fact, the Department of Labor projections identify five service occupations, dominated by women and characterized by low wages, as more likely to experience large-scale growth into the twenty-first century than higher-paying occupations. More women will be employed out of economic necessity for longer periods, but their earnings profile will not necessarily improve. Despite the increased number of women in the paid work force and the relatively greater affluence of some younger women, older women in the future are predicted to remain significantly poorer than older men. Seventy percent of baby-boom women will outlive their husbands by 15 years, but on average will earn only two-thirds of what their husbands earn. When today's 25-year-old woman retires, after having been employed for as long as 35 years, she can expect to receive, on average, the same retirement benefits—adjusted only for inflation—that her mother did even though she will have paid more into Social Security (Older Women's League, 1990).

HEALTH STATUS

Most older people in the future will undoubtedly be healthier than current cohorts, because of the advantages of medical technology, preventive medicine, health promotion, and widely available knowledge about ways to maintain health. Older adults and their health care providers will be less concerned with surviving chronic disease than achieving successful aging and adding years to life (e.g., the quality of life) rather than life to years. As discussed in Chapter 6, there is a growing emphasis on successful aging. Researchers have found that successful agers remain active both physically and mentally in late life, continue their social interactions with a rich network of friends, neighbors, and family members, and maintain a strong sense of "self-efficacy," or the feeling that they can achieve whatever they set their minds to do (Rowe and Kahn, 1998). It is noteworthy that studies of successful aging have concluded that heredity is not the determining factor, but the individual's own determination and desire to live well in old age. Furthermore, the number of people who achieve successful aging continues to grow. An underlying focus will be better understanding or differentiating the effects of disease from the declines of aging alone and developing interventions that postpone aging-related dysfunction. As we have seen in Chapter 1, there will be more emphasis on identifying methods to extend the quality of life, including research on growth hormones, caloric restriction, cell repair, gene therapy to forestall disease, and cell therapy to replace dying or dead cells instead of replacing entire organs.

Recent developments in cell biology have been heralded as "the discovery of the fountain of youth." Indeed, the discovery of a method to force cells to continue producing an enzyme called "telomerase" (useful for keeping a cell alive, but which normal cells can no longer produce as they age) catapulted the researchers to sudden fame and the biotech company producing it to increase its value on the stock market (de Lange, 1998)! This is an example of new methods in gene therapy that will not necessarily add years to life, but will add life to years. By extending the life of specific cells through the production of telomerase, scientists, and eventually medical geneticists, can prevent the rapid deterioration caused by many diseases affecting older people, including cancer and atherosclerosis.

These new developments in cell biology and genetic engineering will someday allow more people to achieve successful or robust aging. Even today there are numerous examples of older people achieving milestones that were previously believed to be impossible beyond a certain age. For example, an organization calling itself "United Flying Octogenarians" (UFOs) is made up of pilots over the age of 80 who are still flying small planes. Although airline pilots are among the few professionals today who must retire at a certain age—in this case, from flying for the airline by age 60—there is no restriction on flying small private planes. UFO boasts 1000 members over the age of 80 who have valid medical certificates to fly small planes. They are required to obtain a physical exam and perform a test ride with an instructor every 2 years. Currently the oldest active pilot who is a member of UFOs is 94!

The recent decision by NASA to invite Senator John Glenn, a former astronaut, on an upcoming space mission is an exciting achievement in gerontology. Not only does this signal the end of defining physiological capacities in terms of chronological age, but the mission will provide a natural experiment in helping us understand the effects of aging on the ability to function in space. It will also give scientists an understanding of the impact of weightlessness on aging. The increase in the number of "master athletes," described in Chapter 3, including marathon runners, mountain climbers, and long-distance cyclists, is no longer a phenomenon but a reality for newer cohorts of older people. This pattern will certainly continue to grow as the baby boomers become senior boomers.

For the majority of older people, however, access to adequate health care will continue to contribute to disparities in health status. Those with adequate health care will enjoy longer periods of functionality followed by more rapid decline. Those who do not have access to good health care will endure years, even decades, of a long and slow decline from chronic illness. If disability rates remain what they are today, the number of older persons needing help with basic tasks is expected to double between 1990 and 2030, and the number of older individuals requiring nursing home care will more than triple (Weiner, Illston, and Hanley, 1994).

The difference in life expectancy between women and men may be narrowed by younger women's tendency to engage in riskier behaviors and life styles as well as the trend of more young men pursuing healthier lifestyles by avoiding smoking, limiting alcohol and fat intake, and increasing exercise levels. This has served to reduce death rates due to heart disease and hypertension. On the other hand, if AIDS continues to affect more younger men than women, there could be a much greater sex differential in life expectancy. Although the interaction of these different trends is unknown, it is clear that women will continue to live longer and will consequently predominate among the frailest and sickest (Cornman and Kingson, 1996).

In addition to the higher rates of chronic illness and mortality among ethnic minorities and women, there are other populations of concern. These include people who are affected by AIDS and those facing long-term developmental disabilities or mental illness. Although the AIDS epidemic affects only about 1 percent of the current cohort of older adults, this proportion will grow, given the probability of baby boomers who have contracted the infection earlier in their lives. The onset of AIDS may occur when senior boomers are experiencing other age-related changes, since the median interval between HIV infection and full-blown AIDS is nearly 10 years.

As noted in Chapter 9, another population that will require specialized care are older persons with developmental disabilities (e.g., cerebral palsy or Down syndrome). Earlier generations of people with developmental disabilities frequently did not survive until old age. As a result of improved health care, life expectancy for persons with Down syndrome has increased dramatically, from 9 years in 1929 to 18.3 years in 1963, to 55 years today (Adlin, 1993). The population with developmental disabilities over age 65 is projected to double by 2030. They may require services from agencies serving older adults and persons with developmental disabilities, as well as care by family members who may be among the old-old (Kelly and Kropf, 1995). What old age will be like for the growing number of adults who are chronically mentally ill or homeless is also unknown and of concern to planners and policymakers.

HEALTH CARE DELIVERY IN THE FUTURE

Baby boomers as a group face considerable uncertainty about health care expenditures in the future. Although they are tremendously concerned about costs, they are not well informed about paying for health and long-term care. Boomers who have been employed part-time as temporary workers or have been self-employed lack access to employer-funded health care benefits. Fortunately, most boomers are likely to be healthier than prior cohorts. Those who face chronic illness will probably cope with a longer lifetime of disability in different ways than previous generations have. Boomers, compared to earlier generations, are more likely to view health care as a responsibility shared by government and the individual, and to place a higher value on individual responsibility for health (Blanchette and Valcour, 1998). The increasingly high costs of hospitalization and nursing homes have already resulted in the growth of various community-based options in health and long-term care, many of which are private pay.

As noted in Chapters 10 and 16, a major area of expansion is home health care provided by hospitals, private and nonprofit agencies, local governments, or privately contracted by the older person. These programs allow older people to remain as self-sufficient as possible in their homes—values that future generations may be more likely to hold because of their greater opportunities for choice. Not surprisingly, home health care aides are predicted to be one of the fastest-growing industries in the coming years, although many aides are only minimally trained and poorly paid for their hard work. Adult day centers and adult day health programs help frail older people remain in the community while providing family members with respite from full-time caregiving. As noted in Chapter 16, however, public funding for such community-based options is relatively limited. More comprehensive, coordinated in-home and community-based supportive services accessible to the older person are needed, along with changes in public financing of long-term care. What is unknown is the extent to which Medicare and Medicaid will be modified to cover more such programs in the future. The current cost-containment mood in Congress, however, suggests that this is unlikely, at least in the next decade.

The growth in the number of hospitals, along with the surplus of physicians and an excess of hospital beds, has led to greater competition for older patients. At the same time, financial limitations on the provision of care have resulted in an increase in ambulatory services. We have moved from an era of reduced hospital days following major surgery to no hospital stays following many surgical procedures. Along with a growth in multi-hospital systems involving proprietary, nonprofit, and public hospitals, many hospitals have developed special geriatric units for both acute and chronic care. Some have established satellite clinics and provide health screening, foot care, and other health-promotion activities in senior centers and senior housing; others offer health education and health promotion for older persons and for family members of frail elders in hospitals and in community settings. Still others provide emergency-response systems, home health care, information and referral, and free transportation to the hospital for older patients. The number of hospitals with long-term care beds, or those planning to establish such beds or to convert acute care to long-term care beds, has also increased significantly.

A growing number of hospitals sponsor membership programs that provide a package of special services such as health screening, annual exams at reduced costs, telephone reassurance, and help with complex insurance forms. Such "health clubs" as Eldermed, Goldencare Plus, and Health Wise have sprung up around the country. Most are aimed at the financially better-off portion of the older population who have Medicare Parts A and B, *and* supplementary "medigap" insurance. They do not address the needs of uninsured people, nor do they generally reduce the cost of outpatient medical care or hospitalization. As competition among hospitals increases, these clubs may eventually lead to lower costs for older people.

Whatever changes occur will probably happen within the context of managed care. As shown in Chapter 16, managed care seeks to control health costs through coordinating and limiting resources, particularly through reducing hospital stays. There will be greater pressures to move Medicare beneficiaries into private managed care systems and for the Health Care Financing Administration, which administers Medicare and Medicaid, to operate more like a private business "managed choice model." Although the overall percent of HMO (Health Maintenance Organization) enrollees over age 65 is currently low compared to younger populations, HMOs are actively recruiting older adults as members by offering comprehensive health care at lower average costs than private hospitals and physicians can offer. Many existing private hospitals are converting to HMOs and will provide attractive health-promotion and health-education programs. The federal demonstration projects, SHMOs, add home care to the standard managed care package and allow earlier discharge from acute-care facilities; whether these will prove to be cost-effective and therefore more widely available in the future is unknown. Pressures to discharge patients as quickly as possible have created demands for a new type of facility for the person who is too sick to go home but not sick enough for a hospital. As a result, subacute care facilities are growing, whereby nursing homes are becoming less like homes and more like hospitals, to provide stroke rehabilitation, cardiac care, and intravenous feeding. This shift, however, means that in many facilities, spaces for long-term Medicaid patients are being filled by higher-paying Medicare patients, furthering inequities in access to health care (Fritz, 1995).

Health care service delivery will continue to be dramatically changed through rapid innovations in computer applications. Already, consumers and professionals alike can access data bases that contain medical information about chronic conditions, care needs, and products through the Internet and Websites to enhance their health care. Health-education and promotion projects, decision-support programs, access to technical expertise, and mutual support from other patients and family members are all available "on line." In fact, over 25,000 Websites relate to health information and mutual support, a number that will grow dramatically in the next century. In addition, a 1997 study found more than 3.5 million Web documents using health-related key words. Some health care organizations maintain the Internet exclusively for members, providing plan information and directories of plan providers (Kelly, 1997). An example of an effective stand-alone system is CHESS, the Comprehensive Health Enhancement Support System. By entering the system through a personal computer from home, users can obtain brief answers to standard health questions as well as detailed articles and descriptions of services. They can anonymously ask questions of experts and communicate and read personal stories of people with similar problems. Preliminary evaluations indicate that CHESS has been extensively used, even by underserved ethnic minority patients with low levels of education (Gustafson, Gustafson, and Wackerbarth, 1997). One advantage of such stand-alone systems is that patients do not need to learn how to navigate the Internet. The Senior-Med Project, which creates a network to help manage and monitor medications, adds accessing the Internet to a stand-alone system with basic information about medications (Deatrick, 1997). All these technology-based approaches to health care point to a collaborative or partnership model between health care providers and older people and their families for their care. The concepts of client empowerment and breaking down traditional boundaries between health care providers and patients are furthered when a client can readily access information from physicians or nurses via e-mail.

The use of technology will undoubtedly affect the training and allocation of health care providers. Even without technology, we have seen increasing use of personnel such as geriatric nurse practitioners who are less costly than traditional physician-based care. The growth of geriatric education in colleges of medicine, nursing, dentistry, social work, pharmacy, and in other areas such as nutrition and physical therapy suggest that a well-trained cadre of health care providers will become increasingly available to future older adults. Most of them will be trained in the use of information technology as a way to communicate with patients. Since the potential for misuse and misinformation on the Internet is high, health care providers will need to be aware of the sources and type of computer-based information accessed by their clients. Nevertheless, all of these developments offer hope for cost containment and quality of care in the absence of national health care reform.

More broadly, there is increasing recognition of the need to expand our intellectual and conceptual approaches to health and healing. This

The Internet is making health care information accessible to both consumers and providers.

encompasses a multidimensional approach to health care that takes account of both physical and psychosocial factors, such as self-efficacy. A striking indicator of people's desire for different health care modalities is the decline in the number of individuals who rely solely on modern Western medicine. In fact, 33 percent of people in the United States (even though they often pay out-of-pocket), 50 percent of those in Europe, and 80 percent worldwide use some type of alternative medicine (Micozzi, 1997). Complementary and alternative medicine (CAM) is generally understood as diagnostic or therapeutic techniques considered to be outside mainstream Western medicine but which may enhance conventional treatment. This represents a "reverse technology transfer" whereby useful medical systems and techniques from other countries make their way into popular usage in the United States.

Alternative medicines encompass two broad types: (1) healing systems, such as homeopathy, herbal treatments, chiropractic medicine, osteopathy, and acupuncture, and (2) well-developed systems represented by ancient health traditions such as tai chi and massage therapy. These techniques are generally considered less invasive, lower tech, and less expensive than traditional medicine. For example, acupuncture or chiropractic techniques rather than surgery may be used to treat chronic back pain. Tai chi, the fluid meditative movement routine from China, has been found to be effective in preventing falls by keeping older people limber and improving their balance; it also has been used in nursing homes and by people in wheelchairs (Jahnke, 1997). Nontraditional approaches may be especially effective with long-term conditions for which there is no cure (e.g., Alzheimer's, arthritis, living with chronic pain and depression). Research to assess the effectiveness of alternative medicine is growing. In fact, institutions, such as the University of California at San Francisco, Stanford, and Columbia are integrating complementary and alternative medicine into their medical curricula and examining the use of alternative treatments for musculoskeletal diseases, cancer,

and heart disease. An Office of Alternative Medicine within the National Institutes of Health is funding scientific studies to understand why many alternative therapies are effective.

Changing Family Relationships

The baby-boom generation has been characterized by a wide variety of family forms and life styles. Family structures have become more diverse because of higher rates of divorce, remarriage, step-family relationships, and never-married adults; more couples or single mothers delaying child-bearing until their 30s or 40s, choosing to have fewer children or not to have children at all; more households with both adults working; more children being raised in single-parent households; and more gay and lesbian partners raising children. Such diversity creates more choices and options for members (Pillemer and Suitor, 1998; Cornman and Kingson, 1996). Family diversity also characterizes family structure by ethnicity and class, as well as by life stage. In addition, "family" no longer simply means co-residents of the same household, particularly in the later phases of the life cycle. As these changes take place, more consideration needs to be given to life course variations in household and kinship arrangements as men and women move in and out of various communities, living and work situations, and primary relationships (Moen, 1998; Moen and Forest, 1995).

Increases in life expectancy complicate the diversity of family structures. The added years due to increased life expectancy serve to prolong a person's relationships to others—spouse, parents, offspring, friends—whose lives are also extended. In the year 2000, a 50-year-old will have an 80 percent chance of having at least one parent alive and a 27 percent chance of both alive. In fact, a 60-year-old will have a 44 percent chance of having a parent alive (Cutler, 1997). It will not be unusual to find retired people in their 70s and 80s caring for a centenarian parent. These dramatic changes mean that a growing proportion of parents and children and perhaps even grandchildren within multigenerational families will share such critical adulthood experiences as work, parenthood, and even retirement and widowhood. For example, for current generations of young women, the death of a mother and the last child leaving home for college may occur close to the daughter's retirement age. Similarly, grandparents or great-grandparents may survive to experience many years of their grandchildren's or great grandchildren's adulthood. Women will experience more years of the "empty nest," with more post-parenting years than active parenting. However, the "empty nest" is likely to be filled by caregiving responsibilities for older relatives, many of whom desire to "age in place" (Dennis and Migliaccio, 1997). With the delay in the onset of morbidity and need for care among the old-old, caregivers of the future are likely to be young-old themselves. They will also be more likely to remain in the work force, given improved health status, higher living standard expectations, a smaller pool of younger workers, and a lower likelihood of caring for young children at home.

As members of a person's social network survive longer, there is an increase in the complexity and the vertical links that cross generational lines of the networks. Individuals in a multigenerational family line interact in a much more complex set of family identities than is the case in a lineage with only two generations, those of parent and child. Kinship networks in the future will become even more attenuated and diffuse than currently. The verticalized or "beanpole family structure" will grow; that is, an increasing number of living generations in a family (though they probably will not physically live together), accompanied by a decreasing number of family members within the same generation due to declining fertility rates. Increased life expectancy combined with reduced fertility means that future cohorts of adult children will have a greater number of aging parents and grandparents to care for, at the same time that they have fewer siblings to call on for assistance. Kin networks, as a result, will be top-heavy. At the same time, intergenerational relations are to a

much greater extent voluntary and individually negotiated (Pillemer and Suitor, 1998; Uhlenberg, 1996; Bengtson, Rosenthal, and Burton, 1990). Such patterns raise questions about multigenerational responsibilities. For example, who is responsible for a great-grandparent who falls and needs daily care—the grandparents who may themselves be frail, the parents who may both be employed, or grandchildren who are often still in school? These trends of declining family size, combined with increases in the number of unmarried persons and childless couples (the "truncated family"), are likely to continue, reducing the pool of potential family caregivers.

Delayed childbearing and smaller family size have resulted in a larger-than-average age difference between each generation and a blurring of demarcations between generations, particularly among Caucasian families. For example, active involvement in the daily demands of raising children is now likely to be fully completed by the time women are grandmothers. Women who marry and give birth later in life are less likely to divorce, and more likely to have economic, educational, and emotional advantages that benefit their children. However, generational differences of 30 to 40 years may, over time, contribute to difficulties in building affective bonds across multiple generations due to different values or life orientations (George and Gold, 1991). In contrast to this phenomenon of later-life marriage and childbearing is the age-condensed family, where young women are bearing children in the teenage years accompanied by higher rates of divorce. This may result in a blurring of roles and relationships, particularly the growth of young grandmothers and great-grandmothers who are the primary caregivers for grandchildren. Some of these differences in family structure vary by socioeconomic status.

Another change with reduced fertility rates is that there are fewer individuals within each generation in which to invest emotionally. As a result, intergenerational relationships are not only more extensive, but also more emotionally intensive (Bengtson et al., 1990). At the same time, siblings who are closer in age and think of themselves as peers may be more likely to share caregiving tasks than to expect the oldest child or the unmarried daughter to be the primary caregiver—a pattern more common in large families in the past. In turn, adults may experience richer social relationships with their peers and be more likely to form nontraditional intimate relationships (Silverstone, 1996).

The increase in longevity has also significantly changed grandparent–grandchildren roles. For example, we now anticipate that our grandparents will not die until our early adulthood, but until quite recently most grandparents did not live long enough to know their grandchildren well. Now, as more women have their first children anywhere from the early teens until their mid-40s, first-time grandparenthood occurs for persons ranging in age from 35 to 75. Accordingly, grandchildren encompass both infants and retirees, and grandparents include active middle-aged adults as well as frail, very old persons. For the first time in history, a woman can be both a granddaughter and a grandmother simultaneously. Additional complicating factors are that grandparents and grandchildren are often separated by geographic distance, and by divorce and remarriage of the grandchildren's parents. This results, at the extremes, in the two generations rarely seeing each other. These patterns, which are likely to increase in the future, raise questions about grandparents' rights and obligations. Without historical precedence, there are few clear culturally shared expectations about grandparent–grandchildren relationships.

The widened gap between the mortality rates of men and women is another demographic change that influences family relationships. Chapters 9 and 14 demonstrated that the world of the very old is a world of women, both in society and within families. Some five-generation families may include three generations of widows. Most older women are widows living alone; most older men live with their wives. Such differences in widowhood and remarriage mean that men are more likely to maintain horizontal, intragenerational ties, primarily through their wives, until the end of

their lives. In contrast, women turn more to intergenerational relationships for help and support throughout their lives, especially in old age. Although more women are entering the marketplace traditionally dominated by men, they continue to put greater emphasis on interpersonal relationships. This, combined with the value placed by the women's movement on friendships and social support, suggests that women will continue to build diverse and extensive social networks to which they can turn in old age. For example, more older women in the future may choose to live with other women, forming intergenerational households as a way to reduce housing costs and strengthen their support networks. Another factor that may contribute to this trend is the growing number of women who choose not to marry or who are lesbians. For these women, friends often represent a stronger social bond than relatives.

A social trend that interacts with these demographic changes is the increasing divorce rate. This increase may be inevitable in aging societies, because modern longevity makes marriage a greater long-term commitment than in the past. The chance of couples who married in the 1930s and 1940s reaching their golden wedding anniversary is less than 5 percent. In spite of increased life expectancy, no more couples reach this 50-year marker nowadays than did a century ago. But whereas before 1974, most marriages ended with death, after 1974, more marriages ended with divorce. As noted in Chapter 9, at least 50 percent of the people currently marrying (and entering old age around the year 2020) will divorce. And the numbers of older people who are divorced will grow among the baby-boom cohort (Hobbs and Damon, 1996). Currently, 50 percent of children under the age of 18 live in single-parent households (Cornman and Kingson, 1996). Children have always faced family disruptions, but now divorce is more common than death as the cause of such disruptions. Furthermore, among the 75 percent of men and 60 percent of women who remarry, more than 40 percent are estimated to divorce yet again, creating complex step-family relationships (U.S. Bureau of the Census, 1992b).

An increasing number of children, parents, and grandparents will thus devote substantial effort toward building reconstituted families and step-relationships, only to find them eventually dissolved.

These trends in divorce and remarriage raise difficult questions. How will children of divorce, remarriage, and re-divorce approach relationships during their own adult years? What patterns of support will exist between aging parents and children in families disrupted by divorce? To what extent will younger members of "blended" families and those unrelated by blood, but joined by years of sharing familial responsibilities, assume the role of caregivers?

Trends in divorce and remarriage are shaping the life course and social networks of young and old, but they differentially affect men and women. For women, divorce reduces their standard of living and creates an uncertain financial future. The more resources (e.g., education and income) that a divorced woman has available, the less likely she is to remarry, whereas this is reversed for men (Choi, 1995; Goldscheider, 1994). Therefore, men and women who have divorced but not remarried will differ from today's population. Among women divorcing in the future will be growing numbers of resourceful individuals who will already have lived for many decades on their own as they face old age at the turn of the century. Although they may experience financial struggles as single mothers, they also may be innovative and adept at coping with the changes that aging brings.

For men, the primary consequence of divorce is disruption of intergenerational family networks. Most common is reduced contact with and financial support for children, because most mothers, whether by choice or out of necessity, assume primary childrearing responsibility. Divorced fathers, for example, are less likely to keep in touch with their children or to be named as a source of support (Bulcroft and Bulcroft, 1991). This reduced responsibility also translates into less involvement across generations, such as diminished interaction between paternal grandparents and grandchildren. Social values toward gender equality have increased in recent years, but demographic and social changes have created very different family worlds for men and women. An increasing proportion of men have only tenuous vertical ties along generational lines, yet women have retained strong links to both young and old generations. These trends pose troubling questions: What will be the nature of relationships between aging fathers and their children with whom they have had only sporadic contact for many years? What sort of responsibility will adult children feel toward an aging father who never paid child support? Will the mother–daughter relationship become even more important as the mainstay of family cohesion? And how will these changes affect the development of policies regarding the care of frail elders?

At the same time that more women, both as single parents and as adult caregivers for older relatives, are assuming more intergenerational responsibilities, their employment demands are expanding. The expectation and necessity for women to enter the paid work force have grown, without any significant diminution in women's family responsibilities, as evidenced by the fact that women devote as much time to household tasks as they did 50 years ago (Twigg and Atkin, 1994). Seventy-five percent of married mothers with children work outside the home, and women with children under age 6 are the fastest-growing component of the female labor force (Coontz, 1997). At the same time, however, traditional expectations about family caregiving have not changed, and the demands on working women can become an unbearable burden. Although such sex-based roles are slowly changing in terms of child care, the fact that women still assume primary care for children tempers any unrealistic expectations that men will soon become the primary caregivers of frail elders.

Who will provide what care for older dependents is a critical policy issue currently and for the future. Federal cutbacks and the devolution of responsibility for services to the states suggest that there will be even fewer publicly funded supports for family caregivers in the future. At the same time, the need for policies conducive to family well-being at all stages of the life course and to sustaining ties within and across generations is likely to grow in the twenty-first century (Moen and Forest, 1995). Fortunately, the private sector is beginning to respond to the growing number of employees who have caregiving responsibilities, and elder care will be an important employee benefit in the next century. Corporations have responded out of recognition of the relationship between caregiving demands and productivity, since elder care is estimated to cost businesses about $29 billion a year. These costs, which include replacing employees, absenteeism, workday interruptions, and supervisory time, will increase in the twenty-first century (De Martino, 1997). A growing number of corporations have initiated elder-care referral and counseling services, especially for caregivers at a geographic distance. A small number of companies have begun on-site day care programs for older parents and young children of employees. Because of the federal Family and Medical Leave Act, more private companies and universities are offering flexible hours and unpaid leave options for their employees with care responsibilities. However, these modifications in the workplace are the exception, not the norm; the trend toward cost-cutting and reduction of employee benefits in many businesses may counteract such improvements.

Elder-care services are increasingly provided by for-profit geriatric care management businesses, which coordinate services by home health aides, geriatric nurses, gerontological social workers, or psychologists. Most often it is the adult children, typically at a geographic distance, who will contract for a private care manager to locate services for an aging parent, visit regularly, and handle emergencies. However, their fees range from $150 to $500, thereby limiting their service to middle- and upper-class families. These marketplace initiatives will undoubtedly expand in the future as parental caregiving responsibilities increase. Closely related to the growth of for-profits serving older adults will be an increase in public–private partnerships. For example, Area Agencies on Aging, faced with reduced federal funds, are likely to reach out increasingly to for-profits to

Growing numbers of younger women will assume both elder-care and employment responsibilities.

establish collaborative initiatives that improve or expand services to older adults (Gray, 1995). It should also be noted that such "caregiving at a distance" does not absolve adult children, most often women, from continued involvement in coordinating and assuring that appropriate services are provided as needed.

Another trend that is likely to increase is the use of information technology to forge intergenerational communities and to provide family caregivers with information and mutual support. Use of e-mail and the Internet provides ways for older adults to communicate with family members and peers around the country who share similar concerns. Intergenerational programs, such as Generations United, can be accessed through the World Wide Web (Ward and Smith, 1997). The aging baby boomers, who have used computers throughout most of their adult lives, are likely to be even more comfortable accessing information and support from others through computer-based technology. In fact, older users of the Internet already do so more than younger users. Accordingly, the computer-based resources available to family caregivers are likely to increase and provide a means to reduce feelings of isolation, particularly in light of the declining pool of potential family caregivers in the future. One example of a rapidly growing resource is the Family Caregiver

Alliance for caregivers of cognitively impaired adults, offering Factsheets, a Website of resources and peer support (Kelly, 1997). Another illustration of what it means to live in a networked society is the Cleveland Free-Net Alzheimer's Forum, which provides free e-mail, question-and-answer functions, and a bulletin-board structure. Users appear to have benefited from the 24-hour-a-day mutual support available through other caregivers even more than from their access to medical information (Hunt, 1997).

The growth of assistive technology, as described in Chapter 10, will enable more and more older people to remain in their own homes. These include devices such as pagers, tracking devices, and emergency call buttons in private homes and apartments. All of these technological developments will have profound implications for how family members relate both to each other as well as to health care professionals. Indeed, as they age, baby boomers will have more electronic access to medical information and for communicating with their physicians as needed.

NEW DEFINITIONS OF WORK AND PRODUCTIVITY

Despite current fears that the baby-boom cohort will not benefit proportionately from Social Security, on average this cohort is likely to enter old age in a better economic position than did pre-boom cohorts. This is because of economic and demographic adjustments, such as deferred marriage, reduced childbearing, increased labor-force participation of wives, and greater pension coverage, all of which have compensated for the baby boomers' relatively lower wages in their earlier years. The majority of older adults in the future will also be better educated. Because of the association between education, occupation, and income, those with degrees are likely to earn more during their lifetimes. More people over age 70 may choose to continue to be employed, preferably on a part-time basis, although the pattern of early retirement will probably persist. In fact, baby

boomers indicate that their preferred retirement age is 58 (Merrill Lynch, 1995)! Despite these projections, most baby boomers express little confidence about their financial futures and are concerned about outliving their retirement savings (Cutler, 1998). Paradoxically, however, relatively few of this cohort are actively planning financially for their retirement. In fact, they are saving only about one-third of what they will need to maintain their current standard of living (Cutler, 1997; Manchester, 1997; Merrill Lynch, 1995). Whether the extent of financial planning will increase with the dramatic growth of planning resources available on the Internet and Websites is as yet unclear (Sherman, 1997).

Nevertheless, there will be a growing proportion of affluent older adults who will participate in the labor market or enjoy the pension benefits of their lifetime employment and who can pay through the private sector for most of their needs. Some baby boomers who are financially secure will want to see Social Security privatized through investment in high-performance stocks and will be able to purchase private long-term care insurance. The projections of a healthier and wealthier older population have resulted in the growth of companies that offer products and services specifically geared to them. Popular periodicals such *50 Plus* and *Mature Outlook* offer a prime medium for advertising these products, such as adaptive technologies to support older adults' remaining in their own homes. In addition, computer-based technology will increasingly provide ways for older people to access information about and order products on-line through the Internet. There are many Websites about products specifically for older people, including the Alliance for Technology Access that focuses on assistive technology for older persons with chronic illness. Third Age.com offers chat rooms, bulletin boards, speak-outs, a Market Square on quality products, and Invest Tools for financial planning. It is important to recognize, however, that many of these computer-based services will be available only to higher-income elders, since government regulations and medical reimbursement programs have not kept pace with the growth of technology and rarely reimburse for such products (Bowe, 1995).

Along with the growth of products specifically geared to older adults, a leisure industry has developed, particularly in retirement communities, to meet the recreational needs of more affluent and healthy older adults. An increasing variety of social activities and recreational sports is offered in many planned retirement communities. The increase in specialized exercise equipment and aerobic classes for older persons is a tangible indicator of the growing number of older people who can purchase the health and psychological benefits of exercise. Such continued opportunities to maintain physical activity in old age will help more baby boomers achieve successful aging than previous cohorts.

At the same time, however, these differential opportunities will benefit middle- and upper-class older persons more than those with limited financial resources. Despite the overall improvement in economic and health status of future cohorts of older adults, the numbers who are economically vulnerable will not diminish dramatically. Instead, it is projected that there will be a permanent underclass of boomers, with disproportionate representation of African Americans, those with a sporadic work history, single women, and the poorly educated (Dennis and Migliaccio, 1997). In contrast to their better-off counterparts, they will want the continuation of Social Security as a risk-free contributory system and will worry about Medicare's and Medicaid's co-payments and deductibles. Not surprisingly, many of the computer-based options described throughout this text will not be available to them, at least until changes are made in Medicaid reimbursement. The extent to which the public sector will focus on the needs of this underclass is unclear, given the increasingly more conservative political climate and the trends toward less federal support and devolution of responsibility to the states. And those in the middle, the "tweeners" who have too many resources to qualify for public programs, yet are unable to pay fully for their health and long-term care needs, will increase. In fact, it is the expansion of the "tweeners" that is predicted to create future intergenerational competition for scarce resources (Smeeding, 1990).

Overall, an imbalance persists between a population of increasingly long-lived people and decreasing opportunities for them to participate fully in society. Perhaps the most striking area in which social and cultural structures lag behind demographic changes is in employment. Since 1900, the labor-force participation of older people has been eroding, and the competence of older workers for productive performance has been consistently underrated. Pension systems, employer-initiated "downsizing" and "restructuring," and the growth of a contingency or secondary workforce have encouraged early retirement. The trend toward early retirement, combined with increased longevity, means that retiring from work often occurs during the same period as children pursue increasingly expensive undergraduate or graduate education. Accordingly, retirement as a stage of life is becoming even more protracted. Today, people find that they are spending over 20 percent of their adult lives in retirement, compared with only 3 percent in 1900 (U.S. Senate Special Committee on Aging, 1992). Increasingly, questions are being raised about whether people should retire and under what conditions and for what purposes. As people begin to comprehend how much of the adult lifetime is spent in retirement, there is growing awareness that formal retirement does not end the need for involvement in the larger society. With declines in work opportunities for older adults, pressures have mounted for socially rewarding, productive roles in the larger community.

The concept of the "Third Age" has been developed by gerontologists at Fordham University to denote that stage in life which occurs after middle age but before the final stage; it is conceptualized as a time of continued involvement and development in areas of life beyond work and family. With increased recognition of the potential of older people to contribute to society in a wide range of ways, new public values regarding their opportunities and responsibilities are needed (Fahey, 1996). Increasingly, questions will be raised about how "work" should be defined and "contributions" measured. For example, volunteer effort may be perceived as contributing more to the common good than paid work and therefore as deserving greater rewards than currently exists. The concept of productive aging, defined in Chapter 11 as paid and unpaid activities that contribute to society in diverse ways, is consistent with that of the Third Age. As noted in Chapters 4 and 5, health-promotion programs aimed at improving older people's physical and functional health and cognitive abilities have grown. However, there has been less emphasis on providing flexible options for productive activity by older persons in all sectors of society (Caro, Bass, and Chen, 1993).

As members of successive cohorts retire at younger ages, are better educated, and perhaps healthier than their predecessors, it seems predictable that pressures from organizations representing older people and from the general public will modify existing work, retirement, and leisure roles. In fact, modifications in the workplace are underway to offset the lag between changes in social structures and the recognition of older people's skills and productivity, as well as to take account of the rapid growth among the older workforce. Many of these efforts seek to encourage people to work longer without undermining the self-esteem of those no longer able to work. A very pragmatic reason for developing incentives for older workers is the projected labor shortage among youth, particularly in the service sector. From 1993 to 2004, the population comprised of workers over age 40 will increase by over 28 million; the aging of the baby boomers will raise the median age of the labor force by 3 years. By 2005, 15.1 percent of workers will be over age 55, compared to 11.9 percent currently (Moen, 1998).

More companies are beginning to modify the workplace in order to retain older workers longer and to encourage multiple careers. These workplace changes include both incentives to maintain the older workers' productivity and ways to ease the transition to retirement. They involve redesigning jobs (e.g., job sharing, flexible and part-time schedules, and conducting work at home) to accommodate older workers' abilities and needs.

They offer retraining in new technologies such as computers and robotics; provide counseling and other support services for new careers; and give additional forms of compensation such as health benefits or tax credits. Some companies, such as Travelers Insurance, have set up data banks of retiree skills for temporary employment and job sharing. Local and federal government agencies have developed programs to make use of retirees' skills in voluntary and paid employment (Moen, 1998). To date, however, such workplace changes do not adequately meet many older people's growing interest in part-time employment. This suggests the need for new forms of public–private collaboration in the future to create viable options for older adults.

It may be more useful in the future to view retirement not as a single and irreversible event, but as a process involving successive decisions. The transition to retirement can be eased through financial planning and comprehensive retirement-preparation programs, although as noted above, baby boomers have thus far not fully utilized such programs. For example, IBM has a Retirement Education Assistance plan that provides tuition to employees and their spouses 3 years prior to retirement eligibility and 2 years after retirement; the plan aims to enable employees to develop new interests and prepare for new careers. Another model, common in some European countries and in Japan, is a "gliding out" plan of phased retirement that permits a gradual shift to a part-time schedule. Some Scandinavian countries give workers year-long sabbaticals every 10 years as a time to reevaluate their careers or to take a break instead of working straight through to retirement. Jobs can also be restructured, gradually allowing longer vacations, shorter work days, and more opportunities for community involvement during the pre-retirement working years.

Volunteer opportunities that draw upon retirees' competence as well as provide them with chances to learn new skills can also blur the line between paid employment and retirement. In recognition of these challenges, the Administration on Aging, a federal agency traditionally concerned with the planning and delivery of services, funded the "Redefining Retirement Initiative: The Baby Boomer Challenge." This initiative seeks to resocialize and inspire baby boomers and middle-aged individuals to prepare for their retirement and projected longer life and to help boomers recognize that they have the ability to reshape U.S. society (Dennis and Migliaccio, 1997). This emphasis on individual and community responsibility reflects the changing ethos about the role of government.

Other changes in occupational patterns are the increased number of people in their forties and fifties who are electing to move into second and even third careers. As noted above, more organizations are allowing their employees opportunities for growth in their jobs by providing sabbaticals, extended vacations and leaves, retraining programs, and career-development alternatives. More of these adult education opportunities will become available through distance-learning formats that use information-based technology. Such educational options benefit employees by allowing them to explore new careers and volunteer and leisure interests; this, in turn, can serve to prevent job burnout or boredom, so that early retirement is not perceived as the only viable option. These programs also benefit employers in companies that are undergoing rapid technological changes, such as automobile manufacturing, where robotics and computerized assembly lines are already in place. By retraining their older, more experienced workers, such organizations can retain employees who have proven capable in the past.

A work–retirement continuum for a population with a longer life span will involve lifelong education and training. Changing social values about the "appropriate age" for education, employment, retirement, and leisure demand a reexamination of employment policies and norms. The traditional linear life cycle of education for the young, employment for the middle aged, and retirement for the old is already undergoing major changes as more middle-aged and older persons enter college for the first time, move into a new career, or begin their studies for a graduate or professional degree. From a developmental perspective, temporary "retirement" may be a more viable option for the young worker just starting a family; employment may be desirable for the teenager who is bored with school; and education may be attractive to the older person who can integrate his or her life experiences with the knowledge gained in a formal learning situation. Instead of the linear career trajectory traditionally followed in our society, movement in and out of the workforce, schooling, and family care may all need to be defined as legitimate options in a cyclical life plan.

Women have moved in and out of the workforce for years, largely because of assuming family responsibilities; but, as described in Chapter 11, they have often been penalized for their discontinuous work patterns through lower salaries and retirement benefits, which reflects the feminization of poverty. However, with increasing numbers of career-oriented women who are committed to an ideology of shared family responsibilities, and with growing awareness of the possibility of two or three careers over the life course, movement in and out of the workforce may come to be viewed as a legitimate alternative for both men and women. This trend may also encourage individuals to better integrate their work and family lives.

Modifications in work patterns and organizational opportunities for career development, described above, suggest that traditional definitions of leisure will also undergo major changes. Employment and leisure are becoming less compartmentalized and more evenly distributed across the life span through modified work schedules, sabbaticals, job sharing, lifelong education, and phased retirement, as well as the increasing number of retirees who work part-time and engage in regular volunteer activities. This "blurring" of work and leisure is reinforced by increased organizational awareness of employee needs, such as on-the-job exercise and fitness programs, child care, staff training, and psychological counseling. To some extent, these factors are an outgrowth of the shift from the traditional work ethic to a more balanced view of employment and leisure in this society. Therefore, future cohorts of older adults may view leisure in retirement merely as a continuation of their leisure activities during their younger years and not regard it as a new stage in life. Such integration of leisure throughout the life span will undoubtedly mean a smoother transition to retirement for many older people.

There is disagreement, however, on the economy's ability to create such work and leisure alternatives, despite dramatic declines in unemployment and a general economic boom in the late 1990s. Many of these new jobs are in the service sector (e.g., health and social services, food, and recreation), rather than in manufacturing. As a result, these new jobs are less likely to provide older workers with financial security. There are also uncertainties about the potential impact of technological advances on job opportunities—whether these will produce new jobs or result in net job losses. What is certain, given the rapid growth of the older population, is that there will be greater labor-market diversity among the older population and greater variations in reasons for retirement. There will also be more diversity among the unemployed by social class and in economic well-being before and after retirement.

Rather than focusing on altering work roles, a more humanistic approach, consistent with the politics of productivity discussed in Chapter 11, is to ask how we can develop and use our human potential in old age as part of a productive society. The vitality of the older population must be recognized out of a need to involve their skills and wisdom, through both paid and unpaid positions, in the enrichment of our society. Advocates of a productive aging society suggest that national policies and attitudes must be changed. They point to the need to develop a national consensus that encourages older people to continue or create their own roles in society, thereby opening doors to interested and capable elders. Changes must include placing a real value on unpaid volunteer and caregiving activities, and taking practical steps such as publicly emphasizing that

technology does not necessarily displace older workers. Finally, these advocates emphasize the need to provide settings where older people can use their talents more productively and in a more satisfying manner (Morris, 1993). As noted by Torres-Gil (in Dennis and Migliaccio, 1997, p. 46): "my vision is to use the aging of this cohort as the way to educate and inspire them to think about themselves and others, plan ahead to grow old with the sense of responsibility not just to themselves but to their community and to the nation." This perspective also reflects the goals of the federally funded Redefining Retirement Initiative, which emphasizes individual behavioral change and responsibility within a larger public policy framework.

Such redefinitions of old age and aging could move citizens and policymakers beyond the artificially framed policy debates about young and old competing for scarce resources. As suggested in Chapter 15, the interdependence of generations across the life span can provide a future framework for policy and program development if it is made more explicit. Older people are becoming more aware of the creative and central roles that they can play in moving beyond their own needs and leaving a legacy for future generations—for example, through their active participation in environmental and energy issues. Likewise, intergenerational programs in schools, community centers, nursing homes, retirement facilities, and adult day care centers are growing. Such programs serve to utilize older adults' skills, as well as to provide children and youth with opportunities to interact with diverse older people. In other words, these interactions can build on the reciprocity that exists between generations. Such cooperative, intergenerational efforts may have the long-term effect of reducing ageism and competition among age groups, so that young and old work together to benefit the most needy in our society, regardless of age. These interactions can also enhance the older person's developmental needs for generativity, as noted in Chapter 6. Such alliances between young and old formed around the need for long-term care reform in the early

1990s. Perhaps in the future it will be less necessary to develop age-based social and health policies, but rather to establish programs that address special needs across the life span.

CHANGES IN LIVING ARRANGEMENTS

The movement away from farms and city centers to the suburbs has also resulted in the graying of the suburbs, with many people who had moved to these areas after World War II reaching retirement. Older residents in these older suburbs have lower average incomes and lower home values than those in newer communities, as seen in Chapter 10.

These trends will continue as the children of these migrants to the suburbs, who, in turn, built their homes in the suburbs and worked in nearby satellite communities, themselves age. Until now, most health and social services, such as clinics, hospitals, senior centers, and nutrition sites, have been built near city centers with high concentrations of older people. Future cohorts will expect these services to be located closer to their homes in the suburbs, just as shopping centers, banks, and jobs have been moved outward from urban centers to these areas to accommodate the needs of this population. Boomers with adequate resources, however, are likely to move to retirement communities that offer numerous amenities, leisure activities, and a moderate climate. These communities will eventually expand to include assisted living and health services to maintain the independence of baby boomers as they approach their 80s and 90s (Longino, 1998).

Regardless of geographic location, there is an increasing demand for "flexible housing" by new home buyers. Indeed, at the 1998 annual meeting of the National Association of Home Builders, which represents small and large companies engaged in new home construction as well as remodeling, a major theme was the issue of designing housing that can be used throughout a lifetime. This interest on the part of home builders is clearly more than academic; it reflects the trend of first-time buyers to select neighborhoods where they will want to live for many years, and the decline in relocation rates among all ages (in 1997 only 15 percent of the U.S. population moved) (Longino, 1998). As a result, architects and builders are already designing homes with movable walls that can expand or shrink a room as needs change, or plumbing that can convert a small room on the main floor of the house into a bathroom. This gives families the flexibility to adapt their homes as they assume caregiving roles for older family members, or if one of the current residents needs long-term care in the future (as a result not only of their own aging, but because of accidents or chronic diseases that result in a disability). Other options that can be built into a home are modifiability in the number and size of bedrooms, using a cluster design so that multiple generations and even unrelated people such as renters can live under the same roof while retaining their privacy.

Perhaps because of their experiences with the requirements of the Americans with Disabilities Act (ADA), builders and architects are becoming aware of the need to make main-floor hallways and doorways in private homes wide enough for future access by a wheelchair. Even though the ADA does not require accessibility in private homes, these trends are occurring because builders recognize the growing market for such housing features. Other features that are too costly for most home buyers today, but which will become more prevalent in homes of the future, are computerized controls for heat, artificial lighting, window coverings, and music. With portable keypads, these features can help frail older persons maintain ambient temperatures, lighting, and music at levels that are comfortable and in ways that are congruent with the older person's competence level.

Although these trends in home building will help future cohorts of older adults, there is a need to make low-cost structural modifications, communication, and transportation systems to help current cohorts of older people remain independent for as long as possible. Consistent with the person-environment model described in Chapter 1, and illustrated throughout this book, the home environment of older people can be modified to reduce the level of environmental press and enhance the aging person's level of competence and quality of life. For example, currently nearly 35 percent of individuals age 75 and older use at least one assistive device or have their home modified for accessibility. This proportion is expected to increase dramatically with newer cohorts of older persons (Emerman, 1994). With the trends toward computerized home-based banking and shopping services, future cohorts may not need to leave their homes to obtain many services. As more older people strive to remain independent, the market for home-based services will expand.

Computer programs have also been developed to describe potential side effects of various medications and interactions among them. Currently, these software programs are aimed at physicians, pharmacists, and other health professionals; it may be possible in the near future to buy such a program written in layman's language, type in the names and doses of medications one is taking, and then obtain a printout of potential side effects and special precautions. This would be particularly useful to the many older adults who are using numerous prescriptions and over-the-counter medications. Although too costly to implement at present, it is technically possible to conduct remote monitoring between a patient's home and a local health care facility for such things as blood pressure and heart-rate measures.

Technology also can be used to enhance options for recreation and enrichment for older people. For example, computers are increasingly being used for leisure, such as games linked by telecommunication channels or books read on microchips. Interactive television, CD-ROM and video discs, special TV programming, and open university via television can greatly expand the social worlds of homebound elders and stimulate the older person's intellectual functioning through active participation in learning. For example, Senior Net is a nationwide computer network that encourages discussion on diverse topics and offers hands-on classes in computer use. It is aimed at people age 55 and older. In addition, for a small membership fee, users can attend local classes on computer literacy, word processing, database management, and how to access useful sites on the Internet.

Technological advances will also benefit younger family caregivers. As robotics and computer systems become more cost-effective and user-friendly, they will be used by frail older people who would otherwise need to rely on family or paid caregivers or to move to a long-term care facility. They may also be freer to use assisted living or other less-intensive and less-costly housing options if these facilities offer such technological assistance to their residents. Communication via FAX machines, video telephones, and e-mail will also reduce the physical distance among older people and their families. These developments will be easier for future generations of elders to adopt, because they will have grown up with computers and rapid technological advances in their work and leisure. On the other hand, older people do not necessarily want technology that saves time or replaces activity, such as automatic tellers or shopping via television. As noted in Chapter 11, for many older adults, household tasks and shopping are not necessarily seen as onerous, but rather as interesting time-fillers. As a result, older people may be most interested in technology that makes life easier, safer, and improves their quality of life (Gitlin, 1995; Markle Foundation, 1989).

Although equipment will increasingly be used to supplement or replace personal assistance, there are financial barriers to the use of these technologies. Currently, third-party sources (private insurance, Medicare, Medicaid, Veterans Administration, or other private or public sources) cover about 50 percent of the assistive devices in use, with the rest paid by those in need or their families out-of-pocket. More than 75 percent of home-accessibility features are paid for entirely by the user and family. The reason that older people most often give for not utilizing needed assistive devices is financial. Since reimbursement and regulatory issues are also a barrier to companies entering this marketplace, producers and consumers may share common goals in changing reimbursement mechanisms. Advocates

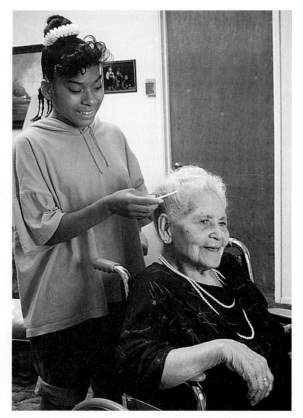

Shared housing between young and old can benefit both generations.

for these new products and designs will also find support for their cause in federal legislation such as the Americans with Disabilities Act (ADA), described earlier. The ADA emphasizes the social desirability of increasing the use of assistive technologies and accessible environmental design (Emerman, 1994).

Shared housing is another means of helping older people remain in their own homes, as discussed in Chapter 10. Community programs that match older homeowners with other elders, or with college students and younger working people who need housing, serve a useful function in making the cost of housing affordable to a wider cross-section of persons. These intergenerational programs also provide security for frail older peo-

ple who need occasional assistance from their healthier peers or younger people, but who do not require the 24-hour care provided by nursing homes. Future cohorts of elders may also continue the trends of their younger years by sharing housing with an unmarried companion. As society has become more accepting of unmarried couples and gay and lesbian partners living together, the advantages of such arrangements for older couples have become more evident. Thus, for example, sharing a home without marrying can reduce an older couple's expenses while they maintain their separate incomes from pensions and Social Security benefits. Most important, shared housing provides much-needed social companionship.

This growth in the number and variety of long-term care options and ways to maintain older people in their own homes is exciting. However, it raises a major policy dilemma for the twenty-first century: What should be the role of government, the private sector, and the family in meeting long-term care needs? Within these roles, what should be done to ensure the autonomy of older individuals? These policy issues inevitably raise ethical dilemmas about the distribution of resources among various segments of society.

ETHICAL DILEMMAS

At the forefront of ethical dilemmas in an aging society is the issue of the prolongation of life at a time of escalating medical costs, increasing use of high-technology treatments, and fears that managed care will foster rationing of services. As a society, we have valued finding cures for dreaded diseases and forestalling death as long as possible. As noted in Chapter 1, medical technology has made it possible to extend life expectancy, but not necessarily to assure quality of life. Many older people are now saved, often at considerable cost, from diseases that previously would have killed them, only to be guaranteed death from another disease at equally high or even higher costs. Physicians have been taught to spare no effort in keeping a patient alive, but increasingly both health professionals and lay persons are questioning whether dying should be prolonged indefinitely when there is no possibility of recovery. Life-support systems, organ transplants, and other advances in medical technology have made it possible to prolong the life of the chronically and terminally ill and have blurred definitions of when life ends. For example, technology now allows the transplantation of various human organs, and life can be prolonged by machines that keep the body functioning even if the conscious mind has died. But these advances have not necessarily ensured better quality of life. In other words, as a society, we have done a better job of adding years to life than life to years.

The timing, place, and conditions of death are increasingly under medical control. For almost any life-threatening condition, some interventions can now delay the moment of death, but not its inevitability. Doctors and nurses have always dealt with dying, but not until the present technical advances have they had so much power and responsibility to control how long life lasts and to determine when treatment is medically futile (Schneiderman, 1994). At the same time, technology has made it more difficult to draw a clear line between living and dying. As a result, these new medical capabilities demand a new set of ethics and practices. As noted in Chapter 12, the field of *bioethics* was born out of the dilemmas that often confront health care providers, family members, and patients regarding the introduction and withdrawal of invasive treatments, the patient's decision-making capacity to participate in treatment decisions, and the quality of the patient's life. It is a field that will grow in the twenty-first century, encompassing a wider range of professionals in debates about end-of-life care.

At the core of these ethical issues is the question of who decides what for whom, and thus issues of power and authority (Scofield, 1994). Decisions about whether and how to intervene in a terminal illness can be excruciating for doctors, nurses, family members, and older patients. At what point should efforts to prolong life be stopped, when the alternative is so final? How much suffering is "worth it" to stay alive? Which is more important: quality or quantity of life? And how do we measure or determine quality of life? Under what conditions and for which decisions should the wishes of the patient supersede those of his or her family members? What institutional mechanisms should be employed to resolve ethical conflicts? Proponents of the right to die maintain that no public interests are served by prolonging pain and shredding dignity in prolonging hopeless situations. These decisions become even more complex when the older person is mentally incompetent, as in the case of patients with advanced Alzheimer's disease. Cross-cultural differences can also affect how patients, family members, and health care providers interpret life-sustaining treatment (Michel, 1994).

Increasingly, there are concerns about when and whether health professionals should withhold treatment (American Geriatrics Society, 1995). Health care facilities are now required to have the capacity to address such bioethical issues for patients, families, and staff, typically through ethics committees. As noted in Chapter 12, all 50 states now have laws authorizing the use of *advance directives*. These are supplemented by a federal law, the Patient Self-Determination Act. Nevertheless, these laws have not necessarily been successfully operationalized, suggesting that ethical issues surrounding the dying process cannot easily be legislated.

One result of the increased visibility of medicine and the media attention on bioethical issues is that more people know about their legal rights as patients and have thought about the personal moral principles that govern their individual choices. Accordingly, there is growing public support for individual determination regarding life-sustaining treatment through advanced directives such as living wills. Citizen initiatives and bills in state legislatures have increased the debate surrounding the "right to die" or "death with dignity." In most cases, the debate centers not on *if* such activity should be condoned but *under what circumstances* and what is meant by terminal and medical finality. In June 1997, the Supreme Court unanimously determined that physician-assisted suicide is not a fundamental right guaranteed by the U.S. Constitution. By this decision, the Supreme Court moved the debate about a person's right to die from the national level back to the states. Even so, the Supreme Court left open the possibility of future appeals. Justice Sandra Day O'Connor echoed four more liberal justices who said that in the future the court may well find that a hastened death might be entitled to constitutional protection. The Supreme Court decision also put at the forefront of the debate the issue of aggressive pain management and how well health care professionals are trained in end-of-life care.

Although less than 1 percent of total health care expenditures go to individuals in the last year of life, economic issues often get raised along with ethical considerations (Alliance for Aging Research, 1997). Many policymakers and the lay public, concerned about scarce public resources, continue to raise questions about how benefits should be distributed among various groups in society. Critics of costly life-saving techniques for older adults, such as transplants, argue that with over 40 million people under age 65 without health care insurance and many more who cannot afford high-tech care, our health care system should first address such basic needs rather than spending disproportionate resources for expensive procedures for only a few. Yet studies to date suggest that the total savings achieved by denying high-cost acute care to older people would have little impact on overall health care expenditures (National Academy on Aging, 1994). Nevertheless, intense debates continue regarding who should decide, in the aggregate and in individual instances, who receives what type of health care. Some fear that in the absence of legal protection for the right to die, economic considerations will override compassionate concerns, especially under managed care with its fixed fees and capitation as incentives to save costs.

Rationing decisions tend to be made at a societal level, while decisions about whether treatment is *medically futile* are made at the patient's bedside. In other words, rationing specifically ac-

knowledges that a treatment offers a benefit, but the issue is how to distribute beneficial but limited resources fairly, while medical futility signifies that a treatment offers no therapeutic benefit to a patient (Schneiderman, 1994). Some would argue that states already ration health care through physicians who refuse to treat Medicaid recipients. In fact, the state of Oregon has already implemented a federally authorized policy experiment in which it operates with a fixed Medicaid budget and classifies specific categories of health care as not reimbursable (Binstock, 1994). This program is being watched by other states as a model for their own Medicaid systems. Even if rationing is not formal policy, there is evidence to suggest that physicians sometimes ration the use of medical care to the oldest-old. As doctors attempt to provide adequate care within the context of limited budgets such as capitated systems of care, they tend to be pressured by colleagues and administrators not to make available the same expensive tests and medical specialties as exist for younger patients, resulting in underservice for some older patients (Kane and Kane, 1994; Binstock, 1994). Debates about an equitable provision of services versus targeting lifesaving interventions for a few will undoubtedly intensify in the future.

Those who argue against rationing maintain that a major cost would be the destruction of moral barriers against placing any group of human beings in a category apart from humanity in general. If older people can be denied access to health care categorically, then this action could happen to other groups as well. They argue that suggesting that older people are unworthy of lifesaving care starts us down a "slippery slope" (Binstock, 1994, p. 40). Not only are the moral costs of rationing too great, but the potential contributions of older people to society are lost. They argue that alternatives other than rationing should be attempted as a way to contain health care costs.

Ultimately, these larger ethical questions translate into daily practice dilemmas for those who are faced with the reality of caring for chronically ill and dying older people, as well as for children with acute medical needs, in an era of diminishing resources of social and health services. As noted by Zuckerman (1994), much of health care is carried out in settings where the need for timely, practical solutions outweighs the need for abstract philosophical debate about patients' ethical and legal rights. The question of who should control decisions about life and death will continue to be argued among doctors, families, and often lawyers. Conflicting pressures for change will likely give way to the creation of new norms, whereby more people will support the removal of life supports for the terminally ill and will want to have control over their own deaths.

One reflection of the growing national debate at the grass-roots level is the increased number of Internet resources on death and dying. The Website of Choices in Dying offers a comprehensive resource for those wanting to understand the right-to-die movement and a way to download advance-directive packages geared to the laws and regulations in a particular state. Death-NET, founded by Derek Humphry, offers the largest collection of "right to die" material and services on the Internet. A smaller number of Websites are maintained by the anti-euthanasia groups, such as LifeWEB of the International Anti-Euthanasia Task Force. Such Internet resources will undoubtedly proliferate in the twenty-first century.

As the older population continues to increase, the decisions regarding the allocation and withholding of health care to individuals will assume greater importance. These decisions must be made by an informed and humanistic society; they cannot be left only to policymakers, physicians, and attorneys. What many today consider to be medical or geriatric issues will increasingly influence the lives of most Americans, young and middle-aged, not just the old. For these reasons and consistent with the underlying assumptions of this book, it is important to understand the processes of aging, as well as the policies and services that affect the older population and how these policies are made, so that society as a whole can make informed choices. In the final section, we will review

some of the many opportunities for careers in gerontology. Whether or not gerontology is chosen as a career, however, it is essential for all of us to become informed about this field so that we can become better consumers, citizens, advocates, and caregivers to frail elders within our families and in our communities.

CAREERS IN GERONTOLOGY

One reason for studying social gerontology is to determine the types of career opportunities in this field. It should be clear by now that gerontology holds great promise for practitioners, researchers, and teachers in diverse aspects of the field. As we have seen throughout this book, specialists in geriatric health care will assume a greater role in helping the growing population of older people to maintain their quality of life, both in terms of treating chronic diseases and in preventing health problems. The increasing number of geriatric training programs in schools of medicine, nursing, dentistry, pharmacy, social work, and public health attest to the importance of this field. While there has been a growth in the number of universities offering courses in aging, these are not necessarily part of the core curriculum and rarely taught in depth to students in the health professions.

Specialists in geriatric nutrition and in physical and occupational therapy will be in greater demand in the future as options expand in housing and long-term care. Attorneys with special training in medical ethics and aging will become critical members of the gerontological team. The increased interest in leisure activities in old age will call for more recreation specialists. Architects and planners will be urged to design housing that is sensitive to the needs of an aging population. Social workers and psychologists will be needed to work with older people and their families as counselors, advocates, support group facilitators, and care or case managers who coordinate services. Program planners, developers, and managers will have opportunities in a myriad of areas such as assisted living, senior centers, adult day health programs, chore services, home health care, and respite care. There will even be opportunities for computer programmers and designers, as well as specialists in electronic communication, to design new products to help maintain older people's independence for as long as possible.

In addition, there will be an ongoing need for low-tech workers, such as nursing aides and home health workers, who provide most of the personal daily long-term care services to older clients. This need must be addressed by better pay, training, and working conditions for these critically needed but low-paid workers. Figure E.1 illustrates the broad

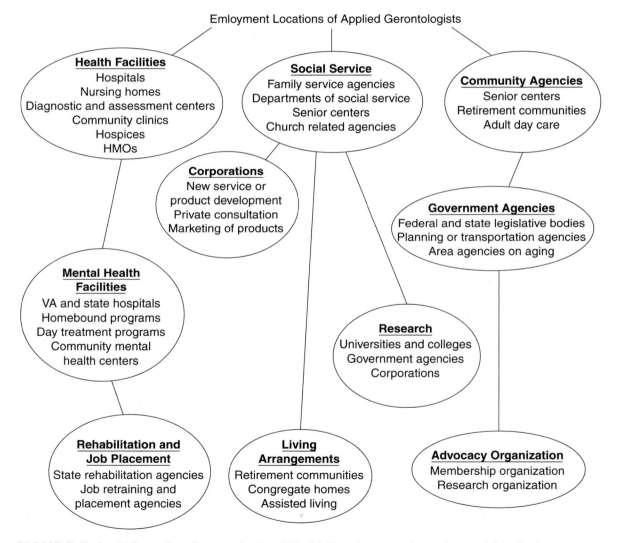

FIGURE E.1   Where Do Gerontologists Work? Employment Locations of Applied Gerontologists

SOURCE: Developed by M. Klein, University of Southern California: Used with permission of the author.

FIGURE E.2 What Do Gerontologists Do?

1. *Direct Service*
   - Assesses client needs
   - Provides services directly to the older client and family
   - Coordinates services with other agencies and institutions
   - Works to assure that the older client and family receive appropriate services that are of a high quality
   - Evaluates and modifies the services needed
   - Conducts outreach to expand and enhance client base
   - Carries out advocacy on behalf of older persons

2. *Program Planning and Evaluation*
   - Identifies the needs of the community
   - Plans the programs and facilities
   - Determines the level and timing of funds required
   - Develops the staffing and management plans
   - Determines the evaluation plan for the program
   - Consults and coordinates with other agencies and programs

3. *Education and Training*
   - Plans and conducts educational programs for older persons, their caregivers, and families
   - Plans and conducts continuing education programs for paraprofessionals and professionals interested in serving older people
   - Instructs preprofessionals
   - Intergenerational programs

4. *Administration and Policy*
   - Designs the structure, motivates and supervises the activities of staff members
   - Determines, monitors, and modifies organizational expenditures
   - Coordinates activities within the organization and with outside organizations
   - Conducts analyses of current and proposed programs
   - Increases public awareness of needs and services

5. *Research*
   - Designs and carries out evaluations and academic studies to clarify aspects of aging and program interventions

array of work settings for gerontologists. These range from government and community agencies to corporations and universities (Klein, 1994). These settings provide tremendous opportunities for significant contributions to improving the quality of life for older persons, as shown in Figure E.2.

As noted throughout this book, more research is needed on the normal and pathological aspects of aging and on how age-related changes influence older people's social functioning. Researchers trained in sociology, psychology, economics, and political science must work with biologists, geneticists, nutritionists, and others in the basic and clinical sciences to understand and develop models of the interactive effects of biological, psychological, and social influences on helping people age successfully. In many ways, the field of gerontology is limited only by one's imagination. For those of you motivated and concerned about improving the quality of life for current and future generations of older people, we hope that the issues raised in this book will encourage you to join this exciting and challenging field.

REFERENCES

Adlin, M. Health care issues. In E. Sutton, A. Factor, B. Hawkins, T. Heller, and G. Seltzer (Eds.) *Older adults with developmental disabilities.* Baltimore, MD: Paul H. Brookes Publishing, 1993.

Alliance for Aging Research. *Seven deadly myths: Uncovering the facts about the high cost of the last year of life.* 2021 K Street, Washington, DC: 1997.

American Geriatrics Society. The care of dying patients: A position paper from the American Geriatrics Society. *Journal of the American Geriatrics Society,* 1995, 43, 577–578.

Bengtson, V. C., Rosenthal, C. J., and Burton, C. Families and aging: Diversity and heterogeneity. In R. H. Binstock and L. K. George (Eds.), *Handbook of aging and the social sciences* (3rd ed.). New York: Academic Press, 1990.

Binstock, R. H. Old-age-based rationing: From rhetoric to risk? *Generations,* 1994, 18, 37–41.

Blanchette, P. L. and Valour, V. G., Health and aging among baby boomers, *Generations,* 1998, 22, 76–80.

Bowe, F. Is it medically necessary: The political and economic issues that drive and derail assistance technology development. *Generations,* Spring 1995, 19, 37–40.

Bulcroft, K. A., and Bulcroft, R. A. The timing of divorce effects on parent child relationships in later life. *Research on Aging,* 1991, 13, 226–243.

Callahan, D. *The troubled dream of life: Living with mortality.* New York: Simon & Schuster, 1993.

Caro, F. G., Bass, S. A., and Chen, Y. P. Introduction. In S. A. Bass, F. G. Caro, and Y. P. Chen (Eds.), *Achieving a productive society.* Westport, CT: Auburn House, 1993.

Choi, N. Long-term elderly widows and divorcees: Similarities and differences. *Journal of Women and Aging,* 1995, 7, 69–72.

Coontz, S. *The way we really are: Coming to terms with America's changing families.* New York: Basic Books, 1997.

Cornman, J. M., and Kingson, E. R. Trends, issues, perspectives and values for the aging of the baby boom cohorts. *The Gerontologist,* 1996, 36, 15–26.

Cutler, N. E. The false alarms and blaring sirens of financial literacy: Middle-agers' knowledge of retirement income, health finance, and long-term care. *Generations,* Summer 1997, 21, 34–40.

Cutler, N. E. Preparing for their older years: The financial diversity of aging boomers. *Generations,* Spring 1998, 22, 81–86.

Day, J. Population projections of the United States by age, sex, race and Hispanic origin: 1992 to 2050. *Current Population Reports,* Series P25, No. 1092, Washington, DC: U.S. Government Printing Office, 1992.

Deatrick, D. Senior-Med: Creating a network to help manage medications. *Generations,* Fall 1997, 21, 59–60.

de Lange, T. Telomeres and senescence: Ending the debate. *Science,* 1998, 279, 334–335.

De Martino, B. *The MetLife study of employee costs for working caregivers.* Westport, CT: MetLife Mature Market Group, 1997.

Dennis, H., and Migliaccio, J. Redefining retirement: The baby boomer challenge. *Generations,* Summer 1997, 21, 45–50.

Emerman, J. Demand grows for technology that helps. *Aging Today.* September/October 1994, XV, 11.

Fahey, Msgr. Charles J. Social work education and the field of aging. *The Gerontologist,* 1996, 36, 36–41.

Fritz, M. Nursing homes chase big profits in subacute care. *The Seattle Times,* March 19, 1995, A4.

Furlong, M. Creating on-line community for older adults. *Generations,* Fall 1997, 21, 33–35.

George, L. K., and Gold, D. T. Life course perspectives on intergenerational and generational connections. *Marriage and Family Review,* 1991, 16, 1–2.

Gitlin, L. Why older people accept or reject assistive technology. *Generations,* Spring 1995, 19, 41–47.

Goldscheider, F. K. Divorce and remarriage: Effects on the elderly population. *Reviews in Clinical Gerontology,* 1994, *4,* 258–259.

Gray, J. What the business community and the aging network can learn from each other. *Generations,* Spring 1995, *19,* 20–25.

Gustafson, D., Gustafson, R. and Wackerbarth, S. CHESS: Health information and decision support for patients and families. *Generations,* Fall 1997, *21,* 56–58.

Hobbs, F., and Damon, B. C. *65+ in the United States.* Washington, DC: U.S. Bureau of the Census, Current Population Reports, 1996.

Hunt, G. C. Cleveland Free-net Alzheimers Forum. *Generations,* Fall 1997, *21,* 37–39.

Jahnke, A. Hospital offers integrated therapies. *Aging Today,* Nov/Dec 1997, *6,* 11–12.

Kane, R. L., and Kane, R. A. Effects of the Clinton health reform on older persons and their families: A health care systems perspective. *The Gerontologist,* 1994, *34,* 598–606.

Kelly, K. Building aging programs with on-line information technology. *Generations,* Fall 1997, 21, 15–18.

Kelly, T., and Kropf, N. Stigmatized and perpetual parents: Older parents caring for adult children with lifelong disabilities. *Journal of Gerontological Social Work,* 1995, 24, 3–17.

Klein, M. *Where do gerontologists work and what do gerontologists do? A model illustrating alternative careers in gerontology.* Unpublished manuscript, University of Southern California: Andrus Gerontology Center, 1994.

Longino, C. Geographic mobility and the baby boom. *Generations,* Spring 1998, *22,* 60–65.

Lubitz, J. D., and Riley, G. F. Trends in Medicare payments in the last year of life. *New England Journal of Medicine,* 1993, *328,* 1092–1096.

Manchester, J. Aging boomers and retirement: Who is at risk? *Generations,* Summer 1997, *21,* 19–22.

Markle Foundation, *Pioneers on the frontier of life: Aging in America.* New York: New York, 1989.

Matthews, J. The retirement crisis. *The Seattle Times,* January 6, 1995, B5.

McGregor, M. Technology and the allocation of resources. *New England Journal of Medicine,* 1989, *320,* 118–120.

Merrill Lynch. *The seventh annual Merrill Lynch retirement and financial planning survey: Confronting the savings crisis.* Princeton, NJ: 1995.

Michel, V. Factoring ethnic and racial differences into bioethics decision making. *Generations,* 1994, *18,* 23–26.

Micozzi, M. Exploring alternative health approaches for elders. *Aging Today,* Nov/Dec 1997, *18,* 9–12.

Moen, P. Recasting careers. *Generations,* Spring 1998, *22,* 40–45.

Moen, P., and Forest, K. B. Family policies for an aging society: Moving to the twenty-first century. *The Gerontologist,* 1995, *35,* 825–830.

Morgan, D. Introduction: The aging of the baby boom. *Generations,* Spring 1998, *22,* 5–10.

Morris, R. Conclusion: Defining the place of the elderly in the twenty-first century. In S. A. Bass, F. G. Caro, and Y. P. Chen (Eds.), *Achieving a productive society.* Westport, CT: Auburn House, 1993.

National Academy on Aging. *Old age in the 21st century.* Syracuse University and the Administration on Aging, 1994.

Older Women's League. *Heading for hardship: Retirement income for American women in the next century.* Washington, DC: Older Women's League, 1990.

Pillemer, K. and Suitor, J. Baby boom families: Relations with aging parents. *Generations,* Spring 1998, *22,* 65–69.

Rix, S. *Older workers: How do they measure up? An overview of age differences on employee costs and performances.* Washington, DC: AARP, 1994.

Rowe, J. W., and Kahn, R. L. *Successful aging.* New York: Pantheon Books, 1998.

Sachs, G. A. Improving care of the dying. *Generations,* 1994, *18,* 19–22.

Schmidt, R. HIV and aging-related disorders. *Generations,* 1989, *13,* 6–15.

Schneiderman, L. J. Medical futility and aging: Ethical implications. *Generations,* 1994, *18,* 61–65.

Scofield, G. R. Medical futility: Can we talk? *Generations,* 1994, *18,* 66–70.

Sherman, R. Sources of help in financial preparation for retirement: AAAs to Web sites. *Generations,* 1997, *21,* 55–60.

Silverstone, B. Older people of tomorrow: A psychosocial profile. *The Gerontologist,* 1996, *36,* 27–32.

Smeeding, T. Economic status of the elderly. In R. H. Binstock and L. K. George (Eds.), *Handbook of ag-*

ing and the social sciences (3rd ed.). New York: Academic Press, 1990.

Sullivan, S., and Gilmore, J. Employers begin to accept eldercare as a business issue. *Personnel,* 1991, *68,* 3.

Twigg, J., and Atkin, K. *Carers perceived: Policy and practice in informal care.* Buckingham, UK: Open University Press, 1994.

Uhlenberg, P. I. Mortality decline over the twentieth century and supply of kin over the life course. *The Gerontologist,* 1996, *36,* 681–685.

U.S. Bureau of the Census. Population projections of the United States by age, sex, race and Hispanic origins: 1992–2050. *Current Population Reports,* P-25, No. 1092. Washington, DC: U.S. Government Printing Office, 1992a.

U.S. Bureau of the Census. Population projections of the U.S. by age, sex, race and Hispanic origin data: 1996–2050. *Current Population Reports,* P25, No. 1130. Washington, DC: U.S. Government Printing Office, 1996.

U.S. Bureau of the Census. Marital status and living arrangements: March 1992. *Current Population Reports,* Series P-20, No. 468. Washington, DC: U.S. Government Printing Office, 1992b.

U.S. Senate Special Committee on Aging. *Aging America: Trends and projections, 1991 edition.* Washington, DC: U.S. Department of Health and Human Services, 1992.

Ward, C. R., and Smith, T. Forging intergenerational communities through information technology. *Generations,* Fall 1997, *21,* 38–42.

Weiner, J. M., Illston, J., and Hanley, F. J. *Sharing the burden: Strategies for public and private long-term care insurance.* Washington, DC: The Brookings Institute, 1994.

Zuckerman, C. Clinical ethics in geriatric care settings. *Generations,* 1994, *18,* 9–12.

INDEX